W9-COO-694

PROMOTION MANAGEMENT & MARKETING COMMUNICATIONS

Third Edition

PROMOTION MANAGEMENT & MARKETING COMMUNICATIONS

Third Edition

Terence A. Shimp
University of South Carolina

The Dryden Press
Harcourt Brace Jovanovich College Publishers

Fort Worth   Philadelphia   San Diego   New York   Orlando   Austin   San Antonio
Toronto   Montreal   London   Sydney   Tokyo

Editor in Chief	Robert A. Pawlik
Acquisitions Editor	Lyn Keeney Hastert
Developmental Editor	Bill Teague
Project Editor	Jennifer Johnson
Production Manager	Marilyn Williams
Book Designer	Nick Welch
Photo/Permissions Editors	Annette Coolidge and Steven Lunetta
Copy Editor	Judi McClellan

Printed in the United States of America

Library of Congress Catalog Number: 92-070973

ISBN: 0-03-076748-2

3 4 5 6 7 8 9 0 1 2   0 3 9   9 8 7 6 5 4 3 2 1

The Dryden Press
Harcourt Brace Jovanovich

In memory of my father and to Judy, John, Julie, Susan, my mother, and brothers Vince, Mac, Jack, and Doug. All of you provide me with the best things in life.

THE DRYDEN PRESS SERIES IN MARKETING

PREFACE

Promotion Management and Marketing Communications, Third Edition, is intended for use in undergraduate or graduate courses in promotion management, promotion strategy, or marketing communications. The text integrates marketing-communications theory, concepts, and research with in-depth treatment of all elements of the promotion mix—advertising, sales promotions, point-of-purchase communications, direct marketing communications, public relations and sponsorship marketing, and personal selling. Thorough yet accessible treatment of theoretical concepts and academic research serve to frame the issues faced daily by marketing communications practitioners.

Organization

The text is organized to cover first the fundamentals of marketing communications and then to treat in detail the various promotion-mix elements. **Part 1,** including Chapters 1 and 2, introduces the topic of integrated marketing communications and reviews the communication-theory fundamentals that apply to all forms of marketing communications.

Part 2 covers the behavioral foundations of marketing communications and promotion management. Chapter 3 overviews buyer behavior theory and research pertinent to a better understanding of marketing communications messages and promotional efforts. Subsequent chapters discuss the role of attitudes and persuasion in marketing communications (Chapter 4) and examine marketing communications in facilitating product adoption and diffusion (Chapter 5).

Part 3 introduces various environmental influences that influence all aspects of marketing communications. Chapter 6 covers demographic forces such as age, income, minority population developments, and changing household characteristics. Chapter 7 treats environmental, ethical, and regulatory issues that confront marketing communicators.

Part 4 focuses on promotion management. Chapter 8 introduces the promotion management process with a conceptual framework that provides a useful model for understanding the elements of the process and their interrelations. Chapter 9 presents two detailed case histories that show how organizations develop creative solutions to achieve marketing-communications objectives. These cases present students with a moving picture of the forest (an integrated marketing communications program) prior to studying individual trees such as advertising, sales promotion, and point-of-purchase communications.

Part 5 focuses solely on media advertising. Chapter 10 overviews the advertising process and describes the activities of objective setting and budgeting. Chapter 11 provides detailed coverage of various message factors (such as humor, fear, and comparative ads) and endorser characteristics that are important ingredients in the advertising creative process. Chapter 12 reviews the message-development and creative-strategy aspects of advertising. Media selection is the topic of Chapter 13, while Chapter 14 describes the objectives and methods used for measuring advertising effectiveness.

Sales promotion is the focus of **Part 6**. Chapter 15 overviews the functioning and growing role of sales promotions, while Chapters 16 and 17 examine trade-oriented and consumer-oriented sales promotion topics, respectively.

Part 7 covers three topics that are growing in importance in today's marketing communications programs: point-of-purchase communications (Chapter 18), direct marketing communications (Chapter 19), and public relations and sponsorship marketing (Chapter 20).

Finally, **Part 8** contains two chapters that examine personal selling (Chapter 21) and sales management (Chapter 22).

Special Features

Several noteworthy features characterize *Promotion Management and Marketing Communications*, Third Edition.

Balance. Balance has been a key consideration in writing this third edition of *Promotion Management and Marketing Communications*. This textbook has attempted to fully incorporate the most positive aspects of the philosophy that "nothing is better than a good theory." At the same time, the approach reflects the equally strong belief that "nothing is better than a good example." A conscientious attempt has been made to bridge the gap between academe and practice. For every academic article referenced, at least two or more relevant citations are presented to practical publications such as *Advertising Age*, *Adweek's Marketing Week*, and *The Wall Street Journal*.

Timeliness. Another noteworthy feature of this third edition is the timeliness of its coverage. Theories and concepts are state of the art, and practical examples are drawn from the most current applications.

Examples, Examples. The text is replete with practical examples drawn from marketing-communications applications. Real-world examples enhance students' understanding of key promotional and marketing-communications concepts. In addition, practical examples drawn from magazine advertisements and other materials are used throughout the textbook to illustrate concepts and to heighten reading interest and comprehension.

Opening Vignettes and Focus on Promotion Sections. To further enhance student interest, each chapter opens with a vignette that sets the stage for the subsequent discussion. A "Focus on Promotion" feature in each chapter elevates reading enthusiasm and highlights specific issues relevant to the topical coverage.

Global Focus Boxes. To interest students in the global dynamics of marketing communications, each chapter includes a feature that illustrates a key concept in an international context.

Full-Color Insert. Eye-catching advertisements in a 16-page, full-color insert highlight the special role of color in advertising.

Transparencies. A set of 80 color acetate transparencies is available to instructors who adopt the text.

Video Tape. Video tapes bringing to life the various fields of promotion management will be available to all adopters.

Instructor's Manual. The Instructor's Manual for the third edition of *Promotion Management and Marketing Communications* includes lecture notes and outlines, comments on transparency acetates, and answers to end-of-chapter questions. The manual also contains numerous new multiple-choice and true-false questions and, where necessary, revises questions contained in the previous manual.

Changes in the Third Edition

The third edition of *Promotion Management and Marketing Communications* represents another very thorough revision. Most of the changes have been made to reflect the dynamic character of marketing communications theory and practice. This edition includes the following specific changes:

Chapter 1. This chapter provides many new examples and a more detailed discussion of integrated marketing communications.

Chapter 2. The chapter deletes some of the more abstract aspects of semiotics that were covered in the previous edition and improves the quality of presentation.

Chapter 3. In the previous edition, Chapter 3 applied a marketing communications perspective to the nonpromotional aspects of the marketing mix. Instead of remaining a freestanding chapter, that material has now been integrated into other chapters. The present Chapter 3 is an updated version of Chapter 4 in the previous edition. Examples and relevant research are updated, with a new section on consumption values and consumer choice behavior.

Chapter 4. This chapter is an updated version on attitudes and persuasion that was treated as Chapter 5 in the prior edition. A major new section has been added on the tools of persuasion (such as reciprocation, social proof, and scarcity). A new model of persuasion is covered that combines features of Petty and Cacioppo's elaboration likelihood model with MacInnis and Jaworski's integrative advertising framework.

Chapter 5. This chapter is a significant revision of material on adoption and diffusion processes, which previously appeared in Chapter 7.

Chapter 6. Material on demography, which previously was covered with other topics in Chapter 9, is the sole focus of this new chapter. The coverage of demographic topics is updated and expanded.

Chapter 7. This new chapter covers environmental, ethical, and regulatory issues in marketing communications. "Green" marketing communications and ethical issues receive in-depth coverage involving their influence in all aspects of marketing communications. Governmental and self-regulation topics are updated from their coverage in Chapter 9 of the previous edition.

Chapter 8. Like its predecessor in the second edition, this chapter presents an integrative model of promotion management.

Chapter 9. This chapter presents two case histories that illustrate fully integrated promotion programs. Their purpose is to present students with a moving picture of the forest prior to studying specific trees in subsequent chapters devoted to each separate promotion mix element.

Chapter 10. This overview of advertising corresponds to Chapter 11 in the second edition. The most notable changes are the removal of material on the social aspects of advertising and greater focus on managerial issues, particularly objective setting and budgeting.

Chapter 11. The treatment of creative strategy in this chapter is an updated treatment of the coverage in the second edition's Chapter 12.

Chapter 12. This new chapter covers material relating to various message factors and endorser considerations in advertising. Some of this material previously appeared as Chapter 6.

Chapter 13. This chapter's discussion of media selection in advertising improves upon its corresponding treatment in the second edition. The explanations of reach, frequency, and rating points are clarified, and a computerized media model is introduced. Descriptions of each medium's strengths, weaknesses, and special characteristics are updated.

Chapter 14. The subject of this chapter, assessing advertising effectiveness, is presented in a readily comprehensible fashion and illustrated with many examples of current measurement techniques, some of which are new since the previous edition.

Chapter 15. This introductory chapter on sales promotion is a reworking of the previous Chapter 18. This chapter, along with two additional chapters on sales promotions, has been moved to come immediately after the advertising chapters.

Chapter 16. This chapter focuses exclusively on trade-oriented sales promotions. The coverage updates and improves the presentation of material previously covered in Chapter 19.

Chapter 17. The topic of this chapter, consumer-oriented sales promotions, updates Chapter 20 from the second edition with current examples concerning objectives, methods, and trends.

Chapter 18. A variety of new examples of point-of-purchase communications are included in this revised version of Chapter 16. A major new addition is the inclusion of a broadened section on packaging and brand naming, material that had been presented in Chapter 3 of the last edition.

Chapter 19. The treatment of direct marketing communications in this chapter updates and expands on the coverage in Chapter 15 of the second edition.

Chapter 20. Public relations and sponsorship marketing are the topics of this revised chapter. The coverage of public relations is improved with new illustrations and recent examples.

Chapters 21 and 22. The treatment of personal selling and sales management in these chapters corresponds to their coverage in the second edition. The changes and updates in these new chapters provide students with a much better understanding of the nature and importance of personal selling and sales management.

ACKNOWLEDGMENTS

I am grateful to a number of people for their assistance in this project. I sincerely appreciate the thoughtful comments from the following people, who provided constructive feedback regarding their experiences in using the second edition:

Craig Andrews, *Marquette University;* Charles S. Areni, *Texas Tech University;* Guy R. Banville, *Creighton University;* Barbara M. Brown, *San Jose State University;* Gordon C. Bruner II, *Southern Illinois University;* P. Everett Fergenson, *Iona College;* James Finch, *University of Wisconsin—La Crosse;* Linda L. Golden, *University of Texas at Austin;* Clayton Hillyer, *University of Connecticut;* Patricia F. Kennedy, *University of Nebraska;* Russell Laczniak, *Iowa State University;* Monle Lee, *Indiana University—South Bend;* J. Daniel Lindley, *Bentley College;* Therese A. Maskulka, *Lehigh University;* Darrel D. Muehling, *Washington State University;* Darrel Nasalroad, *University of Central Oklahoma;* Jeffrey Stoltman, *Wayne State University;* John A. Taylor, *Brigham Young University;* Carolyn Tripp, *Western Illinois University;* Josh Wiener, *Oklahoma State University.*

Also greatly appreciated are the many valuable suggestions made by reviewers of the first and second editions:

Newell Chiesl, *Indiana State University;* Robert Dyer, *George Washington University;* Denise Essman, *Drake University;* Stephen Grove, *Clemson University;* Robert Harmon, *Portland State University;* Ronald Hill, *Villanova University;* Geoffrey Lantos, *Bentley College;* John McDonald, *Market Opinion Research;* John Mowen, *Oklahoma State University;* Kent Nakamoto, *University of California, Los Angeles;* Edward Riordan, *Wayne State University;* Alan Sawyer, *University of Florida;* Stanley Scott, *Boise State University;* Douglas Stayman, *Cornell University;* and Linda Swayne, *University of North Carolina, Charlotte.*

Several other individuals deserve special thanks. Craig Andrews (Marquette University), Paula Bone (West Virginia University), and Elnora Stuart (Winthrop University) are former Ph.D. students who have shared with me their experiences in using the textbook and have provided useful suggestions for change. Angie Davis provided invaluable assistance on the second edition.

Finally, my great appreciation goes out to Lyn Keeney Hastert, Bill Teague, Jennifer Johnson, Marilyn Williams, Nick Welch, Annette Coolidge, and Steven Lunetta at The Dryden Press for their understanding, cooperation, and expertise throughout this project.

Terence A. Shimp
University of South Carolina
August 1992

ABOUT THE AUTHOR

Terence A. Shimp, D.B.A. (University of Maryland), is Professor of Marketing and Distinguished Foundation Fellow in the College of Business Administration, University of South Carolina, Columbia. Professor Shimp teaches undergraduate and graduate courses in marketing communications and research philosophy and methods. He has published widely in the areas of marketing, consumer behavior, and advertising. His work has been published in the *Journal of Consumer Research, Journal of Marketing Research, Journal of Marketing, Journal of Advertising Research, Journal of Advertising,* and elsewhere.

Professor Shimp is President-Elect of the Association for Consumer Research and President of the *Journal of Consumer Research Policy Board.* He is on the editorial boards of five journals.

CONTENTS

INTRODUCTION

Part 1 introduces the student to the fundamentals of promotion management and integrated marketing communications. **Chapter 1** overviews the nature of marketing communications and promotion management and discusses their importance in modern marketing. The section  on the three modes of marketing provides a conceptual framework for understanding the various forms of marketing communications and the interrelationships among them. Chapter 1 emphasizes the importance of integrating all marketing communications elements rather than treating them as separate and independent practices.

Chapter 2 helps the student understand the fundamental and underlying concepts of communications. The chapter discusses the basic elements of the communications process, explains the definition and dimensions of meaning, describes how meaning is learned, and presents a semiotics perspective on marketing communications. Each of these topics is related to marketing communications and promotion through illustrations and examples.

CHAPTER ONE

Overview of
Promotion Management and
Integrated Marketing Communications

WHEN KNOWING THE CONSUMER IS AN OBSESSION

Americans annually consume an average of six pounds of potato chips per person. The choices of flavors, sizes, and brands are voluminous. Competition is intense and consumers are persnickety. How does a company successfully compete in such a market? Frito-Lay, owned by PepsiCo, is an illustrious example. The marketing people at Frito-Lay realize that the secret is to thoroughly understand what people want and to successfully communicate that understanding. Their effort to know the consumer has paid off in earning approximately one-third share of U.S. potato chip sales.

   Here are some of the things Frito-Lay does to keep ahead of the competition and on top of consumer tastes:

1. It spends over $20 million per year on research and development and conducts nearly 500,000 consumer interviews.

2. All 10,000 of Frito-Lay's salespeople are equipped with hand-held computers that are used in stores to monitor stock levels and competitive activity; the central office is notified immediately of any shortages in individual stores or of competitive developments.

3. Frito-Lay's quality control standards assure that potato chips deviate only slightly from consumers' preferred thickness and that flavors match what

consumers desire; indeed, each new flavor goes through hundreds of taste tests.

4. Because consumers' tastes differ throughout the United States, Frito-Lay markets different varieties of potato chips in different regions. For example, darker chips are marketed in the North to suit northerners' taste for chips fried longer.

5. Great detail goes into package design to assure that the package matches the desired image that Frito-Lay wants for its individual brands. Numerous focus groups were conducted to identify the right shades of blue and gold for the Ruffles package.

Source: Adapted from Robert Johnson, "In the Chips—At Frito-Lay, the Consumer Is an Obsession," *Wall Street Journal*, March 22, 1991, sec. B, 1.

This vignette for Frito-Lay identifies some of the many developments in marketing that are relevant to the topics treated in this text. Recent years have witnessed a time of unprecedented change in marketing. Four such changes are noted here. First, observe the incredible developments in technology. The use of hand-held computers by Frito-Lay's salesforce is just one example. Other examples include interactive compact-disc players and electronic scanners at the point of purchase. Second, marketers have increasingly realized the importance of targeting their efforts at specific segments of consumers—such as regional marketing in Frito-Lay's case—and pinpointing their efforts so as to prevent wasted expenditures and to maximize impact. Indeed, the 1990s has been dubbed the decade of **micromarketing,** the customizing of products and communications to smaller segments compared to past practices of mass marketing products. Third, economic pressures such as the recession of 1991 have led to budget cutbacks and a corresponding search for economical yet effective methods of communicating with customers. Finally, competition, often from global rivals, has intensified to the point where only those companies that truly understand their customers and competitors can expect to make it successfully into the twenty-first century.

The subjects of this text, promotion management and marketing communications, are key determinants of whether companies and their individual brands succeed. Effective communication and promotion do not ensure success, but they certainly increase the odds. Coverage in this text includes all major marketing practices that communicate with customers and promote a firm's offerings. Illustrative topics and issues include the following:

- How can advertising and sales promotion be better integrated to achieve overall corporate goals?

- Why do companies such as Gatorade pay celebrities like basketball star Michael Jordan millions of dollars to endorse their products?

- What are the characteristics of effective salespeople? What are the best ways to reward and motivate salespeople?

- What impact are growing environmental concerns having on marketing communications?

- What kind of consumer redeems coupons? Why do companies use coupons rather than simply lowering prices?

- Why are companies spending proportionately less of their promotional budgets on advertising and proportionately more on trade- and consumer-oriented sales promotions?

- What makes for a good package, a good brand name? How important are the choices of package design and brand name to a new product's success?

- Why is direct marketing (i.e., nonstore retailing) growing so rapidly in the United States and elsewhere?

- What point-of-purchase techniques are especially effective in encouraging consumers to choose particular brands? What is the proportion of product and brand choice decisions that are made at the point of purchase?

- What is the role of background music in advertising?

- How much do companies invest in advertising? How do they determine how much to spend?

- What factors influence the speed with which new products are adopted?

- What is the Federal Trade Commission's role in regulating advertising?

- What demographic developments have implications for marketing communicators?

- What are the ethical dilemmas that marketing communicators confront?

- How should a company handle accusations that one of its products represents a health or safety problem?

THE INCREASING IMPORTANCE OF MARKETING COMMUNICATIONS

Along with marketing in general, marketing communications has dramatically increased in importance in recent years.[1] Indeed, effective communications with customers is critical to the successful functioning of any organization, business or otherwise.

A major factor contributing to the increased importance of marketing communications is the fact that the various communication elements (e.g., advertising and publicity) are practiced against a backdrop of ever-changing social, economic, and competitive forces. Consider, for example, the following major developments and the implications they hold for marketing communications and promotion management practices:

■ **WIDESPREAD GOVERNMENTAL DEREGULATION OF MANY INDUSTRIES.** Deregulation in the airline industry, for example, has led to numerous mergers and, thus, fewer competitors. These developments have influenced marketing and promotion practices through changes such as increased advertising expenditures and a multitude of special promotions such as frequent-flyer programs. Deregulation in the financial industry has encouraged banks and other financial institutions to undertake aggressive advertising practices and to use many forms of special events and giveaways to attract and hold customers.

■ **INTENSIFIED GLOBAL COMPETITION AND INCREASED OPPORTUNITIES.** Companies have altered their marketing and promotional programs as markets and competitors have begun to span the globe.[2] Advertising goals and budgets are formulated with world markets in mind; media are selected from around the world rather than restricted to domestic markets; advertising messages are often formulated to appeal to consumers in different cultures; and salesforces, which once were located only domestically, are now scattered across various world markets.

---

[1]The following articles are just a few of the many publications that have chronicled marketing's growing importance: "Marketing: The New Priority," *Business Week*, November 21, 1983, 96–106; "To Market, To Market," *Newsweek*, January 9, 1984, 70–72; "A New Survival Course for CEOs," *Marketing Communications*, September 1985, 21–26, 94; "Marketing's New Look," *Business Week*, January 26, 1987, 64–69.

[2]For an interesting discussion of competition in the United States from Asian competitors, see "The 'Four Tigers' Start Clawing At Upscale Markets," *Business Week*, July 22, 1985, 136, 138, 142. (Note: The "four tigers" represent competitors from Korea, Taiwan, Hong Kong, and Singapore.)

■ **INCREASED CONCERN FOR PHYSICAL FITNESS AND HEALTH.**   Rising interest in personal fitness and well-being has resulted in the rapid growth of a fitness and health industry (including health clubs and aerobic centers), changes in eating habits (such as eating more poultry and seafood and less red meat), and increases in the marketing of products that promise consumers better health and physical appearance (e.g., weight-loss products). Consumers have changed how they eat, how they play, when they engage in recreational activities, and what they expect from life and from products. All told, dramatic societal changes have created many challenges and opportunities for responsive and creative marketing and marketing communications practices.

Hospitals, which used to passively wait for patients to show up, now actively promote their services. A New Orleans hospital developed a promotional program aimed directly at men. (They decided to direct their program at men because men are more likely than women to neglect their health care.) The hospital's two-pronged program consisted of (1) aggressive television advertising that encouraged men to seek medical checkups and (2) a force of well-trained telephone personnel who received advertising-prompted inquiries and arranged for appointments with appropriate physicians.[3]

■ **INTENSIFIED TIME PRESSURES.**   With well over 60 percent of married American women now in the work force and with the rapid growth of two-income households, both women and men have less time available for traditional shopping and consumption behavior. The result has been a trend toward seeking greater *time control*. Consumers now are more determined than ever to tailor daily schedules to their needs rather than having schedules imposed on them.[4] The tremendous popularity of the videocassette recorder and the widespread use of automatic teller machines for conducting banking activities reflect this trend. In both instances, the consumer engages in behavior *when* she or he wants to rather than having a television network or bank dictate that time. Now companies are marketing fax machines designed for home use. Among other applications, consumers are expected to use fax machines for placing grocery orders for home delivery by food stores and for making restaurant and travel reservations.[5] There are a multitude of other manifestations of time control, all of which have created further challenges and opportunities for promotion managers and marketing communicators.

---

[3]"Marketing Medicine to Men," Cable News Network's "Healthwatch," January 16, 1988.

[4]"31 Major Trends Shaping the Future of American Business," *The Public Pulse* (a publication of the Roper Organization), 2, no. 1, 1986, 1.

[5]Christy Fisher, "Murata Puts Fax in Home," *Advertising Age*, June 10, 1991, 16.

THE NATURE OF MARKETING COMMUNICATIONS AND PROMOTION MANAGEMENT

Business enterprises, ranging from the smallest retailers to the largest manufacturers as well as not-for-profit organizations (such as churches, museums, and symphony orchestras), continuously promote themselves to their customers and clients in an effort to accomplish a variety of purposes: (1) *informing* prospective customers about their products, services, and terms of sale, (2) *persuading* people to prefer particular products and brands, shop in certain stores, attend particular entertainment events, and perform a variety of other behaviors, and (3) *inducing action* from customers such that buying behavior is directed toward the marketer's offering and is undertaken immediately rather than delayed. These and other objectives are achieved by using advertisements, salespeople, store signs, point-of-purchase displays, product packages, direct-mail literature, free samples, coupons, publicity releases, and other communications and promotional devices.

Collectively, the preceding activities are called promotion management and marketing communications. Promotion management tends to be the preferred term among marketing educators, whereas marketing practitioners typically prefer the term marketing communications. Your text employs both terms in its title, *Promotion Management and Marketing Communications*. It is important that we properly distinguish their fundamental differences before moving on to more specific issues. It will be helpful to first review briefly the concept of marketing mix.

The **marketing mix** consists of four sets of decisions: (1) *product decisions* (e.g., the choice of product design, shape, color, package, and brand symbolism), (2) *pricing decisions* (e.g., price level and discount structure), (3) *distribution decisions* (e.g., choice of channel length and dealer network), and (4) *promotion decisions* (e.g., advertising and personal selling). Note that the last marketing mix element, **promotion,** is the aspect of general marketing that promotion management deals with explicitly. In comparison, marketing communications is a more encompassing term that includes communications via any and all of the marketing mix elements.

Marketing Communications

Marketing communications can be understood best by examining the nature of its two constituent elements, communications and marketing. **Communications** is the process whereby commonness of thought is established and meaning is shared between individuals or between organizations and individuals. **Marketing** is the set of activities whereby businesses and other organizations create transfers of value (*exchanges*) between themselves and their customers. Of course, marketing is more general than marketing communications per se, but much of marketing involves communications activities. Taken together, **marketing communications** represents the collection of all elements in an organization's marketing mix that facilitate exchanges by establishing shared meaning with the organization's customers or clients.

Central to the definition of marketing communications is the notion that *all marketing mix variables*, and not just the promotional variable alone, communicate with customers. The definition permits the possibility that marketing communications can be either intentional, as in the case of advertising and personal selling, or unintentional (though impactual nonetheless), as when a product feature, package cue, or price symbolizes something to customers that the marketing communicator may not have intended.

The definition further recognizes that a marketing organization is both a sender and a receiver of messages. In its role as sender, a marketing communicator attempts to inform, persuade, and induce the marketplace to take a course of action that is compatible with the communicator's interests. As receiver, the marketing communicator attunes itself to the marketplace in order to align its messages to its present market targets, adapt messages to changing market conditions, and spot new communication opportunities. The discussion of Frito-Lay in the opening vignette typifies a company that actively studies market conditions to develop effective new products and communication strategies.

Promotion Management

In its broadest sense, promotion means "to move forward."[6] In marketing, promotion has a similar meaning, namely, to motivate (or move, in a sense) customers to action. Promotion management employs a variety of tools for this purpose: advertising, publicity, sales promotions, point-of-purchase communications, event marketing, and personal selling. To avoid later confusion, the following brief definitions will clarify the specific sense in which each of these terms is used.

Advertising involves either mass communication via newspapers, magazines, radio, television, and other media (e.g., billboards) or direct-to-consumer communication via direct mail. Both forms of advertising are paid for by an identified sponsor, the advertiser, but are considered to be nonpersonal because the spon-

---

[6]*Promotion* is derived from the Latin word *promovere; pro* meaning forward and *movere* meaning to move.

soring firm is simultaneously communicating with multiple receivers, perhaps millions, rather than talking with a specific person or small group.

Publicity, like advertising, is nonpersonal communication to a mass audience, but unlike advertising, publicity is not paid for by the company. Publicity usually comes in the form of news items or editorial comments about a company's products or services. These items or comments receive free print space or broadcast time because media representatives consider the information pertinent and newsworthy for their reading or listening audiences. It is in this sense that publicity is "not paid for" by the company receiving the benefits of the publicity.

Sales promotion consists of all marketing activities that attempt to stimulate quick buyer action, or, in other words, attempt to promote immediate sales of a product (thereby yielding the name *sales promotion*). In comparison, advertising and publicity are designed to accomplish other objectives such as creating brand awareness and influencing customer attitudes. Sales promotions are directed both at the trade (wholesalers and retailers) and at consumers. *Trade-oriented sales promotion* includes the use of various types of display allowances, quantity discounts, and merchandise assistance that are used to activate wholesaler and retailer response. *Consumer-oriented sales promotion* includes the use of coupons, premiums, free samples, contests/sweepstakes, and rebates.

Point-of-purchase communications encompass displays, posters, signs, and a variety of other materials that are designed to influence buying decisions at the point of purchase. Two additional and very integral elements of point-of-purchase communications are packaging and brand naming.

Event marketing is the practice of promoting the interests of a company and its brands by associating the company with a specific activity (such as a tennis tournament or festival) or charitable cause (e.g., United Way).

Personal selling is person-to-person communication in which a seller attempts to persuade prospective buyers to purchase the company's products or services. Historically, personal selling involved primarily face-to-face interactions but, increasingly, telephone sales and other forms of electronic communication are being used.

The blend of the promotional elements just described is referred to as the **promotional mix. Promotional management** is, then, the practice of coordinating the various promotional mix elements, setting objectives for what the elements are intended to accomplish, establishing budgets that are sufficient to support the objectives, designing specific programs (e.g., advertising campaigns) to accomplish objectives, evaluating performance, and taking corrective action when results are not in accordance with objectives.

Thus, marketing communications and promotion management both contain the notion of communicating with customers. However, whereas promotion management is restricted to communications undertaken by the subset of mechanisms cataloged under the promotion variable in the marketing mix, marketing communications is a general concept that encompasses communications via *all of the marketing mix variables.*

INTEGRATED PROMOTION AND MARKETING COMMUNICATIONS

Some companies erroneously view the promotional mix as the sole communications link with customers. This view often leads to *suboptimization* of an organization's total communications effort. If viewed in isolation, the various promotional elements and other nonpromotional marketing mix elements may actually work against one another. Successful marketing requires careful integration of all promotional and nonpromotional elements.

The trend toward **integrated marketing communications**—the *coordination* of advertising, publicity, sales promotion, point-of-purchase communications, direct marketing, and event marketing with each other and with other elements of a brand's marketing mix—is one of the most important marketing developments of the 1990s. In the past, companies often treated the communication elements as virtually separate activities whereas current marketing philosophy holds that integration is absolutely imperative for success, as clearly summarized in the following quote: "The marketer who succeeds in the new environment will be the one who coordinates the communications mix so tightly that you can look from [advertising] medium to medium, from program event to program event, and instantly see that the brand is speaking with one voice."[7]

Integrating the various communications elements seems so elementary that the student may think: Why is this such a big deal? The reason it *is* a big deal is because many organizations traditionally have resisted integrating the various communication elements. The reluctance to change is due to managers' fears that change might lead to budget cutbacks and reductions in their authority and power. Moreover, corporations' advertising agencies have resisted change due to reluctance to broaden their function beyond just advertising. However, advertising agencies have recently taken on expanded roles by merging with existing companies or creating new departments that specialize in the growth areas of sales promotions, event marketing, and direct marketing.[8]

Reluctance to change notwithstanding, an imperative for marketing success in this last decade of the twentieth century is that the various elements of the promotion mix must be integrated among themselves and be coordinated with all other marketing mix elements. Indeed, it is critical in adopting an integrated

---

[7]Quoting Spencer Plavoukas, chairman of Lintas: New York, and cited in Laurie Petersen, "Pursuing Results in the Age of Accountability," *Adweek's Marketing Week*, November 19, 1990, 21.

[8]For further discussion of the resistance to integrate, see Scott Hume, "New Ideas, Old Barriers," *Advertising Age*, July 22, 1991, 6.

marketing-communications mindset for the student to recognize that all of the marketing mix elements are communication devices and that *all must speak with one voice*. The following examples show how the various nonpromotional elements communicate with customers.

A *product* itself communicates much through its size, shape, brand name, package design, package color, and other features. These product cues provide the customer with subtle ideas about the total product offering. Consider, for example, the advertisement for Ralph Lauren's Safari perfume (see Figure 1.1). The Safari brand name (suggesting adventure and affluence) and bottle configuration (with a look of leaded crystal) portray this brand as special, high in quality, and, indeed, fit for consumers who seek adventure and have the money to pay for it.

Price is another important communication mechanism. The price level can suggest savings, a deal, or indicate quality, luxury, and prestige. The experience of a jewelry store merchant in Arizona illustrates price's communication role. During the peak of tourist season, a merchant was having difficulty selling turquoise jewelry. She attempted various merchandising and selling techniques with no success. Finally, while preparing to depart for an out-of-town buying trip, she scribbled the following note to one of her salesclerks: "Everything in this display case, price × 1/2." Upon returning several days later, she was delighted to find that every turquoise item in the shop had sold. Her delight turned to amazement when she learned that the salesclerk had misread the note and *doubled* the price of each item rather than cutting each price in half. It appears that when the turquoise was merchandised at double its original price, tourists perceived it as more valuable and therefore more worthy as a gift or for personal ownership.[9]

Retail stores also have significant communications value for consumers. Stores, like people, possess personalities which consumers readily perceive and associate with the merchandise located in the stores. Two stores selling similar products can project entirely different images to prospective customers. A brand of clothing sold exclusively through "high-class" specialty shops would project a higher-quality image than if it were sold in a discount department store. What would happen to Safari's image if, in addition to being sold in Saks Fifth Avenue stores (see lower-right corner in Figure 1.1), it were also available in Kmart and Wal-Mart stores?

---

[9]This illustration is presented in Robert B. Cialdini, *Influence: How and Why People Agree to Things* (Glenview, IL: Scott Foresman, 1988, 2d. ed.), 1.

FIGURE 1.1   Use of Packaging and Branding to Communicate Prestige

Review This

THE THREE MODES OF MARKETING

To this point, the chapter has presented a general introduction to the nature of marketing communications and promotion management. It is now appropriate to tie the concepts discussed previously into a more thorough framework called the **three modes of marketing.**[10]

According to this perspective, the overall marketing function consists of three overlapping sets of activities, or modes, whereby marketers seek to *manage the demand* for their offerings. The three modes are the basic offer (Mode 1), persuasive communications (Mode 2), and promotional inducements (Mode 3).

Figure 1.2 illustrates the relations among the three modes and presents a connection between the traditional marketing concept and the promotion concept. The **marketing concept** embodies the notion that the marketer *adapts the company's offering to the customer's needs and wants.* The basic offer is the mode that is primarily responsible for fulfilling the marketing concept. By comparison, the **promotion concept** attempts to *adapt the customer to the marketer's needs and wants.* This is accomplished by the other two modes, persuasive communications and promotional inducements.

There must be a meaningful coordination of efforts to satisfy both the marketing and promotion concepts. Excessive emphasis on customer fulfillment (the marketing concept) may lead to unnecessary expenditures and lost profits. Similarly, excessive emphasis on marketer fulfillment (the promotion concept) can lead to disgruntled customers and lost business.

Mode 1: The Basic Offer

The **basic offer** is "the regular or standard substantive benefits which the marketer offers to his targets as a possible solution to some problem."[11] The role of the basic offer is to satisfy customers' needs and to move customers to action by offering superior value in comparison to substitute offerings. In general, superior value results from providing customers with more wanted gains or fewer unwanted costs. There are two components to the basic offer: (1) the product itself and (2) associated terms of sale.

To illustrate how the basic offer can be improved by changing **the product itself,** consider the case of watermelons and some of the traditional problems with this product. In years past, watermelons fit nicely into Americans' summertime lifestyles: families tended to be large, and people spent much more time outdoors during the summer months. A watermelon was sliced and split among family members and friends, who then discarded the watermelon seeds on the ground as they ate their slice.

---

[10]Eugene R. Beem and H. Jay Shaffer, *Triggers to Customer Action—Some Elements in a Theory of Promotional Inducement* (Cambridge, MA: Marketing Science Institute, December 1981, Report No. 81–106).

[11]Ibid., 4.

FIGURE 1.2

The Three Modes of Marketing

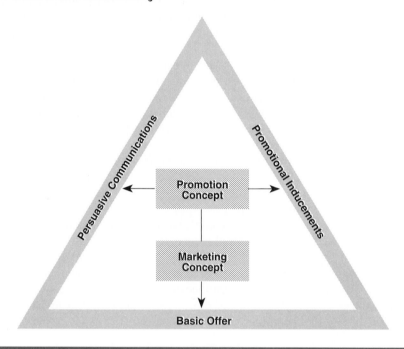

Source: Adapted from Eugene R. Beem and H. Jay Shaffer, *Triggers to Customer Action—Some Elements in a Theory of Promotional Inducement.* (Cambridge, MA: Marketing Science Institute, December 1981), p. 8. Reprinted with permission.

American society has changed dramatically over the past two decades, and watermelon sales have plummeted. The culprits are twofold: (1) today's families are smaller and have no need for an average-sized melon weighing 22 to 25 pounds; and (2) people today, who tend to spend less time outdoors, find eating watermelon indoors messy because of the seeds.

The watermelon industry has responded by altering the basic offer. Researchers have produced mini-sized seedless melons, which are advertised by emphasizing watermelon's high vitamin-C content, low calories, and good taste. The industry hopes that the new mini-sized and seedless watermelons will bring the fruit indoors, possibly making it a year-round item rather than a product that is consumed once a year at the annual family picnic.[12] The *Global Focus* provides an example of enhancing the basic offer by providing a technologically advanced package.

[12]Adapted from Hannah Miller, "Seedless Watermelons Sprout," *Advertising Age*, May 16, 1988, 66S.

GLOBAL FOCUS

THE USE OF PACKAGING TO ENHANCE THE BASIC OFFER

Guiness is a brand name that is well-known and respected by beer drinkers around the world. The Guiness brewery in Ireland dates back to the 1700s. Guiness stout is best known for the creamy head that tops a pint glass when poured from the tap of a keg. Remove the creamy head and Guiness beer is no longer Guiness; it's just another beer. Now comes the interesting question: How do you package Guiness stout in a can and still produce the famous creamy head? This may seem a simple matter to us laypeople, but for packaging engineers at Guiness it took years to develop a special can that would produce a head like the one produced from a tap.

Why the interest in developing such a package? The answer is simple: sales of draft beer (or draught beer in Britain) have experienced a boom. Consumers in Great Britain are increasingly drinking beer at home and not just in pubs; moreover, sales of draft beer have increased rather dramatically in the United States. For example, total U.S. beer sales fell by over 2 percent in 1991, while sales of Miller Genuine Draft increased by 10 percent and Busch Light Draft jumped by 40 percent.

To produce a creamy head from a can, Guiness' packaging engineers developed the "smoothifier," a device inserted at the bottom of each 14.9-ounce can that turns the can into a mini keg. When the top is opened, the can is pressurized with a gas mixture of 75 percent nitrogen and 25 percent carbon dioxide. The resulting agitation results in the creation of tight, swirling bubbles which form the thick Guiness head.

The new product, called Pub Draught Guiness, has been a huge success in the United Kingdom. Also, test market results in the United States (in San Francisco, Chicago, and Washington, D.C.) far exceeded projected volume.

We see in this success story a situation where the basic offer is much more than the actual substance consumed, which in this case is the beer itself. Rather, the basic offer includes the substance *plus* its package, brand name, and associated terms of sale. For example, distribution permitting, you may be able to enjoy Pub Draught Guiness beer, but you will have to pay $1.50 per can or $6.00 for a four-pack.

Source: Adapted from Eric Hollreiser, "Keg in a Can," *Adweek's Marketing Week,* January 20, 1992, 41, 44.

The basic offer also can be enhanced by improving the **terms of sale,** which includes price, credit terms, warranties, and availability and delivery promises. It is not the product per se that people buy, or refuse to buy, but rather the product as *augmented* by its terms of sale. Easy credit terms, attractive warranties, and speedy delivery all serve to enhance the basic offer. Home-delivery pizza services have experienced rapid growth, not just because the pizza is good but also because of the convenience of not having to leave your home, apartment, or dormitory. The warranty is another way to augment the basic offer. The Oldsmobile Edge (see Figure 1.3) is an innovative program that augments the basic offer in several ways: by giving the consumer a trial period of 30 days or 1,500 miles to test the automobile and return it if not completely satisfied; by providing a warranty that extends for 3 years or 50,000 miles; and by offering a 24-hour roadside assistance service that takes care of road breakdowns (such as flat tires) without cost to the owner.

Another illustration of augmenting the basic offer through terms of sale is a program from Sears, Roebuck and Co., called KidVantage. The KidVantage program has terms whereby Sears replaces any clothing a child wears out provided the child's clothing size has not changed. KidVantage also offers a discount program to encourage repeat purchasing. Discounts are offered on the next purchase of children's clothing for consumers who on a previous occasion purchased more than $50 of children's clothing from Sears.[13]

A final and particularly innovative approach to enhance the basic offer is presented in the following *Focus on Promotion.*

Mode 2: Persuasive Communications

Mode 2, **persuasive communications,** consists of various forms of messages designed to enhance customers' impressions of the basic offer.[14] Persuasive communications consist of *impersonal verbal* messages (advertising and publicity), *personal verbal* messages (personal selling and word-of-mouth), and *nonverbal* messages (such as branding and packaging cues).

Whereas the basic offer is designed to meet customer needs, persuasive communications are intended to *stimulate wants* by encouraging customers to

---

[13]"Sears to Guarantee Kids' Clothes," *Marketing News*, August 19, 1991, 7.

[14]Beem and Shaffer, 6.

Use of Warranty to Augment the Basic Offer   FIGURE 1.3

Jump into just any new car or truck and who knows where you'll land. Jump into a new Oldsmobile® and you'll land with the most comprehensive owner satisfaction program in the industry, the Oldsmobile Edge. No other automaker gives you the protection of Guaranteed Satisfaction, Bumper-to-Bumper Plus Warranty and 24-hour Roadside Assistance, as standard equipment on all retail sales.

We're so confident you'll love your new Oldsmobile, we'll give you up to 30 days or 1,500 miles, whichever comes first, to return it for any reason.* You'll be given credit toward the purchase of another new 1991 Oldsmobile.

Our Bumper-to-Bumper Plus Warranty covers your new Olds for 3 years or 50,000 miles, whichever comes first.**

And with 24-hour Roadside Assistance, you can get help anywhere in North America, any time of day or night. So, for instance, if you ever find yourself with a flat tire or out of gas, you won't be out of luck. Just call our toll-free hotline and we'll send someone out at no extra charge.†

So before you jump into that new car or truck, Oldsmobile suggests that you look before you leap. For more information, call 1-800-242-OLDS, Mon.-Fri., 9 a.m.-7 p.m. EST.

The Oldsmobile Edge
A New Generation of Owner Satisfaction.

*Must return to selling dealer. See your dealer for details and restrictions. **Tires covered by their manufacturer. A deductible will apply after 12 months/12,000 miles. See your Oldsmobile dealer for terms of this limited warranty. †Roadside Assistance applies during term of warranty. Services provided by Cross Country Motor Club, Inc., Boston, MA, and in California, by Cross Country Motor Club of California, Inc., Boston, MA. See your participating dealer for details.

FOCUS ON PROMOTION

RAIN INSURANCE

Imagine yourself planning a summer vacation at the beach. This is your chance to work on a great suntan, to fine-tune your golf game, or to play set after set of tennis. Of course, all of this recreation and fun will not come cheaply; you will probably be paying more than $100 per day for this once-a-year opportunity.

You arrive at your vacation destination. The hotel is great, right on the beach. You awaken early with plans of walking on the beach and watching the sunrise. But your plans are dashed when you see that it is pouring rain. Returning to your room, you hear what the weather forecaster has to say. Bad news; rain all day today and tomorrow with chances of thunderstorms the remainder of the week. Your golfing plans are ruined; forget the suntan; what a waste of money.

Hopefully this has never happened to you. But it has to thousands of other beachgoers. To offset the loss of vacation money, one resourceful resort operation (Sands Oceanfront Resorts of Myrtle Beach, SC) is offering rain insurance backed by Lloyd's of London. Insurance purchasers pay a $5 premium for every $100 of coverage. The insuree receives a payment of up to $500 if it rains half of the day during daylight hours. This offer certainly cannot make up for a day of lost fun at the beach; yet an insurance payoff of 20-to-1 takes some of the misery out of the loss.

Source: Adapted from Hannah Miller, "Rain, Rain Go Away," *Advertising Age*, April 15, 1991, 8.

imagine the benefits of the basic offer. Marketers attempt to stimulate wants by supplying *facts* or by appealing to the customer's *fancy* (imagination).[15]

An advertisement for the Magnavox EasyCam 8 camcorder illustrates an *appeal to fact* in persuasive communications (see Figure 1.4). The advertising copy presents one reason after another for purchasing this product.

---

[15]Beem and Shaffer, *Triggers to Customer Action*, p. 9, use the fact versus fancy terminology. Similar distinctions in the marketing literature use factual versus evaluative and objective versus subjective. For more discussion, see Ivan L. Preston, "Contrasting Types of Advertising Content—A Case of Terminology Gone Wild," in *Proceedings of the 1987 Conference of the American Academy of Advertising*, ed. Florence Feasley (Columbia, SC: American Academy of Advertising, 1987), R25–R30.

Use of Fact to Persuade FIGURE 1.4

By comparison, Figure 1.5 illustrates an *appeal to fancy* in its attempt to encourage readers to purchase a Hummel figurine for a spouse or perhaps a special friend. The contemplative, expectant mother thinks about how she will break the news of her pregnancy to her husband and imagines how he might respond upon learning that a new addition will enter their lives. This special moment no doubt reminds many mothers of their own pregnancies and excites the imagination of mothers-to-be. There is no need for this advertisement to talk about specific product features such as was done in the Magnavox ad; readers are persuaded merely by drawing on their own imaginations.

Mode 3: Promotional Inducements

Promotional inducements comprise "extra substantive benefits, beyond the benefits of the basic offer, intended to motivate particular customer actions."[16] *Promotional inducements* is a descriptive way of referring to what is more commonly called sales promotion. Marketing practitioners use three forms of promotional inducements: those representing the *character of the basic offer* (free samples, trial usage, extra goods at the same price), *price-related inducements* (discounts, money-off coupons, trade allowances for dealers), and *inducements that are external to the basic offer* (premiums, contests, trading stamps).

The purpose of all three forms of promotional inducements is to *induce retailers and consumers to adopt the marketer's plan of action.* In the case of retailers, this means stocking more of the marketer's product, providing better display space, and promoting the marketer's product more aggressively. In the case of consumers, this means buying more of the marketer's product, buying it sooner than originally planned, and buying it more frequently. Marketers induce these actions by providing retailers and consumers with rewards such as price savings and free merchandise.

Figures 1.6 and 1.7 illustrate promotional inducements. A standard *price inducement* is reflected in the advertisement for Tombstone® pizza shown in Figure 1.6. Included are two coupons for $0.40 and $0.75 off the regular price. The subheadline (What Do You Want *Off* Your Tombstone®?) is a catchy tie-in to the coupon offer.

The advertisement for Kraft Macaroni & Cheese Dinner includes two forms of promotional inducement, as shown in the ad in Figure 1.7. First, a *price inducement* provides the customer with a $0.25 savings on the purchase of Kraft's Macaroni & Cheese Dinner. In addition, an inducement *external to the basic offer* includes a free mail premium offer for Cheesasaurus Rex™ dinosaur characters—something to delight every child's heart and to drive his or her parents to insanity until all four characters are collected.

Table 1.1 summarizes the three modes of marketing and the specific components of each mode.

---

[16]Beem and Shaffer, *Triggers to Customer Action,* 7.

Use of Fancy to Persuade

FIGURE 1.6 A Price-Related Inducement

An Inducement External to the Basic Offer

FIGURE 1.7

TABLE 1.1	Examples of the Three Modes of Marketing

BASIC OFFER	PERSUASIVE COMMUNICATIONS	PROMOTIONAL INDUCEMENTS
■ Product Itself ■ Terms of Sale 　　Availability and delivery 　　Price 　　Credit terms 　　Guarantees or warranties	■ Impersonal Verbal Messages 　　Publicity 　　Measured advertising–radio, 　　　TV, newspaper, magazine 　　Unmeasured advertising– 　　　direct mail, catalog, trade 　　　shows, point of purchase ■ Personal Verbal Messages 　　Personal selling messages 　　Word-of-mouth support ■ Nonverbal Messages 　　Packaging of product 　　Inherent in delivery of verbal 　　　message 　　Symbolism derived from 　　　resellers, customers, 　　　pricing, etc.	■ Character of Basic Offer 　　Free sample 　　Free trial use 　　Extra goods at same price 　　Special terms of sale (other 　　　than price) ■ Price Related 　　Introductory discounts 　　Money-off coupons 　　Price specials 　　Buy-back allowances to dealers ■ External to Basic Offer 　　Premium promotions–trading 　　　stamps, contests, 　　　sweepstakes, games, free 　　　gift in pack, continuity 　　　coupons 　　"Free" offers to customers 　　"Right to buy" other products– 　　　"self-liquidator," "commodity 　　　continuities" 　　Cash awards–sales contests, 　　　"spiffs" to dealers

Source: Eugene R. Beem and H. Jay Shaffer, Triggers to *Customer Action–Some Elements in a Theory of Promotional Inducement* (Cambridge, MA: Marketing Science Institute, December 1981), 5. Reprinted with permission.

Each Mode Reinforces the Other Modes

It now should be apparent that the three modes of marketing overlap and reinforce each other.[17] As the previous examples have illustrated, persuasive communications and promotional inducements serve to augment the basic offer; reciprocally, the basic offer provides the distinctiveness that persuasive communications can feature and the foundation for effective promotional inducements.

For example, the advertisement for the Magnavox EasyCam 8 camcorder (Figure 1.4) is possible in this form only *because the product* itself (the basic offer) possesses some unique features and competitive advantages. The basic

---

[17]Ibid., 14.

offer also reinforces promotional inducements; inducements alone cannot create product acceptance. The promotional inducement for Kraft macaroni & cheese (Figure 1.7) is designed to encourage consumers to purchase this brand repeatedly, but this will not happen on a large scale unless consumers are satisfied both with the macaroni & cheese dinners and the Cheesasaurus Rex™ dinosaur characters.

Finally, promotional inducements and persuasive communications are mutually reinforcing. When placed strategically in an advertisement, a promotional inducement (such as Kraft's premium offer) can draw attention to the brand itself and remind consumers to again purchase a product they may be out of the habit of buying.

SUMMARY

This chapter introduces the fundamentals of promotion management and integrated marketing communications. *Marketing communications* represents the collection of all elements in an organization's marketing mix that facilitate exchanges by bringing about shared meaning with the organization's customers or clients. This description emphasizes that all marketing mix variables, and not just the promotional variable alone, communicate with customers. Product features, package cues, store image, and price are just some of the nonpromotional variables that perform important marketing communications functions.

Promotion, in its broadest sense, means "to move forward." However, its general meaning in marketing is confined to those communications activities that include advertising, personal selling, sales promotion, publicity, and point-of-purchase communications. The blend of these promotional activities is referred to as the *promotional mix. Promotion management* is the practice of coordinating the various promotion mix elements, setting objectives, establishing budgets, designing specific programs to accomplish objectives, and taking corrective actions when results are not in accordance with objectives.

The *three modes of marketing* serve as a useful conceptual framework to tie together the various marketing communications and promotion mix elements. According to this framework, there are three overlapping sets of activities or modes whereby marketers seek to manage the demand for their offerings: (1) the basic offer, which is the product itself and its associated terms of sale; (2) persuasive communications, which consist of personal and impersonal messages that are designed to enhance customers' impressions of the basic offer; and (3) promotional inducements, which are extra substantive benefits (free samples, coupons, bonus packs) that are used to motivate particular customer actions. All three modes overlap and reinforce each other.

Discussion Questions

1. Offer your opinion regarding the encouragement of consumers to eat water-melons as an indoor fruit throughout the year, as described earlier in this chapter. What would you do to increase watermelon sales if you were the marketing manager for the Florida Department of Agriculture?

Nutritional value

2. Provide your views on the potential success of the "rain insurance" described in the *Focus on Promotion* box. What kind of person will invest in this insurance? Will it increase the number of people who vacation at Myrtle Beach?

Cost conscious people

3. Compare and contrast the marketing concept and the promotion concept. What modes of marketing are used to actualize each? Explain why it is essential to find a proper balance between the marketing and promotion concepts.

4. Explain the meaning of integrated marketing communications and provide several examples of instances where well-known brands appear to have integrated their various communications activities.

Beef, even point-of-purchase

5. Japanese companies now command approximately a one-third market share of automobiles sold in the United States. From a three modes of marketing perspective, explain why Japanese cars have grown from virtually a zero market share two decades ago to their present status.

affordable price - quality - Discounts

- Basic offer persuasive communication promotional inducements

6. American automobile companies often use rebates, a form of promotional inducement, to sell automobiles. Japanese and European companies rarely, if ever, do this. Why not? *priced right the first time, may cheapen the product. Tariffs on imports - can't go over quotas*

7. You have just been appointed VP of Marketing for Chevrolet. Using the three modes of marketing framework, what would you do differently to increase Chevrolet's market share? *good quality product that does the job - media - priced right, not rebates. image*

8. Compare and contrast Reebok's, Nike's, and LA Gear's marketing strategies using the three modes of marketing framework.

9. Assume you have just formed a company to manufacture a new brand of tennis shoes to compete against the likes of the entrenched firms listed in the previous question. What would you do to establish a foothold in this highly competitive industry?

10. What is the basic offer that your college or university presents to students? What persuasive communications does it use to recruit students? Does it use any promotional inducements?

CHAPTER TWO

The Communications Process and the Meaning of Meaning

IS IT "FLIP YOUR BIC" OR "SPRITZ YOUR BIC"?

Several years ago the Bic Corporation introduced pocket-sized perfume spritzers to the United States. The product was heralded by Bic officials as the first inexpensive, quality French perfume. The spritzers, which came in scents with names such as Parfum Bic Jour and Parfum Bic Sport, were packaged in the same shape as Bic's highly successful disposable cigarette lighters.

An initial promotional campaign was split between $15 million on advertising and $7 million on sales promotions. The theme of the campaign was "Four crazy little pocket perfumes. From Paris straight to you." Advertisements carrying this theme appeared in twenty major magazines, and television commercials were run on the three big networks and major cable stations. Sales promotions backed up the advertising by offering a $35 French scarf for only $5 with any Bic perfume purchase. Ten million scent strips were made available in stores so that consumers could sample the product.

Public-relations efforts generated further promotion for Bic's pocket-sized perfumes. Video news releases were made available to 150 television stations in the United States and Canada. These news releases generated influential air time at no cost to the Bic Corporation, except for the expense of developing the videos. Special-event marketing also took place by promoting the product in shopping malls and at fashion shows.

Company officials projected first-year sales of $15 million and sales between $50 to $100 million over the long term. The product never achieved these ambitious goals. In fact, company profits fell by over 20 percent, largely due to the perfume's poor sales performance. Experts posited that sales would have been better had the product been marketed more like a perfume than a cigarette lighter. As mentioned, the perfume's package resembled the traditional Bic lighter. In the final analysis, the close association between Bic lighters and Bic perfumes left consumers unclear as to the specific meaning and image of this perhaps overextended brand.

Source: Adapted from Pat Sloan, "$22M Campaign Urges: Spritz Your Bic," *Advertising Age*, February 20, 1989, 3, 69; Cara Appelbaum, "Overextending a Brand," *Adweek's Marketing Week*, November 5, 1990, 21.

The preceding vignette for Bic Parfum describes an unfortunate outcome for an otherwise successful company. It also illustrates many of the topics covered in this text—advertising, sales promotion, public relations, and package design—all of which involve *communicating* with a company's prospective or current customers to convey desired *meanings*. Therefore, an understanding of the communication process and the nature of meaning and meaning transfer are basic to an appreciation of promotion management and marketing communications.

The chapter begins with discussions of communication objectives and brand-concept management, turns next to a formal description of the communication process, and then discusses the nature of meaning and the semiotics of marketing communications.

COMMUNICATION OBJECTIVES

All marketing communications efforts are directed at accomplishing any one or more of the following objectives:

1. Building product category wants.

2. Creating brand awareness.

3. Enhancing attitudes and influencing intentions

4. Facilitating purchase.[1]

------

[1]These objectives were delineated by John R. Rossiter and Larry Percy, *Advertising & Promotion Management* (New York: McGraw-Hill, 1987), 131.

Objective 1: Building Category Wants

Every marketing organization is interested ultimately in having people select its specific offering rather than choosing a competitive offering. However, consumers have to want the general product category before they buy a specific brand in that category. This is what marketers mean by building category wants, which is also called creating *primary demand*.

Every new product introduction brings with it the responsibility for the innovator to aggressively promote the product to build consumer wants. For example, as mentioned in Chapter 1, consumers are becoming increasingly concerned with their health and physical well-being. Marketers have successfully created health-related category wants for many food items that are fiber-enriched, fat-free, calcium-enhanced, and so forth. Marketers also have been successful in creating consumer wants for a variety of athletic shoes to accommodate the special requirements demanded by each specialized sport. Whereas weekend athletes used to be satisfied with a single pair of "sneakers," consumers are now convinced they need a different pair of shoes for each activity—jogging, tennis, cycling, aerobics, walking, and hiking, to name a few. Beyond performing a specific function, each shoe type is rich in symbolic meaning, a topic for a later section in this chapter.[2]

Objectives 2 and 3: Creating Brand Awareness, Enhancing Attitudes, and Influencing Purchase Intentions

Once category wants are created, marketers compete against one another for shares of total customer expenditures, each attempting to establish *secondary demand* for its particular brand. Each marketer must direct its efforts at creating awareness for its brand and favorably influencing attitudes and intentions. Consider sports drinks. Long dominated by the innovator brand, Gatorade, recent years have seen a variety of new entrants: 10-K from Japan, PowerBurst, Go!, and Mountain Dew Sport, to name just a few. Successfully eating into Gatorade's dominant market share (over 90 percent in 1990) requires aggressive promotion from each new entrant to create awareness for its brand and to influence consumers' attitudes and purchase intentions in a positive direction.[3]

Awareness involves familiarizing consumers—via advertising, sales promotion, and other marketing communications methods—with the company's brand, informing people about its special features and benefits, and showing how it is

---

[2]For an interesting discussion of the meaning and social significance of all types of shoes, see Susan B. Kaiser, Howard G. Schutz, and Joan L. Chandler, "Cultural Codes and Sex-Role Ideology: A Study of Shoes," *The American Journal of Semiotics*, 5, 1 (1987), 13–34.

[3]For further discussion, see "The Gatorade Wars," *Newsweek*, September 3, 1990, 56.

different and hopefully superior to competitive brands. Considering sports drinks again, the issue from the consumer's perspective is: Why should I buy 10-K or PowerBurst rather than Gatorade? If the marketer is successful in creating consumer awareness, consumers may form favorable *attitudes* toward the company's brand and possibly develop an *intention* to purchase that brand the next time a product want arises.

Objective 4: Facilitating Purchase

Whether consumers ultimately purchase the marketer's brand depends on whether the promotion and marketing communications variables *facilitate purchasing*. That is, advertising may generate consumer awareness and build favorable attitudes, but if a new brand is unavailable at the point of purchase or if consumers evaluate it as, say, over-priced compared to competitive brands, then the likelihood of that brand being purchased is reduced. But if a company's marketing communications efforts are really effective, consumers will understand why the brand is higher priced and perhaps will find it more desirable because of its premium price. Effective advertising, packaging, and other marketing communications variables therefore serve to facilitate purchasing and possibly overcome impediments created by the nonpromotional marketing mix variables (product, price, and distribution).

BRAND-CONCEPT MANAGEMENT

Achieving the latter communication objectives—from creating brand awareness to facilitating purchase—requires successful brand-concept management throughout a brand's life cycle. **Brand-concept management** is "the planning, implementation, and control of a brand concept throughout the life of the brand."[4] A **brand concept** is the specific *meaning* that marketing managers create for a brand and then communicate to the target market. A brand concept, or brand meaning, is accomplished by promoting a brand as appealing to any of three categories of basic consumer needs: functional needs, symbolic needs, and experiential needs.[5]

Consumers' **functional needs** are those involving current consumption-related problems, potential problems, or conflicts. Brand-concept management directed at functional needs attempts to provide solutions by communicating that

---

[4]C. Whan Park, Bernard J. Jaworski, and Deborah J. MacInnis, "Strategic Brand Concept-Image Management," *Journal of Marketing*, 50 (October 1986), 136.

[5]This discussion is based on Park et al., ibid.

the brand possesses specific attributes or benefits that will solve consumers' problems. The advertisement for the Gillette Sensor razor (see Figure 2.1) illustrates a functional appeal. The ad emphasizes that the Sensor accommodates a man's need for close and comfortable shaves (the key functions) by virtue of its blade system that senses and adjusts to each face's unique features and curves. Appeals to functional needs are prevalent. In industrial selling, for example, salespeople typically appeal to their customers' functional needs—needs for higher-quality products, faster delivery time, better service, and so forth.

Symbolic needs are those involving psychological needs such as the desire for self-enhancement, role position, or group membership. Brand-concept management directed at symbolic needs attempts to establish meaning by *associating* a brand with people, places, or other symbolically rich objects. Marketers of personal beauty products, alcoholic beverages, and cigarettes are frequent users of appeals to symbolic needs. For example, Marlboro ads invariably portray lone cowboy characters who serve to symbolize that brand as the one for individuals who view themselves, or wish to be viewed by others, as masculine and individualistic.[6]

The advertisement for Lincoln cars (see Figure 2.2) is another illustration of an advertising campaign that appeals to symbolic needs. Unlike many automobile advertisements, this one makes no appeal to functional needs by describing Lincoln's product features and benefits. Rather, it appeals to symbolic needs by directly associating itself with the famous and prestigious Fabergé eggs— Fabergé is luxurious, and so is Lincoln. Other ads in the Lincoln campaign have associated the car with other symbolically rich objects including Ming Dynasty vases, the Concorde jetliner, and famous golfer Jack Nicklaus. In each instance, the advertisers at Lincoln hope to endow that brand with the meaning already contained in these well-known symbols of opulence and achievement. A section later in the chapter elaborates on this by describing a *meaning-transfer process* whereby advertisers draw meaning from the culturally constituted world and attach that meaning to their brands.

Consumers' **experiential needs** are those representing desires for products that provide sensory pleasure, variety, and stimulation. A product such as Levi's 501 jeans satisfies many consumers' experiential needs; the jeans are extraordinarily rich in experiential significance because most people have vivid memories, associated with wearing their favorite pair of worn jeans.[7] Brand-concept management directed at experiential needs promotes brands as being out of the ordinary and high in sensory value (tasting good, feeling wonderful, smelling great, sounding divine, etc.). Look at the ad for Memorex in Figure 2.3. The only verbal

---

[6]This long-standing advertising campaign has been extraordinarily successful. In an incredibly fragmented industry with over 250 brands, Marlboro sells nearly 25 percent of all the cigarettes sold in the United States. See "Here's One Tough Cowboy," *Forbes*, February 9, 1987, 108.

[7]See Michael R. Solomon, "Deep-Seated Materialism: The Case of Levi's 501 Jeans," in *Advances in Consumer Research*, 13, ed. Richard J. Lutz (Provo, UT: Association for Consumer Research, 1986), 619–622.

FIGURE 2.1   An Appeal to Functional Needs

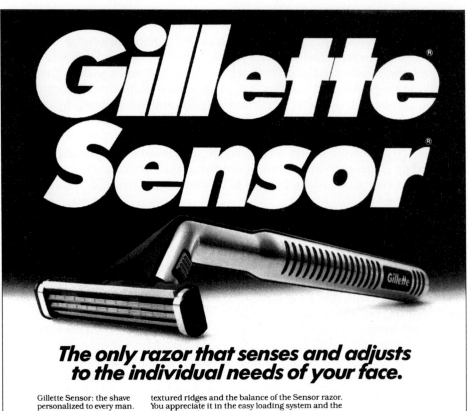

Gillette Sensor®

The only razor that senses and adjusts to the individual needs of your face.

Gillette Sensor: the shave personalized to every man. It starts with twin blades, individually and

independently mounted on highly responsive springs. So they continuously sense and automatically adjust to the individual curves and unique needs of your face.

Innovation is everywhere. You can feel it in the

textured ridges and the balance of the Sensor razor. You appreciate it in the easy loading system and the convenient shaving organizer.

Even rinsing is innovative. The new blades are 50% narrower than any others—allowing water to flow freely around and through them, for effortless cleaning and rinsing.

All these Sensor technologies combine to give your individual face a personalized shave—the closest, smoothest, safest, most comfortable.

The best shave a man can get.

© 1991 The Gillette Company   [USA]

Gillette

The Best a Man Can Get™

An Appeal to Symbolic Needs   FIGURE 2.2

FIGURE 2.3   ## An Appeal to Experiential Needs

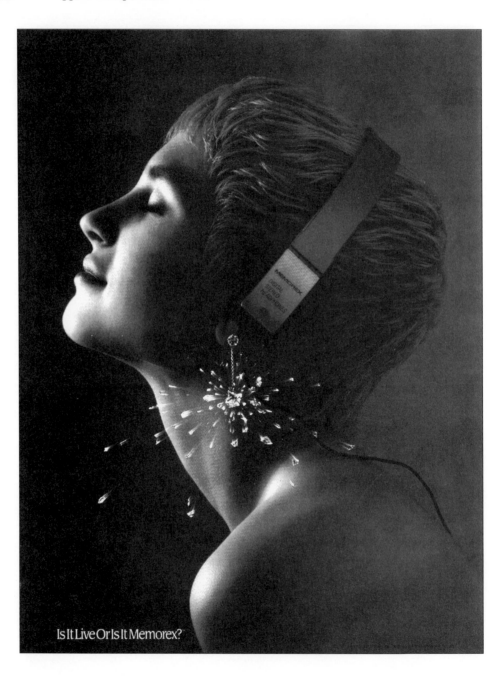

content in the ad is the familiar line, "Is it live or is it Memorex?" The real appeal is to the listener's desire for pure music. The model's enraptured expression and the shattering earring work together to dramatically promise the consumer a special listening experience.

In summary, this section has provided an overview of the various communication objectives that marketing communicators attempt to accomplish. Also described are the various consumer needs towards which companies direct their efforts in managing brand concepts and accomplishing communication objectives. It now will be instructive to review the fundamental process involved in all forms of marketing communications.

THE COMMUNICATIONS PROCESS

The word **communications** is derived from the Latin word *communis*, which translated means "common." Communications then can be thought of as *the process of establishing a commonness or oneness of thought between a sender and a receiver.*[8] The key point in this definition is that there must be a commonness of thought developed between sender and receiver if communication is to occur. Commonness of thought implies that a *sharing* relationship must exist between sender (an advertiser, for instance) and receiver (the consumer).

Consider a situation in which an industrial salesperson is delivering a presentation to a purchasing agent who appears to be listening to what the salesperson is saying but who actually is thinking about a personal problem. From an observer's point of view, it would appear that communication is taking place; however, communication is *not* occurring because thought is not being shared. The reason for the lack of communication in this instance is, of course, the inattentiveness of the intended receiver. Although sound waves are bouncing against his eardrums, he is not actively receiving and thinking about what the salesperson is saying.

An analogy can be drawn between a human receiver and a television set. A television set is continuously bombarded by electromagnetic waves from different stations; yet it will only receive the station to which the channel selector is tuned. Human receivers are also bombarded with stimuli from many sources, and like the television set, people are selective in what information they choose to process.

Both sender and receiver must be active participants in the same communicative relationship in order for thought to be shared. Communications is something one does *with* another person, not something one does *to* another person. A

---

[8]Wilbur Schramm, *The Process and Effects of Mass Communications* (Urbana, IL: University of Illinois Press, 1955), 3.

British advertising researcher conveys the same idea when she reminds us that the question for advertisers is not "What does advertising do to people?" but rather "What do people do with advertising? What do people use advertising for?"[9]

Elements in the Communications Process

All communication activities involve the following eight elements:

1. a source

2. encoding

3. a message

4. a channel

5. a receiver

6. decoding

7. the possibility of noise

8. feedback potential

As shown in the model in Figure 2.4, the **source** (or sender) is a person or group of people (such as a business firm) who has thoughts (ideas, sales points, etc.) to share with some other person or group of people. The source encodes a message to accomplish the communication objectives described previously. **Encoding** is the process of putting thought into symbolic form. The source selects specific *signs* from a nearly infinite variety of words, sentence structures, symbols, and nonverbal elements to encode a message that will communicate effectively with the target audience. The **message** itself is a symbolic expression of a sender's thoughts. In marketing communications, the message takes the form of advertisements, a sales presentation, prices, package designs, point-of-purchase cues, and so on.

The **message channel** is the path through which the message moves from source to receiver. Companies use broadcast (radio and television) and print media (newspapers and magazines) to channel advertising messages to current and potential customers. Messages also are transmitted to customers directly via salespeople, by telephone, direct-mail brochures, and point-of-purchase displays.

The **receiver** is the person or group of people with whom the sender attempts to share thoughts. In marketing communications, receivers are the

[9]Judie Lannon, "New Techniques for Understanding Consumer Reactions to Advertising," *Journal of Advertising Research*, 26 (August/September 1986), sec. R, 6–9.

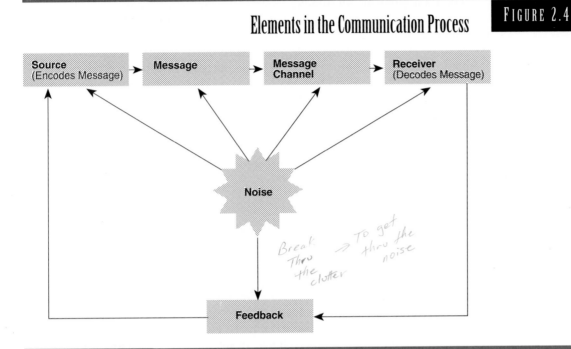

Elements in the Communication Process
FIGURE 2.4

prospective and present customers of an organization's product or service. **Decoding** involves activities undertaken by receivers to interpret marketing messages, that is, to derive meaning from the messages. Because the meaning formation process plays such a crucial role in all marketing communications, the last major section in this chapter discusses in detail the nature of meaning.

A message moving through a channel is subject to the influence of extraneous and distracting stimuli. These stimuli interfere with reception of the message in its pure and original form. Such interference and distortion is called **noise.** Noise may occur at any stage in the communication process (see Figure 2.4). For example, at the point of message encoding, the sender may be unclear about what the message is intended to accomplish. A likely result is a poorly focused and perhaps even contradictory message rather than a message that is clear-cut and integrated. Noise also occurs in the message channel—a fuzzy television signal, a crowded magazine page on which an advertisement is surrounded by competitive clutter, and a personal sales interaction that is interrupted repeatedly by telephone calls. Noise also can be present at the receiver/decoding stage of the process. An infant might cry during a television commercial and block out critical points in the sales message; passengers in an automobile might talk and not listen to a radio commercial; or the receiver simply may not possess the knowledge base needed to fully understand the promotional message.

The final element, **feedback,** affords the source a way of monitoring how accurately the intended message is being received. Feedback allows the source to determine whether the original message hit the target accurately or whether it needs to be altered to evoke a clearer picture in the receiver's mind. Thus, the feedback mechanism offers the source some measure of control in the communications process. Advertisers frequently discover that their target markets do not interpret campaign themes exactly as intended. Using research-based feedback from their markets, management can reexamine and often correct ineffective or misdirected advertising messages. The Frito-Lay example in Chapter 1 illustrated how one successful company invests heavily in marketing research in order to better understand consumers and deliver products and messages that will be well received.

SEMIOTICS OF MARKETING COMMUNICATIONS

The process described in the preceding section focused on promotion management and marketing communications in general terms of how marketers communicate with their customers. Fundamental to the communications process is the concept of meaning. Marketers attempt to convey meaning and consumers receive or interpret meanings, which may or may not be the same as the meaning intended by the marketing communicator. This section discusses the nature of meaning in marketing communications using a semiotics perspective. **Semiotics,** broadly speaking, is the study of meaning and the analysis of meaning-producing events.[10] The fundamental concept in semiotics is the sign.

The Nature of Signs

Marketing communications in all of its various forms uses signs to create messages and convey meanings. A **sign** is something physical and perceivable by our senses that represents, or signifies, something (the *referent*) to somebody (the *interpreter*) in some *context*.[11] Consider the word *pickup truck*. The primary and explicit, or *denotative*, meaning of pickup truck is straightforward; that is, a vehicle with a cab compartment for passengers and space in the rear for hauling

---

[10]For an in-depth treatment of semiotics in marketing communications and consumer behavior, see David Glen Mick, "Consumer Research and Semiotics: Exploring the Morphology of Signs, Symbols, and Significance," *Journal of Consumer Research*, 13 (September 1986): 196–213. For an interesting application of a semiotic analysis, see Morris B. Holbrook and Mark W. Grayson, "The Semiology of Cinematic Consumption: Symbolic Consumer Behavior in Out of Africa," *Journal of Consumer Research*, 13 (December 1986): 374–381.

[11]This description is based on John Fiske, *Introduction to Communication Studies* (New York: Routledge, 1990), and Mick, 198.

people and objects. The secondary and implicit, or *connotative*, meaning of pickup truck is considerably more diverse. Perhaps when hearing or reading the word pickup truck you conjure up an image of a farmer hauling animals, crops, or farm equipment. Possibly you think of unshaven men drinking beer in a vehicle that has a gun rack in the back window. Or maybe you think of a suburban aristocrat who uses the truck primarily for driving to work Monday through Friday and for hauling plants, rubbish, kids, and golf clubs on the weekend.

The same sign, pickup truck, means different things to different people and different things at different times. The image of the pickup truck has changed dramatically in recent years. Historically, pickups were owned almost exclusively by rural people and craftsmen (such as plumbers) and were used primarily for work and secondarily for pleasure, but in more recent times (due largely to effective marketing efforts) the pickup truck has taken on meaning as a dual-purpose vehicle, used first for pleasure and only secondarily for work.

Effective communication takes place when signs are common to both the sender's and the receiver's fields of experience. A field of experience, also called the *perceptual field*, is the sum total of all experiences a person has had during his or her lifetime. Signs contained in the perceptual field are numerous. The larger the *overlap* or *commonness* in their perceptual fields, the greater the likelihood that signs used by the sender will be decoded by the receiver in the manner intended by the sender.

Advertisers, salespersons, and other marketing communicators sometimes employ signs that are not part of their target audience's perceptual field. Effective communication is severely compromised when, for example, marketing communicators use words that customers do not understand.

The Meaning of Meaning

Although we use signs to share meaning with others, the two terms (signs and meanings) should not be construed as synonymous.[12] Signs are simply stimuli that are used to evoke an intended meaning within another person. But words and nonverbal signs do not have meanings per se; instead, *people have meanings for signs*. Meanings are internal responses people hold for external stimuli. Many times people have different meanings for the same words. There is simple proof of this. Ask five of your friends who have never taken a marketing course to define what marketing means to them. You will probably receive five decidedly different responses. The discussion of neckties in the *Focus on Promotion* offers further insight into the difference between signs and meaning.

---

[12]The subsequent discussion is influenced by the insights of David K. Berlo in *The Process of Communication* (San Francisco: Holt, Rinehart & Winston, 1960), 168–216.

FOCUS ON PROMOTION

WHAT IS THE MEANING OF *NECKTIE*?

What comes to mind when you hear the word *necktie*? An initial thought, no doubt, is that a necktie is simply a decorative piece of material that is wrapped around a person's neck and is shaped into a knot. Most people, at least in the Western world, would share this same denotative meaning for necktie.

But there's much more below the surface. Despite the fact that ties serve absolutely no function, the average tie wearer has a collection of 25 to 30 ties.[1] Ties come in a wide variety of colors, designs (geometric, stripe, paisley, foulard), materials (silk, wool, cotton, polyester), shapes (wide, narrow, straight bottom, pointed bottom, bow), and prices. What do ties say about their wearers? What do they mean?

The exact meaning conveyed depends on a combination of factors: the tie's design, its color and material, the context in which it is worn (at the office or after work), and the clothes it is worn with (a suit, a blazer, or simply with a shirt). The necktie sign may connote power (a silk, yellow, foulard tie worn with a charcoal grey suit), preppiness (a silk, striped tie worn with a navy blue blazer), daring (a brightly colored Italian tie worn with a double-breasted suit), conformity, conservatism, and a variety of other meanings.

Men were faced with many new choices starting in 1990, when the rules of tie selection were altered by a flood of bolder and more unusual colors and designs. Newer tie categories include whimsical and clever "conversationals," floral and tropical themes, tossed medallions, and brightly printed jacquards.[2]

What is the meaning of the newer fashions? At least one writer associated the newly exuberant styles with the start of a "post-yuppie era."[3] Several writers suggested that changing tie fashions signal or reflect emerging economic trends. Wild neckties sell when the economy is slow, and bland ones sell when it speeds up. Wide neckties with bold graphics were popular during the Great Depression of the 1930s and 1940s and again in the stagflation of the 1970s.[4]

The diversity of meanings people have for neckties illustrates what makes the study of marketing communications so fascinating. A product as physically simple as the necktie —a virtually useless strip of material—is incredibly rich in meaning.

[1]Lucy Kaylin, "The Semiotics of the Tie," *Gentleman's Quarterly*, July, 1987, 112.
[2]Jules Abend, "Neckwear: Tie It Up!" *Stores*, December 1990, 41.
[3]Michael Norman, "Decision, Decisions," *The New York Times Magazine*, June 10, 1990, sec. G, 41.
[4]See Katarzyna Wandycz, "Recovery Ties," *Forbes*, July 22, 1991, 306–308; and "Fit to Be Tied," *Christian Science Monitor*, October 7, 1991, 20.

If signs have no meaning, it follows that meaning cannot be transmitted. "Only messages are transmittable, and meanings are not in the message, they are in the message-users."[13] Good communicators are people who select verbal and nonverbal signs that elicit intended meanings. Marketing communicators must be especially careful to use signs that will evoke the intended meaning in prospective buyers. All too often companies communicate their product offerings in terms familiar to themselves but not in terms familiar to their potential customers.

Up to this point we have referred to meaning in the abstract. Now a definition is in order. **Meaning** can be thought of as the *subjective perceptions (thoughts) and affective reactions (feelings)* to stimuli evoked within a person when presented with a sign or stimulus object.[14] It should be clear at this point that meaning is internal, rather than external, to an individual. Meaning, in other words, is *subjective*.

Imagine, for example, two consumers seated in front of a television set watching a commercial for a new brand of cat food. For one consumer, the commercial represents a display of adorable animals consuming a brand that this consumer now will consider buying for her own cat. For the other, who is not a pet lover, the commercial represents a disgusting portrayal of unappealing animals and an unappetizing product. It is clear: the identical message has decidedly different meanings for these two consumers.

Meaning Transfer: From Culture, to Object, to Consumer

The culture and social systems in which marketing communications take place are loaded with meaning. Through socialization, people learn cultural values, form beliefs, and become familiar with the physical manifestations, or *artifacts*, of these values and beliefs. The artifacts of culture are charged with meaning and this meaning is transferred from generation to generation. For example, the Lincoln monument and Ellis Island are signs of freedom to Americans. To Germans and many other people throughout the world, the now-crumbled Berlin wall signified oppression and lack of hope. Comparatively, yellow ribbons signify crises and hopes for hostage release and the safe return of military personnel.

Marketing communicators attempt to *draw meaning from the culturally constituted world* (i.e., the everyday world filled with artifacts such as the preceding examples) and transfer that meaning to consumer goods. Advertising is an especially important instrument of meaning transfer. The role of advertising in transferring meaning has been described in this fashion:

---

[13]Berlo, *The Process of Communication*, 175.

[14]Roberto Friedmann and Mary R. Zimmer, "The Role of Psychological Meaning in Advertising," *Journal of Advertising*, 17, 1 (1988), 31.

GLOBAL FOCUS

JAPLISH: MEANING TRANSFER IN JAPANESE COMMERCE

The process of meaning transfer is universal; however, the specific signs that are used to transfer meaning are highly variable. Take the practice of using foreign language or foreign-sounding language for domestic marketing purposes. In the United States, foreign languages are used sparingly in advertising and other marketing communications. By comparison, much package labelling, brand naming, and advertising in Japan uses English names or combines English and Japanese language; this combination of languages is called "Japlish". Products are marketed in Japan with names like *deodoranto* (deodorant), *appuru pai* (apple pie), and *Pocari Sweat* (a sports drink). Japanese automobiles are marketed with English-sounding names such as *Bongo Wagon* and *Cherry Vanette*.

The use of English names or English transmutations symbolizes Japanese people's desire for modernization and cosmopolitanism. The use of English in Japanese promotional efforts involves consumers with a product by investing that product with connotations that the native Japanese language is less able to achieve. English-sounding words and phrases connote positive notions such as modernity. Japanese marketers hope that such positive connotations will transfer to the consumer goods they promote.

(continued)

Advertising works as a potential method of meaning transfer by bringing the consumer good and a representation of the culturally constituted world together within the frame of a particular advertisement. . . . The known properties of the culturally constituted world thus come to reside in the unknown properties of the consumer good and the transfer of meaning from world to [consumer] good is accomplished.[15]

When exposed to advertising, the consumer is not merely drawing information from the ad but is actively involved in assigning meaning to the advertised product.[16]

[15]Grant McCracken, "Culture and Consumption: A Theoretical Account of the Structure and Movement of the Cultural Meaning of Consumer Goods," *Journal of Consumer Research*, 13 (June 1986), 74.

[16]For further discussion, see Grant McCracken, "Advertising: Meaning or Information," in *Advances in Consumer Research*, 14, eds. Melanie Wallendorf and Paul F. Anderson (Provo, UT: Association for Consumer Research, 1987), 121–124.

Japanese marketing communicators' use of English sometimes approaches the bizarre. In beverage advertising, for example, cans are frequently adorned with poetic statements in English. The following examples are illustrative:

Give Cheers to
Asahi Draft Beer! and
May your life be Marvelous.
Natural taste is alive
Asahi Draft Beer.
(From the label of *Live* beer)

Welcome to heaven
As Time brings
softness
found in this can.
(*Mild* coffee)

Pokka White Sour is refreshing and white like Alpine snow.
Its sour taste of yogurt will extend on your tongue softly
 and be a sweetheart.
(*Pokka White Sour* yogurt)

Source: Based on John F. Sherry, Jr., and Eduardo G. Camargo, "'May Your Life Be Marvelous:' English Language Labelling and the Semiotics of Japanese Promotion," *Journal of Consumer Research*, 14 (September 1987), 174–188.

To demonstrate the preceding points, consider the two similar advertising executions for the Alfa Romeo Spider Veloce (see Figure 2.5). These ads for this self-proclaimed "official car of summer" embed the Alfa Romeo in context of two well-known summer artifacts, the Adirondack chair and the Hobie surfboard. Many consumers (especially baby boomers raised during the fifties, who are one of the probable markets for this car) recall the Hobie surfboard from their youths and associate the Adirondack chair with summers at the shore. Alfa Romeo's advertising agency has drawn on these well-known summer symbols as a way of saying that the Alfa Romeo Spider, like the chair and surfboard, is a part of summer. As such, the ad may rekindle thoughts of long-ago summer vacations and the pleasant memories of lost youth—swimming, being carefree, partying, and so on. Oh to be young again!

FIGURE 2.5   Illustrations of Drawing Meaning from the Culturally Constituted World of Artifacts

SIGNALS, SIGNS, AND SYMBOLS

As noted earlier, the sign concept is basic to semiotics and the study of meaning. The term *sign* itself is a bit too general, however. This section presents a more fine-tuned treatment of signs by distinguishing among "signals," "signs," and "symbols."[17] Although it may seem a bit confusing, it is important to note that all three concepts are forms of signs; that is, sign is the general concept that encompasses the three more finely delineated forms.

---

[17]These distinctions and the following discussion are based on Jeffrey F. Durgee, "Richer Findings from Qualitative Research," *Journal of Advertising Research*, 26 (August/September 1986), 36–44.

Signal Relations

A product or specific brand is a signal of something if it is *causally related to it*. For example, consumers have learned in recent years that certain foods are high in fat content and cause obesity and coronary artery disease. Because red meats for many consumers have come to represent *signals* of poor eating habits and bad health, poultry consumption has increased while beef and pork consumption have declined. It is for this reason that the beef and pork industries have mounted campaigns to change people's beliefs and to alter the signaling relation. The beef industry claims that beef is "real food for real people," while the pork industry proclaims that pork is "the other white meat." These campaigns have been responsible for regaining some lost sales to poultry.[18]

Because marketing communicators typically attempt to develop brand concepts that signal only positive relations, it sometimes is necessary for public policy officials to offset these efforts. For example, marketers of disposable trash bags erroneously implied in their package claims that trash bags are biodegradable, even in landfills. The implicit signal relation established was that these brands benefit the environment. The Federal Trade Commission and some states challenged these claims and effectively forced manufacturers to discontinue this misleading communication.

Sign Relations

Signs are used here in a more specific sense than the earlier discussion. Specifically, a product or brand is a sign of something if both product/brand and referent belong to the *same cultural context*. A sign gets its meaning from other items in its context and vice versa. For example, the Polo logo (see Figure 2.6) signifies a sense of high status, financial well-being and even royalty, because the sport of polo is associated with the British royalty. Ralph Lauren was obviously well aware of this when he selected the word Polo to signify his company's products. When buying a sign, one is buying the whole sign context, which brings some degree of truth to the aphorism: "you are what you own."

Another illustration of a sign relation can be seen in Figure 2.7, which is the package front for Vegetable Thins crackers made by Nabisco. The most prominent feature of these crackers is their vegetable shape. It is widely recognized that eating plenty of vegetables is necessary for a healthy diet, so it seems reasonable to assume that Nabisco intended to suggest that Vegetable Thins are

---

[18]Cyndee Miller, "Beef, Pork Industries Have Met the Enemy, and It Is Chicken," *Marketing News*, August 5, 1991, 1,7.

FIGURE 2.6   Illustration of a Well-Known Sign Relation

healthy. This possibility acquires added credence when noting in the bottom righthand corner the conspicuous "no cholesterol" and "low saturated fat" claims, along with the assertion in the top corner that the crackers are "baked, not fried." In short, the package places Vegetable Thins crackers in context of good health.

Another Illustration of a Well-Known Sign Relation   **FIGURE 2.7**

Symbol Relations

A product, or brand, is a **symbol** of something (a referent) when the product and referent have no prior intrinsic relationship but rather are put together arbitrarily or metaphorically. Examples of symbolic usage abound. Prudential Insurance advertises itself as *The Rock* and portrays itself in the context of the Rock of Gibraltar. The rock metaphor symbolizes strength and security. Merrill-Lynch features a bull in its advertising, undoubtedly because in financial circles the bull is a symbol of growth and prosperity.

Figurative or nonliteral language is widely used by marketing communicators when establishing symbolic relations. Three forms of figurative language used in advertising are simile, metaphor, and allegory.[19]

Simile uses a comparative term such as *like* or *as* to join items from different classes of experience. "Love is like a rose" exemplifies the use of simile.[20] For many years, viewers of the soap opera "Days of Our Lives" have listened to the program open with the intonation of the simile: "Like sands through an hourglass, so are the days of our lives." The advertisement for Jekyll Island (Figure 2.8) illustrates the use of simile in advertising. Simile is contained in the passage in the upper left hand corner, which states: "Jekyll Island, Georgia. Like the tide, it draws you back again and again." Of course, the suggestion being made by the Jekyll Island Convention & Visitors Bureau, the sponsor of this ad, is that satisfied tourists return again and again to Jekyll Island, the same way that the drifting tide returns inexorably to the shore.

Metaphor differs from simile in that the comparative term (as, like) is omitted (Love is a rose; She has a heart of gold; He has stone hands). Metaphor applies a word or a phrase to a concept or object that it does not literally denote in order to suggest a comparison. For example, Jaguar XJ-S is claimed to be "the stuff of legends"; Wheaties is the "cereal of champions"; Budweiser is the "king of beers"; and Chevrolet is "the heartbeat of America." The advertiser in using metaphor hopes that by repeatedly associating its brand with a well-known and symbolically meaningful referent, the meaning contained in the referent will eventually carry-over (rub off, so to speak) from the referent to the brand. Kids who identify with sports stars eat Wheaties in hopes that they too can become champions.

---

[19]The following discussion is based on four articles by Barbara B. Stern: "Figurative Language in Services Advertising: The Nature and Uses of Imagery," in *Advances in Consumer Research*, 15, ed. Michael J. Houston (Provo, UT: Association for Consumer Research, 1987), 185–190; "How Does an Ad Mean? Language in Services Advertising," *Journal of Advertising*, 17, 2 (1988), 3–14; "Medieval Allegory: Roots of Advertising Strategy for the Mass Market," *Journal of Marketing*, 52 (July 1988), 84-94; and "Other-Speak: Classical Allegory and Contemporary Advertising," *Journal of Advertising*, 19, 3 (1990), pp. 14–26.

[20]Stern, "Figurative Language in Services Advertising."

Illustration of Simile in Advertising

FIGURE 2.8

Allegory, a word that derives from a Greek term meaning *other-speak*, represents a form of *extended metaphor*. Allegorical presentation equates the objects in a particular narrative (such as the advertised brand in a television commercial) with meanings lying outside the narrative itself—thus the basis for being referred to as *other-speak*."[21] In other words, "allegory conveys meaning in a story-underneath-a-story, where something other than what is literally represented is also occurring."[22] In addition to the use of metaphor, another determining characteristic of allegorical presentation is *personification*.[23]

Through personification, the abstract qualities in a narrative are treated as person-like. For example, the character *Mr. Clean* personifies heavy-duty cleaning ability; *Mr. Goodwrench* exemplifies professional, efficient car service; and *Betty Goodeal* (see Figure 2.9) embodies Toyota's effort to make the ever-growing segment of women automobile purchasers feel more comfortable when visiting a Toyota showroom.

Allegory is often used in promoting taboo or sensitive products that are difficult to advertise without upsetting or offending audiences. Advertisers have found that using personifications (e.g., human-like animals or person-like product characters) makes advertising of these potentially offensive or risque products more palatable to audiences. Consider the case of Rubber Ducky condoms, a product that premiered on Florida and Texas beaches during spring breaks in the late 1980s. The marketers of the product selected the name *Rubber Ducky* to lighten up a serious subject in view of the AIDS epidemic. Aimed at teens, Rubber Ducky condom packages featured an animated duck character dressed in a Miami Vice-type outfit. The condoms themselves were available in colors such as "hundred-dollar green" and "hot pink." Advertising support was based on the theme "protection is cool." Sold in gas stations, surf shops, record stores, and other outlets typically frequented by teens, Rubber Ducky's creative marketing-communications techniques conveyed the very important health message that, indeed, protection *is* cool.[24]

We see in this example the use of extended metaphor and personification. In the same metaphorical way that companies refer to their brands in terms such as "the breakfast of champions," and "the heartbeat of America," Rubber Ducky

---

[21]Stern, "How Does an Ad Mean? Language in Services Advertising," 186.

[22]Stern, "Other-Speak: Classical Allegory and Contemporary Advertising," 15.

[23]Stern, "Medieval Allegory: Roots of Advertising Strategy for the Mass Market," 86. (Stern also recognizes moral conflict as an additional characteristic but notes that moral conflict is less relevant to the use of allegory in advertising than in the historical application of allegory. See Stern, "Other-Speak: Classical Allegory and Contemporary Advertising.")

[24]The details in this description are based on Shannon Thurmond, "Ducky Bills Condoms As 'After-Party Animal'," *Advertising Age*, May 2, 1988, 96. Stern, in "Other-Speak," also used this product as an illustration of the "reification" form of allegory. This article is a good reference for further discussion of the distinctions between the reification and typological forms of allegory and their advertising implications.

Use of Personification in Advertising FIGURE 2.9

presents itself as "the condom of cool people." Because using a real person to deliver this claim would seem phoney to teenagers, the use of a Miami-Vice duck personification overcomes that glibness and allows this allegorical representation to accomplish its purpose.

Another example of allegory is the successful, albeit much-criticized, advertising campaign for Camel cigarettes employing the Smooth Joe personification of the camel that has emblazoned the Camel cigarette package since 1913. Joe and his Hardpack cronies are the embodiment of hip. In the many executions of this campaign Joe is always portrayed as a cool, adventurous, swinging-single type character. The story-underneath-a-story is that smoking Camels is itself the with-it thing to do and Camel cigarettes are the hip brand for guys who are interested in appealing to gorgeous women (caricatures of which are typically included in Smooth Joe ads).

Although there are distinct ethical issues with this campaign (as discussed later in Chapter 7), there is no questioning its effectiveness. From its introduction in 1988 to 1990, Camel shipments rose 11.3 percent and market share increased from 3.9 to 4.3 percent.[25] This may seem a pittance, but every share point in the cigarette industry amounts to sales in the hundreds of millions of dollars.

Wrap-Up

This section has provided a detailed discussion of the nature of meaning in marketing communications and the elements involved in meaning transfer. Perhaps the most important lesson to learn is that marketers utilize a variety of different signs, nonverbal as well as verbal, in their efforts to accomplish communication objectives. In the final analysis, marketing communicators hope to *manage brand concepts* by creating *desired meanings* for their brands. *Meaning is the fundamental concept in all of marketing communications.* Because meaning resides in the minds of people and not in messages per se, it is important to understand the psychological factors that determine how consumers derive meaning from messages. Accordingly, the following two chapters elaborate on some of the issues only alluded to in this chapter.

SUMMARY

The promotional arm of marketing is geared toward achieving various communication objectives. These include building product category needs, creating brand awareness, enhancing brand attitudes, influencing purchase intentions, and facili-

---

[25]Laura Bird, "Joe Smooth for President," *Adweek's Marketing Week*, May 20, 1991, 20–22.

tating purchase. These objectives are realized by managing brands throughout their life cycles. Brand concepts are managed by appealing to customers' functional, symbolic, and experiential needs through effective communications.

Communications is the process of establishing a commonness or oneness of thought between a sender and a receiver. The process consists of the following elements: a source who encodes a message; a channel that transmits the message; a receiver who decodes the message; noise, which interferes with or disrupts effective communications at any of the previous stages; and a feedback mechanism that affords the source a way of monitoring how accurately the intended message is being received.

The concept of *signs* is introduced to explain how thought is shared between senders and receivers and how meaning is created. The larger the overlap, or commonness, in their perceptual fields, the greater the likelihood that signs used by the sender will be decoded by the receiver in the manner intended by the sender.

Signs are used to share meaning, but signs and meaning are not synonymous. *Meanings* are internal responses people hold for signs. Meaning is found within an individual's perceptual field. No two people have exactly the same meaning for the same sign; each sign elicits a meaning specific to each individual's field of experience.

Meaning is acquired through a process whereby stimuli (signs in the form of words, symbols, etc.) become associated with physical objects and evoke within individuals responses that are similar to those evoked by the physical objects themselves. Marketing communicators use a variety of techniques to make their brands stand for something, to embellish their value, or, in short, to give them meaning. This is accomplished by (1) relating the brand to a referent in a cause-effect relation (*signal*), (2) relating the brand to a desirable referent in some context (*sign*), or (3) relating the brand to a symbolic referent that has no prior intrinsic relation to the brand (*symbol*). Simile, metaphor, and allegory are forms of figurative language that perform symbolic roles in marketing communications.

Discussion Questions

1. Discuss the nature and importance of feedback. In what ways do marketing communicators get feedback from present and prospective customers?

2. Assume you are a key marketing executive with Chrysler Corporation. What forms of feedback would be most important to you as a way of assessing the long-run success potential of a new automobile you introduced to the market six months ago?

3. A reality of communication is that the same sign often means different things to different people. The Confederate flag, for example, means dramatically

different things to different groups. Provide a good example from your own personal experience where the same sign had different meanings. What are the implications for marketing communications?

4. Some magazine advertisements show a picture of a product, mention the brand name, but have virtually no verbal content except, perhaps, a single statement about the brand. Locate an example of this type and explain what meaning you think the advertiser is attempting to convey in each instance. Ask two friends to offer their interpretations of the same ad and then compare their responses to determine the differences in meaning that these ads have for you and your friends.

5. How can a marketing communicator (such as an advertiser or salesperson) reduce noise when communicating a product message to a customer?

6. The famous California Raisins commercial humanized raisins by using claymatic characterizations. Raisins dressed in sunglasses and sneakers were shown dancing to "I Heard It through the Grapevine." Explain how this ad illustrates allegorical presentation in advertising.

7. Provide one example each of advertisements that appeal to functional, symbolic, and experiential needs. Then describe specifically how each ad represents the form of need that you believe it illustrates.

8. Give one example each of the use of signal-, sign-, and symbol-relations in marketing communications.

9. Provide one example each of the use of simile and metaphor in marketing communications.

10. In the late 1980s Seven-Up introduced a line extension called 7Up Gold, a caffeinated drink with a ginger-ale taste, a cinnamon-apple overtone, and a reddish caramel hue. 7Up Gold was not a cola or a lemon-lime drink; in fact, it fit no established soft-drink category. Seven-Up executives had high hopes that 7Up Gold would capture around 1 percent of the estimated $26.6 billion annual U.S. soft-drink market. Unfortunately, after Seven-Up invested as much as $10 million to advertise and promote 7Up Gold, the brand had gained only one-tenth of 1 percent of the market. After 7Up Gold had been on the market for less than one year, the Seven-Up Company decided to discontinue heavy advertising and promotional support. Using concepts presented in this chapter, offer your explanation of why 7Up Gold failed.

BEHAVIORAL
FOUNDATIONS of
MARKETING COMMUNICATIONS

Part 2 builds a foundation for a better understanding of the nature and function of marketing communications and promotion management by examining three important topics: theory and research regarding buyer behavior, attitude and persuasion theory, and adoption and diffusion processes.

Part 2

Chapter 3 examines two perspectives on consumer behavior: first, the logical, thinking person as embodied in the consumer information processing approach, and second, the hedonic-experiential perspective of the pleasure-seeking, feeling person. Chapter 4 continues the overview of buyer behavior by discussing the central concepts of attitudes and persuasion. These topics are important because marketing communications and promotion represent organized efforts to influence and persuade customers to make choices that are compatible with the marketing communicator's interests while simultaneously satisfying the customer's needs. Chapter 5 looks at the adoption and diffusion processes and the role of promotion management in facilitating these processes and achieving acceptance for new products.

CHAPTER THREE

Behavioral Foundations of
Marketing Communications

TWO CONTRASTING AUTOMOBILE PURCHASES

Successful marketing communications strategy requires an understanding of consumer behavior. This understanding is complicated by the fact that at times consumers differ rather dramatically in how and why they make purchase choices. The automobile purchase decisions of Doug and Jack illustrate this point.

Doug, a high-level state government official, became extremely dissatisfied with his two-year old automobile and reached the point where he had to find a replacement. He began actively searching for another car by reviewing articles in *Consumer Reports*, visiting dealerships, paying close attention to automobile advertisements, and talking with friends and acquaintances. He knew exactly what he wanted in a new car—durability, good gas mileage, suitable passenger and luggage space, good resale value, and an automatic transmission that shifted smoothly. Doug narrowed the choice to three possibilities: a Chevrolet Caprice, a Ford Taurus, and a Honda Accord. After test driving all three cars and negotiating with the three respective dealers, he selected the Ford Taurus because he considered that model to be the best value for the money and would best accommodate his purchase needs. We see from this brief description that Doug was deliberate, logical, and systematic in his purchase.

Consider by comparison the automobile choice made by Jack, a free-spirited artist who has been driving a Toyota pickup truck for the past five years. Jack had been fully satisfied with his Toyota and was recently overheard saying "I'll hang onto the old truck until it falls apart." To the surprise of his friends, Jack showed up at a party one evening driving a new, British racing-green Mazda

Miata. With virtually no prior thought about buying a new car, Jack, on a whim, stopped at a Mazda dealership one evening after work, fell in love with the Miata, and decided on the spot to purchase it. When asked at the party why he bought a new car and why in particular the Miata, Jack's rationale was straightforward: "I want to change my image." When pressed for further reasons why he chose the Miata, Jack simply stated that the car excited him and brought back a lot of pleasant dreams of when he was a kid in high school.

Marketing communicators direct their efforts toward influencing *consumer choice behavior*. To accomplish this goal, appropriate advertising messages, packaging cues, brand names, sales presentations, and other communications activities are designed to stimulate the intended market to action. Because a fundamental understanding of consumer behavior is essential to a full appreciation of the intricacies of marketing communications, the ideas presented in this chapter lay an important foundation to subsequent topical chapters.

This chapter examines how consumers respond to marketing communications stimuli and make choices among consumption alternatives (such as products and specific brands). Much of the discussion focuses on two models that describe how consumers go about choosing from among the many alternatives typically available in the marketplace. Before describing these models, it first will be useful to examine the general *consumption values* that consumers seek to acquire when making choices.

CONSUMPTION VALUES AND CONSUMER CHOICE BEHAVIOR

Consumers' choices are influenced by five forms of *perceived utility*, called **consumption values,** that individually or collectively are acquired when choosing an alternative: functional value, social value, emotional value, epistemic value, and conditional value (see Figure 3.1).[1]

Functional value represents the consumer's perception of an alternative's capacity to fulfill *utilitarian or functional requirements*. An alternative obtains its functional value by possessing certain attributes and providing benefits. Doug, in the opening vignette, perceived the Ford Taurus as having greater functional value (in terms of durability, resale value, etc.) than the other alternatives considered.

Social value is the perceived utility acquired when an alternative has been associated with a *stereotyped group* such as a demographic group (e.g.,

[1]These values and the definitions that follow are based on Jagdish N. Sheth, Bruce I. Newman, and Barbara L. Gross, "Why We Buy What We Buy: A Theory of Consumption Values," *Journal of Business Research*, 22 (1991), 159–170.

FIGURE 3.1   Consumption Values and Consumer Choice Behavior

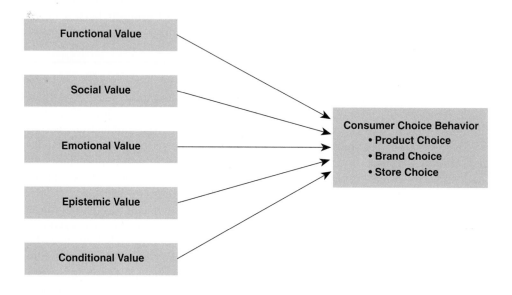

teenagers), an ethnic group (e.g., Hispanics), a group based on some distinct cultural characteristic (e.g., environmentalists), or some other type of group. Regardless of the group's specific identifying characteristic, products and brands often are perceived as more desirable merely due to their association with a group.

Emotional value is acquired when a consumption alternative precipitates or perpetuates *specific feelings*. For example, Jack in the opening vignette may have purchased the Miata because it reminded him of his youth when he deeply wanted to own, but could not afford, a sports car. The Alfa Romeo Spider described in the previous chapter (see Figure 2.5) is an additional reminder of the emotional value that might be aroused by a product.

An alternative acquires **epistemic value** when it is perceived as yielding utility by arousing *curiosity*, providing *novelty*, or satisfying a desire for *knowledge*. For example, traveling to another continent may be valued primarily for the novel opportunity it affords while providing cultural and intellectual stimulation.

The fifth consumption value, **conditional value,** is acquired when an alternative is perceived as having greater utility due to *situational factors* that enhance its functional or social value. These situational factors include emergencies, infrequent events (e.g., overseas travel), and gift-giving occasions. Consider, for example, a consumer who is traveling to Scotland for a once-in-a-lifetime opportunity to tour that beautiful country and play its great golf courses. In this situation, the purchase of a rain suit for playing golf would acquire conditional value since it rains frequently in Scotland.

It should be apparent that these five consumption values have differential impact on any particular choice behavior. The exact impact is clearly an empirical question that can be answered only by conducting marketing research.[2] Moreover, the relative importance of these consumption values varies across market segments and consumption contexts.

Hence, to design successful marketing communication messages requires that the advertiser (or salesperson, or point-of-purchase communicator, or package designer, and so forth) possess an understanding of which values are particularly crucial and how these values can be imparted to potential customers. This, in turn, necessitates that the marketing communicator possess a fundamental understanding of how consumers acquire and use marketplace information so as to obtain those alternatives that will allow them to realize prized consumption values.

Toward this end, the following presentation focuses on two alternative perspectives, or models, of how consumers process and respond to marketing communications stimuli. These are the *consumer processing model (CPM)* and the *hedonic, experiential model (HEM)*.[3] From a consumer-processing perspective, behavior such as Doug's in the opening vignette is seen as logical, highly cognitive, systematic, and reasoned. The hedonic, experiential perspective, on the other hand, views consumer behavior like Jack's as driven not by rational and purely logical considerations, but rather by emotions in pursuit of "fun, fantasies, and feelings."[4]

A very important point needs to be emphasized before moving on to discussions of each model. In particular, it must be recognized that consumer behavior is much too complex and diverse to be captured perfectly by two extreme models. Rather, you should think of these models as *bipolar perspectives that anchor a continuum* of possible consumer behaviors. At one end of the continuum is consumer behavior that is based on *pure reason*—cold, logical, and rational; the behavior best described by the CPM perspective. At the other end is consumer behavior that is based on *pure passion*—hot, spontaneous, and perhaps even irrational; the behavior best described by the HEM perspective. In between

---

[2]For further discussion on this matter, see ibid.

[3]What is being called the consumer processing model (CPM) is more conventionally called the consumer information processing model (CIP). CPM is chosen over CIP for two reasons: (1) it is nominally parallel to the HEM label and thus simplifies memory; (2) the term information is too limiting inasmuch as it implies that only verbal claims (information) are important to consumers and that other forms of communications (e.g., nonverbal statements) are irrelevant. This latter point was emphasized by Esther Thorson, "Consumer Processing of Advertising," *Current Issues & Research in Advertising*, 12, eds. J. H. Leigh and C. R. Martin, Jr. (Ann Arbor, MI: University of Michigan, 1990), 198–199.

[4]Elizabeth C. Hirschman and Morris B. Holbrook, "Hedonic Consumption: Emerging Concepts, Methods, and Propositions," *Journal of Marketing*, 46 (Summer 1982), 92–101; Morris B. Holbrook and Elizabeth C. Hirschman, "The Experiential Aspects of Consumption: Consumer Fantasies, Feelings, and Fun," *Journal of Consumer Research*, 9 (September 1982), 132–140.

these extremes rests the bulk of consumer behavior, most of which is not based on pure reason or pure passion, neither hot nor cold. Rather, most behavior ranges, in metaphorical terms, from cool to warm. In the final analysis, we will examine the rather extreme perspectives of consumer behavior but recognize that oftentimes both perspectives are applicable to understanding how and why consumers behave as they do.

THE CONSUMER PROCESSING MODEL (CPM)

The information-processing situation faced by consumers and the corresponding communications imperatives for marketing communicators have been described in the following terms:

> The consumer is constantly being bombarded with information which is potentially relevant for making choices. The consumer's reactions to that information, how that information is interpreted, and how it is combined or integrated with other information may have crucial impacts on choice. Hence, [marketing communicators'] decisions on what information to provide to consumers, how much to provide, and how to provide that information require knowledge of how consumers process, interpret, and integrate that information in making choices.[5]

The following sections discuss consumer information processing in terms of eight interrelated stages:[6]

1. *Exposure* to information.

2. *Selective attention.*

3. *Comprehension* of attended information.

4. *Agreement* with comprehended information.

5. *Retention in memory* of accepted information.

6. *Retrieval* of information from memory.

7. *Consumer decision making* from alternatives.

8. *Action* taken on the basis of the decision.

----

[5]James B. Bettman, *An Information Processing Theory of Consumer Choice* (Reading, MA: Addison-Wesley, 1979), 1.

[6]William J. McGuire, "Some Internal Psychological Factors Influencing Consumer Choice," *Journal of Consumer Research*, 4 (March 1976), 302–319.

Exposure to Information

The marketing communicator's fundamental task is to deliver messages to consumers, who, it is hoped, will process the messages and be persuaded to undertake the course of action advocated by the marketer. By definition, **exposure** simply means that consumers come in contact with the marketer's message (they see a magazine ad, hear a radio commercial, and so on). Exposure does not ensure that a message will have any impact; it is, however, an essential preliminary step to subsequent stages of information processing. From the marketing communicator's perspective, gaining exposure is a necessary but insufficient condition for success.

Selective Attention

Attention means to focus on and think about a message that one has been exposed to. Consumers attend to only a small fraction of marketing communications stimuli because demands placed on attention are great; therefore, attention must be highly *selective*. Selectivity is necessary because information-processing capacity is limited, and effective utilization of this capacity requires the consumer to allocate mental energy (processing capacity) to only messages that are *relevant and of interest to current goals*.[7] For example, once their initial curiosity is satisfied, most nonsmokers will pay relatively little attention to cigarette advertisements, because the product is less relevant to them than it is to smokers.

There are three kinds of attention: involuntary, nonvoluntary, and voluntary. **Involuntary attention** requires little or no effort on the part of a receiver. A stimulus intrudes upon a person's consciousness even though he or she does not want it to. In this case, attention is gained on the basis of the intensity of the stimulus—examples include a loud sound and a bright light. **Nonvoluntary attention,** sometimes called spontaneous attention, occurs when a person is attracted to a stimulus and continues to pay attention because it holds interest for him or her. A person in this situation neither resists nor willfully attends to the stimulus initially. However, once the individual's attention is attracted, he or she continues to give attention because the stimulus has some benefit or relevance. Generally, advertisers create messages to gain the nonvoluntary attention of an audience, since in most situations consumers do not willfully search out advertising messages. Therefore, advertisements must attract and maintain attention by being interesting and, often, entertaining. Finally, **voluntary attention** occurs when a person willfully notices a stimulus. Consumers who are considering the purchase of, say, new furniture will consciously direct their attention to furniture advertisements. Also, people who have recently made important purchase decisions will voluntarily attend to messages to reassure themselves of the correctness of their decision.

---

[7]Bettman, *An Information Processing Theory of Consumer Choice*, 77.

As this discussion indicates, attention is highly selective. The following discussion reviews four factors that explain selectivity; the first two represent message characteristics and the remaining two reflect consumer characteristics. In other words, attention selectivity is determined both by properties of the marketing stimulus itself and by factors that rest in the consumer's background and psychological makeup.

STIMULUS INTENSITY.   Intense stimuli (those that are louder, more colorful, bigger, brighter, etc.) are more likely than less intense stimuli to attract attention. This is because it is difficult for consumers to avoid intense stimuli, thus leading to involuntary or nonvoluntary attention. One need only walk through a shopping mall, department store, or supermarket and observe the various packages, displays, sights, sounds, and smells to appreciate the special efforts marketing communicators take to attract consumers' attention.

Advertisements, too, utilize intensity to attract attention. For example, the advertisement for Jolly Rancher fruit-flavored candy (see Figure 3.2) catches the reader's attention by highlighting a huge apple against the Manhattan skyline and playing on the consumer's recognition that New York City is known as the *Big Apple*.

STIMULUS NOVELTY.   Novel marketing communications using unusual, distinctive, or unpredictable stimuli are effective attention-attracting devices. Unusual stimuli tend to produce greater attention than those that are familiar. This phenomenon is based on the behavioral concept of *human adaptation*. People tend to adapt to the conditions around them. As a stimulus becomes more familiar, people become desensitized to it. Psychologists refer to this as *habituation*. For example, if you drive past a billboard on the way to school or work each day, you probably notice it less on each occasion. If the billboard were removed, you probably would notice it was no longer there. In other words, we *notice by exception*.

Figure 3.3 illustrates the use of a novel, eye-catching advertisement. In a long-running magazine campaign, Oneida has used novel layouts to advertise its flatware pieces. This particular execution is novel insofar as we rarely see a butterfly perched on a spoon. Looking carefully at the ad, you will see that the butterfly ties in with the spoon's rose pattern and the heading "Sometimes it's nice to fool Mother Nature."

NEED STATES.   Consumers are most likely to attend those stimuli that are congruent with their current goals and needs. A student who wants to move out of a dormitory and into an apartment, for example, will be constantly on the lookout for information pertaining to apartments. Classified ads and overheard conversations about apartments will be attended even when the apartment seeker is not actively looking for information.

Use of Intensity to Attract Attention

FIGURE 3.2

FIGURE 3.3   Use of Novelty to Attract Attention

In similar fashion, advertisements for food products are especially likely to be attended when people are hungry. For this reason, many restaurant and fast-food marketers advertise on radio during drive time when people are leaving work. Fast-food advertisers also promote their products on late-night television. You may recall the late-night television commercials for Burger King restaurants that asked rhetorically, "Aren't You Hungry?" and then proceeded to announce the expanded, late-night operating hours of many Burger King outlets. McDonald's followed with a campaign featuring a moon-headed caricature of a man (Mac Tonight) seated at a piano crooning a rendition of Bobby Darin's classic song "Mack the Knife." Both campaigns were attempts to increase late-night consumption of fast food.

PAST REINFORCEMENT AND PERSISTENT VALUES. People are most likely to attend those stimuli that have become *associated with rewards* and that relate to *those aspects of life that they value highly*. Those rewards and values often are related to the *social and emotional consumption values* described earlier in the chapter. For example, attractive people, babies, idyllic locations, appetizing food items, and gala events are some of the commonly used stimuli in advertisements. These symbols are inherently appealing to most people because they are firmly associated in our memories with past good times and enjoyment and with things we value in life (family, warm relations, relaxation, freedom, and so on). Pepsi-Cola's most successful commercial ever until the Ray Charles "Uh-Huh" campaign showed an adorable little boy rollicking on the ground with puppies licking his face. Viewers could not help but pay attention to this commercial; its gaiety reminded people of their own children or perhaps of their own childhood.

The magazine ad for Haggar slacks (see Figure 3.4) appeals to various aspects of life that are important and good—family, sharing, and permanence of relations. The advertisement uses metaphor to juxtapose these sentiments with Haggar slacks, which, like family, are claimed to be a product that men want to hold onto forever.

In sum, attention involves allocating limited processing capacity in a selective fashion. Effective marketing communications are designed to activate consumer interests by appealing to those consumption values that are most relevant to a market segment. This is no easy task; marketing communications environments (stores, advertising media, noisy offices during sales presentations) are inherently cluttered with competitive stimuli and messages that also vie for the prospective customer's attention. Research shows that *clutter* in television advertising reduces the effectiveness of individual commercials. Commercials appearing later in a stream of multiple commercials and those for low-involvement products are particularly susceptible to clutter effects.[8]

---

[8]Peter H. Webb, "Consumer Initial Processing in a Difficult Media Environment," *Journal of Consumer Research*, 6 (December 1979), 225–236; Peter H. Webb and Michael L. Ray, "Effects of TV Clutter," *Journal of Advertising Research*, 19 (June 1979), 7–12.

FIGURE 3.4   An Appeal to Persistent Values

A beautiful Sunday morning. The simple joy of being together as a family.

Making time for the important things in life. These are the things that last. The things that feel good.

And once you find them, you want to hold on to them forever. Haggar has a feel for the way you live.

Maybe that's why more men take comfort in Haggar than any other brand of slacks.

To find out where you can buy Haggar, call 1-800-4HAGGAR.

Comprehension of What Is Attended

To comprehend is to understand and create meaning out of stimuli and symbols. The term **comprehension** often is used interchangeably with *perception;* both terms refer to *interpretation.* Because people respond to their perceptions of the world and not to the world as it actually is, the topic of comprehension, or perception, is one of the most important subjects in marketing communications.

The perceptual process of interpreting stimuli is called **perceptual encoding.** Two main stages are involved.[9] **Feature analysis** is the initial stage whereby a receiver examines the basic features of a stimulus (such as size, shape, color, and angles) and from this makes a preliminary classification. For example, a consumer is able to distinguish a motorcycle from a bicycle by examining such features as size, presence of an engine, and the number of controls.

The second stage of perceptual encoding, **active synthesis**, goes beyond merely examining physical features. The *context* or situation in which information is received plays a major role in determining what is perceived and interpreted. In other words, stored in consumers' memories are expectations of which stimuli (products, brands, people) are likely to be associated with certain contexts. Interpretation results from combining, or *synthesizing*, stimulus features with expectations of what should be present in the context in which a stimulus is perceived. For example, a simulated fur coat placed in the window of a discount clothing store (the context) is likely to be perceived as a cheap imitation; however, the same coat, when attractively merchandised in an expensive boutique (a different context), might now be looked upon as a high-quality, stylish garment.

A humorous way to better understand the difference between feature analysis and active synthesis is by examining cartoons. Witty cartoonists often use humor in subtle ways. They insert characters and props in cartoons that require the reader to draw from his or her own past experiences and recollections in order to perceive (comprehend) the humor. Consider the cartoon in Figure 3.5 from Gary Larson's "The Far Side." (Look at it now before reading on.) The readily recognized features in this cartoon (feature analysis) are three Neanderthal characters, a mammoth, and a spear that has fallen short of the mammoth. These features are not humorous per se; rather, humor is comprehended via active synthesis on the reader's part. Some people immediately pick up on the humor, while others see no humor at all. Understanding the cartoon requires that one *generalize* to the situation in the cartoon from what happens in a basketball game. Specifically, when a player fires up a shot that completely misses the basket, fans spontaneously hoot in unison: "Airrrr ball . . . airrrr ball." Gary Larson has generalized to the plight of the Neanderthal man who has failed to reach the mammoth with his spear and who then is ridiculed by his chums: "Airrrr spearrrr . . . airrrr spearrrr! . . . "

---

[9]Bettman, *An Information Processing Theory of Consumer Choice*, 79.

FIGURE 3.5 Humorous Illustration of Active Synthesis

The important point in the preceding discussion is that consumers' comprehension of marketing stimuli is determined by stimulus features *and* by characteristics of the consumers themselves. Expectations, needs, personality traits, and past experiences all play important roles in determining consumer perceptions. Due to the subjective nature of the factors that influence our perceptions, comprehension is oftentimes *idiosyncratic*, or peculiar to each individual. Figure 3.6 provides a humorous, albeit revealing, illustration of the idiosyncracy of perception. "The Investigation" illustrates that each individual's personal characteristics and background influence how he or she perceives someone else.

An individual's *mood* also can influence his or her perception of stimulus objects. Research has found that when people are in a good mood they are more likely to retrieve positive rather than negative material from their memories; are more likely to perceive the positive side of things; and, in turn, are more likely to respond positively to a variety of stimuli.[10] These findings have potentially important implications for both advertising strategy and personal selling activity. Both forms of marketing communications are capable of placing consumers in positive moods and may enhance consumer perceptions and attitudes toward marketers' offerings.

MISCOMPREHENSION.   People occasionally *misinterpret* or *miscomprehend* messages so as to make them more consistent with their existing beliefs, expectations, or other cognitive-structure elements. This typically is done without conscious awareness; nonetheless, distorted perception and message miscomprehension are facts of life.

A tragic case that points out the prevalence of selective perception and misinterpretation occurred in 1988 when the crew of the USS Vincennes shot down an Iranian commercial airliner in the Persian Gulf, killing 290 people. The crew, under stress, had been warned that Iranian F-14 warplanes were in the area; therefore, they expected to see an F-14 warplane attacking their ship. They *saw* a warplane (actually a commercial airliner) and shot it down—a tragic case of human error.[11]

An example of selective perception in a marketing context can be seen in a study that examined viewer miscomprehension of three forms of televised communication: programming content, commercials, and public-service announcements (PSAs). Nearly 3,000 people from test sites throughout the United States were exposed to two communication units from a pool of 60 units (25 commercials, 13 PSAs, and 22 program excerpts). Respondents answered six true-false questions immediately after viewing the communication units. Two of the six statements were always true, and the remainder were always false; half related

---

[10]Alice M. Isen, Margaret Clark, Thomas E. Shalker, and Lynn Karp, "Affect, Accessibility of Material in Memory, and Behavior: A Cognitive Loop," *Journal of Personality and Social Psychology*, 36 (January 1978), 1–12; Meryl Paula Gardner, "Mood States and Consumer Behavior: A Critical Review," *Journal of Consumer Research*, 12 (December 1985), 281–300.

[11]"A Case of Human Error," *Newsweek*, August 15, 1988, 18–19.

> FIGURE 3.6   Humorous Illustration of Selective Perception

Source: Courtesy of John Jonik in *Psychology Today.*

to objective facts, and half were inferences. A high rate of miscomprehension was uncovered across all three forms of communications, with an average miscomprehension of nearly 30 percent. Surprisingly, advertisements were not miscomprehended any more than the other communication forms.[12]

Agreement with What Is Comprehended

A fourth information-processing stage involves the manner by which individuals *yield to*, that is, agree with, what they have comprehended in a message. Comprehension by itself does not ensure that the message will change consumers' attitudes or influence their behavior. Agreement depends on whether the message is credible and whether it contains information and appeals that are compatible with the *consumption values* (the functional, social, and other values discussed earlier) that are important to consumers. For example, a consumer who is more interested in the social-value implications of consuming a particular product than in acquiring functional value is more likely to be persuaded by a message that associates the advertised brand with a desirable group than one that talks about product features.

Retention of What Is Accepted and Search and Retrieval of Stored Information

Retention and search/retrieval are discussed together because both involve *memory* factors relevant to consumer choice. The subject of memory is a complex topic that has been studied extensively. Theories abound and research findings are sometimes contradictory. These technicalities need not concern us here, however, because our interest in the subject is considerably more practical.[13]

---

[12]Jacob Jacoby and Wayne D. Hoyer, "Viewer Miscomprehension of Televised Communication: Selected Findings," *Journal of Marketing*, 46 (Fall 1982), 12–26. It is relevant to note that the Jacoby and Hoyer research has stimulated considerable controversy. See Gary T. Ford and Richard Yalch, "Viewer Miscomprehension of Televised Communications—A Comment," *Journal of Marketing*, 46 (Fall 1982), 27–31; Richard W. Mizerski, "Viewer Miscomprehension Findings Are Measurement Bound," *Journal of Marketing*, 46 (Fall 1982), 32–34; and Jacob Jacoby and Wayne D. Hoyer, "On Miscomprehending Televised Communications—A Rejoinder," *Journal of Marketing*, 46 (Fall 1982), 35–43.

[13]Several valuable sources for technical treatments of memory operations are available in the advertising and marketing literatures. See Bettman, *An Information Processing Theory of Consumer Choice*, Chapter 6; James B. Bettman, "Memory Factors in Consumer Choice: A Review," *Journal of Marketing*, 43 (Spring 1979), 37–53; Andrew A. Mitchell, "Cognitive Processes Initiated by Advertising," in *Information Processing Research in Advertising*, ed. R. J. Harris (Hillsdale, NJ: Lawrence Erlbaum Associates, 1983), 13–42; Jerry C. Olson, "Theories of Information Encoding and Storage: Implications for Consumer Research," in *The Effect of Information on Consumer and Market Behavior*, ed. A. A. Mitchell (Chicago: American Marketing Association, 1978), 49–60; Thomas K. Srull, "The Effects of Subjective Affective States on Memory and Judgment," in *Advances in Consumer Research*, 11, ed. T. C. Kinnear (Provo, UT: Association for Consumer Research, 1984); Kevin Lane Keller, "Advertising Retrieval Cues on Brand Evaluations," *Journal of Consumer Research*, 14 (December 1989), 316–333.

From a marketing-communications perspective, memory involves the related issues of what consumers remember (recognize and recall) about marketing stimuli and how they access and retrieve information when making consumption choices. The subject of memory is inseparable from the process of *learning*, so the following paragraphs first discuss the basics of memory, then examine learning fundamentals, and, finally, place special emphasis on the practical application of memory and learning principles to marketing communications.

Memory consists of long-term memory *(LTM)*, short-term, or working, memory *(STM)*, and a set of sensory stores *(SS)*. Information is received by one or more sensory receptors (sight, smell, touch, and so on) and passed to an appropriate SS, where it is rapidly lost (within fractions of a second) unless attention is allocated to the stimulus. Attended information is then transferred to STM, which serves as the center for current processing activity by bringing together information from the sense organs and from LTM. **Limited processing capacity** is the most outstanding characteristic of STM; individuals can process only a limited amount of information at any one time. An excessive amount of information will result in reduced recognition and recallability. Furthermore, information in STM that is not thought about or rehearsed will be lost from STM in about 30 seconds or less.[14] (This is what happens when you get a phone number from a telephone directory but then are distracted before you have an opportunity to dial the number. You must refer to the directory a second time and then repeat the number to yourself—rehearse it—so that you will not forget it again. Telephone companies have recognized this problem and have placed a redial feature on many new telephone models.)

Information is transferred from STM to LTM, which cognitive psychologists consider to be a virtual storehouse of unlimited information. Information in LTM is organized into coherent and associated cognitive units, which are variously called *schemata, memory organization packets,* or *knowledge structures.* All three terms reflect the idea that LTM consists of *associative links* among related information, knowledge, and beliefs.[15] Figure 3.7 presents Jack's (the consumer described earlier in the chapter) knowledge structure for the Mazda Miata. It can be seen that Jack's structure for this model contains elements that relate to functional, social, and emotional consumption values.

The marketing practitioner's job is to provide positively valued information that consumers will store in long-term memory and that will increase the odds of ultimately choosing the marketer's offering over competitive options. Stated differently, the marketing communicator's task is to facilitate consumer learning. **Learning** represents changes in the content or organization of information in consumers' long-term memories.[16] Marketing communicators continuously attempt

---

[14]Richard M. Shiffrin and R. C. Atkinson, "Storage and Retrieval Processes in Long-Term Memory," *Psychological Review,* 76 (March 23, 1969), 179–193.

[15]See Mitchell, "Cognitive Processes Initiated by Advertising."

[16]Ibid.

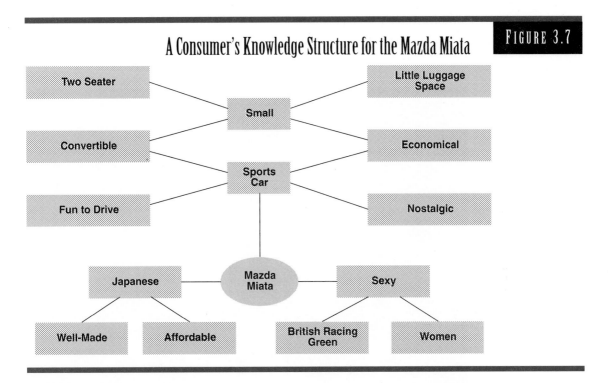

A Consumer's Knowledge Structure for the Mazda Miata   FIGURE 3.7

to alter consumers' long-term memories by facilitating learning of information that is compatible with the marketer's interest. For example, the advertisement for Claussen pickles (Figure 3.8) is an ingenious attempt to have consumers learn two points: that this brand of pickles is available only in refrigerated cases, and that Claussen pickles are fresher and tastier than competing, nonrefrigerated brands that are "parked on a grocer's warm shelf."

Two primary types of learning are relevant to marketing communications activity.[17] One type is the *strengthening of linkages among specific memory concepts*. The Ford Motor Company has invested heavily in promoting the theme "Quality is Job 1" (see Figure 3.9). The purpose is to affix in consumers' memories a strong linkage between two concepts, Ford cars and quality. In general, linkages are strengthened by *repeating* claims, presenting them in more *concrete* fashion (a topic treated in some detail shortly), and being *creative* in conveying a product's features.

Marketing communicators facilitate a second form of learning by *establishing entirely new linkages*. Consider, for instance, what happens when scientists or government researchers report that a product has certain beneficial effects not heretofore known about. Companies quickly capitalize on these scientific findings by aggressively advertising the new product benefits. For example, during the past decade researchers reported that aspirin taken daily in small quantities

---

[17]Ibid.

FIGURE 3.8   Facilitating Consumer Learning

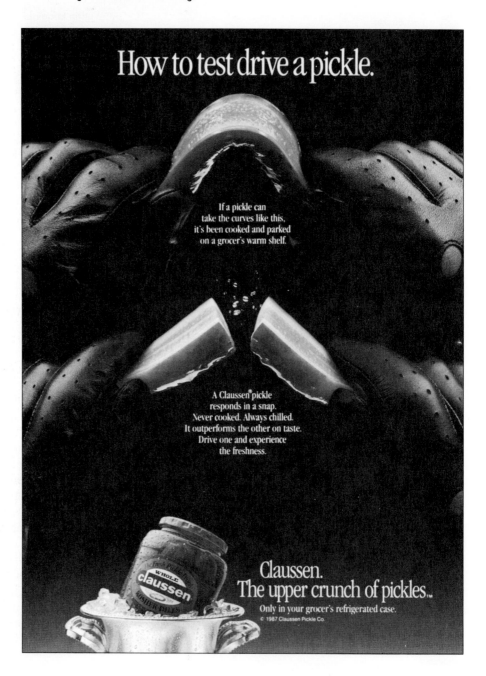

Strengthening the Linkage between Two Memory Concepts

FIGURE 3.9

reduces the likelihood of heart attacks. With this information, advertisers began actively promoting their brands as "heart-attack fighters." This was done in a semi-subtle fashion, but the point was clear: aspirin advertisers wanted consumers to establish an entirely new linkage, namely, that this product has benefits other than relieving headaches.

The category of nonalcohol brews provides a more recent example of how marketers attempt to establish new linkages in consumers' minds (see Figure 3.10). The advertisement for Sharp's (one in a series of similar advertising executions for this brand) is attempting to build a link in beer drinkers' minds between the brand, Sharp's, and the promise that it enables the thirsty participant to enjoy the "refreshing taste of real beer in a non-alcoholic brew" yet "keep your edge." The message, in other words, is that by drinking Sharp's the beer drinker can have it all—the desirable taste of beer without the drawbacks of feeling sluggish. In order for Miller Brewing Company, the makers of Sharp's, to successfully establish this linkage requires that Sharp's basic offer (its taste) live up to the persuasive claim that Sharp's does in fact taste like real beer.

Information that is learned and stored in memory has an impact on consumer choice behavior only when it is searched and retrieved. Precisely how retrieval occurs is beyond the scope of this chapter.[18] Suffice it to say that retrieval is facilitated when a new piece of information is linked, or associated, with another concept that is itself well known and easily accessed. Procter & Gamble used a simple but creative strategy to make it easy for consumers to remember that new Luvs diapers come in separate designs for boys and girls (see the *Focus on Promotion*).

FOCUS ON PROMOTION

THE USE OF COLOR TO IDENTIFY A DISTINCT PRODUCT BENEFIT

Marketing personnel at Procter & Gamble Co. faced a major challenge when they replaced unisex Luvs Deluxe diapers with diapers designed differently for boys and girls. P&G hoped that consumers would regard the specially designed diapers as superior to competitors' brands of unisex diapers. But how could they get that point across? The answer was simple: just take advantage of the widely recognized cue that blue signifies a boy and pink stands for a girl. P&G gave new Luvs diapers two different colors and packaged them in pink and blue boxes, thereby successfully conveying the point that their diapers for boys and girls are truly distinct.

---

[18]A good discussion is provided by Darlene V. Howard, *Cognitive Psychology* (New York: Macmillan, 1983), Chapter 6.

Establishing a New Memory Linkage   **FIGURE 3.10**

THE USE OF CONCRETIZING AND IMAGERY.   Concretizing and imagery are used extensively in marketing communications to facilitate both consumer learning and retrieval of product and brand information. **Concretization** is based on the straightforward idea that it is easier for people to remember and retrieve concrete rather than abstract information. Product claims become more concrete when they are made more tangible and vivid. Examples of concretizing abound. Here are a few illustrations:

1. An advertisement for Johnson's baby powder positioned the brand to be capable of making the user's body feel "as soft as the day you were born." To concretize this claim, a series of age-regression scenes revealed, first, a shot of a woman in her thirties, then a shot as she looked in her twenties, next as an early teenager, and finally as a baby. Accompanying music was played throughout to the lyrics "make me, make me a baby." This beautiful and somewhat touching ad made concrete Johnson's claim that its baby powder will make the user feel "as soft as the day you were born."

2. The makers of Anacin tablets needed a concrete way to present that brand as "strong pain relief for splitting headaches." The idea of a splitting headache was concretized by showing a hard-boiled egg splitting with accompanying sounds of a splitting egg.

3. Tinactin, an athlete's foot product, concretized its relief properties by showing a person's pair of feet literally appearing to be on fire (representing the fiery sensation of athlete's foot), which is "extinguished" by an application of Tinactin.

4. To demonstrate how easy it is to seal a Ziplock plastic bag, the Ziplock "finger man" (an index finger with a face drawn on it) was created to dramatize the claim that it takes only one finger to seal a Ziplock bag.

5. To demonstrate the argument that Tums E-X is "twice as strong as Rolaids," the commercial showed a sledge hammer behind Tums and a regular-sized hammer behind Rolaids. The commercial then showed the sledge hammer driving in a nail twice as quickly as the regular hammer. This nail-driving comparison concretized Tums' claim of being twice as strong as Rolaids.

6. The makers of Fab-1-Shot detergent needed to convey the selling point that the brand contains detergent and softener all in one convenient and easy-to-use package. They accomplished this by showing people in a laundry room listening to "Sweet Georgia Brown" music (the theme song of the Harlem Globetrotters and symbolic of basketball in general) and shooting packets of Fab-1-Shot into washing machines. This commercial enabled consumers to imagine themselves also using this convenient and labor-saving laundry product.

The preceding examples highlight the important role of concretization in advertising. Underlying some of the illustrations, especially the last one, is the use of imagery. **Imagery,** by definition, represents a mental event involving visualization of a concept or relationship.[19] To better understand the notion of imagery, think of the following words: pencil, tennis racket, dancing, duck-billed platypus, satisfaction, and standard deviation. The first two, pencil and tennis racket, no doubt evoke distinct images in your mind; dancing also probably elicits a visualization, and some of you might even possess a visual concept for platypus. It is doubtful, however, that you have an image for satisfaction or standard deviation, both of which are inherently abstract concepts.

Mental imagery plays an important role in various aspects of consumer information processing (comprehension, recall, retrieval). For practical purposes, the issue is this: What can marketing communicators do to elicit imagery? Three different strategies are possible: (1) using visual or pictorial stimuli, (2) presenting concrete verbal stimuli, and (3) providing imagery instructions.[20] Only the first two of these will be discussed, as the third is not used extensively in marketing communications, although advertisers occasionally instruct listeners or readers to imagine themselves engaged in some behavior.

Pictures and visuals are best remembered (compared with abstract or concrete verbalizations) because pictures are best able to elicit imagery. A more formal explanation is provided by the **dual-coding theory,** which holds that pictures are represented in memory in verbal as well as visual form, whereas words are less likely to have visual representations.[21] It would be expected, therefore, that visual imagery would play an important role in advertising, point-of-purchase stimuli, and other marketing communications. Research has shown that information about product attributes is better recalled when the information is accompanied with pictures than when presented only as words.[22] The value of pictures is especially important when verbal information is itself low in imagery.[23]

---

[19]Kathy A. Lutz and Richard J. Lutz, "Imagery–Eliciting Strategies: Review and Implications of Research," in *Advances in Consumer Research*, 5, ed. H. Keith Hunt (Ann Arbor, MI: Association for Consumer Research, 1978), 611–620. For a more recent in-depth treatment of imagery see Deborah J. MacInnis and Linda L. Price, "The Role of Imagery in Information Processing: Review and Extensions," *Journal of Consumer Research*, 13 (March 1987), 473–491.

[20]Lutz and Lutz, "Imagery-Eliciting Strategies," 611–620.

[21]Allan Paivio, "Mental Imagery in Associative Learning and Memory," *Psychological Review*, 76 (May 1969), 241–263; John R. Rossiter and Larry Percy, "Visual Imaging Ability as a Mediator of Advertising Response," in *Advances in Consumer Research*, 5, ed. H. Keith Hunt (Ann Arbor, MI: Association for Consumer Research, 1978), 621–629.

[22]Michael J. Houston, Terry L. Childers, and Susan E. Heckler, "Picture-Word Consistency and the Elaborative Processing of Advertisements," *Journal of Marketing Research*, 24 (November 1987), 359–369.

[23]H. Rao Unnava and Robert E. Burnkrant, "An Imagery-Processing View of the Role of Pictures in Print Advertisements," *Journal of Marketing Research*, 28 (May 1991), 226–231.

Consumer researchers have found that people remember significantly greater numbers of company names when the names are paired with meaningful pictorials. The name "Jack's Camera Shop," for example, is better remembered when the store name is presented along with a jack playing card shown holding a movie camera to its eye.[24] Many marketing communicators use similar pictorials, as can be proven by a perusal of the yellow pages of any city telephone directory.

Visual imagery also reinforces the verbal content of an advertisement to create a favorable brand attitude and a desire to buy. The verbal message may stimulate short-run sales with price-off statements, but the nonverbal message sets the stage for long-term brand attitudes and sales.[25] Thus, a retailer may use more highly verbalized messages for immediate sales, whereas the manufacturer would be more likely to opt for the visual imagery (nonverbal), long-term sales approach.[26]

Finally, effective visual imagery in advertising can place the audience member in a number of imagined or fantasy-like situations that are conducive to sales of the marketer's product. For example, the advertisement may place the consumer behind the wheel of a powerful sports car cruising down a beautiful country road; in a pair of new basketball shoes leaping high off the floor over an opponent to make an acrobatic, Jordanesque dunk shot; in a dazzling gown attending an important social event; basking in the sun on an ocean liner cruising toward the Caribbean; rushing toward an important meeting carrying a new leather briefcase; or delivering packages of food and toys to needy people on Christmas Eve.

There is no doubt that imagery and concretization have numerous potential applications for advertising, point-of-purchase displays, personal selling, and other marketing communications practices.[27] Much of what we feel and visualize internally is what we see. Perhaps as much as 70 to 80 percent of what we learn is visual.[28]

Deciding among Alternatives

The six preceding stages have examined how consumers receive, encode, and store information that is pertinent to making consumption choices. Stored in consumers' memories are numerous information packets for different consumption

---

[24]Kathy A. Lutz and Richard J. Lutz, "The Effects of Interactive Imagery on Learning: Application to Advertising," *Journal of Applied Psychology*, 62 (August 1977), 493–498.

[25]John R. Rossiter and Larry Percy, "Visual Imaging Ability as a Mediator of Advertising Response," 621–629.

[26]Ibid.

[27]For an extensive list of visual imagery "principles," see John R. Rossiter, "Visual Imagery: Applications to Advertising," in *Advances in Consumer Research*, 9, ed. A. A. Mitchell (Ann Arbor, MI: The Association for Consumer Research, 1982), 101–106.

[28]Roger N. Shepard, "The Mental Image," *American Psychologist*, 33 (February 1978), 125–137.

alternatives. This information is in the form of bits and pieces of *knowledge* (e.g., Nike is a brand of tennis shoes), *specific beliefs* (e.g., the Mazda Miata is an attractive sports car), and *evaluations of purchase consequences* (e.g., manufacturer reputability is more important than price when buying sophisticated electronic equipment).

The issue for present discussion is this: When contemplating a purchase from a particular product category, how does a consumer decide which brand to purchase? The simple answer is: she or he simply chooses the best brand. However, it is not always clear what the best brand is, especially when considering that the consumer likely has stored in long-term memory a wide variety of information (facts, beliefs, etc.) about each brand. Some of the information is positive, and some of it is negative; occasionally the information is contradictory; oftentimes the information is incomplete.

The following discussion provides some insight into how consumers deal with the situation described above. It will become clear that consumers often resort to simplifying strategies, or *heuristics*, to arrive at decisions that are at least satisfactory if not perfect. Before describing specific heuristics, it should be instructive to review a decision that all of us have made and which, in many respects, is one of the most important decisions we will ever make—namely, the choice of which college or university to attend.

For some of you, there really was no choice—you went to a school you had always planned on attending, or perhaps your parents insisted on a particular institution. Others, especially those of you who work full- or part-time or have family responsibilities, may have selected a school purely as a matter of convenience or affordability; in other words, you really did not seriously consider other institutions. But some of you actively evaluated several or many colleges and universities before making a final choice. The process was probably done in the following manner: you received information from a variety of schools and formed preliminary impressions of these institutions; you established criteria for evaluating schools (academic reputation, distance from home, cost, curricula, availability of financial assistance, quality of athletic programs, etc.); you formed weights regarding the relative importance of these various criteria; and you eventually integrated this information to arrive at the all-important choice of which college to attend. Now, let's use this example to better understand the different types of heuristics and the terminology that follows.

The simplest of all decision heuristics is **affect referral.**[29] With this strategy the individual simply calls from memory his or her attitude, or affect, toward relevant alternatives and picks that alternative for which the affect is most positive. In the college decision, for example, you may decide that you like a school simply because your friends attend it. There is no need to go through a rigorous decision-making process. In general, this type of choice strategy would be

---

[29]Peter L. Wright, "Consumer Choice Strategies: Simplifying vs. Optimizing," *Journal of Marketing Research*, 11 (February 1975), 60–67.

expected for frequently purchased items where risk is minimal. Such items typically are regarded as *low-involvement* purchases.

Consider, by comparison, the use of a **compensatory heuristic.** To understand how and why compensation operates, it is important to realize that rarely is a particular alternative completely superior or *dominant* over other consumption alternatives. Although a brand may be preferable with respect to one, two, or several benefits, it is unlikely that it is superior to its alternatives in terms of all attributes or benefits that consumers are seeking. (If you're having trouble appreciating the idea that alternatives are rarely dominant, consider the situation with people. Have you ever known another person who is more intelligent, more honest, more attractive, more athletic, more caring, and who has a better sense of humor than everyone else?)

When making choices under *nondominant* circumstances, consumers must give something up in order to get something else. That is, high-involvement decision making most always requires that *trade-offs* be made. If you want more of a particular benefit, you typically have to pay a higher price; if you want to pay less, you often give something up in terms of performance, dependability, or durability. Returning to the university choice decision, illustrative trade-offs are between tuition cost and the quality of education and between size of school and quality of athletic programs.

In general, when applying principles of compensation, the chosen alternative probably is not the best in terms of all criteria, but its superiority on some criteria offsets, or compensates for, its lesser performance on other criteria.[30] In terms of the consumption values described earlier in the chapter, the outcome of compensatory decision making may mean that the consumer acquires, say, an alternative which might yield the most functional value but not the most social or emotional value, or vice versa. In short, the consumer typically cannot have it all.

In addition to compensatory choice behavior, consumers use a variety of so-called **noncompensatory heuristics.** The only one to be discussed here is the **conjunctive heuristic,** which is derived from the word *conjoin*, which means to unite or combine.[31] In using this heuristic, the consumer establishes cutoffs, or minima, on all pertinent choice criteria. An alternative is retained for further consideration only if it meets or exceeds *all* minima. As seen in the hypothetical

---

[30]The best known illustration of compensation in consumer behavior is Fishbein and Ajzen's theory of reasoned action, which states that one's attitude toward performing an act is the sum of one's beliefs regarding the outcomes of the act weighed by one's evaluations of those outcomes. Further discussion of the attitudinal component of this model will be delayed until the next chapter, which describes attitude formation and change in the context of the general topic of persuasion.

[31]For discussion of other noncompensatory heuristics, see Bettman, *An Information Processing Theory of Consumer Choice* or any standard consumer behavior text.

university choice, for example, a particular consumer may establish these cutoffs: a viable school must have a respected undergraduate major in advertising, be no farther than approximately 500 miles from home, and cost no more than $6,000 per year. All schools meeting these criteria receive further consideration.

The foregoing discussion should not be misinterpreted as meaning that consumers invariably use only a compensatory or only a noncompensatory choice heuristic. On the contrary, a more likely possibility, especially in high-involvement decisions, is that **phased strategies** are used—that is, a combination of heuristics are used in sequence (in phase) with one another.[32] For example, after the future university student has applied a conjunctive strategy to eliminate schools that do not satisfy all of his or her minima, he or she might then apply a compensatory heuristic to arrive at a choice from the remaining options that do satisfy all the minima.

Acting on the Basis of the Decision

It might seem that consumer choice behavior operates in a simple, lock step fashion. This, however, is not necessarily the case. People do not always behave in a manner consistent with their preferences.[33] A major reason is the presence of events that disrupt, inhibit, or otherwise prevent a person from following through on his or her intentions.[34] Situational factors are especially prevalent in the case of low-involvement consumer behavior. Stock-outs, price-offs, in-store promotions, and shopping at a store other than where one regularly shops are just some of the factors that lead to the purchase of brands that are not necessarily the most preferred and which would not be the predicted choice based on some heuristic, such as affect referral.

What all this means for marketing communications and promotion management is that the three modes of marketing (as discussed in Chapter 1) must be coordinated and integrated in order to get consumers to act favorably toward the marketer's offering. That is, marketers must design a *basic offer* that is congruent with consumer wants, employ *persuasive communications* that consumers will process and that will be persuasive, and devise *promotional inducements* that will influence consumers to choose the marketer's offering at the point of purchase.

---

[32]Bettman, *Information Processing Theory*, 184.

[33]Martin Fishbein and Icek Ajzen, *Beliefs, Attitude, Intention, and Behavior: An Introduction to Theory and Research* (Reading, MA: Addison Wesley, 1975).

[34]For further reading on the role of situational variables, see Russell W. Belk, "Situational Variables and Consumer Behavior," *Journal of Consumer Research*, 2 (December 1975), 157–164.

A CPM Wrap-Up

A detailed account of consumer information processing has been presented to this point. As noted in the introduction, the CPM perspective provides an appropriate description of consumer behavior when the behavior is deliberate, thoughtful, or, in short, highly cognitive. Much consumer behavior and much of the behavior of industrial and organizational buyers is of this nature. Doug's selection of the Ford Taurus (in the opening vignette) typifies this type of behavior. On the other hand, much behavior is motivated by emotional, hedonic, and experiential considerations. Therefore, we need to consider the HEM perspective and the implications it holds for promotion managers and marketing communicators.

THE HEM PERSPECTIVE

The hedonic, experiential model (HEM) is an alternative view to the CPM framework, though the two are not necessarily mutually exclusive. Whereas the CPM perspective looks upon consumers as pursuing such objectives as "obtaining the best buy," "getting the most for the money," and "maximizing utility," the HEM perspective recognizes that people often consume products for the sheer fun of it or in the pursuit of amusement, fantasies, or sensory stimulation.[35] Product consumption from the hedonic perspective results from the *anticipation* of having fun, fulfilling fantasies, or having pleasurable feelings. Comparatively, product choice behavior from the CPM perspective is based on the thoughtful evaluation that the chosen alternative will be more functional and provide better results than will other alternatives.

Thus, viewed from an HEM perspective, products are more than mere objective entities (a bottle of perfume, a stereo system, a can of soup) and are, instead, subjective symbols that precipitate *feelings* (love, pride) and promise *fun* and the possible realization of *fantasies.* Products most compatible with the hedonic perspective include the performing arts (opera, modern dance), the so-called plastic arts (photography, crafts), popular forms of entertainment (movies, rock concerts), fashion apparel, sporting events, leisure activities, and recreational pursuits (wind surfing, hang gliding, golf, tennis).[36] It is important to realize, however, that *any* product, and not just these exemplars, may have hedonic and experiential elements underlying its choice and consumption. For example, the *Global Focus* illustrates the fun, feeling, and perhaps fantasy that Levi jeans hold for Japanese consumers.

---

[35]Hirschman and Holbrook, "Hedonic Consumption."
[36]Ibid., 91.

GLOBAL FOCUS

THE PRICE OF FANTASY: LEVI'S IN JAPAN

Jeans made by Levi Strauss in the 1950s now are selling in Japan for as much as $4,000 a pair! Wearing old American jeans is a fashion craze in Japan, where a growing number of retail outlets are selling used American clothing. Over 2 million pounds of used American clothes were imported into Japan during the first five months of 1991 alone.

Why the used-clothing rage? It seems that many Japanese consumers have a fascination for the American cowboy and are obsessed with Western style. Clearly, this passionate interest with American fashion is not something easily explained in terms of the CPM formulation. To the contrary, Japanese consumers are willing to pay outrageously high prices in their pursuit of fun and the realization of fantasies. Could it be that many prosperous and hard-working (overworked?) Japanese consumers relish the freedom they envision in the storybook version of American cowboy life?

Some Americans have gone into business to support the Japanese demand for old jeans. For example, one California buyer of old jeans pays between $50 to $200 for a high-quality pair; he then sells them to Tokyo stores for $150 to $500. The store then sells them for around $1,000. (One pair of unworn pre-1960 503 jeans—which designates a boy's size—commanded a price of about $4,000 because this size was perfect for smaller Japanese men.) An Arizona company actively uses TV ads, billboards, radio, and direct mail to attract suppliers. It pays $10 per pair of relatively new (less than 10 years old) 501 jeans that are not soiled or torn.

Source: Adapted from Nina Darnton and Hideko Takayama, "An Heirloom You Can Sit On," *Newsweek*, December 23, 1991, 61.

The differences in these two perspectives, HEM and CPM, hold meaningful implications for marketing communications practice. Whereas verbal stimuli designed to affect consumers' product knowledge and beliefs are most appropriate for communicating CPM-relevant products, the communication of HEM-relevant products emphasizes nonverbal content or emotionally provocative words and is intended to generate images, fantasies, and positive emotions and feelings.

A vivid contrast between the CPM and HEM orientations is illustrated in the differences in two food advertisements, one for Louis Rich® sausage (see Figure 3.11) and the other for Campbell's vegetable soup (see Figure 3.12). The

FIGURE 3.11   An Ad Exemplifying the CPM Approach

An Ad Exemplifying the HEM Approach

FIGURE 3.12

former ad uses verbal content in describing objective product benefits, with the intent of convincing consumers that Louis Rich® sausage is delicious and also 90 percent fat free.[37] The ad exemplifies the CPM approach in that it attempts to move the consumer through all the CPM stages discussed previously. That is, Louis Rich® expects the consumer to attend the message arguments (especially the claim of 90 percent fat free), agree with them, retain them in memory, use this information to form a favorable attitude, and, ultimately, choose this brand over competitive offerings.

Comparatively, the Campbell's soup ad (see Figure 3.12) offers no explicit information about product attributes and benefits. Rather, the ad merely appeals to the fun of eating soup. (See the word "fun" spelled with alphabet letters in the spoon?)

Another HEM-oriented advertisement is shown in Figure 3.13. This ad, unlike many advertisements for milk, says nothing about calcium or nutrition. Rather, its appeal is to that special feeling people share when enjoying hot chocolate together. Little sister, in this case, is recalling a moment of friendship enjoyed with her big brother years ago. The nostalgia is enhanced by giving the scene the look of an old photo. All in all, the ad is a touching reminder to parents of their childhoods and a subtle suggestion to serve hot chocolate to their own children.

The prior discussion and examples have emphasized advertising, but it should be apparent that the differences between CPM and HEM perspectives apply as well to other forms of marketing communications, especially to personal selling. A salesperson may emphasize product features and tangible benefits in attempting to sell a product, or he or she may also attempt to convey the fun, fantasies, and pleasures that prospective customers can enjoy with product ownership. Successful salespersons employ both approaches and orient the dominant approach to the consumer's specific "hot buttons." That is, successful salespersons know how to adapt their presentations to different customers—hopefully, of course, doing it honestly and maintaining standards of morality.

Finally, no single marketing-communications approach, whether CPM or HEM, is effective in all instances. What works best depends on the specific character and needs of the targeted market segment. In general, appeals to *functional values* are most congenial with the CPM perspective, whereas the HEM perspective offers a more appropriate approach for appealing to *social, emotional*, or *epistemic* values.

---

[37]It is interesting to note that this claim (90 percent fat free) is *framed* in a positive fashion compared to the equally true but negative claim (contains 10 percent fat). Research has demonstrated that claims framed in positive terms have more favorable effects on consumer attitudes than do claims framed in negative terms. For further discussion, see Irwin P. Levin and Gary J. Gaeth, "How Consumers Are Affected by the Framing of Attribute Information Before and After Consuming the Product," *Journal of Consumer Research*, 15 (December 1988), 374–378; and Ajit Kaicker and Brian D. Till, "The Framing Effect: Attribute Information and Product Experience," in *Proceedings of Winter Educators' Conference*, eds. Terry L. Childers and Scott B. MacKenzie (Chicago: American Marketing Association, 1991), 404–410.

Another Ad Exemplifying the HEM Approach

FIGURE 3.13

SUMMARY

This chapter describes the fundamentals of consumer choice behavior. First, consumer choice behavior is conceptualized as being influenced by five *consumption values:* economic, social, emotional, epistemic, and conditional values. Next, two relatively distinct perspectives of choice behavior are presented: the consumer processing model (CPM) and the hedonic, experiential model (HEM). The CPM approach views the consumer as an analytical, systematic, and logical decision maker. According to this perspective, consumers are motivated to achieve desired goal states. The CPM process involves attending, encoding, retaining, retrieving, and integrating information so that a person can achieve a suitable choice among consumption alternatives.

The HEM perspective views consumer choice behavior as resulting from the mere pursuit of fun, fantasy, and feelings. Thus, some consumer behavior is based on emotional considerations rather than on objective, functional, and economic factors.

The distinction between the CPM and HEM views of consumer choice is an important one for marketing communications and promotion management. The techniques and creative strategies for affecting consumer choice behavior clearly are a function of the prevailing consumer orientation. Specific implications and appropriate strategies are emphasized throughout the chapter.

Discussion Questions

1. Using a compact-disc player for illustration, explain how you (as a presumably representative consumer) might perceive this product as providing functional, social, emotional, epistemic, and conditional values.

2. Assume you are the marketing communications director for your college or university. The president has asked you to develop an advertising program that will attract more students. For each of the five consumption values listed in the previous question, prepare an appropriate one-sentence headline for placement in high school newspapers which would appeal to each consumption value.

3. The metaphors *hot* and *cold* were used in describing the CPM and HEM perspectives on consumer behavior. Describe and provide a label for the type of consumer behavior that might fall at a midpoint between these extremes.

4. When discussing exposure as the initial stage of information processing, it was claimed that gaining exposure is a necessary but insufficient condition for success. Explain.

5. There are numerous examples of marketing communicators' use of bright colors, loud sounds, and other intense stimuli to attract consumers' attention. Can you think of any drawbacks in using intense stimuli? Be specific.

6. Explain why attention is highly selective and what implications selectivity holds for marketing communicators.

7. All marketing communications environments are cluttered. Explain what this means and provide several examples.

8. Explain each of the following related concepts: perceptual encoding, feature analysis, and active synthesis. Using a supermarket product of your choice, explain how package designers for that industry implicitly use concepts of feature analysis in designing packages.

9. Present an example of misperception based on your personal experience that conceptually parallels the USS Vincennes example given in the text.

10. Figure 3.7 represents Jack's knowledge structure for the Mazda Miata. Explain how functional, social, and emotional consumption values are all contained in Jack's structure.

11. Linkages between memory concepts (for example, between a brand and a product benefit) are strengthened by frequently repeating a claim, presenting the claim in concrete fashion, or conveying it in a creative manner. Considering only the latter two ways (being concrete or creative), illustrate how you would use these approaches in advertising the following claim: "With Macmadden's non-alcohol brew, you don't have to give up taste when you give up alcohol." (Be careful not to confuse the Macmadden's claim with the Sharp's campaign described in this chapter.)

12. Distinguish between compensatory and noncompensatory heuristics.

13. In what sense would attending a Saturday afternoon college football game represent an hedonic- or experiential-based behavior?

14. Overpopulation is a major problem for much of the developing world. Complicating government efforts to reduce birth rates is the fact that many men, perhaps especially in Latin American countries, consider fathering children a sign of their virility. Thus, efforts to reduce populations by encouraging men to have vasectomies often fall on deaf ears. Using concepts from this chapter, with particular attention to concretizing, what kind of promotional campaign would you develop to encourage Latin men to consider having a vasectomy?

CHAPTER FOUR

Attitudes and Persuasion in Marketing Communications

WILL THE IMPACT HAVE AN IMPACT?

The 1990s has been dubbed the *green decade*—a period when intelligent companies and educated consumers around the globe are finally starting to deal with environmental abuses heaped on the earth throughout the twentieth century. Needless to say, initial environmental efforts by companies are those which are the easiest and the least costly, such as producing and merchandising environmentally safe packages. The same can be said of consumers, who have accepted the concept of being more environmentally conscious and have undertaken modest alterations in their consumption behavior. However, the real test of consumers' willingness to engage in more environmentally safe behavior involves what for many is one of their most prized possessions, the automobile. For example, can consumers be persuaded to switch from gasoline-powered cars to electric-powered vehicles?

General Motors is predicting they can. Possibly by 1993 GM will launch impact, a two-seater electric-powered car. Consider the implications for consumers. Foremost, the Impact eliminates gasoline emissions. The Impact, additionally, is noiseless and has a rapid pickup, going from 0 to 60 miles per hour in 8 seconds. However, these primary advantages in the Impact's basic offer are not without some pain for consumers. This car is battery charged, and goes only 120 miles per charge, with a full recharge requiring up to 8 hours. Although new battery designs are under development, current lead-acid batteries must be replaced every 20,000 miles or so and cost as much as $1,500. Also, the Impact's price tag is expected to be somewhere around $25,000.

Can many consumers be persuaded to purchase an Impact? Who are the most likely candidates for this innovative automobile concept? What is your attitude toward the Impact?

Source: Based on David Woodruff and Thane Peterson, "The Greening of Detroit," *Business Week,* April 8, 1991, 54-60, especially p. 58.

The opening vignette touches on the two interrelated topics treated in this chapter, *attitudes* and *persuasion.* Attitudes and persuasion are closely related topics. To understand one requires an understanding of the other. Attitude is a mental property of the consumer. Persuasion is an effort by a marketing communicator to influence the consumer's attitude and behavior in some manner.

The analogy of an automobile race should clarify the distinction between attitude and persuasion and their mutual interdependence. An automobile race consists of a driver with a vehicle who has the objective of beating competitive drivers to the finish line. Analogously, so it is in promotion management and marketing communications. The driver (marketing communicator) has a vehicle at his disposal (the markets' thoughts about and opinions of—attitude toward— his brand). He is trying to accelerate the vehicle (persuade the market) toward the finish line before fellow drivers (the competition) get there. Thus attitude is the *object* and persuasion the *objective* of the marketing communications race.

For example, the opening vignette indicated that General Motors is introducing the Impact electric-powered automobile. Most consumers will resist changing from conventional cars to battery-operated ones. Yet there will be a segment of early adopters (discussed more in the next chapter) who will accept this innovative vehicle. Along with this acceptance will come competition from other American, European, and Japanese automobile makers. All firms will thereafter compete for market share, and marketing communications activities will strive to build brand preference for each firm's offering and persuade consumers to buy their brand rather than competitive alternatives.

This chapter first describes the core attitude concept and then discusses several frameworks that explain how attitudes are formed and changed and how persuasion occurs. In effect, what we are doing in this chapter is studying marketing communications from the consumer's perspective. This chapter builds upon the fundamentals treated in the previous two chapters and provides insight into why marketing communicators' messages sometimes succeed and at other times fail to influence consumers' attitudes and behavior.

THE NATURE AND ROLE OF ATTITUDES

Attitude is one of the most extensively examined topics in all of marketing. The reason is simple: Understanding how people feel toward different objects (such as brands within a product category) makes it possible to predict and influence behavior so that it is compatible with the marketing communicator's interests.

What Is an Attitude?

Attitudes are *hypothetical constructs;* they cannot be seen, touched, heard, or smelled. Because attitudes cannot be observed, a variety of perspectives have developed over the years in attempting to describe what they are.[1] The term **attitude** will be used here to mean a general and enduring positive or negative *feeling toward or evaluative judgment of* some person, object, or issue.[2]

Beyond this basic definition, three other notable features of attitudes are that they are *learned, relatively enduring*, and they *influence behavior*.[3] Consider the following examples of consumer attitudes that express feelings and evaluations with varying degrees of intensity: "I like Diet Pepsi," "I detest Madonna," "Mike Tyson is a creep," "I favor recycling," and "I love the Chicago Bulls." All of these attitudes are learned and will likely be retained until there is some strong reason to change them; moreover, it can be expected that the holders of these attitudes would behave consistently with their evaluations—drinking Diet Pepsi, turning the channel when Madonna or Tyson appear on TV, recy-

[1]A number of major theories of attitudes and attitude-change processes have developed over the last half century. Seven particularly significant theories are reviewed in Richard E. Petty and John T. Cacioppo, *Attitudes and Persuasion: Classic and Contemporary Approaches* (Dubuque, IA: Wm. C. Brown Company, 1981). For a more recent review, see Richard E. Petty, Rao H. Unnava, and Alan J. Strathman, "Theories of Attitude Change," in *Handbook of Consumer Behavior*, eds. T. S. Robertson and H. H. Kassarjian (Englewood Cliffs, NJ: Prentice-Hall, 1991), 241–280.

[2]This definition adheres to Petty and Cacioppo, ibid., 7, and also reflects the concept of attitude popularized in recent years by Fazio and his colleagues. See, for example, Russell H. Fazio, Jeaw-Mei Chen, Elizabeth C. McDonel, and Steven J. Sherman, "Attitude Accessibility, Attitude-Behavior Consistency, and the Strength of the Object-Evaluation Association," *Journal of Experimental Social Psychology*, 18, 1982, 339–357. On a technical note, the definition makes no distinction between what some authors properly consider to be the distinct constructs of *affect* (or feeling states) and *attitude* (or evaluative judgments). For discussion, see Joel B. Cohen and Charles S. Areni, "Affect and Consumer Behavior," in *Handbook of Consumer Behavior*, eds. T. S. Robertson and H. H. Kassarjian (Englewood Cliffs, NJ: Prentice-Hall, 1991), 188–240.

[3]Daniel J. O'Keefe, *Persuasion: Theory and Research* (Newbury Park, CA: Sage Publications, 1990), 18.

cling aluminum cans, jumping at an opportunity to attend a Chicago Bulls game, and so on.

The preceding description focuses on feelings and evaluations, or what is commonly referred to as the **affective** component of an attitude. The affective component is what is generally referred to when people use the word *attitude*. However, attitude theorists recognize two additional components, cognitive and conative.[4] The **cognitive** component refers to a person's *beliefs* (i.e., knowledge and thoughts, which sometimes are erroneous) about an object or issue ("Reebok shoes are more stylish than Nike"; "Nike Air Jordans are high-quality basketball shoes"). The **conative** component represents one's *behavioral tendency*, or *predisposition to act*, toward an object. In consumer-behavior terms, the conative component represents a consumer's intention to purchase a specific item. Gordon W. Allport integrated these two components when formulating his classic definition: "Attitudes are learned predispositions to respond to an object or class of objects in a consistently favorable or unfavorable way."[5]

A clear progression is implied: from initial cognition, to affection, to conation. An individual becomes aware of an object, such as a new product, then acquires information and forms beliefs about the product's ability to satisfy consumption needs (*cognitive* component). Beliefs are integrated, and feelings toward and evaluations of the product are developed (*affective* component). On the basis of these feelings and evaluations, an intention is formed to purchase or not to purchase the new product (*conative* component). An attitude, then, is characterized by progressing from thinking (cognitive), to feeling (affective), to behaving (conative).[6]

An illustration will help clarify the notion of attitude progression. Consider the description in the previous chapter of Doug's purchase of a Ford Taurus. Doug knew precisely what he wanted in a new automobile: economy, reasonable passenger and luggage space, good resale value, and a smooth-shifting automatic transmission. He acquired a variety of information about the Ford Taurus and other models from friends and acquaintances, from advertisements, and from his

---

[4]See, for example, Richard P. Bagozzi, Alice M. Tybout, C. Samuel Craig, and Brian Sternthal, "The Construct Validity of the Tripartite Classification of Attitudes," *Journal of Marketing Research*, 16 (February 1979), 88–95; Richard J. Lutz, "An Experimental Investigation of Causal Relations among Cognitions, Affect, and Behavioral Intention," *Journal of Consumer Research*, 3 (March 1977), 197–208.

[5]Gordon W. Allport, "Attitudes," in *A Handbook of Social Psychology*, ed. C. A. Murchinson (Worcester, MA: Clark University Press, 1935), 798–844.

[6]The view that this strict progression applies to all behavior and that cognition must necessarily precede affect is not uncontested. Various alternative "hierarchies of effect" have been postulated. For further discussion, see Michael L. Ray, "Marketing Communication and the Hierarchy of Effects," in *New Models for Mass Communication Research*, ed. P. Clarke (Beverly Hills, CA: Sage Publications, 1973), 147–175. For a thorough recent review see Thomas E. Barry, "The Development of the Hierarchy of Effects," in *Current Issues and Research in Advertising*, eds. James H. Leigh and Claude R. Martin, Jr. (Ann Arbor, MI: Division of Research, Graduate School of Business, University of Michigan, 1987), 251–296.

own shopping experiences. He formed beliefs about product features and about specific automobile models as a result of this information search and processing activity. These beliefs (representing the cognitive-attitude component) led Doug to form specific feelings toward and evaluations of (affective component) various automobile models. He liked the Honda Accord, except for what he considered to be a rather jerky-shifting automatic transmission. Overall, his most positive affect was toward the Ford Taurus, and his intention to purchase this model (conative component) finally materialized when he drove the new automobile away from the Ford dealership.

PERSUASION IN MARKETING COMMUNICATIONS

The foregoing discussion of attitudes, the *object*, provides us with useful concepts as we turn now to the strategic issue of how marketing communicators influence customers' attitudes and behaviors through persuasive efforts, the *objective*. Salespeople attempt to convince customers to purchase one product rather than another; advertisers appeal to consumers' reason or to their fantasies and feelings in attempting to create desired images for their brands in hopes that consumers will someday purchase their brands; brand managers use coupons, samples, rebates, and other devices to induce consumers to try their products and to purchase now rather than later.

Persuasion is the essence of marketing communications. Marketing communicators—as well as all persuaders (politicians, theologians, parents, teachers)—attempt to guide people toward the acceptance of some belief, attitude, or behavior by using reasoning or emotional appeals.[7] The actual process by which this occurs is a matter of later discussion. It first will be useful to provide some brief discussion on the ethics of persuasion inasmuch as the word *persuasion* may suggest to you something manipulative, exploitative, or unethical.

The Ethics of Persuasion

At times, marketing communicators' persuasion efforts are undeniably unethical. Shrewd operators bamboozle the unsuspecting and credulous into buying products or services that are never delivered. Elderly consumers, for example, are occasionally hustled into making advance payments for household repairs (e.g., roof repairs) that are never performed. Unscrupulous realtors sell swamp land in

---

[7]A similar account is offered by Kathleen Kelley Reardon, *Persuasion in Practice* (Newbury Park, CA: Sage Publications, 1990), 2.

Florida. Telemarketers sometimes get our attention under the pretense that they are conducting marketing research and then try to sell us something.

Yes, persuasion by *some* marketing communicators is unethical. Of course, so sometimes are persuasive efforts by government officials, clergymen, teachers, your friends, and even you. Persuasion is a part of daily life in all its facets. The practice of persuasion can be noble or deplorable. There is nothing wrong with persuasion per se; it is the practitioners of persuasion who sometimes are at fault. To paraphrase an old adage: Don't throw the persuasion baby out with the bath water; just make sure the water is clean.

Multitude of Persuasion Possibilities

It would be erroneous to think that persuasion is a single method, practice, or technique. Rather, there are as many persuasion methods in theory as there are persuasion practitioners. This is a bit of an exaggeration, but it serves to emphasize that persuasion practices are highly diverse.

Another important point is that the topic of persuasion can be looked at from two perspectives. One perspective involves examining persuasion from the perspective of the *persuader* and studying the persuasive techniques used by practitioners. The other perspective treats persuasion from the perspective of the *persuadee* by exploring the factors that determine how recipients of persuasive efforts are persuaded. The next section looks at persuasion from the persuader's perspective, and the following section then takes a persuadee-oriented view.

TOOLS OF INFLUENCE: THE PERSUADER'S PERSPECTIVE

Persuaders in all capacities of life routinely use a variety of tools to influence people. These influence tactics have evolved throughout the millenia and are widely understood by many persuaders, if only tacitly. Robert Cialdini, a social psychologist, has spent much of his professional career studying the persuasive tactics used by car dealers, insurance salespeople, fund-raisers, waiters, and other persuasion practitioners. His studies, involving both work in the field (as car salesman, fund-raiser, etc.) and laboratory research, have identified six tools of influence that cut across persuasion practices.[8] These are (1) reciprocation, (2) commitment and consistency, (3) social proof, (4) liking, (5) authority, and (6) scarcity.

---

[8]Cialdini actually discusses seven influence tactics, but the seventh, instant influence, actually cuts across all the others and need not be discussed separately. Also, he refers to influence tactics as "weapons" of influence. Because the term weapons implies that the persuadee is an adversary, I prefer instead the term "tool" insofar as many modern marketing practitioners view their customers as participants in a long-term relation-building process and not as adversaries or victims. The following sections are based on Cialdini's insightful work. See Robert B. Cialdini, *Influence: Science and Practice* (Glenview, IL: Scott, Foresman, 1988, 2d ed.).

Before discussing each of these influence tools, it is important to note that these tactics work because much of our behavior occurs in a rather automatic, noncontrolled, and even mindless fashion. In other words, due to limitations on our information processing capacities (as discussed in the previous chapter) and time pressures, we often make judgments and choices without giving a great deal of thought to the matter. Cialdini refers to this as *click, whirr* behavior.[9] He uses this term in reference to patterns of behavior (called *fixed-action patterns*) that appear throughout the animal kingdom. Many animal species (including *Homo-sapiens*) will, under special circumstances, engage in patterns of scripted behavior in response to some *trigger feature* that activates the behavior. For example, mother hens will automatically act motherly on hearing the sound cheep-cheep.[10] That single sound activates maternal behavior; if a football could emit the sound cheep-cheep, a mother turkey would act motherly toward it, taking it under her wing and nurturing it; however, she will not nurture her own offspring if they are unable to make that sound.

Humans sometimes also operate in a click, whirr fashion. Something triggers a response (click) and then an automatic, scripted pattern of behavior follows (whirr). We are not aware of this happening (if we were, it would not happen), but, as we will see, persuaders know how to click on, or trigger, our behavior and out whirrs a response that results in our purchasing a product, making a donation, or doing something else that favors the persuader's best interests.

Reciprocation

As part of the socialization process in all cultures, people acquire a *norm of reciprocity.* As children we learn to return a favor with a favor, to respond to a nicety with another nicety. Knowing this, marketing communicators sometimes give gifts or samples with hopes that customers will reciprocate by purchasing products. We see this with in-store sampling of food items in supermarkets. Also, anyone who has ever attended a Tupperware party (or other product party of this sort) knows that the hostess often distributes free gifts at the beginning with designs that attendees will reciprocate with big purchases. Click-whirr: "Something nice was done for me; I should return the favor."

You would be correct if you are thinking that reciprocation tactics do not always work. The reason they do not is because we as consumers sometimes "see through" the tactic and realize that the nicety is not really a sincere offering but rather a come-on to get us to respond in kind. In saying this, an important theme carries through the entire discussion of influence tactics. This theme is that no influence tactic is equally effective under all circumstances. Rather, the effectiveness of a tactic is *contingent on the circumstances:* Whether and when a tactic is

---

[9]Ibid., 2.

[10]Ibid.

effective depends on the persuasion circumstances and the characteristics of the persuader and persuadee. As a student of marketing communications, it is critical that you incorporate this *it-depends* thinking into your understanding of marketing practices. No influence tactic is universally effective. Rather, the situation or circumstances determine whether and when a tactic might be effective.

With regard to reciprocation, this tactic is most effective when the persaudee perceives the gift-giver as honest and sincere. Party plans like the Tupperware parties typify this situation in that the persuader (the host or hostess) is often friends with the persuadees.

Commitment and Consistency

After people make a choice (a commitment), there often is a strong tendency to remain faithful to that choice. Consistency is a valued human characteristic. We admire people who are consistent in their opinions and actions. We sometimes feel ashamed of ourselves when we say one thing and do something differently. Hence, the marketing communicator might attempt to click-whirr the consumer by getting him or her to commit to something (commitment is the click or trigger) and then hope that the consumer will continue to act in a manner consistent with this commitment.

Consider the tactic often used by automobile salespeople. They get the consumer to commit to a price and then say they have to get their sales manager's approval. At this point the consumer has psychologically committed to buying the car. The salesperson, after supposedly taking the offer to the sales manager, returns and declares that the manager would not accept the price. Nevertheless, the consumer, now committed to owning the car, will often increase the offer. In the trade this is referred to as *low balling* the consumer, a tactic that is widespread because it is effective (albeit not entirely ethical).

When would you expect commitment and consistency to be most effective in marketing communications? (Think first before reading on.) Again, the apparent sincerity of the persuader would play a role. The tactic is unlikely to work when it is obviously deceitful and self-serving. From the persuadee's perspective, it would be expected that consumers are most likely to remain consistent when they are highly ego-involved in their choices. In other words, it is hard not to be consistent when a great amount of thought and psychological energy have gone into a choice.

Social Proof

What do I do? How should I behave? The principle of social proof is activated in circumstances where appropriate behavior is somewhat unclear. Not knowing exactly what to do, we take leads from the behavior of others; their behavior provides *social proof* of how we should behave. For example, suppose someone asks you for a charitable donation. The appropriate amount to give is unclear, so you might ask the fund raiser what amount others are giving and then contribute a like amount. As discussed in the following chapter, new-product developers sometimes encourage widespread adoption by giving new products to opinion leaders and trend setters, who, it is hoped, will provide social proof for others to adopt the same behavior. In general, people are most likely to accept the actions of others as correct "when we are unsure of ourselves, when the situation is unclear or ambiguous, when uncertainty reigns."[11]

Liking

This influence tactic deals with the fact that we are most likely to adopt an attitude or undertake an action when a likable person promotes that action. There are various manifestations of likability. Two of the more prominent in marketing communications are *physical attractiveness* and *similarity*. Research (described in detail in Chapter 11) has shown that people respond more favorably to others who they perceive to be like themselves and physically attractive. This explains why models in advertising, individuals on magazine covers, and celebrity endorsers are typically attractive people who consumers can relate to and like. In the next major section, which looks at persuasion from the persuadee's perspective, we will elaborate on the likability tactic when discussing the role of classical conditioning.

Authority

Most people are raised to respect authority figures (parents, teachers, coaches, etc.) and to exhibit a sense of duty toward them. It therefore comes as no surprise to realize that marketing communicators sometimes appeal to authority. Because marketers cannot invoke the types of sanctions that real authority figures can (e.g., parents witholding allowances), appeals to authority in the marketplace typically use surrogates of real authority figures. For example, advertisers sometimes use medical authorities to promote their products' virtues. During late-night television programming and at other fringe times, broadcasters often air so-called long commercials, or infomercials, that devote 30-minute programs to weight-loss, skin-care, and hair-restoration products. Frequently these products are endorsed by medical doctors, upon whose authority the consumer is promised the product will perform its function.

---

[11]Ibid., 123.

A humorous version of an appeal to authority can be seen in Figure 4.1. In this ad for America West Airlines, which appeared in 1991 shortly after the successful Desert Storm campaign against Iraq, Jonathan Winters is portrayed in a Stormin'-Norman Schwarzkopf pose. At that time, hardly anyone in America had as much authority as the general who led the military campaign in the Persian Gulf.

Scarcity

This influence tactic is based on the principle that things become more desirable when they are in great demand but short supply. Simply put, if an item is rare or becoming rare it is more valued. Salespeople and advertisers use this tactic when encouraging people to buy immediately with appeals such as "only a few are left," "we won't have any more in stock by the end of the day," and "they're really selling fast."

The theory of **psychological reactance** helps explain why scarcity works.[12] This theory suggests that people react against any efforts to reduce their freedoms or choices. Removed or threatened freedoms and choices are perceived as even more desirable than previously. Thus, when products are made to seem less available, they become more valuable in the consumer's mind. Of course, appeals to scarcity are not always effective. But if the persuader is credible and legitimate, then an appeal may be effective. (Click-whirr: "Not many of this product remain, so I better buy now and pay whatever it takes to acquire it.") In contrast, the *Global Focus* demonstrates what can happen when consumers do not believe that the persuader (advertiser) is credible.

THE INFLUENCE PROCESS: THE PERSUADEE'S PERSPECTIVE

To motivate the following discussion, it will be useful to consider examples of persuasive efforts by two advertisers. In the advertisement for Light n' Lively (see Figure 4.2), model Cheryl Tiegs is surrounded by children who seem delighted with the product. The body copy, a personal statement from Ms. Tiegs, provides several reasons (message arguments) why parents should consider buying Light n' Lively for their children: "It's more nutritious than some other snacks"; "[Kids] really like its fruity, creamy taste"; "Sometimes, what kids don't know can only help them." In short, parents are being informed that their kids will like the taste of Light n' Lively and that it will be good for them.

---

[12]Jack W. Brehm, *A Theory of Psychological Reactance* (New York: Academic Press, 1966). See also Mona Clee and Robert Wicklund, "Consumer Behavior and Psychological Reactance," *Journal of Consumer Research*, 6 (March 1980), 389–405.

FIGURE 4.1   A Humorous Appeal to Authority

GLOBAL FOCUS

ADVERTISING: THE PRICE OF ECONOMIC FREEDOM

When communism collapsed in Europe and the Berlin Wall literally came tumbling down, East Germany's consumers were confronted with something they had not experienced since World War II: advertising. The reunification of Germany brought with it a blanketing of the East with western-style advertisements. After two years of advertising, the consumers from what was formerly East Germany are overwhelmingly mistrustful and fed up.

Why such negative attitudes? Under a communist regime for over four decades, the consumers of East Germany were taught that capitalism and its lightning rod (i.e., advertising) are evil. A recent survey determined that 87 percent of consumers from the east sector of reunified Germany think advertising makes people buy things they don't need, and 64 percent regard advertising as giving people a misleading impression of products.

It probably is to be expected that these consumers eventually will grow to develop a greater trust and appreciation of advertising. But just as western consumers dislike excessive amounts of advertising and misleading tactics, it is certain that East German consumers will remain skeptical. Advertising (both fortunately and unfortunately) is the price people must pay to realize economic freedom.

Source: Adapted from Joanne Lipman, "Eastern Germans Distrust Deluge of Ads," *The Wall Street Journal*, October 4, 1991, sec. B, 4.

A second illustration of persuasive techniques is the ad for American Express shown in Figure 4.3. Though presented here on a single page, this ad ran on two pages when it appeared in magazines. The interesting thing about the ad is that it says virtually nothing about the advertised service. Rather, it simply portrays two well-known sports personalities, Wilt Chamberlain (the celebrated basketball player who once scored 100 points in a single game) and Willie Shoemaker (the famous jockey who rode hundreds of horses to victory, many after passing the age when most jockeys follow their horses to pasture). The verbal content simply notes how long each athlete has held "membership" in the American Express "club."

FIGURE 4.2   Persuasive Advertisement for Light n' Lively

"Don't tell them
how good it is for them,
and they'll love it even more."

"Growing up, I was just a normal kid. I didn't like anything that was good for me. These days, kids have it so much better. Because now there's Light n' Lively" 6 pack Lowfat Yogurt. It's more nutritious than some other snacks. But the best part is, they really like its fruity, creamy taste.

Sometimes, what kids don't know can only help them."

AN EARLY START TO EATING SMART.

Not available in all areas. © 199' Kraft General Foods Inc.

Persuasive Advertisement for American Express

FIGURE 4.3

Wilt Chamberlain. Cardmember since 1976.
Willie Shoemaker. Cardmember since 1966.

*Membership
has its privileges.*

Don't leave home without it.
Call 1-800-THE CARD to apply.

These contrasting persuasive efforts highlight the fact that there are different ways to skin the persuasion cat. The following section identifies four factors that are fundamental in the persuasion process. Two factors (message arguments and peripheral cues) deal with persuasion vehicles under the marketing communicator's control. The other two (receiver involvement and receiver's initial position) deal with characteristics of persuadees.

MESSAGE ARGUMENTS.   The *strength or quality of message arguments* (e.g., the reasons for buying Light n' Lively) is often the major determinant of whether and to what extent persuasion occurs. Consumers are much more likely to be persuaded by convincing and believable messages than by weak arguments. It may seem strange, then, that much advertising fails to present substantive information or compelling arguments. The reason is that the majority of advertising, particularly television commercials, is for product categories (like soft drinks) in which interbrand differences are modest or virtually nonexistent.[13] There is not a lot American Express can say to encourage people to use their bank card. The ingenious idea of card *membership*, serves, however, to give consumers a sense of selectivity and status by implying that the user will possess something that celebrities use.

PERIPHERAL CUES.   A second major determinant of persuasion is the presence of cues that are *peripheral to the primary message arguments*. These include such elements as the message source (celebrity endorsers such as Cheryl Tiegs in the Light n' Lively ad, "The Stilt" and "The Shoe" in the American Express ad), background music, scenery, and graphics. As will be explained in a later section, under certain conditions these cues may play a more important role than message arguments in determining the outcome of a persuasive effort.

RECEIVER INVOLVEMENT.   The *personal relevance* that a communication has for a receiver is a critical determinant of the extent and form of persuasion. Highly involved consumers (people who are in the market for an expensive, risky product) are motivated to process message arguments when exposed to marketing communications, whereas uninvolved consumers are likely to exert minimal attention to message arguments and to perhaps only examine peripheral cues. The upshot is that involved and uninvolved consumers have to be persuaded in different ways. This will be detailed fully in a following section titled "An Integrated Model of Persuasion."

---

[13]Leo Bogart, "Is All This Advertising Necessary?" *Journal of Advertising Research*, 18 (October 1978), 17–26.

FOCUS ON PROMOTION

MEASURING CONSUMER INVOLVEMENT

The concept of involvement, which has been mentioned several times to this point in the text, is fundamental to all consumer behavior and marketing communications. You may be wondering "How is involvement measured?" One measure, called the **Personal Involvement Inventory,** consists of the 20 items below. Involvement is measured with regard to a specific product that is placed at the top of the 20 semantic differential scales. All items are scored from "1" to "7" (left to right) except for the reverse-coded items (with asterisks) which are scored from "7" to "1" (left to right). A consumer's responses to all 20 scales are summed to form a total involvement score, with a range of scores from 20 (low involvement) to 140 (high involvement).

(insert name of object to be judged)

important	_:_:_:_:_:_:	unimportant*
of no concern	_:_:_:_:_:_:	of concern to me
irrelevant	_:_:_:_:_:_:	relevant
means a lot to me	_:_:_:_:_:_:	means nothing to me*
useless	_:_:_:_:_:_:	useful
valuable	_:_:_:_:_:_:	worthless*
trivial	_:_:_:_:_:_:	fundamental
beneficial	_:_:_:_:_:_:	not beneficial*
matters to me	_:_:_:_:_:_:	doesn't matter*
uninterested	_:_:_:_:_:_:	interested
significant	_:_:_:_:_:_:	insignificant*
vital	_:_:_:_:_:_:	superfluous*
boring	_:_:_:_:_:_:	interesting
unexciting	_:_:_:_:_:_:	exciting
appealing	_:_:_:_:_:_:	unappealing*
mundane	_:_:_:_:_:_:	fascinating
essential	_:_:_:_:_:_:	nonessential*
undesirable	_:_:_:_:_:_:	desirable
wanted	_:_:_:_:_:_:	unwanted*
not needed	_:_:_:_:_:_:	needed

*Indicates item is reverse scored.

Source: See Judith Lynne Zaichkowsky, "Measuring the Involvement Construct," *Journal of Consumer Research*, 12 (December 1985), 341–352.

RECEIVER'S INITIAL POSITION.   Scholars now agree that persuasion results not from external communication per se but from the *self-generated thoughts* that consumers produce in response to persuasive efforts. Persuasion, in other words, is self-persuasion, or, stated poetically, "thinking makes it so."[14]

Marketing and consumer behavior scholars have identified various forms of self-generated thoughts, which they refer to as **cognitive and emotional responses.** These responses may be directed at message arguments, at executional elements (e.g., thoughts about Cheryl Tiegs), or may involve emotional reactions and images related to using the promoted product.[15]

Three specific forms of cognitive responses that are directed at message claims are supportive arguments, counter arguments, and source derogations.[16] **Supportive arguments** occur when a receiver agrees with a message's arguments. For example, a father reading the Light n' Lively ad may entertain the thought that a good-tasting but nutritious snack food is just what he wants to buy for his kids. **Counter arguments** occur when the receiver challenges message claims (counterargues with those claims). **Source derogations** arise when the receiver disputes the source's ability to make such claims (belittles the source). A mother reading the Light n' Lively ad may counterargue that yogurt is not nutritious, or she may react against the use of Cheryl Tiegs on grounds that "she's just a model who doesn't know anything about nutrition or what kids like or dislike."

Whether a persuasive communication accomplishes its objectives depends on the balance of cognitive and emotional responses. If the combination of counter-arguments and source derogations exceeds supportive arguments, it is unlikely that many consumers will be convinced to undertake the course of action advocated. Marketing communications, however, may effectively persuade consumers if more supportive than negative arguments are registered or if emotional responses are predominately positive.

The preceding point, though stated in terminology different from that previously used in this text, should not come as any great surprise. You may recall that in Chapter 2 a similar point was made concerning the communications process, namely that communications is *not* something you do *to* people; it is something done *with* people.

---

[14]Richard M. Perloff and Timothy C. Brock, "'And Thinking Makes It So': Cognitive Responses to Persuasion," in *Persuasion: New Directions in Theory and Research*, eds. M. E. Rioloff and G. R. Miller (Beverly Hills, CA: Sage Publications, 1980), 67–99.

[15]For further discussion, see Deborah J. MacInnis and Bernard J. Jaworski, "Information Processing from Advertisements: Toward an Integrative Framework," *Journal of Marketing*, 53 (October 1989), 8.

[16]Peter L. Wright, "The Cognitive Processes Mediating the Acceptance of Advertising," *Journal of Marketing Research*, 10 (February 1973), 53-62. Also see Amitava Chattopadhyay and Joseph W. Alba, "The Situational Importance of Recall and Inference in Consumer Decision Making," *Journal of Consumer Research*, 15 (June 1988), 1–12.

AN INTEGRATED MODEL OF PERSUASION

The various factors that play a role in the persuasion process can be combined into a coordinated theory of persuasion. Figure 4.4 presents a model of the alternative mechanisms, or routes, by which persuasion occurs.[17] This explanation is based on psychologists Petty and Cacioppo's *elaboration likelihood model* (ELM) and on marketing scholars MacInnis and Jaworski's integrative framework.[18]

It should be clear by this point in the chapter that there is no single mechanism by which persuasion occurs. Instead, there are a variety of possibilities. Understanding why this is so requires that you understand the concept of elaboration. **Elaboration** deals with mental activity in response to a persuasive message. Elaborating on a message involves thinking about what the message is saying, evaluating the arguments in the message, agreeing with some, disagreeing with others, reacting emotionally to some of the claims, and so on.

Whether and to what extent a person engages in elaboration depends on that person's motivation, ability, and opportunity to process (i.e., to attend and comprehend) a marketing message's selling claims. **Motivation** is high when a message relates to a person's present goals and needs and is thus relevant to that individual. Generally speaking, consumers are more motivated to process messages the more *involved* they are in the subject matter of a message. **Ability** deals with whether a person is familiar with message claims and is capable of comprehending them. Consumers, on occasion, are motivated but unable to process message claims. **Opportunity** involves the matter of whether it is physically possible for a person to process a message; opportunity is restricted when a message is presented too quickly, when the sound is too low, or when an individual is distracted.

Together, these three factors (which, for mnemonic convenience, can be thought of as **AMO** factors—ability, motivation, and opportunity[19]) determine each individual's *elaboration likelihood* for a particular message. **Elaboration likelihood** is the chance or prospect that a message receiver will add to, or elaborate on, a message by thinking about and reacting to it and comparing it with his or her preexisting memory bank of thoughts and beliefs regarding the product category, the advertised brand, and competitive brands. (The student will note

---

[17]Readers familiar with Petty and Cacioppo's ELM model may wonder why their model is not presented. Although suitable for guiding academic research and graduate study, my own experience in teaching the ELM has revealed that undergraduate students often have some difficulty in following the model. The reworking of Petty and Cacioppo's model is intended to provide a more accessible structure for students without doing disservice to their theory.

[18]Petty and Cacioppo, *Attitudes and Persuasion;* MacInnis and Jaworski, "Information Processing from Advertisements: Toward an Integrative Framework."

[19]MacInnis and Jaworski, "Information Processing from Advertisements: Toward an Integrative Framework."

FIGURE 4.4

An Integrated Model of Persuasion

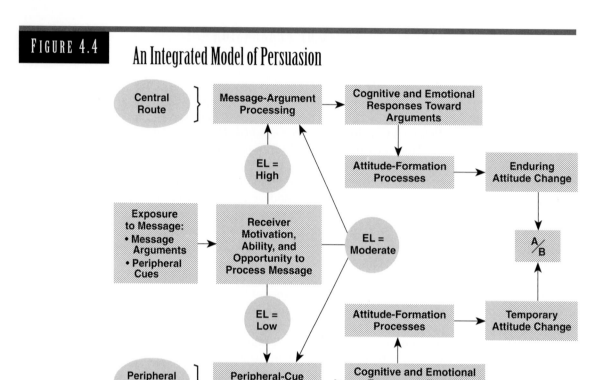

here a close similarity between elaboration likelihood and the concept of *active-synthesis* that was discussed in the previous chapter.) We can envision an *elaboration likelihood continuum* ranging from a low likelihood at one end to a high likelihood at the other.

The elaboration likelihood (*EL*) is *low* when the AMO factors are themselves low. This would be the case when a consumer is confronted with an advertisement for a product that she or he is not interested in (hence low motivation). The elaboration likelihood is *high* when the AMO factors are high. Doug back in Chapter 2 exhibited a high elaboration likelihood for information about automobiles because he had an urgent need to purchase a new car. In many marketplace situations, consumers' ELs for messages are at a *moderate* level rather than being low or high. Note in Figure 4.4 that these three EL levels are shown in circles extending from the box labeled "Receiver Motivation, Ability, and Opportunity to Process Message."

In general, the strength of one's elaboration likelihood will determine the type of process by which attitudes are formed toward the advertised brand. The model in Figure 4.4 shows two mechanisms by which persuasion occurs—at the top a *central route* and at the bottom a *peripheral route*. There is also a *dual route* which results from a moderate elaboration likelihood level and combines features of both the central and peripheral routes.

The Central Route

Upon *exposure* to a message consisting of message arguments and peripheral cues (see Exposure to Message box in Figure 4.4), the receiver's level of motivation, ability, and opportunity will determine the elaboration-likelihood level. When EL is high, the receiver will focus predominantly or exclusively on message arguments rather than peripheral cues (see the Message-Argument Processing box in Figure 4.4). This situation defines the activation of the so-called **central route.**

When the central route is activated, the receiver will listen to, hear, or read about a brand's attributes and benefits but will *not* necessarily accept them at face value. Rather, because the consumer is motivated to acquire information about the product category, she or he will react to the arguments with subvocal thoughts and emotions called cognitive and emotional responses (see the Cognitive and Emotional Responses Toward Arguments box in Figure 4.4). The consumer may accept some of the arguments but counterargue with others. She or he may also emit emotional reactions to the arguments—"That's a lie!" or "Who do they think they're kidding?"

The nature of the cognitive and emotional processing—whether predominantly favorable (support arguments and positive emotional responses) or predominantly unfavorable (counterarguments, source derogations, and negative emotional reactions)—will both determine whether the persuasive communication influences attitudes and the direction of that influence. This takes us to the box labeled Attitude-Formation Processes in Figure 4.4. The issue now addressed is one of how under the central route attitudes are formed or changed. There are, in fact, several possibilities, two of which are discussed in the following sections: *emotion-based persuasion* and *message-based persuasion.*[20]

EMOTION-BASED PERSUASION.   When a consumer is highly involved in a marketing communications message, say a TV commercial, there is a tendency to relate aspects of the message to his or her personal situation. The consumer may vicariously place him or herself into the commercial, relate him or herself to the product and people in the commercial, and *empathically* experience positive emotions (e.g., patriotic feelings of pride, romantic feelings) or negative emotions (e.g., anguish, fear). Under these circumstances, attitudes toward the advertised brand (depicted as A_B in Figure 4.4) stand a good chance of being changed in the direction of the experienced emotion—positive emotional reactions leading to positive brand attitudes and negative reactions leading to negative attitudes. Moreover, because the consumer's elaboration likelihood is high, it is to be expected that any attitude change experienced under the central route

---

[20]The basis for distinguishing these two forms of central-route persuasion is in MacInnis and Jaworski, 13–15. The discussion of what is termed here emotion-based persuasion is guided by MacInnis and Jaworski's presentation.

will be relatively permanent or enduring (see Enduring Attitude Change box in Figure 4.4).

Consider for example an award-winning advertising campaign undertaken by the South Carolina Department of Highways. This ongoing campaign is directed at persuading people (especially teenagers and young adults) not to drink and drive. Commercials graphically depict the aftermath of accidents and the personal tragedy suffered by the driver and the victims of his or her drunken driving. Many viewers of these commercials find themselves emotionally involved with the people and situations depicted. They vicariously experience the anguish that the drama presents. Research indicates that the campaign has successfully influenced many people in the target audience to hold negative attitudes toward driving after drinking or riding with someone who has been drinking.

MESSAGE-BASED PERSUASION.   The second central-route attitude-formation process results from processing message arguments. When consumers are sufficiently motivated and able to process a message's specific arguments or selling points, their cognitive and emotional responses to the selling points (e.g., support and counterarguments) may lead to changes in *beliefs* about the advertised brand or changes in *evaluations* of the importance of brand attributes and benefits. In either or both cases, the result is a change in attitudes toward the brand.

The process just described has been fully developed in the well-known theory of reasoned action (TORA). This theory proposes that all forms of planned and reasoned human behavior (versus unplanned, spontaneous, impulsive behavior) have two primary determinants: attitudes and normative influences.[21] Many of you previously have been exposed to this theory in a psychology or consumer behavior course, so rather than explaining the entire theory, the present discussion is limited to describing just the attitudinal component.[22]

Attitude formation according to TORA can best be described in terms of the following equation.

EQUATION 4.1

$$A_B = \sum_{i=1}^{n} b_i \cdot e_i$$

where:

A_B = *attitude* toward a particular brand

b_i = the expectation or *belief* that owning that brand will lead to desired outcome i

e_i = the positive or negative *evaluation* of the ith outcome

---

[21] Fishbein and Ajzen, *Belief, Attitude, Intention, and Behavior.*
[22] The normative component of the theory deals with the influence that important others (also called referent groups) have on our intentions and behavior.

In words, the equation says that a consumer's attitude toward a brand (or, more technically, toward the act of owning and consuming the brand) is determined by his or her beliefs regarding the outcomes, or consequences, of owning the brand weighed by the evaluations of those outcomes. **Outcomes** (expressed in Equation 4.1 as i = 1 through n, where n is typically fewer than 7) involve those aspects of brand ownership that the consumer either desires to obtain (e.g., good gas mileage with an automobile) or to avoid (e.g., frequent breakdowns). **Beliefs,** the b_i term in Equation 4.1, are the consumer's subjective probability assessments regarding the likelihood that performing a certain act (e.g., buying Brand X automobile) will lead to a certain outcome. In theory, the consumer who is in the market for a product has in memory a separate belief associated with each potential outcome for each brand he or she is considering buying (e.g., Honda has really good resale value; Taurus's resale value is fairly good). Doug, the CPM-oriented consumer in the last chapter's opening vignette, considered outcomes such as durability, gas mileage, and resale value to be the most important factors in choosing a car. Doug formed specific beliefs on each of these attributes for each car that he considered purchasing.

Because all outcomes are not equally important or determinant of consumer choice, we need to introduce a term that recognizes this differential influence. This term is the evaluation component, e_i, in Equation 4.1. **Evaluations** represent the subjective value or importance that consumers attach to consumption outcomes. For example, Doug may have considered durability to be the most important consideration in selecting an automobile, followed by resale value, and then gas mileage.

Hence, Equation 4.1 and the corresponding discussion represent the attitudinal-formation process that results from the *integration* (see the summation symbol in Equation 4.1) of beliefs regarding individual outcomes of brand ownership weighed by their relative importance to the consumer. Attitudes toward a brand are more positive when a brand is perceived favorably with respect to valued outcomes and less positive when a brand is perceived unfavorably on these outcomes.

ATTITUDE CHANGE STRATEGIES.   With Equation 4.1 in mind, we can identify three different strategies that marketing communicators employ in attempting to change consumer attitudes.[23] First are attempts to *influence existing beliefs* (the b_i term in Equation 4.1). As an example, consider the advertisement for the Subaru Legacy in Figure 4.5. Subaru in this comparative advertisement is attempting to influence consumer beliefs regarding the Legacy's overall level of safety.

A second strategy is to *change existing evaluations* (the e_i term in Equation 4.1). This amounts to getting consumers to reassess a particular outcome associated with brand ownership and to alter their evaluations of the outcome's value.

[23]Richard J. Lutz, "Changing Brand Attitudes through Modification of Cognitive Structure," *Journal of Consumer Research*, 1 (March 1975), 49-59.

FIGURE 4.5

An Effort to Influence Consumers' Beliefs

Volvo Has Built A Reputation For Surviving Accidents. Subaru Has Built A Reputation For Avoiding Them.

The Volvo 240 has done a fine job of surviving accidents. And we, at Subaru, have always admired that.

So we gave the new Subaru Legacy unibody construction like the Volvo 240.

But at Subaru, we think there's something even better than surviving accidents. And that's not getting into them in the first place.

So unlike the 240, the Subaru Legacy offers an optional anti-lock braking system (ABS). A feature that pumps your brakes automatically for maximum maneuverability and gives you much greater steering control during heavy braking.

Unlike the 240, the Subaru Legacy

is available with full-time four wheel drive. A more civilized form of four wheel drive giving you greater traction on smooth high speed highways as well as on washboard dirt roads.

And unlike most cars in the world, the Subaru Legacy comes with both four wheel disc brakes and independent suspension.

At Subaru, we know that even cars not involved in accidents can eventually come apart. So every Subaru is put together to stay together through conditions which drive other cars into the ground. Of course, we can't guarantee how long every one of our cars will last. But we do know 93% of all Subaru cars registered in America

since 1979 are still on the road.*

And the new Subaru Legacy may even surpass that record for durability. A Subaru Legacy has broken the FIA World Speed/Endurance record by running 19 days at an average speed of 138.8 mph for more than 62,000 miles.**

So you see, it wasn't just accidents the Subaru Legacy was designed to avoid. But junk yards as well.

*R.L. Polk & Co. Statistics, July 1, 1988. **Validated by the Federation Internationale De L'Automobile.

Subaru® Legacy™

We Built Our Reputation By Building A Better Car.

Figure 4.6 illustrates this strategy. Tylenol is advertising the fact that it, unlike some competitive brands of pain reliever, contains no caffeine. In effect, Tylenol is attempting to get consumers to place a negative value on the presence of caffeine in pain relievers and by doing so to have a more favorable attitude toward Tylenol and less favorable attitudes toward brands that are not caffeine free.

A third strategy marketing communicators use to change the attitude component is to get consumers to *add an entirely new outcome* into how they judge brands in a product category. This outcome, of course, would be one on which the marketer's product fares especially well. We see in Figure 4.7 an effort by Kraft to introduce the property "fat free" into consumers' evaluations of what it takes to be a good mayonnaise. This advertisement hopes to reach consumers who previously never thought about a fat free mayonnaise and to encourage them to hold a more favorable attitude toward Kraft and a less favorable attitude toward Hellmann's.

The Peripheral Route

When the AMO factors (see Figure 4.4) are at low levels, a different form of persuasion process is involved. Specifically, when the consumer is *not* motivated to attend and comprehend message arguments, she or he may nonetheless attend nonmessage, or peripheral, features of an advertisement, a sales presentation, or other forms of marketing communications. The peripheral route is shown at the bottom of Figure 4.4, where it can be seen that attention is focused on processing peripheral cues rather than message arguments.

As previously noted, peripheral cues in a marketing communications message involve elements of the message gestalt that are unrelated (and hence peripheral) to the primary selling points in the message. For example, in a TV commercial peripheral cues might include the background music, the scenery, or attractive models. In the case of a sales presentation, peripheral cues would include a salesperson's physical appearance, how he or she is dressed, and his or her accent.

The consumer, having attended a peripheral cue, may experience thoughts or emotions in response to the cue ("That music excites me"; "That's a beautiful dress she's wearing"; "The scenery is gorgeous"). These responses (labeled "Cognitive and Emotional Responses Toward Peripheral Cues" in Figure 4.4) might produce an attitude toward the advertisement itself and/or an attitude toward the advertised brand.[24] Classical conditioning provides one account of how attitudes toward a brand (A_B) are formed via the peripheral route.

---

[24]For a thorough review of research involving the attitude toward the ad construct, see Scott B. MacKenzie and Richard J. Lutz, "An Empirical Examination of the Structural Antecedents of Attitude Toward the Ad in an Advertising Pretesting Context," *Journal of Marketing*, 53 (April 1989), 48–65.

FIGURE 4.6   An Effort to Change Consumers' Evaluations

An Effort to Get Consumers to Add a New Outcome   FIGURE 4.7

CLASSICAL CONDITIONING OF ATTITUDES.   You are no doubt familiar with the experiments in which Ivan Pavlov, the famous Russian scientist, trained dogs to salivate on hearing a bell ring or seeing a metronome click back and forth. What makes this interesting is that these objects are inherently incapable of evoking a salivation response from dogs. The way Pavlov accomplished this was by establishing a systematic *contingency relation* between a neutral object (a bell) and a nonneutral object that by itself *was* able to make dogs salivate (meat powder). Trial after trial, dogs would hear a bell ring and then would be presented with meat powder. In this situation, meat powder was an *unconditioned stimulus (US)* and salivation was an *unconditioned response (UR)*. By repeatedly pairing the bell (a *conditioned stimulus*, or *CS*) with the meat powder, the bell itself eventually caused the dog to salivate. The dog, in other words, had been trained to emit a *conditioned response (CR)* upon hearing the bell ring. The dog had learned that the bell regularly preceded meat powder, and thus the ringing bell caused the dog to predict that something desirable—the meat powder—was forthcoming.

Something analogous to this happens with consumers when processing peripheral cues. For example, brand advertisements that include adorable babies, sexy people, and majestic scenery can elicit positive emotional reactions. (Think of these peripheral cues as analogous to meat powder [the US], the emotional reactions as analogous to the dog's salivation [the UR], and the advertised brand as analogous to the bell in Pavlov's experiment [the CS].) The emotion contained in the cue may become associated with the brand, thereby influencing consumers to like the brand more than they did prior to viewing the commercial. In other words, through their association, the CS (advertised brand) comes to elicit a conditioned response (CR) similar to the unconditioned response (UR) evoked by the US itself (the peripheral cue).[25]

TEMPORARY VERSUS ENDURING ATTITUDE CHANGE. According to the ELM theory on which the foregoing discussion is based, people experience only temporary attitude change when persuaded via the peripheral route in comparison to the relatively enduring change experienced under the central route. Thus, in circumstances in which receivers think about and process message arguments (i.e., when the elaboration likelihood is high), attitudes that are formed will be relatively enduring and somewhat resistant to change. Comparatively, when the elaboration likelihood is low (because the communication topic is not particularly relevant to the message recipient), attitude change may nevertheless occur (by virtue of receivers' processing peripheral cues) but will only be temporary unless consumers are exposed continuously to the peripheral cue.

---

[25]For a more detailed account of classical conditioning see Terence A. Shimp, "Neo-Pavlovian Conditioning and Its Implications for Consumer Theory and Research," in *Handbook of Consumer Behavior*, eds. T. S. Robertson and H. H. Kassarjian (Englewood Cliffs, NJ: Prentice-Hall, 1991), 162–187.

Dual Routes

The central and peripheral paths represent endpoints on a continuum of persuasion strategies and are not intended to imply that persuasion is an either-or proposition. In other words, in many cases there is a combination of central and peripheral processes operating simultaneously. This is shown in Figure 4.4 under the situation where the AMO factors produce a moderate elaboration likelihood level. In this instance, which no doubt captures the majority of situations in marketing communications, consumers can be expected to process *both* message arguments and peripheral cues. As such, attitudes toward the promoted brand result from a combination of central- and peripheral-route attitude-formation processes.

An Empirical Illustration

A theory is only as good as the empirical evidence that supports it. In fact, considerable empirical evidence has been marshalled in support of the ELM theory. It will be instructive to review one such study.

Researchers performed an experiment that encouraged college student subjects to engage in central-route or peripheral-route processing.[26] This was accomplished by motivating subjects in one group to want to process message arguments (high-involvement subjects) and those in another group not to want to process arguments but to instead focus only on peripheral cues (low-involvement subjects). Four different advertisements were created for "Edge," a fictitious brand of disposable razor, by varying advertising messages both in terms of the quality of arguments presented in the ad (strong or weak selling claims) and the attractiveness of the endorser (either celebrity athletes as endorsers or a group of ordinary citizens). Thus, the four advertisements created for this experiment included (1) an ad containing all strong arguments and displaying the pictures of two celebrity endorsers (golfer Jack Nicklaus and tennis player Tracy Austin), (2) an ad containing all strong arguments and displaying a picture of ordinary citizens, (3) an ad containing all weak arguments and displaying the pictures of two celebrity endorsers, and (4) an ad containing all weak arguments and displaying the picture of ordinary citizens.

The selling points in the *strong arguments* ads included claims such as: Edge is scientifically designed, provides unsurpassed sharpness, eliminates nicks and cuts, and offers the smoothest shave possible. These points reflect the qualities most shavers look for in a good razor. By comparison, subjects exposed to the

[26]Richard E. Petty, John T. Cacioppo, and David Schumann, "Central and Peripheral Routes to Advertising Effectiveness: The Moderating Role of Involvement," *Journal of Consumer Research*, 10 (September 1983), 135-146.

weak arguments ad received selling points such as these: Edge is designed with the bathroom in mind, floats in water, and can only be used once but will be memorable.

According to the ELM's prediction, under the *central route*, the high-involvement subjects should be motivated to process message arguments about Edge razor and be persuaded by the strength of message arguments. That is, positive attitude change would be expected in the group presented with strong, believable arguments, and no change, or possibly negative attitude change, would be expected in the group exposed to weak, specious arguments. By comparison, under the *peripheral route* low-involvement subjects would be expected to concentrate on the message source and be more persuaded by the celebrity than by the noncelebrity presenters. (Before reading on, think about how the results of the experiment should have turned out.)

Experimental results (summarized in Table 4.1) were generally in accordance with the ELM predictions. Specifically, the nature of the endorser had a significant impact on product attitudes *only under low-involvement, or peripheral-route, conditions.* Argument quality had an impact on product attitudes under both low and high involvement, but the impact on attitudes was significantly greater under high than low involvement. Thus, this study supports the proposition that different features of a marketing communications effort may be more or less effective, depending on receivers' information–processing involvement.[27]

Practical Implications

In recognizing alternative paths to attitude formation and thus to persuasion, the ELM points out that the form of persuasion will depend both on the *characteristics of the market* (consumers' motivation and ability to process marketing messages) and the *strengths of the marketing communicator's relative market position.* If consumers are interested in learning about a product, and a company's brand has clear advantages over competitive brands, then the persuasion tact to be taken is obvious: *Design a message telling people explicitly why your brand is superior.* The result should be equally clear: Consumers will be swayed by your arguments, which will lead to enduring attitude change and a strong chance they will select your brand over competitors' brands.

However, the marketplace reality is that most brands in a product category are similar and, because of this, consumers generally are not anxious to devote mental effort toward processing messages which provide little new information. Thus, the marketing communicator, faced with this double whammy (only slightly-involved consumers and a me-too brand), has to find ways to create

---

[27]For reviews of other ELM studies, see Petty, Cacioppo, and Schumann, "Central and Peripheral Routes" and Petty, Unnava, and Strathman, "Theories of Attitude Change."

Summary of Results for Edge Razor Experiment: Means and Standard Deviations for Each Experimental Cell on the Attitude Index

TABLE 4.1

| | LOW INVOLVEMENT | | HIGH INVOLVEMENT | |
	Weak Arguments	Strong Arguments	Weak Arguments	Strong Arguments
Citizen Endorser	-.12 (1.81)	.98 (1.52)	-1.10 (1.66)	1.98 (1.25)
Celebrity Endorser	1.21 (2.28)	1.85 (1.59)	-1.36 (1.65)	1.80 (1.07)

Note: Attitude scores represent the average rating of the product on three nine-point semantic differential scales anchored at-4 and +4 (bad-good, unsatisfactory-satisfactory, and unfavorable-favorable). Standard deviations are in parentheses.

Source: R.E. Petty, J. T. Cacioppo, and D. Schumann, "Central and Peripheral Routes to Advertising Effectiveness: The Moderating Role of Involvement," *Journal of Consumer Research*, 10, September 1983, 141.

interest, excitement, and sometimes trivial reasons for differentiating his brand from competitors' offerings. Here, peripheral cues take on added significance. It matters not only what a salesperson has to say but also how professionally she appears and whether she has style. It is not just what a television commercial says but how it is said, what props are used, what music is played in the background, how attractive the models are, and so on.

In practice, then, persuasive marketing communications efforts include a combination of message arguments and peripheral cues. Returning to the analogy at the beginning of the chapter, the winners in the persuasion race typically have either a better *basic offer* (back to Mode 1 in Chapter 1), employ better *persuasive communications* (Mode 2), use more enticing *promotional inducements* (Mode 3), or have some superior combination of all of these.

USING ATTITUDES TO PREDICT BEHAVIOR

Marketing researchers regularly measure consumers' attitudes with expectations of being able to use these attitude measures to accurately predict how consumers will subsequently behave. Whether attitudes do, in fact, predict behavior accurately has been controversial in the study of consumer behavior as well as in the more general study of psychology.

Although a number of studies by psychologists and marketing researchers have questioned whether attitudes predict behavior, the prevailing contemporary view is that measures of attitudes do predict behavior reasonably accurately *under the right conditions*.[28] Thus, the issue is not whether attitudes predict behavior, but, rather, *when* attitudes accurately predict behavior.[29] There are two major determinants: (1) measurement specificity and (2) whether people have direct or indirect experience with the object of the attitude measurement.

MEASUREMENT SPECIFICITY.   A fundamental problem in much attitude research has been invalid data resulting from the measurement of attitudes and behavior *at different levels of specificity*. Four important components of any overt behavior must be considered in order to obtain specific and accurate measures: the target of the behavior, the specific action, the context in which the behavior occurs, and the time when it occurs.[30]

To illustrate these four aspects of measurement specificity, assume a researcher wanted to predict clothing purchase behavior at a future time based on measures of attitudes at some earlier time. More specifically, do senior-level college students' attitudes toward navy blue suits accurately predict whether they purchase navy blue suits? In this situation, the *target* of interest is a navy blue suit; buying is the *action* (rather than borrowing or stealing); the *context* is for the purpose of job interviewing; and the *time* is during the senior year in college.

In general, attitudes do *not* predict behavior very accurately unless both are measured *at the same level of specificity*. For example, if at the beginning of the semester the hypothetical researcher asked, "What is your opinion of navy blue suits?" your response might have been, "I don't like suits very much, and navy blue suits are particularly boring." If, then, at a later date you actually purchased a navy blue suit, your behavior would be inconsistent with your previously announced unfavorable attitude toward navy blue suits. This inconsistency would result because the measure of your attitude was too general and lacked specificity. Your expressed attitude would probably have been considerably different if the question had been, "What is your opinion of buying a navy blue suit for job interviewing this semester?" Because this question is specific with regard to the

---

[28]For a classic review of the psychology literature on attitude-behavior predictiveness, see A. W. Wicker, "Attitudes Versus Actions: The Relationship of Verbal and Overt Behavioral Responses to Attitude Objects," *Journal of Social Issues*, 25 (Autumn 1969), 41–78. An interesting marketing study that found weak attitude-behavior prediction is George S. Day and Terry Deutscher, "Attitudinal Predictions of Choices of Major Appliance Brands," *Journal of Marketing Research*, 19 (May 1982), 192–198.

[29]D. T. Regan and R. H. Fazio, "On the Consistency between Attitudes and Behavior: Look to the Method of Attitude Formation," *Journal of Experimental Psychology*, 13 (1977), 28–45; see also Deborah L. Roedder, Brian Sternthal, and Bobby J. Calder, "Attitude-Behavior Consistency in Children's Responses to Television Advertising," *Journal of Marketing Research*, 20 (November 1983), 337–349.

[30]Martin Fishbein and Icek Ajzen, *Belief, Attitude, Intention, and Behavior: An Introduction to Theory and Research* (Reading, MA: Addison-Wesley, 1975).

purpose and timing of purchasing a navy blue suit, your response would probably reflect a somewhat favorable attitude because you know that navy blue suits are generally regarded as appropriate attire for job interviewing. This response would then be consistent with your subsequent act of purchasing a navy blue suit.

Thus, in order to predict a specific behavior accurately, the attitude measurement must also be specific with regard to target, action, context, and time. The strength of the attitude-behavior relationship is strengthened appreciably when these requirements are satisfied. (To fully understand the material just covered, it would be beneficial for you to construct a personal example that illustrates a situation involving an action, target, context, and time.)

DIRECT VERSUS INDIRECT EXPERIENCE.   The other determinant of attitude-behavior consistency is whether people have had direct or indirect experience with the attitude object. *Direct experience* is gained by the consumer when he or she has actually tried or used the attitude object, whereas *indirect experience* refers to any product knowledge or experience short of actual use.

A series of psychological experiments demonstrated that attitudes based on direct experience predict behavior better than attitudes based on indirect experience.[31] The researchers in one study attempted to predict the proportion of time people would play with different puzzles based on their attitudes toward the puzzles. One group of subjects (the direct-experience group) played with sample puzzles *prior* to indicating their attitudes toward the puzzles. Another group (the indirect-experience group) received verbal descriptions of the various puzzles but did not actually play with them prior to revealing their attitudes. Both groups, after indicating their attitudes, then played with the various puzzles. The researchers recorded subjects' puzzle-playing behavior in terms of the proportion of time they devoted to each puzzle. The correlation between attitudes and behavior was predictably higher for the direct-experience group ($r = .53$) than for the indirect-experience group ($r = .21$).[32]

In a similar but more practical marketing study, researchers performed an experiment with a new cheese-filled pretzel as the experimental product. Undergraduate business students were divided into two experimental groups: a direct-experience group, which actually sampled the pretzels, and an indirect-experience group, which read an advertisement about the pretzels but did not sample them. The results indicated considerably higher levels of attitude-behavior consistency for the direct-experience subjects than for the indirect-experience subjects.[33]

[31]R. H. Fazio, M. P. Zanna, and J. Cooper, "Direct Experience and Attitude-Behavior Consistency: An Information Processing Analysis," *Personality and Social Psychology Bulletin*, 4 (Winter 1978), 48–52; R. H. Fazio and M. P. Zanna, "On the Predictive Validity of Attitudes: The Roles of Direct Experience and Confidence," *Journal of Personality*, 46 (June 1977), 228–243.

[32]Regan and Fazio, "On the Consistency between Attitudes and Behavior."

[33]Robert E. Smith and William R. Swinyard, "Attitude-Behavior Consistency: The Impact of Product Trial Versus Advertising," *Journal of Marketing Research*, 20 (August 1983), 257–267.

In sum, the most notable conclusion from the research findings cited and from the prior discussion on measurement issues is that attitudes can and do predict behavior fairly accurately, but only under the appropriate conditions—when measurements of attitudes are as specific as the predicted behavior, and when consumers have direct rather than indirect experience with the attitude object.

SUMMARY

Marketing communications in its various forms (advertising, personal selling, point-of-purchase displays, and so on) involves efforts to persuade consumers by influencing their attitudes and ultimately their behavior. This chapter describes the role and nature of attitudes and different mechanisms by which they are formed and changed. From the marketing communicators' perspective, attitude formation and change represent the process of persuasion.

The nature of persuasion is discussed with particular emphasis on the *elaboration likelihood model (ELM)*. Two alternative persuasion mechanisms are described: A *central route*, which explains persuasion under conditions where the receiver is involved in the communication topic, and a *peripheral route*, which accounts for persuasion when receivers are not highly involved.

Three attitude-formation processes are described in some detail: emotion-based persuasion, message-based persuasion, and classical conditioning. The first two are mechanisms for attitude change under the central route, whereas classical conditioning is a peripheral-route process.

Discussion Questions

1. Explain the cognitive, affective, and conative components of an attitude and provide examples of each using your attitude toward the idea of personally pursuing a career in selling and sales management.

2. Accurate attitude measurement requires specificity with regard to action, target, context, and time. Using a campus blood drive as an illustration, explain how each of these criteria applies.

3. Distinguish between message arguments and peripheral cues as fundamental determinants of persuasion. Provide several examples of each from actual television commercials.

4. Receiver involvement is the fundamental determinant of whether people may be persuaded via a central route or via a peripheral route. Explain.

5. There are three general strategies for changing attitudes. Explain each, using a hotel chain as your illustration.

6. Respond to the questions posed early in the chapter regarding Impact, the battery-powered automobile described in the opening vignette. Specifically, do you think many consumers will be persuaded to purchase an Impact? Who are the most likely candidates for this innovative automobile concept? What is your attitude toward the Impact?

7. Assume that your target audience is comprised of people who can afford to purchase the Impact but who have negative attitudes toward electric-powered vehicles. Using material from the chapter, how would you attempt to change their attitudes if you were the advertising agency responsible for this campaign? Be specific.

8. Have you personally experienced unethical persuasive efforts from marketing communicators? Under what circumstances would you most expect to find unethical marketing communications, and when would unethical communications most likely be effective in marketing?

9. In the discussion of the influence tactic of reciprocation, you were introduced to the concept of contingency, or it-depends, thinking. Apply this concept to the *scarcity* tactic in explaining the it-depend factors which might explain when this tactic would and would not be effective.

10. Assume that you are the fund-raising chairperson for a social or professional fraternity or sorority. Explain how you might use each of the six influence tactics discussed in the text. Be specific.

11. Describe the similarity between active-synthesis (discussed in the prior chapter) and the concept of elaboration described in the present chapter.

CHAPTER FIVE

Adoption and Diffusion Processes: The Role of Marketing Communications

----

HOT SOFT-DRINK SALES CHALLENGED BY COLD COFFEE

American preferences for beverages have changed dramatically over the last third of the twentieth century. It used to be that Americans drank a lot of coffee and some soft drinks. Americans now drink incredible quantities of soft drinks, a lot of bottled water, but relatively little coffee compared to the past. Indeed, annual sales in the soft-drink industry total over $45 billion, whereas coffee sales are not much larger than bottled-water sales, both of which are less than 10 percent of the soft-drink total.

Beverage makers are introducing one new product after another in hopes of stealing sales from the soft-drink companies. Consider, for example, that there are some 600 brands of bottled water marketed in the United States. New varieties of sparkling waters are being introduced all the time.

Perhaps the most interesting new beverage product to be introduced to the United States is iced coffee. Brands like Maxwell House's Cappio, Coca-Cola's Georgia, Nescafe's Mocha Cooler, and Original New York Express are being marketed in cans, bottles, and other containers with hopes of obtaining $1 billion in sales by the end of the decade. The idea for marketing iced coffee in the United States came from Japan, where sales annually exceed $4 billion.

Iced coffee is most popular among young Japanese consumers and also is expected to appeal to younger American consumers. The interesting question, however, is whether chilled coffee will meet resistance in the United States. Many younger American consumers are not fond of the taste of coffee and, in addition to this, the idea of drinking cold coffee is incompatible with the way that product has always been consumed in the United States.

Sources: Robert McMath, "Adrift in a Sea of Bottled Water," *Adweek's Marketing Week*, November 19, 1990, 42; Judann Dagnoli, "Iced Coffee Next for Coke, Nestle," *Advertising Age*, May 21, 1990, 4; Dorian Friedman and Jim Impoco, "Get Your Iced, Cold Java," *U.S. News & World Report*, April 29, 1991, 59.

NEW PRODUCTS AND INNOVATIVENESS

For most industries and companies, introducing a stream of new products is absolutely essential for success and long-term growth. Likewise, the continued viability of many nonbusiness organizations (such as charitable groups, religious organizations, and political parties) depends on introducing new ideas to their constituencies on a regular basis.

Despite the huge investments and concerted efforts to introduce new products and ideas, many are never successful. It is impossible to pinpoint the percentage of new ideas and products that eventually fail because organizations vary in how they define a success; estimates range from as high as 90 percent to as low as a 33 percent failure rate among new product introductions.[1]

This chapter describes the processes involved in the acceptance of product innovations. Discussion focuses on the characteristics of people who are more and less likely to be innovative, the role of personal influence in facilitating new product acceptance, and the role of marketing communications in ensuring that new products are successful.

The Degree of Innovativeness

An **innovation** is an idea, practice, product, or service that an individual *perceives* to be new. How people view an object determines whether it is innovative. People who believe something is an innovation behave differently toward the object than people who do not perceive the object as new.

The degree of newness is an important dimension of innovation. Innovations can be classified along a continuum according to their degree of impact on established consumption patterns. Table 5.1 presents an innovativeness continuum,

[1]"Survey Finds Sixty-Seven Percent of New Products Succeed," *Marketing News*, February 8, 1980, 1.

TABLE 5.1	The Innovation Continuum		
CONTINUOUS INNOVATIONS			DISCONTINUOUS INNOVATIONS
Line Extensions (For example, new flavors, sizes, packages)	Minor Product Modifications (For example, annual new models in cars or new fashions)	Major Product Modifications (For example, compact cars when first introduced or color television vs. black & white)	New Technologies (For example, the invention of the computer or jet aircraft)

Source: Thomas S. Robertson, Joan Zielinski, and Scott Ward, *Consumer Behavior* (Glenview, IL: Scott, Foresman and Company, 1984), 369.

labels the end points *continuous* and *discontinuous,* and provides examples of different degrees of innovativeness along the continuum.[2] It is important to realize that there are many gradations along this continuum. The categories described next are merely convenient end-and mid-points along the continuum.

A **continuous innovation** is one that generally represents a *minor change* from existing products and which has *limited impact on customers' consumption patterns.* That is, the consumer can buy and use the new product in much the same way that he or she has used another product to satisfy the same need. Table 5.1 shows that new flavors, sizes, and packages represent typical continuous innovations. Companies routinely introduce new flavors of food products (for instance, regular potato chips, then barbecue flavored, then Cajun spiced, etc.), new scents for cleaning products (e.g., lemon scented), new package designs, and many other slight product modifications. All of these are continuous innovations.

In comparison, a **discontinuous innovation,** which anchors the other extreme of the innovation continuum (see Table 5.1), requires *substantial relearning and fundamental alterations in basic consumption patterns.* The automobile, computer, birth-control products, and television are perhaps the most significant mass-marketed discontinuous innovations of the twentieth century.

Most new products are continuous innovations or **dynamically continuous innovations.** This latter term represents innovations that require some disruption in established behavioral patterns rather than fundamental alterations. Compact disc (CD) players, digital audiotape (DAT) players, disposable cameras,

[2]The innovation continuum notion is attributable to Thomas S. Robertson, *Innovation Behavior and Communication* (New York: Holt, Rinehart and Winston, 1971), 7.

disposable contact lenses, cellular phones, and electric-powered automobiles (such as GM's Impact described in the prior chapter) are some of the more notable dynamically continuous innovations that have appeared in recent years.

The Role of Marketing Communications

Regardless of a product's degree of innovativeness, an organization's marketing-communications specialists have major roles in ensuring new product success. Perhaps this can best be appreciated by conceptualizing the new-product adoption process.[3] The model in Figure 5.1 indicates with circles the three main stages through which an individual becomes a new-brand consumer: awareness class, trier class, and repeater class. The blocks surrounding the circles are marketing mix and promotion elements that are responsible for moving consumers through the three classes and ultimately creating new product users.

Model of New-Product Adoption Process

FIGURE 5.1

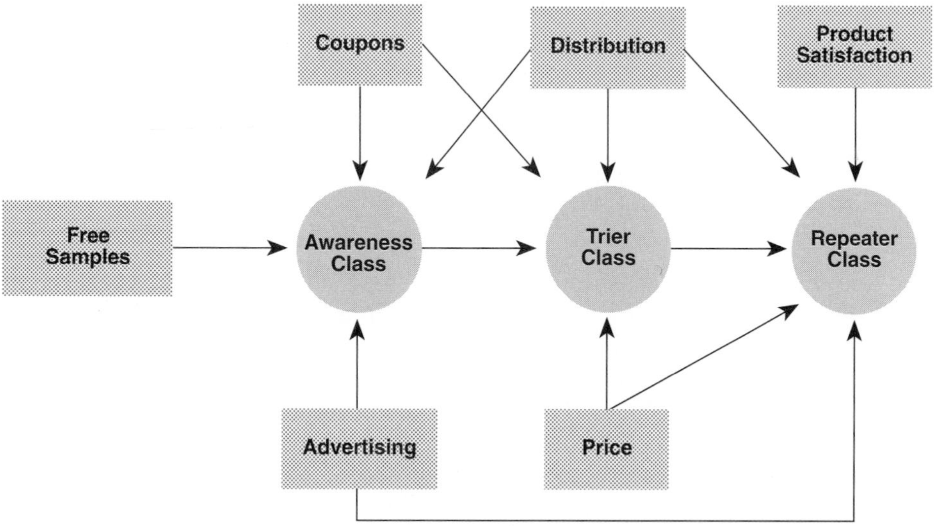

Sources: Chakravarthi Narasimhan and Subrata K. Sen, "New Product Models for Test Market Data," *Journal of Marketing*, 47, (Winter 1983), 13. Reprinted with permission from *Journal of Marketing*, published by the American Marketing Association.

---

[3]The following discussion is adapted from Chakravarthi Narasimhan and Subrata K. Sen, "New Product Models for Test Market Data," *Journal of Marketing*, 47 (Winter 1983), 13, 14.

The first step in facilitating adoption is to make the consumer aware of a new product's existence. Figure 5.1 shows that four marketing-mix variables influence the **awareness class:** free samples, coupons, advertising, and distribution. The first three variables are distinctly promotion-mix variables, and the fourth, distribution, is closely allied with promotion in that the sales force is responsible for gaining distribution, providing reseller support, and making point-of-purchase materials available to the trade.

Once a consumer becomes aware of a new product or brand, there is an increased probability that the consumer will actually try the new offering. Coupons, distribution, and price are the variables that affect the **trier class.** Only the first of these, coupons, is a direct element of marketing communications, but as mentioned in Chapter 1, price and distribution variables perform important communications functions in addition to their more basic economic roles.

Repeat purchasing, the **repeater class,** is a function of four primary forces: advertising, price, distribution, and product satisfaction. That is, consumers are more likely to continue to purchase a particular brand if advertising reminds them about the brand, if the price is considered reasonable, if the brand is accessible, and if product quality is considered satisfactory.

It is evident from this discussion that marketing communications is essential to new product success. The following sections explain in greater detail the processes by which innovations are adopted by individual consumers and diffused throughout the marketplace.

THE ADOPTION PROCESS

The **adoption process** consists of the mental stages an individual goes through in accepting and becoming a repeat purchaser of an innovation. Marketing communicators play a role in accelerating the rate of new-product adoption and thereby increasing the probability of product success. As firms have become more sophisticated marketers, the rate of adoption in consumer markets has increased.[4]

Although consumers are accepting new products more readily than ever, there is still a high percentage of failure in the introduction of new products. Understanding the factors that facilitate or impede successful adoption is crucial to a full appreciation of the role of marketing communications in modern marketing.

---

[4]Richard W. Olshavsky, "Time and Rate of Adoption of Innovations," *Journal of Consumer Research*, 6 (March 1980), 425–428; William Qualls, Richard W. Olshavsky, and Ronald E. Michaels, "Shortening of the PLC—An Empirical Test," *Journal of Marketing*, 45 (Fall 1981), 76–80.

There are five stages of the adoption process: (1) knowledge, (2) persuasion, (3) decision, (4) implementation, and (5) confirmation.[5] As Figure 5.2 indicates, each stage is a necessary precondition to a subsequent stage. The figure also shows various conditions and characteristics that act to increase or retard the innovation-decision process. Among the broad groups of variables that influence the various stages are *prior conditions* (e.g., the consumer's previous consumption practices), *characteristics of the decision-making unit* (e.g., socioeconomic characteristics), and *perceived characteristics of the innovation* (e.g., relative advantages).

Knowledge Stage

In the knowledge stage, which is similar to the awareness class mentioned previously, the individual becomes aware of an innovation and learns something about

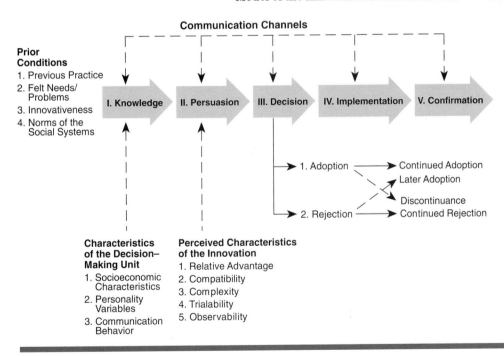

Model of the Innovation-Decision Process

FIGURE 5.2

Source: Reprinted with permission of The Free Press, a Division of Macmillan, Inc., from *Diffusion of Innovations*, Third Edition, by Everett M. Rogers, p.165. Copyright 1962, 1971, 1983 by The Free Press.

[5] Everett M. Rogers, *Diffusion of Innovations*, 3d ed. (New York: The Free Press, 1983), 7.

how the innovation functions. For example, an individual learns that digital audiotape players cost anywhere from $500 to $2,000, that they play cassettes that are smaller than the tapes used in conventional tape players, and that they combine the features of conventional audiotape with the advantages of compact disc players.

Distinct differences exist between those who know about an innovation early and those who are late in recognizing it. On average, those who recognize an innovation early have a higher level of education, a higher social status, a greater exposure to mass media and interpersonal channels of communications, and greater social participation; they are also more cosmopolitan.[6] VCR owners in the United States, for example, are better educated and better-off financially than most Americans.[7]

Advertising plays a crucial role in making consumers aware of and knowledgeable about new products. Sometimes advertising can be irritating, but without it product adoption would be much slower. Salespersons also perform an important role in making customers knowledgeable about new products. In the pharmaceutical industry, for example, salespersons (called *detailers*) inform physicians about new drug products and provide details about product features, benefits, side effects, and so on.

Persuasion Stage

The mental activity at the knowledge stage was mainly cognitive (or thinking), but at the persuasion stage it is mainly affective (or feeling). Though an individual may be aware of an innovation for a long period of time and may know how to use it, he or she may not have developed any feeling or affect (i.e., attitude) toward the innovation. The persuasion stage begins when the individual develops an *attitude* toward the innovation.

In forming an attitude, a consumer often goes through a *vicarious trial* of the product. This helps the consumer to reduce the uncertainty of using the new product or service. The advertisement back in Chapter 3 (see Figure 3.8) for Claussen pickles illustrates an effort to create a vicarious trial experience. (Take a moment to review the ad on page 74 before reading on.) With the catchy headline ("How to test drive a pickle") and the picture showing a man's hands in driving gloves bending a pickle, the reader is provided with a *vivid* reason for adopting the attitude that this brand indeed is fresher than other pickles.[8]

---

[6]Ibid., 168–169.

[7]"VCRs: Coming on Strong," *Time*, December 24, 1984, 45.

[8]It is worth noting that vivid information is more interesting, more able to draw attention and to provoke thoughts, and more likely to influence attitudes than is pallid, or nonvivid, information. For further discussion see Paul M. Herr, Frank R. Kardes, and John Kim, "Effects of Word-of-Mouth and Product-Attribute Information on Persuasion: An Accessibility-Diagnosticity Perspective," *Journal of Consumer Research*, 17 (March 1991), 454–462.

Marketing communications plays a major role in ensuring that consumers form positive attitudes toward innovative products and services. This is done by influencing five innovation-related characteristics that undergird consumers' attitudes toward new products and services: relative advantage, compatibility, complexity, trialability, and observability.

RELATIVE ADVANTAGE.   The degree to which an innovation is perceived as better than an existing idea or product is termed **relative advantage.** Relative advantage is a function of whether a person *perceives* the new product to be better than competitive offerings, not a function of whether the product is objectively better. Relative advantage is positively correlated with an innovation's adoption rate; that is, the greater an innovation's relative advantages vis-a-vis existing offerings, the more rapid the rate of adoption to be expected.

In general, relative advantages exist to the extent that a new product offers (1) increases in comfort, (2) savings in time and effort, and (3) immediacy of reward. Figure 5.3 is a vivid illustration of a relative advantage due to *increased comfort.* The Tracer from Schick is claimed to be the first razor with a blade that flexes and thus is able to trace the curvature of the shaver's face. Microwave ovens epitomize the relative advantage achieved by providing an option which *saves the user's time and effort. Immediacy of reward* advantages are achieved in an endless variety of creative ways. For example, scientists in California have developed a tennis-ball size head of lettuce that tastes like normal lettuce but which can be consumed in a single sitting, thus eliminating the problem of spoiled, leftover lettuce. A maker of barbecue accessories has introduced Hot Stix, an ethanol-based charcoal product that is smokeless and odorless and therefore preferable to petroleum-based charcoals that smoke and stink.[9] Procter & Gamble is introducing a 100 percent compostable disposable diaper that will completely disintegrate and thus help alleviate the landfill problem.[10]

Relative advantages depend on the inherent characteristics of the product itself but can also be influenced by persuasive communications. For example, overnight package delivery (such as provided by Federal Express) offers the real relative advantage of quicker delivery in comparison to conventional mailing; however, advertising must accentuate this real advantage in order for potential users to fully appreciate the advantages of using overnight delivery. Advertising also serves to negate the relative advantages claimed by marketers of new competitive products. For example, Schick's competitors will undoubtedly advertise that their brands provide an even more comfortable shave than does the Tracer.

---

[9]Robert McMath, "Tie a Yellow Ribbon 'Round the Barbecue," *Adweek's Marketing Week*, February 18, 1991, 33.

[10]Laurie Freeman, "Disposable Solution," *Advertising Age*, October 15, 1990, 24.

FIGURE 5.3   An Illustration of Relative Advantage

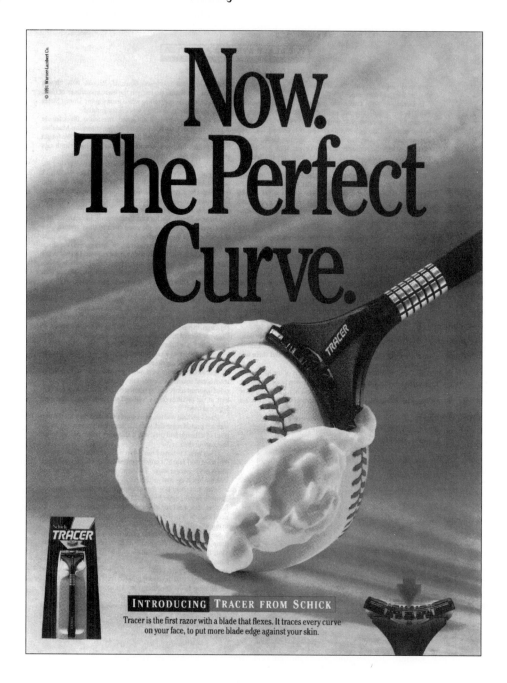

COMPATIBILITY.   The degree to which an innovation is perceived to fit into a person's way of doing things is termed **compatibility.** In general, the more compatible an innovation is with a person's needs, personal values, beliefs, and past experiences, the more rapid its rate of adoption. Innovations that are compatible with a person's existing situation are less risky, more meaningful, and require less effort to incorporate into one's consumption lifestyle. Anheuser-Busch, the makers of O'Doul's Non-Alcoholic Brew, is well aware of the importance of compatibility, as can be seen in the advertisement in Figure 5.4. This ad positions O'Doul's as being compatible with people's need for a non-alcohol beverage that fits into their busy working—and working out—lifestyles.

Establishing compatibility is largely a function of product design. The rebirth of polyester as a fashion item illustrates how physical features of the product itself can accomplish greater compatibility with consumers' lifestyles and thus enhance the rate of adoption (see the *Focus on Promotion*). Beyond this, marketing communicators are largely responsible for ensuring compatibility in the minds of customers by choosing promotional appeals that serve to position a brand as compatible with the target market's beliefs, past experiences, and needs. An interesting illustration of this is the marketing of grapefruit by the Florida Department of Citrus, which has attempted to reposition this product so that it better fits into consumers' workday lives. Many people consider the time required to prepare a grapefruit to be incompatible with the hectic pace of their lives. Advertisements were developed to convince consumers that slicing a grapefruit in half and scooping out the fruit with a spoon is *not* the only way to eat grapefruit. Potential adopters are informed, as simple as it may seem, that grapefruit can be quickly peeled and eaten much like an orange. If successful, these efforts will make the grapefruit more compatible with the hectic pace of many people's lives.[11]

COMPLEXITY.   The degree of perceived difficulty of an innovation is termed **complexity.** The more difficult an innovation is to understand or use, the slower the rate of adoption. Home computers have been adopted slowly because many homeowners perceive computers as too difficult to understand and use. Advertisers have confronted this by creating subtle (and not-so-subtle) television commercials to convey the idea that anyone can easily learn to use a computer, even little kids. Companies have also redesigned their products and introduced new computers that *are* easier to use. The same can be said of VCRs. The current generation of videocassette recorders are easy enough for even adults to use. (Kids, raised in an electronic age, had no trouble using the earlier generations of VCRs, but adults were slow to learn how to do much more with their VCRs than play a prerecorded cassette.)

---

[11]Elaine Underwood, "A New Way to Think about Grapefruit," *Adweek's Marketing Week*, January 28, 1991, 17.

FIGURE 5.4   Establishing Compatibility

FOCUS ON PROMOTION

POLYESTER: ITTTTTTT'S BACK

If you are younger than 30, you, fortunately, have possibly never worn a pair of 100 percent polyester slacks or a fully polyester blouse, shirt, or suit. But throughout much of the 1960s and 1970s polyester was *the* fabric of choice. Nearly every imaginable garment was made of 100 percent polyester fabrics. Fiber companies developed polyester fabrics that were considerably cheaper than natural fabrics. Apparel companies could produce polyester garments much less expensively than cotton, wool, or other natural fibers. Retailers stocked their racks and shelves with polyester garments, and consumers oftentimes had little choice but to purchase items made of polyester.

It was only a matter of time, however, before polyester would die a natural (or unnatural) death. The fabric was unattractive, uncomfortable, and, frankly, downright cheap. By the late 1980s "king" cotton returned to a commanding market share of over 50 percent compared to a low of around only 34 percent during polyester's heyday.

But now polyester is coming back, potentially in a big way. Fiber companies like DuPont and Hoechst Celanese are repositioning polyester to appeal to the upper end of the clothing market. These companies have developed polyester fibers that are just 10 percent the thickness of the old double-knit polyesters. These fibers can be spun into cotton-like and silk-like fabrics so as to appear entirely natural and unsynthetic. DuPont's own research involving 5,000 consumers determined that 77 percent preferred the feel of that company's synthetic fabric to natural fibers. Because the thin fibers are more expensive than cotton itself, they will be marketed to the upper end of the market and not the masses. To avoid undesirable connotations associated with polyester, these new fibers, called *microdeniers*, are being marketed with trade names such as MicroSpun, Micronesse, and Micromatique. And hence polyester has come full cycle—from compatible with American consumers' lifestyles in the 1960s and 1970s, to incompatible in the 1980s, to perhaps compatible again in the 1990s.

Source: The statistics and much of the information in this section are from Elaine Underwood, "Can a Reborn Polyester Dethrone King Cotton?" *Adweek's Marketing Week,* April 15, 1991, 16.

TRIALABILITY.   The extent to which an innovation can be used on a limited basis is referred to as **trialability.** In general, products that lend themselves to trialability are adopted at a more rapid rate. Trialability is tied closely to the concept of *perceived risk*. Test drives of new automobiles, free samples of food products at local supermarkets, and small packages of new detergents all permit the consumer to try a new product on an experimental basis. The trial experience serves to reduce the risk of a consumer's being dissatisfied with a product after having permanently committed to it through an outright purchase.

Facilitating trial is typically more difficult with durable products than with inexpensive packaged goods. Automobile companies allow consumers to take test drives, but what do you do if you are, say, a computer manufacturer or a lawn-mower maker? If you are creative, you do what companies like Apple Computer and John Deere did in novel efforts to give people the opportunity to try their products. Apple developed a "Test Drive a Macintosh" promotion that gave interested consumers the opportunity to try the computer in the comfort of their own homes for 24 hours at no cost. Approximately 200,000 Macintoshes were "test driven" during the promotional period, and dealers attributed 40 percent of their sales volume during this period to the promotion.[12] Figure 5.5 shows an advertisement for a John Deere mower and describes a 30-day free test period whereby the consumer can try the mower for this period and then return it, no questions asked, if not fully satisfied.

OBSERVABILITY.   The degree to which other people can observe one's ownership and use of a new product is referred to as observability, or *visibility*. The more a consumption behavior can be sensed by other people (seen, smelled, etc.), the more visible it is said to be. Thus, driving an automobile with a new type of engine is less visible than driving an automobile with a unique body design; wearing a new perfume fragrance is less visible than adopting a hairstyle that is avant-garde. In general, innovations that are high in visibility lend themselves to rapid adoption if they also possess relative advantages, are compatible with consumption lifestyles, and so on. Products whose benefits lack observability are generally slower in adoptability.

The important role of product observability is illustrated by Nike Shoe Co.'s use of Air Pockets in its athletic shoes marketed in the late 1980s. These highly visible inserts in the heel section of Nike shoes clearly conveyed the product benefit of comfort by showing that running and jumping in Nike shoes is like landing on a protective mattress. Nike could have designed their shoes so that the air pocket was concealed from observation; instead, they decided to make the feature conspicuous and in so doing provided themselves with the easily communicable point that Nike shoes are more comfortable than competitive brands.

---

[12]William A. Robinson and Kevin Brown, "Best Promotions of 1984: Back to Basics," *Advertising Age*, March 11, 1985, 42.

Achieving Trialability

FIGURE 5.5

Even after mowing from Chicago to Amarillo, you could still get your money back.

When you buy just about any John Deere mower, you get 30 days to test it out. If you're not happy, you can get your money back. No questions asked.

So why not give it a *real* test? With our fast, new LX172 (and its 14-hp OHV engine), you could

mow a 38-inch swath all the way from the Great Lakes to the Texas panhandle inside 30 days.

For shorter test runs, our affordable STX30 mows nearly an acre an hour. Or about 250 football fields in a single month of dawn-to-dusk operation.

We've also got a new line of rear engine riders. From the economical GX models, to the deluxe SRX75. With a top speed of 5 mph, you could manicure an entire nine-hole golf course just working four weekends.

Like to walk? All six John Deere walk-behinds come with our money-back guarantee, and start at around $400. After testing one out on your own lawn, you may as well accept the inevitable and let your neighbors borrow it.

To see the full line, just visit your nearest John Deere dealer. (Call 1-800-544-2122.)

He'll help you pick a mower and give you 30 days to try it. The rest is up to you.

NOTHING RUNS LIKE A DEERE.

Reebok's Pump shoe is further illustration of how the product benefit is made visible. In the athletic shoe industry, this is called *exposing the technology*.[13] By any name, this practice simply recognizes the basic fact that consumers are more likely to adopt a new product when its advantages are observable.

In sum, the persuasion stage represents an important area of concern for marketing communicators. In this stage, the potential adopter is making up his or her mind about the innovation. Many times an individual will mentally or vicariously try the innovation to see how it applies to his or her present situation. Advertisers facilitate this vicarious trial by showing the new product being used by people with whom the target audience identifies positively. Sales representatives do the same by informing prospective customers of other desirable individuals who have already purchased the product. Through the right choice of symbols and appeals, marketing communicators can assist product designers in expediting the rate of product adoption and in increasing the chances of product success.

Decision and Implementation Stages

The **decision stage** (return to Figure 5.2) represents the period during which a person mentally chooses either to adopt or reject an innovation. For example, a long-time wearer of contact lenses decides to discard her old, permanent contacts in favor of new, disposable contacts. Another consumer rejects the idea of disposable contacts on the grounds that they are too expensive and that it would be extravagant for her to buy this new product when her old contacts are still in good condition.

The **implementation stage** occurs when a person puts the new product or idea to use. In the previous stage (decision), the individual simply makes a mental commitment either to use the product or sample it on a *trial basis*. However, no full-scale commitment is made. In the implementation stage, the individual wants answers to questions such as, "How do I use this product?" and "How do I solve these operational problems?" Salespersons and professionals (e.g., optometrists) perform important functions in such instances by providing technical assistance and by giving the customer helpful suggestions for using the product.

Confirmation Stage

People often seek additional information after making an important adoption decision in an attempt to confirm the wisdom or appropriateness of their decision. The **confirmation stage** represents the time period in which postdecisional

---

[13]E. M. Swift, "Farewell My Lovely," *Sports Illustrated*, February 19, 1990, 84.

dissonance, regret, and dissonance reduction occur. People seek out friends in hopes of being told how wise their choice was and they also respond to impersonal sources of information (such as magazine ads) that buttress their decision. If a person cannot be adequately assured of the correctness of an adoption decision, he or she may discontinue the adoption. Sales representatives have a special role in this stage. An axiom in personal selling is, "You must continue to sell after the sale."

THE DIFFUSION PROCESS

In comparison to the adoption process, which focuses on the individual consumer (a micro viewpoint), the **diffusion process** is concerned with the broader issue of how an innovation is communicated and adopted *throughout the marketplace* (a macro viewpoint). In simple terms, diffusion is the process of spreading out. In a marketing communications sense, this means that a product or idea is adopted by more and more customers as time passes. By analogy, consider a situation where gas is released into a small room. The fumes eventually spread throughout the entire room. Similarly, product innovations spread ideally to all parts of a potential market. The word *ideally* is used because, unlike the physical analogy, the communication of an innovation in the marketplace is often impeded by factors such as unsuitable communication channels, competitive maneuverings, and other imperfect conditions.

This section deals with the *aggregate behavior* of groups of customers in comparison to the individual mental stages used to describe the adoption process. Specifically, it examines the characteristics that are typical of each group in the diffusion process.[14]

Adopter Categories

As a product spreads through the marketplace over time, different types of consumers adopt the product. The diffusion literature identifies five general groups of adopters: (1) innovators, (2) early adopters, (3) early majority, (4) late majority, and (5) laggards. As a matter of convention, these five categories are presumed to follow a normal (bell-shaped) statistical distribution with respect to each group's average (mean) time of adoption following the introduction of an innovation (see Figure 5.6). That is, in accordance with the properties of a normal distribution, 68 percent of all people who ultimately adopt an innovation fall within plus (late majority) or minus (early majority) one standard deviation of

---

[14]For further discussion, see Hubert Gatignon and Thomas S. Robertson, "A Propositional Inventory for New Diffusion Research," *Journal of Consumer Research*, 11 (March 1985), 849–867.

FIGURE 5.6   Classification of Adopter Groups

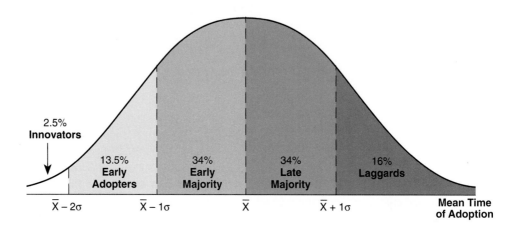

Sources: Reprinted with permission of The Free Press, a Division of Macmillan, Inc., from *Diffusion of Innovations*, Third Edition, by Everett M. Rogers, p. 165. Copyright© 1962, 1971, 1983 by Three Free Press.

the mean time of adoption. The other adopter categories are interpreted in a similar manner. Although the categorization is arbitrary, it has been found meaningful in the study of the diffusion process.

INNOVATORS. The small group of innovators are the first people to accept a new idea or product. Innovators exhibit a *high level of venturesomeness*. They also are more *willing to take risks*, because innovation requires risk taking. That is, being among the first people to adopt a new product, especially if it is expensive, means that the innovator incurs the risk that the product will not work as well as expected, that money will be lost, and possibly that he or she will be embarrassed by a bad decision. Consider, for example, the risk of being among the very first people in a community to own an electric-powered automobile. Not many people are willing to be the first to invest $20,000 or more in a product that may turn out to have little resale value.

Another characteristic of innovators is that they are willing to seek social relationships outside of their local peer group; that is, they are *cosmopolites*. Innovators also tend to be *younger, higher in social status*, and *better educated* than later adopter groups. Innovators interact mostly with other innovators and rely heavily on *impersonal* informational sources, rather than on other people, to satisfy their information needs. Innovators generally have been found to display a broader range of interests than noninnovators.[15]

EARLY ADOPTERS.   Early adopters are the second group to adopt an innovation. The size of this group is defined statistically as 13.5 percent of all potential adopters.[16] Early adopters are *localites*, in contrast to innovators, who were described as cosmopolites. The early adopter is *well integrated* within his or her community and is *respected* by his or her friends.[17] Because of this respect, the early adopter is *often sought for advice and information* about new products and services. The respect he or she commands among peers makes the early adopter a very important determinant of the success or failure of an innovation. *Opinion leaders* come primarily from the early-adopter group. Their characteristics and role in the diffusion process are discussed later in the chapter.

EARLY MAJORITY.   Approximately 34 percent of all potential adopters of an innovation fall into the early-majority group. As shown in Figure 5.6, the early majority adopt the product prior to the mean time of adoption. Members of this group are *deliberate* and *cautious* in their adoption of innovations.[18] They spend more time in the innovation-decision process than the two earlier groups. Though the group displays some opinion leadership, it is well below that shown by early adopters. This group is *slightly above average in education and social status* but below the levels of the early-adopter group.

LATE MAJORITY.   As shown in Figure 5.6, the late majority is depicted as 34 percent of potential adopters just below the average time of adoption. The key word that characterizes the late majority is *skepticism*.[19] By the time they adopt an innovation, the majority of the market has already done so. Peers are the primary source of new ideas for the late majority, who make *little use of mass media*. Demographically, they are *below average* in education, income, and social status.

LAGGARDS.   The final group to adopt an innovation is referred to as laggards; they represent the bottom 16 percent of potential adopters. These people are *bound in tradition*.[20] As a group, laggards *focus on the past* as their frame of reference.

---

[15]Thomas S. Robertson and James N. Kennedy, "Prediction of Consumer Innovators: Application of Discriminant Analysis," *Journal of Marketing Research*, 5 (February 1968), 64-69, citing *America's Tastemakers, Research Reports Nos. 1 and 2* (Princeton, NJ: Opinion Research Corporation, 1959).

[16]That is, the area under the normal curve between one and two standard deviations from the mean.

[17]Rogers, *Diffusion of Innovations*, 248–249.

[18]Ibid.

[19]Ibid.

[20]Ibid., 250.

Their collective attitude may be summarized as, "If it was good enough for my parents, it's good enough for me." Laggards are tied closely to other laggards and to their local community and have limited contact with the mass media. This group, as might be expected, has the *lowest social status and income* of all adopter groups. If and when laggards adopt an innovation, it usually occurs after one or more innovations have replaced the earlier innovation.

Managing the Diffusion Process

The actual course of diffusion for a new product is partly determined by a company's marketing actions (including product quality, sales-force efforts, advertising level, and price strategy) and partly by external forces that are largely beyond a firm's control (such as competitive actions, shifts in consumers' buying moods and desires, and the state of the economy). However, to the greatest possible extent, firms hope to manage the diffusion process so that the new product or service accomplishes the following objectives:[21]

1. Secures initial sales as quickly as possible (achieves a *rapid takeoff*).
2. Achieves cumulative sales in a steep curve (achieves *rapid acceleration*).
3. Secures the highest-possible sales potential in the targeted market segment (achieves *maximum penetration*).
4. Maintains sales for as long as possible (achieves a *long-run franchise*).

Figure 5.7 displays the *desired* diffusion pattern that satisfies the preceding conditions and compares it with the *typical* diffusion pattern. The typical pattern following a product's introduction involves a relatively slow takeoff, a slow rate of sales growth, maximum penetration below the full market potential, and a sales decline sooner than what would be desired.

What can marketing communications do to make the typical pattern more like the desired pattern? First, *rapid takeoff* can be facilitated by having a promotion budget that is sufficiently large to permit (1) aggressive sales force efforts that are needed to secure trade support for new products, (2) intensive advertising to create high product-awareness levels among the target market, and (3) sufficient sales promotion activity to generate desired levels of trial-purchase behavior. Second, *rapid acceleration* may be accomplished (1) by ensuring that product quality is suitable and will promote positive word-of-mouth communication, (2) by continuing to advertise heavily to reach later adopter groups, (3) by ensuring that the sales force provides reseller support,

---

[21]This section is adapted from Thomas S. Robertson, Joan Zielinski, and Scott Ward, *Consumer Behavior* (Glenview, IL: Scott, Foresman and Company, 1984), 380–382.

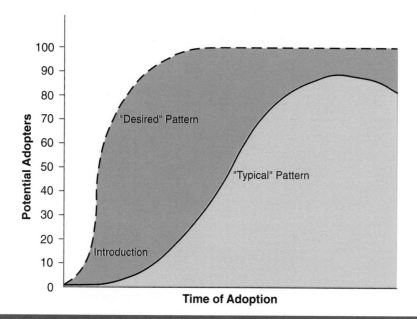

"Desired" and "Typical" Diffusion Patterns   **FIGURE 5.7**

Source: Thomas S. Robertson, Joan Zielinski and Scott Ward, *Consumer Behavior* (Glenview, IL.: Scott, Foresman and Company, 1984), 381.

and (4) by using sales promotion creatively so that incentives are provided for repeat-purchase behavior. Third, *maximum penetration* can be approached (1) by continuing the same strategies that stimulated rapid acceleration and (2) by revising product design and advertising strategies in such a fashion that the product or service appeals to the needs of the later adopters. Finally, a *long-run franchise* can be maintained by ensuring (1) that the old product continues to meet the market's needs, (2) that distribution is suitable to reach the market, and (3) that advertising continues to remind the market about the product.

STIMULATING WORD-OF-MOUTH INFLUENCE

People in all buying capacities—consumers buying automobiles, industrial purchasing agents buying new equipment, physicians ordering drug products, hospitals ordering supplies, athletic teams purchasing equipment, and so on—rely on two major sources of information to assist them in making decisions: impersonal

GLOBAL FOCUS

DIFFUSION OF CONSUMER DURABLES IN PACIFIC RIM COUNTRIES

A fascinating issue for marketing researchers is the question of how adoption and diffusion processes differ in various countries. In a recent study of consumer durable goods, researchers studied four Pacific Rim countries: Japan, South Korea, Taiwan, and the United States. In addition to being the only western country, the United States differs from these other Pacific Rim countries in that its society is much more diverse ethnically, racially, and culturally. Due to the United States' relative diversity, the researchers predicted that the rate of durable-good diffusion would be *faster* in the three Asian countries compared to the United States.

It also was hypothesized that the rate of adoption and diffusion would be *faster* when products are introduced in countries after they have already been adopted and diffused in other countries. The lag period allows the newly adopting country to quickly realize a product's relative advantages (based on the experience of other countries) and to readily see the product's compatibility with the country's needs.

Products examined included black & white TVs, electric washing machines, room air conditioners, passenger cars, electric refrigerators, calculators, vacuum cleaners, and radios. The researchers obtained national statistics on when these products were introduced in each country and annual sales figures on each product. For example, washing machines were marketed in the United States starting in 1927, but did not enter Japan until 1952, Taiwan until 1968, and South Korea until 1975.

Using a mathematical model to test their predictions, the researchers found support for the hypothesis that the rate of product adoption and diffusion in the United States would be significantly slower on average than in the Asian countries. Although most of the researched products were introduced earlier in the United States than in other countries, it took longer for these products to achieve maximum penetration levels in the United States. Apparently, there is a tendency for these other Pacific Rim countries to emulate United States consumption behavior, and the emulation process occurs quickly once *Americanized* products enter these other countries.

Source: Hirokazu Takada and Dipak Jain, "Cross-National Analysis of Diffusion of Consumer Durables Goods in Pacific Rim Countries," *Journal of Marketing*, 55 (April 1991), 48–54.

and personal sources. *Impersonal sources* include information received from television, magazines, and other mass-media sources. *Personal sources*, the subject of this section, include word-of-mouth influence from friends and acquaintances. Research has shown that the more favorable information a potential new-product adopter has received from peers, the more likely that individual is to adopt the new product or service.[22]

Opinion Leaders

An **opinion leader** is a person who frequently influences other individuals' attitudes or overt behavior.[23] Opinion leaders perform several important functions: they *inform* other people (followers) about new products and ideas, they *provide advice* and reduce the follower's perceived risk in purchasing a new product, and they *provide positive feedback to support or confirm* decisions that followers have already made. Thus, an opinion leader is an informer, persuader, and confirmer.

Opinion leadership influence is typically *restricted to one or several consumption topics* rather than applying universally across many consumption domains. That is, a person who is an opinion leader with respect to issues and products in one consumption area (say, movies or skiing or cooking) is not generally influential in other unrelated areas. It would be very unlikely, for example, for one person to be respected for his or her knowledge and opinions concerning all three of the listed consumption topics. Moreover, opinion leaders are found *in every social class*. In most instances, opinion leadership influence moves *horizontally* through a social class instead of vertically from one class to another.

Opinion leaders have profiles that are distinctly different than others' profiles. In general, opinion leaders (1) are more *cosmopolitan* and have greater *contact with the mass media* than do followers, (2) are usually more *gregarious* than the general population and have more *social contacts* and thus more opportunity for discussing and passing information than followers, (3) tend to have slightly *higher socioeconomic status* than followers, (4) are generally more *innovative* than followers, and (5) are willing to act differently than other people, to withstand criticism and rejection, and, in general, have a *need to be unique*.[24]

---

[22]Johan Arndt, "Role of Product-Related Conversation in the Diffusion of a New Product," *Journal of Marketing Research*, 4 (August 1967), 291–295; Dorothy Leonard-Barton, "Experts as Negative Opinion Leaders in the Diffusion of a Technological Innovation," *Journal of Consumer Research*, 11 (March 1985), 914-926.

[23]Rogers, *Diffusion of Innovations*, 271.

[24]This fifth point is based on recent research that has detected a new dimension of opinion leadership termed *public individuation*. In a study of college students' wine-consumption attitudes and behavior, the researchers obtained support that opinion leaders in this category are more publically individuated. See Kenny K. Chan and Shekhar Misra, "Characteristics of the Opinion Leader: A New Dimension," *Journal of Advertising*, 19 (no. 3 1990), 53-60.

What motivates opinion leaders to give information? It seems that opinion leaders are willing to participate in word-of-mouth (WOM) communications with others because they *derive satisfaction* from telling others what their opinions are and what they know about new products and services. In order to share what they know about innovations and thus gain satisfaction from telling others, the opinion leaders continually *strive to keep themselves informed* (often feeling an obligation to do so).

Prestige is at the heart of WOM. "We like being the bearers of news. Being able to recommend gives us a feeling of prestige. It makes us instant experts."[25] Being an expert in marketplace matters does bring prestige. Researchers have recently referred to the marketplace expert as a market maven.[26] **Market mavens** are "individuals who have information about many kinds of products, places to shop, and other facets of markets, and initiate discussions with consumers and respond to requests from consumers for market information."[27] In other words, the market maven is looked upon as an important source of information and receives prestige and satisfaction from supplying information to friends and others.

A vice president of marketing for Paramount Pictures suggests that the key to generating good WOM is by finding cheerleaders, that is, consumers who will "get the talk started." Usually this is a carefully selected target group that is most likely to love a new movie.[28] In the book industry, cheerleading is stimulated by giving free copies of a new book to a select group of opinion leaders. For example, in the case of *Megatrends*, a leading seller by John Naisbitt, the book publisher sent more than 1,000 copies to chief executive officers of major corporations. Within one month of publication, it became a *must read* book by literally thousands of businesspeople.[29]

Thus, positive word-of-mouth communication is a critical element in a new product's or service's success. Unfavorable WOM can have devastating effects on adoption, because consumers seem to place *more weight on negative information* in making evaluations than on positive information.[30]

---

[25]This quote is from the famous motivational researcher, Ernest Dichter, in Eileen Prescott "Word-of-Mouth: Playing on the Prestige Factor," *The Wall Street Journal*, February 7, 1984, 1.

[26]A *maven* (or mavin) is considered an expert in everyday matters.

[27]Lawrence F. Feick and Linda L. Price, "The Market Maven: A Diffuser of Marketplace Information," *Journal of Marketing*, 51 (January 1987), 83-97.

[28]Prescott, "Word-of-Mouth."

[29]Ibid.

[30]See Herr, Kardes, and Kim, "Effects of Word-of-Mouth and Product-Attribute Information on Persuasion: An Accessibility-Diagnosticity Perspective"; Richard J. Lutz, "Changing Brand Attitudes through Modification of Cognitive Structure," *Journal of Consumer Research*, 1 (March 1975), 49-59; Peter Wright, "The Harassed Decision Maker: Time Pressures, Distractions, and the Use of Evidence," *Journal of Applied Psychology*, 59 (October 1974), 555–561.

Marketing communicators can do several things to minimize the level of negative word-of-mouth:[31] (1) At the minimum, companies need to show customers that they are responsive to legitimate complaints; (2) manufacturers can do this by providing detailed warranty and complaint-procedure information on labels or in package inserts; (3) retailers can demonstrate their responsiveness to customer complaints through employees with positive attitudes, store signs, and inserts in monthly billings to customers; (4) companies can offer toll-free numbers to provide customers with an easy, free way to voice their complaints and suggestions. By being responsive to customer complaints, companies can avert negative WOM and perhaps even create positive WOM.[32]

SUMMARY

The continual introduction of new products and services is critical to the success of most business organizations. The likelihood of success depends in part on the degree of innovativeness. Innovations are classified along a continuum ranging from slightly new at one end (*continuous innovations*) to dramatically different at the other end (*discontinuous innovations*).

The concepts of adoption and diffusion explain the processes by which new products and services are accepted by more and more customers as time passes. The *adoption process* views the mental stages an individual goes through in accepting and becoming a repeat purchaser of an innovation. The process consists of five stages: knowledge, persuasion, decision, implementation, and confirmation. Each of these stages is affected by a wide array of variables, which act to expedite or retard the rate of product adoption.

The *diffusion process* is concerned with the broader issue of how an innovation is communicated and adopted throughout the marketplace. Diffusion, in simple terms, is the process of spreading out. Diffusion scholars have identified five relatively distinct groups of adopters. These groups, moving from the first to adopt an innovation to the last, are *innovators, early adopters, early majority, late majority*, and *laggards*. Research has shown that these groups differ considerably in terms of such variables as socioeconomic status, risk-taking tendencies, and peer relations.

Opinion leadership and word-of-mouth influence are important elements in facilitating more rapid product adoption and diffusion. *Opinion leaders* are

---

[31] Marsha L. Richins, "Negative Word-of-Mouth by Dissatisfied Consumers: A Pilot Study," *Journal of Marketing*, 47 (Winter 1983), 76.

[32] Ibid.

individuals who are respected for their product knowledge and opinions. Opinion leaders inform other people (followers) about new products and services, provide advice and reduce the follower's perceived risk in purchasing a new product, and confirm decisions that followers have already made. In comparison to followers, opinion leaders are more cosmopolitan, more gregarious, have higher socioeconomic status, and are more innovative. Positive word-of-mouth influence is often critical to new-product success. It appears that people talk about new products and services because they gain a feeling of prestige from being the bearer of news. Marketing communicators can take advantage of this prestige factor by stimulating cheerleaders, who will talk favorably about a new product or service.

Discussion Questions

1. Classify the following products and services as continuous, dynamically continuous, or discontinuous innovations: nonalcoholic brew, fat-free mayonnaise, digital audiotape (DAT) players, satellite dishes for homeowner use, metal golf clubs (Pittsburgh persimmon) used as a substitute for wood golf clubs, and electrically powered automobiles.

2. Using nonalcoholic brews for illustration, explain the process by which marketing variables can influence consumers to become part of the awareness, trier, and repeater classes (refer to Figure 5.1).

3. The Double Dog is the brand name for a distinctive hotdog bun that has two cuts and allows two weiners to be eaten at once. Based on what you now know about the adoption process, what is the likelihood that this product will receive wide consumer acceptance?

4. What determines whether a new product or service has relative advantages over competitive offerings? What are the relative advantages of each of the following: disposable cameras, disposable contact lenses, fat-free pastries, electric-powered automobiles? Given that each of the above products also has relative *disadvantages* compared to its predecessor product, present a *general statement* (a statement with universal applicability) that would explain how consumers are willing to adopt new products even though they almost invariably have relative disadvantages.

5. What is meant when we say that a potential adopter of a product or service "vicariously tries" the product before adopting it? What can marketing communicators do to promote vicarious trial?

6. Pick a new product or service (your choice) and describe in detail how that product or service satisfies, or fails to satisfy, the following success requirements: relative advantages, compatibility, communicability, trialability, and observability.

7. Suppose you are the manager of a new restaurant located in your college or university community that caters primarily to the campus population. Your fledgling restaurant cannot yet afford media advertising, so the promotional burden rests upon stimulating positive word-of-mouth communications. Present a *specific* strategy for how you might go about stimulating positive WOM.

8. The researchers who conceived the concept of *market maven* (see footnote 27) devised a six-item scale to measure the concept. Respondents rate each item on a seven-point scale from strongly disagree (= 1) to strongly agree (= 7); thus, total scores range from a low of 6 (strongly disagrees to all items) to 42 (strongly agrees to all items). The items are:

(1) I like introducing new brands and products to my friends.
(2) I like helping people in providing them with information about many kinds of products.
(3) People ask me for information about products, places to shop, or sales.
(4) If someone asked where to get the best buy on several types of products, I could tell him or her where to shop.
(5) My friends think of me as a good source of information when it comes to new products or sales.
(6) Think about a person who has information about a variety of products and likes to share this information with others. This person knows about new products, sales, stores, and so on, but does not necessarily feel he or she is an expert on one particular product. How well would you say that this description fits you?

Administer the scale to two friends whom you regard as market mavens and to two friends who are not market mavens. See if the mavens receive predictably higher scores than the nonmavens. Also, comment on whether you think these six items do a good job of measuring market mavenness. What additions or deletions, if any, would you make?

ENVIRONMENTAL INFLUENCES on MARKETING COMMUNICATIONS

Part 3 examines factors that are beyond marketing communicators' direct control but which nonetheless have considerable influence on the direction and effectiveness of marketing communications practices.

The external, or environmental, factors discussed in the next two chapters include demographic developments (Chapter 6) and ecological, ethical, and regulatory issues (Chapter 7).

Chapter 6 discusses a variety of demographic developments in the United States and their marketing communications implications. The major topics discussed include population growth and geographic developments, changes in the age structure of the United States, changes in household size and composition, changes in the roles of women, income dynamics, and minority population developments.

Chapter 7 first explores major developments relating to the physical environment and implications for marketing communicators. A second section examines a variety of ethical issues involving matters of targeting communications at vulnerable groups, deceptive advertising, and other cases of potentially unethical marketing communications practices. A final section reviews governmental regulation and industry self-regulation of marketing communications practices.

The Demographic Environment

THE WAY IT WAS: A DRAMATICALLY CHANGED MARKETPLACE

Imagine, for the moment, that the year is 1962 and your father is manager of detergent products for Procter & Gamble, the famous multi-product consumer-goods firm located in Cincinnati, Ohio. One of his brands is Tide detergent. Increasing Tide's sales volume is fairly simple because the population is growing rapidly during this baby-boom period and mothers need increasing quantities of detergent to keep their families' clothing clean and respectable. To maintain Tide's image all your father has to do is buy a lot of time on daytime network television and advertise day after day to the millions of housewives who enjoy watching soap operas. Creating TV commercials is relatively simple, because in appealing to the mass market there is no need to bother with customizing messages to small market segments.

Now, let's return to the 1990s. You are the daughter or son of the Tide product manager. By some incredible stroke of coincidence, you also work for P&G and occupy a new position, called category manager, which was established in the late 1980s (to be discussed in Chapter 8). Your job is much more challenging than your father's. Sales volume in the United States is not increasing as rapidly as back in 1962 because the population growth rate has declined. Network television advertising isn't as effective or efficient as it used to be. Now, many mothers no longer are at home during the daytime, and viewers increasingly are watching cable programs. Furthermore, many of your target customers are not members of the traditional household of yesteryear, with father, mother, and two or three kids. Rather, a surprisingly large percentage are singles—people who have been divorced, separated, widowed, or never married. Compared to 1962, a larger percentage of your customers are in the mature age category. There are a lot more minorities in the market—blacks, Hispanics, and Asians—and the television commercial that appealed to the mass audiences of the fifties and sixties no longer is effective for all groups. Moreover, buyers and consumers of detergent are not just the stereotypical homemakers of years past, but now are fathers, older children, and millions of singles.

Your father, detergent products manager circa 1962, was successful in mass marketing Tide because he could reach the multitudes easily and inexpensively. You, the micro marketer, will succeed only if you use marketing communications tools that will effectively and efficiently reach the fragmented market segments of today. Dad's job was a lot easier than yours!

Note: A good overview of micromarketing can be obtained in an article by Zachary Schiller, "Stalking the New Consumer," *Business Week*, August 28, 1989, 54–62. Micro marketing is further discussed in Chapter 8.

OVERVIEW

The opening vignette portrays, from the hypothetical perspective of one company, a very changed marketplace. Some of the points are perhaps overstated, but only slightly. The United States is an extremely dynamic society that has changed dramatically in only a matter of decades. Promotion management and marketing communications are vastly more complicated than they used to be due, in large part, to significant changes in the demographic fabric of American society.

This chapter's purpose is to introduce you to notable aspects of the demographic environment that have relevance to marketing communicators. The task of promotion management is to adapt and respond appropriately to marketplace changes. Firms must stay abreast of demographic developments and be prepared to alter policies, strategies, and tactics in line with changing circumstances.

Demographic variables are measurable characteristics of populations, including characteristics such as age distribution, household living patterns, income distribution, minority population patterns, and regional population statistics. By monitoring demographic shifts, marketers are better able to (1) identify and select market segments, (2) forecast product sales, and (3) select media for reaching target customers.[1]

[1]Thomas S. Robertson, Joan Zielinski, and Scott Ward, *Consumer Behavior* (Glenview, IL: Scott, Foresman and Company, 1984), 340.

Some of the dramatic and profound changes in the demographic structure of the United States include the following:

1. *A maturing society.* There now are more people over age 65 than there are teenagers living in the United States.

2. *Lure of the sunbelt.* Populations in the southern and western sunbelt states have increased dramatically in comparison to population growth elsewhere in the United States.[2]

3. *Women on the move.* In the early 1960s approximately 30 percent of married women worked outside the home. Now the percentage exceeds 65 percent.

4. *Rise of minorities.* The combined population of blacks, Hispanics, and Asian Americans is growing at a disproportionately faster rate than the remainder of the population.

The following sections will focus on six major demographic topics that are important to promotion managers and marketing communicators: (1) population growth and regional geographic developments, (2) the changing age structure, (3) the changing American household, (4) the changing roles of women, (5) income dynamics, and (6) minority population developments.

POPULATION GROWTH AND REGIONAL GEOGRAPHIC DEVELOPMENTS

The world population is experiencing an incredible and alarming increase. In 1960 the population was barely over 3 billion people, in 1984 it approached 5 billion, and by the year 2025 it is projected to exceed 8 billion.[3]

In contrast to much of the rest of the world, the United States is *slow* in population growth. In 1980, the U.S. population was about 226.5 million. It reached almost 250 million in 1990 and is expected to grow to approximately 268 million by 2000. Nearly 23 million people were added to the U.S. population in the 1970s, and a like amount were added in the 1980s.[4] However, only 18 million additional people are expected to be added to the U.S. population in the 1990s.[5] In percent-

[2]Alex Kucherov, "10 Forces Reshaping America," *U.S. News and World Report,* March 19, 1984, 40–52.

[3]"People, People, People," *Time,* August 6, 1984, 24, 25.

[4]Judith Waldrop and Thomas Exter, "What the 1990 Census Will Show," *American Demographics,* January 1990, 20–30.

[5]William Lazer, *Handbook of Demographics for Marketing and Advertising* (Lexington, MA: Lexington Books, 1987), 6.

ages, the U.S. population increased by nearly 10 percent between 1980–1989, whereas it is expected to increase by only 7 percent during the 1990s.[6]

A further interesting facet of the U.S. population is the shifts that are taking place in its *geographical distribution*. Historically, the population was concentrated in the industrial Northeast and Midwest, but by the year 2000 a solid majority of Americans will live in the South or West. In fact, in 1990 the Northeast had the smallest population, with approximately 51 million people residing in states from Pennsylvania to Maine. This compares with 52 million in the West, 60 million residents in the Midwest, and 87 million in the South.[7] Population increases between 1980 and 1990 were modest in the Northeast (3.6 percent) and Midwest (1.8 percent) but explosive in the South (15.4 percent) and West (20.5 percent).

THE CHANGING AGE STRUCTURE

One of the most dramatic features of the American population is its relentless aging; the median age of Americans was 28 in 1970, 30 in 1980, and 33 in 1990; it will rise to 36 by the year 2000.[8] In 1990 there were more than 30 million Americans over the age of 65; by comparison, slightly more than 19 million were under the age of 5. Table 6.1 presents these population figures along with the distribution by age group and, at the bottom, median-age data.

The Baby-Boom Generation

The changing age structure is attributable in large part to what demographers term the **baby boom**—the 75 million Americans born between 1946 and 1964.[9] The effects of the baby boom (and subsequent bust) can be seen in Figure 6.1, which compares age-group population figures for the years 1985 and 1995 and in this comparison portrays three major developments:

1. In 1995 there will be over 5 million more preteenage Americans than in 1985; the original baby boomers are creating a *mini baby boom* as they reach childbearing age.

---

[6]Alecia Swasy, "Changing Times: Marketers Scramble to Keep Pace with Demographic Shifts," *Wall Street Journal*, March 22, 1991, sec. B, 6.

[7]Waldrop and Exter, "What the 1990 Census Will Show," 24.

[8]"The Year 2000: A Demographic Profile of the Consumer Market," *Marketing News*, May 25, 1984, 8.

[9]Bryant Robey and Cheryl Russell, "The Year of the Baby Boom," *American Demographics*, May 1984, 19.

| TABLE 6.1 | Projections of the Population of the United States by Age: 1985–2000 |

Population (numbers in thousands)

Age		1985	1990	1995	2000
Under 5		18,453	19,198	18,615	17,626
5–9	Children	16,611	18,591	19,337	18,758
10–14	and Teens	16,797	16,793	18,772	19,519
15–19		18,416	16,968	16,968	18,943
20–24	Young	21,301	18,580	17,142	17,145
25–29	Adults	21,838	21,522	18,882	17,396
30–34		19,950	22,007	21,698	19,019
35–39		17,894	20,001	22,052	21,753
40–44	Middle	14,110	17,846	19,945	21,990
45–49	Agers	11,647	13,980	17,678	19,763
50–54		10,817	11,422	13,719	17,356
55–59	Olders	11,245	10,433	11,040	13,280
60–64		10,943	10,618	9,883	10,487
65–69	Elders	9,214	9,996	9,736	9,096
70–74		7,641	8,039	8,767	8,581
75–79	The	5,556	6,260	6,640	7,295
80–84	Very Old	3,501	4,089	4,671	5,023
85 and over		2,697	3,313	4,074	4,926
Total		238,631	249,657	259,559	267,955
Median Age		31.4	33.2	34.7	36.3

Source: U.S. Bureau of the Census (1984), "Projections of the Population of the United States by Age, Sex and Race: 1983–2080." *Current Population Reports* Series P-25 (No. 952), Table 6, Washington, D.C.: U.S. Government Printing Office.

2. The number of teenagers and young adults is *declining.* In 1995 there will be 8.8 million fewer Americans aged 14 to 30 than in 1985. This is due to the low birth rate during the 1960s and 1970s, which resulted in relatively few people (the baby busters) to move through those age groups.

3. As the baby-boom generation ages, the number of people aged 31 to 56 will grow by 20.9 million between 1985 and 1995. This maturing of the baby boomers is perhaps the most significant demographic development confronting marketers in the United States.

The preceding developments hold considerable promise for many marketers but may cause problems for others. First, consider the problems. Marketers who appealed to the teenage and young-adult markets during the 1970s and 1980s have suffered as the size of these markets declined. The blue jeans industry is a

FIGURE 6.1

The Legacy of the Baby Boom and Bust
(U. S. Population by Age: 1985 and 1995, in Millions)

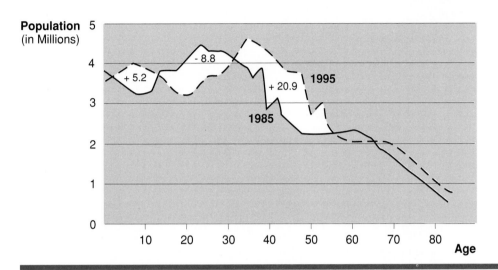

Population (in Millions)

Source: U.S. Census Bureau. Reprinted in Bryant Robey and Cheryl Russell, "The Year of the Baby Boom," *American Demographics*, May 1984, p. 20.

case in point. Blue jeans sales reached a tremendous peak in 1981, when an estimated 600 million pairs were sold in the United States alone.[10] Since then, sales have declined, due in large part to the baby-boom generation's changing tastes and preferences as they have matured and turned to other types of clothing. This explains why Levi Strauss, for example, introduced and actively promotes Dockers apparel, a line aimed at aging baby boomers. Not many years ago Levi's corporate revenues were obtained primarily through sales of jeans; now Dockers represent about 20 percent of total sales.[11]

On the positive side, the baby-boom generation offers tremendous potential for many marketers. Research shows that baby boomers are an attractive market for high-tech products, branded merchandise, quality durable goods (like the Mazda Miata in Figure 6.2), and investments such as securities, insurance, and real estate.[12] Moreover, just because baby boomers are aging does not

[10]"Beyond the Blue Horizon," *Time*, August 20, 1984, 106.

[11]Gary Levin, "Boomers Leave a Challenge," *Advertising Age*, July 8, 1991, 1, 14.

[12]For a discussion of the psychology underlying baby boomers' purchasing behavior, see Robert B. Settle and Pamela L. Alreck, "The Psychology of Expectations," *Marketing Communications*, March 1988, 19–27.

FIGURE 6.2 An Appeal to Baby Boomers

necessarily mean that they are getting psychologically old or are significantly altering their consumption patterns from a younger age. Rather, there are indications that baby boomers are retaining many of their more youthful consumption habits and, in a sense, are taking longer to grow up.[13] For example, baby boomers still purchase blue jeans, but the jeans have been cut for larger, redistributed bodies.

Middle-Aged and Mature Consumers

The 1980s was the decade of marketing to youthful baby boomers and the subsegment of affluent boomers known by the now-passe term, yuppies. With the aging of the U.S. population, however, the 1990s is the decade of marketing to middle-aged baby boomers and mature consumers. Where is the dividing line between middle age and maturity? Although somewhat arbitrary, we can think of middle age starting at age 35 and ending at age 54. Actually, there is some disagreement over the dividing point between middle age and maturity.[14] Sometimes a 65 and over classification is used, since age 65 normally marks retirement. In this text we will use the U.S. Bureau of the Census's designation, which classifies mature people as those who are *55 and older*. Hence, *middle age* should be thought of as including all people between the ages 35-54, whereas *maturity* includes people aged 55 and older. In 1995 there will be approximately 73 million Americans between the middle ages of 35-54. Because most of these individuals are the baby boomers described above who were born between 1946 and 1964, no further commentary about middle-aged consumers is needed at this point.

Turning to mature consumers, there will be in 1995 nearly 55 million U.S. citizens aged 55 or older who will represent approximately 21 percent of the total U.S. population (refer again to Table 6.1). Historically, many marketers have ignored the mature market or have treated them in unflattering ways by focusing on "repair kit products" such as dentures, laxatives and arthritis remedies.[15] Not only are mature consumers numerous, they also are wealthier and more willing to spend than ever before. Mature Americans control about $7 trillion

---

[13]See Ken Dychtwald and Greg Gable, "Portrait of a Changing Consumer," *Business Horizons*, January–February 1990, 62–73.

[14]William Lazer, "Dimensions of the Mature Market," *The Journal of Consumer Marketing*, 3 (Summer 1986), 24.

[15]The expression "repair kit" is from Charles D. Schewe, "Marketing to Our Aging Population: Responding to Physiological Changes," *The Journal of Consumer Marketing*, 5 (Summer 1988), 61–73. For further discussions of marketers' unflattering treatment of older consumers and recommendations for avoiding such treatment, see Randall Rothenberg, "Ad Industry Faulted on Over-50's," *The New York Times*, May 11, 1988, 42, and Melinda Beck, "Going for the Gold," *Newsweek*, April 23, 1990, 74–76.

of wealth, which is nearly 70 percent of the net worth of all U.S. households.[16] Mature consumers are less likely to shop by price alone and are more concerned with product quality and store service. In addition, they are more likely to purchase expensive items.[17]

A variety of implications accompany marketing communications efforts that are directed at the mature market. In advertising directed at this group, it is advisable to portray them as active, vital, busy, forward looking, and concerned with looking attractive and being romantic.[18] (See Figure 6.3 for Freedent chewing gum, which represents a good application of this advice.) Advertisers are beginning to appeal to the mature market in a flattering fashion as typified by the use of attractive, middle-aged models to represent clothing, cosmetics, and other products that had been the exclusive advertising domain of youthful models.

In closing this section, it is important to point out that just because mature consumers share a single commonality (i.e., they are age 55 or older), they by no means represent a homogeneous market segment. Indeed, the Bureau of the Census divides the 55 and over people into four distinct age segments: 55 to 64 (olders); 65 to 74 (elders); 75 to 84 (the very old); and 85 and over.[19] On the basis of age alone, consumers in each of these groups differ—sometimes dramatically—in terms of lifestyles, interest in the marketplace, reasons for buying, and spending ability. Moreover, it is important to realize that age alone is not the best indicator of how an individual lives or what role consumption plays in that lifestyle. The *Focus on Promotion* elaborates on this point and describes four groups of mature consumers based on a combination of health and self-image characteristics.

Children and Teenagers

At the other end of the age spectrum are children and teenagers. The group of young Americans aged 19 and younger has fallen dramatically from 40 percent of the population in 1965 (during the baby-boom heyday) to approximately 29 percent of the population in 1990. Yet, this is a substantial group with over 70 million occupants. (See Table 6.1 for specific breakouts by age group; that is, under 5, 5 to 9, 10 to 14, and 15 to 19.)

Preschool-age children represent a substantial market for many obvious products. The size of this group has grown considerably in recent years. More babies were born in the United States in 1990 (4.2 million) than at any time since the baby boom peak of 4.3 million babies born in 1957.[20] Products and services appealing to the family and home have increased to cater to this mini baby boom.

---

[16]Peter Petre, "Marketers Mine for Gold in the Old," *Fortune*, March 31, 1986, 70. Also, Beck, "Going for the Gold."

[17]" 'Fifty-Ups'—The Next Wave?" *Marketing Communications*, January 1988, 11.

[18]"Market Profile: The Graying of America's Consumer," *POPAI News*, 7, 1 (1983), 5. Also, see ibid.

[19]Lazer, "Dimensions of the Mature Market," 24.

[20]Christy Fisher, "Wooing Boomers' Babies," *Advertising Age*, July 22, 1991, 3, 30.

An Appeal to Mature Consumers   FIGURE 6.3

Go ahead. Get close.

If you've got dental work, there's only one gum you can be confident chewing.

Freedent won't stick to your dental work. And because it also moistens your mouth and keeps your breath really fresh, it's in a class by itself. So go ahead—with Freedent you can get close with confidence.

Non-stick Freedent.
Moistens mouth.
Freshens breath.

FREEDENT and WON'T STICK TO MOST DENTAL WORK are registered trademarks of the Wm. Wrigley Jr. Co. © 1991.

FOCUS ON PROMOTION

FROM HEALTHY INDULGERS TO FRAIL RECLUSES

A national mail survey received completed questionnaires from 1,000 people aged 55 and older. Respondents were classified into four groups based on how they answered the survey questions: Healthy Hermits, 38 percent; Ailing Outgoers, 34 percent; Frail Recluses, 15 percent; and Healthy Indulgers, 13 percent. These categories are unrelated to age per se, because people vary greatly in terms of how fast they age physically as well as their self-image related to age.

Healthy Hermits, though in good health, are psychologically withdrawn from society. They represent a good market for various services such as tax and legal advice, financial services, home entertainment, and do-it-yourself products. Direct mail and print media are the best media for reaching this group.

Ailing Outgoers are diametrically opposite to Healthy Hermits. Though in poor health, they are socially active, health conscious, and interested in learning to do new things. Home health care, dietary products, planned retirement communities, and entertainment services are some of the products and services most desired by this group. They can be reached via sales promotions and through select mass media tailored to their positive self-image and active, social lifestyle.

Frail Recluses are withdrawn socially and are in poor health. Various health and medical products and services, home entertainment, and domestic-assistance services (e.g., lawn care) can be successfully marketed to this group. They can be reached by mass media and special-assistance services.

Healthy Indulgers are in good health, are relatively wealthy, and are socially active. They are independent and want the most out of life. They are a good market for financial services, leisure-travel-entertainment, clothes, luxury goods, and high-tech products and services. They are accessible via in-store promotions, direct mail, and specialized print media.

Source: The research was performed by George P. Moschis and is reported in "Survey: Age Is Not Good Indicator of Consumer Need," *Marketing Communications*, November 21, 1988, 6.

Elementary-school-age children, aged 6 to 11, are influential consumers. These children have direct influence on product purchases and indirect influence on what their parents buy.[21] Figure 6.4 presents data on products children aged 6 to 11 buy with their own money and purchases they influence. For example, nearly 60 percent of all children in this age group buy candy and gum, and approximately 30 percent buy toys, soft drinks, and presents. Over 80 percent influence their parents' choice of clothing and toys. Approximately 30 percent influence the brand choice of products such as toothpaste. This explains why many companies have introduced products aimed at children which in past years were not segmented on this basis. For example, companies like My Own Meals and Hormel market microwaveable children's meals that do not require refrigeration.[22] The advertisement for IronKids bread (see Figure 6.5) is another illustration of this trend.

Advertising and other forms of marketing communications aimed at young children have increased substantially in recent years. More than $350 million is spent annually on network, cable, and syndicated television to reach children.[23] Gatorade, for example, aims special ads at kids and their "purchasing agent" mothers.[24] In addition to Channel One, a daily TV news program in schoolrooms, marketing communicators have encroached on classrooms at all grade levels with promotional messages often disguised as learning tools.[25] In the next chapter we will examine the ethical issues associated with these types of marketing communications.

Teenagers, including 12-year-olds as well as conventional teens between the ages of 13 and 19, are estimated to have spent $78 billion for personal and household purchases in one year alone.[26] With nearly two-thirds of all mothers in the work force, teenagers now have purchasing influence and power far greater than ever before, which, again, accounts for the growth of Channel One and other communications programs aimed at this group as well as younger children. Teenagers are noted for several outstanding characteristics: they are highly conformist, narcissistic, and fickle consumers.[27] These characteristics pose great

[21]See Horst H. Stipp, "Children As Consumers," *American Demographics*, February 1988, 27-32; Ellen Graham, "As Kids Gain Power of Purse, Marketing Takes Aim at Them," *The Wall Street Journal*, January 19, 1988, 1; John Schwartz, "Portrait of a Generation," *Newsweek Special Issue*, Summer 1991, 6–9; Monte Williams, "'Parental Guidance' Lost on This Crop," *Advertising Age*, July 30, 1990, 1, 28.

[22]"My Own Meals Makes Microwaveable History," *Adweek's Marketing Week*, November 26, 1990, 22.

[23]Jon Berry, "The New Generation of Kids and Ads," *Adweek's Marketing Week*, April 15, 1991 25, 28.

[24]See Laura Bird, "Gatorade for Kids," *Adweek's Marketing Week*, July 15, 1991, 4–5.

[25]"Selling to Children," *Consumer Reports*, August 1990, 518–521.

[26]Graham, "As Kids Gain Power of Purse, Marketing Takes Aim at Them."

[27]Ibid. Also, Selina S. Guber, "The Teenage Mind," *American Demographics*, August 1987, 42–44.

FIGURE 6.4   Children's Purchases and Purchase Influences

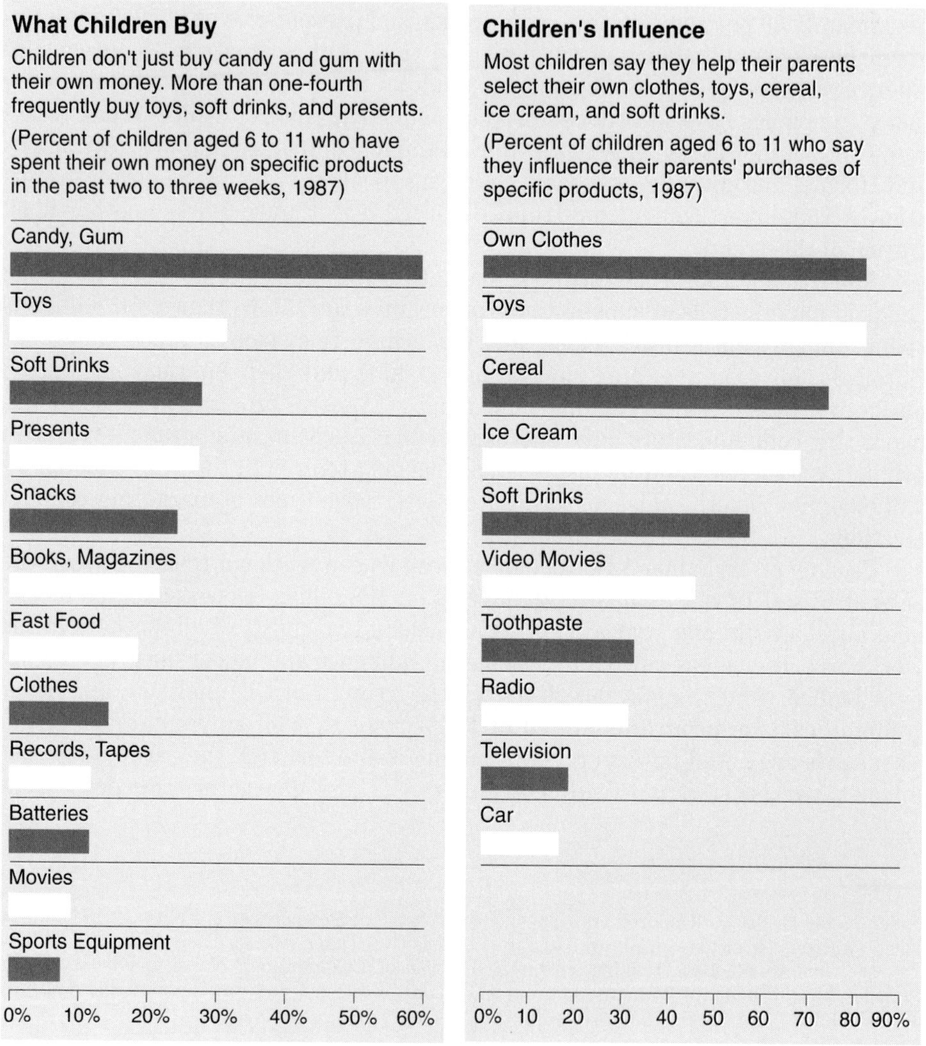

What Children Buy

Children don't just buy candy and gum with their own money. More than one-fourth frequently buy toys, soft drinks, and presents.

(Percent of children aged 6 to 11 who have spent their own money on specific products in the past two to three weeks, 1987)

Candy, Gum
Toys
Soft Drinks
Presents
Snacks
Books, Magazines
Fast Food
Clothes
Records, Tapes
Batteries
Movies
Sports Equipment

0%   10%   20%   30%   40%   50%   60%

Children's Influence

Most children say they help their parents select their own clothes, toys, cereal, ice cream, and soft drinks.

(Percent of children aged 6 to 11 who say they influence their parents' purchases of specific products, 1987)

Own Clothes
Toys
Cereal
Ice Cream
Soft Drinks
Video Movies
Toothpaste
Radio
Television
Car

0% 10   20   30   40   50   60   70   80 90%

Source: Youth Monitor, Winter 1987, Yankelovich, Skelly and White/Clancy, Shulman, Inc.

A Product for Children

FIGURE 6.5

© 1991 Campbell Taggart, Inc.

opportunities and challenges for marketers and promotion managers. An accepted product can become a huge success when the teenage bandwagon selects a brand as a personal mark of the *in* crowd. However, today's accepted product or brand can easily become tomorrow's passé item.

THE CHANGING AMERICAN HOUSEHOLD

By way of background, a **household** represents an independent housing entity, either rental property (e.g., an apartment) or owned property (a condominium or house). As of 1991, there were approximately *93 million* households in the United States, which means that there are about two and two-thirds residents, on average, per household. The traditional American household—as portrayed stereotypically in television programs such as *Leave It to Beaver*—was a family consisting of mother, father, and two or three children. Millions of such households still exist in the United States, but the percentage of these households is declining and American households are changing rather dramatically.

In 1950, *families* (such as a married couple with or without children) constituted 90 percent of all households; this percentage fell to 72.3 percent in 1985 and is projected to fall to 68.2 percent by 2000.[28] *Nonfamily households*, that is, a person living alone or with one or more unrelated person(s), are experiencing a huge increase, jumping from approximately 24 million in 1985 to nearly 34 million nonfamily households by the year 2000.[29] Indeed, slightly over 40 percent of the adult population is now unmarried compared to only 28 percent unmarried adults just two decades ago.[30]

American households have been altered forever by the combined effects of changes in marriage patterns, widespread birth control, working women, and rising divorce rates.[31] Households are growing in number, shrinking in size, and changing in character. The number of new households has grown twice as fast as the population, while household size has declined rapidly in all 50 states.[32] In 1970 there were 3.14 persons per household in the United States; this number is expected to fall to 2.48 by the year 2000.[33]

The changing composition of the American household has tremendous implications for marketing communicators, especially advertisers. Advertising will

[28]Richard Kern, "USA 2000," *Sales and Marketing Management*, October 27, 1986, 8–30.
[29]Ibid.
[30]Jon Berry, "Forever Single," *Adweek's Marketing Week*, October 15, 1990, 20–24.
[31]Peter Francese, "Baby Boom's Echo Keeps Economy Moving," *Advertising Age*, July 19, 1984, 12.
[32]Ibid.
[33]Kern, "USA 2000," 8–30.

have to reflect the widening range of living situations that exist. This is particularly true in the case of the "singles market."[34] Singles represent a large and ever-growing group. For example, one-fourth of men aged 30–34 and one-sixth of men aged 35–39 have never been married. The percentage of unmarried women is also increasing dramatically.[35]

Many advertisers make special appeals to the buying interests and needs of singles, appealing in food ads, for example, to such needs as ease and speed of preparation, maintenance simplicity, and small serving sizes. Reaching singles requires special media-selection efforts because (1) singles tend not to be big prime-time television viewers but are skewed instead toward the late-fringe hours (after 11 p.m.); (2) singles are disproportionately more likely than the rest of the population to view cable television; and (3) singles are disproportionately heavy magazine readers.[36]

Singles not only differ in household size in comparison to their married counterparts but also in terms of their buyer behavior. Recent consumer research found that singles are more brand loyal, apparently because buying brands associated with their childhoods makes them feel less lonely.[37] There also is some indication that singles are more innovative insofar as they are more inclined to turn to products and services as a source of stimulation.[38] The following *Global Focus* describes a worldwide trend away from traditional households.

THE CHANGING ROLES OF WOMEN

Historically, marketing communicators portrayed women in stereotypical roles as wife, mother, homemaker, and hostess or as single girls preparing for these roles.[39] Women are no longer "just" housewives; indeed, only 3.5 percent of American families portray the traditional stereotype where the husband works and the wife is homemaker.[40] Major changes over the past two decades in the

----

[34]The "singles" label is certainly too crude to constitute a true market segment because a variety of different groups are included in the general category (people who have never been married, divorced people, widowed people, etc.).

[35]Berry, "Forever Single," 20.

[36]Gay Jervey, "Y & R Study: New Life to Singles," *Advertising Age*, October 4, 1982, 14.

[37]Berry, "Forever Single," 21.

[38]Ibid.

[39]Alladi Venkatesh, "Changing Roles of Women—A Lifestyle Analysis," *Journal of Consumer Research*, 7 (November 1980), 189.

[40]Jerry Goodbody, "America's Vanishing Housewife," *Adweek's Marketing Week*, June 24, 1991, 28–29.

GLOBAL FOCUS

WORLDWIDE DECLINE OF TRADITIONAL HOUSEHOLDS

Traditional households are declining throughout the world—not just in the United States. Four primary factors account for the trend toward greater numbers of singles and other forms of nontraditional households: women are having fewer children; more children are being born out of wedlock; the average age of the populace is continuing to increase in developed countries; and the rate of divorce continues to increase while marriage declines.

A major study performed by the U. S. Bureau of Labor Statistics found the following specific information regarding nontraditional households in several countries:

1. Sweden and Germany have the largest proportions of single-person households of all the developed countries investigated. This is due in part to these countries' older populations.

2. Sweden and Denmark have the largest shares of births by unmarried women. However, these Scandinavian countries do not have the largest numbers of single parents, because many unmarried mothers live with their partners.

3. The United States has the highest proportion of single parents. This is due to high divorce rates and because American single mothers are more likely to live on their own rather than cohabitate.

4. It is estimated that virtually all young Swedes cohabitate before they marry.

5. Japan is the most traditional of all developed countries. It has the largest share of married couples and low rates of divorce and out-of-wedlock births.

Source: Adapted from "Traditional Households Are Fading World-Wide." *The Wall Street Journal*, May 4, 1990, Sec. B, 1.

roles of women have forced marketing communicators to develop a wider range of appeals that reflect women's changing needs and status.

Some of the most notable changes are the following: (1) the number of women in the nation's work force increased from under 25 million in 1960 to over 50 million today; fully 70 percent of the women between the ages of 25 and 54 are in the labor force [41]; (2) today, women head almost one-third of all households compared with one in seven in 1950[42]; and (3) a larger share of women are remaining single into their thirties; this trend results from more educational and occupational opportunities, as well as disenchantment with marriage because of the divorce rate.[43]

Although marketing communicators have made strides in reflecting women's changing roles, it is probably fair to conclude that women are still being portrayed in a limited range of roles that do not fully reflect the actual working position and status of women in today's society.[44] Fortunately, this is changing, albeit slowly, as advertisers begin to recognize the importance of women as major decision makers. The advertisement for Diet Coke (see Figure 6.6) reflects a contemporary appeal to today's sophisticated, professional working woman. The following passage characterizes the modern woman to whom advertisers must appeal in the future.

Advertising which remains locked into the traditional roles of mother/homemaker will play to a decreasing audience in the future. Although a woman may fulfill these roles in a partial capacity, the desire to shed this image will lead to dual roles, role switching, and role blending. Thus, both women and men can be expected to be portrayed in roles which show a person in more than one capacity; a man doing "woman's" work, and men and women jointly deciding on a purchase decision. In short, the modern woman is not, and will not, accept a thrusting into traditional roles, and expects to be found in an expanding number of positions replacing her male counterpart.[45]

Because of women's involvement in the labor force, the choice of advertising media used to reach women has changed. Traditional media, like daytime television, are ineffective for reaching vast numbers of working women. Outdoor advertising, direct mail, radio, and magazines are increasingly important media for getting advertising messages to working women.

---

[41]Susan E. Shank, "Women and the Labor Market: The Link Grows Stronger," *Monthly Labor Review*, 111 (March 1988), 3–8.

[42]Daphne Spain and Suzanne M. Bianchi, "How Women Have Changed," *American Demographics*, May 1983, 18–25.

[43] Ibid.

[44]A number of studies have detected stereotypical role portrayal of women. For a review, see Roger A. Kerin, William J. Lundstrom, and Donald Sciglimpaglia, "Women in Advertisements: Retrospect and Prospect," *Journal of Advertising*, 8, 3 (1979), 37–42.

[45]Ibid., 41.

FIGURE 6.6   ## An Appeal to Modern Women

INCOME DYNAMICS

American society is characterized by increasing numbers of people at both extremes of the income distribution. At the low end, there are, incredibly, more than 30 million Americans living below the poverty level.[46] The situation is particularly bleak for blacks and Hispanics, whose poverty rates far exceed that for whites.

At the other end of the distribution, a number of American households are enjoying continually rising incomes. *Affluent households* are defined as the top 10 percent of households in the United States. The threshold for recognition into the affluent category was a disposable income of $62,000 in 1989, whereas in 1983 the threshold was just $47,000.[47] This $15,000 jump in the requirement for top 10 percent status is due in large part to the increasing numbers of dual-income households.

Automobile companies, financial services, home-construction firms, and many other companies are interested in the affluent consumer because of his or her spending power. Yet despite this emphasis on spending power, there appears to be a subtle shift taking place in many consumers' attitudes toward consumption. There has been a transition from a "disposable psychology" to an "investment psychology." Many affluent and relatively affluent Americans are showing much more enthusiasm for quality merchandise, things that will last, and values that will grow. This shift has been referred to as the "Europeanization of America."[48]

Special marketing communications efforts are required to reach and motivate the affluent market. In terms of advertising claims, appeals to elegance, quality, and durability are especially effective. Media selection is critical because research shows that media-behavior patterns change with increases in income—television viewing and radio listening decrease and magazine readership increases.

MINORITY-POPULATION DEVELOPMENTS

America has always been a melting pot, and it became even more so in the 1980s and especially the 1970s, known as the "decade of the immigrant." The numbers

---

[46]"A Portrait of America, " *Newsweek*, January 17, 1983, 31.

[47]"They're in the Money: A Look at America's Affluent Market," *Sales & Marketing Management*, June 1990, 34.

[48]"The Rich, the Very Rich, and the Super Rich," *Marketing Communications*, November/ December 1982, 25.

of immigrants admitted to the United States in the 1970s surpassed any year since 1924.[49] The largest minorities in the United States are blacks and Hispanics, both of which are experiencing rapid growth. By the year 2010, minorities will represent one of three people in the United States.[50] In recognition of the growing role of minorities, the following sections examine population developments and marketing communications implications for blacks, Hispanics, and America's most affluent minority group, Asians.

Black Americans

By the year 2000, black people in the United States will total approximately 36 million, or 13.4 percent of the U.S. population.[51] Black Americans are characterized more by their common heritage than by skin color. This heritage "is conditioned by an American beginning in slavery, a shared history of discrimination and suffering, confined housing opportunities, and denial of participation in many aspects of the majority culture."[52] Although many black Americans share a common culture in that they have similar values, beliefs, and distinguishable behaviors, blacks do not represent a single culture or a single market any more than whites do. Although blacks' incomes are skewed to the low end of the U.S. income distribution, nearly 40 percent of blacks have incomes that place them in middle-class status or above. [53]

Black Americans represent an attractive market for many companies. Several notable reasons account for this: (1) the aggregate income of black consumers exceeds $140 billion; (2) the average age of black Americans is considerably younger than that for whites; (3) blacks are geographically concentrated; approximately two-thirds of all blacks live in the top 15 U.S. markets; (4) black consumption in some product categories is disproportionately greater than general population usage (e.g., blacks purchase over one-third of all hair-conditioning products); and (5) blacks tend to purchase prestige and name-brand products in greater proportion than do whites.[54]

These impressive figures notwithstanding, many companies make no special efforts to communicate with blacks. This is foolish, for research indicates that blacks are responsive to advertisements placed in black-oriented media and to

[49]"Lands of Our Fathers," *Newsweek*, January 17, 1983, 22.

[50]Christy Fisher, "Ethnics Gain Market Clout," *Advertising Age*, August 5, 1991, 3, 12.

[51]Lazer, *Handbook of Demographics for Marketing and Advertising*, 92.

[52] James F. Engel, Roger D. Blackwell, Paul W. Miniard, *Consumer Behavior*, 5th ed. (Hinsdale, IL: The Dryden Press, 1986), 410.

[53]Jon Berry, "6 Myths about Black Consumers," *Adweek's Marketing Week*, May 6, 1991, 16–19.

[54]David Astor, "Black Spending Power: $140 Billion and Growing," *Marketing Communications*, July 1982, 13–14.

advertisements that make personalized appeals by using black models and advertising contexts with which blacks can identify.[55] Major corporations are developing effective programs for communicating with black consumers. For example, the Eastman-Kodak Company recognizes the importance of black consumers and reflects this by advertising on network black radio, on Black Entertainment Television, and in black magazines such as *Ebony* and *Essence.*

Although greater numbers of companies are realizing the importance of directing special marketing communications efforts to black consumers, it is important to emphasize that the black consumer market is *not* homogeneous. Blacks exhibit different purchasing behaviors according to their lifestyles, values, and demographics. Therefore, companies must use different advertising media, distribution channels, advertising themes, and pricing strategies as they market to the various subsegments of black Americans.

Hispanic Americans

The U.S. Hispanic population grew by nearly 8 million people between 1980 and 1990, a 53 percent increase, and now represents nearly 10 percent of the U.S. total population.[56] The largest percentage of Hispanics are Mexican Americans (63 percent), followed by Puerto Rican Americans (12 percent), Latin Americans from Central and South America (11 percent), Cuban Americans (5 percent), and other Hispanic Americans (9 percent).[57] It is projected that Hispanics will make up over 11 percent of the U.S. population by the year 2000 and total over 34 million people.[58] About 75 percent of U.S. Hispanics are concentrated in five states: California, Texas, New York, Florida, and Illinois.

According to the U.S. Bureau of the Census, Hispanics in the United States have several outstanding characteristics in comparison with other members of the American population. They are younger, have larger families, tend to live in urban clusters, and are becoming increasingly mobile as they begin to fan out from the five states in which they are concentrated.[59]

Marketing communicators need to be aware of several important points when attempting to reach Hispanic consumers:

---

[55]Ibid.

[56]Jon Berry, "The New 'Multilingual' Pitch," *Adweek's Marketing Week*, April 22, 1991, 35; Christy Fisher, "Ethnics Gain Market Clout," 3.

[57]Joe Schwartz, "Hispanics in the Eighties," *American Demographics*, 10 (January 1988), 42–45.

[58]Lazer, *Handbook of Demographics for Marketing and Advertising*, p. 92; Christy Fisher, "Hispanic Explosion," *Advertising Age*, August 26, 1991, 30.

[59]Craig Endicott, "Marketing to Hispanics: Making the Most of Media," *Advertising Age*, March 19, 1984, Sec. M, 10.

1. Over 40 percent of Hispanic Americans speak only Spanish or just enough English to get by; consequently, many Hispanics can be reached only via Spanish-language media.[60]

2. A further reason for using Spanish-language media is that over one-half of Hispanics use Spanish media primarily; 70 percent watch, listen to, or read Spanish media every week.[61]

3. Over 70 percent of Hispanics report resenting ads that appear to be little more than perfunctory adaptations of English ads.[62]

4. Advertisers must be very careful in using the Spanish language. A number of snafus have been committed when advertisers translate their English campaigns to Spanish. For example, Frank Perdue, an East Coast marketer of chickens, had his famous slogan ("It takes a strong man to make a tender chicken") translated into Spanish so he could read it to Hispanics. Amusingly (probably to everyone except Frank), the Spanish version erroneously substituted "a sexually excited man" for "a strong man."[63]

The Spanish-speaking market represents a golden opportunity for many companies. Yet it is estimated that as many as 80 percent of U.S. companies make no special efforts to reach Hispanic consumers.[64] Many companies consider Anglo advertising to be sufficient for reaching Hispanic consumers. Research has shown that television commercials fail to portray Hispanics as often as their numbers would suggest, and when they are portrayed in commercials it is typically in crowd scenes.[65] However, marketers such as Coca-Cola, Pepsi, and McDonald's, to name some of the more prominent, are now investing heavily in Hispanic-oriented advertising and sales promotions.[66]

Asian Americans

Asians in the United States include many nationalities, the major ones being Chinese, Filipinos, Indians, Japanese, Koreans, and Vietnamese. Asian

---

[60]"Hispanic Ethnic Market: 27,000,000 by 2000," *POPAI News*, 6, 2 (1982), 7.

[61]Ibid.

[62]Ibid.

[63]"Snafus Persist in Marketing to Hispanics," *Marketing News*, June 24, 1983, 3.

[64]Robert E. Mack, "A Golden Growth Opportunity," *Marketing Communications*, March 1988, 54–57.

[65]Robert E. Wilkes and Humberto Valencia, "Hispanics and Blacks in Television Commercials," *Journal of Advertising*, 18, 1 (1989), 19–25.

[66]Fisher, "Hispanic Explosion"; Christy Fisher, "Bringing Down the House," *Advertising Age*, October 15, 1990, 44.

Americans have been heralded as the newest "hot ethnic market."[67] The demographics support this optimistic outlook. Over 7 million Asians live in the United States, and early in the next century the Asian population will reach 15 million or more.[68] Asian Americans on average are better educated, have higher incomes, and occupy more prestigious job positions than any other segment of American society including whites.[69] According to 1989 Census Bureau figures, Asians' median income was $36,102 compared with $30,406 for whites, $21,921 for Hispanics, and $18,083 for blacks.[70]

It is important to emphasize that just as there is no single black or Hispanic market, there certainly does not exist a single Asian market. Between Asian nationalities there are considerable differences in product choices and brand preferences.[71] Even within each nationality there are variations in terms of English-language skills and financial well-being.

Some firms have been successful in marketing to specific Asian groups by customizing marketing programs specifically to Oriental values and lifestyles rather than merely translating Anglo programs. For example, Metropolitan Life, an insurance company, conducted research that determined that Asian parents' top priority was their children's security and education. Metropolitan translated this finding into a successful campaign targeted to Koreans and Chinese. An advertisement portrayed a baby in a man's arms with the heading: "You protect your baby. Who protects you?" This ad along with the attraction of Asians to Metropolitan Life's sales force resulted in a substantial increase in insurance sales to Asians.[72] Reebok's sales among Asian Americans increased substantially after that company used tennis star Michael Chang in its advertisements.[73] The growing appreciation of Asian Americans is perhaps typified by the advertisement in Figure 6.7 portraying a beautiful Indian woman. This advertisement was directed not at Asian Indians but to affluent Americans in general and was placed in *Newsweek* and other mainstream magazines.

---

[67]John Schwartz, Dorothy Wang, and Nancy Matsumoto, "Tapping into a Blossoming Asian Market," *Newsweek*, September 7, 1987, 47–48.

[68]Cyndee Miller, "'Hot'" Asian-American Market Not Starting Much of a Fire Yet," *Advertising Age*, January 21, 1991, 12.

[69]Richard Kern, "The Asian Market: Too Good To Be True?" *Sales and Marketing Management*, May 1988, 39–42.

[70]Fisher, "Ethnics Gain Market Clout," 12.

[71]For an interesting discussion of differences in brand preferences across Asian nationalities, see Jerry Goodbody, "Taking the Pulse of Asian-Americans, *Adweek's Marketing Week*, August 12, 1991, 32.

[72]Schwartz, Wang, and Matsumoto, "Tapping into a Blossoming Asian Market."

[73]Miller, "'Hot' Asian-American Market Not Starting Much of a Fire Yet."

FIGURE 6.7   Growing Appreciation for Asian Americans

SUMMARY

Six major demographic developments are reviewed in this chapter: (1) population growth and regional geographic developments, (2) the changing age structure, (3) the changing American household, (4) the changing roles of women, (5) income dynamics, and (6) minority population developments.

The presentation covers a variety of topics relevant for promotion managers. Some of the major demographic developments discussed are (1) the fact that the U.S. population is growing at a slow rate; (2) the population is continuing to shift from the Northeast and Midwest to the South and West; (3) the U.S. population is getting progressively older, increasing from an average age of 33 in 1990 to a projected 36 in 2000; (4) the number of teenagers and young adults is declining, whereas the numbers of middle-aged and mature Americans are increasing; (5) more babies were born in the United States in 1990 than at any time since the baby boom peak in 1957; (6) the percentage of single American adults has increased dramatically in the past two decades; and (7) there has been an explosive growth of minorities in the United States, particularly Hispanics, and by early in the next century minorities will represent one of three people in the United States.

Discussion Questions

1.   Demographers tell us that households in the United States are growing in number, shrinking in size, and changing in character. Assume that you are the vice president of marketing for a corporation that manufactures refrigerators and other kitchen appliances. What implications do these changes hold for your company? Be specific.

2.   As a percentage of the total population, young Americans aged 19 and younger represent a much smaller percentage of the total population today (approximately 29 percent) than they did a quarter of a century ago (approximately 40 percent in 1965). In light of this development, what would you do if you were the CEO of a firm that markets exclusively youth-oriented products?

3.   References are often made to the childrens market, the singles market, and the mature market. Are these truly markets in the rigorous sense of market segmentation? Start your response by identifying the requirements that a market segmentation basis must satisfy, and then respond to the question.

4.   Black, Hispanic, and Asian consumers do not represent three homogeneous markets; rather, they represent many markets composed of people who merely share a common race and/or language. Explain.

5. The text drew a distinction between *disposable* and *investment* psychologies of consumption and also discussed the Europeanization of America. Describe these developments in detail and explain what implications they hold for marketing and marketing communications.

6. Explain why the U.S. population is undergoing relentless aging and discuss some implications this will have on marketing and marketing communications.

7. Some prognosticators contend that the 1990s will be reminiscent of the 1950s with its emphasis on traditional values and family. Do you agree, and if so why?

8. If the 1980s was the decade of the baby boomers and yuppies and the 1990s the decade of mature consumers, who will the first decade of the next millenium pay tribute to?

9. Based on your understanding of the communications process covered in Chapter 2 and the elaboration likelihood model covered in Chapter 4, explain why you think the Channel One news program in schools would be an effective or ineffective medium for delivering advertisements.

10. The opening vignette to the chapter ended with the statement that marketing communications back in the early 1960s was a lot easier than it is in the 1990s. From your reading of the chapter, provide five reasons to support this assertion.

11. Assume you are brand manager of a food product that is consumed by all Americans—blacks, whites, Hispanics, Asians, and others. You are considering running an extended advertising campaign on primetime television that uses Hispanic actors and appeals to Hispanic consumers. Aside from cost considerations, what reservations might you have in running this campaign?

Environmental, Ethical, and Regulatory Issues in Marketing Communications

---

TRASH BAGS, DEGRADABILITY, ETHICS, AND REGULATION

Assume the year is 1988 and you are the vice president of marketing and sales for the consumer-products division of a large chemical company. One of your products, plastic trash bags, is likely to experience lost sales because your competitors are promoting their brands as degradable. To nontechnical consumers, the word degradable implies that these trash bags will literally disintegrate within a relatively short period after they leave the consumer's curbside and are buried in a landfill. Although these bags *are* photodegradeable (they will degrade if left out in the sun and rain for an extended period), they are not biodegradable. That is, they will not disintegrate when placed in landfills; rather, like most everything else that is buried in landfills, these so-called degradable bags will remain intact for decades.

As vice president of marketing and sales, you know your competitors' bags are not biodegradable and you know your own yet-to-be introduced degradable brand is not biodegradable. However, your predicament is that your regular brand of nondegradable trash bags may lose shelf space to competitive brands and sales to environmentally concerned consumers who think they are serving the environment by using your competitors' degradable bags. You could introduce a photodegradable bag, but you know that it, like the competitors' bags, is not truly degradable and will not solve the solid waste problem. Hence, if you introduce a new bag labeled degradable you can prevent potential lost sales to competitors, but, at the same time, you will be misleading consumers into thinking that they are purchasing a truly degradable bag.

What would you do if you were placed in this position? Would you introduce your own brand of degradable trash bag, or would you be willing to suffer the consequences of lost sales to unethical competitors? Perhaps available to you are alternatives other than the choice between merely introducing or not introducing a degradable bag. Before reading on, think about what you would have done if you had been the key decision maker in this situation. Think about the consequences of your decision for your company, its employees, and for your career. Attempt, as best you can, to balance idealistic and practical considerations. Write down what you would do and fully justify your choice.

The situation described in the opening vignette is *not* hypothetical. Something very similar to this confronted the Mobil Chemical Co. in the late 1980s, a time when many American consumers were just beginning to be concerned with saving the environment. It also was a time when many marketers were beginning to respond to consumers' concerns, sometimes in exploitative ways. Mobil's brand of regular Hefty trash bags was, in fact, losing shelf space in supermarkets and experiencing lost sales to brands such as First Brands' degradable Glad bags. Nonetheless, Mobil fully recognized that degradable bags were no panacea. Mobil's general manager of solid-waste-management solutions was quoted as stating: "Mobil has concluded that biodegradable plastics will *not* (emphasis added) help solve the solid waste problem."[1]

This acknowledgment notwithstanding, Mobil in 1989 introduced its own line of degradable trash bags. No advertising was undertaken; rather, the promotional burden fell entirely on the Hefty package itself. The package was labeled Hefty® Degradable*, with the asterisk qualifying the degradable property as photodegradable (*"Activated by Exposure to the Elements"). The package front included a scene of a pine tree with bright sunlight shining through and an eagle preparing to land on the tree—all presumably chosen as emblematic of the implied claim that Hefty bags are themselves compatible with the environment. The back of the package made additional claims about Hefty bags' degradability.

Shortly after Mobil introduced Hefty® Degradable, the Federal Trade Commission requested both Mobil and First Brands (Glad bags) to provide substantiation for the degradability claims. By the spring of 1990 Mobil voluntarily decided to discontinue using degradability claims on its trash bag packages. Nonetheless, in the summer of 1990 the attorneys general of seven states (California, Massachusetts, Minnesota, New York, Texas, Washington, and

---

[1]Quoted at p. 12 in Jennifer Lawrence, "Mobil," *Advertising Age*, January 29, 1991, 12–13. Many of the facts in the following description are based on this article.

Wisconsin) brought suits against Mobil on grounds that it had engaged in deceptive communications and consumer fraud by falsely claiming that trash bags degrade in landfills. Although refusing to admit wrongdoing, Mobil settled the suits out of court and agreed to pay the states $150,000 to fund environmental educational programs.[2]

This case encapsulates much of the material covered in this chapter. In particular, the chapter addresses three major topics: (1) environmental matters and their implications for marketing communications, (2) ethical issues in marketing communications, and (3) the regulation of marketing communications practices. All three topics are interrelated: Many ethical issues confronting contemporary marketing communicators occur over environmental marketing efforts, and regulation (from federal and state governmental bodies and by industry self-regulators) is needed in large part due to unethical marketing communications practices, many of which are now occurring in the area of *green* marketing.

THE ENVIRONMENT AND GREEN MARKETING COMMUNICATIONS

The United States, as well as much of the industrialized world, is in the throes of a garbage crisis. More than 70 percent of the 180 million tons of trash disposed each year in the United States is buried in landfills, and the landfills are reaching capacity.[3] On top of this, a hole in the ozone layer threatens people with skin cancer. Increasing numbers of Americans are showing concern for the physical environment and are more stringent than ever in their demands that companies do something to ensure a cleaner and safer environment.[4] Over three-fourths say they are willing to pay more for products that do not harm the environment.[5]

It is easy to understand why so many companies have responded to environmental concerns by introducing environmentally oriented products and undertaking aggressive marketing communications programs to promote these products. These actions are referred to as *green marketing*. Unfortunately, for every truly green product there are probably two or more bogus entries. This is why green marketing is sometimes referred to in such unflattering terms as "greenscam," "greenwashing," and "big green lies."[6] Companies have jumped on the green bandwagon and exploited consumers' sensitivity to products claiming

---

[2]Jennifer Lawrence and Christy Fisher, "Mobil, States Settle Degradability Suits," *Advertising Age*, July 1, 1991, 4.

[3]William L. Rathje, "Once and Future Landfills," *National Geographic*, May 1991, 117–134.

[4]"How to Deal with Tougher Customers," *Fortune*, December 3, 1990, 38–48.

[5]Stefan Bechtel, *Keeping Your Company Green* (Emmaus, PA: Rodale Press, 1990), 1.

[6]Alecia Swasy, "Color Us Green," *Wall Street Journal*, March 22, 1991, sec. B, 4.

to be recyclable, degradable, safe for the ozone layer, and so on. One authority estimates that only 15 percent of all green claims are true, 15 percent are outright false, and the remainder fall into a gray area.[7]

It is not enough for companies to merely claim they are environmentally sensitive; consumers are becoming increasingly skeptical and are turned off by exploitative efforts that do not deliver on environmental-safety promises. As one journalist put it: "Declarations of environmental sensitivity cannot be taken at face value. Everybody wears green on St. Patrick's Day, too—but it doesn't make them Irish."[8]

Responses to Environmental Problems

There have been a number of legitimate responses by companies to environmental problems. Some of these responses have been in the form of new products such as the Impact electric-powered automobiles discussed in Chapter 4.[9] Of more relevance here are the marketing communications efforts that appeal to environmental sensitivities. In addition to advertisements which promote green products, the major green communications efforts include (1) new packages, (2) seal-of-approval programs, (3) cause-oriented programs, and (4) point-of-purchase displays.

PACKAGING RESPONSES.   Consumers are more concerned about packaging materials than ever, and a number of positive corporate responses have been forthcoming. (What type of consumer most likely responds to biodegradable packages and other environmental initiatives? See Figure 7.1 for an interesting profile.) Consider the following examples: McDonald's switched from polystyrene clamshell containers to paperboard packages. Hanes, the country's leading maker of panty hose with its L'eggs brand, changed from the famous plastic egg container to a cardboard container that maintains the egg silhouette though not its shape. This changeover from plastic to cardboard cost millions of dollars in packaging materials and displays.[10] The major detergent makers have all introduced concentrated detergents as a way of achieving smaller packages. Spic and Span® Pine cleaner promotes in a freestanding insert (Figure 7.2) that its bottle is made from 100 percent recycled plastic, which is projected to reduce annual landfill accumulation in the United States by 14 million 2-liter soda bottles.

SEAL-OF-APPROVAL PROGRAMS.   In Germany the Blue Angel seal has been a promise to consumers that a product carrying an environmental

---

[7]Penelope Wang, "Going for the Green," *Money*, September 1991, 98.

[8]Bob Garfield, "Beware: Green Overkill," *Advertising Age*, January 29, 1991, 26.

[9]David Woodruff and Than Peterson, "The Greening of Detroit," *Business Week*, April 8, 1991, 54–60.

[10]"L'eggs to Scrap Plastic 'Egg' Package," *Marketing News*, August 19, 1991, 20.

Profile of a Green Consumer   FIGURE 7.1

Green consumer: Concern for environment no fad

Who's the "green" consumer?

Here's a profile of one, developed from DDB Needham Worldwide's Life Style data by matching women who said they "make a special effort to buy products in biodegradable packages" with their answers to various other questions.

This sketch is much less detailed than the full profiles typically produced by the agency.

I'm a 46-year-old mother. I am a homemaker, and I take my role as the "family caretaker" seriously, but I have a professional career outside the home, too. I certainly don't hold the "traditional" view of women's role in society.

I'm keenly interested in news and politics. I try to be active in the community.

I'm not reluctant to express my opinion, sometimes by writing letters to newspapers.

I like to cook and bake and think it's important to do so. I am nutrition- conscious and avoid foods high in salt, sugar or fat. I feel guilty about serving my family convenience foods.

I make a detailed shopping list. I check ingredients and prices carefully.

I like to discuss products with friends. I consult *Consumer Reports* and other published information for comparative product information.

In advertising, I look for useful information. I don't like sex in advertising. I believe a lot of advertising, especially that on TV, is condescending to women. Insult me and I won't buy your product.

I believe commercials for beer and wine and commercials aimed at children should be taken off TV. I also think there's too much sex and violence on TV.

I think pollution is a serious threat to our health. Even if it means reducing our standard of living, we should toughen our pollution standards.

I believe the individual can make a difference in cleaning up the environment. To me, environmentalism isn't a fad that will go away. Portray it as a hip or trendy thing and you'll turn me off.

Joseph M. Winski

Source: DDB Needham Worldwide.

FIGURE 7.2 An Environmental Appeal

claim is in fact legitimate. More recently in the United States two certification programs, Green Seal and Green Cross, have begun to provide American consumers with assurance that the products carrying these seals truly are environmentally friendly.[11] These licensing programs charge manufacturers to verify environmental claims but only for the actual cost of testing.[12]

[11]Laurie Freeman, "Ecology Seals Vie for Approval," *Advertising Age*, January 29, 1991, 30.

[12]Ibid.

CAUSE-ORIENTED PROGRAMS.   Cause-oriented marketing is practiced when companies sponsor or support worthy causes. (See Chapter 20 for further details.) In doing so, the marketing communicator anticipates that associating the company and its brands with a worthy cause will generate goodwill. It is for this reason that companies sponsor causes such as the annual Earth Day. Figure 7.3 is the front page of an Amway advertising brochure that describes (inside the brochure) a program offering over $50,000 in awards to schools. Cash prizes were awarded in the name of classes for developing original campaigns or fund-raisers that demonstrated outstanding devotion to the environment. Cause-oriented programs can be effective if not overused and if they come across to consumers as reflecting a company's sincere involvement in an environmental cause and not just naked commercialism.

POINT-OF-PURCHASE PROGRAMS.   In-store displays provide an ideal setting to communicate a brand's environmental merits. A display, called Environmental Centers, developed by the makers of Arm & Hammer illustrates a creative application. These end-of-aisle units merchandise Arm & Hammer products along with select other brands of environmentally safe products. The displays also provide shoppers with free pamphlets from environmental groups.[13] A particularly interesting illustration of environmental marketing at the point of purchase is provided in the *Global Focus*, describing green marketing at Loblaws, an innovative Canadian supermarket chain.

What Does the Future Hold for Green Marketing?

Green marketing is here to stay. As described by a Harvard Business School professor, green products are to the 1990s what *lite* products were to the 1980s.[14] The significance of the issue demands that marketing communicators do everything possible to ensure that environmental claims are credible, realistic, and believable.

To assist marketing communicators and to serve society and consumers, a task force of attorneys general from ten states developed a set of recommendations for environmental marketers. These recommendations provide guidelines for labeling, packaging, and advertising products on the basis of environmental attributes.[15] Marketing communicators are provided with four general

---

[13]Laura Bird, "Arm & Hammer Stakes Its Name on the Environment," *Adweek's Marketing Week*, November 19, 1990, 4.

[14]Bechtel, *Keeping Your Company Green.*

[15]Julie Vergeront (principal author), *The Green Report: Findings and Preliminary Recommendations for Responsible Environmental Advertising* (St. Paul, MN: Minnesota Attorney General's Office, November 1990). See also Jennifer Lawrence, "State Guides Define Green Terms," *Advertising Age*, May 27, 1991, 3, 34. The following discussion is a summary of the recommendations in *The Green Report.*

FIGURE 7.3   An Illustration of Cause-Oriented Marketing

GLOBAL FOCUS

LOBLAWS' LINE OF GREEN PRODUCTS

Major corporate initiatives typically require bold leadership from an individual who is committed to accomplishing an ideal or grand vision. This certainly was the situation at the Canadian supermarket chain, Loblaws, when it embarked on a program to introduce a complete line of private-branded products under the GREEN name. Mr. Dave Nichol got the idea from a monograph, *The Green Consumer Guide*, he picked up on a visit to England in 1989. Within months, Loblaws' GREEN line of environmentally friendly products became a reality.

All GREEN products are packaged in bright green packages made from recycled paper. And all provide environmental information along with the logo: SOMETHING *CAN* BE DONE! In the first year alone, GREEN products generated nearly $52 million in sales for Loblaws'. One of the most interesting products carried in Loblaws' stores under the GREEN label is a high-efficiency light bulb that sells for $20. Although costing 10 times more than conventional bulbs, these high-efficiency bulbs save customers about $32 over their life by reducing energy costs and the cost of bulb replacement. Customers can't get enough of the bulbs. Ideas for adding new GREEN products come from all over the world; indeed, according to Mr. Nichol, most of the new ideas come from outside North America.

Source: This description is based on Carolyn Lesh, "Loblaws," *Advertising Age*, January 29, 1991, 38.

recommendations for making appropriate environmental claims: (1) make the claims specific, (2) have claims reflect current disposal options, (3) make the claims substantive, and (4) make supportable claims.

MAKE SPECIFIC CLAIMS.   This guide is intended to prevent marketing communicators from using meaningless claims such as "environmentally friendly" or "safe for the environment." The use of specific environmental claims enables consumers to make informed choices, reduces the likelihood that claims will be misinterpreted, and minimizes the chances that consumers will think that a product is more environmentally friendly than it actually is. In general, it is recommended that environmental claims be as specific as possible, not general, vague, incomplete, or overly broad.

REFLECT CURRENT DISPOSAL OPTIONS.   This guide is directed at preventing environmental claims which are technically accurate but practically unrealizable due to local trash-disposal practices. For example, most communities dispose trash by burying it in public landfills. Because paper and plastic products do *not* degrade when buried, it is misleading for businesses to make environmental claims that their products are degradable, biodegradable, or photodegradable. As illustrated in the opening vignette, products such as trash bags may be photodegradable, but once buried in a landfill they do not experience further degradation.

MAKE SUBSTANTIVE CLAIMS.   Some marketing communicators use trivial and irrelevant environmental claims to convey the impression that a promoted brand is environmentally sound. An illustration of a nonsubstantive claim is a company promoting its polystyrene foam cups as "preserving our trees and forests." Another trivial claim is when single-use products such as paper plates are claimed to be "safe for the environment." Clearly, a paper plate is not unsafe to the environment in the same sense that a toxic chemical is unsafe; however, paper plates and other throwaways do not actually benefit the environment but rather exacerbate the landfill problem.

MAKE SUPPORTABLE CLAIMS.   This recommendation is straightforward: environmental claims should be supported by competent and reliable scientific evidence. The purpose of this recommendation is to encourage businesses to make only those environmental claims that can be backed by facts. The injunction to businesses is clear: Don't claim it unless you can support it!

Some companies are indeed showing restraint in making environmental claims. Such restraint not only benefits consumers and society at large, but it also supports the long-run interest of businesses themselves. Misleading consumers with false environmental claims is a short-run tactic that provides a company a Pyrrhic victory at best. Long-term growth achieved from consumer allegiance is obtained only by developing legitimate basic offers (Mode 1 of the three modes of marketing in Chapter 1) and promoting these offers with honest and supportable claims.

ETHICAL ISSUES IN MARKETING COMMUNICATIONS

The foregoing discussion has made it clear that green marketing is fraught with ethical predicaments. But such is the case with all aspects of promotion management and marketing communications. Advertisers, sales promoters, package designers, sales personnel, telemarketers, public relations people, and point-of-purchase designers regularly make decisions that have ethical implications. This section examines many of the ethical issues involved with all elements of the promotions mix.

In this chapter, **ethics** is to be considered as involving matters of right and wrong, or *moral*, conduct pertaining to any aspect of marketing communications. Hence, for our purposes, ethics and morality will be used interchangeably and considered synonymous with societal notions of *honesty, honor, virtue,* and *integrity* in matters of marketing communications conduct.

It is relatively easy to define ethics, but it is difficult to identify what is or is not ethical conduct in marketing communications. Indeed, throughout the field of marketing there is an absence of consensus about what is ethical conduct.[16] Consensus notwithstanding, we nevertheless can identify marketing communications' practices that are especially susceptible to ethical challenges. The following sections examine, in order, ethical issues in (1) the targeting of marketing communications efforts, (2) advertising, (3) public relations, (4) personal selling and telemarketing, (5) packaging communications, and (6) sales promotions.

The Ethics of Targeting

According to widely accepted dictates of the marketing concept (see Chapter 1) and sound marketing strategy, firms should direct their offerings at specific segments of customers rather than use a scatter or shotgun approach. Nonetheless, ethical dilemmas are sometimes involved when special products and corresponding promotional efforts are directed at particular segments.[17] Especially open to ethical debate is the practice of targeting products and promotional efforts at segments which, for various psychosocial and economic reasons, are vulnerable to marketing communications. Children and minorities are frequently the targets of marketing communications actions.

TARGETING TO CHILDREN. Advertising and in-school marketing programs continuously urge kids to desire various products and brands. Critics often contend that many of the products targeted to children are unnecessary and that the communications are exploitative. Because it would involve debating personal values to discuss what kids do or do not need, the following presentation merely presents the critics' position and allows you to draw your own conclusion.

Consider the advertising of Gatorade to kids. Advertisements claimed that Gatorade is the "healthy alternative for thirsty kids." Nutritionists and other critics charged that Gatorade is unnecessary for kids and no better than water— no harm or no benefit arising from its consumption.[18] If indeed Gatorade does *not*

---

[16]O. C. Ferrell and Larry G. Gresham, "A Contingency Framework for Understanding Ethical Decision Making in Marketing, *Journal of Marketing,* 49 (Summer 1985), 87–96.

[17]For a provocative discussion of the dysfunctional social effects resulting from implementations of the marketing concept, see Steven H. Star "Marketing and Its Discontents," *Harvard Business Review,* 67 (November–December 1989), 148–154.

[18]Laura Bird, "Gatorade for Kids," *Adweek's Marketing Week,* July 15, 1991, 4–5.

benefit kids, is it ethical to urge them to encourage their gatekeeping parents to purchase this product?

Another criticized aspect of children-directed marketing communications is the practice of businesses using posters, book covers, free magazines, advertising (such as the Channel One school news program mentioned in Chapter 6), and other so-called learning tools.[19] Disguised as *educational* materials, these communications oftentimes are little more than attempts to persuade school children to want the promoted products and brands. Critics contend these methods are unethical because they use children's trust in educational materials as a deceptive means of hawking merchandise.[20]

In addition to classroom tactics, critics also question the ethics of practices such as placing products in movies (for instance, the famous Reese's Pieces in the movie *E.T.*) and backing up the product-movie connection with tie-in merchandise programs. Another criticized practice is the use of magazine *advertorials*, that is, an advertisement disguised as an editorial opinion. For example, *Seventeen* magazine runs a personal-advice column providing answers to make-up and wardrobe questions. Sometimes, however, the editorial-appearing advice is little more than a product plug.[21]

TARGETING TO MINORITIES.   Makers of alcohol and tobacco products frequently employ billboards and other advertising media to target brands to blacks and Hispanics. Billboards advertising alcohol and tobacco are disproportionately more likely to appear in inner-city areas.[22] Two celebrated cases illustrate the concerns involved. A national uproar ensued in 1990 when R. J. Reynolds was preparing to introduce Uptown, a brand of menthol cigarette aimed at blacks and planned for test marketing in Philadelphia where blacks make up 40 percent of the population.[23] Because blacks have over a 50 percent higher rate of lung cancer than whites, many critics, including the U.S. government's secretary for Health and Human Services, were incensed by the product launch.[24] In response to the public outcry, RJR canceled test marketing and the brand died.[25]

Following in the wake of Uptown's demise, critics challenged another firm, the Heileman Brewing Co., for introducing its PowerMaster brand of high-alcohol malt liquor targeted to inner-city residents—a brand containing 5.9 percent alcohol compared to the 4.5 percent content of other malt liquors.[26] Brewing

[19]"Selling to Children," *Consumer Reports* (August 1990), 518–519.

[20]Ibid.

[21]Ibid.

[22]"Fighting Ads in the Inner City," *Newsweek*, February 5, 1990, 46.

[23]Dan Koeppel, "Insensitivity to a Market's Concerns," *Adweek's Marketing Week*, November 5, 1990, 25.

[24]"A 'Black' Cigarette Goes Up in Smoke," *Newsweek*, January 29, 1990, 54.

[25]"RJR Cancels Test of 'Black' Cigarette," *Marketing News*, February 19, 1990, 10.

[26]Laura Bird, "An 'Uptown' Remake Called PowerMaster," *Adweek's Marketing Week*, July 1, 1991, 7.

industry supporters claimed that rather than being exploitative, PowerMaster and other malt-liquors merely meet the demand among blacks and Hispanics who buy the vast majority of malt liquor.[27] Nonetheless, the U.S. Treasury Department's Bureau of Alcohol, Tobacco, and Firearms (BATF)—which regulates the brewing and liquor industries—would not permit the Heileman Brewing Co. to market malt liquor under the name PowerMaster. The BATF arrived at this decision because it considered the name PowerMaster as promoting the brand's alcoholic content in violation of federal regulations.

OTHER INSTANCES OF TARGETING.   The controversy over targeting is not restricted to children and minorities. The R. J. Reynolds tobacco company was again widely criticized when preparing to introduce its Dakota brand of cigarettes to young, economically downscale women. RJR's plans to test market Dakota in Houston were squashed when critics created an outcry in response to what was considered to be exploitative marketing.

Another area of criticism is the practice of beer companies' promoting their brands to college students during spring breaks at beaches. Beer companies have curtailed their sponsorships of spring break events.[28]

IS TARGETING UNETHICAL OR JUST GOOD MARKETING? The foregoing discussion points out instances where advertising and other forms of marketing communications are criticized because they are directed at specific target markets. Proponents of targeting practices respond to such criticisms by arguing that targeting is good for consumers, not bad. Targeting, according to the proponents' view, tailors products to consumers and provides them with products best suited to their particular needs and wants. Not to be targeted, according to the advocates' position, is to have to choose a product that better accomodates someone else's needs.[29]

The issue is, of course, more complicated than whether targeting is good or bad. Sophisticated marketing practitioners and students fully accept the strategic justification for target marketing. There is the possibility, however, that some instances of targeting are concerned not with fulfilling consumers' needs and wants but rather with exploiting consumer vulnerabilities to the gain of the targeting marketer, but not to the gain of society. Herein rests the ethical issue which cannot be dismissed with a mere claim that targeting is sound marketing. You should discuss the ethical ramfications of targeting in class and benefit from the views of your professor and fellow students.

---

[27]"Fighting Ads in the Inner City."

[28]Jeffery D. Zbar, "Spring Break: Inflatable Beer Bottles Gone, But Other Marketers Move In," *Advertising Age*, April 1, 1991, 16.

[29]See Jahn E. Calfee, "'Targeting' the Problem: It Isn't Exploitation, It's Efficient Marketing," *Advertising Age*, July 22, 1991, 18.

Ethical Issues in Advertising

The role of advertising in society has been debated for centuries. Advertising is claimed by its practitioners to be largely responsible for much of what is good in life and is criticized by its opponents as being responsible for the bad. Following is a succinct yet elegant account of why advertising is so fiercely criticized:

> As the voice of technology, [advertising] is associated with many dissatisfactions of the industrial state. As the voice of mass culture it invites intellectuals' attack. And as the most visible form of capitalism it has served as nothing less than a lightning-rod for social criticism.[30]

A variety of ethical criticisms have been leveled against advertising. Because the issues are complex, it is impossible in this chapter to treat each criticism in great detail. The purpose of this discussion is merely to introduce the basic issues.[31] The following criticisms are illustrative rather than exhaustive.

ADVERTISING IS DECEPTIVE.   As discussed in detail in the following regulatory section of the chapter, deception occurs when an advertisement falsely represents a product and consumers believe the false representation. Is advertising deceptive according to this general definition? Some advertising *is* deceptive—the existence of governmental regulation and industry self-regulation attests to this fact. It would be naive, however, to assume that most advertising is deceptive. The advertising industry is not much different from other institutions in a pluralistic society. Lying, cheating, and outright fraud are universal, occurring at the highest levels of government (recall Watergate) and in the most basic human relationships (e.g., unfaithful husbands and wives). Advertising is not without sin, but neither does it hold a monopoly on sin.

ADVERTISING IS MANIPULATIVE.   The criticism of manipulation asserts that advertising has the power to influence people to behave in certain ways that they would not otherwise were it not for advertising. Taken to the extreme, this suggests that advertising is capable of moving people against their own free wills. What psychological principles would account for such power to

---

[30]Ronald Berman, "Advertising and Social Change," *Advertising Age*, April 30, 1980, 24.

[31]The interested reader is encouraged to review the following three articles for an extremely thorough, insightful, and provocative debate over the social and ethical role of advertising in American society. Richard W. Pollay, "The Distorted Mirror: Reflections on the Unintended Consequences of Advertising," *Journal of Marketing*, 50 (April 1986), 18–36; Morris B. Holbrook, "Mirror, Mirror on the Wall, What's Unfair in the Reflections of Advertising?" *Journal of Marketing*, 51 (July 1987), 95–103; Richard W. Pollay, "On the Value of Reflections on the Values in 'The Distorted Mirror'," *Journal of Marketing*, (July 1987), 104–109. Professors Pollay and Holbrook present alternative views of whether advertising is a "mirror" that merely reflects societal attitudes and values or a "distorted mirror" that is responsible for unintended and undesirable social consequences.

manipulate? As will be discussed in detail later in Chapter 11, the evidence certainly does not support subliminal advertising, which has provided advertising critics with the most provocative explanation underlying the claim of manipulation.

In general, the contention that advertising manipulates is without substance. Undeniably, advertising does attempt to persuade consumers to purchase particular products and brands. But persuasion and manipulation are not the same thing. Persuasion is a legitimate form of human interaction that all individuals and institutions in society perform.

ADVERTISING IS OFFENSIVE AND IN BAD TASTE. Advertising critics contend that much advertising is insulting to human intelligence, vulgar, and generally offensive to the tastes of many consumers. Several grounds exist for this criticism: (1) inane commercials of the "ring around the collar" genre, (2) sexual explicitness or innuendo in all forms of advertisements, (3) television commercials that advertise unpleasant products (hemorrhoid treatments, diarrhea products, etc.), and (4) repetitious usage of the same advertisements *ad infinitum, ad nauseam.*

Undeniably, much advertising is disgusting and offensive. Yet, the same can be said for all forms of mass media presentations. For example, many network television programs verge on the idiotic, and theater movies are often filled with inordinate amounts of sex and violence. This certainly is not to excuse advertising for its excesses. Recently, for example, criticism has been leveled against advertising for the increased use of male eroticism. Men are now portrayed as passive sex objects in the same fashion that women have been treated (e.g., in controversial Calvin Klein ads).[32] While this trend is disturbing to some, in advertising's defense it is likely that many consumers are not at all offended but rather enjoy this new form of advertising.[33]

ADVERTISING CREATES AND PERPETUATES STEREOTYPES. The contention at the root of this criticism is that advertising tends to portray certain groups in very narrow and predictable fashion: Blacks and other minorities are portrayed disproportionately in working-class roles rather than in the full range of positions they actually occupy; women too are stereotyped as housewives or as sex objects; and senior citizens are frequently characterized as feeble and forgetful people.

Advertising *is* guilty of perpetuating stereotypes. However, it would be unfair to blame advertising for creating these stereotypes, which, in fact, are perpetuated by all elements in society. Spreading the blame does not make advertising any better, but it does show that advertising is probably not any worse than the rest of society.

---

[32]Andrew Sullivan, "Flogging Underwear," *The New Republic*, January 18, 1988, 20–24.

[33]Ibid., 24.

PEOPLE BUY THINGS THEY DO NOT REALLY NEED.   A frequently cited criticism suggests that advertising causes people to buy items or services that they do not need. This criticism is a value-laden judgment. Do you need a new blouse or shirt? Do you need a college education? Who is to say what you or anyone else needs? Advertising most assuredly influences consumer tastes and encourages people to undertake purchases they may not otherwise make, but is this unethical?

ADVERTISING PLAYS UPON PEOPLE'S FEARS AND INSE-CURITIES.   Some advertisements appeal to the negative consequences of not buying a product—rejection by members of the opposite sex, bad breath, failure to have provided for the family if one should die without proper insurance coverage, and so on. Some advertisers must certainly plead guilty to this charge. However, once again, advertising possesses no monopoly on this transgression.

IN SUM.   The institution of advertising is certainly not free of criticism. What should be clear, however, is that advertising reflects the rest of society, and any indictment of advertising probably applies to society at large. Responsible advertising practitioners, knowing that their practice is particularly susceptible to criticism, have a vested interest in producing legitimate advertisements. Ethical advertising can serve society well. The *Focus on Promotion* (pages 198–199) looks at college marketing students' opinions about the social and economic consequences of advertising.

Ethical Issues in Public Relations

Publicity, which is the one aspect of public relations that is of primary relevance to marketing communications, involves disseminating positive information about a company and its products and handling negative publicity. Because publicity is like advertising in that both are forms of mass communications, many of the same ethical issues apply and need not be repeated. The one distinct aspect of publicity worthy of separate discussion is the matter of dealing with *negative publicity*.

There have been a number of celebrated cases in recent years where companies have been widely criticized for marketing unsafe products. The way firms deal with negative publicity has important strategic as well as ethical ramifications. (Discussion of strategic issues is delayed until Chapter 20.) The primary ethical issue is one of whether firms confess to product shortcomings and acknowledge problems or, instead, attempt to cover up the problems.

Consider, for example, the case of Tylenol capsules. Seven people in the Chicago area died in 1982 after ingesting cyanide-poisoned capsules. The publicity people at Johnson & Johnson, the makers of Tylenol, could have claimed that the problem was not of their making but rather was the workings of an isolated madman in Chicago. Such a position would have led J & J to continue selling Tylenol in all markets except Chicago. However, because it was unknown at the time whether the capsules had been poisoned at the factory or by a deranged person in retail outlets, the cautionary and ethical response was to remove Tylenol from store shelves throughout the country. This is precisely what J & J chose to do in taking the moral high road. It turned out that the problem *was* restricted to Chicago, but the ethics of the situation required caution to prevent the possibility of widespread deaths around the country.

Ethical Issues in Personal Selling and Telemarketing

The possibility for unethical behavior is probably greater in personal selling, including telemarketing, than any other aspect of marketing communications. This is because much of personal selling occurs on a one-on-one basis in the privacy of a customer's office. It is easier under such circumstances, compared to the case of mass communications, to make unsubstantiated claims and undeliverable promises. In other words, a salesperson is in a position to say things that are not subjected to public scrutiny. Each person's moral fiber is the primary determinant of how truthful she or he is behind a customer's closed doors or when delivering a sales pitch by telephone. Companies' penalty and reward structures also have some effect on salespeople's ethical conduct, but largely it is a personal matter.[34]

Ethical Issues in Packaging

Four aspects of packaging involve ethical issues: (1) label information, (2) packaging graphics, (3) packaging safety, and (4) environmental implications of packaging.[35]

  Label information on packages can mislead consumers by providing exaggerated information or by unethically suggesting that a product contains more of desired attributes (e.g., nutrition) or less of undesired attributes (such as cholesterol or fat) than is actually the case. *Packaging graphics* are unethical when the picture on a package is not a true representation of product contents (like when a children's toy is made to appear much bigger on the package than it actually is). Another case of unethical behavior is when a store brand is packaged so that it looks virtually identical to a well-known national brand. *Unsafe packaging* problems are particularly acute with dangerous products that are unsafe for children and the package is not tamper-proof. *Environmental* issues in packaging are typified by the discussion of Hefty trash bags earlier in the chapter. Packaging

---

[34]Joseph A. Bellizzi and Robert E. Hite, "Supervising Unethical Salesforce Behavior," *Journal of Marketing*, 53 (April 1989), 36–47.

[35]These issues were identified by Paula Fitzgerald Bone and Robert J. Corey, "Ethical Dilemmas in Packaging: Beliefs of Packaging Professionals," unpublished working paper, West Virginia University Department of Marketing, 1991. The following discussion is guided by this paper. The authors identified a fifth ethical aspect of packaging (the relationship between a package and a product's price) that is not discussed here.

FOCUS ON PROMOTION

COLLEGE STUDENTS' OPINIONS OF ADVERTISING

Most everyone has a definite opinion about advertising, and views vary widely. Some see advertising as a valuable social and economic force, while others view it in a much less positive light. What do college marketing students think about advertising?

An opinion survey was distributed to over 1,500 marketing students in colleges and universities around the country. Respondents rated seven statements on a seven-point Likert scale ranging from "strongly agree" to "strongly disagree." The survey included three statements about advertising's social implications and four statements about its economic effects:

Statements about Advertising's Social Implications
1. Most advertising insults the intelligence of the average consumer.
2. Advertising often persuades people to buy things they shouldn't buy.
3. In general, advertisements present a true picture of the product being advertised.

Statements about Advertising's Economic Effects
4. Advertising is essential.
5. In general, advertising results in lower prices.
6. Advertising helps raise our standard of living.
7. Advertising results in better products for the public.

(continued)

information is misleading and unethical when it suggests environmental benefits that cannot be delivered.

In a recent study of packaging ethics, completed questionnaires were received from nearly 600 packaging practitioners representing businesses throughout the United States. Respondents shared their opinions regarding various aspects of packaging ethics.[36] Some of the survey highlights include the following practices which practitioners consider *unethical:* (1) using the word *light* in reference to a product's texture and not its caloric content; (2) packaging store brands to mimic national-brand packages; (3) being aware of safety problems with a package's design but doing nothing to remedy the problems; (4) charging

---

[36]Ibid.

Here is what the survey revealed about marketing students' opinions toward advertising:

STATEMENT	AGREE	NEITHER AGREE NOR DISAGREE	DISAGREE
1	42.6%	16.6%	40.8%
2	61.5	14.1	24.4
3	31.0	14.9	54.1
4	94.8	2.4	2.8
5	19.8	20.6	59.6
6	40.6	38.0	21.4
7	53.9	24.1	22.0

Regarding the social and ethical implications of advertising (statements 1 through 3), marketing students are about evenly mixed on the matter of whether advertising insults their intelligence. Most (61.5 percent) agree that advertising is persuasive, while the majority (54.1 percent) do not think that advertising presents a true picture about advertised products. In terms of advertising's economic effects (statements 4 through 7), marketing students around the country overwhelmingly agree (94.8 percent) that advertising is essential. Yet nearly 60 percent do not believe that advertising lowers prices. A majority (53.9 percent) agree that advertising leads to better products, but only about 41 percent think that advertising raises the standard of living.

These results reveal that even a fairly homogeneous group like marketing students holds a diversity of opinions about the negative and positive consequences of advertising. It is little wonder that society at large is even more divided.

Source: This study was performed by J. Craig Andrews, "Dimensionality of Beliefs about Advertising," *Journal of Advertising,* 18, 1 (1989), 26–35.

more per unit for a large package than a small package; and (5) not attending to environmental problems when packaging materials are available for doing so.

Ethical Issues in Sales Promotions

Ethical considerations are involved with all facets of sales promotions, including manufacturer promotions directed at the trade (wholesalers and retailers) and to consumers. As later discussed in detail in Chapter 16, retailers have recently gained considerable bargaining power vis-a-vis manufacturers. One outcome of this power shift has been increased demands for *deals* imposed by retailers on manufacturers. *Slotting allowances* illustrate the power shift. This practice (thoroughly discussed in Chapter 16) requires manufacturers to pay retailers a per-store fee for their willingness to handle a new stock unit from the manufacturer. Critics of slotting allowances contend this practice represents a form of bribery and is therefore unethical.

Consumer-oriented sales promotions (including practices such as coupons, premium offers, rebates, sweepstakes, and contests) are unethical when the sales promoter offers consumers a reward for their behavior that is never delivered— for example, failing to mail a free premium object or to provide a rebate check. Sweepstakes and contests are potentially unethical when consumers think their odds of winning are much greater than they actually are.[37]

Fostering Ethical Marketing Communications

As alluded to throughout the preceding discussion, primary responsibility for ethical behavior resides within each of us when placed in any of the various roles as marketing communicator. We can take the easy route and do those things which are most expedient, or we can pursue the moral high road and treat customers in the same honest fashion that we expect to be treated. In large part it is a matter of our own personal integrity. *Integrity* is perhaps the pivotal concept of human nature.[38] Although difficult to precisely define, integrity involves avoiding deceiving others or behaving purely in an expedient fashion.[39] Hence, marketing communications itself is *not* ethical or unethical, but rather communication practitioners who exhibit integrity or fail to exhibit integrity and thus are themselves ethical or unethical.

Placing the entire burden on individuals is perhaps unfair, because how we behave as individuals is largely a function of the organizational culture in which we operate. Businesses can foster ethical or unethical cultures by establishing *ethical core values* to guide marketing communications behavior. Two core values that would go a long way toward enhancing ethical behavior are these: (1) treat customers with respect, concern, and honesty, the way you would want to be treated or the way you would want your family treated; and (2) treat the environment as though it were your own property.[40]

---

[37]For an insightful discussion of sales promotion practices and related consumer psychology that result in exaggerated expectations of winning, see James C. Ward and Ronald Paul Hill, "Designing Effective Promotional Games: Opportunities and Problems," *Journal of Advertising*, 20 (September 1991), 69–81.

[38]Jeffrey P. Davidson, "The Elusive Nature of Integrity: People Know It When They See It, But Can't Explain It," *Marketing News*, November 7, 1986, 24.

[39]Ibid.

[40]Donald P. Robin and R. Eric Reidenbach, "Social Responsibility, Ethics, and Marketing Strategy: Closing the Gap Between Concept and Application," *Journal of Marketing*, 51 (January 1987), 44–58.

Firms can facilitate ethical marketing communication behavior from their employees by suggesting that employees apply each of the following tests when faced with an ethical predicament: (1) act in a way that you would want others to act toward you (*the Golden Rule*); (2) take only actions which would be viewed as proper by an objective panel of your professional colleagues (*the professional ethic*); and (3) always ask, would I feel comfortable explaining this action on TV to the general public? (*the TV test*).[41]

REGULATION OF MARKETING COMMUNICATIONS

Advertisers, sales managers, and other marketing communicators are faced with a variety of regulations and restrictions that influence their decision-making latitude. Although regulation is inherently antithetical to the philosophical premises of a free-enterprise society, the history of the past century has shown that regulation is necessary. Regulation protects *consumers and competitors* from fraudulent, deceptive, and unfair practices that some businesses choose to perpetrate.

Regulation is needed most *when consumer decisions are based on false or limited information.*[42] Under such circumstances, consumers are likely to make decisions they would not otherwise make and, as a result, incur economic, physical, or psychological injury. Competitors are also harmed because they lose business they might have otherwise enjoyed.

In theory, regulation is justified if the benefits realized exceed the costs. What are the benefits and costs of regulation?[43] Regulation offers three major *benefits:* First, *consumer choice* among alternatives is improved when consumers are better informed in the marketplace. For example, consider the Alcoholic Beverage Labeling Act, which requires manufacturers to place the following warning on all containers of alcoholic beverages:

GOVERNMENT WARNING: (1) According to the Surgeon General, women should not drink alcoholic beverages during pregnancy, due to the risk of birth defects. (2) Consumption of alcoholic beverages impairs your ability to drive a car or operate machinery, and may cause health problems.[44]

---

[41]Based on Gene R. Laczniak and Patrick E. Murphy, "Fostering Ethical Marketing Decisions," *Journal of Business Ethics*, 10 (1991), 259–271 (264).

[42]Michael B. Mazis, Richard Staelin, Howard Beales, and Steven Salop, "A Framework for Evaluating Consumer Information Regulation," *Journal of Marketing*, 45 (Winter 1981), 11–21.

[43]The following discussion is adapted from Mazis, et al.

[44]Senate bill S.2047, 1988.

This regulation serves to inform consumers that drinking has negative consequences. Pregnant women and their unborn children in particular will benefit if this warning prompts consumers to exercise the alternative not to drink alcoholic beverages.

A second benefit of regulation is that when consumers become better informed, *product quality tends to improve* in response to consumers' changing needs and preferences. For example, when consumers began learning about the dangers of fat and cholesterol, manufacturers started marketing healthier food products. When regulators prevented makers of aspirin and analgesic products from making outrageously false and misleading claims, companies introduced new alternatives such as Tylenol and Advil as a means of taking market share away from entrenched aspirin brands.[45]

A third regulatory benefit is *reduced prices* resulting from a reduction in a seller's "informational market power." For example, prices of used cars undoubtedly would fall if dealers were required to inform prospective purchasers about a car's defects, since consumers would not be willing to pay as much for automobiles with known problems.

Regulation is not costless. One cost incurred by companies is the *cost of complying* with a regulatory remedy. For example, U.S. cigarette manufacturers are required to rotate over the course of a year four different warning messages for three months each. Obviously, this is more costly than the previously required single warning message. *Enforcement costs* incurred by regulatory agencies and paid for by taxpayers represent a second cost category. A third cost is the costs to buyers and sellers of *unintended side effects* that might result from regulations. A regulation may unintentionally harm sellers if buyers switch to other products or reduce their level of consumption after regulation is imposed. The cost to buyers may increase if sellers pass along, in the form of higher prices, the costs of complying with a regulation. In sum, regulation is theoretically justified only if the *benefits exceed the costs*.

The following sections examine the two forms of regulation that affect marketing communications decision making: governmental regulation and industry self regulation.

Federal and State Regulation of Marketing Communications

Governmental regulation takes place both at the federal and state levels. All facets of promotion (personal selling, sales promotion, advertising, telemarketing, etc.) are subject to regulation, but advertising is the one area in which regulators have been most active. This is because advertising is the most conspicuous

---

[45]For a fascinating history of advertising and regulatory activity in the aspirin/analgesic industry, see Charles C. Mann and Mark L. Plummer, "The Big Headache," *The Atlantic Monthly*, October 1988, 39–57.

aspect of marketing communications. The Federal Trade Commission is the government agency that has primary responsibility for regulating promotion at the federal level. The Food and Drug Administration, which regulates product labeling, has in recent years become an active regulator at the federal government level. At the state level, the National Association of Attorneys General has become the most active force.

The **Federal Trade Commission (FTC),** created in 1914, was concerned during its early years with preventing anticompetitive practices; that is, protecting businesses rather than consumers. By 1938, Congress realized that the FTC's mandate should be expanded to offer more assistance to consumers as well as businesses, especially in the area of false and misleading advertising. The *Wheeler-Lea Amendment* of 1938 accomplished this objective by changing a principal section of the original FTC Act of 1914 from "unfair methods of competition" to "unfair methods of competition and unfair or deceptive acts or practices in commerce." This seemingly minor change enhanced the FTC's regulatory powers appreciably and provided a legal mandate for the FTC to protect consumers against fradulent business practices. The FTC's regulatory authority cuts across three broad areas that directly affect marketing communicators: deceptive advertising, unfair practices, and information regulation.

R E G U L A T I O N   O F   D E C E P T I V E   A D V E R T I S I N G .   In a general sense, consumers are deceived by an advertising claim or campaign when (1) the impression left by the claim or campaign is false; that is, there is a claim-fact discrepancy, and (2) the false claim or campaign is believed by consumers. The important point is that a false claim is not necessarily deceptive by itself. Rather, consumers must *believe* a claim in order to be deceived by it. As Russo et al. have asserted, "A false claim does not harm consumers unless it is believed, and a true claim can generate harm if it generates a false belief."[46]

Although the FTC makes deception rulings case by case, it does employ some general guidelines in deciding whether deceptive advertising has occurred in a particular case. Deception policy at the FTC is not inscribed in granite but rather is subject to shifts, depending on the regulatory philosophy of different FTC chairpersons and the prevailing political climate. Under the Reagan Administration, lasting from 1980–1988, the FTC's enforcement policy against deception reflected the conservative political mood and the corresponding opposition to business regulation. However, in recent years the FTC has become more vigorous in opposing advertisers who make false and misleading claims.[47]

---

[46]J. Edward Russo, Barbara L. Metcalf, and Debra Stephens, "Identifying Misleading Advertising," *Journal of Consumer Research*, 8 (September 1981), 120. See also for a thorough review of advertising deception David M. Gardner and Nancy H. Leonard, "Research in Deceptive and Corrective Advertising: Progress to Date and Impact on Public Policy," *Current Issues & Research in Advertising*, 12 (1990), 275–309.

[47]"Suddenly, Green Marketers Are Seeing Red Flags," *Business Week*, February 25, 1991, 74–75.

The current deception policy declares that the FTC will find a business practice deceptive "if there is a representation, omission or practice that is likely to mislead the consumer acting reasonably in the circumstances, to the consumer's detriment.[48] The three elements that follow undergird this policy.[49]

1. *Misleading.*   There must be a representation, omission, or a practice that is likely to mislead the consumer. A *misrepresentation* is defined by the FTC as an express or implied statement contrary to fact, whereas a *misleading omission* is said to occur when qualifying information necessary to prevent a practice, claim, representation, or reasonable expectation or belief from being misleading is not disclosed.

2. *Reasonable Consumer.*   The act or practice must be considered from the perspective of the reasonable consumer. The FTC's test of reasonableness is *whether the consumer's interpretation or reaction to an advertisement is reasonable.* That is, the commission determines the effect of the advertising practice on a reasonable member of the group to which the advertising is targeted. The following quote indicates that the FTC evaluates advertising claims case by case in view of the target audience's unique position—its education level, intellectual capacity, mental frame of mind, and so on.

> For instance, if a company markets a cure to the terminally ill, the practice will be evaluated from the perspective of how it affects the ordinary member of that group. Thus, terminally ill consumers might be particularly susceptible to exaggerated cure claims. By the same token, a practice or representation directed to a well-educated group, such as a prescription drug advertisement to doctors, would be judged in light of the knowledge and sophistication of that group.[50]

3. *Material.*   The representation, omission, or practice must be material. A material representation involves *information that is important to consumers and which is likely to influence their choice or conduct regarding a product.* In general, the FTC considers information to be material when it pertains to the central characteristics of a product or service (including performance features,

---

[48]Public copy of letter dated October 14, 1983, from FTC Chairman James C. Miller III to Senator Bob Packwood, Chairman of Senate Committee on Commerce, Science, and Transportation.

[49]For a thorough and insightful discussion of these elements and other matters surrounding FTC deception policy, see Gary T. Ford and John E. Calfee, "Recent Developments in FTC Policy on Deception," *Journal of Marketing,* 50 (July 1986), 82–103.

[50]Chairman Miller's letter to Senator Packwood.

size, price). Hence, if an athletic-shoe company falsely claimed that its brand possesses the best shock-absorption feature on the market, this would be a material misrepresentation to the many runners who make purchase choices based on this factor. On the other hand, for this same company to falsely claim that it has been in business for 25 years—when in fact it has been in business for only 18 years—likely would not be regarded as material, since most consumers would not make a purchase choice based on this claim.

An important case involving the issue of materiality was brought by the FTC against Kraft, Inc., and its advertising of Kraft Single American cheese slices.[51] The FTC challenged Kraft on grounds that advertisements for Kraft Singles falsely claimed that each slice contains the same amount of calcium as five ounces of milk. Kraft responded that its $11 million advertising campaign did not influence consumer purchases. Kraft's legal counsel argued that advertisements (1) did not convey the misleading representation claimed by the FTC, but (2) even if this representation had been conveyed, it would not have mattered because calcium is a relatively unimportant factor in consumer's decision to purchase Kraft Singles. (Out of nine factors rated by consumers in a copy test, calcium was rated no higher than seventh.)

Kraft's defense, in other words, was that its calcium claim, whether false or not, is nondeceptive because that product attribute is *immaterial* to consumers. Or, in other words, Kraft's defense amounted to the following: (1) Yes, we (Kraft) may have made claims about the calcium benefits of Kraft Singles, but (2) our advertising was ineffective; (3) therefore, the issue of deceptiveness is moot because (4) calcium, the product attribute our advertising made claims about, is immaterial to consumers.[52]

After hearing detailed testimony on the matter and following an appeal process, the five commissioners of the FTC determined that Kraft's advertising claim was material.[53] Accordingly, the FTC ordered Kraft to *cease and desist* (literally, "stop and go no more," or discontinue) further misrepresentations of Kraft Singles' calcium content.

REGULATION OF UNFAIR PRACTICES.   As noted at the beginning of this section, the Wheeler-Lea Amendment of 1938 gave the Federal Trade Commission authority to regulate **unfair,** as well as deceptive, acts or practices in commerce. Unfairness is necessarily a somewhat vague concept. For this reason, the unfairness doctrine received limited use by the FTC until 1972, when in a famous judicial decision (*FTC v. Sperry & Hutchinson Co.*) the

---

[51]The advertising campaign ran in 1984 and 1985, but the FTC did not file a complaint until 1987.

[52]This interpretation is based on Julie Liesse Erickson, "Kraft Takes on FTC, Cites 'Ineffective' Ads," *Advertising Age*, July 4, 1988, 39.

[53]Ruling of the Federal Trade Commission, Docket No. 9208, January 30, 1991.

Supreme Court noted that consumers as well as businesses must be protected from unfair trade practices.[54] Unlike deception, a finding of unfairness to consumers may go beyond questions of fact and relate merely to public values.[55] The criteria used to evaluate whether a business act is unfair involve such considerations as whether the act (1) offends public policy as it has been established by statutes, (2) is immoral, unethical, oppressive, or unscrupulous, and (3) causes substantial injury to consumers, competitors, or other businesses.[56]

The FTC has applied the unfairness doctrine in three major areas: (1) advertising substantiation, (2) promotional practices directed to children, and (3) trade-regulation rules.[57]

Advertising Substantiation.   The ad-substantiation program is based on a simple premise: It is unfair for advertisers to make claims about their products without having a *reasonable basis* for making the claims. According to the FTC, unfairness results from imposing on the consumer the unavoidable economic risk that the product may not perform as advertised if neither the consumer nor the manufacturer has a reasonable basis for belief in the product claim. In other words, the ad-substantiation program requires advertisers to have documentation (test results or other data) indicating that they have a "reasonable basis" for making a claim *prior to the dissemination of advertisements.*[58]

The FTC charged Walgreen, a large retail drugstore chain, with making unsubstantiated claims for Advil pain reliever. Walgreen had advertised Advil as a "prescription pain reliever . . . " and "an anti-inflammatory . . . source of comfort for people who experience arthritis pain." The FTC ruled that Walgreen did not have a reasonable basis for this claim. The case was dropped when Walgreen consented not to make unsubstantiated claims for Advil or other analgesic drug products.[59]

---

[54]For further discussion, see Dorothy Cohen, "Unfairness in Advertising Revisited," *Journal of Marketing,* 46 (Winter 1982), 74.

[55]Dorothy Cohen, "The Concept of Unfairness as It Relates to Advertising Legislation," *Journal of Marketing,* 38 (July 1974), 8.

[56]Cohen, "Unfairness in Advertising Revisited," 8.

[57]Ibid., 75–76.

[58]For further discussion, see Dorothy Cohen, "The FTC's Advertising Substantiation Program," *Journal of Marketing,* 44 (Winter 1980), 26–35; and Debra L. Scammon and Richard J. Semenik, "The FTC's 'Reasonable Basis' for Substantiation of Advertising: Expanded Standards and Implications," *Journal of Advertising,* 12, 1 (1983), 4–11.

[59]Cited in the "Legal Developments in Marketing" section of the *Journal of Marketing,* 52 (January 1988), 131.

Unfairness Involving Children.   Because children are more credulous and less well-equipped than adults to protect themselves, public-policy officials are especially concerned with protecting youngsters. When applied to cases involving children, the unfairness doctrine is especially useful because many advertising claims are not deceptive per se but are nonetheless potentially unethical, unscrupulous, or inherently dangerous to children. For example, the FTC considered a company's use of Spider Man vitamin advertising unfair because such advertising was judged capable of inducing children to take excessive and dangerous amounts of vitamins.[60]

Trade-Regulation Rules.   Whereas most Federal Trade Commission actions are taken on a case-by-case basis, the use of trade-regulation rules (TRRs) enables the FTC to issue a regulation that restricts an entire industry from some unfair and objectional practice. For example, the FTC issued a TRR to vocational schools that would have required the schools to disclose enrollment and job placement statistics in their promotional materials. The rule was later rejected by a court of appeals on grounds that the FTC had failed to define the unfair practices that the rule was designed to remedy.[61] In recent years the FTC has used industry-wide trade-regulation rules sparingly.

INFORMATION REGULATION.   Although the primary purpose of advertising regulation is the prohibition of deceptive and unfair practices, regulation also is needed at times to provide consumers with information they might not otherwise receive.[62] Many believe that the corrective advertising program is the most important of the FTC's information provision programs.[63]

Corrective advertising is based on the premise that a firm that misleads consumers should have to use future advertisements to rectify any deceptive impressions it has created in consumers' minds. In other words, the purpose is to prevent a firm from continuing to deceive consumers; the purpose is not to punish the firm. The texts of four early corrective advertisements are shown in Table 7.1. In parentheses at the bottom of each corrective ad is the FTC's

---

[60]Cohen, "Unfairness in Advertising Revisited," 74.

[61]Ibid., 75.

[62]Ivan L. Preston, "A Review of the Literature on Advertising Regulation," in James H. Leigh and Claude R. Martin, eds., *Current Issues and Research in Advertising* 1983 (Ann Arbor, MI: University of Michigan, 1983), 14.

[63]The following discussion borrows heavily from the excellent review article by William L. Wilkie, Dennis L. McNeill, and Michael B. Mazis, "Marketing's 'Scarlet Letter': The Theory and Practice of Corrective Advertising," *Journal of Marketing*, 48 (Spring 1984), 11. See also Gardner and Leonard, "Research in Deceptive and Corrective Advertising."

TABLE 7.1	**Texts of Four Early Corrective Ads**

Profile Bread

"Hi, (celebrity's name) for Profile Bread.
   Like all mothers, I'm concerned about
   nutrition and balanced meals. So, I'd like
   to clear up any misunderstanding you
   may have about Profile Bread from its
   advertising or even its name."

"Does Profile have fewer calories than any other
   breads? No. Profile has about the same
   per ounce as other breads. To be exact,
   Profile has seven fewer calories per slice.
   That's because Profile is sliced thinner.
   But eating Profile will not cause you to
   lose weight. A reduction of seven calories
   is insignificant. It's total calories and
   balanced nutrition that count. And Profile
   can help you achieve a balanced meal
   because it provides protein and B
   vitamins as well as other nutrients."

"How does my family feel about Profile? Well,
   my husband likes Profile toast, the
   children love Profile sandwiches, and I
   prefer Profile to any other bread. So you
   see, at our house, delicious taste makes
   Profile a family affair."

(To be run in 25% of brand's advertising, for one
   year.)

Amstar

"Do you recall some of our past messages saying
   that Domino Sugar gives you strength,
   energy, and stamina? Actually, Domino is
   not a special or unique source of strength,
   energy, and stamina. No sugar is, because
   what you need is a balanced diet and
   plenty of rest and exercise."

(To be run in one of every four ads for one year.)

Ocean Spray

"If you've wondered what some of our earlier
   advertising meant when we said Ocean
   Spray Cranberry Juice Cocktail has more
   food energy than orange juice or tomato
   juice, let us make it clear: we didn't mean
   vitamins and minerals. Food energy
   means calories. Nothing more."

"Food energy is important at breakfast since
   many of us may not get enough calories,
   or food energy, to get off to a good start.
   Ocean Spray Cranberry Juice Cocktail
   helps because it contains more food
   energy than most other breakfast
   drinks."

"And Ocean Spray Cranberry Juice Cocktail
   gives you and your family Vitamin C plus
   a great wake-up taste. It's . . . the other
   breakfast drink."

(To be run in one of every four ads for one year.)

Sugar Information, Inc.

"Do you recall the messages we brought you in
   the past about sugar? How something
   with sugar in it before meals could help
   you curb your appetite? We hope you
   didn't get the idea that our little diet tip
   was any magic formula for losing weight.
   Because there are no tricks or shortcuts;
   the whole diet subject is very
   complicated. Research hasn't established
   that consuming sugar before meals will
   contribute to weight reduction or even
   keep you from gaining weight."

(To be run for one insertion in each of seven
   magazines.)

Source: William L. Wilkie, Dennis L. McNeill, and Michael B. Mazis, "Marketing's 'Scarlet Letter': The Theory and Practice of Corrective Advertising," *Journal of Marketing*, 48, Spring 1984, 13. Reprinted with permission from *Journal of Marketing*, published by the American Marketing Association.

stipulation for how often the corrective ad was to appear. For example, the stipulation for Profile Bread required the corrective statement to be printed or aired in 25 percent of Profile's ads for one full year.

   The most prominent corrective advertising order to date is the case of Warner-Lambert's Listerine mouthwash. According to the FTC, Warner-

Lambert had over a number of years misled consumers into thinking that Listerine was able to prevent colds and sore throats or lessen their severity. The FTC required Warner-Lambert to run this corrective statement: "Listerine will not help prevent colds or sore throats or lessen their severity." The corrective campaign ran for 16 months at a cost of $10.3 million to Warner-Lambert, most of which was spent on television commercials.

Several studies evaluated the effectiveness of the Listerine corrective advertising order.[64] The FTC's own study revealed only partial success for the Listerine corrective campaign. On the positive side, there was a 40 percent drop in the amount of mouthwash used for the misconceived purpose of preventing colds and sore throats; on the negative side, 57 percent of Listerine users continued to rate cold and sore throat effectiveness as a key attribute in their purchasing decision (only 15 percent of Scope users reported a similar goal), and 39 percent of Listerine users reported continued use of the mouthwash to relieve or prevent a cold or sore throat.

The FTC walks a fine line when issuing a corrective advertising order and specifying the remedial action a deceptive advertiser must take. The objective is to restore the marketplace to its original position prior to the deceptive advertising so that a firm does not continue to reap the rewards of its past deceptive practices. However, there is always the possibility that the corrective advertising effort may go too far and severely damage the firm and perhaps, unintentionally, hurt other companies in the industry. Fortunately, a national study of a corrective advertising order against STP oil additive determined that corrective advertising action in this case worked as intended: False beliefs were corrected without injuring the product category or consumers' overall perceptions of the STP Corporation.[65]

REGULATION OF PRODUCT LABELING.   The **Food and Drug Administration,** or **FDA,** is the federal body responsible for regulating information on the packages of food and drug products. The FDA was inactive until recent years. Under a new director, the FDA in 1991 took action against Procter & Gamble's Citrus Hill brand of concentrated orange juice. Citrus Hill's package falsely represented the brand as being *fresh* orange juice when in fact the product is concentrated. The FDA made a point of showing its revived regulatory vigilance by literally seizing 2,000 cases of Citrus Hill orange juice from a Minnesota warehouse. Just two days after the FDA action, P&G agreed to remove all references to *fresh.*[66]

---

[64]See ibid. for review.

[65]Kenneth L. Bernhardt, Thomas C. Kinnear, and Michael B. Mazis, "A Field Study of Corrective Advertising Effectiveness," *Journal of Public Policy & Marketing*, 5 (1986), 146–162. This article is "must reading" for anyone interested in learning more about corrective advertising.

[66]Steven W. Colford, "FDA Getting Tougher," *Advertising Age*, April 29, 1991, 1, 53; David Kiley, "FDA Seizes Citrus Hill," *Adweek's Marketing Week*, April 29, 1991, 6–7.

The action against P&G's Citrus Hill had strong symbolic impact and notified other marketers that the FDA is prepared to again regulate deceptive and misleading package labeling. The FDA has been looking into potentially misleading claims for supposedly fat-free products. In fact, a consortium of four major U.S. food manufacturers are working with the FDA to establish more graphic ways to better present nutritional information on package labels.[67]

REGULATION OF PROMOTION BY THE STATES.   Individual states have their own statutes and regulatory agencies to police the marketplace from fraudulent business practices. Most if not all states have departments of consumer affairs or consumer protection. During the sweeping deregulation climate in Washington under the Reagan Administration, states became more vigorous in their own regulatory activities. The **National Association of Attorneys General (NAAG),** which includes attorneys general from all 50 states, has played a particularly active role. For example, NAAG issued guidelines directed at advertising practices in the airline and car-rental industries. In another instance, attorneys general from 22 states filed a complaint against Honda of America, alleging that Honda's three-wheel, all-terrain vehicles are "rolling death traps."[68]

A particularly interesting case involved a lawsuit filed in 1990 by the Texas attorney general against Volvo North America. Volvo had produced a television commercial showing Bear Foot, a monster truck with huge wheels, running over a string of automobiles. All of the automobiles collapsed except the Volvo station wagon. An investigation revealed, however, that the Volvo had been reinforced with steel and wood while the other cars had their roof supports severed.[69] What makes this case so interesting is that it is reminiscent of similar advertising practices that were chastised two decades ago. For example, Campbell Soup Co. produced a commercial in which marbles were placed at the bottom of the bowl so that the food stock would rise to the top and give the soup a hearty appearance.

There is every indication that states will become even more active in their efforts to regulate advertising deception and other business practices.[70] This poses a potentially significant problem for many national advertisers who might

---

[67]Laura Bird, "Kessler Turns His Sights to 'Fat-Free'," *Adweek's Marketing Week*, June 10, 1991, 5–6.

[68]Paul Harris, "Will the FTC Finally Wake Up?" *Sales and Marketing Management*, January 1988, 57–59.

[69]David Kiley, "Candid Camera: Volvo and the Art of Deception," *Adweek's Marketing Week*, November 12, 1990, 4–5; Raymond Serafin and Gary Levin, "Ad Industry Suffers Crushing Blow," *Advertising Age*, November 12, 1990, 1, 76–77; Raymond Serafin and Jennifer Lawrence, "Four More Volvo Ads Scrutinized," *Advertising Age*, November 26, 1990, 4.

[70]See Andrew J. Strenio, Jr., "The FTC in 1988: Phoenix Or Finis?" *Journal of Public Policy & Marketing*, 7 (1988), 21–39.

find themselves subject to multiple, and perhaps inconsistent, state regulations. It is somewhat ironic that many national companies would prefer to see a stronger Federal Trade Commission. In other words, these firms are better off with a single regulatory agency that (1) institutes uniform national guidelines and rules, and (2) keeps the marketplace as free as possible from the fly-by-night operators that tarnish the image of all businesses.

Advertising Self-Regulation

Self-regulation, as the name suggests, is undertaken by advertisers themselves rather than by governmental bodies. Thus, self-regulation is in a sense a form of *private government* whereby peers establish and enforce voluntary rules of behavior.[71] Advertising self-regulation has flourished in many countries, particularly in highly developed countries such as Canada, France, and the United Kingdom.[72] In the United States self-regulation has resulted in response to heightened consumer criticism of advertising and stricter government controls.[73] Four major groups sponsor self-regulation programs: (1) advertising associations (e.g., American Association of Advertising Agencies, Association of National Advertisers), (2) special industry groups (e.g., the Council of Better Business Bureaus), (3) media associations, and (4) trade associations.[74]

The *advertising clearance process* is a form of self-regulation that takes place behind the scenes before a commercial or other advertisement reaches consumers. A magazine advertisement or television commercial undergoes a variety of clearance steps prior to appearing in media. Clearance includes (1) advertising agency clearance, (2) approval from the advertiser's legal department and perhaps also from an independent law firm, and (3) media approval (such as television networks' guidelines regarding standards of taste).[75] A finished ad that makes it through the clearance process and appears in advertising media is then subject to the possibility of post hoc regulation from the FTC, NAAG, and the National Advertising Review Board.

---

[71]Jean J. Boddewyn, "Advertising Self-Regulation: True Purpose and Limits," *Journal of Advertising*, 18, 2 (1989), 19–27.

[72]Jean J. Boddewyn, "Advertising Self-Regulation: Private Government and Agent of Public Policy," *Journal of Public Policy & Marketing*, 4 (1985), 129–141.

[73]Priscilla A. LaBarbera, "Analyzing and Advancing the State of the Art of Advertising Self-Regulation," *Journal of Advertising*, 9, 4 (1980), 27.

[74]Ibid., 28. See also Martha Rogers, "Advertising Self-Regulation in the 1980s: A Review," *Current Issues & Research in Advertising*, 13 (1991), 369–392.

[75]For a thorough discussion, see Eric J. Zanot, "Unseen But Effective Advertising Regulation: The Clearance Process," *Journal of Advertising*, 14, 4 (1985), 44–51, 59.

THE NATIONAL ADVERTISING REVIEW BOARD.   Self-regulation by the Council of Better Business Bureaus' National Advertising Division (NAD) and **National Advertising Review Board (NARB)** has been the most publicized and perhaps most effective form of self-regulation. The NAD and NARB were established with the goal of sustaining "high standards of truth and accuracy in national advertising."[76] NARB is the umbrella-like term applied to the combined NAD/NARB self-regulatory mechanism; however, by strict definition, *NARB* is a court of appeals consisting of 50 representatives who are formed into five-member panels to hear appeals of NAD cases when one or more of the involved parties is dissatisfied with the initial verdict.[77] *NAD* is the investigative arm of NARB and is responsible for "receiving or initiating, evaluating, investigating, analyzing and holding initial negotiations with an advertiser on complaints or questions from any source involving truth or accuracy of national advertising."[78]

The number of cases investigated and resolved each year varies, but NAD/NARB often becomes involved in 100 or more cases. Cases are brought to the NAD by competing advertisers, initiated by the NAD staff itself, or originate from local Better Business Bureaus and consumer groups. Food and beverages and child-directed ads are the categories most frequently involved.[79] A review of three advertising cases will demonstrate the nature of NAD/NARB activities.

Kellogg's Special K.   Kellogg agreed to modify advertising for its Special K brand cereal after the NAD questioned one aspect of Kellogg's claims. Television spots claimed that Special K's "200-calorie breakfast helps you keep the muscle while you lose the fat." Kellogg substantiated its claim that Special K contains the highest protein of all breakfast cereals, but NAD contested the advertising on grounds of whether it was appropriate for Kellogg to direct the claims to quick weight-loss dieters, the intended audience, who may benefit more from supplementary protein "of higher biological value." Kellogg complied by redirecting subsequent advertisements to state that Special K contributes to a nutritionally balanced diet and exercise program.[80]

---

[76]*Statement of Organization and Procedures of the National Advertising Review Board* (Washington, D.C.: National Advertising Review Board, June 19, 1980).

[77]Eric J. Zanot, "A Review of Eight Years of NARB Casework: Guidelines and Parameters of Deceptive Advertising," *Journal of Advertising*, 9, 4 (1980), 20.

[78]*Statement of Organization and Procedures.*

[79]"NAD Tackles 103 Cases in '88," *Advertising Age*, January 16, 1989, 49.

[80]"NAD Slaps Kellogg Over Special K Ads," *Advertising Age*, March 21, 1988, 70.

Nuprin.   A chiropractor questioned a claim that Nuprin "works at the site of pain." NAD investigated the claim and found that Bristol-Myers Squibb Co., the makers of Nuprin, could substantiate the claim.[81]

Beech-Nut Nutrition Corp.   Gerber Products, a competitor, challenged three Beech-Nut print ads which claimed that "the other leading brand also adds sugar to their instant fruit cereals, but Beech-Nut adds only fruit. We wouldn't dream of adding sugar or salt or other things your baby doesn't need." Gerber claimed its products do not contain salt or sugar. Beech-Nut agreed to comply with NAD's recommendation that future ads should be modified to indicate that Beech-Nut does not add any refined sugar to its cereals.

NAD/NARB COMPLAINT RESOLUTION PROCESS.   The preceding cases illustrate some of the fundamentals of the NAD/NARB self-regulatory process. This section details the specific activities that are involved from the time a complaint is initiated until it is resolved.[82]

Step 1: Complaint Screening and Case Selection.   The self-regulatory process begins with the NAD screening complaints against allegedly deceptive or misleading advertising. Complaints originate from four major sources: (1) competitors, (2) consumers and consumer groups, (3) Better Business Bureaus, and (4) NAD's own monitoring activities. The NAD pursues those complaints that it regards as having merit.

Step 2: Initial NAD Evaluation.   Some cases are administratively closed because they fall outside NAD's jurisdiction, but in most cases NAD contacts the advertiser and opens a dialogue. There are three possible outcomes from this dialogue: (1) the disputed advertisement is found acceptable; (2) the advertisement is considered questionable; or (3) the advertisement is deemed unacceptable because NAD feels it violates a precedent or may be misinterpreted by consumers.

Step 3: Advertiser's Initial Response.   Advertisers can respond to NAD by providing sufficient substantiation to show that the disputed advertising claim is justified (as in the Nuprin case) or by discontinuing or modifying the claim (as in the Kellogg's and Beech-Nut cases).

---

[81]Janice Kelly, "Texaco Sparks NAD Action," *Advertising Age*, February 25, 1991, 42.

[82]The following discussion borrows heavily from the thorough presentation by Gary M. Armstrong and Julie L. Ozanne, "An Evaluation of NAD/NARB Purpose and Performance," *Journal of Advertising*, 12, 3 (1983), 19–23.

Step 4: NAD's Final Evaluation.   All ads that have been discontinued or modified are publicly reported by NAD. For example, the cases described above were reported in *Advertising Age*, a publication that has wide distribution in the advertising community. Ads for which advertisers have provided substantiation are then reviewed by NAD to assess the adequacy of the evidence provided. In most instances NAD rules that the disputed claims have been adequately substantiated. Claims that NAD considers insufficiently substantiated are subject to appeal to NARB.

Step 5: Advertiser's Final Response.   The NAD's ruling may be upheld, reversed, or dismissed by NARB. However, because NAD/NARB is merely a self-regulatory body without legal jurisdiction or power, the ultimate resolution of disputed cases depends on voluntary cooperation between advertisers and NAD/NARB.

In conclusion, self-regulation has a variety of potential benefits to consumers and businesses. It can strengthen effectiveness by "discouraging exaggerated or misleading promises which lower the believability and selling power of advertising."[83] Self-regulation may also reduce the need for government regulation. Furthermore, because advertisers are strongly motivated to point out their competitor's deceptive advertising practices, their efforts to protect themselves help to maintain the general integrity of advertising and, in so doing, to protect consumers. Thus, the evidence seems to indicate that consumers have benefited substantially from NAD/NARB's self-regulatory efforts.[84]

SUMMARY

This chapter examines a variety of issues related to the physical environment, ethical behavior, and the regulation of marketing communications. In the first section, environmental marketing, or *green* marketing, is described and implications for marketing communications are discussed. Marketing communicators have responded to society's environmental interests by developing more environmentally friendly packaging and undertaking other communication initiatives. Recommendations provided to marketing communicators for making appropriate environmental claims are: (1) make the claims specific, (2) have claims reflect current disposal options, (3) make the claims substantive, and (4) make supportable claims.

---

[83]LaBarbera, "Analyzing and Advancing the State of the Art of Advertising Self-Regulation."

[84]Armstrong and Ozanne, "An Evaluation of NAD/NARB Purpose and Performance," 25.

The second major section examines ethical marketing communications behavior. The ethics of each of the following marketing communications activities are discussed: the targeting of marketing communications efforts, advertising, public relations, personal selling and telemarketing, packaging communications, and sales promotions. A concluding discussion examines how firms can facilitate ethical behavior.

The final section looks at the regulation of marketing communications activities. The regulatory environment is described with respect to both government regulation and industry self-regulation. The Federal Trade Commission's role is explained in terms of its regulation of deception, unfair practices, and information regulation. Specific topics covered include the advertising substantiation program, trade-regulation rules, and the corrective advertising program. Self-regulation by the Council of Better Business Bureaus' National Advertising Division (NAD) and National Advertising Review Board (NARB) are discussed, with emphasis placed on the process by which the NAD/NARB regulates national advertising.

Discussion Questions

1. The opening vignette concluded by asking you to think about the following questions: If you were the manager in this situation, would you introduce your own brand of degradable trash bag, or would you be willing to refrain from introducing a falsely claimed degradable trash bag and, consequently, to suffer lost sales to unethical competitors? Identify other marketing alternatives besides *introduce* versus *don't introduce* that might have been available to the Mobil Chemical Co. in the Hefty trash bag situation.

2. Increasing numbers of Americans are showing concern for the physical environment. However, all consumers are not equally concerned. Provide a specific profile of what in your opinion would be the socioeconomic and psychographic characteristics of the "environmentally concerned" consumer.

3. Using concepts from the elaboration likelihood model discussed in Chapter 4, provide a conceptual explanation of why seal-of-approval programs (Green Cross and Green Seal) may effectively persuade consumers.

4. The chapter quoted a Harvard Business School professor as claiming that *green* products would be to the 1990s what *lite* products were to the 1980s. Can you offer any reasons why this assertion may be overstated?

5. Some nutritionists claim that Gatorade is neither helpful nor harmful to children. If indeed Gatorade for children is little more than an inert substance, is it unethical in your opinion for that company to actively advertise the product?

6. What is your opinion regarding the ethics of product placements in movies targeted at children? Identify the arguments on both sides of the issue, and then present your personal position.

7. What is your opinion regarding the ethics of advertorials in magazines targeted to teenagers? Identify the arguments on both sides of the issue, and then present your personal position.

8. Marketers of malt liquor claim they focus on inner cities because blacks and Hispanics are the heavy consumers of this product. Is this practice ethical? Identify the arguments on both sides of the issue, and then present your personal position.

9. Advertising is often accused of various ethical violations. The criticisms of advertising mentioned in the chapter include claims that advertising is deceptive, manipulative, offensive, and that it plays on people's insecurities and fears. Provide evidence from your own personal experience and memory in support of any of these claims.

10. Theoretically, one benefit of business regulation is improvement in product quality. The chapter cited lower cholesterol and fat content in food products as one illustration of this. Identify two additional instances in which regulation has improved product quality.

11. What is the distinction between a deceptive and an unfair business practice?

12. In your opinion, should a firm be required to have substantiating evidence (test results or other data) for an advertising claim prior to making the claim? Why or why not?

13. Give examples of advertising claims which, if found false, probably would be considered material and claims which probably would be evaluated as immaterial.

14. What is your opinion of the defense Kraft used in claiming that calcium is an immaterial product attribute?

15. In theory, corrective advertising represents a potentially valuable device for regulating deceptive advertising. In practice, however, corrective advertising must perform a very delicate balancing act by being strong enough without being too strong. Explain the nature of this strong-enough-without-being-too-strong dilemma.

OVERVIEW of the PROMOTION MANAGEMENT PROCESS and ITS EXECUTION

The purpose of the two chapters in Part 4 is to provide a bridge between the general marketing communications topics covered in Parts 1–3 and the specific promotion practices (advertising, sales promotion, and so on) that are covered in the remaining chapters.

Part 4

Chapter 8 overviews the promotion management process by structuring promotion in terms of an integrative framework. Chapter 9 applies the framework and presents two detailed illustrations of integrated promotion management. The DuPont Stainmaster case shows how a manufacturer of carpeting profited from borrowing advertising programs and other promotional practices more typically observed in the marketing of consumer packaged goods. The second case involves a program undertaken by the United States Agency for International Development. This program used creative marketing communications practices to teach mothers in undeveloped countries how to deliver oral rehydration therapy to save the lives of their dehydrated children. This case provides a socially meaningful application of marketing communications in a nontraditional situation.

CHAPTER EIGHT

The Promotion Management Process

CONTEMPORARY BRAND MANAGEMENT: THE ART OF RECONCILIATION

The brand management form of marketing organization prevailed in American packaged-goods firms for over a half century. Introduced by Procter & Gamble in 1931, this organizational arrangement placed individual brand managers in charge of each brand in a company's various product lines. The traditional brand manager literally served as the brand champion who fought for budget dollars to support the brand and pushed for periodic sales promotions and point-of-purchase programs to boost the brand's sales volume. Brand managers typically were recruited from prestigious MBA programs. After serving apprenticeships as assistant managers for periods as short as two years, the "stars" among this pool of young MBAs—typically in their late twenties or early thirties—moved into the position of brand manager.

The brand management system of marketing organization worked well for many companies for years. However, major developments in the 1980s created pressures for significant organizational changes. Three forces in particular forced packaged-goods companies to reorganize their marketing functions: (1) the realization that consumer preferences often differ considerably across regions of the country; (2) the availability of immediate sales-performance data from optical scanners, which made it possible for manufacturers and retailers alike to determine which brands were meeting sales objectives and which marketing programs were effective in achieving manufacturers' and retailers' separate objectives; and (3) the power shift from manufacturers to retailers which afforded retailers a greater say in how brands are marketed by manufacturers.

The old brand management system was no longer adequate because long-term brand equity often was subordinated to short-term interests. Individual managers faced various conflicts that oftentimes were resolved in ways that were expedient but not compatible with long-term corporate welfare. Consider the following typical conflicts faced by brand managers:

■ Should I (the brand manager) focus on boosting the brand's short-term sales volume or should I work toward building long-term brand equity?

■ Should I do those things that will most benefit my career (such as increasing the brand's short-term sales and market share) or should I take a company-wide perspective and undertake actions that will be in the company's best long-term interests?

■ Should I focus more on providing price deals and other sales promotions to final consumers or should I be more concerned with developing promotions for my wholesaler and retailer customers?

■ Should my orientation be more national or regional in scope?

■ Should I spend my time working more on tactical maneuvers (i.e., devising day-to-day programs) or on developing long-range strategic plans?

In most every instance, the opponent on the left side of the conflict won out over the one on the right. That is, brand managers were excessively short-term oriented, too tactical, too national, too consumer rather than customer oriented, and probably too interested in enhancing self interests. For these reasons, many package-goods companies have recently reorganized their marketing organizations in order to better reconcile the right-side and left-side interests. The operative word here is *reconcile*, not supplant. Successful brand management necessitates that both sides of the various conflicts receive due accord. A later section in the chapter elaborates on the reorganization of marketing departments and discusses the trend toward category management structures replacing the traditional brand management system.

Note: See also Laurie Petersen, "Brand Managing's New Accent," *Adweek's Marketing Week*, April 15, 1991, 18-22.

INTRODUCTION

This chapter's purpose is to develop a comprehensive framework that fully integrates the various aspects of the promotion management process. Chapters hereafter will separately examine the various promotion-mix elements—advertising (Chapters 10–14), sales promotion (Chapters 15–17), point-of-purchase communications (Chapter 18), direct marketing communications (Chapter 19), public relations and sponsorship marketing (Chapter 20), and personal selling and sales management (Chapters 21–22). A unifying framework is needed to *appreciate* the fact that these elements must be fully integrated rather than treated as separable; indeed, as noted previously in Chapter 1, the integration of all the elements of marketing communications and promotion management is one of the most important marketing developments of the 1990s.

A MODEL OF INTEGRATED PROMOTION MANAGEMENT

Figure 8.1 lays out the elements and relations of promotion management. The model contains four general components, which are designated by Roman numerals: (I) Marketing Structure, (II) Monitoring and Managing the Environment, (III) Customer Satisfaction, and (IV) Promotion Decision Process. This last element, the decision process, consists of a set of general choices (selection of target markets, objectives, budgets, modes and mixture), specific plans (messages, media, and momentum), and program evaluation (measured results). It is very important at this point that you scan the model in Figure 8.1 and achieve a basic understanding in preparation for the following discussion that will flesh out the model skeleton.

Overview

The *Promotion Decision Process (PDP)* is the cornerstone of the model and represents the bulk of this chapter's discussion. Initially, however, it will be helpful to overview the general relations portrayed in Figure 8.1. Note first that the PDP is shown to be influenced by *Marketing Structure* (relation [A] in Figure 8.1). As subsequently will be described in detail, marketing structure represents the organizational arrangement employed by a firm for performing its marketing and promotional functions. Thus, the way a company is organized has great influence on how it makes promotional decisions and how these decisions are implemented.

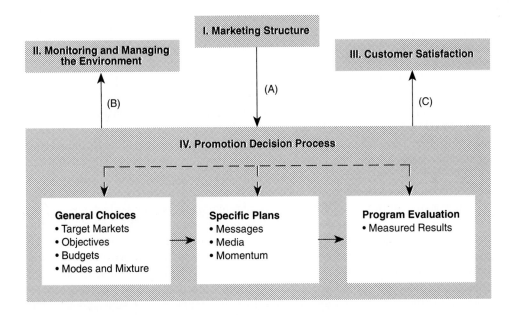

FIGURE 8.1

Integrated Promotion Management Model

The PDP involves proactive efforts directed at *Monitoring and Managing the Environment* (competition, social developments, economic trends, and so on) in order to achieve *Customer Satisfaction* (relations [B] and [C] in Figure 8.1).

Marketing Structure

Marketing structure is the *organizational arrangement* employed in a company to achieve its overall marketing and promotional objectives. As suggested in the opening vignette, a company's organizational structure is instrumental in determining how well it is able to manage its environment, satisfy its customers, and implement effective promotion decisions. In recent years many well-known companies (including Procter & Gamble, Campbell Soup, Coca-Cola, Pepsi-Cola, and IBM) have revamped their marketing structures in order to (1) better serve their immediate *customers* (wholesalers, brokers, and retailers), (2) do a better job in satisfying their ultimate *consumers'* needs, and (3) outperform *competitors*.

All three *C*s (customers, consumers, and competitors) have placed pressure on companies to reorganize.[1] Retailers have become more sophisticated and better informed—largely due to the advent of optical-scanning devices and the near-instantaneous information that they provide—and, as a result, expect more service and support from their manufacturer suppliers than they received in past years. Greater choices than ever are available to consumers, thereby forcing each company to do a better job in order to win the consumer's loyalty and beat competitors.

For example, Pepsi-Cola used to organize its marketing of soft drinks by channel of distribution—retail (e.g., grocery stores), vending machines, and fountain sales. Three separate organizations marketed Pepsi-Cola nationally to customers within each channel. Pepsi accordingly reorganized its marketing department into four large regions. The staff in each region is responsible for marketing to all customers (retail, vending, and fountain) within the region. The advantage of such *regionalized marketing structures* is that they enable marketing staffs to be more responsive to customer needs and competitive actions.[2]

Increasing numbers of firms are reorganizing to better reflect special regional demands. For example, Campbell Soup has reorganized its marketing department into more than 20 regional units. Each unit contains a combined marketing and sales force and has its own promotional budget, media-buying power, and discretion over marketing and promotional strategies. In the past these decisions were made at Campbell Soup by a centralized national office.[3] Another company, Frito-Lay—the well-known marketer of snack foods—has carved its market into seven regions. As with other regional marketing efforts, this has permitted Frito-Lay to target its programs more finely than ever before and to better accommodate regional differences in taste preferences.[4]

The most dramatic marketing restructuring in many years occurred recently at Procter & Gamble. This marketing superstar of packaged goods (detergents, soaps, snacks, cookies, paper products, etc.) has altered (not abolished) the traditional brand-management system that it innovated in 1931 and has established a **category management** structure. Under this new system, each of P&G's 39 product categories (detergents, paper products, etc.) is managed by a *category manager*. Advertising, sales, manufacturing, research, engineering, and other staffs report directly to the category manager, who has direct profit responsibility.[5]

The reorganization has reduced internal bickering for resources among brand managers and curtailed the tendency toward excessive short-term orienta-

---

[1]Laurie Freeman, "Why Marketers Change," *Advertising Age*, February 22, 1988, 24.

[2]"The Marketing Revolution at Procter & Gamble," *Business Week*, July 25, 1988, 72–76.

[3]"Marketing's New Look," *Business Week*, January 26, 1987, 64–69.

[4]Jennifer Lawrence, "Frito Makes Regional Advances," *Advertising Age*, July 4, 1988, 21. For further reading on the trend toward regional marketing, see Thomas W. Osborn, "Opportunity Marketing," *Marketing Communications*, September 1987, 49–63.

[5]"The Marketing Revolution at Procter & Gamble," 73.

tion fostered by the brand-management system discussed in the opening vignette. All brand managers (for example, the managers of Tide and Cheer) within a particular product category report directly to a category manager (detergent in this example), who has responsibility for allocating resources among brand managers and seeing that long-term objectives and overall corporate welfare are paramount over short-term expediencies and individual brand performance.

In sum, an organization's marketing structure is its direct link with the environment, plays an instrumental role in determining customer satisfaction, and has great influence on the promotion decision-making process.

Monitoring and Managing the Environment

Every organization operates in a dynamic relation with its environment. You will recall from an introductory marketing course that a variety of external forces constitute the environment for marketing decisions. These include economic, competitive, technological, social-cultural-demographic, and regulatory influences.

The relationship between promotion management and the various environmental influences is illustrated in Figure 8.2. The figure shows, via double-headed arrows, that all marketing-mix decisions (product, distribution, etc.) are subject to environmental influences. Specific decisions with respect to the six components of the promotional mix also must be adjusted in order to be compatible with environmental conditions and must be formulated in a way that enables a firm to manage environmental forces rather than merely react to these forces. Promotion managers must continuously monitor environmental developments and undertake actions with the intent of managing the environment.

MONITORING THE ENVIRONMENT.   Developing successful marketing communications necessitates continual monitoring of the environment: competitors, societal events, economic developments, regulatory activity, and even the company's internal situation. **Environmental monitoring,** or what also is referred to as performing a *situation analysis*, involves two general activities. First, an *internal analysis* must be made of an organization's *strengths and weaknesses*. Financial considerations and personnel matters are the primary issues in an internal analysis. A company with strong financial reserves and a talented team of promotion specialists has numerous opportunities for developing creative and impactual promotional programs, whereas an impoverished firm is limited in what it can accomplish.

An *external analysis* is the second component of a situation analysis. This analysis involves a thorough review of environmental factors that are likely to influence promotional effectiveness and product success. The economic situation, competitive activity, sociocultural developments, the legal climate, and channel of distribution considerations are typical factors involved in an external situation

FIGURE 8.2   **Monitoring and Managing Environmental Influences**

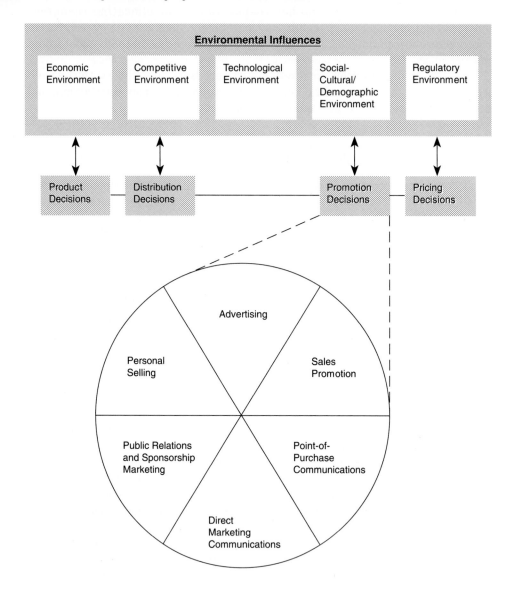

analysis. In effect, an external analysis examines the *opportunities and threats* that confront a brand at a point in time. Hence, analyzing a company's strengths and weaknesses in the internal analysis and environmental opportunities and threats in the external analysis, leads to the well-known acronym, *SWOT*—the analysis of a company's (or brand's) strengths, weaknesses, opportunities, and threats.

To illustrate the nature of an external analysis, consider the Dutch Boy brand of paint that has been marketed for over 80 years. This brand, which historically was directed at a mass audience rather than to any particular segment, was not doing well until it was purchased by the more financially secure Sherwin Williams company. Sherwin Williams' marketing research revealed that nearly 40 percent of all paint purchases are made by younger, fashion-oriented consumers in the 18 to 34 age group. Dutch Boy was repositioned to appeal to this particular target market. Advertising expenditures were increased and a series of MTV-type ads set to fast-paced music were designed. The commercials emphasized consumers' lifestyles by showing users painting with Dutch Boy and then enjoying the fruits of their labor—fashionable high-sheen results emulating the European decorating style that has become increasingly popular in the United States.[6]

MANAGING THE ENVIRONMENT. **Environmental management** captures the idea that through its promotional efforts and other marketing activities a firm can attempt to modify existing environmental conditions.[7] In other words, managers in specific areas of promotion (advertising, sales promotion, and so on) must attempt to influence and alter environmental circumstances so that the organization's interests are best served. Organizations are not able to completely manage their environments. It is critical, nevertheless, that they monitor their environments and are prepared to alter policies, strategies, and tactics to be compatible with environmental circumstances and developments. Successful companies anticipate environmental developments and prepare in advance, rather than simply reacting to significant changes after they have occurred.

For example, athletic-shoe companies have been remarkably effective in managing their environments. Changes in the cultural and social environment (e.g., the increased emphasis on health and fitness) have provided opportunities for new types of athletic shoes that are customized to meet the demands of specific sports (e.g., aerobic shoes). Nike's initial success was largely attributed to being in the vanguard of the running trend, while Reebok's early success was due in large part to spotting the need for special aerobic shoes. These companies have also effectively withstood the competitive inroads of many domestic and foreign competitors by building prestigious and quality brand images through a combination of effective advertising and good product performance.

---

[6]Adapted from Cyndee Miller, "Dutch Boy Repositions Itself to Reach Upscale, Fashion-Oriented Consumers," *Marketing News*, July 4, 1988, 1.

[7]Carl P. Zeithaml and Valarie A. Zeithaml, "Environmental Management: Revising the Marketing Perspective," *Journal of Marketing*, 48 (Spring 1984), 46–53; "Kotler: Rethink the Marketing Concept," *Marketing News*, September 14, 1984, 1ff.

The operative theme in the foregoing discussion is that organizations must be *proactive* in dealing with their various environments and not simply reactive. Effective environmental management requires anticipation of forthcoming changes and anticipatory action rather than belated reaction after competitors have already responded to the changes. Many declining industries in the United States (such as women's dress shoes and steel manufacturing) were notoriously slow in responding to environmental changes.

Customer Satisfaction

The touchstone of all marketing and promotional activities is ultimately the degree of **customer satisfaction.** Satisfying customers depends, of course, on the suitability of all marketing-mix elements, not just the promotional components. Nevertheless, the promotional components play an important role by informing customers about new products and brands and their relative advantages and by avoiding the tendency to over-inflate customer expectations. The cost of not satisfying customers can be great. For example, persistent complaints of poor-quality cars forced General Motors to introduce a "Bumper to Bumper" warranty on many of its models. The warranty covers virtually the entire car for three years or 50,000 miles and is estimated to cost GM up to $500 million per year.[8]

Companies that have a true commitment to *long-term customer satisfaction* do things that build long-term relationships with customers. These companies, according to one observer, realize that "you do not manage a company by focusing on R&D (an input), production (an output), or finance (a scoreboard), but rather by a thorough driving orientation toward the market and the customer."[9]

Delivering greater customer satisfaction can be accomplished in a number of ways. In general, it involves listening to the customer and focusing on retaining existing customers and *building relations* rather than always going after more and more new customers.[10] The sales force has a critical role in ensuring customer satisfaction and retention. Directing advertising and other promotional efforts at well-defined market segments is another way to enhance customer satisfaction. This requires concentrating on clearly defined target markets and developing real or imagined advantages over competitive offerings. The *Focus on Promotion* describes a form of relation building called *micromarketing*, which is one of the major marketing developments of the 1990s.

---

[8]"The High Cost of Selling Quality," *Fortune*, August 29, 1988, 11.

[9]"A New Survival Course for CEO's," *Marketing Communications*, September 1985, 21–26, 94.

[10]For further discussion of retention marketing, see Laura A. Liswood, "Once You've Got 'Em, Never Let 'Em Go," *Sales and Marketing Management*, November 1987, 73–77. For a theoretical yet highly readable account of relational marketing, see F. Robert Dwyer, Paul H. Schurr, and Sejo Oh, "Developing Buyer-Seller Relationships," *Journal of Marketing*, 51 (April 1987), 11–27.

THE PROMOTION DECISION PROCESS

Having now overviewed the general factors that give rise, influence, or constrain promotion-management activities in all of their various forms, attention now turns to the specific elements of the decision process. The following discussion is keyed to Figure 8.1. It will be helpful to briefly overview the PDP before proceeding with discussions of specific features. The model shows that *General Choices* (selection of target markets, objectives, budgets, modes and mixture) influence *Specific Plans* regarding messages, media, and momentum. *Program Evaluation* in the form of measured results follows from the general choices made and specific plans implemented. The evaluation results, in turn, feed back (dashed lines in Figure 8.1) to the general choices and specific plans. Corrective actions (increased sales-promotion expenditures, new advertising campaigns and so on) are called for when measured results indicate that performance has fallen below expectations.

General Choices

As shown in Figure 8.1, promotion managers have five general choices: the choice of target markets, objectives, budgets, the choice of modes to reach the targets, and choice of relative influence, or mixture, of modes.

TARGET MARKETS.   A pivotal concept in all of marketing is *market segmentation*. As described in the *Focus on Promotion*, marketing to specific targets is a fundamental requirement for successful micromarketing. Targeting allows marketing communicators to more precisely deliver their messages and to prevent wasted coverage to people falling outside the targeted market. Hence, selection of target segments is a critical first step toward effective and efficient marketing communications.

Companies identify potential target markets in terms of various characteristics—demographics, lifestyle characteristics, product usage patterns, and geographic location. It is crucial to recognize, however, that most profitable segments are based *not* on a single characteristic (such as people sharing just the same gender, just a particular age category, just the same race, and so on). Rather, meaningful market segments generally possess a *combination of characteristics* that result in consumers who share these characteristics acting in a similar fashion.

Consider, for example, the segmentation implications of a new brand of premium-priced, nonfat ice cream. The market segment for this new brand is not just women, not just men, not just younger people or older people, and, in general, not any group of people sharing any single characteristic. Rather, a meaningful segment would possess several or more shared characteristics, defined, for

FOCUS ON PROMOTION

THE DECADE OF MICROMARKETING

The three decades following World War II (1950 through 1970) represented a time when companies could easily achieve sales growth and profits. The population was growing, consumers had increasingly greater disposable incomes, and competition from abroad was not very strong; many foreign competitors were recovering from the economic devastation of World War II. Needless to say, those unprecedented prosperous days are long gone. Marketers now must fight for every percentage point of market share and for every dollar of profit. Competitive pressures demand that marketers be efficient with every dollar invested in marketing communications. The world of modern marketing has moved from the mass marketing of yesteryear to the micromarketing of today.

To fully appreciate the changes that have occurred, it is necessary to examine the nature of *mass marketing* during its heyday in the 1950s through the 1970s. During this period, marketers directed their advertising and other communications efforts at rather crudely designated target markets and relied on network television to reach general audiences across the United States. Much of the advertising was wasted because many message recipients were not strong prospects for the advertised product. However, for the reasons noted earlier (growing population size, etc.), mass marketing efforts were still profitable in spite of their crudeness and imprecision. Intensified competition now

(continued)

example, as people living in urban or suburban areas, earning incomes above $40,000, who are aging (over 35) and are health and weight conscious.

In general, a meaningful market segment is one consisting of people who exhibit *relatively homogeneous response tendencies* to a brand's marketing mix elements and who are *economically accessible* via distribution and media channels. People who respond in a similar way to marketing mix variables (e.g., prefer non-fat to regular ice cream and are willing to pay a premium price) and who shop in similar outlets and read, listen to, and view similar programs do so because of their similar interests in life, not because they share a single common characteristic. Hence, meaningful and profitable market segmentation efforts typically require that segment members share various demographic, lifestyle, and possibly geographical characteristics. Advertisers and other marketing communicators sometimes pretend to be segmenting markets when they designate an audience in terms such as *women aged 18-49*, but such broad groupings are much too crude to satisfy the characteristics described above.

demands more precise target market specification. The availability of precise and detailed marketing information makes it possible to implement and pinpoint communication efforts.

The practice of **micromarketing** involves focusing marketing communications on targets that provide the greatest opportunity and attempting to minimize messages aimed at the wrong targets.[1] The micromarketer operates by answering three fundamental questions: *Who* exactly are the consumers most likely to become users of a brand? *Where* are they located? *How* most efficiently can they be reached with marketing communications tools?[2]

Answering the *who* and *where* questions is facilitated by the ready availability to brand managers of information both about product movement at retail and customers' product-usage patterns. For example, massive computerized databases containing check-out scanner data inform managers of the volume of brand movement from retail shelves. This information plus rich databases on household characteristics and purchase patterns reveal the prime targets for marketing communications efforts. Marketers know who (in terms of demographic and socioeconomic characteristics) their best customers are and where they are to be found (in terms of geographic locations and specific retail outlets where they shop).

Answering the *how* question amounts to determining the most efficient ways to reach the most opportune customers. The trend is away from national network advertising and toward more spot advertising, more focused couponing efforts, greater usage of direct mailings, and more selectively placed in-store promotions. In general, the micromarketer of the 1990s is seeking ways to accomplish greater impact with more selectively placed marketing communications dollars.[3]

---

[1]This definition is based on Danny L. Moore, "What Is Micromarketing?" *Aim*, 2, 2 (1990), 7. Note: *Aim* is a publication of the Nielsen research company.

[2]Ibid. See also Howard Hunt, "How to Become a Micromarketer," *Aim*, 2, 2 (1990), 13–16.

[3]See Richard Gibson, "Marketers' Mantra: Reap More with Less," *The Wall Street Journal*, March 22, 1991, sec. B, 1.

OBJECTIVES.   Promotion managers' general and specific choices are grounded in underlying *goals* or **objectives.** Promotion managers base their decisions on specific organizational objectives to be accomplished. Of course, the content of these objectives varies within specific areas of the promotion mix because the components of the mix have different capabilities. For example, whereas mass-media advertising is ideally suited for creating consumer awareness of a new or improved brand, point-of-purchase communications are perfect for influencing in-store brand selection, and personal selling is unparalleled when it comes to informing buyers about product improvements.

Specific chapters later in the text detail the objectives that each component of the promotion mix is designed to accomplish; for present purposes it will suffice to merely list various objectives that promotion managers hope to accomplish:

■ Facilitate the successful introduction of new products.

■ Build sales of existing products by increasing frequency of use, variety of uses, or the quantity purchased.

■ Inform the trade and consumers about product improvements.

■ Build the company's image.

■ Generate sales leads.

■ Persuade middlemen (dealers, distributors, etc.) to handle the company's brands.

■ Stimulate point-of-purchase sales.

■ Develop brand awareness, acceptance, and insistence.

■ Increase customer loyalty.

■ Let consumers know where to buy a new product.

■ Improve corporate relations with special-interest groups.

■ Offset bad publicity about a company's products.

■ Generate good publicity.

■ Counter competitors' marketing and promotional efforts.

■ Provide customers with reasons for buying now rather than delaying a purchase choice.

BUDGETS.   An organization's financial resources are budgeted to specific promotion elements in order to accomplish the communications objectives established for its various brands. The amount of resources allocated to specific promotion elements is typically the result of an involved process in most sophisticated corporations. Companies use different budgeting processes in allocating funds to promotion managers and other organizational units. At one extreme is *top-down budgeting (TD)*, in which senior management decides how much each subunit receives. At the other extreme is *bottom-up budgeting (BU)*, in which managers of subunits (brand managers and category managers) determine how much is needed to achieve their objectives; these amounts are then combined to establish the total marketing budget.

Most budgeting practices involve a combination of top-down and bottom-up budgeting. For example, in the *bottom-up/top-down process (BUTD)*, subunit managers submit budget requests to a chief marketing officer (say, a vice president of marketing), who coordinates the various requests and then submits an overall budget to top management for approval. This is the form of budgeting used at Procter & Gamble with its 39 new category managers. Within each product category, brand managers submit budgets to the category manager, who in turn coordinates an overall category budget. The 39 category budgets are coordinated by a vice president of marketing and then are submitted to top management for approval. The *top-down/bottom-up process (TDBU)* reverses the flow of influence by having top managers first establish the total size of the budget and then divide it among the various subunits.

Research has shown that combination budgeting methods (BUTD and TDBU) are used more often than the extreme methods (TD or BU).[11] The BUTD process is by far the most frequently used, especially in more sophisticated firms where marketing-department influence is high compared to finance-department influence.[12]

MODES AND MIXTURE.   The term modes is used here in the three-modes-of-marketing sense described in Chapter 1. As you will recall, the three modes are: Mode 1, the *basic offer* (the product itself and associated terms of sale); Mode 2, *persuasive communications* (verbal and nonverbal messages such as advertisements and point-of-purchase displays); and Mode 3, *promotional inducements* (extra substantive benefits beyond the benefits of the basic offer, which are also referred to as sales promotions).

Although the three modes overlap and reinforce each other, only Modes 2 and 3 are discussed further because Mode 1, the basic offer, is a determination of general marketing management and not promotion management per se. Mode 2, *persuasive communications*, consists of messages directed to target customers (via a combination of personal selling, advertising, publicity, and point-of-purchase devices) that are intended to enhance the impression of the basic offer and to stimulate wants for it. Mode 3, *promotional inducements*, are used to induce customers and consumers to adopt the marketer's plan of action. This is accomplished by using free samples, trial usage, coupons, discounts, rebates, allowances, and other promotional inducements.

A fundamental issue confronted by all companies is deciding exactly how to allocate resources between the two general modes, persuasive communications and promotional inducements. The mix in *industrial-goods companies* typically emphasizes personal selling with supplementation from trade advertising, technical literature, and trade shows.[13]

---

[11]Nigel F. Piercy, "The Marketing Budgeting Process: Marketing Management Implications," *Journal of Marketing*, 51 (October 1987), 45–59.

[12]Ibid. See Figure 2, 55.

[13]Donald W. Jackson, Jr., Janet E. Keith, and Richard K. Burdick, "The Relative Importance of Various Promotional Elements in Different Industrial Purchase Situations," *Journal of Advertising*, 16, 4 (1987), 25–33.

For *consumer-goods companies*, the mix issue is, in many respects, more complicated and controversial because greater options are available. Personal selling is important in a consumer-goods company's *push efforts*, but the real difficulty and controversy arises when deciding how best to *pull* a product through the channel.[14] The issue boils down to a decision of how much to allocate to advertising and to sales promotion. Over the past decade, the trend has been in the direction of greater expenditures on sales promotion. Indeed, sales-promotion expenditures increased at an average rate of 13 percent, while advertising expenditures grew annually by only 10 percent.[15] Sales promotion's share of the total promotional budget has grown from less than 60 percent in the late 1970s to nearly 70 percent today.

What is the *optimum mixture* of expenditures between advertising and sales promotion? Unfortunately, no specific answer is possible because the promotion-mix decision is what is called an *ill-structured problem*.[16] This means that for a given level of expenditure there is no way of knowing what the mathematical optimum allocation between advertising and sales promotion should be in order to maximize sales or profit. At least four factors account for this inability to determine a mathematically optimum mix.[17]

First, advertising and sales promotion are somewhat *interchangeable* in that both tools can accomplish some of the same promotional objectives. Because of this, it is impossible to know exactly which tool or combination of tools is better in every situation.

Second, the fact that the combined effect of these two promotional tools is greater that what they would achieve individually (a *synergistic effect*) makes it difficult to determine the exact effects that different combinations of advertising and sales promotion might generate.

Third, advertising and sales promotion not only operate synergistically with each other, they also *interact with other elements of the marketing mix*. Thus, the effectiveness of these tools is impossible to evaluate without considering the overall marketing mix.

---

[14]The terms push and pull are metaphors, as you probably recall from your introductory marketing course, that characterize the nature of the promotional thrust through the channel of distribution. The *push* metaphor suggests a forward thrust from manufacturer to the trade (wholesalers or retailers) on to the consumer. Personal selling to the trade is the primary push technique. *Pull* means that a manufacturer promotes directly to consumers with intentions they will pressure retailers to stock the promoted product. In actuality, manufacturers use a combination of pull and push techniques. These techniques complement one another and are not perfectly substitutable.

[15]Nathaniel Frey, "Ninth Annual Advertising and Sales Promotion Report," *Marketing Communications*, August 1988, 9–19.

[16]Thomas A. Petit and Martha R. McEnally, "Putting Strategy into Promotion Mix Decisions," *The Journal of Consumer Marketing*, 2 (Winter 1985), 41–47.

[17]This discussion is based on Petit and McEnally, 43.

Fourth, the optimum advertising and sales-promotion mix is affected by various *market forces*—the nature of the buying process, characteristics of the market, the extent of competition, and so on.

The result is that there simply is no way to take all of the preceding factors into account to determine which combination of advertising and sales promotion is the best among the many possibilities.[18] Thus, rather than seeking an optimum mixture, it is more reasonable to develop a workable, satisfactory mixture. Achieving a *satisfactory mixture* of advertising and sales promotion requires that the following key considerations be addressed:[19]

1. A careful *cost-value analysis* of each proposed mix has to be performed to determine whether distribution, sales, and profit objectives can be achieved in view of the intended expenditure.

2. An evaluation must be made of how well the proposed levels of advertising and sales promotion *fit with each other and complement one another.*

3. *Strategic considerations* in determining the differing purposes of advertising and sales promotion must be studied carefully. A key strategic consideration is whether short-term or long-term considerations are more important given a brand's life-cycle stage. An appropriate mixture for mature brands is likely to be much different than the mixture for brands recently introduced. New brands require a proportionately much larger investment in sales promotions (such as couponing and sampling) in order to generate trial purchases, whereas mature brands require proportionately greater advertising investment to maintain or enhance a brand's image.

4. *Brand equity* represents a final consideration in evaluating a satisfactory combination of advertising and sales promotion. **Brand equity** represents the goodwill (equity) that an established brand has built up over the period of its existence. Poorly planned or excessive sales promotions can seriously damage a brand's equity by cheapening its image. If a brand is frequently placed on sale or if some form of promotional inducement is regularly offered, consumers will delay purchasing the brand until they can get a deal. The effect is that the brand becomes an object purchased more for its price discount or promotional inducement than for the value of its basic offer.

---

[18]Ibid.

[19]The following key issues are adapted from Joseph W. Ostrow, "The Advertising/Promotion Mix: A Blend or a Tangle," *AAAA Newsletter*, August 1988, 6–7. Parenthetically, note this article title refers to advertising versus promotion. Mr. Ostrow, like other marketing practitioners, drops the leading word *sales* when referring to sales promotion. Whereas in the academic marketing community we refer to promotion in a general sense to include all forms of promotional tools (advertising, personal selling, sales promotion, etc.), practitioners use the word *promotion* in reference to sales promotion per se.

The matter of properly mixing advertising and sales promotion is aptly summarized in the following quote by Joseph W. Ostrow:

> As one views the opportunities inherent in ascertaining the proper balance between advertising and [sales] promotion, it should be quite clear that both should be used as one would play a pipe organ, pulling out certain stops and pushing others, as situations and circumstances change. Rigid rules, or continuing application of inflexible advertising-to-promotion percentages, serve no real purpose and can be quite counterproductive in today's dynamic and ever-changing marketing environment. A short-term solution that creates a long-term problem is no solution at all.[20]

The short-term *solution* alluded to is spending excessive amounts on sales promotion to create quick sales while failing to invest sufficiently in advertising to build a brand's long-term image. That is, excessive sales promotion can rob a brand's future. An appropriate mixture involves spending enough on sales promotion to ensure sufficient sales volume in the short term while simultaneously spending enough on advertising to ensure the growth or preservation of a brand's equity position. Many brand managers seem to be unaware of or disregard the damage that short-term thinking can have. For example, the marketing of Schlitz beer excessively emphasized price discounts and promotions, and the effect in five years was a transition from a profitable brand earning $48 million to one losing $50 million.[21]

Specific Choices

The general choice of segments and mixture of promotional modes is just the beginning. Within each mode there are many choices to be made regarding (1) the types of *messages* to use, (2) the *media* to deliver messages, and (3) the *momentum* backing up the media effort (see Figure 8.1).

M E S S A G E S .   As established in Chapter 2 on communications fundamentals, the message is a critical component of marketing communications effectiveness. Managers of every promotional element have choices to make regarding how best to present their persuasive arguments to achieve established objectives. Consider the following examples:

Sales managers decide on the form and content of sales presentations. One important consideration, for example, is whether the presentation should follow a fixed script (a *canned* presentation) or vary from prospect to prospect. *Public-relations directors*, when faced with adverse publicity, choose how best to defend their company's products without appearing excessively contrite or defensive.

---

[20]Ostrow, "The Advertising/Promotion Mix: A Blend or a Tangle," 7.

[21]Cited in "The Purest Treasure," *The Economist*, September 7, 1991, 67. For a detailed discussion of brand equity, see David Aaker, *Managing Brand Equity: Capitalizing on the Value of a Brand Name* (New York: The Free Press, 1991).

The public relations person walks a fine line between being an apologist and a dogmatist. Effective public relations people are able to come across sincerely but forcefully in support of their company's products that are under attack. *Advertising creative directors* have numerous message choices. What image to create, how to position the brand, and what specific types of appeals to employ (such as sex, humor, or fear) are just some of the many choices. Subsequent chapters will deal with specific message issues as they relate to each promotional element.

M E D I A .   All marketing communications messages require an agency or instrument (a medium) for transmission. Though the term media is typically applied to advertising media (television, magazines, radio, etc.), the concept of **media** is relevant to all promotional tools. For example, personal sales messages can be delivered via face-to-face communications or by telemarketing; these media alternatives have different costs and effectiveness. Point-of-purchase materials are delivered in a variety of ways—via in-store signs, electronically, musically, and otherwise. Each of these represents a different medium.[22]   Detailed discussions of media are reserved for specific chapters that follow.

M O M E N T U M .   The word **momentum** refers to an object's force or speed of movement, its *impetus*. The same idea can be applied to marketing communications. Simply developing an advertising message, personal sales presentation, or publicity release is insufficient. The effectiveness of each of these message forms depends on their *timing* (speed, so to speak) and *force* (amount of effort). Insufficient momentum, that is, poorly timed messages and insufficient investment, is ineffective at best and a waste of money at worst.

As is the case with almost every decision faced by promotion managers, momentum is a relative matter: There is no level of momentum equally appropriate for all situations. For example, the amount of investment appropriate for one advertiser may be woefully inadequate for another. L.A. Gear spends a much larger portion of its sales on advertising than either of its much larger competitors, Nike and Reebok. This is because L.A. Gear is a relatively new and unestablished brand; a very strong commitment to advertising is therefore required in order to build its brand name and create a desired image.

Critical to the concept of momentum is the need to *sustain an effort* rather than starting and stopping—advertising for a while, then discontinuing the effort for a longer while, and so on. In other words, some companies never create nor sustain momentum because their marketplace presence is inadequate "Out of

---

[22]You no doubt have noted the switch in this paragraph between *media* and *medium*. The former is plural, the latter singular. Thus, *medium* is the appropriate descriptor when referring only to, say, television; however, *media* is the correct usage when referring to television, magazines, and radio as a collection of advertising vehicles.

sight, out of mind" is probably a more relevant saying in reference to brands in the marketplace than to people. We generally do not forget our friends and family, but today's product friend is tomorrow's stranger unless it is kept before our consciousness. The *Global Focus* describes some momentum-building efforts by Pepsi and Coca-Cola in their global market warfare.

Program Evaluation

Communication objectives are set, modes are selected and mixed, messages and media are chosen, programs are implemented and possibly sustained, and then the programs must be evaluated. This is accomplished by measuring results of promotional programs against the objectives that were established at the outset. For a local advertiser, say a sporting-goods store that is running an advertised special on athletic shoes for a two-day period in May, the results are the number of Nike, Reebok, and other brands sold. If you tried to sell an old automobile through the classified pages, the results would be the number of phone inquiries you receive and whether you ultimately sold the car. For a national manufacturer of a branded product, results typically are not so quick to occur. Rather, a company invests in point-of-purchase communications, sales promotions, and advertising, and then waits, often for many months, to see whether these programs deliver the desired sales volume.

Regardless of the situation, it is critical to **evaluate** (or measure) **the results** of marketing communications efforts. The preceding discussion suggests that results are measured solely in terms of *sales volume.* In actuality, results of promotional programs more typically are measured in terms of *communication outcomes* rather than sales. This is because sales volume is determined by *all* of the elements of the marketing mix, not just the promotional elements, as well as by various environmental forces. Consequently, increases in sales volume cannot be attributed solely to sales promotion, advertising, or other promotional elements. Communication outcomes provide a more precise measure of promotional effectiveness.

Detailed discussions of communication measures are postponed until appropriate chapters (e.g., Chapter 14 on measuring advertising effectiveness), but a few comments are in order at this time. A *communication measure* is one that deals with a nonsales target: brand awareness, message comprehension, attitude toward the brand, and purchase intentions are typical communication measures. All of these are communication (rather than sales) objectives in the sense that an advertiser has attempted to communicate a certain message argument or overall impression. Thus, the goal for an advertiser of a relatively unknown brand may be to increase brand awareness in the target market by 30 percent within six months of starting a new advertising campaign. This objective (a 30 percent increase in awareness) would be based on knowledge of the awareness level prior to the campaign's debut. Post-campaign measurement would then reveal whether the target level was achieved.

GLOBAL FOCUS

INTERNATIONAL WARFARE BETWEEN COCA-COLA AND PEPSI-COLA

International competition between Coke and Pepsi is just as intense as their legendary domestic battles. This is quite understandable considering the huge opportunity for relatively easy growth in cola sales offered by the international arena. Indeed, Coca-Cola presently receives about 60 percent of its soft-drink sales from abroad and earns approximately 80 percent of its operating income from outside the United States. Pepsi historically has been less successful internationally, but in recent years has begun to intensify its overseas efforts.

Outside the United States, Pepsi is aiming its efforts at building brand loyalty among youths. This explains why Pepsi has paid millions of dollars to Michael Jackson for his Pepsi-sponsored international tours. In 1983, Pepsi first signed Jackson to a $5 million endorsement deal for his *Victory* tour. Then in 1987 Pepsi paid Jackson $10 million for an international deal tied into his *Bad* album. In 1992, Pepsi sponsored the *Dangerous* tour in the most lucrative sponsorship ever between a corporation and a music entertainer.

Coca-Cola also is intensifying its marketing efforts throughout the world. For example, in Moscow, a market historically dominated by Pepsi-Cola, Coca-Cola is in the process of erecting 2,000 kiosks to sell Coke and Fanta soft drinks fountain-style throughout the city.

Marketing communicators at Coca-Cola and Pepsi-Cola fully appreciate the fact that achieving success internationally requires creating distinct brand identities and building customer loyalty. These goals, in turn, demand that advertising and promotional momentum be maintained—otherwise, a competitor will be prepared to step in and steal sales volume and market share.

Source: Adapted from Alison Fahey, "Pepsi's Concerts Vs. Coke's Games," *Advertising Age,* February 10, 1992, 47.

It is essential to measure results of all promotional programs. Failure to achieve targeted results prompts corrective action (see dashed lines, or *feedback loops,* in Figure 8.1). Corrective action might call for greater investment, a different combination of modes, revised creative strategy, different media allocations, or a host of other possibilities. Only by systematically setting targets (objectives) and measuring results is it possible to know whether promotional programs are working as well as they should.

SUMMARY

This chapter provides a model of the promotion management process to serve as a useful integrative device for understanding the overall promotion process. The model (Figure 8.1) contains four general components: marketing structure, monitoring and managing the environment, customer satisfaction, and the promotion-decision process.

The *marketing structure*, which involves the organizational arrangement for accomplishing a firm's marketing task, plays an instrumental role in determining how important promotion is in the overall marketing mix and how promotion decisions are made and implemented. The *guts* of promotion management is the *promotion-decision process*. The process is aimed at ultimately *managing the environment* and achieving *customer satisfaction*. The latter objective is the embodiment of the marketing concept covered in Chapter 1. The former objective involves anticipating and responding to environmental forces (especially competitive maneuvers) rather than merely reacting belatedly to changes in the marketplace—changes that might disrupt or seriously impede a company's success. The promotion-decision process consists of a set of general choices, specific plans, and program evaluation. General choices include choosing *target markets, objectives, budgets*, and *mixing modes* (persuasive communications and promotional inducements). Specific plans entail decisions about *messages, media*, and *momentum*. These decisions are evaluated by comparing *measured results* against program objectives.

Discussion Questions

1. Discuss the difference between the brand-management and category-management organizational structures at Procter & Gamble. Describe what implications the change from brand to category management will have for decisions at Procter & Gamble regarding *general choices* in Figure 8.1.

2. Changes in the so-called *three Cs of marketing* (customers, consumers, and competitors) have imposed pressures on companies to alter their marketing organizational structures. Explain.

3. Explain the concept of *environmental management*. Compare this idea with the notion presented in many introductory marketing texts that the environment is *uncontrollable*.

4. Objectives and budgets are necessarily interdependent. Explain this interdependency and provide a supportive example to illustrate your point.

5. What is the distinction between top-down (TD) and bottom-up (BU) budgeting? Why is BUTD budgeting used in companies that are more marketing ori-

ented, whereas TDBU budgeting is found more frequently in finance-driven companies?

6. Promotion management has been described as an ill-structured problem. Explain what this means.

7. Describe why you think the balance of power has moved from advertising toward sales promotion in many companies' promotional budgets.

8. Two of the most important considerations in achieving a balance between advertising and sales promotion are strategic and brand equity factors. Explain precisely how these considerations are relevant to the decision about the relative influence placed on advertising and sales promotion. Select a brand of a well-known grocery product as a basis for motivating your discussion.

9. Explain the concept of *momentum*. Using the same brand that you selected for answering the previous question, describe your understanding of how this brand accomplishes a suitable level of momentum

10. Assume you are the fund-raising chairperson for an organization on your campus, say a student chapter of the American Marketing Association. It is your job to identify a suitable project and to manage the project's promotion. For the purpose of this exercise, identify a fund-raising project idea and apply the model in Figure 8.1 to show how you might go about promoting this project. Be sure to address all aspects of the model but place special focus on the elements in the Promotion-Decision Process component of the model.

11. Select a well-known brand from a packaged-good product sold in grocery stores, drug stores, or other mass-merchandise outlets. Analyze this brand's promotional activities at the general-choice and specific-plan levels. Describe the specific promotional choices and programs this brand has employed in the past year or so. You cannot be expected to know exactly how the brand is promoted, but your casual observations should provide some idea. Moreover, by reviewing the Business Periodical Index in your library, you should be able to identify various articles in business periodicals that describe your chosen brand's promotional activities (you can look for articles published in *Advertising Age, Business Week, Drug Store Age, Fortune, Forbes, Grocery World*, and *The Wall Street Journal*).

Two Case Illustrations of Promotion Management Practices

OOPS . . . NAIL POLISH ON THE NEW CARPET

Imagine that you have recently installed light-colored carpeting throughout your home. The carpeting looks great. Your home looks entirely different than it did with the outdated, soiled carpeting that you replaced. Imagine now that a family member decides to paint her fingernails in the living room. Reaching for a soft drink, she knocks over the nail-polish bottle, and polish spills everywhere. Disaster has struck—the carpeting is ruined!

This would have been the outcome several years ago, but now there are carpets that resist stains such as nail polish. One stain-resistant brand is marketed by Du Pont under the name Stainmaster. Its ability to resist stains has surprised even people who purchased Stainmaster carpeting mainly for this reason. For example, a Massachusetts woman did indeed spill bright red nail polish on her new wheat-colored carpet and thought it was ruined, but, using only soap and water, she had the stain out in less than five minutes. A Michigan family installed off-white carpeting throughout their new house. Around Easter, the mother and her children were coloring eggs when a cup of bright green egg coloring was accidentally spilled. "I was sick," the mother commented. "I was sure it would never come out of the carpet. But I blotted up as much as I could, then saturated the stained area several times with warm water. Every bit of the coloring came out without the need of any cleaning agent."

Note: Stainmaster is Du Pont's registered certification mark.
Source: Based on "What Are They Saying about 'Stainmaster'?" *Du Pont Magazine*, March/April 1988, 24–25.

This stain-resistance feature provided the Du Pont Corporation with a distinct relative advantage over competitors. It also posed a major challenge inasmuch as prior to the Stainmaster introduction, Du Pont had relatively little experience in attempting to create consumer demand for its branded products.[1] The following pages chronicle the evolution of the Stainmaster marketing communications program and describe the steps taken to accomplish the company's marketing communications objectives.

In general, this chapter has two purposes: first, to show how the Integrated Promotion Management Model (Figure 8.1) presented in the previous chapter can be applied in real situations, and, second, to acquaint students with the big picture of promotion management as a prelude to subsequent chapters' specialized treatment of specific promotion topics. Up to this point in the text, you have been introduced to the general aspects of promotion management and marketing communications and the behavioral foundations that undergird their practical implementation. The chapters that follow provide in-depth treatments of each of the promotion-mix elements. There is a danger that the element-by-element coverage might convey the idea that each of the promotion mix tools is self-sustaining and independent of the other elements. Nothing could be further from the truth. In practice, all of the tools must be coordinated to achieve overall marketing communications objectives.

To minimize the tendency for students to study the trees but lose sight of the forest, this chapter will show what the forest—that is, an integrated marketing communications program—looks like before individual trees (advertising, sales promotion, etc.) are examined. Two practical case histories accomplish this purpose. The first examines Du Pont's highly successful introduction of Stainmaster carpeting.[2] The second deals with a fascinating application of marketing communications undertaken in the public sector by the United States Agency for International Development.

DIFFERENTIATING CARPETING THROUGH EFFECTIVE MARKETING COMMUNICATIONS

The Integrated Promotion Management Model presented in the previous chapter (Figure 8.1) provides a useful framework for analyzing Du Pont's marketing communications program for Stainmaster carpeting. (It would be useful to spend a few minutes reviewing Figure 8.1 before reading on.)

---

[1] Edward E. Messikomer, "Du Pont's 'Marketing Community'," *Business Marketing*, October 1987, 90.

[2] I am extremely grateful to Mr. Gary A. Johnston, Du Pont's Advertising Manager, for providing many of the materials for this case-history discussion.

Monitoring and Managing the Environment

To fully appreciate Du Pont's introduction of Stainmaster carpeting, it will be informative to briefly review the business perspective that prevailed at Du Pont preceding Stainmaster's introduction. Three fundamental factors capture this perspective.[3] First, the company was dominated by *technologically driven* decision making. In other words, new product and other major decisions typically had their genesis in Du Pont's chemical laboratories rather than originating from the marketplace. Second, Du Pont's marketing orientation was almost exclusively *business to business*. That is, very few of Du Pont's 2,500 or so products were marketed to final consumers; rather, most were marketed to other companies. Historically business-to-business marketing has been far less sophisticated than consumer marketing.

A final factor characterizing Du Pont's past business perspective was its *premier economic and technological position around the world.* Until the 1970s, Du Pont, like many other U.S. industrial firms, had distinct technological and economic advantages over its international competition. This enabled Du Pont to achieve financial success without having to concentrate on sophisticated marketing methods. However, as international competition has intensified during the past two decades, Du Pont (as well as other business-to-business oriented firms) has been forced to elevate the quality and sophistication of its marketing efforts. Du Pont remains a very profitable and successful enterprise, but its recent gains are attributable largely to the fact that it has evolved into a truly marketing-oriented organization. This corporate-mindset change set the stage for the development and introduction of Stainmaster carpet.

To understand how Stainmaster came about, it is necessary first to understand Du Pont's role in the carpet business.[4] Du Pont is not a carpet manufacturer per se. Rather, it manufactures carpet *fiber*. It markets fiber to carpet mills who spin the fiber into yarn, tuft and dye it, and produce finished carpet. These mills (companies such as Bigelow, Milliken, and West Point Pepperell) market finished carpeting to architects and decorators, wholesalers, and directly to larger retailers.

Synthetic carpeting had experienced sustained growth for nearly four decades following World War II, but sales reached a plateau in 1979. The product was in the late maturity stage of its life cycle. On top of this, carpet had become basically a *commodity product* (i.e., an undifferentiated good).[5] The result was that consumers typically bought carpet on the basis of price. Brand name had

---

[3]This discussion is adapted from Messikomer, 90.

[4]The following comments are based partially on an outline of a lecture delivered by Andrew Ballentine, a retired Du Pont marketing communications executive. I am deeply grateful to Mr. Ballentine for bringing this material to my attention and acting as my mentor in the area of business-to-business marketing.

[5]"Branding Builds Business for Stainmaster Carpets," *Marketing Communications*, February 1988, 42.

relatively little influence on the buying decision. To break out of this commodity trap, Du Pont's Strategic Business Team was charged in 1982 with developing a greatly improved carpet that would provide Du Pont with distinct competitive advantages.

Before the marketing revolution at Du Pont, the team would have sent company chemists back to the lab to come up with something. Under the new marketing mindset, they decided to ask consumers what was important to them when purchasing carpet. A major marketing research study revealed that consumers regarded stain and soil resistance to be just as important considerations when purchasing carpeting as color, styling, and price.

This information gave Du Pont's chemists something specific to work on. By 1985 they had a solution. The new product ultimately became Stainmaster, which essentially is a *stain-blocking chemical* that is applied to the fiber at the carpet mill during the dyeing process. Carpet manufactured with the Stainmaster process has superior stain resistance ability. Most household stains—including fruit drinks, blueberry pie, and tomato juice (but not shoe polish, mustard, or India ink)—can be removed completely from Stainmaster with water and mild detergent.

In light of this situation, it was concluded that substantial profits could be made by being the first fiber producer to offer a revolutionary new anti-stain fiber system for carpet. It was also concluded that the only way Stainmaster would be successful was by differentiating the product at the consumer level. Stainmaster was introduced in the fall of 1986.

General Choices

Women between the ages of 25–54 with annual household incomes of at least $30,000 were identified as the primary *target market* for Stainmaster's communications efforts. The marketing communications challenge was to come up with a way to promote the stain-resistance advantage and convince homeowners to ask for a Du Pont certified Stainmaster carpet. To an unprecedented degree, Du Pont sought to encourage final consumers to demand carpet made with Stainmaster and thereby *pull* the product through the distribution channel. This required familiarizing consumers with Stainmaster's distinct stain-resistance feature and convincing them that stain resistance made Stainmaster an excellent investment. Another readily promotable benefit was the fact that consumers no longer needed to avoid purchasing carpet in light colors, since the ability to resist stains made such colors safer than ever.

Overriding marketing objectives were to gain widespread distribution for Stainmaster, to promote it as a premium product, and to ensure that the product performed exactly as claimed. Toward this end, agreements were reached with a select group of 21 carpet mills who were licensed to manufacture carpet with the Stainmaster process. A licensing and certification program ensured that these mills would produce Stainmaster carpet exactly as specified by Du Pont.

Specific communications *objectives* were designed for retailers and consumers. At the retail level, Du Pont's primary objectives were to convince dealers of the volume and profit benefits associated with stocking and selling Stainmaster carpet. For consumers, the primary objective was to create strong consumer awareness of the Stainmaster name and its stain-resistance feature. Awareness was expected to reach 50 percent of all target customers within 60 days after product launch and 70 percent in one year.

Du Pont *budgeted* $50 million to Stainmaster's introductory marketing communications campaign.[6] The budget was allocated accordingly:

BUDGET CATEGORY	PERCENT OF BUDGET
Consumer advertising	48
Cooperative advertising	27
Point-of-purchase materials	20
Publicity	3
Trade advertising	2

Specific Plans

TELEVISION ADVERTISING.   Television advertisements recreated common household disasters, all with a humorous twist. An initial Clio (the "Oscar" for television commercials) award-winning commercial portrayed a mischievous red-haired boy throwing a tray of food onto the floor. His mother was shown easily removing the peas, carrots, and cherries from the carpet without a trace of stain. (See this commercial's storyboard in Figure 9.1.)

Another introductory commercial that you may recall seeing depicted a party scene in which someone accidentally dropped a piece of chocolate cake. As the cake descended in slow motion, an elegantly dressed woman raced through the crowd and intercepted the cake just before it hit the carpet. In a subsequent repeat performance during the party, she was unsuccessful in preventing a wine glass from reaching the carpet. While this action took place, an announcer's voice-over reminded viewers that sooner or later every household will need Stainmaster carpet to prevent the inevitable stain-producing accidents.

POINT-OF-PURCHASE DISPLAYS.   In addition to television advertising, which served to invigorate consumer interest in carpet and prompt visits to carpet outlets, Du Pont used effective point-of-purchase displays to demonstrate Stainmaster's stain-resistant properties. Displays were placed in 10,000 retail outlets throughout the United States. The display consisted of one beaker filled with a red fruit drink, another filled with water, and a supply of

---

[6]"Branding Builds Business for Stainmaster Carpets," 42.

DuPont's "Landing" Commercial for Stainmaster Carpet

FIGURE 9.1

E-86847

BBDO

Batten, Barton, Durstine & Osborn, Inc.

Client: DU PONT CARPET FIBERS		Time: 30 SECONDS
Product: STAINMASTER	Title: "LANDING"	Comml. No.: DDTC 6023

CONTROL TOWER: Flight 124 fly runway heading to

3,000. Right turn to two-seven-zero. You are cleared for take-off.

AVO: Introducing Du Pont

certified Stainmaster carpet.

Stainmaster gives you

a revolutionary new level of protection

against stains and spills

that's better than any other carpet you can buy today.

Because you never know . . .

STARTER: Gentlemen, start your engines.

AVO: New Stainmaster.

AVO: From Du Pont Carpet Fibers.

swizzle sticks. Affixed to each stick was a patch of Stainmaster carpet at one end and a nonstain-resistant patch at the other end. Consumers were instructed to dip a swizzle stick first in the fruit juice beaker and then to swish the stick in the beaker of clear water. Result: the Stainmaster patch emerged stain free, whereas the other patch remained stained with fruit juice. The swizzle-stick illustration represented a dramatic reinforcement of Stainmaster's advertising claims and provided consumers with concrete support that Stainmaster carpeting would indeed fulfill its claimed advantages.

DIRECT MAIL.   Du Pont further appealed to consumers with direct-mail letters that invited store visitations at local Stainmaster dealers. Visitations were encouraged with the inducement of free home-decorating books. Needless to say, this form of direct approach provides an unsurpassed micromarketing opportunity by directing mailings to only those households which match Du Pont's targeting criteria.

DEALER PROGRAMS.   Beyond reaching final consumers and encouraging store visitations, it was imperative that Du Pont also provide retail dealers with sufficient incentive to actively promote Stainmaster carpet. Du Pont's biggest promotion ever was designed with this purpose in mind. Participating dealers received 100 free copies of the *Carpet Decorating Ideas* book along with the swizzle stick point-of-purchase display discussed above. Throughout the six-week promotion period, Du Pont ran commercials on the three major television networks and on cable television. Print ads appeared in 19 consumer magazines and hundreds of Sunday newspapers; all of the ads included a toll-free number for dealer information.

Du Pont provided dealers with promotion kits that included newspaper advertising copy and radio scripts. The retailer's advertising was partially paid for by Du Pont through its cooperative advertising program.[7] In addition to supporting dealers' advertising, Du Pont awarded retail salespeople for their sales of Stainmaster carpet during the promotional period.

Program Evaluation

The marketing communications program that introduced Stainmaster carpet was an overwhelming success. Consumer awareness registered 29 percent just 90 days after product launch, an impressive level for a product category that only a short time ago had been a commodity item. After 18 months, consumer awareness reached 78 percent. Retailer awareness was 100 percent, and Stainmaster

---

[7]Cooperative advertising involves an arrangement between manufacturer and retailer whereby the manufacturer reimburses the retailer for all or some of the costs incurred by the retailer when advertising the manufacturer's brands in local media. Chapter 16 provides a detailed description of this form of advertising.

was stocked in virtually all carpet stores. Shipments of Stainmaster were nearly three times larger than the company's optimistic forecast. Large retailers pressured carpet mills to buy into the Stainmaster program. Ultimately, Du Pont was able to significantly differentiate itself from competitors and create consumer name recognition and preference for Du Pont Stainmaster carpet; in so doing, Du Pont realized a substantial market share increase and was able to command a premium price.

Returning to the product-adoption concepts covered in Chapter 5, it can be seen that much of Du Pont's early success was due to Stainmaster's unique *relative advantage*. However, that technological feature alone would not have facilitated a successful introduction. It was necessary to make the advantage *observable* (visible and concrete rather than abstract). This was accomplished through a combination of attention-getting creative advertising and the swizzle stick point-of-purchase display. Successful introduction also required that Stainmaster be promoted as a product that is *compatible* with consumers' needs and past experiences. This was accomplished through creative television advertising showing carpet-staining circumstances that most or all consumers could readily imagine happening in their own lives. All in all, Du Pont's marketing communications efforts were creative, well targeted, carefully integrated, and undoubtedly well worth the $50 million introductory investment.

Post-Introduction Developments

Within five years of its introduction, Stainmaster had become the best-known and best-selling carpet brand of all time. Ninety-five percent of eligible carpet-purchasing consumers in the United States had become aware of the Stainmaster name.[8] Over six million households had purchased Stainmaster carpet. This success was accomplished with heavy and continuous network television and magazine advertising (strong *momentum*). In fact, Stainmaster's consumer advertising exceeded the total spending by all other carpet advertisers combined.

This success made it possible for Du Pont to extend its basic offer with additional brands. Stainmaster Luxura, appealing to less price-sensitive consumers, and Stainmaster Xtra Life, a superior carpet offering a comprehensive five-year warranty, were introduced to reach the top-end of carpet purchasers. Heavy advertising continued with humorous television executions such as the food fight commercial shown in storyboard form in Figure 9.2. To enhance *customer satisfaction*, Du Pont provides consumers and retailers with a 24-hour 800-number service. Consumers are encouraged to call with questions about cleaning

---

[8]As a general point, it is important to realize that for most brands the *awareness asymptote*, or upper limit, is below 100 percent. Some consumers simply are not exposed to much advertising or are unaffected by it.

FIGURE 9.2   DuPont's "Dinner for Two" Commercial for Stainmaster Carpet

H 28398

BBDO

Client: DU PONT

Product: STAINMASTER

Title: "DINNER FOR TWO"

Time: 30 SECONDS

Comml. No.: DDTC 1013

(SFX: JAZZY MUSIC)

ANNCR. V.O.: Underneath every

spotless evening

lies a Du Pont Certified Stainmaster Carpet.

BUTLER: Dessert?

ANNDR. V.O.: It's not a Stainmaster

if it doesn't say Du Pont.

emergency spills; retailers are invited to call for advice in answering challenging questions from shoppers.

COMBATTING DEHYDRATION IN UNDERDEVELOPED COUNTRIES

This section presents a detailed case history of an extraordinarily effective communications program designed by the United States Agency for International Development. The program was implemented in Honduras and Gambia to combat what may at first strike you as a trivial and rather disgusting issue, namely the problem of diarrheal dehydration among children in developing countries. It is hoped that after reading the case you will see it as a rather ingenious application of marketing communication techniques to an important, indeed lifesaving, situation. This case illustrates the application of conventional marketing communications methods in a nonbusiness situation. This is an important lesson insofar as societal problems (such as drug abuse, AIDS, and environmental protection) can hopefully be combatted with the same marketing communications techniques that traditionally have been applied to promote goods and services.

As surprising as it may seem to those of us living in advanced post-industrial countries, diarrhea is one of the world's leading killers. Every year, millions of children under the age of five die due to diarrheal dehydration.[9] Children in developing countries typically have diarrhea several times a year. Local practice often leads mothers to purge their children and to withhold food or stop breast-feeding when they realize that the diarrhea bout is more severe than usual. The mother does not realize that dehydration, caused by the diarrhea, is the problem. Dehydration advances rapidly, and the child loses his or her appetite and the capacity to absorb vital liquids. Death can follow within hours.

Working with the Ministries of Health in Honduras and Gambia, the U.S. Agency for International Development and its contractors (experts in health, communications, anthropology, evaluation and behavioral psychology) developed a public health education program to deliver *oral rehydration therapy (ORT)* to large numbers of rural and isolated people threatened by diarrheal dehydration. Using mass media, simple printed materials, and health-worker training, rural women were taught what ORT is, how to use it in the home, and how to monitor their child's progress during the diarrheal episode.[10]

---

[9]Anthony J. Meyer, Clifford H. Block, and Donald C. E. Ferguson, "Teaching Mothers Oral Rehydration," *Horizons*, 2 (April 1983), 14–20. The remaining discussion borrows liberally from this source.

[10]*After Twelve Months of Broadcasting: A Status Report on the Project in Honduras and The Gambia* (Washington, D.C.: Academy for Educational Development, Inc., January 1984), 1.

Monitoring and Managing the Environment

Oral rehydration therapy (ORT) is an established medical treatment for combatting an infant's loss of body fluid and electrolytes during a diarrheal episode. The therapy involves having mothers administer an oral rehydration solution that is prepackaged or can be made at home by mixing appropriate portions of sugar, salt, and water. The solution is administered to a dehydrated child at the rate of approximately one liter per day.

The key to effective ORT is the correct preparation and administration of the oral rehydration solution (ORS). Mothers must know how to mix the ingredients in exact proportions to avoid ineffective or potentially dangerous concentrations of sodium. They must also know how to give the solution correctly—that is, slowly and continuously over a 24-hour period, even if the child vomits or refuses the liquid.

The challenge confronting the Agency for International Development was to design a communications program that would teach mothers *a new form of behavior*, namely, mixing and administering ORS to their sick children. Environmental monitoring indicated that such behavior, although fully within the mothers' capacities, was not being performed. Hence, the Agency's environmental-management task was to develop a program that would lead to alterations in mothers' diarrheal-treatment behaviors. A number of important questions had to be answered: (1) Who in the total population should be selected as the principal target audience? (2) What communication channels are most appropriate? (3) What behaviors should be advocated? (4) What resources are needed to conduct the program?

Preprogram research was conducted in both Honduras and Gambia to assist planners in thoroughly understanding the problem that the subsequent communication and promotion programs would address.[11] Focus-group interviews, surveys, and product-preference trials were conducted to provide answers to the preceding questions. Among the many findings, the research uncovered some traditional health beliefs that the communications programs would have to address. Rural Gambian mothers most often attributed diarrhea to some natural cause, such as dirt or wind, or to some supernatural cause. In Honduras, there was widespread belief that diarrhea is caused by *la bolsa*, a sack believed to exist in everyone and to contain worms that leave the sack after becoming agitated.

An important research question involved the proper method for delivering the ORS solution: as a new medicine, a traditional tea, or a new local remedy. Prior to the research, it was assumed that mothers would prefer a product that

---

[11]The following description of the preprogram research is from Elizabeth M. Booth and Mark Rasmuson, "Traditional and Empirical Inputs in Program Design: The Role of Formative Evaluation in the Mass Media and Health Practice Project," Washington, D.C.: Academy for Educational Development, Inc., May 1984.

was similar to their existing method for treating diarrhea, namely, a herbal tea solution. The research evidence indicated that this assumption was incorrect— mothers seemed to prefer a modern medicine rather than the herbal tea.

Contrary to preresearch doubts, the research further revealed that mothers were able to mix the ORS solution in the correct proportions. They learned the mixing instructions very quickly, after only one or two explanations, even when the instructions were delivered via a tape recorder.

Overall, the preprogram research resulted in a detailed communications program consisting of (1) behavioral objectives, (2) target-audience selection, (3) specific instructional messages, (4) culturally appropriate message formats, (5) plans for media use and integration, and (6) a complete plan of action.

General Choices

In the final analysis, the success of the program depended on providing a large number of people with information they would find important and practical. To be successful, the program had to

> make an impact on the consciousness of the intended audience by rising above the everyday clutter of advice and suggestions to become an important new priority in their lives. It must change what people do as well as what they think and believe.. . . It requires: a sensitive understanding of how people are affected by specific health problems, articulate crafting of useful and practical educational messages, and a coordinated distribution network that reaches each individual through various channels simultaneously.[12]

Several local practices and beliefs that contributed to dehydration were singled out for modification. These included the practice of mothers purging and withholding food from infants and the belief that breast milk causes diarrhea. Most important of all was the goal to get mothers to administer the proper oral rehydration solution and thereby reduce the number of infant deaths caused by diarrhea.

As will be seen shortly, the communications programs in Honduras and Gambia were remarkably successful. Yet the results were accomplished with very small budgets. Figure 9.3 illustrates the total costs and specific cost categories for each country. Costs exclude technical assistance from the U.S. Agency for International Development but include local salaries, benefits, travel, transportation, research, printing, production, and broadcast. Costs were significantly lower in Gambia because (1) air time was provided free, (2) commercial printing

---

[12]*After Twelve Months of Broadcasting,* 8.

FIGURE 9.3   First-Year Budgets for Honduras and Gambia

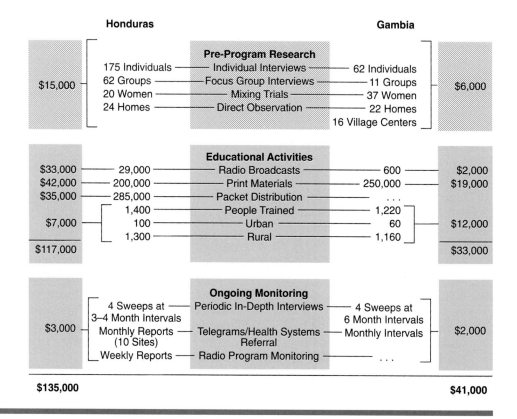

	Honduras		Gambia
Pre-Program Research			
$15,000	175 Individuals — Individual Interviews — 62 Individuals		$6,000
	62 Groups — Focus Group Interviews — 11 Groups		
	20 Women — Mixing Trials — 37 Women		
	24 Homes — Direct Observation — 22 Homes		
		16 Village Centers	

Honduras		Educational Activities		Gambia
$33,000	29,000	Radio Broadcasts	600	$2,000
$42,000	200,000	Print Materials	250,000	$19,000
$35,000	285,000	Packet Distribution	. . .	
$7,000	1,400	People Trained	1,220	$12,000
	100	Urban	60	
	1,300	Rural	1,160	
$117,000				$33,000

Honduras		Ongoing Monitoring		Gambia
$3,000	4 Sweeps at 3–4 Month Intervals	Periodic In-Depth Interviews	4 Sweeps at 6 Month Intervals	$2,000
	Monthly Reports (10 Sites)	Telegrams/Health Systems Referral	Monthly Intervals	
	Weekly Reports	Radio Program Monitoring	. . .	

$135,000   **$41,000**

Source: After Twelve Months of Broadcasting: A Status Report on the Project in Honduras and The Gambia, (Washington, D.C.: Academy for Education Development, January 1984).

costs were much lower, and (3) preprogram research costs were lower because the prior experience in Honduras permitted significant savings.[13]

The first-year expenditures in Honduras amounted to $135,000, of which $18,000 (approximately 13 percent) involved the combination of expenses for preprogram research and ongoing monitoring. The remaining $117,000 was spent on various communication media that were used to educate Honduran mothers about oral rehydration therapy. There were, for example, 29,000 radio broadcasts aired at a cost of $33,000 during the first year in Honduras.

[13]Ibid., 25.

Total first-year expenditures in Gambia amounted to $41,000. Approximately 20 percent ($8,000) was invested in preprogram research and ongoing monitoring, and the remaining $33,000 was spent on educational activities.

Specific Plans

Success in Honduras and Gambia depended on the combination of three communication media: radio broadcasts, print materials, and person-to-person communications using health workers and community volunteers. The careful integration of broadcast, print, and face-to-face support was essential. Radio alerted hundreds of thousands of Hondurans and Gambians about ORT. In Honduras, radio taught mothers how to measure a liter using local bottles. In Gambia, radio taught mothers to understand the printed mixing instructions. Printed materials and graphics (posters and flags) helped mothers recall what to do at the actual time of using ORT. Health workers, who contacted mothers individually or in small groups, provided the needed credibility for key messages delivered by radio and in print.

PROGRAM IMPLEMENTATION IN HONDURAS.[14]   The communications program in Honduras was aimed at two target groups: (1) a primary audience of rural mothers/grandmothers with children under the age of five along with community volunteer health-care workers (called guardians) and (2) a secondary audience of physicians, nurses, fathers of children under five, rural schoolteachers and schoolchildren, and regional health promoters. The program was designed to teach the primary audience the proper preparation and administration of a prepackaged oral rehydration solution (Litrosol) and to teach the secondary audience to support the primary audience by encouraging the use of ORT.

Litrosol, the prepackaged oral rehydration formula, was widely publicized through posters, pamphlets, and radio programs. A central campaign theme was developed around the concept of a loving image—a red heart was chosen as the central visual symbol to signify the love that mothers have for their children. Thousands of spot radio broadcasts and dozens of weekly programs were broadcast on carefully selected local stations. The programs built on the loving theme that was used in print materials. Local health workers and health professionals were trained to use and promote Litrosol. A simple flag with the red heart symbol was given to each trained health worker. Radio programs announced that Litrosol was available at houses that displayed the red heart flag.

---

[14]The following discussion summarizes the presentation found in two sources: *After Twelve Months of Broadcasting,* 10–32, and Meyer, Block, and Ferguson, "Teaching Mothers Oral Rehydration," 16-20.

PROGRAM IMPLEMENTATION IN GAMBIA.   The primary audience for the program in Gambia was rural mothers, grandmothers, and older female siblings of children under five. The secondary market consisted of various health-care workers (such as health inspectors and nurses). The communication program was designed (1) to teach the primary audience to mix a simple sugar and salt (S/S) rehydration solution properly and to administer the solution along with breast milk and soft foods during episodes of diarrhea and (2) to teach the secondary audience to mix and administer the S/S solution properly and to take care of moderate and severe diarrhea in the health centers.

Accomplishing these objectives required some creative thinking, because most people in Gambia are unfamiliar with print materials of any kind. The solution involved a national contest, which began with the distribution of 200,000 copies of a color-coded flyer that provided instructions for the correct mixing and administering of the S/S solution. In conjunction with the flyers, radio announcements literally led listeners through each panel of the color-coded flyer. Mothers were repeatedly told how to mix the formula, how to administer it, what to do in the case of vomiting, and how to tell if the child was improving. Radio announcers also told them about other mothers with "happy baby" flags flying over their homes. These flags served as a symbol to people of the village that the "happy baby" home was a source of information on the diarrhea medicine.

Another element in the program was a promotional inducement in the form of a prize giveaway contest. Any mother could win a prize—a plastic liter container or a bar of soap wrapped in a label with the happy baby symbol printed on it—by demonstrating to a health-care worker that she could mix the S/S solution correctly. Winning mothers' names were included in a drawing for 15 radios. Follow-up radio programs used the testimonials of happy baby winners to continually reinforce the value and importance of the sugar, salt, and water solution. There was also a community prize each week for the village that had the greatest number of mothers participating in the contest. The contest was concluded with a one-hour radio broadcast in which the Gambian president's wife announced the names of grand-prize winners.

Program Evaluation

Evaluation research was conducted at six-month intervals to determine the amount of learning among target audiences and to identify strengths and weaknesses in the promotional campaign. Program monitoring in Honduras, for example, detected that mothers did not understand the concept of dehydration nor did they associate it with diarrhea and Litrosol. Therefore, subsequent promotional activity deemphasized the abstract concept of dehydration and focused instead on the physical manifestations of dehydration. This change in emphasis resulted in an increase from 20 percent to 77 percent of mothers who understood the signs of dehydration.[15]

The integration of radio, graphics, and health workers proved to be a powerful combination in Honduras.[16] Several dramatic results occurred within in a year: (1) nearly half of the entire sample of mothers had tried Litrosol at least once; (2) recognition of Litrosol as a diarrheal remedy went from 0 percent to 93 percent; (3) knowledge levels concerning the procedure for mixing Litrosol received over 90 percent correct responses; (4) nearly 90 percent of mothers knew to continue breastfeeding during diarrheal bouts; and (5) a 40 percent decrease in the percentage of deaths involving diarrhea was achieved.

The integrated communications program in Gambia yielded some dramatic results, just as it had in Honduras. After eight months of the program, 66 percent of mothers knew the correct home mix solution, and 47 percent reported having used the solution to treat their children's diarrhea.

A Wrap-up

The ORT programs in Honduras and Gambia illustrate the use of some very sophisticated communications efforts. There are, in fact, four features of the oral rehydration program that could serve as models for any marketing communications endeavor.

COMMUNICATIONS GROUNDED IN ENVIRONMENTAL MONITORING.   Marketing communicators sometimes jump immediately to the tasks of creating messages and selecting media before they have a thorough understanding of the marketplace. Such an approach stands a good chance of failing unless the marketing communicator has had extensive prior experience with the intended audience. Many communication programs are doomed because companies have not done their homework in adequately understanding the marketplace in terms of its culture, values, beliefs, stereotypes, and behavioral habits.

The project directors for the ORT program avoided such a mistake. They conducted extensive preprogram research in both Honduras and Gambia prior to designing communication programs for these countries. The information acquired from this research enabled the project directors to develop communication programs that were compatible with the beliefs, attitudes, and health-care practices of both mothers and health-care workers.

---

[15]Booth and Rasmuson, "Traditional and Empirical Inputs."

[16]Summative evaluation was conducted under an Agency for International Development contract to Stanford University Institute for Communication Research. These data are from their extensive evaluation activities, not from the AEP formative research.

USE OF UNIFYING CREATIVE MESSAGE THEMES. Another mistake committed by many marketing communicators is the failure to design communication programs around a central creative theme. In the absence of a unifying theme, programs tend to flounder because they lack direction and meaning.

Such a mistake was not made in Honduras or Gambia. The loving theme with the red heart symbol in Honduras and the happy baby theme in Gambia provided unifying forces for the communication programs in these countries. By directing communication efforts around these themes, the chances were increased substantially that mothers would gain awareness of the ORT programs and become sufficiently motivated to learn how to mix the oral rehydration solution properly and administer it when necessary.

COORDINATION OF COMMUNICATIONS EFFORTS. Three communication channels—radio, print, and interpersonal—were carefully coordinated to accomplish communication objectives. Mothers learned about the oral rehydration solution through radio; pamphlets and flyers provided instructions for proper mixing and administration of the rehydration therapy; and the availability of trained health-care workers—with red heart and happy baby flags flying over their homes—enhanced the credibility of the ORT program and provided another source of information for mothers who required additional assistance.

EVALUATING PROGRAM PERFORMANCE. Another error marketing communicators sometimes commit is the failure to monitor communication programs to determine whether they are working as originally intended. Project directors in Honduras and Gambia avoided this mistake by performing ongoing research to ensure that the programs were accomplishing their objectives. This periodic monitoring identified several problems that were quickly corrected. Due to midcourse corrections, the ultimate results were much more effective than they otherwise would have been.

SUMMARY

This chapter provides an aerial view of the *forest* as a prelude to subsequent chapters' in-depth, ground-level analysis of specific *trees*—that is, components of the promotion mix. Two case histories, one from the private sector and the other from the public sector, are presented to show how organizations plan and integrate various marketing communications techniques and promotion management tools to achieve marketing objectives.

The example of Du Pont's Stainmaster carpeting illustrates how a historically business-to-business oriented company was able to break out of the commodity trap it confronted in the early 1980s by introducing an innovative new type of carpeting. Du Pont's creative use of television advertising, point-of-purchase displays, and direct mail created consumer pull for Stainmaster, while its use of attractive dealer incentives accomplished the necessary trade push. All in all, this integrated marketing communications program resulted in unprecedented levels of consumer brand awareness for this product category and led to a substantial increase in Du Pont's market share.

The remainder of the chapter describes a program developed by the U.S. Agency for International Development to combat diarrheal dehydration in Honduras and Gambia. This program is an outstanding example of how conventional marketing practices can be applied to not-for-profit situations.

Discussion Questions

1. Why is environmental monitoring (or situation analysis) a critical first step in the process of developing a marketing communications program?

2. Analyze the television commercial used in introducing Stainmaster carpeting (see Figure 9.1). Specifically, explain what the commercial attempts to convey and why you think it was or was not effective. Use concepts from Chapter 3 (e.g., stages of the CPM process) as formal grounding for your response. Compare the introductory commercial (Figure 9.1) with the brand extension commercial (Figure 9.2) and explain how these commercials reflect different target markets.

3. In your own words, describe what a commodity product is. From the marketer's perspective, explain why it is undesirable to be involved in marketing a commodity product.

4. Analyze Du Pont's swizzle-stick promotion. Using concepts from Chapter 3, explain why this promotion was effective. Also, comment on the following statement by someone who is critical of point-of-purchase displays: "The Stainmaster display was a waste; it simply duplicated what consumers already learned from Du Pont's television advertising."

5. What was the importance of using the red heart theme in Honduras and the happy baby theme in Gambia as symbols of the ORT programs?

6. The Academy for Educational Development, the chief consultant to the U.S. Agency for International Development in the ORT program, characterized their task as one of changing mothers' behavior rather than attitudes. On the other hand, marketers of conventional products frequently place their promotional emphasis on creating favorable images for their brands. How can you account for this apparent contrast in communication objectives?

7. It could be argued that the communications task in, say, Gambia was simpler than the promotional task faced by marketers of conventional products such as shampoo and personal computers. Take a position on this point and thoroughly support your position.

8. The communications program in Gambia included a giveaway contest in which mothers could receive a prize by demonstrating an ability to mix the salt, sugar, and water solution correctly. Winners then became eligible to win a bigger prize in a drawing. Moreover, there was a community prize each week for the village that turned out the most mothers for the contest. With reference to material presented in Part 2 of the text, what are the social-psychological principles that would justify the use of these promotional techniques?

9. Analyze current Stainmaster advertising and visit a Stainmaster dealer to determine the more recent marketing communications efforts that are being used to promote this brand. Comment on the suitability of these efforts.

10. Choose any not-for-profit issue or organization that interests you and analyze the marketing communications program that is being used to market (or perhaps demarket) greater (or less) consumption of the behavior in question.

MEDIA ADVERTISING

Part 5 contains five chapters on media advertising. **Chapter 10** first overviews the advertising management process and then provides detailed discussions of advertising objective setting and budgeting.

Chapter 11 provides a detailed study of the creative-strategy aspect of the advertising-management process. Topics include requirements for effective advertising messages, advertising planning, means-end chains and MECCAS models, creative message strategies, and corporate image/issue advertising.

Part 5

Chapter 12 expands the coverage of advertising message creation by examining various message and source factors. These include fear appeals, humor, sex, subliminal messages, comparative ads, and source credibility.

Media strategy is the focus of **Chapter 13.** The chapter provides thorough discussions of the four major activities involved in media strategy: target-audience selection, objective specification, media and vehicle selection, and media-buying activities. The chapter also evaluates the strengths and weaknesses of five major advertising media: television, radio, magazines, newspapers, and outdoor.

The last chapter in Part 5, **Chapter 14,** examines the measurement of advertising effectiveness. The chapter describes four general categories of advertising-research methods: measures of advertising exposure, awareness, persuasion, and action. Research methods that are widely used by advertising practitioners are explained.

CHAPTER TEN

Advertising Management Overview

WHAT DO ADVERTISING AND EXERCISE HAVE IN COMMON?

Advertising is costly, often its effects are uncertain, and sometimes it takes a while before it has any impact on customers' buying behavior. It is for these reasons that many companies think it appropriate to reduce expenditures on advertising and redirect spending toward sales promotions, direct mail, sponsorship of events, and other forms of marketing communications. Companies find it particularly seductive to pull funds out of advertising during economic downturns—every dollar not spent on advertising is one more dollar added to the bottom line.

Such behavior implicitly fails to consider the fact that advertising is not just a current expense (as the term is used in accounting parlance) but rather is an *investment*. Although businesspeople fully appreciate the fact that building a new, more efficient production facility or purchasing a new computer system are investments in their companies' futures, many of these same people often think advertising is an expense that can be reduced or even eliminated when financial pressures call for cost-cutting measures.

However, Procter and Gamble, the world's largest advertiser with global advertising spending in 1990 exceeding $3 billion, is one company that fully appreciates advertising's investment role. P&G's chairman and CEO, Edwin L. Artzt, considers advertising a long-term investment that shouldn't be intruded upon by short-term needs. Artzt aptly draws an analogy between advertising and exercise in that both provide long-term benefits. Moreover, like exercise, it is easy to stop advertising or postpone it because there is no immediate penalty for not exercising or not advertising. According to Artzt, "If you want your brand to be fit, it's got to exercise regularly. When you get the opportunity to go to the movies or do something else instead of working out, you can do that once in a while—that's [equivalent to] shifting funds into [sales] promotion. But it's not a good thing to do. If you get off the regimen, you will pay for it later."[1]

The opening vignette makes an important point regarding the long-term role of advertising. As hinted back in Chapter 8, a trend over the past 10 years or so has been in the direction of companies shifting marketing communications funds out of advertising and into sales promotions, direct mail, and elsewhere. This trend notwithstanding, advertising in one form or another will continue to play an important, albeit perhaps reduced, role in most firms' promotional mixes. This chapter, the first of five chapters devoted to advertising, first overviews the general advertising management process and then focuses on two advertising management tasks: establishing advertising objectives and setting advertising budgets.

OVERVIEW

In its most basic sense, advertising is an economic investment, an investment regarded very favorably by numerous businesses and not-for-profit organizations. Advertising expenditures in the United States exceeded $130 billion in 1990.[2] This amounts to over $500 in advertising expenditures for each of the 250 million men, women, and children in the United States. The biggest advertising spenders following the United States are Japan, the United Kingdom, West Germany, Canada, and France. However, advertising expenditures in these countries are small compared to those in the United States, amounting to less than 15 percent of the amount spent on advertising in the United States.[3]

Some American companies invest over $1 billion a year on domestic advertising. In 1990, for example, Procter & Gamble spent $2.3 billion, Philip Morris $2.2 billion, and Sears, Roebuck & Co. and General Motors both invested $1.5 billion in domestic advertising.[4] Even the U.S. government advertises to the tune of

---

[1]Jennifer Lawrence, "P&G's Artzt on Ads: Crucial Investment," *Advertising Age*, October 28, 1991, 1, 53.

[2]"Tracking Ad Dollars," *The Wall Street Journal*, March 22, 1991, sec. B, 4.

[3]Lena Vanier, "U.S. Ad Spending Double All Other Nations Combined," *Advertising Age*, May 16, 1988, 36.

[4]R. Craig Endicott, "P&G Spends $2.28 Billion, Surges to Head of Top 100," *Advertising Age*, September 25, 1991, 1.

over $300 million. The government's advertising goes to efforts such as military recruiting, the Postal Service, Amtrak rail services, the U.S. Mint (e.g., commemorative coins), and AIDS awareness.

These massive investments suggest that many firms have faith in the effectiveness of advertising. Consider the incredible results advertising has generated for a product like Marlboro cigarettes. At a time when American consumers are reducing their consumption of cigarettes, with annual sales declining at a rate of 1.5 to 2 percent annually, Marlboro sales have grown more than 3 percent per year since 1980. This one product accounts for 28 percent of Philip Morris' $25 billion in revenues and earns $2 billion operating profit on sales of $7 billion. Approximately one out of every four packs of cigarettes consumed in the United States is Marlboro; the brand is also experiencing great growth outside the United States.[5]

In general, advertising is valued because it is recognized as performing a variety of critical communications *functions:* (1) informing, (2) persuading, (3) reminding, (4) adding value, and (5) assisting other company efforts.[6]

I N F O R M I N G .   Advertising makes consumers aware of new products, informs them about specific brands, and educates them about particular product features and benefits. Because advertising is an *efficient form of communication,* capable of reaching mass audiences at a relatively low cost per contact, it facilitates the introduction of new products and increases demand for existing products.

P E R S U A D I N G .   Effective advertising persuades customers to try advertised products. Sometimes the persuasion takes the form of influencing *primary demand*, that is, creating demand for an entire product category. More frequently, advertising attempts to build *secondary demand*, that is, demand for a specific company's brand.

R E M I N D I N G .   Advertising also keeps a company's brand fresh in the consumer's memory. When a need arises that is related to the advertised product, past advertising impact makes it possible for the advertiser's brand to come to the consumer's mind as a purchase candidate.

A D D I N G   V A L U E .   There are three basic ways by which companies can add value to their offerings: by innovating, by improving quality, or by altering

---

[5]Jeffrey A. Trachtenberg, "Here's One Tough Cowboy," *Forbes*, February 9, 1987, 108. For an informative and sobering report on the magnitude and strategic direction of cigarette advertising, see Ronald M. David, "Current Trends in Cigarette Advertising and Marketing," *The New England Journal of Medicine*, 316 (March 19, 1987), 725–732.

[6]These functions are similar to those identified by the noted advertising pioneer James Webb Young. See, for example, "What Is Advertising, What Does It Do," *Advertising Age*, November 21, 1973, 12.

consumer perceptions. These three value-added components are completely interdependent.

> Innovation without quality is mere novelty. Consumer perception without quality and/or innovation is mere puffery. And—both innovation and quality, if not translated into consumer perceptions, are like the sound of the proverbial tree falling in the empty forest.[7]

Advertising adds value to products and specific brands by influencing *consumers' perceptions*. Effective advertising causes brands to be viewed as more elegant, more stylish, more prestigious, perhaps superior to competitive offerings, and, in general, of *higher perceived quality*. Hence, advertising is an important value-adding function, because, when done effectively, brands are perceived as higher quality, which in turn can lead to increased market share and greater profitability.[8] It is little wonder why, as discussed in the opening vignette, the world's largest advertiser, Procter & Gamble, fully appreciates advertising's value-added role.

ASSISTING OTHER COMPANY EFFORTS.   Advertising is just one member of the promotion team. The advertising player is at times a *scorer* who accomplishes goals by itself. At other times advertising's primary role is that of an *assister* who facilitates other company efforts in the marketing communications process. For example, advertising may be used as a *vehicle for delivering sales promotions*. That is, advertisements are the physical vehicles for delivering coupons and sweepstakes and attracting attention to these sales promotion tools.

Another crucial role of advertising is to *assist sales representatives*. Advertising presells a company's products and provides salespeople with valuable introductions prior to their personal contact with prospective customers. Sales effort, time, and costs are reduced because less time is required to inform prospects about product features and benefits. Moreover, advertising legitimizes or makes more credible the sales representative's claims.[9]

Advertising also *enhances the results of other marketing communications*. For example, consumers can identify product packages in the store and recognize the value of a product more easily after seeing it advertised on television or in a magazine.

---

[7]*The Value Side of Productivity: A Key to Competitive Survival in the 1990s*, (New York: American Association of Advertising Agencies, 1989), 12.

[8]Ibid., 13–15.

[9]The synergism between advertising and personal selling is not always a one-way flow from advertising to personal selling. In fact, one study has demonstrated a reverse situation, in which personal sales calls sometimes pave the way for advertising. See William R. Swinyard and Michael L. Ray, "Advertising-Selling Interactions: An Attribution Theory Experiment," *Journal of Marketing Research*, 14 (November 1977), 509–516.

THE ADVERTISING-MANAGEMENT PROCESS

A completed advertisement, such as a television commercial or a magazine advertisement, results from the collective efforts of various participants. Four major groups are involved in the total advertising process: (1) companies and other organizations that advertise (Procter & Gamble, the U.S. Government, and so on), (2) advertising agencies (such as Ogilvy and Mather, J. Walter Thompson, and Tokyo-based Dentsu), which are responsible for creating and placing ads for their clients, (3) advertising production companies (i.e., independent businesses that photograph, film, and otherwise produce advertisements), and (4) advertising media (newspapers, television, etc.).

Although the advertising industry involves a number of collective efforts, the following discussion is restricted to the first group, the advertisers themselves.

The discussion of the advertising-management process is based on the framework in Figure 10.1. The figure shows that *advertising strategy* extends from a company's overall marketing strategy. *Marketing strategy* involves the plans, budgets, and controls needed to direct a firm's product, promotion, distribution, and pricing activities. Marketing strategy (1) is formulated in view of a brand's inherent strengths and weaknesses and (2) is based on analyses of economic, competitive, social, and other pertinent factors that represent opportunities and

The Advertising-Management Process   FIGURE 10.1

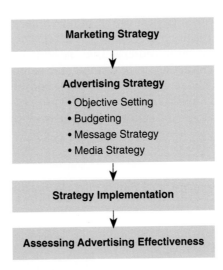

threats. *Strategy implementation* represents the execution of advertising messages in specific media. *Assessing advertising effectiveness* determines whether advertising results have met preestablished objectives and whether corrective action is necessary.

Advertising Strategy

Advertising strategy involves four major activities (see Figure 10.1). The first two, *objective setting* and *budgeting*, are described later in this chapter. A third aspect of advertising strategy is *message strategy*, which is the subject of Chapters 11 and 12. *Media strategy*, the topic of Chapter 13, involves the selection of media categories and specific vehicles to deliver advertising messages.

Strategy Implementation

Strategy implementation deals with the tactical, day-to-day activities that must be performed to carry out an advertising campaign. For example, whereas the decision to emphasize television over other media is a strategic choice, the selection of specific types of programs and times at which to air a commercial is a *tactical* implementation matter. Likewise, the decision to emphasize a particular brand benefit is a strategic message consideration, but the actual way the message is delivered is a matter of creative implementation.

Assessing Advertising Effectiveness

Assessing effectiveness is a critical aspect of advertising management inasmuch as only by evaluating results is it possible to determine whether objectives are being accomplished. This often requires that baseline measures be taken before an advertising campaign begins (to determine, for example, what percentage of the target audience is aware of the brand name) and then afterwards to determine whether the objective was achieved. Because research is fundamental to advertising control, Chapter 14 is devoted exclusively to evaluating advertising effectiveness.

SETTING ADVERTISING OBJECTIVES

Advertising objectives are goals that advertising efforts attempt to achieve. Setting advertising objectives is possibly the most difficult task of advertising management, yet these objectives provide the foundation for all remaining advertising decisions.[10] There are three major reasons for setting advertising objectives:[11]

1. Advertising objectives are an *expression of management consensus*. The process of setting objectives literally forces top marketing and advertising management to agree upon the course advertising is to take for the following planning period as well as the tasks it is to accomplish for a product category or specific brand.

2. Objective setting *guides the budgeting, message strategy, and media strategy* aspects of advertising strategy. Objectives determine how much money should be spent and provide guidelines for the kinds of message strategy and media choice needed to accomplish the objectives.

3. Advertising objectives provide *standards against which results can be measured*. As will be detailed later, good objectives set precise, quantitative yardsticks of what advertising hopes to accomplish. Subsequent results can then be compared with these standards to determine whether the advertising accomplished what it was intended to do.

Who, What, Where, When, and How Often?

Several categories of advertising objectives guide advertising strategy—the Who? What? Where? When? and How Often? of setting objectives.[12]

WHO?   The most basic consideration underlying advertising-strategy formulation is the *choice of target market*. Objectives related to the *who* question specify the target market in terms of demographics, lifestyle, or other characteristics that influence choice behavior. For example, General Motors' Cadillac division undertook a bold advertising campaign in 1991 by aiming the redesigned Seville and Eldorado models at affluent babyboomers who historically have preferred imports.[13]

WHAT?   The *what* question involves two sets of considerations: (1) what emphasis? and (2) what goals? The *emphasis* issue relates to the features and

[10]Charles H. Patti and Charles F. Frazer, *Advertising: A Decision-Making Approach* (Hinsdale, IL: The Dryden Press, 1988), 236.

[11]Ibid., 237–239.

[12]This formulation has its origins in a broadly similar scheme constructed by John R. Rossiter and Larry Percy, "Advertising Communication Models," Working Paper, N.S.W. Institute of Technology, Sydney, Australia, September 22, 1983.

[13]David Kiley, "A Bold Push for Cadillac's New Models," *Adweek's Marketing Week*, August 26, 1991, 7. Raymond Serafin, "Cadillac Takes Youthful Turn," *Advertising Age*, August 26, 1991, 3, 38.

benefits to be emphasized and the emotions to be evoked when advertising a brand. For example, Cadillac's marketing of the Seville and Eldorado focuses on performance and how well these models fare against imported luxury cars. The *goals* issue deals with the specific communication or sales objectives that need to be accomplished at the present stage in a brand's life cycle.

Advertising may be designed to accomplish several goals: (1) to make the target market aware of a new brand, (2) to facilitate consumer understanding of a brand's attributes and its benefits compared to competitive brands, (3) to enhance attitudes, (4) to influence purchase intentions, and (5) to encourage product trial. We will return to these *what-goal* issues shortly for more detailed discussion.

WHERE? WHEN? HOW OFTEN?   Which geographic markets need to be emphasized, what months or seasons are best, and how often the product should be advertised are additional issues that need to be addressed when setting advertising objectives.

Although advertising practitioners must take all of the preceding categories into consideration when setting objectives, subsequent attention focuses exclusively on the *what-goal* category. The reason is that the other considerations are all situation specific, but the goal issue is relevant to all situations and brands.

A full appreciation of how advertising goals (objectives) are set requires that we first look at advertising from the customer's perspective. That is, advertisers establish objectives that are designed to move customers to eventually purchase the advertiser's brand. To understand how advertisers set objectives is, thus, to first understand the fundamental process by which customers move ever closer toward a brand purchase decision. The *hierarchy-of-effects* concept provides an appropriate framework for accomplishing this understanding.

The Hierarchy of Effects

The **hierarchy-of-effects** metaphor implies that for advertising to be successful it must move consumers from one goal to the next goal, much in the same way that one climbs a ladder—one step, then another, and another until the top of the ladder is reached.

Although a variety of hierarchy-of-effects models have been formulated,[14] all are predicated on the idea that advertising moves people from an initial state of

---

[14]For thorough discussions see Thomas E. Barry, "The Development of the Hierarchy of Effects: An Historical Perspective," *Current Issues and Research in Advertising*, 10, eds. James H. Leigh and Claude R. Martin, Jr. (1987), 251–296 (Ann Arbor, MI, Division of Research, Graduate School of Business Administration, University of Michigan); Ivan L. Preston, "The Association Model of the Advertising Communication Process," *Journal of Advertising*, 11, 2 (1982), 3–15; and Ivan L. Preston and Esther Thorson, "Challenges to the Use of Hierarchy Models in Predicting Advertising Effectiveness," in *Proceedings of the 1983 Convention of the American Academy of Advertising*, ed. Donald W. Jugenheimer (Lawrence, KS: American Academy of Advertising, 1983).

unawareness about a brand to a final stage of *purchasing* that brand. Intermediate stages in the hierarchy represent progressively closer steps to purchase. Consider the following hierarchy:

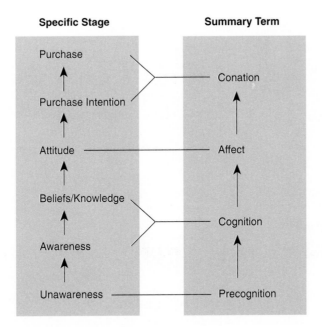

The meaning of each of these stages is best understood by examining an actual advertisement. Consider the Twist and Shoot camcorder from Hitachi depicted in Figure 10.2. When this brand was first introduced to the market, consumers were initially *unaware* of the brand's existence and of its special features (some no doubt remain unaware to this day). The initial advertising imperative, therefore, was to make people *aware* of the Twist and Shoot brand name. (Creating brand awareness is absolutely essential for success; see the following *Focus on Promotion* for elaboration.) However, mere awareness would not have been enough to get people to buy the Twist and Shoot camcorder. Advertising had to persuade consumers that the Twist and Shoot is somehow different and better than competitive brands. The ad attempts to accomplish this by informing consumers that the Twist and Shoot is the thinnest video camcorder on the market—so thin, in fact, that it will fit into a purse or coat pocket. In addition to its convenient size, the Twist and Shoot claims to produce sharp, true-to-life pictures every time (*beliefs/knowledge*). These distinctive advantages are designed to create favorable *attitudes* toward the Twist and Shoot with the expectation that many consumers will be sufficiently impressed to want to buy this brand (*purchase intention*). This intention may develop into an actual *purchase* of a Twist and Shoot camcorder for those consumers who eventually become camcorder buyers.

FIGURE 10.2   Hitachi's Twist and Shoot Camcorder

Twist and Shoot.

The engineers at Hitachi have just come up with a remarkable new twist in video technology. It's called the Twist and Shoot and it's the only camcorder that twists open for instant shooting.

Closed, its super-thin, 2⅜″ profile makes it the world's thinnest video camcorder. It'll fit eas-ily into a purse or a coat pocket.

Open, it's fully automatic. Revolutionary twin beam auto focus produces a precise, clear, stable picture. At the same time, shutter speed, lens opening and white balance are adjusted auto-matically for the best possible exposure.

In addition to all its conve-nience, the Twist and Shoot pro-duces sharp, true-to-life pictures every time.

To appreciate this revolu-tionary new kind of camcorder, call 1-800-HITACHI for your nearest dealer. Then shoot on down and twist one for yourself.

⊚ HITACHI
© 1991 Hitachi Home Electronics (America), Inc.

FOCUS ON PROMOTION

CREATING BRAND AWARENESS IS THE NAME OF THE GAME

Political pollsters tell us there is a strong relationship between a politician's name recognition and the number of votes he or she receives. The same type of relationship applies to brand names: Consumers don't often purchase brands which barely scratch the surface of name recognition. Awareness is the name of the game for both politicians and brands.

For example, would you spend $75 on a brand of athletic shoes named Avia (pronounced ah-Vee-ah)? Only 4 percent of U.S. consumers associate the name Avia with sneakers.[1] Avia's marketing vice president notes that consumers do not purchase that brand because "they don't know who we are." By comparison, he notes that Reebok and Nike are known by more than 70 percent of U.S. consumers. This comes as little surprise, because these companies spend 7 to 10 times more on advertising than Avia.[2] Can you recall seeing any Avia ads?

Further complicating matters for lesser-known brands is the fact they, compared to well-known brands, must spend a disproportionately large percentage of revenue on advertising to avoid being forgotten. In order to build that all-important brand awareness, smaller companies

(continued)

The Integrated Information-Response Model

The preceding traditional view of how advertising works has been widely criticized because it suggests there is a single response pattern (i.e., cognition leading to affect and then to conation). However, the pattern in the traditional hierarchy applies only in instances of *high-involvement behavior,* in which the purchase decision is important to the consumer and has significant risks associated with it. A more comprehensive model is needed to capture fully the diversity of purchase decisions and consumer behavior in response to advertising.

The **integrated information-response model** (see Figure 10.3) provides the needed comprehensiveness.[15] The model takes its name from the idea that consumers *integrate information* from two sources—advertising and direct product-usage experience—in forming attitudes and purchase intentions toward products and brands.

---

[15]Robert E. Smith and William R. Swinyard, "Information Response Models: An Integrated Approach," *Journal of Marketing,* 46 (Winter 1982), 81–93.

have to resort to ingenuity to accomplish the job. For example, when Nevica USA, a Colorado distributor of a British skiwear line, entered the market, it could not afford to advertise its distinctive neon-colored clothing in major ski magazines. Nevica's president, not to be deterred, had her staff identify those photographers whose work appeared most frequently in ski magazines. She then offered each photographer free skiwear and a fee for each time one of their pictures with a Nevica-clad skier appeared in a ski magazine. Needless to say, skiers wearing neon-colored Nevica skiwear began appearing in ski magazines with some frequency.[3]

Other ways of creating brand name awareness without investing heavily in advertising include giving products to opinion leaders with hopes they will influence others to purchase the product. For example, the makers of the Millenium line of high-priced cookware sent $70 sauté pans to about 100 chefs and cooking-school operators. One recipient, the host of a cable television cooking program, gave a cooking demonstration on the *Today* show and used the Millenium sauté pan.[4] Millenium's distinctive blue-lined pan received a level of exposure for only a small fraction of what the advertising cost would have been.

The moral is simple: Name recognition is imperative! If you cannot afford to invest heavily in advertising, then you either have to be ingenious or suffer the consequences—namely, the absence of large scale brand awareness and probably eventual brand failure.

[1]Joseph Pereira, "Name of the Game: Brand Awareness," *The Wall Street Journal*, February 14, 1991, sec. B, 1.
[2]Ibid.
[3]William M. Bulkeley, "It Needn't Always Cost a Bundle to Get Consumers to Notice Unknown Brand Names," *The Wall Street Journal*, February 14, 1991, sec. B, 1, 8.
[4]Ibid.

It will be useful first to overview the model's general characteristics. Note carefully the five column headings labeled information source, information acceptance, cognitions, affect, and conation. Two *information sources* are available to the consumer: advertising and one's own direct experience in using a particular product or brand. *Information acceptance* (due to factors such as source credibility as discussed in the following chapter) ranges between low and high levels. Extending from information acceptance are *cognitions*, which are shown in Figure 10.3 as either lower- or higher-order beliefs. Lower-order beliefs represent the consumer's mere awareness or recognition that an advertiser has claimed that its brand possesses some feature or benefit. For example, having read the advertisement for the Twist and Shoot camcorder, you now know that it is thin and convenient and promises to produce true-to-life pictures. This knowledge is a lower- rather than higher-order belief because merely registering what

---

Integrated Information-Response Model FIGURE 10.3

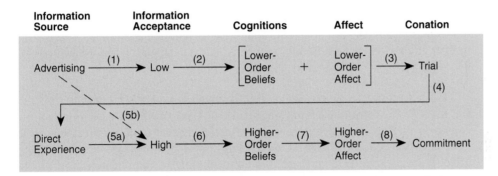

Detailed Sequence

Source: Adapted from Robert E. Smith and William R. Swinyard, "Information Response Models: An Integrated Approach," *Journal of Marketing*, Vol. 46, Winter 1982; p. 85. Adopted with permission from *Journal of Marketing*, published by the American Marketing Association.

---

an advertiser has said a product will do is not the same as experiencing the product actually doing what the advertisement said it would.

Higher-order beliefs, which result from direct product-usage experience, represent the consumer's acceptance that a brand does in fact do (or fail to do) what the advertiser has claimed. (If you used the Twist and Shoot and it performed exactly as Hitachi, its maker, claimed, you then would really believe the product advantages—this is what is meant by higher-order belief.) *Affect* is also shown to be lower- or higher-order. Lower-order affect is little more than a favorable (or unfavorable) disposition toward a brand after having learned about it from, say, a magazine advertisement. For example, one consumer's response to learning about the Twist and Shoot camcorder might be "That's a great idea. The old camcorders were too cumbersome, inconvenient, and conspicuous. I like the thought that I can keep the Twist and Shoot in my purse until I'm ready to use it." Higher-order affect, on the other hand, represents the consumer's actual feelings about a product after using it. "The Twist and Shoot is a fantastic camcorder. It's the easiest-to-use camcorder I've ever tried, and it takes great pictures!" Finally, *conation* ranges from a one-time trial purchase (as with an inexpensive packaged good) all the way to a commitment to regularly incorporate a product or brand into one's consumption lifestyle.

Having laid out the terminology of the integrated information-response model, we can now discuss the three patterns of consumer response to advertising that are implied by the model.

PATTERN 1: COGNITION → AFFECT → COMMITMENT. The pattern of cognition to affect to commitment is the traditional hierarchy-of-effects model previously described. This is shown in Figure 10.3 by the dashed arrow from advertising to high information acceptance (path 5b) and then, in turn, to higher-order beliefs (path 6), to higher-order affect (path 7), and ultimately to commitment (path 8).

This pattern is applicable when consumers fully accept advertising message claims, form attitudes toward the advertised brand, and become firmly committed to purchasing the advertised product. Because advertising has limited ability to form higher-order beliefs, this response pattern, though a theoretical possibility, is the exception rather than the rule.

PATTERN 2: COGNITION → TRIAL → AFFECT → COMMITMENT. The sequence from cognition to trial to affect to commitment is captured in Figure 10.3 by the flow of solid arrows from advertising to low information acceptance (path 1), on through lower-order beliefs and lower-order affect (path 2), then to trial (path 3), and ultimately to commitment as a function of direct experience and the higher-order beliefs and affect that result (paths 5a through 8).

This response pattern typifies *low-involvement learning*. When consumers are passive learners of information (as typically is the case with most products), higher-order affect results only *after* one has acquired direct, or firsthand, experience using a product. A true attitude (i.e., higher-order affect) typically follows rather than precedes direct product usage experience. In other words, actual product usage experience (eating a food product, drinking a beverage, or using a camcorder) is extremely informative and convincing, whereas merely learning from advertising about how a product is supposed to taste or perform is far less revealing.

Think of it this way: Upon learning about a new food product from a television commercial, you may develop a favorable impression, or tentative attitude, toward it. This impression is considered lower-order affect—it is held tentatively awaiting support or refutation based on actual product usage. However, after buying and tasting the new food, you have firsthand knowledge (direct experience) to inform you how good the product actually is. Your attitude formed from actual product usage represents higher-order affect. In plain terms, the tongue knows! We have more faith in sensory impressions received from our tongues (or other sensory receptors) than we have in promises obtained from advertisers.

PATTERN 3: COGNITION → TRIAL → TRIAL → TRIAL. The pattern from cognition to multiple trials is implicit in Figure 10.3 and suggests that in the case of relatively homogenous product categories there may be no such thing as higher-order affect either before or after direct-usage experience. In such instances consumers may consistently switch brands and never form a strong preference for any one brand. The consumer, in other words, learns about several brands in a product category but never develops strong affect or preference for any one brand. Rather, the consumer continuously shifts his or her allegiance from one brand to the next, constantly trying, trying, and trying but never developing a strong commitment or preference for any particular brand. Consumer behavior can be like dating; some people continue to "play the field" but never become committed to anyone.

Back to the What-Goal Issue

The alternative response patterns in the integrated information-response model point out that advertising objectives must be set in accordance with the response pattern that characterizes the advertiser's particular product and market situation. For example, because the information response pattern for consumers who are in the market for a new automobile is different than the pattern for consumers choosing a brand of toothpaste, advertising objectives must also differ.

To more fully understand the implications that the alternative response pattern holds for objective setting, let us continue the discussion of advertising goals alluded to previously. As noted, advertising accomplishes goals such as (1) making consumers aware of a new brand, (2) facilitating their knowledge and beliefs about a brand's attributes and benefits, (3) enhancing their attitudes toward the brand, (4) influencing purchase intentions, and (5) encouraging them to try the brand.

The first goal, *awareness*, is essential for all three response patterns. That is, creating high levels of awareness is an important prerequisite to swaying consumer choice toward the marketer's brand. Though important under all circumstances, the awareness goal is relatively more important for patterns 2 and 3 than pattern 1. In other words, consumers may be willing to try a new brand of an inexpensive packaged good merely because they have seen it advertised on television, but few consumers would ever purchase a new automobile model simply because they learned of its existence.

Other goals are more critical for achieving success under high- than low-involvement situations. Accomplishing the second goal, *forming knowledge and favorable beliefs* toward the advertised brand, is essential for advertising success when consumers are highly involved in product choice. In this situation, advertising must persuade highly involved consumers that the advertised product possesses features and benefits that make it superior to competitive offerings or a better value for the price. Consumer acceptance of the advertiser's claims leads to higher-order beliefs (refer again to Figure 10.3), then on to higher-order affect, and perhaps finally to a preference for and commitment (loyalty) to the advertised brand.

Requirements for Setting Good Advertising Objectives

Advertising objectives are *statements* of what advertising must accomplish to overcome problems or realize opportunities facing a brand. However, not all statements represent good advertising objectives. Consider the following examples:

Example A: The advertising objective this year is to increase Brand X's sales.

Example B: The advertising objective is to increase by July 31st the target audience's awareness of Brand X from 60 percent to 90 percent.

These extreme examples differ in two important respects. First, Example B is obviously more specific. Second, whereas Example A deals with a sales objective, Example B involves a nonsales goal. The sections that follow describe the specific criteria that good advertising objectives must satisfy.[16]

OBJECTIVES MUST INCLUDE A PRECISE STATEMENT OF WHO, WHAT, AND WHEN.   Objectives must be *stated in precise terms.* At a minimum, objectives should specify the target audience (who), indicate the specific goal to be accomplished (what; e.g., awareness level), and indicate the relevant time frame (when) in which to achieve the objective.

For example, the advertising campaign for the Twist and Shoot camcorder might include objectives such as these: "Within six months from the beginning of the campaign, research should show that 60 percent of middle-income households with children are familiar with the Twist and Shoot name and that at least 40 percent know that it is the thinnest camcorder on the market."

Advertising objectives provide valuable agendas for communication between advertising and marketing decision makers and offer benchmarks against which to compare actual performance. These functions can be satisfied, however, only if objectives are stated precisely.

Example B, above, represents the desired degree of specificity and, as such, would give executives something meaningful to direct their efforts toward as well as a clear-cut benchmark for assessing whether the advertising campaign has accomplished its objectives. Example A, by comparison, is much too general. Suppose sales have actually increased by 2 percent during the course of the ad campaign. Does this mean the campaign was successful since sales have in fact increased? If not, how much increase is necessary for the campaign to be regarded as a success?

OBJECTIVES MUST BE QUANTITATIVE AND MEASURABLE.   This requirement implies that ad objectives should be stated in quantitative terms, as are the hypothetical objectives given for Twist and Shoot in the preceding example. A nonmeasureable objective for the Twist and Shoot would be a vague statement such as "Advertising should increase consumer's knowledge of product features." This objective lacks measurability

---

[16]The following discussion is influenced by the classic work on advertising planning and goal setting by Russell Colley. His writing, which came to be known as the DAGMAR approach, set a standard for advertising objective setting. See Russell H. Colley, *Defining Advertising Goals for Measured Advertising Results* (New York: Association of National Advertisers, 1961).

because it fails to specify the product features for which consumers are to possess knowledge.

OBJECTIVES MUST SPECIFY THE AMOUNT OF CHANGE. In addition to being quantitative and measurable, objectives must specify the amount of change they are intended to accomplish. Example A (to increase sales) fails to meet this requirement. Example B (to increase awareness from 60 to 90 percent) is satisfactory because it clearly specifies that anything less than a 30 percent awareness increase would be considered unsuitable performance.

OBJECTIVES MUST BE REALISTIC. Unrealistic objectives are as useless as having no objectives at all. An unrealistic objective is one that cannot be accomplished in the time allotted to the proposed advertising investment. For example, a brand that has achieved only 15 percent consumer awareness during its first two years on the market could not realistically expect a small advertising budget to increase the awareness level to, say, 65 percent.

OBJECTIVES MUST BE INTERNALLY CONSISTENT. Advertising objectives must be compatible (internally consistent) with objectives set for other components of the promotional mix. It would be incompatible for a manufacturer of packaged goods to proclaim a 25 percent reduction in sales force size while simultaneously stating that advertising's objective is to increase retail distribution by 20 percent. Without adequate sales force effort, it is doubtful that the retail trade would give a brand more shelf space.

OBJECTIVES MUST BE CLEAR AND IN WRITING. For objectives to accomplish their purposes of fostering communication and permitting evaluation, they must be stated clearly and in writing so that they can be disseminated among their users and among those who will be held responsible for seeing that the objectives are accomplished.

Using Direct versus Indirect Advertising Objectives

Direct objectives are those that seek an *overt behavioral response* from the audience. **Indirect objectives** are aimed at communication tasks that need to be accomplished before overt behavioral responses can be achieved.[17] We will see in the following discussion that direct objectives are appropriate and realistic under certain advertising circumstances, while indirect (communication) objectives must be used in other instances.

---

[17]Patti and Frazer, *Advertising: A Decision-Making Approach*, 241.

Direct objectives are appropriate when the purpose of the advertising is to accomplish a specific *action-forcing activity*. There are four primary instances of this form of advertising:[18]

1. *Advertising by retailers.*   Sometimes retail advertising merely informs prospective customers about a new store or attempts to elevate a store's image. This type of advertising would be regarded as *indirect* in that the purpose is not to generate immediate buyer action. On the other hand, much of the advertising undertaken by supermarkets, mass merchandisers (e.g., Kmart), and other retailers promotes new or sale items and is designed to bring customers to the store. This type of advertising has a direct objective—to sell merchandise immediately or in the very near future. With such a short time frame in mind and with knowledge of product sales volume when the merchandise is not on special, it is reasonable for the retail advertiser to state the ad objective in terms of a direct measure such as *sales volume*.

For example, assume that Circuit City, a specialty electronics store, has past sales records indicating that on a typical Friday-through-Sunday weekend it sells an average of 15 camcorders in each of its stores. Suppose Circuit City runs a 25 percent-off price special on all camcorders for next weekend only. Newspaper ads announcing the special are placed on Thursday and Friday in all markets where Circuit City has retail outlets. The purpose of the sale is to increase store traffic and double the number of camcorders sold compared to a typical weekend. In this case, the direct advertising objective—to sell an average of 30 camcorders in each store next weekend—represents a precise, quantitative (measurable), and possibly realistic advertising objective.

2. *Direct-response advertising.*   Much advertising via the mail or in mass media (e.g, television or newspapers) is designed to generate immediate action. When an advertiser of inexpensive apparel runs an ad in the *Parade* supplement to the Sunday newspaper announcing the availability of three pairs of slacks for a total price of $29.95, the purpose is plain and simple: to sell tons of slacks. The purpose is not to create brand awareness or to enhance the company's image; rather, the objective is for thousands of consumers to place an order within the next week or so.

In general, direct-response advertising is designed to generate immediate sales volume. Therefore, it is reasonable to set a planned volume level as the advertising objective.

Similarly, when World Vision, a charitable organization, runs newspaper advertisements throughout the United States informing the public that 28 million people in Bangladesh are homeless following devastating floods, the purpose is to generate donations for the Bangladesh Flood Relief. World Vision's advertising objective is to generate an immediate overt response—financial donations.

---

[18]Ibid.

3. *Sales-promotion advertising.*   Sales promotions in the form of coupons, con-tests, premium offers, and other techniques are delivered via advertisements in media such as newspapers and magazines. This form of advertising is expected to generate quick buyer action as indicated by the number of coupons redeemed or the number of people who enter a contest. In such instances, it is appropriate for the advertiser/sales promoter to establish a direct objective such as "obtain a 5 percent coupon redemption level" or "encourage 100,000 people to enter a contest."

4. *Business-to-business advertising.*   Businesses that market their products to other businesses rather than to final consumers often use advertising as a means of generating prospects for their salespeople. Thus, the effectiveness of the advertising can be gauged by the number of telephone or mail inquiries received from prospective customers.

Consider the case of a manufacturer of medical equipment that announces its most recent product innovation in a trade publication read by the manufacturer's primary prospects. The advertisement requests interested parties to call 1-800-555-1111 for further information. The number of expected inquiries represents an appropriate advertising objective, and the number actually received within, say, the next two months indicates how successful the advertisement is.

Indirect, or communication, objectives are appropriate, indeed necessary, in all advertising situations other than the four just described. This is especially the case for *national advertisers*, in contrast to local advertisers such as the neighborhood supermarket, whose reason for advertising typically is indirect rather than direct. For example, the local McDonald's franchise near your campus advertises to generate immediate store traffic, but McDonald's corporate advertising at the national level is typically designed to accomplish indirect objectives such as announcing new menu items, conveying the idea that McDonald's is a good corporate citizen via practices such as hiring older people, or creating the impression that McDonald's is a fun place to take your family.

Direct objectives such as sales volume or profit goals typically are unsuitable goals for advertising efforts by national advertisers because these outcomes are the *consequence of a host of factors* in addition to advertising. A brand's sales and profits in a given period result from the prevailing economic climate, competitive activity, and all marketing-mix variables—price level, product quality, distribution efficiencies, personal-selling activity, and so forth. It is virtually impossible to determine precisely what role advertising has had in influencing sales and profits in a given period, because advertising is just one of many possible determinants of sales and profit performance. The following quote uses an American football analogy to accent the foregoing point.

Some argue that evaluating advertising only by its impact on sales is like attributing all the success (or failure) of a football team to the quarterback. The fact is that many other elements can affect the team's record—other players, the competition, and the bounce of the ball. The implication is that the effect of the quarterback's performance should be measured by the things he alone can influence, such as how he throws the ball, how he calls the plays, and how he hands off. If, in a real-world situation, all factors remained constant except for advertising (for example, if competitive activity were static), then it would be feasible to rely exclusively on sales to measure advertising effectiveness. Since such a situation is, in reality, infeasible, we must start dealing with response variables that are associated more directly with the advertising stimulus.[19]

A second reason that sales response is an unsuitable objective for advertising effort is that the effect of advertising on sales is typically *delayed or lagged*. That is to say, advertising during any given period influences sales during later periods. Hitachi's current advertising of the Twist and Shoot camcorder may have an immediate impact on consumers' awareness of and lower-order beliefs about this brand, but it may not influence purchases until a later date when consumers are actively in the market for a camcorder. Thus, advertising may have a decided impact on consumers' brand awareness, product knowledge, attitudes, and, ultimately, purchase behavior, but this influence may not be evident during the period when advertising's effect is measured.

Direct objectives are therefore not suitable measures of advertising effectiveness when the purpose of the advertising is to generate product awareness, influence attitudes, enhance the corporate image, or accomplish other indirect (communication) objectives.

In sum, if an overt behavioral response can be attributed with reasonable certainty to a particular advertising placement or to an overall campaign, then the objective should be stated in terms of sales volume or some other direct indicator of advertising effectiveness. If, on the other hand, the advertising's objective is to increase awareness levels, favorably influence attitudes, or perform other indirect functions, then sales volume may not be an appropriate objective.

VAGUELY RIGHT VERSUS PRECISELY WRONG. The previous sentence intentionally ended on a somewhat noncommittal note concerning the matter of when it is appropriate to use sales as the advertising objective. The preceding discussion has presented the *traditional* view of the appropriateness of using indirect versus direct advertising objectives.

However, some advertising specialists contend that advertisers should *always* state objectives in terms of sales volume and that failure to do so is a *copout*. The logic of this *nontraditional* view is that advertising's purpose is not just to create awareness, or to enhance attitudes, or to influence purchase intentions, but rather to generate sales. Thus, according to this position, it is always possible

[19]David A. Aaker and John G. Myers, *Advertising Management*, 2d ed. (Englewood Cliffs, NJ: Prentice-Hall, 1982), 93–94.

to measure, if only vaguely and imprecisely, whether advertising has contributed to increased sales. Indirect objectives and corresponding measures (e.g., awareness levels) are claimed to be "precisely wrong" in contrast to sales measures that are "vaguely right."[20]

This position, albeit somewhat heretical, makes a very important point—namely that advertisers, and perhaps especially their agencies, might be deceiving themselves into thinking that advertising is effective when it leads to increases in consumer awareness or some other indirect objective. However, Leonard Lodish, the author of the vaguely right versus precisely wrong concept, argues that advertising is not accomplishing its job unless sales and market share are increasing. The fact is that some advertising may create higher awareness levels but accomplish little more than this. Certainly such advertising is not effective. There is no simple resolution to the matter of whether direct (sales) or indirect (communication) objectives are more appropriate. However, one thing is certain: Companies are beginning to demand more from advertising than ever before. Increasing pressure is being placed on advertising agencies to develop campaigns that produce bottom-line results—increases in sales, market share, and return on investment.[21]

BUDGETING FOR ADVERTISING

The advertising budgeting decision is, in many respects, the most important decision advertisers make. If too little money is spent on advertising, sales volume will not be as high as it could be, and profits will be lost. If too much money is spent, expenses will be higher than they need to be, and profits will be reduced.

Budgeting is also one of the most difficult advertising decisions. This difficulty arises because it is hard to determine precisely how effective advertising has been or might be in the future. The sales-response function to advertising is influenced by a multitude of factors (quality of advertising execution, intensity of competitive advertising efforts, customer taste, and other considerations), thereby making it difficult if not impossible to know with any certainty what amount of sales advertising will generate.

Another reason that advertising budgeting is a complicated process is the fact that advertising budgets are largely the result of *organizational political processes*.[22] Separate organizational units view the advertising budget

---

[20]Leonard M. Lodish, *The Advertising and Promotion Challenge: Vaguely Right or Precisely Wrong?* (New York: Oxford University Press, 1986), chap. 5.

[21]See Kevin J. Clancy, "The Coming Revolution in Advertising: Ten Developments Which Will Separate Winners from Losers," *Journal of Advertising Research*, February/March 1990, 47–52.

[22]Nigel Piercy, "Advertising Budgeting: Process and Structure as Explanatory Variables," *Journal of Advertising*, 16, 2 (1987), 34–40.

differently. "For the accounting department, it's an expense, usually the largest after rent and payroll. For the marketing team, it's the big push that make the phones ring and it's never big enough. For top management, it's an investment, a speculation formulated to bring in the most revenue for the least amount of cash."[23] Research has shown that the size of the advertising budget is positively influenced by the political power of the marketing department.[24]

Advertising Budgeting in Theory

In theory, advertising budgeting is a simple process, provided one accepts the premise that the best (optimal) level of any investment is the level that maximizes profits. This assumption leads to a simple rule for establishing advertising budgets: continue to invest in advertising as long as the marginal revenue from that investment exceeds the marginal cost. Profits are maximized at the point where marginal revenue is equal to marginal cost.

The reader may recall from basic economics that marginal revenue (MR) and marginal cost (MC) are the change in total revenue and total cost, respectively, that result from producing and selling an additional item. The profit-maximization rule is then a matter of simple economic logic: Profit maximization can occur only at the point where MR = MC. At any quantity level below this point (where MR > MC), profits are not maximized because at a higher level of output more profit can be earned. Similarly, at any level above this point (where MC > MR), there is a marginal loss.

In practical terms, this means that advertisers should continue advertising as long as it is profitable to do so. For example, suppose a company is currently spending $1 million on advertising and is considering the investment of another $200,000. Should the investment be made? The answer is simple: only if the additional advertising generates more than $200,000 revenue. Now say the same company is contemplating an additional advertising expenditure of $300,000. Again, the company should go ahead with the advertising if it can be certain that the investment will yield more than $300,000 in additional revenue.

It is evident from this simple exercise that setting the advertising budget is a matter of answering a series of if-then questions—if $X are invested in advertising, then what amount of revenue will be generated? Because budgets are set before the fact, this requires that the if-then questions have advance answers. In order to employ the profit-maximization rule for budget setting, the advertising decision maker must know the advertising-sales response function for every brand for which a budgeting decision will be made. Because such knowledge is

[23]Kathleen Weeks, "How to Plan Your Ad Budget," *Sales and Marketing Management*, September 1987, 113.

[24]Piercy, "Advertising Budgeting: Process and Structure as Explanatory Variables."

rarely available, theoretical (profit maximization) budget setting is an ideal that is generally nonoperational in the real world of advertising decision making.

Budgeting Considerations in Practice

Advertising decision makers must consider several different factors when establishing advertising budgets. The most important consideration should be the *objectives* that advertising is designed to accomplish. That is, the level of the budget should follow from the specific objectives established for advertising; more ambitious objectives require larger advertising budgets. If advertising is intended to increase a brand's market share, then a larger budget is needed than would be required if the task were simply to maintain consumer awareness of the brand name.

Competitive advertising activity is another important consideration in setting ad budgets. In highly competitive markets, more must be invested in advertising in order to increase or at least maintain market position. Pepsi and Coke, for example, spend huge sums on advertising because each poses such intense competition for the other. In 1990 Coke spent nearly $160 million to advertise its various soft drinks and Pepsi nearly matched this with $156 million in expenditures.[25]

A third major consideration is the *amount of funds available.* In the final analysis, advertising budget setting is determined in large part by decision makers' perceptions of how much they can afford to spend on advertising. Because top management often views advertising budgets with suspicion and considers them to be inflated, advertising managers face the challenge of convincing management officials that proposed budgets are indeed affordable. Because this is no easy task, especially when hard data on advertising effectiveness is unavailable, advertising budget setters have tended to use simple decision rules (heuristics) for making budgeting decisions.

Budgeting Methods

In view of the difficulty of accurately predicting sales response to advertising, companies ordinarily set budgets by using judgment, applying experience with analogous situations, and using simple rules-of-thumb, or heuristics, as guides to setting budgets.[26] Although criticized because they do not provide a basis for advertising budget setting that is directly related to the profitability of the

---

[25]"Top 200 Mega-Brands by 1990 Ad Spending," *Advertising Age*, May 20, 1991, 22.

[26]Gary L. Lilien, Alvin J. Silk, Jean-Marie Choffray, and Murlidhar Rao, "Industrial Advertising Effects and Budgeting Practices," *Journal of Marketing*, 40 (January 1976), 21.

GLOBAL FOCUS

THE INTERNATIONALIZATION OF THE SNEAKER BUSINESS

Athletic shoe companies in the United States—especially Nike and Reebok—experienced tremendous growth rates throughout the 1970s and 1980s. However, the U.S. market is becoming saturated. Growth for individual brands can be obtained only by grabbing market share from competitors or moving into new markets. Because in many respects the latter option is more appealing, American companies are increasing their efforts throughout the world.

Nike expected to receive $800 million in sales from 90 foreign countries in 1991, representing a nearly 25 percent increase over 1990 foreign sales. Even the much smaller L.A. Gear, Converse, and New Balance all had foreign sales in 1991 exceeding $100 million. Part of the success of U.S. sneaker firms overseas is due to the rapid international growth of basketball and the American companies' association with that game. Well-known endorsers in the United States such as Michael Jordan (Nike), Larry Bird and Magic Johnson (Converse), and Kareem Abdul-Jabbar (L.A. Gear) also do well overseas.

Even small companies like New Balance have achieved success in certain foreign markets. New Balance's market share of running shoes is less than 1 percent in the United States, but heavy advertising spending and sponsorship of the Tokyo marathon have given New Balance 12 percent of the Japanese market for running shoes.

Source: Adapted from Matthew Grimm, "To Munich and Back with Nike and L.A. Gear," *Adweek's Marketing Week,* February 18, 1991, 21–22.

advertised brand, these heuristics continue to be widely used.[27] The two most pervasive heuristics used by both industrial advertisers and consumer-goods advertisers are the percentage-of-sales and objective-and-task methods.[28]

[27]Fred S. Zufryden, "How Much Should Be Spent for Advertising a Brand?" *Journal of Advertising Research,* April/May 1989, 24–34.

[28]The extensive use of the percentage-of-sales and objective-and-task methods in an industrial context has been documented by Lilien et al., while support in a consumer context is provided by Kent M. Lancaster and Judith A. Stern, "Computer-based Advertising Budgeting Practices of Leading U.S. Consumer Advertisers," *Journal of Advertising,* 12, 4 (1983), 6.

PERCENTAGE-OF-SALES BUDGETING. In using the **percentage-of-sales method,** a company sets its advertising budget for a particular brand by simply establishing the budget as a fixed percentage of *past* or *anticipated* sales volume. Assume, for example, that a company allocates three percent of anticipated sales to advertising and that the company projects next year's sales to be $10,000,000. Its advertising budget would be set at $300,000.

A survey of the top 100 consumer-goods advertisers in the United States found that 53 percent employ the percentage-of-anticipated sales method and 20 percent use the percentage-of-past-sales method.[29] This is to be expected, since budget setting should logically be set in accordance with what a company expects to do in the future rather than based on what it accomplished in the past.

What percentage of sales revenue do most companies devote to advertising? Actually, the percentage is highly variable. For example, in 1991 the highest percentage of sales devoted to advertising for any industry was 19.4 percent for the industrial inorganic chemical industry (lawn and garden fertilizers). The only other double-digit industries were children's games and toys (16.3%), cleaners and polish preparations (16.3%), motion pictures and videotape production (13.2%), sugar and confectionary products (10.5%), records, audiotapes, and compact discs (10.2%), and perfume, cosmetics, and toilet preparations (10.1%). Most industries average less than 5 percent advertising-to-sales ratios. These, of course, are industry averages, and advertising-to-sales ratios vary considerably across firms within each industry.[30]

The percentage-of-sales method is frequently criticized as being illogical. Criticism is based on the argument that the method *reverses the logical relationship between sales and advertising.* That is, the true ordering between advertising and sales is that advertising causes sales, or, stated alternatively, sales are a function of advertising: Sales = f (Advertising). Contrary to this logical relation, implementing the percentage-of-sales method amounts to reversing the causal order by setting advertising as a function of sales: Advertising = f (Sales). That is, when sales are anticipated to increase, the advertising budget also increases; when sales are expected to decline, the budget is reduced.

The illogic of the percentage-of-sales method is demonstrated by the fact that this method could lead to potentially erroneous budgeting decisions such as cutting the advertising budget when a brand's sales are expected to decline. For example, many firms reduce advertising budgets during recessionary periods. However, rather than decreasing the amount of advertising, it may be wiser to increase advertising to prevent further sales erosion. When used blindly, the percent-of-sales method is little more than an arbitrary and simplistic rule of thumb substituted for what needs to be a sound business judgment. Used without

---

[29]Lancaster and Stern, ibid.

[30]All ratios are based on "Advertising-to-Sales Ratios, 1991," *Advertising Age*, September 16, 1991, 32.

justification, this budgeting method is another application of precisely wrong (versus vaguely right) decision making.[31]

In practice, most sophisticated marketers do *not* use percentage of sales as the sole budgeting method. Instead, they employ the method as an initial pass, or first cut, for determining the budget and then alter the budget forecast depending on the objectives and tasks that need to be accomplished.

THE OBJECTIVE-AND-TASK METHOD.   The **objective-and-task method** is generally regarded as the most sensible and defendable advertising budgeting method. In using this method, advertising decision makers must clearly specify the role they expect advertising to play and then set budgets accordingly. The role is typically identified in terms of a communication objective (e.g., increase brand awareness by 20 percent) but could be stated in terms of sales volume or market-share expectations (e.g., increase market share from 15 percent to 25 percent).

The objective-and-task method is the advertising budget procedure *used most frequently* by both consumer and industrial companies. Surveys have shown that over 60 percent of consumer-goods companies and 70 percent of industrial-goods companies use this budgeting method.[32] These percentages represent a dramatic increase in comparison with the 12 percent of respondents in a 1974 survey who said they used the objective-and-task method.[33]

The following steps are involved when applying the objective-and-task method:[34]

1. The first step is to *establish specific marketing objectives* that need to be accomplished, such as sales volume, market share, and profit contribution.

   To illustrate this and the remaining steps, consider the case of Samsung, a Korean electronics company. Samsung, as of the late 1980s, marketed approximately 13 percent of the camcorders and 20 percent of the microwave ovens sold in the United States, though most of the camcorders and microwave ovens were marketed under private names (such as J. C. Penney and Sears brands manufactured by Samsung).[35] Samsung's marketing objective in the United States is to substantially increase its market share,

[31]See Lodish, *The Advertising and Promotion Challenge: Vaguely Right or Precisely Wrong?*, chap. 6.

[32]Charles H. Patti and Vincent J. Blasko, "Budgeting Practices of Big Advertisers," *Journal of Advertising Research*, 21 (December 1981), 23–29; Vincent J. Blasko and Charles H. Patti, "The Advertising Budgeting Practices of Industrial Marketers," *Journal of Marketing*, 48 (Fall 1984), 104–110.

[33]Andre J. San Augustine and William F. Foley, "How Large Advertisers Set Budgets," *Journal of Advertising Research*, 15 (October 1975) 13.

[34]Adapted from Lilien et al., "Industrial Advertising and Budgeting," 23.

[35]These figures are based on Ira Teinowitz, "Koreans Dial Up Ad Spending," *Advertising Age*, June 13, 1988, 12.

especially sales of products under Samsung's own brand name rather than under private labels. Samsung aspires to be the Korean equivalent of the extremely successful Japanese Panasonic.

2. The second step in implementing the objective-and-task method is *to assess the communication functions that must be performed* to accomplish the overall marketing objectives.

   Samsung must accomplish two communication functions in order to realize its overall marketing objective: It must increase U.S. consumer awareness of the Samsung brand name and persuade consumers that Samsung manufactures quality products and not just low-price items.

3. The third step is *to determine advertising's role in the total communication mix* in performing the functions established in step two.

   Given the nature of its products and communication objectives, advertising is a crucial component in Samsung's mix.

4. The fourth step is *to establish specific advertising goals in terms of the levels of measurable communication response* required to achieve marketing objectives.

   Samsung might establish goals such as (1) increasing awareness from the present level of, say, 45 percent of the target market, to 75 percent, and (2) expanding the percentage of survey respondents who rate Samsung products as high quality from, say, 15 percent to 30 percent.

5. The final step is *to establish the budget* based on estimates of expenditures required to accomplish the advertising goals.

In view of Samsung's challenging objectives, it was decided in 1988 to increase the advertising budget by 50 percent to approximately $10 million. Most of this was spent on television advertisements that ran during the coverage of the 1988 Summer Olympics.[36]

OTHER BUDGETING HEURISTICS.   The match-competitors (also known as competitive parity) and affordability methods are additional heuristics used by industrial and consumer-goods advertisers. The **match-competitors method** sets the ad budget by basically following what competitors are doing. A company may learn that its primary competitor is devoting 10 percent of sales to advertising and then decide next year to spend the same percentage advertising its own brand. In the **affordability method,** the funds that remain after budgeting for everything else go into advertising. Only the most unsophisticated and impoverished firms would be expected to budget in this manner.

These techniques are used most frequently by smaller firms, who tend to follow industry leaders. However, affordability and competitive considerations

---

[36]Ibid.

influence the budgeting decisions of all companies. In reality, most advertising budget setters combine a variety of methods rather than depending exclusively on one heuristic. For example, an advertiser may have a fixed percentage-of-sales figure in mind when starting the budgeting process but subsequently adjust this figure in light of anticipated competitive activity, funds availability, and other considerations.

Companies often find it necessary to adjust their budgets during the course of a year in line with sales performance. Many advertisers operate under the belief that they should "shoot when the ducks are flying."[37] In other words, advertisers spend most heavily during periods when products are hot and cut spending when funds are short; however, they should always maintain a decent ad budget even when sales take a downturn.

SUMMARY

This chapter offers an introduction to advertising, an overview of the advertising-management process, and detailed discussions of advertising objective setting and budgeting. Advertising is shown to perform five major functions: informing, persuading, reminding, adding value, and assisting other company efforts.

Advertising objective setting depends on the specific response pattern to advertising. In this chapter, the integrated information-response model is presented, and three different response patterns are described. Requirements for developing effective advertising objectives are discussed. A final section describes the problems associated with using sales volume or other financial goals as the advertising objectives.

The chapter concludes with an explanation of the advertising budgeting process. The budgeting decision is one of the most important advertising decisions and also one of the most difficult. The complication arises with the difficulty of determining the sales response to advertising. In theory, budget setting is a simple matter, but the theoretical requirements are generally unattainable in practice. For this reason, advertising practitioners use various rules of thumb (heuristics) to assist them in arriving at satisfactory, if not optimal, budgeting decisions. Percentage-of-sales budgeting and objective-and-task methods are the dominant budgeting heuristics.

---

[37]Kathleen Weeks, "How to Plan Your Ad Budget," *Sales and Marketing Management*, September 1987, 114.

Discussion Questions

1. Of the five advertising functions described in the chapter, which is the most important?

2. A manufacturer of office furniture has established the following advertising objective for next year: Increase sales by 20 percent. Comment on this objective's suitability. Provide a better objective.

3. What reasons can you give for certain industries investing considerably larger proportions of their sales in advertising than other industries?

4. Why is it so difficult to measure precisely the specific impact that advertising has on sales and profits?

5. Compare the difference between *precisely wrong* versus *vaguely right* advertising objectives. Give an example of each.

6. Some critics contend that the use of the percentage-of-sales budgeting technique is illogical. Explain.

7. Would it be possible for an advertising budget setter to use two or more budgeting heuristics in conjunction with one another? Describe how this could be done.

8. How do local businesses in your college or university community identify their advertising objectives? Interview three or four local businesses and investigate whether they set formal ad objectives and, if not, whether they have some rather clear-cut, though implicit, objectives in mind.

9. While interviewing the same businesses from the previous question, investigate their advertising budgeting practices. Determine whether they establish formal ad budgets, and identify the specific budgeting methods used.

CHAPTER ELEVEN

Advertising Creative Strategy

- -

DOES SHE . . . OR DOESN'T SHE?

Imagine yourself employed as a creative copywriter in a New York advertising agency some 40 years ago, specifically in the year 1955. You have just been assigned creative responsibility for a product that heretofore (as of 1955) had not been nationally marketed or advertised. The product: hair coloring. The brand: Miss Clairol. Your task: come up with a creative strategy that will convince millions of American women to purchase Miss Clairol hair coloring.

The person assigned this task was Shirley Polykoff, a copywriter for the Foote, Cone & Belding agency. Her story of how she came up with the famous line—"Does she . . . or doesn't she" (see Figure 11.1)—provides a fascinating illustration of the creative process in advertising. At the time of the Miss Clairol campaign, there was no hair-coloring business. In fact, according to Ms. Polykoff, at-home hair-coloring jobs invariably turned out blotchy and women were ashamed to color their hair. A product that provided a natural look stood a strong chance of being accepted, but women would have to be convinced that an advertised hair-coloring product, in fact, would give them that highly desired natural look.

Shirley Polykoff explains how she came up with that famous advertising line that convinced women Miss Clairol would produce a natural look:

> In 1933, just before I was married, my husband had taken me to meet the woman who would become my mother-in-law. When we got in the car after dinner, I asked him, "How'd I do? Did your mother like me?" and he

Original and Recent Versions of Miss Clairol Campaign

THE MOMENT:
1955

THE CLIENT:
Miss Clairol

THE CAMPAIGN:
"Does she...or doesn't she?"

THE AGENCY:
Foote, Cone & Belding

THE CREATOR:
Shirley Polykoff

"Does she...or doesn't she?" lives on. The new version from Grey Advertising Inc. began running in 1988.

told me his mother had said, "She paints her hair, doesn't she?" He asked me, "Well, do you?" It became a joke between my husband and me; anytime we saw someone who was stunning or attractive we'd say, "Does she, or doesn't she?" Twenty years later [at the time she was working on the Miss Clairol account], I was walking down Park Avenue talking out loud to myself, because I have to hear what I write. The phrase came into my mind again. Suddenly, I realized, "That's it. That's the campaign." I knew that [a competitive advertising agency] couldn't find anything better. I knew that immediately. When you're young, you're very sure about everything.

Source: Based on an interview by Paula Champa in "The Moment of Creation," *Agency*, May/June 1991, 32.

What makes a good advertising message? What is the process that leads to the creation of advertising messages? What are the different types of creative strategies, and when and why are they used? How does corporate advertising differ from product- or brand-oriented advertising? What is the role of corporate advertising?

The present chapter surveys these questions. First addressed is the matter of what makes effective advertising and the related subject of creativity advertising. Next covered is the process underlying the formulation of advertising strategy. A third section introduces the concept of means-end chains as a mechanism to bridge the advertiser's creative process with the values that drive consumers' product and brand choices. A following section describes seven creative strategies that are in wide use by advertising practitioners. Finally the discussion moves away from product- and brand-oriented advertising to corporate image and issue advertising.

WHAT MAKES EFFECTIVE ADVERTISING?

It is easy, in one sense, to define effective advertising: Advertising is effective if it accomplishes the advertiser's objectives. This perspective defines effectiveness from the output side, or in terms of what it accomplishes. It is much more difficult to define effective advertising from an input perspective, or in terms of the composition of the advertisement itself. There are many perspectives on the issue of what makes for good advertising, and practitioners are broadly split on the issue. This is because practitioners have a variety of experiential bases from which they have drawn their philosophies. For example, a practitioner of direct-mail advertising probably has a different opinion about what constitutes effective advertising than does Shirley Polykoff, the creator of the Miss Clairol campaign.

Simple definitions of what constitutes good advertising are generally little more than misleading attempts to generalize from a base of limited experiences. For example, the following definition offered by one well-known advertising practitioner is meaningless in its generality: "A good advertisement is one which sells the product without drawing attention to itself."[1] This is equivalent to saying that a newscaster is good only if he or she does not attract attention to him or herself, or that a professor is good if no one notices him or her. Of course, this is unrealistic.

Although it is impractical to provide a singular, all-purpose definition of what constitutes effective advertising, it is meaningful to talk about general characteristics.[2] At a minimum, good (or effective) advertising satisfies the following considerations:

1. It *must extend from sound marketing strategy.* Advertising can be effective only if it is compatible with other elements of an integrated and well-orchestrated marketing communications strategy.

2. Effective advertising *must take the consumer's view.* Consumers buy product benefits, not attributes. Therefore, advertising must be stated in a way that relates to the consumer's needs, wants, and values and not strictly in terms of the marketer's needs and wants.[3]

3. Effective advertising is *persuasive.* Persuasion usually occurs when there is a benefit for the consumer and not just for the marketer.

4. Advertising *must find a unique way to break through the clutter.* Advertisers continuously compete with competitors for the consumer's attention. This is no small task considering the massive number of print advertisements, broadcast commercials, and other sources of information available daily to consumers. Indeed, the situation in television advertising has been characterized as "audio-visual wallpaper," which implies sarcastically that consumers pay just about as much attention to commercials as they do to the detail in their own wallpaper after it has been on the walls for awhile.[4]

---

[1]David Ogilvy, *Confessions of an Advertising Man* (New York: Atheneum, 1986), 90.

[2]The following points are a mixture of the author's views and perspectives presented by A. Jerome Jewler, *Creative Strategy in Advertising* (Belmont, CA: Wadsworth Publishing Company, 1985), 7–8, and Don E. Schultz and Stanley I. Tannenbaum, *Essentials of Advertising Strategy* (Lincolnwood, IL: NTC Business Books, 1988), 9–10.

[3]Note the similarity here to the earlier discussion on the three modes of marketing in Chapter 1, where we distinguished between the *marketing concept* (the marketer adapting to the customer's needs and wants) and the *promotion concept* (attempting to adapt the customer to the marketer's needs and wants).

[4]Stan Freberg, "Irtnog Revisited," *Advertising Age,* August 1, 1988, 32.

5. Good advertising *should never promise more than it can deliver*. This point speaks for itself, both in terms of ethics (recall discussion in Chapter 7) and in terms of smart business sense. Consumers learn quickly when they have been deceived and resent it.

6. Good advertising *prevents the creative idea from overwhelming the strategy*. The purpose of advertising is to persuade and influence; the purpose is not to be cute for cute's sake or humorous for humor's sake. For example, a Diet Pepsi ad in 1990 with blind blues pianist Ray Charles used humor very effectively. You may remember seeing Mr. Charles being tricked into taking a drink of Diet Coke when expecting he would be drinking Diet Pepsi. Immediately realizing he had been fooled, he says, "All right, who's the wise guy?" The off-camera prankster laughs along with Ray Charles, and their laughter is infectious. This ad works because it is enjoyable to watch, attracts attention, and subtly delivers the advertiser's point that Diet Pepsi tastes better, or at least different, than Diet Coke. Comparatively, the ineffective use of humor results in people remembering the humor but forgetting the selling message.

The following quote aptly summarizes the essentials of effective advertising:

[It] is advertising that is created for a specific customer. It is advertising that understands and thinks about the customer's needs. It is advertising that communicates a specific benefit. It is advertising that pinpoints a specific action that the consumer takes. Good advertising understands that people do not buy products—they buy product benefits . . . Above all, [effective advertising] gets noticed and remembered, and gets people to act.[5]

Being Creative

Effective advertising is usually *creative*. That is, it differentiates itself from the mass of mediocre advertisements; it is somehow different and out-of-the-ordinary. Advertising that is the same as most other advertising is unable to break through the competitive clutter and fails to grab the consumer's attention.

It is easier to give examples of creative advertising than to define exactly what it is. Here are three examples of what many advertising practitioners would consider effective, creative advertising:

■   The pink bunny campaign for Energizer batteries. This is the campaign where a pink drum-beating bunny is shown walking across the action

---

[5]Schultz and Tannenbaum, *Essentials of Advertising Strategy*, 75. This quote actually describes what these authors term "creative advertising," but they use creative in the same sense as the present use of good, or effective, advertising.

sequence of what initially appear to be real commercials but are subsequently recognized as bogus. The viewer thinks she or he is watching an ad for a brand such as "Halo" mouthwash, but then along comes the bunny and the viewer realizes the ad is actually for Energizer. This campaign effectively reversed a situation where Energizer had been losing market share to its major competitor, Duracell.[6]

■ The Diet Pepsi campaign with Ray Charles seated at a piano surrounded by a trio of beautiful women singing "You've got the right one baby, uh-huh." This ad scored number one in recall for quite a long period after it was aired.[7]

■ Nike's ads with Bo Jackson. Perhaps the most memorable in the series was the ad aired while Bo was recuperating from a serious hip problem. The ad opens with Bo shown on stage accompanied by a large group of entertainers. Shortly into the routine, the action stops with Bo pronouncing, "I'm an athlete; I don't have time for this." The scene then cuts to Bo frantically working out to get back in shape so he can return to his athletic career. Final action cuts back to the stage where, now, fat, old, lovable boxer George Foreman is on stage where Bo had been saying "But I do [have time for this]."

Most readers probably vividly remember all three commercials. They appealed to you because they offered solid reasons for wanting to watch them, and they made their selling points in an entertaining, creative fashion.

But what is creativity? Unfortunately, there are no simple answers to this elusive aspect of advertising.[8] It is beyond the purpose of this text to attempt a thorough explanation of the creative process. Let the following three accounts suffice. First, Jack Smith, vice chairman and creative director of the Leo Burnett advertising agency in Chicago, describes creativity as "a sensitivity to human nature and the ability to communicate it. The best creative [advertising] comes from an understanding of what people are thinking and feeling."[9] John O'Toole, president of the American Association of Advertising Agencies, describes

---

[6]Julie Liesse, "How the Bunny Charged Eveready," *Advertising Age*, April 8, 1991, 20.

[7]"Pepsi: Memorable Ads, Forgettable Sales," *Business Week*, October 21, 1991, 36.

[8]For an interesting discussion on creativity and the creative process in advertising, see Vincent J. Blasko and Michael P. Mokwa, "Paradox, Advertising and the Creative Process," in *Current Issues and Research in Advertising*, J. H. Leigh and C. R. Martin, Jr., eds. (Ann Arbor, MI: Graduate School of Business Administration, University of Michigan, 1989), 351–366.

[9]Terence Poltrack, "Stalking the Big Idea," *Agency*, June 1991, 26.

advertising creativity as "a new combination of familiar elements that forces involvement and memorability."[10] Perhaps jazz musician Charlie Mingus said it best: "Creativity is more than just being different. Anybody can play weird, that's easy. What's hard is to be simple as Bach. Making the simple complicated is commonplace, making the complicated simple, awesomely simple, that's creativity."[11]

In sum, effective, creative advertising must make a relatively lasting impact on consumers. This means getting past the clutter from other advertisements, activating attention, and giving consumers something to remember about the advertised product. In other words, advertising must *make an impression.* Based on the above perspectives on creativity, this means developing ads that are *empathetic* (i.e., that understand what people are thinking and feeling), that are *involving and memorable,* and that are *"awesomely simple."* The following *Focus on Promotion* describes a brilliant creative advertising campaign for Absolut Vodka.

ADVERTISING PLANS AND STRATEGY

Advertisements can be developed in an ad hoc fashion without much forethought or they can be created systematically. *Advertising plans* provide the framework for the systematic execution of advertising strategies. To appreciate the role of an advertising plan, imagine an analogous situation where a soccer team approaches an upcoming game without any idea of how it is going to execute its offense or defense. Without a game plan, the team would have to play in the same spontaneous fashion as do players in a "pick up" game. Under such circumstances there would be numerous missed assignments and overall misexecution. The team very likely would lose unless they played a badly mismatched opponent.

So it is with advertising. Companies compete against opponents who generally are well prepared. This means that a firm must enter the advertising game with a clear plan in mind. An advertising plan evaluates a product or brand's advertising history, proposes where the next period's advertising should head, and justifies the proposed strategy for maintaining or improving a brand's competitive situation.

To put an advertising plan into action requires (1) careful evaluation of consumer behavior related to the brand, (2) detailed evaluation of the competition, and (3) a coordinated effort to tie the proposed advertising program into the brand's overall marketing strategy.

---

[10]Ibid.

[11]Lou Centlivre, "A Peek At the Creative of the '90s," *Advertising Age,* January 18, 1988, 62.

FOCUS ON PROMOTION

ABSOLUTELY BRILLIANT

Just over a decade ago, imported brands of vodka were virtually nonexistent in the United States. Three brands (Stolichnaya from Russia, Finlandia from Finland, and Wybrowa from Poland) made up less than one percent of the total United States vodka market. In 1980 Carillon Importers, Ltd., began marketing Absolut Vodka from Sweden, a brand that at the time was completely unknown in the United States. In addition to having a great name (suggesting the unequivocally best, or absolute, vodka), the brand's most distinguishing feature was a unique bottle—crystal clear with an interesting shape.

With a small advertising budget and the capability of advertising only in print media, Carillon's advertising agency, TBWA, set about the task of rapidly building brand awareness. The agency's brilliant idea was to simply feature a full-page shot of the bottle with a two-word headline. The first word would always be the brand name, Absolut, used as an adjective followed by a second word that would describe the brand or its consumer. Figure 11.2 presents a recent execution of this strategy.

Business grew rapidly from the very beginning, facilitated somewhat by American consumers temporarily boycotting the major competitive brand of imported vodka, Stolichnaya, after Russia invaded Afghanistan. Sales growth has never abated. This in large part is due to consistently creative advertising and strong budgetary support given the brand. The advertising budget grew from only $750,000 in 1981 to $20 million in 1990. Absolut is the most heavily advertised spirits brand anywhere in the world—and, by 1995, Absolut is expected to be the fourth highest-selling spirit brand of any kind sold in the United States.

Source: This description is based on "Absolut Success," *1990 Winners of the Effie Gold Awards: Case Studies in Advertising Effectiveness* (New York: American Marketing Association of New York and the American Association of Advertising Agencies, 1991), 14–20.

FIGURE 11.2   Illustration of Absolut Vodka's Creative Advertising

Because an advertising plan involves a number of planning steps and details that are beyond the scope of this chapter, attention now turns to the advertising strategy that extends directly from the advertising plan.[12]

Advertising strategy is what the advertiser says about the brand being advertised. It is the formulation of a sales message that communicates the product or brand's primary benefit or how it can solve the consumer's problem.[13]

A Five-Step Program

Formulating an advertising strategy requires the advertiser to undertake a formal, five-step program.[14] Each step is illustrated by discussing a $30 million television advertising campaign undertaken by the Beef Industry Council.[15]

In an attempt to enhance the image of beef and revive sales at a time when American eating habits had moved toward greater consumption of poultry and seafood products, this campaign employed the services of a variety of well-known celebrities (actresses Julia Louis-Dreyfus, Lauren Bacall, and Madeline Kahn; television star Timothy Busfield; model Kim Alexis; country singer Reba McIntire; and basketball players Larry Bird and Michael Cooper).

STEP 1: SPECIFY THE KEY FACT.   The *key fact* in an advertising strategy is a single-minded statement from the *consumer's point of view* that identifies why consumers are or are not purchasing the product/service/brand or are not giving it proper consideration.

Research performed for the Beef Industry Council undoubtedly revealed that many American consumers have reduced their consumption of beef, or eliminated it entirely from their diets, because they regard it as high in fat and cholesterol and not an "in" food. The key fact that the Beef Industry Council probably wanted to convey in developing its advertising strategy was that beef is an *in* food—"Real food for real people."

STEP 2: PRIMARY MARKETING PROBLEM.   Extending from the key fact, this step states the problem from the *marketer's point of view*. The primary marketing problem may be an image problem, a product perception problem, or a competitive problem.

---

[12]For more details on the advertising plan, see Don E. Schultz, Dennis Martin, and William P. Brown, *Strategic Advertising Campaigns* (Lincolnwood, IL: NTC Business Books, 1987), chap. 4; and Schultz and Tannenbaum, *Essentials of Advertising Strategy*, chap. 2.

[13]Schultz and Tannenbaum, *Essentials of Advertising Strategy*, 4.

[14]The following discussion is an adaptation from Schultz, Martin, and Brown, *Strategic Advertising Campaigns*, 240–245.

[15]General information for this discussion is based on Julie Liesse Erickson, "Star-Studded Cast Flavors New Beef Ads," *Advertising Age*, September 12, 1988, 3. Much of the interpretation is conjectural on the author's part, however, and is not based on direct information received from the Beef Industry Council.

The Beef Industry Council was faced with these issues: beef's image was less than desirable, the perception of beef as a non-nutritional product had to be overcome, and beef had to win back sales from poultry and seafood—its product-category competitors.

STEP 3: COMMUNICATIONS OBJECTIVE.   This is a straightforward statement about what effect the advertising is intended to have on the target market and how it should persuade consumers.

The Beef Industry Council's use of famous celebrities who represent the mainstream of American culture undoubtedly was intended to communicate an overall impression such as this: "These celebrities are *in* people; they eat beef and enjoy it greatly; therefore, beef is an *in* food that I, too, should include more often in my diet."

STEP 4: CREATIVE MESSAGE STRATEGY.   The guts of the overall advertising strategy is the creative message strategy, sometimes also called the creative platform.[16] Implementing creative message strategy requires the following:

Defining the Target Market.   The target market for the advertising strategy and related marketing program is defined in terms of demographics, geographics, psychographics, media-consumption habits, and product/brand usage patterns.

The Beef Industry Council defined its market as "light users" of beef, that is, people who eat beef less than six times in any typical two-week period. The predominant choice of female celebrities suggests that the strategy was aimed slightly more at women than men, since women generally hold less-favorable attitudes toward beef. Also, the choice of specific celebrities indicates that the target market consists of people who are likely to be relatively heavy television viewers and who enjoy sporting events.

Identifying the Primary Competition.   Who are the primary competitors in the segment the brand is attempting to tap and what are their advantages and disadvantages? Answering this question enables an advertiser to know exactly how to *position* a brand against consumers' perceptions of competitive brands' advantages and disadvantages.

Choosing the Promise.   This aspect of the creative platform amounts to selecting a brand's *primary benefit or major selling idea*. In most cases, the promise is a consumer benefit or solution to a problem.

Beef cannot hope to compete with poultry and seafood on the basis of good-for-your-health claims, since most consumers are familiar with research that

---

[16]For example, see Jewler, *Creative Strategy in Advertising.*

shows these products to be more healthy. However, the Beef Industry Council can promise that beef is *good* food—a food that is relatively nutritious and that is irreplaceable when, say, the consumer wants a hamburger and will accept no substitute. The promise, then, is actually a collection of hedonistic-experiential eating concepts (taste, convenience, fun, fulfillment) rather than a single product benefit. Consumers are promised that beef fits with their lifestyle and is an *in* food—"Real food for real people." Based on concepts covered in Chapter 3, it should be apparent that this advertising campaign is based more on a HEM- than a CPM-orientation.

Offering Reasons Why. These are the *supporting facts* to back up the promise. In some instances advertisers can back up advertising claims with factual information that is relevant, informative, and interesting to consumers. Many times it is impossible to physically prove or support the promise being made, such as when the promise is symbolic or psychological. In these instances, advertisers turn to authority figures, experts, or celebrities to support the implicit advertising promise.

This is precisely why the Beef Industry Council chose the cast of well-known and respected celebrities, who represent a variety of backgrounds and lifestyles that consumers find appealing.

STEP 5: CORPORATE/DIVISIONAL REQUIREMENTS. The final step in formulating an advertising strategy involves the *mandatory requirements* that must be included in an ad. This aspect of advertising strategy formulation is relatively technical and uncreative. Basically, it reminds the advertiser to include the corporate slogan, a standard tag line ("Beef is real food for real people"), any regulatory requirements (as with cigarette advertising), and so on.

In sum, advertising strategy lays out the details for the upcoming advertising program. It insists on a disciplined approach to analyzing the product/brand, the consumer, and the competition. A single-minded benefit is the outcome. The strategy becomes a blueprint, road map, or guide to subsequent advertising efforts. Every proposed tactical decision is evaluated in terms of whether it is compatible with the strategy.

MEANS-END CHAINS AND ADVERTISING STRATEGY

The consumer is, or at least should be, the foremost determinant of advertising messages. The notion of a means-end chain provides a useful framework for understanding the relationship between consumers and advertising messages. Means-end chaining focuses on the linkages between *attributes* of products (the means), the *consequences* of these attributes for the consumer, and the *personal values* (the ends) that the consequences reinforce.[17]

Attributes are features or aspects of the product or brand to be advertised. For example, attributes of beef include positive features such as taste and ease of preparation, and negative features (real or perceived) such as fat content and cholesterol. **Consequences** are the advantages (*benefits*) or disadvantages (*detriments*) which consumers hope to receive or avoid when consuming products. Good taste, fun times (e.g., enjoying a hamburger with friends), high calories, and fears of heart disease are just some of the consequences that consumers associate with eating beef. **Values** represent those enduring beliefs people hold regarding what is important in life.[18] Values are formed during early childhood but undergo some change throughout life. Table 11.1 provides a list of so-called terminal and instrumental values. *Terminal values* are those aspects of life that are desired for their own sake, whereas *instrumental values* are seen as means (or instruments) for accomplishing the terminal end states. Values related to eating include the terminal values of happiness, pleasure, and self-respect as well as the instrumental value of self-control. In general, values determine the relative desirability of consequences and serve to organize the meanings for products and brands in consumers' memories.[19]

Figure 11.3 diagrams an illustrative means-end chain for beef. This hypothetical chain represents one segment of consumers' perceptions regarding the positive (approach) and negative (avoid) attributes, consequences, and values associated with consuming beef. To the extent that this chain is representative for large numbers of American consumers, it is little wonder that the Beef Industry Council would have great difficulty in its advertising efforts to improve beef's image and increase beef consumption.

The means-end chain in Figure 11.3 is presented from the product's perspective (product attributes→consequences→consumer values). That is, a product (beef in this case) has attributes which have benefits which either enable

---

[17]This discussion is based on various writings by Professors Gutman and Reynolds, who along with several colleagues have popularized means-end theory in advertising. For example, see Jonathan Gutman, "A Means-End Chain Model Based on Consumer Categorization Processes," *Journal of Marketing*, 46 (Spring 1982), 60–72; Thomas J. Reynolds and Jonathan Gutman, "Advertising Is Image Management," *Journal of Advertising Research*, 24 (February-March 1984), 27–36; Thomas J. Reynolds and Jonathan Gutman, "Laddering Theory, Method, Analysis, and Interpretation," *Journal of Advertising Research*, 28 (February/March 1988), 11–31; Thomas J. Reynolds and Alyce Byrd Craddock, "The Application of MECCAS Model to the Development and Assessment of Advertising Strategy: A Case Study," *Journal of Advertising Research*, 28 (April/May 1988), 43–59.

[18]For further discussion of cultural values, see Lynn R. Kahle, Basil Poulos, and Ajay Sukhdial, "Changes in Social Values in the United States during the Past Decade," *Journal of Advertising Research*, 28 (February/March 1988), 35–41; Sharon E. Beatty, Lynn R. Kahle, Pamela Homer, and Shekhar Misra, "Alternative Measurement Approaches to Consumer Values: The List of Values and the Rokeach Value Survey," *Psychology and Marketing*, 2, 3 (1985), 181–200.

[19]J. Paul Peter and Jerry C. Olson, *Consumer Behavior: Marketing Strategy Perspectives* (Homewood, IL: Irwin, 1990).

TABLE 11.1	Terminal and Instrumental Values

TERMINAL	INSTRUMENTAL
1. A comfortable life	14. Ambitious
2. An exciting life	15. Broadminded
3. A sense of accomplishment	16. Capable
4. A world of beauty	17. Cheerful
5. Equality	18. Clean
6. Family security	19. Imaginative
7. Freedom	20. Independent
8. Happiness	21. Intellectual
9. Inner harmony	22. Logical
10. Pleasure	23. Responsible
11. Self-respect	24. Self-control
12. Social recognition	
13. Wisdom	

Source: J. Michael Munson and Edward McQuarrie, "Shortening the Rokeach Value Survey for Use in Consumer Research," *Advances in Consumer Research, XV,* Michael Houston (ed.), Provo, Utah: Association for Consumer Research, 1988, 381–386.

consumers to achieve valued states or, perhaps, threaten the achievement of these states. It is critical, however, that you think of means-end chains in a reverse order from the consumer's vantage point. This perspective (values → consequences → attributes) better captures the process that actually determines consumer choice behavior. That is, every meaningful act of consumption can be seen as an attempt to achieve valued end states. Consumers seek product consequences and attributes only as a means for achieving values. Hence, from the consumer's perspective, the *end* (values) drive the *means* (attributes and their consequences).

Advertising Applications of Means-End Chains

The creation of effective advertisements requires a clear understanding of what consumers value when choosing among brands in a particular product category. This understanding then directs the advertiser's determination of which product attributes and consequences need to be emphasized. A formal model, called **MECCAS,** provides a procedure for applying the concept of means-end chains to the creation of advertising messages. MECCAS is an acronym standing for Means-End Conceptualization of Components for Advertising Strategy.[20]

[20]Jerry Olson and Thomas J. Reynolds, "Understanding Consumers' Cognitive Structures: Implications for Advertising Strategy," in *Advertising and Consumer Psychology,* eds. L. Percy and A. Woodside (Lexington, MA: Lexington Books, 1983), 77–90.

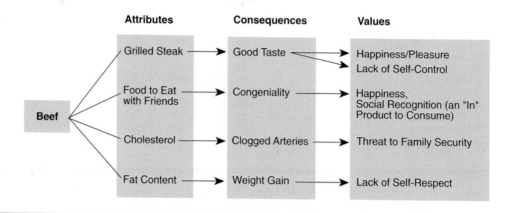

FIGURE 11.3   A Hypothetical Means-End Chain for Beef

Table 11.2 presents and defines the various levels of the MECCAS model. Note that the components (or levels) include a *driving force*, a *leverage point*, *executional framework*, *consumer benefit*, and *message elements*. The driving force is the consumer value or end-level that the advertising strategy focuses on. Every other level is geared toward achieving the end-level. Study the definitions carefully in Table 11.2 before moving on to the following two applications of the MECCAS approach.[21]

ARMSTRONG MAGAZINE AD.   A magazine advertisement for Armstrong's Trim and Fit™ vinyl flooring is shown in Figure 11.4. (Study it carefully before reading on.) This cartoon-like ad is actually a very serious attempt to remove the consumer's fear of making a mistake when installing floor covering. The *driving force* consists of several interrelated values from Table 11.1: independence, a sense of accomplishment, self-respect, and social recognition. That is, a person performing some do-it-yourself home repair is seeking independence from having to pay someone else to perform the work and, as a result, achieves a sense of accomplishment, self-respect, and perhaps social recognition. The *leverage point* is the bottom scene, which shows a man smiling rather smugly as he receives an adoring hug from his wife for a job well done—

---

[21]These illustrations are post hoc interpretations of the two advertisements. It is unknown whether the advertisers in these two cases actually performed formal means-end analyses in developing their ads.

TABLE 11.2	MECCAS—Means-End Conceptualization of Components for Advertising Strategy

Don't bother to memorize MECCA

LEVEL	DEFINITION
Driving Force	The value orientation of the strategy; the end-level to be focused on in the advertising.
Leverage Point	The manner by which the advertising will "tap into," reach, or activate the value or end-level of focus; the specific key way in which the value is linked to the specific features in the advertising.
Executional Framework	The overall scenario or action plot, plus the details of the advertising execution. The executional framework provides the "vehicle" by which the value orientation is to be communicated; especially the Gestalt of the advertisement; its overall tone and style.
Consumer Benefit	The major positive consequences for the consumer that are to be explicitly communicated, verbally or visually, in the advertising.
Message Elements	The specific attributes or features about the product that are communicated verbally or visually.

Source: Advertising and Consumer Psychology edited by Larry Percy and Arch G. Woodside, (Lexington, Mass.: Lexington Books, D. C. Heath and Company, 1983).

thereby tapping into his (and, vicariously, the reader's) sense of accomplishment, self-respect, and recognition. The action plot in the *executional framework* reaches this conclusion by first showing the man in the top scene sweating profusely as he ponders the undesirable consequences of making a bad cut; in the bottom scene, the man is shown receiving the rewards of his endeavors. The major *consumer benefit* is a fail-safe program for installing your own floor covering. *Message elements* point this out in the body copy by stating that "if you goof while cutting or fitting," there is no need for worry: the Armstrong dealer will replace the flooring and the kit.

All-in-all, this no goof guarantee is an extremely effective marketing strategy, and the cartoon advertisement is a very creative way to tap into or activate the basic values associated with using this product. How effective do you think this magazine ad would have been if real people had been portrayed instead of cartoon characters? Might not the use of real people poised in this fashion have made the man seem excessively smug and the wife glaringly subservient?

CANOVISION 8 MAGAZINE AD. A magazine advertisement for Canon's Canovision 8™ camcorder is shown in Figure 11.5. (Study it carefully before reading on.) The *driving force* in this ad, which obviously is directed at parents, focuses on the idea that pleasant memories are easily lost unless efforts are taken (now) to permanently capture them. As such, the ad subtly implies that parents who fail to visually record their children's important accomplishments

MECCAS Illustration for Armstrong

Go on, cut. You'll be brilliant.
Armstrong guarantees it.

Install your new Armstrong sheet vinyl floor with a Trim and Fit ™ kit, and if you goof while cutting or fitting, your Armstrong retailer will replace both the flooring and the kit.

Free. That's the Fail-Safe ™ Guarantee. Just see your local home center or building supply retailer for details.

FREE. For a free Floor Project Planning Pack, call the Armstrong Consumer Line at 1 800 233-3823 and ask for Dept. 69GWD. Or, send this coupon: Armstrong, Dept. 69GWD, P.O. Box 3001, Lancaster, PA 17604

Name _____
        (please print)
Street _____
City _____
State _____ Zip _____

Armstrong
so nice to come home to ™

MECCAS Illustration for Canovision 8

FIGURE 11.5

lack wisdom and jeopardize future family happiness and pleasure. The *leverage point* is the wording in the headline—"2 out, bottom of the 9th. You'd better catch it." On the surface, this headline seems merely to be describing the fact that a baseball game is almost completed (there is only one out remaining in the bottom of the ninth inning). But, of course, the statement really is suggesting to parents that their children are getting older and precious moments (like exploits during a baseball game) might be lost forever unless they purchase a camcorder—not just any camcorder, but a Canovision camcorder.

The *executional framework* (a boy who appears to have just completed a baseball game—probably in a hero role) is simply a meaningful way for Canon to place a child in a summer situation (the time when this ad was run) that many parents can identify with and would like to savor when their sons or daughters are grown. The major *consumer benefit* is the promise that the Canovision 8™ will deliver clear, sharp images. *Message elements* point this out in the body copy by describing the interchangeable lenses, autofocus, wireless remote control, and expert-crafted lenses.

In conclusion, the important point to remember about the MECCAS approach is that it provides a systematic procedure for linking the advertiser's perspective (the possession of brand attributes and consequences) with the consumer's perspective (the pursuit of products to achieve desired end states, or values). Effective advertising does *not* focus on product attributes/consequences per se; rather, it is directed at showing how the advertised brand will benefit the consumer and enable him or her to achieve what he or she most desires in life—comfort, excitement, a sense of accomplishment, and the other values listed in Table 11.1. Products vary in terms of which values they are capable of satisfying; nonetheless, all products are capable of fulfilling some value(s), and it is the role of sophisticated advertising to learn just what these values are and how best to tap into them.

ALTERNATIVE CREATIVE STRATEGIES

The use of advertising to tap consumer values leaves open the possibility of a variety of different creative approaches to provide the executional framework and leverage the value orientation of the advertising strategy. Several relatively distinct creative advertising strategies have evolved over the years. In fact, the bulk of contemporary advertising falls into seven creative categories. These are summarized in Table 11.3 and are described in detail in the following sections.[22]

---

[22]The following discussion is based on Charles F. Frazer, "Creative Strategy: A Management Perspective," *Journal of Advertising*, 12, 4 (1983), 36–41. For other perspectives on creative strategies, see Henry A. Laskey, Ellen Day, and Melvin R. Crask, "Typology of Main Message Strategies for Television Commercials," *Journal of Advertising*, 18, 1 (1989), 36–41; Christopher P. Puto and William D. Wells, "Informational and Transformational Advertising: The Differential Effects of Time," in *Advances in Consumer Research*, 11 (1989), T. C. Kinnear, ed., Provo, UT: Association for Consumer Research, 638–643.

Summary of Creative Strategy Alternatives

TABLE 11.3

ALTERNATIVE	MOST SUITABLE CONDITIONS	COMPETITIVE IMPLICATIONS
Generic Straight product or benefit claim with no assertion of superiority.	Monopoly or extreme dominance of product category.	Serves to make advertiser's brand synonymous with product category; may be combated through higher-order strategies.
Preemptive Generic claim with assertion of superiority.	Most useful in growing or awakening market where competitive advertising is generic or nonexistent.	May be successful in convincing consumer of superiority of advertiser's product; limited response options for competitors.
Unique Selling Proposition Superiority claims based on unique physical feature or benefit.	Most useful when point of difference cannot be readily matched by competitors.	Advertiser obtains strong persuasive advantage; may force competitors to imitate or choose more aggressive strategy (e.g., "positioning").
Brand Image Claims based on psychological differentiation, usually symbolic association.	Best suited to homogeneous goods where physical differences are difficult to develop or may be quickly matched; requires sufficient understanding of consumers to develop meaningful symbols/associations.	Most often involves prestige claims which rarely challenge competitors directly.
Positioning Attempts to build or occupy mental niche in relation to identified competitor.	Best strategy for attacking a market leader; requires relatively long-term commitment to aggressive advertising efforts and understanding consumers.	Direct comparison severely limits options for named competitor; counterattacks seem to offer little chance of success.
Resonance Attempts to evoke stored experiences of prospects to endow product with relevant meaning or significance.	Best suited to socially visible goods; requires considerable consumer understanding to design message patterns.	Few direct limitations on competitor's options; most likely competitive response is imitation.
Emotional Attempts to provoke involvement or emotion through ambiguity, humor, or the like, without strong selling emphasis.	Best suited to discretionary items; effective use depends upon conventional approach by competitors to maximize difference; greatest commitment is to aesthetics or intuition rather than research.	Competitors may imitate to undermine strategy of difference or pursue other alternatives.

Source: Charles F. Frazer, "Creative Strategy: A Management Perspective," *Journal of Advertising,* 12, 4, 1983, 40.

Generic Strategy

An advertiser employs a **generic strategy** when making a claim that could be made by any company that markets the product. The advertiser makes no attempt to differentiate its brand from competitive offerings or to claim superiority. This strategy is particularly appropriate for *a company that dominates a product category*. In such instances, the firm making a generic claim will enjoy a large share of any primary demand stimulated by advertising.

For example, Campbell's dominates the prepared-soup market in the United States, selling nearly two-thirds of all soup. Any advertising that increases overall soup sales naturally benefits Campbell's. This explains its "Soup is good food" campaign that extolled the virtues of eating soup without arguing why people should buy Campbell's soup. Along similar lines, AT&T's "Reach out and touch someone" campaign is a wise strategy in light of this company's grasp on the long-distance phone market.

Preemptive Strategy

Preemptive strategy is employed when an advertiser makes a generic-type claim but does so with an *assertion of superiority*. This strategy is used most often by advertisers in product or service categories where there are few, if any, functional differences among competitive brands. Preemptive advertising by one firm forces competitors into the position of either saying the same thing, and thus being considered copycats, or of finding another advertising alternative.

The maker of Visine eye drops claims that this brand "gets the red out." All eye drops are designed to get the red out, but by making this claim first, Visine made a dramatic statement that the consumer will associate only with Visine. No other company would make this claim now for fear of being labeled a copycat. Likewise, no margarines contain cholesterol, but when one advertiser makes a contains-no-cholesterol claim, competitors have to search for something different to say about their brands.

A particularly clever preemptive campaign was introduced by Nissan Motor Corporation in the late 1980s with its advertising of the Maxima. Preceding the campaign, the Maxima competed against models such as the Ford Taurus and Toyota Cressida in the upper-middle segment of the industry, a segment which at the time had experienced a 25 percent sales decline over a two-year period. To avoid stiff price competition and price rebates, Nissan wanted a more upscale and high-performance image for the Maxima. Based on extensive research, Maxima's advertising agency, Chiat/Day/Mojo, devised a brilliant preemptive line which tauted the Maxima as *the* "Four-Door Sports Car." Of course, other sedans have four doors, but Maxima preempted sports-car status for itself with this one clever claim. Its sales immediately increased by 43 percent over the previous year despite a price increase, and Maxima began appealing to more upscale consumers.[23]

Unique Selling-Proposition Strategy

With the **unique selling-proposition (USP)** strategy, an advertiser makes a superiority claim based on a unique product *attribute that represents a meaningful, distinctive consumer benefit.* The main feature of USP advertising is identifying an important difference that makes a brand unique and then developing an advertising claim that competitors either cannot make or have chosen not to make. The translation of the unique product feature into a relevant consumer benefit provides the unique selling proposition.

The USP strategy is best suited for companies whose products possess relatively lasting competitive advantages, such as makers of technically complex items or providers of sophisticated services.

The Gillette Sensor razor (see Figure 2.1 on p. 32) has a USP when claiming that it is "the only razor that senses and adjusts to the individual needs of your face." A competitive brand, the Schick Tracer (see Figure 5.3 on p. 134), counters with the USP claim that it "is the first razor with a blade that flexes." Advertisers of the Panasonic® Quiet dot matrix printer (see Figure 11.6) claim that only it offers scalable fonts, color, and quiet technology. The Dodge Caravan had a unique selling proposition, if only temporarily, when it was able to claim that it was "the first and the only minivan with a driver's air bag." Kentucky Fried Chicken's unique selling proposition is based on its claim that it knows chicken better than the burger places. The proposition that only Burger King (not McDonald's, Wendy's, or other hamburger chains) broils hamburgers is also unique.

In many respects the unique selling-proposition strategy is the optimum creative technique. This is because it gives the consumer a clearly differentiated reason for selecting the advertiser's brand over competitive offerings. The only reason USP advertising is not used more often is because brands in most product categories are pretty much homogeneous. They have no unique physical advantages to advertise and therefore are forced to use strategies favoring the more symbolic, psychological end of the strategy continuum. It has been suggested that advertisers in the 1990s will use the USP strategy to a much greater degree in comparison to the image-oriented ads so popular in the 1980s.[24]

---

[23]This description is based on "Four-Door Sports Car," *1990 Winners of the Effie Gold Awards: Case Studies in Advertising Effectiveness* (New York: American Marketing Association of New York and the American Association of Advertising Agencies, 1991), 124–131.

[24]"Madison Avenue Is Getting a lot Less Madcap," *Business Week*, October 29, 1990, 78, 82.

FIGURE 11.6   Illustration of USP Advertising Strategy

Brand-Image Strategy

Whereas the USP strategy is based on promoting physical and functional differences between the advertiser's product and competitive offerings, the **brand-image strategy** involves *psychological, rather than physical, differentiation.* Advertising attempts to develop an image or identity for a brand by associating the product with symbols and archetypes.

Developing an image through advertising amounts to giving a brand a *distinct identity or personality.* This is especially important for brands that compete in product categories where there is relatively little physical differentiation and all brands are relatively homogeneous (beer, soft drinks, cigarettes, blue jeans, etc.). Thus Pepsi is the soft drink for the "new generation"; Mountain Dew is for "cool dudes" (see Figure 11.7); Levi's 501 jeans are for "hip" people; and Marlboro stands for rugged individualism (see the *Global Focus*).

Positioning Strategy

According to **positioning strategy,** successful advertising must implant in the customer's mind a *clear meaning of what the product is and how it compares to competitive offerings.* Effective positioning requires that a company be fully aware of its competition and exploit competitive weaknesses. A brand is positioned in the consumer's mind relative to competition. The originators of the positioning concept, Jack Trout and Al Ries, contend that

> to be successful today, a company must be 'competitors' oriented. It must look for weak points in the position of its competitors and then launch marketing attacks against those weak points.[25]

It is important to realize that positioning strategy is *not* mutually exclusive of other strategies and can be implemented using USP, brand-image, or other creative approaches.

Numerous examples are available to illustrate positioning strategies. For example, in the dishwashing-detergent category, Cascade says that it "fights spots," while Sunlight claims that it "cleans dried food from dishes." The automobile industry relies heavily on effective positioning. For example, Pontiac's positioning theme is "We build excitement"; they back this up with exciting stylings and advertising. Volvo positions itself as "a car you can believe in" and supports the claim in advertising by showing how sturdy the product is. Chevrolet uses a patriotic theme in promoting itself as "the heartbeat of America." Toyota positions itself as a maker of quality automobiles ("Who could ask for anything

---

[25]Jack Trout and Al Ries, "The Positioning Era: A View Ten Years Later," *Advertising Age,* July 16, 1979, 39–42.

FIGURE 11.7   Illustration of Brand-Image Advertising

GLOBAL FOCUS

MARLBORO'S IMAGE IN DIFFERENT COUNTRIES

What do college students in different countries think about when considering Marlboro cigarettes? A researcher at Northwestern University posed this question and put it to the test by studying college students in five countries: Brazil, Japan, Norway, Thailand, and the United States. Small samples of students in each country participated in a word-association test by responding to the statement: "Smoking a Marlboro cigarette . . ."

Responses were sharply mixed. Thai students considered smoking a Marlboro cigarette to be relaxing. Norwegian students most closely linked smoking Marlboros to disease, and Brazilians associated the brand with pollution. U.S. students linked Marlboro cigarettes with words like cowboy, horse, and macho—all relating directly to Marlboro's longstanding advertising campaign. The Japanese associated smoking Marlboros with social occasions.

These different images point out that products and brands mean different things around the world because the cultural contexts in which they are interpreted vary greatly. This means that creative advertising needs to be adjusted to accommodate the specific cultural context in which it is placed. For example, because Japanese consumers associate Marlboro cigarettes with sociability, Marlboro advertisements in Japan could show the cowboy chatting with other cowboys rather than by himself. In Thailand, where consumers perceive cigarettes to be suggestive of relaxation, it may be most effective to show the cowboy in a subdued context rather than chasing wild horses.

Source: The research is by Eduardo Camargo and is summarized in Lenore Skenazy, "How Does Slogan Translate?" *Advertising Age*, October 12, 1987, 84.

more?"). BMW, the veritable icon of the now-disdained materialism and yuppieism of the 1980s, *repositioned* the 325i as a car sensitive to consumers' concerns for safety and value. This repositioning came at a time when BMW sales in the United States had fallen nearly 25 percent below the previous-year's sales.[26]

[26]Raymond Serafin, "BMW Puts 30M Behind Ads to Drive Away Yuppie Image," *Advertising Age*, June 24, 1991, 3.

Resonance Strategy

When used in the advertising-strategy sense, the term **resonance** is analogous to the physical notion of resonance, which refers to noise resounding off an object. In similar fashion, an advertisement resonates (*patterns*) the audience's life experiences. Resonant advertising strategy extends from psychographic research and structures an advertising campaign to pattern the prevailing lifestyle orientation of the intended market segment.

Resonant advertising does not focus on product claims or brand images but rather seeks to present circumstances or situations that find counterparts in the real or imagined experiences of the target audience. Advertising based on this strategy attempts to match "patterns" in the commercial or ad with the target audience's stored experiences.[27]

The advertisement for the Pioneer PD-M700 compact disc player illustrates the use of resonance strategy (see Figure 11.8). The ad portrays a situation in which a young father is enjoying the experience of holding his baby and not having to waste time changing discs. Many readers of this ad could easily relate to the benefit of spending less time changing the music and more time enjoying it.

Emotional Strategy

Much contemporary advertising aims to reach the consumer on an emotional level through the use of **emotional strategy.**[28] Many advertising practitioners and scholars recognize that products are bought often on the basis of emotional factors and that appeals to emotion can be very successful if used appropriately and with the right products. The use of emotion in advertising runs the gamut of positive and negative appeals, including appeals to romance, nostalgia, compassion, excitement, joy, fear, guilt, disgust, and regret.[29]

Emotional commercials and ads work especially well for products that naturally are associated with emotions (foods, jewelry, cosmetics, fashion apparel, soft drinks, and long-distance telephoning). However, emotional strategy can be used when advertising any product.

The campaign for Taster's Choice coffee typifies the use of emotion in advertising. This campaign, which is a spin-off of a similar campaign first aired in Great Britain, portrays an ongoing flirtation between two neighbors. The first ad in the

---

[27]Frazer, "Creative Strategy," 39.

[28]Frazer, ibid., refers to this as "affective strategy," but "emotional strategy" is more descriptive and less subject to alternative interpretations.

[29]For a variety of perspectives on the use of emotion in advertising, see Stuart J. Agres, Julie A. Edell, and Tony M. Dubitsky, *Emotion in Advertising: Theoretical and Practical Explorations* (New York: Quorum Books, 1990).

Illustration of Resonance Strategy

FIGURE 11.8

series presented the man and woman meeting when she ran out of coffee during a dinner party and turned to her next door neighbor to borrow coffee. In a second ad the woman returned the jar of Taster's Choice at a time when the man was entertaining another woman. This soap-opera type campaign builds romantic suspense and in doing so attracts consumer attention to the advertised brand.

In Sum

Seven general forms of creative strategy have been discussed. These strategic alternatives, although they overlap to some extent, should provide a useful aid to understanding the different approaches available to advertisers and the factors influencing the choice of creative strategy.

It would be incorrect to think of these strategies as pure and mutually exclusive. Because there is some unavoidable overlap, it is possible that an advertiser may consciously or unconsciously use two or more strategies simultaneously. For example, positioning strategy can be used in conjunction with any of the other strategies. An advertiser can position a brand against competitors' brands using emotional strategy, image strategy, a unique selling proposition, or other possibilities.

It is also worth noting that some advertising experts contend that advertising is most effective when it reflects both ends of the creative advertising continuum—that is, by *addressing both rational product benefits and symbolic/ psychological benefits*. A New York advertising agency, Lowe Marschalk, provided evidence in partial support of the superiority of combined benefits over rational appeals only. The agency tested 168 television commercials, 47 of which contained both rational and psychological appeals and 121 of which contained rational appeals only. Using recall and persuasion measures, the agency found that the ads containing both rational and psychological appeals outperformed the rational-only ads by a substantial margin.[30]

An interesting application of the use of both rational and emotional appeals is a campaign for the Toyota Paseo. The Paseo, which means stroll or pathway in Spanish, appeals to a young, primarily male audience. The advertisement in Figure 11.9 appeals to rationality (the bold words) while simultaneously appealing to emotion (the smaller words aside the bold words). Toyota's corporate marketing manager refers to the ad strategy as a "left brain/right brain approach."[31]

[30]Kim Foltz, "Psychological Appeal in TV Ads Found Effective," *Adweek*, August 31, 1987, 38.

[31]Cleveland Horton, "Toyota Double Talk," *Advertising Age*, June 10, 1991, 53.

Use of Rational and Emotional Appeals

FIGURE 11.9

CORPORATE IMAGE AND ISSUE ADVERTISING

The type of advertising discussed to this point is commonly referred to as product- or brand-oriented advertising. Such advertising focuses on a product (e.g., beef) or, more typically, a specific brand (Absolut, Paseo) and attempts ultimately to persuade consumers to purchase the advertiser's product/brand.

Another form of advertising, termed **corporate advertising,** focuses not on specific products or brands but on a corporation's overall image or on economic/social issues relevant to the corporation's interests. Two rather distinct forms of corporate advertising are discussed in the following sections: (1) image advertising and (2) issue, or advocacy, advertising.[32]

Corporate Image Advertising

This type of corporate advertising has been defined as follows:

> Corporate image advertising is aimed at creating an image of a specific corporate personality in the minds of the general public and seeking maximum favorable images amongst selected audiences (e.g., stockholders, employees, consumers, suppliers, and potential investors). In essence, this type of advertising treats the company as a product, carefully positioning and clearly differentiating it from other similar companies and basically "selling" this product to selected audiences. Corporate image advertising is not concerned with a social problem unless it has a preferred solution. It asks no action on the part of the audience beyond a favorable attitude and passive approval conducive to successful operation in the marketplace.[33]

Corporate image advertising attempts to gain name recognition for a company, establish goodwill for a company and its products, or identify itself with some meaningful and socially acceptable activity. For example, the ad for State Farm Insurance (Figure 11.10) associates this company with the Good Neighbor Award that was developed in cooperation with the National Council of Teachers of Mathematics. Like other corporate image advertisements, this ad attempts to

---

[32]This distinction is based on a classification by S. Prakash Sethi, "Institutional/Image Advertising and Idea/Issue Advertising As Marketing Tools: Some Public Policy Issues," *Journal of Marketing*, 43 (January 1979), 68–78. Sethi actually labels the two subsets of corporate advertising as "institutional/image" and "idea/issue." For reading ease they are shortened here to image versus issue advertising.

[33]Ibid.

Illustration of Corporate Image Advertising

FIGURE 11.10

Mrs. Belsky's Advice To Her Math Students: "Go Fly A Tetrahedron."

Each spring, the math lessons Nancy Belsky's students have learned take to the air over Westmoreland, New Hampshire.

Nancy, a teacher at Westmoreland Elementary School, uses this innovative teaching technique to show her fifth through eighth grade students how math skills can be put to practical use.

Her fifth grade students build "sleds," a type of kite which is easily constructed and flown; the sixth graders go further, creating kites of various sizes with their own designs; the seventh graders use their knowledge of solid geometry to make cellular kites, building complex boxes and tetrahedrons; and the eighth graders are allowed to make any kite they can find or dream up.

It's a challenging task. The students are given limited materials to work with, so they have to be precise in their calculations as they go about building their kites. The older students apply the Pythagorean theorem to aid them in design, as well as other formulas to determine surface areas.

In the end, the sight of these high-flying kites is testimony to Nancy's teaching methods: "Simply giving students the tools of mathematics isn't enough. You have to show students how useful these tools are and how they can be applied in practical ways."

State Farm is honored to present Nancy with our Good Neighbor Award. We are also delighted to make a contribution of $5,000 to Westmoreland Elementary School in her name.

Nancy Belsky. Through her innovative teaching, she's raised her students' understanding of math to the highest level.

STATE FARM INSURANCE COMPANIES
Home Offices: Bloomington, Illinois

Good Neighbor Award

The Good Neighbor Award was developed in cooperation with the National Council of Teachers of Mathematics (NCTM).

advertisements, this ad attempts to accomplish two overriding objectives: increase consumer recognition of the State Farm Insurance name and enhance the company's image as a good corporate citizen.[34]

In general, corporate image advertising is directed at more than merely trying to make consumers feel good about a company. Companies are increasingly using the image of their firms to enhance sales and financial performance.[35] Corporate advertising that does not contribute to increased sales and profits is difficult to justify in today's economic climate.[36]

Corporate Issue (Advocacy) Advertising

The other form of corporate advertising is **issue, or advocacy, advertising.** When using issue advertising a company takes a position on a controversial social issue of public importance "in hopes of swaying public opinion."[37] It does so in a manner that supports the company's position and best interests while expressly or implicitly challenging the opponent's position and denying the accuracy of their facts.[38]

An example of issue (advocacy) advertising is presented in Figure 11.11. The advertisement is just one of several ads undertaken by Philip Morris in a campaign that describes smokers' economic power. Directed at business executives in wake of the backlash against smokers, the ads apparently are designed to encourage greater tolerance of smokers, tolerance grounded in economic interest—"America's 55.8 million smokers are a powerful economic force."

Issue advertising is a topic of considerable controversy.[39] Business executives are divided on whether this form of advertising represents an effective allocation of corporate resources. What, for example, does the Philip Morris ad hope to accomplish? Will it ultimately increase product sales and profits? How?

---

[34]A study of over 200 major U.S. manufacturing and non-manufacturing firms showed that executives regard *image* and *identity* to be the two most important functions of corporate advertising. See Charles H. Patti and John P. McDonald, "Corporate Advertising: Process, Practices, and Perspectives" (1970–1989), *Journal of Advertising*, 14, 1 (1985), 42–49.

[35]See Lewis C. Winters, "Does It Pay to Advertise to Hostile Audiences with Corporate Advertising?" *Journal of Advertising Research*, 28 (June/July 1988), 11–18.

[36]For further discussion, see Lori Kesler, "Merger Craze Colors Image," *Advertising Age*, October 5, 1987, S1–S4.

[37]Bob D. Cutler and Darrel D. Muehling, "Advocacy Advertising and the Boundaries of Commercial Speech," *Journal of Advertising*, 18, 3 (1989), 40.

[38]Sethi, "Institutional/Image Advertising," 70.

[39]For discussion of the First Amendment issues surrounding the use of advocacy advertising, see Cutler and Muehling, "Advocacy Advertising and the Boundaries of Commercial Speech," and Kent R. Middleton, "Advocacy Advertising, The First Amendment and Competitive Advantage: A Comment on Cutler & Muehling," *Journal of Advertising*, 20, 2 (1991), 77–81.

FIGURE 11.11

An Issue Advertisement Promoting the Economic Power of American Smokers

$1 trillion is too much financial power to ignore.

America's 55.8 million smokers are a powerful economic force. If their household income of $1 trillion were a Gross National Product, it would be the third largest in the world. The plain truth is that smokers are one of the most economically powerful groups in this country. They help fuel the engine of the largest economy on the globe.

The American Smoker— an economic force.

PHILIP MORRIS
MAGAZINE

Presented by Philip Morris Magazine in the interest of America's 55.8 million smokers.
Source: The Roper Organization.

Critics question the legitimacy of issue advertising and challenge its status as a tax-deductible expenditure. Further discussion of these points is beyond the scope of this chapter. The interested reader is encouraged to review the sources contained in the following footnote.[40]

SUMMARY

The chapter examines creative advertising, advertising-strategy formulation, creative strategies, means-end models, and corporate image and issue advertising. An important initial question is: What are the general characteristics of effective advertising? Discussion points out that effective advertising must (1) extend from sound marketing strategy, (2) take the consumer's view, (3) be persuasive, (4) break through the competitive clutter, (5) never promise more than can be delivered, and (6) prevent the creative idea from overwhelming the strategy.

Creative advertising formulation involves a multi-step process. The strategy is initiated by specifying the *key fact* advertising should convey to the target market. This key fact is translated, in step 2, into the *primary marketing problem*. Extending from this problem statement is the selection of *specific communications objectives*. The guts of advertising strategy consists, in step 4, of designing the *creative message strategy*. This involves selecting the target market, identifying the primary competition, and choosing the primary benefit to emphasize. The last step in the process involves ensuring that the advertisement meets all *corporate/divisional requirements*.

The next major subject covered in this chapter is the concept of *means-end chains* and the advertising framework extending from the *MECCAS model*. Means-end chains and MECCAS models provide a bridge between product *attributes* (the means), the *consequences* to the consumer of realizing product attributes, and the ability of these consequences to satisfy consumption-related *values* (the end). MECCAS models provide an organizing framework for developing creative ads that simultaneously consider attributes, consequences, and values.

[40]Louis Banks, "Taking on the Hostile Media," *Harvard Business Review*, March-April 1978, 123-130; Barbara J. Coe, "The Effectiveness Challenge in Issue Advertising Campaigns," *Journal of Advertising*, 12, 4 (1983), 27-35; David Kelley, "Critical Issues for Issue Ads," *Harvard Business Review*, July-August 1982, 80-87; Ward Welty, "Is Issue Advertising Working?" *Public Relations Journal* (November 1981), 29. For an especially thorough and insightful treatment of issue advertising, particularly with regard to the measurement of effectiveness, see Karen F. A. Fox, "The Measurement of Issue/Advocacy Advertising," in *Current Issues & Research in Advertising*, 9, eds. James H. Leigh and Claude R. Martin, Jr. (Ann Arbor, MI, Division of Research, Graduate School of Business Administration, University of Michigan, 1986), 61–92.

The use of advertising to tap consumer values leaves open the possibility of a variety of different creative strategies. Seven specific strategies are described and illustrated with real advertising examples. These strategies are: *generic, preemptive, unique selling proposition, brand image, positioning, resonance,* and *emotional*.

The final subject discussed is *corporate advertising*. A distinction is made between conventional product- and brand-oriented strategy and advertising that focuses on facilitating corporate goodwill, enhancing image, and advocating matters of economic or social significance to a corporation. Two forms of corporate advertising, image and issue (advocacy) advertising, are described.

Discussion Questions

1. One requirement for effective advertising is the ability to break through competitive clutter. Explain what this means and provide several examples of advertising methods that successfully accomplish this.

2. Explain the meaning of the MECCAS model and describe an advertising campaign of your choice in terms of this model—i.e., discuss specifically the driving force, leverage point, and so on.

3. Explain the differences between unique selling-proposition and brand-image strategies and indicate the specific conditions under which each is more likely to be used.

4. Positioning strategy is not mutually exclusive of other creative advertising strategies. Explain what this means and discuss how positioning can be achieved using different types of creative strategies. Provide examples of actual advertisements to buttress your points.

5. What is a resonant advertising strategy? Explain the similarity between resonant advertising and what some advertising practitioners call *slice of life* advertising.

6. A television commercial for Miller Draft beer started out by showing scenes of people experiencing a stifling summer day while fantasizing about a cold beer. In a subsequent scene, Miller Draft came into the picture and as people opened cans of beer, the urban setting miraculously changed from a hot summer day to snow-covered streets. Describe how this television commercial represents a form of preemptive strategy.

7. Explain the preceding commercial in terms of means-end chain components (attributes, consequences, and values).

8. Some critics contend that advocacy, or issue, advertising should not be treated as a legitimate tax-deduction expenditure. Present and justify your opinion on this matter.

9. Select two advertising campaigns that have been on television for some time and describe in detail what you think their creative message strategies are.

10. Review magazine advertisements and locate specific examples of the seven creative strategies that were discussed in the chapter. Be sure to justify why each ad is a good illustration of the strategy with which you identify it.

11. Along the lines of the Beef Industry Council case described in the chapter, select an advertising campaign and reconstruct in detail your interpretation of all the steps in the campaign's advertising strategy.

CHAPTER TWELVE

Message Appeals and Endorsers in Advertising

THE PROS AND CONS OF USING CELEBRITY ENDORSERS

Celebrities—chosen primarily from the entertainment business or the athletic field—are mainstays of North American advertising. This is understandable since consumers readily identify with these stars, often regarding them as heroes and heroines for their accomplishments, personalities, and physical appeal.

Advertisers fondly employ celebrities, because their famous attributes—including beauty, courage, talent, athleticism, grace, power, and sex appeal—often represent the appeals desired for the brands they endorse. The repeated association of a brand with a celebrity may ultimately lead consumers to think the brand possesses the same attractive qualities as that celebrity. More generally, consumers may like a brand merely because they like the celebrity who endorses it. Regardless of the specific mechanism by which celebrities enhance the value of brands, the undeniable fact is that they are often worth the millions of dollars advertisers pay for their services.

There is, nevertheless, a distinct downside to using celebrity endorsers. Suppose a celebrity is convicted of a crime or has his or her image blemished in some way during the course of an advertising campaign. What are the potential negative implications for the endorsed brand? Frankly, there are no simple answers to this provocative question, and researchers are just beginning to explore the issue in a sophisticated fashion.

In the meantime, many advertisers and advertising agencies are becoming reluctant to use celebrity endorsers. Their concern is not without justification. Consider some of the celebrity-related incidents making news in the early 1990s:

■ Michael Jordan was accused of paying off large gambling debts to persons of questionable moral stature.

■ Mike Tyson—an active endorser before a series of mishaps—was convicted on a rape charge.

■ Bo Jackson's dual athletic career was terminated (probably along with his lucrative endorsement career) by a serious hip injury.

■ Magic Johnson became HIV positive.

■ Kristi Yamaguchi, who achieved her celebrity by winning a gold medal in the 1992 Winter Olympics, probably will receive fewer endorsement opportunities than the last American to win gold in figure skating (Dorothy Hamill), because Yamaguchi won her medal at the unfortunate time when Japan bashing was prevalent in the United States.

This chapter examines the use of endorsers in advertising. It also discusses six other types of advertising messages that are used to influence consumers attitudes and actions: (1) fear appeals, (2) humor, (3) music, (4) sex appeals, (5) subliminal messages, and (6) comparative ads.

Where possible, an attempt is made to identify some *generalizations* about advertising messages. It is important to realize, however, that generalizations are not the same as scientific laws or principles. These higher forms of scientific truth (such as Einstein's general theory of relativity and Newton's law of gravitation) have not been established in the realm of advertising. Two reasons explain why. First, the buyer behavior that advertising is designed to influence is complex and dynamic; consequently, it is difficult to arrive at straightforward explanations of how communication elements operate in all situations and across all types of market segments. Second, because the scientific knowledge of advertising is based on research that necessarily has been conducted under somewhat artificial conditions (e.g., laboratory experiments with college students), it is impossible to draw clear-cut inferences to applied marketing settings.

Thus, the findings presented and the conclusions drawn should be considered tentative rather than definitive. It is well we heed the philosopher's advice: "Seek simplicity and distrust it."[1] In other words, there are no simple answers to say that a particular advertising technique will be universally effective under all circumstances. Rather, the effectiveness of any technique depends on specific

---

[1]Abraham Kaplan, *The Conduct of Inquiry: Methodology for Behavioral Science* (New York: Intext Educational Publishers, Chandler Publishing Co., 1964).

circumstances such as the nature of the competition and the extent of consumer involvement.

ENDORSERS

The products in many advertisements receive explicit endorsements from a wide variety of popular public figures. In addition to celebrity endorsements, products also receive the explicit or tacit support of noncelebrities. (This latter form of typical-person endorsement will be discussed in a separate section following the presentation of celebrity endorsers.)

Celebrity Endorsers

Television stars, movie actors, and famous athletes are widely used in magazine ads and television commercials to endorse products. By definition, a celebrity is a personality (actor, entertainer, or athlete) who is known to the public for his or her accomplishments in areas other than the product class endorsed.[2] Celebrities are in great demand as product spokespersons. In fact, it is estimated that one-third of all television commercials use endorsements, most often involving entertainment or athletic celebrities.[3] The most popular entertainer and athlete endorsers in TV commercials for one year, 1991, are shown in the *Focus on Promotion.*

Advertisers and their agencies are willing to pay huge salaries to those celebrities who are liked and respected by target audiences and who will, it is hoped, favorably influence consumers' attitudes and behavior toward the endorsed products. This is probably justified in view of research, showing that consumers' attitudes and perceptions of quality are enhanced when celebrities endorse products.[4] The vignette at the beginning of this chapter shows that celebrities such as those presented in the *Focus on Promotion* can have tremendous influence on product sales.

Top celebrities receive enormous payments for their endorsement services. Some top celebrity fees average $2 million to $3 million a year for the

[2]Hershey Friedman and Linda Friedman, "Endorser Effectiveness by Product Type," *Journal of Advertising Research*, 19 (October/November 1979), 63–71.

[3]H. M. Spielman, "Pick Product Presenter Prudently," *Marketing News*, September 8, 1987, 5.

[4]See, for example, R. B. Fireworker and H. H. Friedman, "The Effects of Endorsements on Product Evaluation," *Decision Sciences*, 8 (July 1977), 576–583; and H. H. Friedman, Salvatore Termini, and R. Washington, "The Effectiveness of Advertisements Utilizing Four Types of Endorsers," *Journal of Advertising*, 5 (Summer 1976), 22–24.

FOCUS ON PROMOTION

MOST POPULAR ENDORSERS IN TV COMMERCIALS, 1991

Video Storyboard Tests, Inc., is a New York research company that tests the effectiveness of television commercials. Among the various forms of research performed by this company is an annual survey of consumers' attitudes toward celebrities. The results from the 1991 survey are presented here broken out by entertainers and athletes. The 10 most popular celebrities in each category are listed along with some of the products they endorsed at the time of the survey.

ENTERTAINERS	ENDORSEMENTS
1. Bill Cosby	Jell-O, Kodak Colorwatch
2. Ray Charles	Diet Pepsi
3. Paula Abdul	Diet Coke
4. Candice Bergen	Sprint
5. Linda Evans	Clairol, LensCrafters
6. Ed McMahon	American Family Publishers
7. Angela Lansbury	Bufferin
8. Kathie Lee Gifford	Carnival Cruise Lines, Ultra SlimFast
9. Hammer	Pepsi, British Knights
10. Lynn Redgrave	Weight Watchers

ATHLETES	ENDORSEMENTS
1. Michael Jordan	Nike, McDonald's, Hanes, Wheaties
2. Bo Jackson	Nike
3. Tommy Lasorda	Ultra SlimFast
4. Magic Johnson	Converse, Pepsi, KFC
5. Joe Namath	Flex-All, The Wiz
6. Bob Uecker	Miller Lite
7. Joe Montana	Diet Pepsi
8. Nolan Ryan	Advil
9. Hulk Hogan	Right Guard
10. Arnold Palmer	Jiffy Lube, Hertz, Sears

Source: Joanne Lipman, "Celebrity Pitchmen Are Popular Again," *The Wall Street Journal,* September 4, 1991, sec. B, 5.

endorsement of a single product.[5] For example, Michael Jordan entered into 10-year contract with Gatorade that will pay him $18 million.[6] In fact, Jordan is estimated to earn $11 million to $15 million yearly in endorsement fees in deals with a broad range of local and national advertisers.[7]

What makes a celebrity an effective endorser for a particular product? Basically, there has to be a *meaningful relationship*, or match-up, between the celebrity and the product.[8] Wilford Brimley, star of the television series *Our House*, is a perfect endorser for Quaker Oatmeal cereal, a wholesome product endorsed by a man associated with healthy, happy people. Victoria Principal, of beautiful-flowing-hair fame, is ideal for promoting Jhirmack's Lite shampoo. Dr. J (Julius Erving), the famous basketball player, is a great individual to promote Dr. Scholl's Tritin foot spray. Jimmy Connors is perfect for Nuprin; Bo Jackson was ideal for Nike Cross-Trainer shoes; and Nolan Ryan is a good representative for Advil pain reliever (see Figure 12.1). Can you think of endorsements where the fit between celebrity and brand is inappropriate? Why, in your opinion, is the match-up poor?

Typical-Person Endorsers

A frequent advertising approach is to show regular people using or endorsing products. An illustration is presented in Figure 12.2, a magazine ad for Timex watches. (See Lisa Boyer's fascinating story in the lower-left corner of the ad.) This advertisement is one of many executions in a campaign by Timex using the services of interesting people, albeit noncelebrities, to endorse various models of Timex watches.

Testimonial advertising is widespread. For example, physicians are shown dressed in lab coats to promote one cold capsule over other brands. Audi of America, following negative publicity about problems with automatic transmissions in its model 5000 sedans, used dozens of owner testimonials (as well as celebrity endorsements) in an attempt to stop falling sales.

Many advertisements that portray typical-person users often include multiple people rather than a single individual. Is there any reason why multiple sources should be more effective than a single source? Yes there is: The act of portraying more than one person increases the likelihood an advertisement will generate higher levels of message involvement and correspondingly greater

[5]"Star Turns That Can Turn Star-Crossed," *U.S. News & World Report*, December 7, 1987, 57.

[6]Matthew Grimm, "Gatorade Tries to Steal Jordan from Coke," *Adweek's Marketing Week*, June 24, 1991, 5.

[7]Julie Liesse, "Jordan Jumping for Gatorade," *Advertising Age*, July 15, 1991, 2.

[8]For further reading on the importance of match-up, see Michael A. Kamins, "An Investigation into the 'Match-Up' Hypothesis in Celebrity Advertising: When Beauty May Be Only Skin Deep," *Journal of Advertising*, 19, 1 (1990), 4–13.

FIGURE 12.1   A Celebrity Endorsement

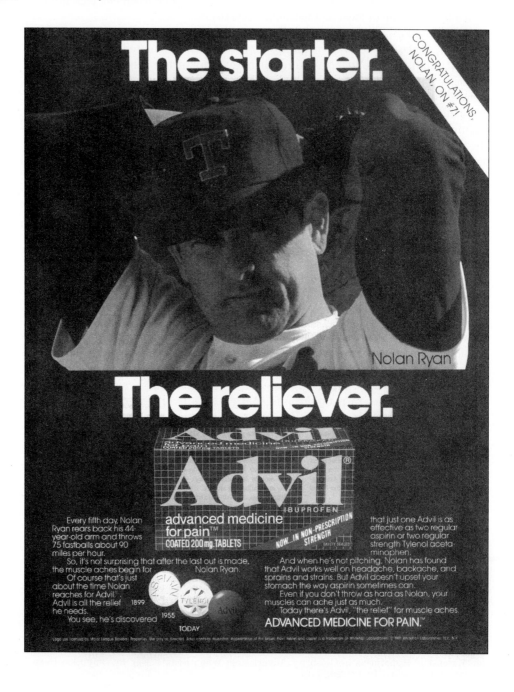

A Typical-Person Endorsement   FIGURE 12.2

Lisa Boyer survived a 12,500-foot free fall while skydiving after her chutes malfunctioned. Luckily, she landed in a four-foot-deep sludge pond at a sewage treatment plant. She hit at more than 80-miles-per-hour and "swam" to safety. Lisa is wearing our water-resistant women's Triathlon watch. It costs about $35.

TIMEX

For the retailer nearest you call 1-800-367-8463.

message *elaboration* (recall the discussion on involvement and elaboration in the context of the Elaboration Likelihood Model in Chapter 4). In turn, greater elaboration increases the odds that strong message arguments will favorably influence attitudes.

This line of reasoning was tested in an experiment that manipulated (1) one versus four person-in-the-street endorsers for a new pizza chain advertisement, and (2) strong versus weak arguments favoring eating this chain's pizza. As theorized, the four-person advertisement was found to be more effective (as measured by cognitive responses and attitude measures) than the single source when message arguments were strong. On the other hand, the single source was superior when weak arguments were offered. The practical implication for advertisers is that increasing the number of endorsers will not necessarily increase persuasive impact; the message arguments themselves must also be impactual.[9]

Endorser Attributes

Now that a distinction has been made between the two general types of advertising endorsers, endorser attributes and the role they play in facilitating effectiveness must be explained. Extensive research has demonstrated that two basic attributes contribute to an endorser's effectiveness: (1) attractiveness and (2) credibility. Each involves a different mechanism by which the endorser affects consumer attitudes and behavior.[10]

ATTRACTIVENESS: THE PROCESS OF IDENTIFICATION. **Attractiveness** does *not* mean simply physical attractiveness but includes any number of virtuous characteristics that receivers may perceive in an endorser: intellectual skills, personality properties, lifestyle characteristics, athletic prowess, and so on. The general concept of attractiveness consists of three related ideas: *similarity, familiarity,* and *liking.*[11] That is, an endorser is considered attractive to receivers if they share a sense of similarity or familiarity with him or her or if they simply like the endorser regardless of whether the two are similar in any respect.

When receivers find something in an endorser that they consider attractive, persuasion occurs via an **identification process.** That is, when receivers perceive a source to be attractive, they *identify with* the endorser and are very likely to adopt the attitudes, behaviors, interests, or preferences of the source.

---

[9]David J. Moore and Richard Reardon, "Source Magnification: The Role of Multiple Sources in the Processing of Advertising Appeals," *Journal of Marketing Research*, 24 (November 1987), 412–417.

[10]It is important to note that although the present discussion is framed in terms of endorser characteristics, more general treatment of the topic refers to *source* characteristics. For a classic treatment of the subject, see Herbert C. Kelman, "Processes of Opinion Change," *Public Opinion Quarterly*, 25 (Spring 1961), 57–78. For a more current treatment, see Daniel J. O'Keefe, *Persuasion Theory and Research* (Newbury Park, CA: Sage, 1990), chap. 8.

[11]H. C. Triandis, *Attitudes and Attitude Change* (New York: John Wiley & Sons, 1971).

Advertising researchers have not studied attractiveness extensively and what little research has been conducted has focused only on the physical-attractiveness dimension.[12] Research has supported the rather intuitive expectation that physically attractive endorsers produce more favorable evaluations of ads and advertised products than do less attractive communicators.[13] However, empirical evidence suggests that attractive endorsers are more effective only when the endorser's *image is compatible with the nature of the endorsed product.*

In other words, an attractive endorser does not necessarily benefit a product if there is a poor *match-up* between the endorser and the product. One experiment tested this possibility by comparing the effectiveness of actors Tom Selleck and Telly Savalas for two products: an attractiveness-related product (luxury automobile) and an attractiveness-unrelated product (home computer). As predicted by the *match-up hypothesis*, when Tom Selleck endorsed the luxury automobile, subjects' attitudes toward the advertisement were significantly more favorable than when Telly Savalas endorsed the same car. However, no significant difference between these two endorsers was detected for the attractiveness-unrelated home computer product.[14]

CREDIBILITY: THE PROCESS OF INTERNALIZATION.   In its most basic sense, **credibility** refers to the tendency to believe or trust someone. When an information source, such as an endorser, is perceived as credible, the source can change attitudes through a psychological process called internalization. **Internalization** occurs when the receiver accepts the endorser's position on an issue as his or her own. An internalized attitude tends to be maintained even if the source of the message is forgotten or if the source switches to a different position.[15]

Two important properties of endorser credibility are *expertise* and *trustworthiness*. **Expertise** refers to the knowledge, experience, or skills possessed by an endorser as they relate to the communications topic. Hence, athletes are expert when it comes to the endorsement of sports-related products. Expertise is a *perceived* rather than absolute phenomenon. Whether an endorser is indeed an expert is unimportant; all that matters is how he or she is perceived by the target audience. An endorser perceived by an audience as an expert on a given subject is more persuasive in changing audience opinions pertaining to his or her

---

[12]For information about how to measure attractiveness, see Roobina Ohanian, "Construction and Validation of a Scale to Measure Celebrity Endorsers' Perceived Expertise, Trustworthiness, and Attractiveness," *Journal of Advertising,* 19, 3 (1990), 39–52.

[13]W. Benoy Joseph, "The Credibility of Physically Attractive Communicators: A Review," *Journal of Advertising,* 11, 3 (1982), 15–24; Lynn R. Kahle and Pamela M. Homer, "Physical Attractiveness of the Celebrity Endorser: A Social Adaptation Perspective," *Journal of Consumer Research,* 11 (March 1985), 954–961.

[14]Kamins, "An Investigation into the `Match-Up' Hypothesis in Celebrity Advertising: When Beauty May be Only Skin Deep."

[15]Richard E. Petty, Thomas M. Ostrom, and Timothy C. Brock, eds., *Cognitive Responses in Persuasion* (Hillsdale, NJ: Lawrence Erlbaum Associates, 1981), 143.

area of expertise than an endorser who is not perceived as possessing the same characteristic. This no doubt explains the extensive use of athletes to endorse sports-related products.

Trustworthiness refers to the honesty, integrity, and believability of a source. While expertise and trustworthiness are not mutually exclusive, often a particular endorser is perceived as highly trustworthy but not particularly expert. An endorser's trustworthiness depends primarily on the audience's perception of his or her endorsement motivations. If the audience believes that an endorser is motivated purely by self-serving motives, he or she will be less persuasive than someone the audience perceives as having nothing to gain or as completely objective.

Advertisers capitalize on the value of trustworthiness by selecting endorsers who are widely regarded as being honest, believable, and dependable people. This probably explains why celebrities such as Candice Bergen, Bill Cosby, Bob Hope, Michael Jordan, and Angela Lansbury are successful endorsers. They simply appear to be individuals who can be trusted.

Advertisers also use the *overheard conversation* technique to enhance trustworthiness. A television advertisement might show a middle-aged person overhearing one man explain to another why his brand of arthritis pain-relief medicine is the best on the market. In this case, the commercial attempts to have audience members place themselves in the position of the person overhearing the conversation. The investment firm E. F. Hutton perfected this technique in a continuing series of ads with the tag line, "When E. F. Hutton talks, people listen."

An experiment tested whether a *hidden-camera endorser* (one who is presumably extolling the virtues of a product without being aware of it) is more persuasive than a typical-person endorser (one who is aware of his or her spokesperson role). The researchers hypothesized that the hidden-camera endorser should be considered more trustworthy because he or she makes favorable product claims but does not come across as having ulterior motives. The hidden-camera spokesperson was, in fact, shown to be more trustworthy.[16]

In general, endorsers must establish that they are not attempting to manipulate the audience and that they are objective in their presentations. By doing so, they establish themselves as trustworthy and, therefore, credible.

FEAR APPEALS

As noted earlier in the chapter, advertisers use a variety of specific appeals to influence consumer behavior, one of which is the negative appeal to people's

[16]James M. Hunt, Theresa J. Domzal, and Jerome B. Kernan, "Causal Attributions and Persuasion: The Case of Disconfirmed Expectancies," in *Advances in Consumer Research*, 9, ed. A. Mitchell (Pittsburgh: Association for Consumer Research, 1982), 287–292.

fears. Advertisers, in attempting to motivate customers to action, sometimes invoke fear appeals by identifying either (1) the negative consequences of *not using the advertised product* or (2) the negative consequences of *engaging in unsafe behavior* (e.g., drinking and driving).

The underlying logic when using fear appeals is that fear will stimulate audience involvement with a message and thereby promote acceptance of message arguments. The appeals may take the form of *social disapproval* or *physical danger*. For example, mouthwashes, deodorants, toothpastes, and other products use fear appeals when emphasizing the social disapproval we may suffer if our breath is not fresh, our underarms are not dry, or our teeth are not cavity free. Smoke detectors, automobile tires (see Figure 12.3), unsafe sex, and driving under the influence of alcohol and other drugs are products and themes that advertisers use to induce fear of physical danger.

Aside from the basic ethical issue of whether fear should be used at all, the fundamental issue for advertisers is determining *how intense* the fear presentation should be. In short, should the advertiser employ a slight amount of threat merely to get the consumer's attention, or should a heavy dose of fear appeal be used so the consumer cannot possibly miss the point the advertiser wishes to make? Numerous fear-appeal studies have been performed by psychologists and marketing researchers, but the fact remains that there still is no consensus on the optimum level of fear. Some studies have reported that a low level of fear is most effective,[17] whereas other researchers contend that a moderate fear level is more effective than levels of fear that are either too low or too high.[18]

In an attempt to reconcile the apparently contradictory findings, two marketing researchers arrived at the conclusion that differences in research findings are probably attributable to the different definitions of high, moderate, and low fear appeals employed in different studies. These researchers summarized the early fear-appeal literature by concluding:

> Neither extremely strong nor very weak fear appeals are maximally effective. It seems that appeals at a somewhat moderate level of fear are best. A simple explanation for this might be that if an appeal is too weak, it just does not attract enough attention. If it is too strong, on the other hand, it may lead people to avoid the message or ignore the message's recommendations as being inadequate to the task of eliminating the feared event.[19]

---

[17]The classic demonstration is a study on dental hygiene practices. See I. Janis and S. Feshbach, "Effects of Fear-Arousing Communications," *Journal of Abnormal and Social Psychology*, 48 (January 1953), 78–92.

[18]Michael L. Ray and William L. Wilkie, "Fear: The Potential of an Appeal Neglected by Marketing," *Journal of Marketing*, 34 (January 1970), 54–62.

[19]Ibid., 55.

FIGURE 12.3   A Fear Appeal

A LOT OF TIRES COST LESS THAN A MICHELIN. THAT'S BECAUSE THEY SHOULD.

To everyone out there looking to save a few dollars on a set of tires, let's not mince words. You buy cheap, you get cheap.

There may be a lot of tires out there that cost less than a Michelin. The only question is, what do you have to give up if you buy one?

Do they handle like a Michelin?

Do they last like a Michelin?

Are they as reliable as a Michelin?

Then ask yourself this: Do you really want to find out?

At Michelin, we make only one kind of tire.

The very best we know how.

Because the way we see it, the last place a compromise belongs is on your car.

As a matter of fact, we're so obsessed with quality we make the steel cables that go into our steel-belted radials. We even make many of the machines that make and test Michelin tires.

And our quality control checks are so exhaustive that they even include x-rays.

These and hundreds of other details, big and small (details that may seem inconsequential to others), make sure that when you put a set of Michelin

tires on your car, you get all the mileage Michelin is famous for.

True, there may be cheaper tires. But if they don't last like a Michelin, are they really less expensive?

So the next time someone tries to save you a few dollars on a tire, tell him this: It's not how much you pay that counts. It's what you get for your money.

And then *he'll* know that *you* know that there's only one reason a tire costs less than a Michelin.

It deserves to.

MICHELIN®
BECAUSE SO MUCH IS
RIDING ON YOUR TIRES.®

This conclusion has been termed the *inverted-U explanation;* unfortunately, it has *not* stood up under scrutiny.[20] An alternative, *degree-of-relevance explanation* holds that the optimum level of fear depends on how much relevance a topic has for an audience—the greater the relevance, the lower the optimal level of fear. In other words, people who are highly involved in a topic can be motivated by a relatively small amount of fear, whereas a more intense level of fear is required to motivate uninvolved people.[21]

To illustrate the relation between fear intensity and issue relevance, let us compare a low-fear campaign for Michelin tires with the much more intense fear-appeal ads in anti-drinking and driving campaigns. As you may recall, the long-standing Michelin campaign contains a series of television commercials that show adorable babies sitting on or surrounded by tires. These commercials are subtle reminders (low levels of fear) for parents to consider buying Michelin tires to ensure their children's safety. A low-level of fear is all that is needed in this situation, because safety for their children is perhaps the most relevant concern for most parents.

Consider by comparison the level of fear needed to reach high school students and other young people who are the targets of anti-drinking and driving public service announcements (PSAs). The last thing many young people want to hear is what they should or should not be doing. Hence, although safety is relevant to most everyone, it is less relevant to young people who consider themselves invulnerable. Consequently, very intense fear-appeal PSAs are needed to impress upon high schoolers the risk they place themselves and their friends in when drinking and driving.[22]

HUMOR

Politicians, actors and actresses, after-dinner speakers, professors, and indeed all of us at one time or another use humor to create a desired reaction. Advertisers also turn to humor in the hopes of achieving various communication objectives— to gain attention, guide consumer comprehension of product claims, influence

---

[20]For further discussion, see Herbert J. Rotfeld, "Fear Appeals and Persuasion: Assumptions and Errors in Advertising Research," *Current Issues and Research in Advertising*, 11, eds., J. H. Leigh and C. R. Martin, Jr. (Ann Arbor, MI: Graduate School of Business Administration, 1988), 21–39.

[21]Peter Wright, "Concrete Action Plans in TV Messages to Increase Reading of Drug Warnings," *Journal of Consumer Research*, 6 (December 1979), 256–269.

[22]For further reading on the use of fear appeals in anti-drinking and driving campaigns, see Karen Whitehill King and Leonard N. Reid, "Fear Arousing Anti-Drinking and Driving PSAs: Do Physical Injury Threats Influence Young Adults?" *Current Issues and Research in Advertising*, 12, eds. J. H. Leigh and C. R. Martin, Jr. (Ann Arbor, MI: Graduate School of Business Administration, 1990), 155–175.

attitudes, enhance recallability of advertised claims, and, ultimately, to create customer action. The use of humor in advertising is extensive, representing approximately 25 percent of all television advertising in the United States and over 35 percent in the United Kingdom.[23]

Whether humor is effective and what kinds of humor are most successful are matters of some debate among advertising practitioners and scholars.[24] A survey of advertising agency executives determined that these practitioners consider the use of humor to be effective for gaining attention and achieving brand awareness, but that humor may harm comprehension and recall.[25] However, when used correctly and in the right circumstances, humor can be an extremely effective advertising technique. The famous "Where's the beef?" campaign for Wendy's hamburgers led to a phenomenal 15 percent increase in sales shortly after the ad was aired.[26] The subtle humor of Tom Bodett in radio ads for Motel 6 has undoubtedly had an impressive impact on that hotel chain's revenue. A survey of college students determined that they liked the humor in Energizer battery's pink-bunny campaign and, in fact, ranked it as their overall favorite TV commercial.[27] You no doubt can think of many other advertising campaigns that achieved their effectiveness through the creative and appropriate use of humor.

Despite the frequent use of humor in advertising, relatively little is known in a definitive scientific sense about its effects on consumer behavior. In fact, humor in advertising has been studied seriously for less than two decades.

Because humorous appeals seem to inhibit comprehension but enhancing message attention and brand awareness, it has been suggested that humor in advertising should be used only in situations in which the audience is familiar with the product—not in situations where the product is substantially new or when there are a large number of facts for consumers to understand.[28]

Furthermore, humorous appeals are not equally effective for all. Using data on magazine readership patterns from the Starch magazine readership database (see Chapter 14 for details about Starch data), researchers determined that men had higher attention scores than women for humorous ads and that magazines with predominantly white audiences had higher attention scores for humorous

[23]Marc Weinberger and Harlan Spotts, "Humor in U.S. Versus U.K. TV Advertising," *Journal of Advertising*, 18, 2 (1989), 39–44.

[24]A thorough review of the issues is provided by Paul Surgi Speck, "The Humorous Message Taxonomy: A Framework for the Study of Humorous Ads," *Current Issues and Research in Advertising*, 13, eds. J. H. Leigh and C. R. Martin, Jr. (Ann Arbor, MI: Graduate School of Business Administration, 1991), 1–44.

[25]Thomas J. Madden and Marc G. Weinberger, "Humor in Advertising: A Practitioner View," *Journal of Advertising Research*, 24, 4 (1984), 23–29.

[26]"Prime Ribbing," *Time*, March 26, 1984, 54.

[27]Janice Steinberg, "Be Sure to Leave 'Em Laughing," *Advertising Age*, February 5, 1990, sec. S, 2.

[28]Brian Sternthal and C. Samuel Craig, *Consumer Behavior: An Information Processing Perspective* (Englewood Cliffs, NJ: Prentice-Hall, 1982), 272.

ads than did those with predominantly black readers.[29] This finding obviously should not be interpreted as meaning that blacks and women lack a sense of humor; rather, what it likely reflects is a bias in advertising that caters more to the special interests of white males over females or minority audiences.

In addition to demographic differences in responsiveness to humor, research evidence also shows that humorous ads are more effective than nonhumorous ads *only when consumers' evaluations of the advertised brand are already positive.* When prior evaluations are negative toward the advertised brand, humorous ads are shown to be less effective than nonhumorous ads.[30] This finding has a counterpart in interpersonal relations: When you like someone, you are more likely to consider his or her attempt at humor to be funny than if you do not like that person.

In sum, humor in advertising can be an extremely effective device for accomplishing a variety of marketing communications objectives. Nonetheless, several findings suggest that advertisers should proceed cautiously when contemplating the use of humor. First, the effects of humor can differ due to differences in audience characteristics; what strikes some people as humorous is not at all funny to others. Second, the definition of what is funny in one country or region of a country is not necessarily the same in another country or region. Finally, a humorous message may be so distracting to an audience that receivers ignore the message content. Advertisers should carefully research their intended market segments before venturing into humorous advertising.

MUSIC

Paula Abdul, Ray Charles, and Hammer are just some of the musicians whose music is used to *move* merchandise. In addition to these well-known celebrities, nonvocal musical accompaniment and unknown vocalists are used extensively in promoting everything from fabric softeners to automobiles.[31]

Many advertising practitioners and scholars think that music performs a variety of useful communication functions. These include *attracting attention,*

---

[29]Thomas J. Madden and Marc G. Weinberger, "The Effects of Humor on Attention in Magazine Advertising," *Journal of Advertising*, 11, 3 (1982), 4–14.

[30]Amitava Chattopadhyay and Kunal Basu, "Humor in Advertising: The Moderating Role of Prior Brand Evaluation," *Journal of Consumer Research*, 27 (November 1990), 466–476.

[31]Julie Candler, "Music Takes a Front Seat in Auto Campaigns," *Advertising Age*, May 5, 1986, sec. S, 32; Christine Demkowych, "Music on the Upswing in Advertising," *Advertising Age*, March 31, 1986, S5; Merle Kingman, "Music Is the Magic for Most of the Best," *Advertising Age*, March 14, 1988, 26.

putting consumers in a *positive mood*, making them more *receptive to message arguments*, and even *communicating meanings* about advertised products.[32]

Although music's role in marketing is an incredibly understudied subject, a few recent experiments have begun to demonstrate the roles that music performs. In one study using classical conditioning procedures, music represented the unconditioned stimulus in an effort to influence experimental subjects' preference for a ballpoint pen, which represented the conditioned stimulus.[33] An *unconditioned stimulus* (US) is one that evokes pleasant feelings or thoughts in people. A *conditioned stimulus* (CS) is one that is emotionally or cognitively neutral prior to the onset of a conditioning experiment. In simple terms, classical conditioning is achieved when the pairing of US and CS results in a transfer of feeling from the US (music in the present case) to the CS (the ballpoint pen).

Experimental subjects in this study were informed that an advertising agency was trying to select music for use in a commercial for a ballpoint pen. Subjects then listened to music while they viewed slides of the pen. The positive US for half the subjects was music from the movie *Grease*, and the negative US for the remaining subjects was classical Asian Indian music. The simple association between music and the pen influenced product preference—nearly 80 percent of the subjects exposed to the *Grease* music chose the advertised pen, whereas only 30 percent of the subjects exposed to the Indian music chose the advertised pen.[34]

Although falling outside of an advertising context, two additional studies of music are noteworthy in that they provide dramatic evidence regarding the potential impact music can have on consumers' buying behavior. A first experiment examined the effects of *background music* in a supermarket setting. A supermarket chain was studied over a nine-week period by comparing sales volume during days when slow-tempo background music was played (72 beats per minute or slower) versus days when fast-tempo music was in the background (94 beats per minute or more). The researcher found that daily sales volume averaged approximately $16,740 on days when slow-tempo music was played but only about $12,113 when fast-tempo music was played—for an average increase of $4,627 per day, or a *38.2 percent increase!* The slow-tempo music apparently *slowed the pace* at which customers moved through the store and increased their total expenditures since they had a longer opportunity to purchase more.[35]

---

[32]Very good reviews of music's various advertising functions are available in Gordon C. Bruner II, "Music, Mood, and Marketing," *Journal of Marketing*, 54 (October 1990), 94–104; Linda M. Scott, "Understanding Jingles and Needledrop: A Rhetorical Approach to Music in Advertising," *Journal of Consumer Research*, 17 (September 1990), 223–236.

[33]Gerald J. Gorn, "The Effects of Music in Advertising on Choice Behavior: A Classical Conditioning Approach," *Journal of Marketing*, 46 (Winter 1982), 94–101.

[34]A replication of this study failed to obtain supporting evidence, thereby calling into question the ability to generalize from Gorn's prior research. See James J. Kellaris and Anthony D. Cox, "The Effects of Background Music in Advertising," *Journal of Consumer Research*, 16 (June 1989), 113–118.

[35]Ronald E. Milliman, "Using Background Music to Affect the Behavior of Supermarket Shoppers," *Journal of Marketing*, 46 (Summer 1982), 86–91.

In a second field experiment, the same researcher examined the effects of background music on restaurant customers' purchase behavior. A restaurant alternated playing slow- and fast-tempo music on Friday and Saturday nights over a one-month period. Slow music increased the amount of time customers remained seated at their tables—an average of 56 minutes per customer group during slow-music nights compared to an average of 45 minutes during fast-music nights. Also, customers during slow-music nights spent significantly larger amounts on alcoholic beverages (an average of $30.47 per customer group) compared to fast-music nights ($21.62 per customer group).[36]

In the final analysis, music appears to be effective in creating customer moods and stimulating buying preferences and choices. Of course, considerably more research is needed to fully understand the scientific role of music in accomplishing different marketing communications functions. Marketplace wisdom, as manifested by marketing communicators' nearly universal use of music in advertisements and in retail settings, clearly suggests that music is an effective form of nonverbal communication.

SEX APPEALS

Sex appeals in advertising are used frequently and with increasing explicitness. Whereas the use of such explicit sex was unthinkable just a few years ago, it now represents a current trend.[37] The trend is not restricted to the United States; indeed, sexual explicitness is more prevalent and more overt elsewhere, for example, in Brazil and Western Europe.

Whether such advertising is effective and under what conditions it may be effective remain largely unexplored issues.[38] Complicating the matter is the fact that sex in advertising actually takes two forms: *nudity* and *suggestiveness*. It is uncertain which form is more effective.[39]

---

[36]Ronald E. Milliman, "The Influence of Background Music on the Behavior of Restaurant Patrons," *Journal of Consumer Research*, 13 (September 1986), pp. 286–289.

[37]A content analysis of magazine advertising for the years 1964 and 1984 indicates that the percentage of ads with sexual content has not changed. What has changed, however, is that sexual illustrations have become more overt. Female models are more likely than male models to be portrayed in nude, partially nude, or suggestive poses. See Lawrence Soley and Gary Kurzbard, "Sex in Advertising: A Comparison of 1964 and 1984 Magazine Advertisements," *Journal of Advertising*, 15, 3 (1986), 46–54.

[38]For a review of the scientific issues involved in studying sex in advertising, see Robert S. Baron, "Sexual Content and Advertising Effectiveness: Comments on Belch et al. (1981) and Caccavale et al. (1981)" in *Advances in Consumer Research*, 9, ed. Andrew Mitchell (Ann Arbor, MI: Association for Consumer Research, 1982), 428–430.

[39]Michael A. Belch, Barbro E. Holgerson, George E. Belch, and Jerry Koppman, "Psychophysiological and Cognitive Responses to Sex in Advertising," in *Advances in Consumer Research*, 9, ed. Andrew Mitchell (Ann Arbor, MI: Association for Consumer Research, 1982), 424–427.

What role does sex play in advertising? Actually, it has several potential roles. First, sexual material in advertising acts as an initial *attentional lure* while also retaining that attention for a longer period—often by featuring attractive models in pleasant surroundings.[40] This is called the *stopping power* role of sex.[41] There is little doubt that the magazine ad for h.i.s.® (Figure 12.4) will attract many readers' attention.

A second potential role is to *enhance recall* of message points. Research suggests, however, that sexual content or symbolism will enhance recall only if it is *appropriate to the product category and the creative advertising execution.*[42] Sexual appeals produce significantly better recall when the advertising execution has an appropriate relationship with the advertised product.[43] A sexual advertising theme for a product such as RED For Men cologne (see Figure 12.5) reflects an appropriate sex appeal in view of the nature of both the product and target market. Comparatively, the use of sex in ads for industrial equipment, a frequent practice in past years, would likely be inappropriate and result in diminished recall of copy points.

A third role performed by sexual content in advertising is to *evoke emotional responses* such as feelings of arousal or even lust.[44] These reactions can increase an ad's persuasive impact, with the opposite occurring if the ad elicits negative feelings such as disgust, embarrassment, or uneasiness.[45]

Whether sexual content elicits a positive reaction or a negative one depends on the *appropriateness or relevance* of the sexual content to the advertised subject matter. An interesting marketing experiment tested this by varying magazine ads for two products, a ratchet wrench set (a product for which a sexual appeal is irrelevant) and a body oil (a relevant sex-appeal product). The study also manipulated three versions of dress for the female model who appeared in the ads: in the demure model version, she was shown fully clothed in a blouse and slacks; in the seductive model version, she wore the same clothing as in the demure version, but the blouse was completely unbuttoned and knotted at the bottom, exposing some midriff and cleavage; in the nude model version, she was completely undressed. Study findings revealed that the seductive model/body oil combination was perceived most favorably by all respondents, whereas the nude

---

[40]Baron, "Sexual Content and Advertising Effectiveness," 428.

[41]B. G. Yovovich, "Sex in Advertising—The Power and the Perils," *Advertising Age*, May 2, 1983, sec. M, 4.

[42]Larry Percy, "A Review of the Effect of Specific Advertising Elements upon Overall Communication Response," in *Current Issues and Research in Advertising*, 2, eds. J. H. Leigh and C. R. Martin, Jr. (Ann Arbor, MI: Graduate School of Business Administration, 1983), 95.

[43]David Richmond and Timothy P. Hartman, "Sex Appeal in Advertising," *Journal of Advertising Research*, 22 (October–November 1982), 53–61.

[44]Michael S. LaTour, Robert E. Pitts, and David C. Snook-Luther, "Female Nudity, Arousal, and Ad Response: An Experimental Investigation," *Journal of Advertising*, 19, 4 (1990), 51–62.

[45]Baron, "Sexual Content and Advertising Effectiveness," 428.

Attention-Luring Use of Sex Appeal

FIGURE 12.5   Illustration of Appropriate Sex Appeal

model/body oil combination was perceived as the least appealing advertisement. Females regarded the nude model/ratchet set as least appealing.[46]

Similar results were obtained from focus-group research involving television commercials for Underalls pantyhose. One commercial focused on the derrieres of two women: one had a "terrific looking rump" (according to the research report) and the other had panty lines that looked awful. The woman with the panty lines tells viewers that "Underalls make you look like I wish I looked." Focus-group tests on this commercial revealed that respondents liked the commercial and did not find it offensive. Reactions were very unfavorable, however, to a second version of this commercial that differed from the first by using the tagline "Underalls make me look like I'm not wearing nothing." This ad was viewed as offensive because looking like one is wearing "nothing" is not regarded as a primary product benefit.[47]

The implication to be drawn from the previously cited research is that sexual content stands little chance of being effective unless it is directly relevant to an advertisement's primary selling point. When used appropriately, sexual content is capable of eliciting attention, enhancing recall, and creating a favorable association with the advertised product.

The Downside of Sex Appeals in Advertising

The presentation to this point has indicated that when used appropriately, sex appeals in advertising can be effective. The discussion would be incomplete, however, if we were not to mention potential hazards in using sex appeals. From the academic front there is evidence to suggest that the use of explicit sexual illustrations in advertisements may *interfere with consumers' processing of message arguments and reduce message comprehension.*[48] There also is considerable anecdotal evidence to suggest that many people are offended by advertisements that portray women as brainless sex objects.[49] For example, an outcry ensued in response to a 1991 advertisement for Old Milwaukee beer featuring the so-called "Swedish Bikini Team"—a boat full of beautiful Scandinavian-looking women wearing blue bikinis who appeared out of nowhere in front of a group of fishermen. Female employees of Stroh's Brewery Co., the makers of Old Milwaukee,

[46]Robert A. Peterson and Roger A. Kerin, "The Female Role in Advertisements: Some Experimental Evidence," *Journal of Marketing*, 41 (October 1977), 59–63.

[47]This research was performed by the research department of what used to be called the Needham, Harper, and Steers advertising agency and is described in B. G. Yovovich, "Sex in Advertising," sec. M, 5.

[48]Jessica Severn, George E. Belch, and Michael A. Belch, "The Effects of Sexual and Non-sexual Advertising Appeals and Information Level on Cognitive Processing and Communication Effectiveness," *Journal of Advertising*, 19, 1 (1990), 14–22.

[49]"Sex Still Sells—But So Does Sensitivity," *Business Week*, March 18, 1991, 100.

sued their employer claiming that the advertisement created an atmosphere conducive to sexual harassment in the workplace.[50] Regardless of the merits of this particular case, the general issue being addressed is that sex in advertising can be demeaning to females (and males), and, for this reason, should be used cautiously. The use of sex in advertising is a matter of concern to people and regulatory bodies throughout the world. For further discussion, see the *Global Focus*.

SUBLIMINAL MESSAGES AND SYMBOLIC EMBEDS

The word *subliminal* refers to the presentation of stimuli at a rate or level that is below the conscious threshold of awareness. An example would be playing self-help messages on audiotapes (e.g., to help one quit smoking) at a decibel level indecipherable to the naked ear. Stimuli that cannot be perceived by the conscious senses may nonetheless be perceived *subconsciously*. This possibility has generated considerable concern from advertising critics and has fostered much speculation from researchers.

Original outcry occurred in response to research by James Vicary in 1957, who claimed to have increased sales of Coca-Cola and popcorn in a New Jersey movie theatre by using subliminal messages. At five-second intervals during the movie *Picnic*, subliminal messages saying "Drink Coca-Cola" and "Eat Popcorn" appeared on the screen for a mere 1/3,000th of a second. Although the naked eye could not possibly have seen these messages, Vicary claimed that sales of Coca-Cola and popcorn increased 58 and 18 percent respectively.[51] Though Vicary's research is *scientifically meaningless* because he failed to use proper experimental procedures, the study nonetheless raised public concerns about subliminal advertising and led to Congressional hearings.[52] Federal legislation was never enacted, but since then subliminal advertising has been the subject of criticism by advertising critics, a matter of embarrassment for advertising practitioners, and an issue of theoretical curiosity to advertising scholars.[53]

---

[50]Ira Teinowitz and Bob Geiger, "Suits Try to Link Sex Harassment Ads," *Advertising Age*, November 18, 1991, 48.

[51]This description is adapted from Martin P. Block and Bruce G. Vanden Gergh, "Can You Sell Subliminal Messages to Consumers?" *Journal of Advertising*, 14, 3 (1985), 59.

[52]Vicary himself acknowledged that the study that initiated the original furor over subliminal advertising was based on too small an amount of data to be meaningful. See Fred Danzig, "Subliminal Advertising—Today It's Just Historic Flashback for Researcher Vicary," *Advertising Age*, September 17, 1962, 42, 74.

[53]For example, see Sharon E. Beatty and Del I. Hawkins, "Subliminal Stimulation: Some New Data and Interpretation," *Journal of Advertising*, 18, 3 (1989), 4–8.

The fires of controversy were fueled again in the early 1970s with the publication of three provocatively titled books: *Subliminal Seduction, Media Sexploitation,* and *The Clam Plate Orgy.*[54] The author of these books, Wilson Key, claimed subliminal advertising techniques are used extensively and have the power to influence consumers' choice behaviors.

Many advertising practitioners and marketing communications scholars discount Key's arguments and vehemently disagree with his conclusions. Part of the difficulty in arriving at clear answers as to who's right and who's wrong stems from the fact that commentators differ in what they mean by subliminal advertising. In fact, there are three distinct forms of subliminal stimulation: A first form presents *visual stimuli* at a very rapid rate by means of a device called a tachistoscope (say, at 1/3,000th of a second such as in Vicary's research). A second form uses *accelerated speech in auditory messages.* The third form involves the *embedding of hidden symbols* (such as a sexual images or words) in print advertisements.

This last form, *embedding,* is what Key has written about and is the form that advertising researchers have studied. However, it is important to remember that embeds (for example, the word SEX airbrushed into an advertisement) are not truly subliminal since they are visible to the naked eye. Nonetheless, the remaining discussion of subliminal messages is restricted to the practice of embedding. For a parody of the practice of embedding, see the ad for Absolut Vodka in Figure 12.6.

To better appreciate embedding, look at the advertisement for Edge shaving cream presented in Figure 12.7. One need not be a Freudian psychologist to realize that the ad contains considerable sexual innuendo. Aside from the symbolism associated with the water tunnel and the look of ecstasy on the man's face, note also that the volcanic-looking mountain below the man's lips is not really a mountain at all; rather, it is a nude woman resting on her back with her knees in a raised position. Notice also that above the man's upper lip are three nude figures that have been airbrushed into the lather (a male with extended arms on the right side of the man's face, a female directly below his nose, and another female to the left of his nose).

Is there proof that embedded symbols in advertisements do in fact influence consumers' product and brand choices? To answer this we first need to examine the process that would have to operate in order for embedding to influence consumer choice behavior. The Edge shaving cream advertisement provides a useful vehicle for motivating this discussion. The first step in the process is that the consumer would have to consciously or subconsciously process the embedded symbol (the nude woman in the Edge magazine ad). Second, as the result of

[54]Wilson B. Key, *Subliminal Seduction: Ad Media's Manipulation of a Not So Innocent America* (Englewood Cliffs, NJ: Prentice-Hall, 1972); *Media Sexploitation* (Englewood Cliffs, NJ: Prentice-Hall, 1976); *The Clam Plate Orgy: And Other Subliminal Techniques for Manipulating Your Behavior* (Englewood Cliffs, NJ: Prentice-Hall, 1980).

GLOBAL FOCUS

WORLDWIDE CONCERN ABOUT SEX AND DECENCY IN ADVERTISING

Many people throughout the world are troubled by advertising they consider indecent. But, of course, what is considered indecent in one country is not necessarily considered indecent in another. The International Chamber of Commerce's (ICC) Code of Advertising Practice states that "advertising should be decent"; that is, "prepared with a due sense of social responsibility . . . [and] not be such as to impair public confidence in advertising."

Three categories of advertising indecency that are matters of concern around the world include advertisements that are sexist, sexy, or sexually objectify their models. *Sexist* ads are those that demean one sex in comparison with the other, particularly through sex-role stereotyping; *sexy* ads use sexual imagery or suggestiveness; and *sexual objectification* occurs when ads use women (or men) as decorative or attention-getting objects with little or no relevance to the product category.

The nature and extent of government regulation of indecent sex-oriented advertising varies considerably, from a relatively laissez-faire attitude in the United States and Western Europe to stringent controls in various Muslim countries. Following are some examples of government regulations of advertising in different countries:

(continued)

processing the cue, the consumer would have to develop a greater desire for Edge shaving cream than he had before seeing the ad. Third, because advertising is done at the brand level and because advertisers are interested in selling their brands and not just any brand in the product category, effective symbolic embedding would require that consumers develop a desire for the specific brand, Edge in this case, rather than just any brand in the category. Finally, the consumer would need to transfer the desire for the advertised brand into actual purchase behavior.

Is there evidence to support this chain of events? Empirical work is just beginning to accumulate. Three recent advertising studies have attempted to tackle the issue. Only one study will be described here, however, because the

■ In Malaysia, the Ministry of Information's Advertising Code states that women should not be the principal objects of an advertisement or intended to attract sales unless the advertised product is relevant to women.

■ The Ministry of Information in Saudi Arabia prevents any advertising depicting veiled or unveiled women.

■ Indian law forbids the depiction of a woman's figure or any female body part if the depiction is derogatory to women or immoral.

■ Portuguese law prohibits sex discrimination or the subordination or objectification of women in advertising.

■ Norway requires that advertising not portray men or women in an offensive manner or imply any derogatory judgment of either sex.

The regulation of advertising (on grounds of decency or otherwise) is complex and controversial, because regulation curtails the rights of advertisers to communicate with their public, and impinges on the rights of people to receive information and images in any form they consider nonobjectionable. Regulators in all countries are placed in a tricky position when attempting to balance the rights and interests of advertisers, consumers, and society at large.

Source: Jean J. Boddewyn, "Controlling Sex and Decency in Advertising Around the World," *Journal of Advertising*, 20 (December 1991), 25–36.

other two, though interesting in their own right, are too far removed from actual advertising practice to have much relevance for the present discussion.[55]

Researchers performed an experiment using an advertisement for Chivas Regal Scotch whiskey.[56] The experiment involved exposing one group of subjects

[55]The other studies are Ronnie Cuperfain and T. K. Clarke, "A New Perspective of Subliminal Perception," *Journal of Advertising*, 14, 1 (1985), 36–41; and Myron Gable, Henry T. Wilkens, Lynn Harris, and Richard Feinberg, "An Evaluation of Subliminally Embedded Sexual Stimuli in Graphics," *Journal of Advertising*, 16, 1 (1987), 26–31.

[56]William E. Kilbourne, Scott Painton, and Danny Ridley, "The Effect of Sexual Embedding on Responses to Magazine Advertisements," *Journal of Advertising*, 14, 2 (1985), 48–56.

FIGURE 12.6   Parody of Embedding Advertising

Actual Use of Embedding

FIGURE 12.7

to an ad containing an embed and another group to a non-embedded, but otherwise identical ad. Figure 12.8 presents both Chivas Regal ads.[57] If you look carefully at the ad in the right panel of Figure 12.8, you will notice that immediately above the label at the point of bottle curvature, there is embedded the image of a nude female's backside. (An arrow has been added to the figure to direct your attention to the exact location.) By comparison, in the control (non-embedded) version in the left panel, the same location on the ad is without a nude image.

Over 400 college students participated in the experiment. Subjects were exposed either to the ad with or without the embedded figure. After viewing the embedded or non-embedded ad, subjects' attitudes toward Chivas Regal were measured. Results indicated that subjects exposed to the embedded version of the ad had significantly more favorable attitudes toward Chivas Regal than did subjects exposed to the non-embedded ad.[58]

The above experimental evidence offers partial support that sexual embeds in magazine advertisements may increase consumers' attitudes toward advertised products.[59] Whether these results generalize to other products is unknown. The fact that the sexual image enhanced attitudes only for the liquor product but not a tobacco product (see footnote 58) goes along with the earlier discussion about the role of relevance for effective non-subliminal sexual appeals. Liquor is arguably a more sexually oriented product than cigarettes and therefore probably a more appropriate product for sexual embeds.

Despite this limited evidence that sexual images may influence consumers' attitudes, there are a variety of practical problems that *probably prevent embedding from being effective in a realistic marketing context.* Perhaps the major reason why embedding in advertising has little effect is because the images have to be concealed to preclude detection by consumers. Many consumers would resent such tricky advertising efforts if they knew they existed. Thus, precluding detection from consumers means that embedding is a relatively weak technique in comparison to more vivid advertising representations. (You probably would have had difficulty spotting the nude embed in the Chivas Regal bottle had the arrow not directed your attention to it.) Because the majority of consumers devote relatively little time and effort in processing advertisements, a weak stimulus means that most consumers could not possibly be influenced.[60]

---

[57]These ads were not presented in the article by Kilbourne et al. but were reproduced in Jo Anna Natale, "Are You Open to Suggestion?" *Psychology Today*, September 1988, 28.

[58]These same researchers also tested embedded and non-embedded versions of a Marlboro cigarettes advertisement, but they were unable to detect a statistically significant difference in the embedded and non-embedded groups' attitudes toward Marlboros.

[59]This article has been criticized on technical grounds that need not concern us here. For an excellent review of the literature and for a discussion of a view opposing subliminal advertising, see Joel Saegert, "Why Marketing Should Quit Giving Subliminal Advertising the Benefit of the Doubt," *Psychology & Marketing*, 4 (Summer 1987), 107–120.

[60]For further discussion of the practical difficulties associated with implementing subliminal advertising, see Timothy E. Moore, "Subliminal Advertising: What You See Is What You Get," *Journal of Marketing*, 46 (Spring 1982), 41.

Subliminally Embedded and Non-Embedded Ads for Chivas Regal

FIGURE 12.8

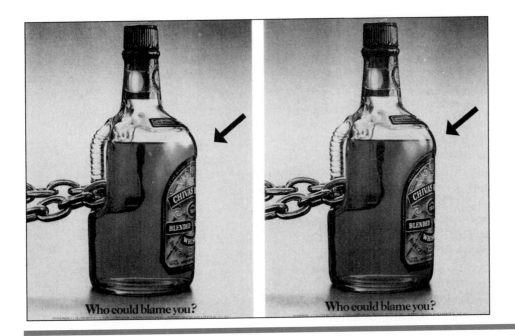

Even if consumers did attend and encode sexual embeds under natural advertising conditions, there remains serious doubt that this information would have sufficient impact to affect product or brand choice behavior. Standard (superliminal) advertising information itself has a difficult time influencing consumers. There is no theoretical reason to expect that subliminal information is any more effective. For example, do you really think that men would run out to buy Edge shaving cream just because they consciously or subconsciously spot a nude woman in the advertisement for that product?

In sum, the topic of subliminal advertising (particularly the Wilson Key variety of symbolic embeds) makes for interesting speculation and discussion, but scientific evidence in support of its practical effectiveness is virtually nonexistent. The following quotation appropriately sums up the issue:

A century of psychological research substantiates the general principle that more intense stimuli have a greater influence on people's behavior than weaker ones. While subliminal perception is a bona fide phenomenon, the effects obtained are subtle and obtaining them typically requires a carefully structured context. Subliminal stimuli are usually so weak that the recipient is not just unaware of the stimulus but is also oblivious to the fact that he/she is being stimulated. As a result, the potential effects of subliminal stimuli are easily nullified by other ongoing stimulation in the same sensory channel or by attention being focused on another modality. These factors pose serious difficulties for any possible marketing application.[61]

COMPARATIVE ADVERTISING

The practice in which advertisers directly compare their products against competitive offerings, typically claiming that the promoted item is superior in one or several important purchase considerations, is called **comparative advertising.** Comparative ads differ both with regard to the explicitness of the comparisons and with respect to whether the target of the comparison is named or referred to in general terms.[62] Salespeople have always used comparative messages in arguing the advantages of their products over competitors' products. Likewise, print advertisers (newspapers, magazines) have used comparative claims for decades. It was not until the early 1970s, however, that television commercials began making direct-comparison claims. Since then all media have experienced notable increases in the use of comparative advertising.

Advertisers face a number of difficult questions when deciding whether to use comparative advertising. The following questions are involved in evaluating the use of comparative advertising:

- Is comparative advertising more effective than noncomparative advertising?

- How do comparative and noncomparative advertisements compare in terms of differential impact on awareness, believability, credibility, comprehension and advertiser identification?

- Do they differ with regard to effects on purchase intentions, brand preferences, purchase behavior?

- What are the effects of copy claim variation and substantiation on the performance of competitive advertisements?

- Is effectiveness influenced by factors such as prior brand loyalty or competitive position?

[61]Ibid., 46.

[62]See Darrell D. Muehling, Donald E. Stem, Jr., and Peter Raven, "Comparative Advertising: Views from Advertisers, Agencies, Media, and Policy Makers," *Journal of Advertising Research,* 29 (October/November 1989), 38–48.

■ Should companies use comparative advertisements and, if so, under what conditions?[63]

Researchers have performed a number of comparative-advertising studies since the mid-1970s.[64] Findings are inconclusive and even contradictory at times. Lack of definitive results is to be expected, however, because advertising is a complex phenomenon that varies greatly from situation to situation in terms of executional elements, audience characteristics, media characteristics, and other factors. The research does, however, permit the following general observations:[65]

1. *Situational factors* (characteristics of audience, media, message, company, and product) play an important role in determining whether comparative advertising is more effective than noncomparative advertising. For example, one study found that product superiority claims in a comparative advertisement were evaluated significantly less favorably by subjects who had a prior preference for the comparison brand (i.e., the brand that the advertised brand was compared against) than for subjects who did not have a prior preference for the comparison brand.[66]

2. Comparative advertising may be more suitable for *low-involvement products* (like convenience goods) than for durable goods, certain services, and other high-involvement products. This observation is speculative because the research support is limited, but it is not without logical support. Specifically, advertisements for low-involvement products have difficulty attracting the consumer's attention; therefore, comparative advertisements may be more effective for these products because the relative novelty of comparative advertising provides a means of attracting viewer attention. High-involvement products, on the other hand, are more concerned with conveying information and influencing purchase intentions than with merely attracting attention.

3. Comparative advertising may be particularly effective for promoting *new brands that possess distinct advantages relative to competitive brands.* One

[63]Stephen B. Ash and Chow-Hou Wee, "Comparative Advertising: A Review with Implications for Further Research," in *Advances in Consumer Research*, 10, eds. R. P. Bagozzi and A. M. Tybout (Ann Arbor, MI: Association for Consumer Research, 1983), 374.

[64]For especially good examples of comparative advertising research, see Cornelia Pechmann and David W. Stewart, "The Effects of Comparative Advertising on Attention, Memory, and Purchase Intentions," *Journal of Consumer Research*, 17 (September 1990), 180-191; Cornelia Pechmann and S. Ratneshwar, "The Use of Comparative Advertising for Brand Positioning: Association Versus Differentiation," *Journal of Consumer Research*, 18 (September 1991), 145–160.

[65]The following comments are adapted from Ash and Wee, "Comparative Advertising," primarily 374.

[66]V. Kanti Prasad, "Communications Effectiveness of Comparative Advertising: A Laboratory Analysis," *Journal of Marketing Research*, 13 (May 1976), 128–137.

study found that comparative advertising is more effective for a new market entrant, whereas noncomparative advertising appears to be more effective for established brands.[67] When a new brand has a distinct advantage over competitive brands, comparative advertising provides a powerful method to convey this advantage. As compared to noncomparative advertising, comparative advertising has also been shown to increase the perceived similarity between a challenger brand in a product category and the category leader.[68]

4. The effectiveness of comparative advertising increases *when comparative claims are made to appear more credible.* There are various ways to accomplish this: (1) have an independent research organization support the superiority claims, (2) present impressive test results to back up the claims, and (3) use a trusted endorser as spokesperson.

5. Because comparative advertising is generally perceived by consumers to be more interesting than noncomparative advertising, comparative advertising may also be appropriate for *established brands that have experienced static sales using noncomparative advertising.*

6. *Print media* appear to be better vehicles than broadcast media for comparative advertisements. Print lends itself to more thorough comparisons, and consumers have control over the time needed to process the large amount of information that is usually found in comparative ads.

SUMMARY

This chapter discusses both the role of celebrity endorsers and the nature and effectiveness of specific advertising techniques such as humor and fear appeals. Discussion of celebrity and typical-person endorsers indicates that endorsers have influence on consumers via the attributes of attractiveness and credibility. Attractiveness operates through an identification mechanism, whereas credibility functions via the process of internalization.

Widely used advertising techniques discussed in this chapter include fear appeals, humor, music, sex appeals, subliminal messages, and comparative advertisements. Discussion covers empirical research and indicates when each of these advertising techniques is most effective.

---

[67]Terence A. Shimp and David C. Dyer, "The Effects of Comparative Advertising Mediated by Market Position of Sponsoring Brand," *Journal of Advertising,* 7, 3 (1978), 13–19.

[68]Gerald J. Gorn and Charles B. Weinberg, "The Impact of Comparative Advertising on Perception and Attitude: Some Positive Findings," *Journal of Consumer Research,* 11 (September 1984), 719–727.

Discussion Questions

1. Using the concepts of attractiveness, expertise, and trustworthiness, explain what makes Bo Jackson an effective endorser for Nike products.

2. Identify two product categories where Michael Jordan would *not* make an effective endorser. Justify your reasoning and do not use ridiculous products which Jordan nor any other man would endorse.

3. The *Focus on Promotion* section listed the 10 outstanding endorsers in 1991 from both the entertainment and athletic fields. It will be noted that Bill Cosby endorses Jell-O. Assume for some reason that Cosby needs to be replaced as the endorser for this product. What one person on the entertainer or athlete list would you replace Mr. Cosby with if you were in charge of this account? Fully justify the rationale behind your choice.

4. Magic Johnson announced to the world in November 1991 that he had just tested positive for HIV, a precursor to AIDS, and would be retiring from professional basketball. Try to place yourself in the position of Converse's Vice President of Marketing in November 1991. Would you have allowed Magic to continue endorsing Converse (his contract was written through 1995), or would you have amicably terminated the contract and sought another endorser?

5. Is Lisa Boyer (in Figure 12.2) actually endorsing Timex watches, or, alternatively, is she simply an attractive prop around which Timex is able to tell a story about its watches? What exact role is Lisa Boyer performing in this ad?

6. A relatively new form of advertising is referred to as the long commercial or informercial. These commercials typically are aired during fringe times and frequently promote products such as diet aids and balding cures. Invariably these infomercials turn to physicians and other health professionals to buttress claims about the promoted brand's efficacy. Using concepts from the text, explain why health professionals are used in this form of advertising.

7. You have probably seen a number of anti-drinking and driving public service announcements along the lines described in the fear-appeals section. In your opinion, is this form of advertising effective in altering the behavior of people your age? Be specific in justifying your answer.

8. The fear of getting AIDS should be relevant to many college students. Accordingly, would you agree that a relatively weak fear appeal should suffice in influencing students to either abstain from sexual relations or practice safe sex? If you disagree, then how can you reconcile your disagreement with the degree-of-relevance explanation?

9. Develop a list of products for which you feel fear appeals might be a viable approach to persuading consumer acceptance of a brand. What kinds of products do

not lend themselves to fear appeals? Explain why you feel these products are not appropriate for fear appeals.

10. Consumers occasionally find television commercials to be humorous and enjoyable. Some advertising pundits claim that such commercials may capture attention but are frequently ineffective in selling products. What is your stance on this issue? Justify your position.

11. The advertising agency for an automobile-tire manufacturer is considering using a fear-appeal message to promote its client's tires. What would you suggest to the advertising agency in terms of fear-appeal strength?

12. Industrial advertisers sometimes use magazine advertisements with decorative models—that is, scantily clad females who are there to adorn the ad but who serve no function in terms of the sales message. Why do you think industrial advertisers use decorative models? Present arguments explaining why you think such advertising is effective or ineffective.

13. Explain why an advertiser would prefer to change consumer attitudes through an internalization process rather than through compliance or identification.

14. Distinguish between an attractive and a credible source. Provide two or three examples of well-known product spokespersons who, in your opinion, are high in both attractiveness and credibility. Justify why you consider these individuals to possess both attributes.

15. Provide two or three examples of music in advertisements that you think are particularly effective. For each example, explain why you think the music is effective.

16. Clip several examples of comparative advertisements from magazines. Analyze each ad in terms of why you think the advertiser used a comparative-advertising format and whether you think the advertisement is effective. Justify your position.

17. Collect advertisements from magazines and locate two or three illustrations of each of the following: credible sources, attractive sources, and trustworthy sources. Explain why you chose each example to illustrate a particular source characteristic.

18. In an article entitled "Understanding Jingles and Needledrop: A Rhetorical Approach to Music in Advertising," (see footnote 32) it has been suggested that music in commercials is able to communicate specific meanings to listeners and viewers. In other words, music can talk (communicate) to people by conveying a sense of speed, excitement, sadness, nostalgia, and so on. Identify two commercials where the music is communicating a specific emotion or other state or action to consumers.

19. Too much sex is used in advertising. Comment.

20. Do you have any reservations about the findings in the Chivas Regal experiment? In other words, can you provide an alternative explanation for these findings other than the proferred explanation that the embedded nude created more positive attitudes?

CHAPTER THIRTEEN

Media Strategy

THE VIDEOCART: A PROMISING NEW ADVERTISING MEDIUM

Manufacturers use traditional advertising media (magazines, television, etc.) to inform consumers about new brands and to encourage trial and repeat purchases. Such advertising, albeit essential, is less than ideal inasmuch as it is received by consumers in their homes or at other locations *prior* to the time when they are at the point of purchase. Clearly, the best time to reach a customer with your advertising message is when she or he is actually shopping. But how? How, as an advertiser of a nationally marketed brand, could you reach consumers at the actual time when they are doing their grocery shopping?

The VideOcart is an advertising medium explicitly designed for this purpose. The VideOcart is nothing more than a shopping cart with a liquid-crystal display screen on its handle. As the shopper moves through grocery aisles, advertisements for brands on the shelves being passed are triggered. This is accomplished with a main computer in each supermarket that directs a low-power FM transmitter to send advertisements to each cart's computer memory. This is made technologically possible by placing satellite dishes on supermarket roofs (see Figure 13.1).

Manufacturers who buy the VideOcart's advertising space receive exclusive advertising rights. That is, for any particular time period only one brand in a product category is advertised on the VideOcart. Well-known companies such as Kraft, Pepsi, RJR Nabisco, Procter & Gamble, and Ralston Purina have purchased VideOcart space.

Graphic Illustration of the VideOcart's Operation | FIGURE 13.1

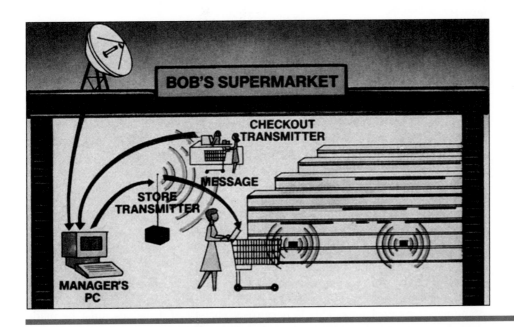

Source: "VideOcart Shopping Cart with Computer Screen Creates New Ad Medium That Also Gathers Data," *Marketing News*, Vol. 22, May 9, 1988, p. 2. Reprinted with permission from *Marketing News*, published by the American Marketing Association.

The marketers of the VideOcart advertising program charge participating manufacturers $4 per 1,000 supermarket customers. This cost compares with an average primetime TV cost of around $11 per thousand people. It is projected that by the end of 1994 VideOcarts will be in 5,000 stores in the top 25 U.S. markets and will reach about half of all U.S. households. The marketers of VideOcarts claim that test results have shown that stores installed with VideOcarts have realized sales increases averaging $1 per transaction, or between $20,000–$30,000 more in weekly sales than comparable stores without VideOcarts.

Supermarket chains have accepted VideOcarts into their stores because of the potential for added sales. Chains pay nothing to get the computer screens installed; their only responsibility is to replace damaged screens. A supplemental benefit of the VideOcarts to supermarkets is that the VideOcarts' computer memories enable the tracking of shopper-movement patterns through the supermarket aisles. This information should be invaluable to supermarkets in making better product-placement decisions.

Sources: David Kiley, "After a Successful Test, VideOcart Rolls East, *Adweek's Marketing Week,* November 12, 1990, 46; and Scott Hume, "Improved VideOcart Starts Test," *Advertising Age,* November 12, 1990, 66.

Creative advertising messages, the subject of the previous two chapters, are necessary for advertising success. Outstanding message execution is to no avail, however, unless the messages are delivered to the right customers at the right time and with sufficient frequency. In other words, advertising messages stand a chance of being effective only if the media strategy itself is effective. Good messages and good media go hand in hand; they are inseparable—a true marriage. Improper media selection can doom an otherwise promising advertising campaign.

Creative advertisements are more effective when placed in media whose characteristics enhance the value of the advertising message and reach the advertiser's targeted customers at the right time. For example, the VideOcart is a promising advertising medium because it will deliver messages to shoppers at the time when they are prepared to make a product/brand purchase decision.

In many respects, media strategy is the *most complicated* of all marketing communications decisions. This is because a variety of decisions must be made when choosing media. In addition to determining which *general media* categories to use (television, radio, magazines, etc.), the media planner must also pick *specific vehicles* within each medium (e.g., select specific magazines) and decide how to *allocate the available budget* among the various media and vehicle alternatives. Additional decisions involve determining *when to advertise,* choosing specific *geographical locations,* and deciding how to *distribute the budget over time and across geographic locations.* The complexity of media selection is made clear in the following commentary:

An advertiser considering a simple monthly magazine schedule, out of a pool of 30 feasible publications meeting editorial environment and targeting requirements, must essentially consider over one billion schedules when narrowing the possibilities down to the few feasible alternatives that maximize campaign goals within budget constraints. Why over one billion possible schedules? There are two outcomes for each monthly schedule, either to use a particular publication or not to do so. Therefore, the total number of possible schedules equals two raised to the 30th power (i.e., $2^{30} = 1,073,741,800$). If ten *weekly* magazines are involved in a monthly schedule, the choices for each are not to run any advertisement or to run up to 4.3, the average number of weeks in a month. Technically, this presents the planner with over 17 million possible schedules from which to choose (i.e., 4.3+1)[10]. Now imagine how the options explode when one is also considering 60 prime time and 25 daytime broadcast television network programs, 12 cable television networks, 16 radio networks, four national newspapers, and three newspaper supplements, with *each vehicle* having between 4.3 and perhaps as many as 30 or more possible insertions per month.[1]

This chapter first reviews the media-planning process and then provides detailed analyses of five major advertising media: television, radio, magazines, newspapers, and outdoor advertising. Discussion of a sixth major medium—direct mail—is delayed until Chapter 19.

THE MEDIA-PLANNING PROCESS

Media planning is "the process of designing a course of action that shows how advertising time and space will be used to contribute to the achievement of marketing objectives."[2] As shown in Figure 13.2, media planning involves coordination of three levels of strategy formulations: marketing strategy, advertising strategy, and media strategy. The overall *marketing strategy* (consisting of target-market identification and marketing-mix selection) provides the impetus and direction for the choice of both advertising and media strategies. The advertising objectives, budget, and message, and media strategies thus extend naturally from the overall marketing strategy. For example, the advertisement for the Toyota Paseo presented in Figure 11.9 (p. 319) naturally extends from Toyota's strategy to sell approximately 40,000 Paseos per year to young, primarily male consumers who desire both practicality and sexiness in a new car.[3]

Media strategy necessarily evolves from the more general *advertising strategy* involving budgeting, objective setting, and message considerations. Let us assume that the Paseo received a $10 million advertising budget in 1991, its introductory year, with the objectives of creating brand awareness among young males and conveying the ideas that the Paseo is a practical yet exciting car. Advertising strategy decisions simultaneously impose constraints on media strategy ($10 million is the maximum amount to be spent on the 1991 Paseo

---

[1]Kent M. Lancaster, "Optimizing Advertising Media Plans Using ADOPT on the Microcomputer," Working Paper, University of Illinois, December 1987, 2–3.

[2]Arnold M. Barban, Steven M. Cristol, and Frank J. Kopec, *Essentials of Media Planning: A Marketing Viewpoint* (Lincolnwood, IL: NTC Business Books, 1987), 1.

[3]Cleveland Horton, "Toyota Double Talk," *Advertising Age*, June 10, 1991, 53.

FIGURE 13.2   Overview of the Media-Planning Process

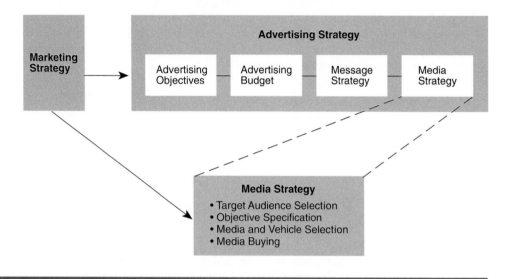

campaign) and provide direction for media selection. The *media strategy* itself consists of four sets of interrelated activities:

1. selecting the target audience,

2. specifying media objectives,

3. selecting media categories and vehicles, and

4. buying media.

The following sections discuss the first three activities in detail. No discussion is devoted to media buying because it is a specialized topic more appropriately treated in texts devoted exclusively to media planning.

Selecting the Target Audience

Successful media strategy requires first that the target audience be clearly pinpointed. Failure to precisely define the audience results in wasted exposures; that is, some nonpurchase candidates are exposed to advertisements while some prime candidates are missed.

Four major factors are used in segmenting target audiences for media strategy purposes: (1) geographic, (2) demographic, (3) product usage (e.g., heavy, medium, and light product users), and (4) lifestyle/psychographics. Product usage information typically provides the most meaningful basis for segmenting target audiences.[4]

Geographic, demographic, and psychographic considerations are typically combined for purposes of target-audience definition. For example, Toyota would define the target audience for the Paseo in terms such as the following: young men and women (but primarily men) between the ages of 18 and 34 (a demographic variable) who have incomes exceeding $25,000 (demographic), who are concerned with their sex appeal but are unwilling to indulge themselves to the point of excess (psychographic), and are avid sports fans (psychographic). A target audience defined in such specific terms has obvious implications for both message and media strategy. Magazines appealing to this group (such as *Sports Illustrated*) and televised sports programs would represent two attractive media possibilities.

Specifying Media Objectives

A second aspect of media strategy is establishing specific objectives. Four objectives are fundamental to media planning: reach, frequency, continuity, and cost. Media planners seek answers to the following types of questions: (1) What proportion of the target audience do we want to see (or read, or hear) the advertising message? (a *reach* issue); (2) How often should the target audience be exposed to the advertisement? (a *frequency* issue); (3) When is the best time to reach the target audience? (a *continuity* issue); (4) What is the least expensive way to accomplish the other objectives? (a *cost* issue). Each of these objectives is now discussed in detail.

R E A C H . The *percentage of a target audience* that is exposed *at least once* to the advertiser's message during an established time frame (usually *four weeks*) represents **reach.** In other words, reach represents the number of target customers who receive the advertiser's message *one or more times during a four-week time period*. Other terms used by media planners for describing reach are *1+* (read one-plus) *net coverage, unduplicated audience,* and *cumulative audience* (or *cume*). Later it will become clear why these terms are interchangeable with reach.

A number of factors determine the reach of an advertising campaign. Generally speaking, more people are reached when a media schedule uses *multiple media* rather than a single medium. For example, if the Paseo were advertised only on network television, its advertisements would reach fewer people

---

[4]Henry Assael and Hugh Cannon, "Do Demographics Help in Media Selection?" *Journal of Advertising Research,* 19 (December 1979), 7–11; Hugh M. Cannon and G. Russell Merz, "A New Role for Psychographics in Media Selection," *Journal of Advertising,* 9, 2 (1980), 33–36, 44.

than if it were advertised in magazines and on radio in addition to television. A second factor influencing reach is the *number and diversity of different media vehicles used.* For example, more of the target audience for the Paseo would be reached by advertising on different television programs compared to advertising exclusively on, say, *NFL Monday Night Football.* Third, reach can be increased by *diversifying the day parts* used to advertise a program. For example, radio advertising during drive time and television advertising during prime time would reach more potential Paseo purchasers than advertising exclusively during daytime.

Reach by itself is an inadequate objective for media planning because it tells nothing about *how often* target customers are exposed to the advertiser's message. Frequency of advertising exposures must also be considered.

F R E Q U E N C Y .   The number of times, on average, within a four-week period that members of the target audience are exposed to (see, read, or hear) the advertiser's message is referred to as *average frequency* (or **frequency,** for short). To better understand the concept of frequency and how it relates to reach, consider the simplified example in Table 13.1. This example provides information about ten hypothetical members of the target audience for the Toyota Paseo and their exposure to Paseo advertisements placed in *Rolling Stone* magazine over four consecutive weeks. Member **A,** for example, is exposed to Paseo ads twice, on weeks 2 and 3; **C** is never exposed to a Paseo ad in *Rolling Stone;* **F** is exposed only once, on week 4; and so on. Notice also in Table 13.1 that for each week, only five of ten households (50 percent) are exposed to the Paseo ad in *Rolling Stone.* This reflects the dual fact that (1) a single vehicle (*Rolling Stone* in this case) rarely reaches the full target audience and (2) exposure to a vehicle does not guarantee that consumers will see a particular advertisement.

The frequency distribution and summary reach and frequency statistics are also presented in Table 13.1. The frequency distribution (designated as **f**) represents the percentage of audience members (i.e., % **f**) exposed 0, 1, 2, 3, or 4 times to the Paseo advertisement. The column labeled % **f +** (the cumulative frequency distribution) indicates the percentage of the ten-member audience exposed at a certain level of exposures or greater than that level. For example, 70 percent were exposed two or more times to the magazine ad for the Paseo.

With this background, we now are in a position to illustrate how reach and frequency are calculated. It can be seen in Table 13.1 that 90 percent of the hypothetical audience for the Paseo have been exposed to one or more ads (i.e., with **f** = 1, %**1+** = 90%). This figure, 90 percent, represents the reach for this advertising effort. Ninety percent of the target audience have been exposed to the ad one or more times during the four-week advertising period. When discussing reach statistics, advertising practitioners drop the percent and simply refer to the number. In this case, reach is expressed simply as 90.

Frequency is the average of the frequency distribution. In this situation, frequency equals 2.2. That is, 90 percent of the target audience is reached 1 or more

Hypothetical Frequency Distribution for Toyota Paseo Advertised in Rolling Stone   TABLE 13.1

Week	TARGET-AUDIENCE MEMBER										Total Exposures
	A	B	C	D	E	F	G	H	I	J	
1		X		X	X		X		X		5
2	X	X			X		X		X		5
3	X	X		X				X		X	5
4		X		X		X	X			X	5
Total Exposure	2	4	0	3	2	1	3	1	2	2	

SUMMARY STATISTICS

Frequency Distribution (f)	% f	% f+	Audience Members
0	10%	100%	C
1	20%	90%	F, H
2	40%	70%	A, E, I, J
3	20%	30%	D, G
4	10%	10%	B

Reach (1 + exposures) = 90
Frequency = 2.2
GRPs = 200

times—20 percent are reached 1 time, 40 percent are reached 2 times, 20 percent are reached 3 times, and 10 percent 4 times. Or, arithmetically,

$$\frac{(1 \times 20) + (2 \times 40) + (3 \times 20) + (4 \times 10)}{90} = \frac{200}{90} = 2.2.$$

Hence, this hypothetical situation indicates that 90 percent of the Toyota Paseo's ten-member target audience are exposed an average of 2.2 times during the four-week advertising schedule in *Rolling Stone*.

GROSS RATING POINTS (GRPS).   Notice at the bottom of Table 13.1 that this hypothetical schedule yields 200 GRPs. **Gross rating points (GRPs)** are an indicator of the amount of impact, or gross weight, of an advertising schedule. The term *gross* is the key. The number of GRPs indicates the *gross coverage* or *duplicated audience* that is exposed to a particular advertising schedule. Compare these terms with the alternative terms given earlier for reach, that is, *net coverage* or *unduplicated audience*.

Returning to our hypothetical example, the reach (net coverage, unduplicated audience) is 90. The gross rating points (gross coverage, duplicated audience) amount to 200, because audience members on average are exposed multiple times (2.2 times) to the Paseo advertisement during the four-week ad schedule.

It should be apparent from this discussion that GRPs represent the arithmetic product of reach times frequency.

$$
\begin{aligned}
\text{GRPs} \;&=\; \text{Reach (r)} \times \text{Frequency (f)} \\
&=\; 90 \times 2.2 \\
&=\; 200^5
\end{aligned}
$$

It should be apparent that by simple algebraic manipulation the following additional relations are obtained:

$$
\begin{aligned}
r &= \text{GRPs/f} \\
\text{and } f &= \text{GRPs/f}
\end{aligned}
$$

Determining GRPs in Practice.   In actual advertising practice, media planners make media purchases by deciding how many GRPs are needed to accomplish established objectives. However, because the frequency distribution and reach and frequency statistics are unknown commodities before the fact (i.e., at the time when the media schedule is determined), media planners need some other way to determine how many GRPs will result from a particular schedule.

There is, in fact, a simple way to make this determination. GRPs are determined (before the fact!) by simply summing the *ratings* obtained from the individual vehicles included in a prospective media schedule. REMEMBER: Gross rating points are nothing more than *the sum of all vehicle ratings in a media schedule.*

But what exactly is meant by ratings? A **rating** is simply the proportion of the target audience presumed to be exposed to a single issue of an advertising vehicle. For example, considering the hypothetical target audience specifications for the Toyota Paseo given earlier, assume there are approximately 17 million consumers who satisfy the age and income specifications that define this product's target audience. Assume further that approximately 2.59 million members of this predominantly male audience read *Rolling Stone (RS)*. *RS's* rating for this target audience would therefore be 15.2 (2.59/17 = .152, or 15.2). Finally, assume that one full-page ad for the Paseo is to be placed in each of the following maga-

----

[5]The reader may think an arithmetic error has been committed inasmuch as $90 \times 2.2 = 198$ and not 200. In actuality, this is simply due to a rounding error. The exact frequency in this case is 2.22, which multiplied times 90 gives 200. However, media practitioners round frequency figures to a single decimal place.

zines during a single week. Although GRPs are typically determined for a full, four-week period, this simplified one-week schedule would yield 103.8 GRPs.

Magazine	Hypothetical Rating
Sports Illustrated	48.4
Playboy	28.6
Rolling Stone	15.2
Ebony	11.6
	103.8

EFFECTIVE REACH AND EFFECTIVE RATING POINTS (ERPS). Alternative media schedules are usually compared in terms of the number of GRPs each generates. It is important to realize, however, that more GRPs does not necessarily mean better. Consider, for example, two alternative media plans, X and Z, both of which require the same budget. Plan X generates 90 percent reach and an average frequency of 2, thereby yielding 180 GRPs. (Note again that reach is defined as the proportion of the audience exposed one or more times to an advertising vehicle during the course of the four-week campaign. Again, reach is referred to in shorthand terms as 1+.) Plan Z provides for 166 GRPs from a reach of 52 percent and a frequency of 3.2. Which plan is better? Plan X is clearly superior in terms of total GRPs and reach, but Plan Z has a higher frequency level. If the product/brand in question requires a greater number of exposures for the advertising to have an impact, then Plan Z may be the superior plan even though it yields fewer GRPs.

It is for the reason suggested in the preceding comparison that many advertisers and media planners have become critical of the GRP concept, contending that "it rests on the very dubious assumption that every exposure is of equal value, that the 50th exposure is the same as the tenth or the first."[6] Media analysts are beginning to think more in terms of effective reach.[7]

Effective reach is based on the idea that an advertising schedule is effective only if it does not reach members of the target audience too few or too many times. In other words, there is a theoretical optimum range of exposures to an advertisement with minimum and maximum limits. But what constitutes too few or too many exposures? This, unfortunately, is one of the most complicated issues in all of advertising. The only statement that can be made with certainty is: "It depends!"

It depends, in particular, on considerations such as the advertised brand's competitive position, audience loyalty to the brand, message creativity, and what objectives advertising is attempting to accomplish. In fact, high levels of weekly

---

[6]A quote from advertising consultant Alvin Achenbaum cited in B. G. Yovovich, "Media's New Exposures," *Advertising Age*, April 13, 1981, sec. S, 7.

[7]As a side note, the term *effective exposure* and *effective frequency* are often used in lieu of *effective reach*. However, the term *effective reach* is preferred here because it creates less confusion when discussing the calculation of *effective rating points (ERPs)*, a concept discussed later.

exposure to a brand's advertising may be unproductive for loyal consumers because of a leveling off of ad effectiveness.[8] Specifically, brands with higher market shares and greater customer loyalty typically require fewer advertising exposures to achieve minimal levels of effectiveness. Likewise, it would be expected that the more creative and distinctive a brand's advertising is, the fewer exposures would be needed. The higher up the hierarchy of effects the advertising is attempting to move the consumer, the greater the number of exposures needed to achieve minimal effectiveness. For example, more exposures probably are needed to successfully convince consumers that the Toyota Paseo provides the dual advantages of practicality and excitement than merely to make them aware of the Paseo's presence on the market.

In the final analysis, the minimum and maximum numbers of effective exposures can be determined only by conducting sophisticated research. Because research of this nature is time consuming and expensive, advertisers and media planners have relied on rules of thumb to indicate minimum and maximum levels of effective advertising exposure. On the low end, *fewer than three exposures* during a four-week media schedule is generally considered ineffective, while *more than ten exposures* during this period is considered excessive.

It cannot be overemphasized that what is effective (or ineffective) for one product/brand may not necessarily be so for another. Although effective reach planning is widely practiced by large consumer-product advertisers, media planners remain divided on the matter of what constitutes effective reach.[9]

The use of effective reach rather than gross rating points as the basis for media planning can have a major effect on overall media strategies. In particular, effective reach planning generally leads to using *multiple media* rather than depending exclusively on television, which is often the strategy when using the gross rating point criterion. Prime-time television is especially effective in terms of generating high levels of reach (1+ exposures), but may be deficient in terms of achieving effective reach (i.e., 3+ exposures). Thus, using effective reach as the decision criterion often involves giving up some of prime-time television's reach to obtain greater frequency (at the same cost) from other media.

This is illustrated in Table 13.2, which compares four alternative media plans involving different combinations of media expenditures from an annual advertising budget of $12 million. Plan A allocates 100 percent of the budget to network television advertising; Plan B allocates 67 percent to television and 33 percent to network radio; Plan C splits the budget between network television and magazines; Plan D allocates 67 percent to television and 33 percent to outdoor advertising.

[8]Gerard J. Tellis, "Advertising Exposure, Loyalty, and Brand Purchase: A Two-Stage Model of Choice," *Journal of Marketing Research*, 25 (May 1988), 134–144.

[9]Peter B. Turk, "Effective Frequency Report: Its Use and Evaluation by Major Agency Media Department Executives," *Journal of Advertising Research* (April/May, 1988), 55–59.

Alternative Media Plans (Based on a $12 Million Annual Budget and Four-Week Media Analysis)

TABLE 13.2

	Plan A: TV (100%)	Plan B: TV (67%) Radio (33%)	Plan C: TV (50%) Mags.(50%)	Plan D: TV (67%) Outdoor (33%)
Reach[a]	69%	79%	91%	87%
Effective Reach[b]	29%	48%	53%	61%
Frequency	2.8	5.5	3.2	6.7
GRPs	193	435	291	583
ERPs	81	264	170	409
$ per GRP	$62,176	$27,586	$41,237	$20,583
$ per ERP	$148,148	$45,455	$70,588	$29,340

[a]Based on 1+ exposures.
[b]Based on 3+ exposures.

Source: Adapted from "The Muscle in Multiple Media," *Marketing Communications*, December 1983, 25.

Notice first that Plan A (the use of network television only) leads to the lowest levels of reach, effective reach, frequency, and GRPs. An even split of 50 percent to network television and 50 percent to magazines generates an especially high level of reach (91 percent), while combinations of network television with network radio and network television with outdoor advertising are especially impressive in terms of frequency, GRPs, and the percentage of consumers exposed three or more times.

More to the point, notice that the network-television-only plan yields far fewer GRPs (reach × frequency) and considerably fewer effective rating points, ERPs (effective reach × frequency) than any of the other plans. Plan D, which combines 67 percent network television and 33 percent outdoor advertising, is especially outstanding in terms of the numbers of GRPs and ERPs generated. This is because outdoor advertising is seen frequently as people travel to and from work.

Should we conclude from this discussion that Plan D is the best and Plan A is the worst? Not necessarily! Clearly, the impact from seeing one billboard advertisement is probably far less than being exposed to a captivating television commercial. This points out a fundamental fact in media planning: *subjective factors* also must be considered when allocating advertising dollars. The numbers, on the surface, do favor Plan D. However, judgment and past experience may speak in favor of Plan A on the grounds that the only way to effectively advertise this particular product is by presenting dynamic action shots of people consuming and enjoying the product. Only television could satisfy this requirement.

It is useful to return again to a point established in Chapter 11: *It is better to be vaguely right than precisely wrong.*[10] Reach, frequency, effective reach, GRPs, and ERPs are precise in their appearance, but in application, if used blindly, may be precisely wrong. Intelligent decision makers never become slaves to numbers by relying on numbers to make the decisions for them. Rather, the numbers should be used solely as additional inputs into a decision that ultimately involves insight, wisdom, and judgment.

CONTINUITY.   A third general objective the media planner deals with is the timing of advertising. **Continuity** involves the matter of how advertising is allocated during the course of an advertising campaign. The fundamental issue is this: Should the media budget be distributed uniformly throughout the period of the advertising campaign, should it be spent in a concentrated period to achieve the most impact, or should some other schedule between these two extremes be used? As always, the determination of what is best depends on the specific product/market situation. In general, however, a uniform advertising schedule suffers from too little advertising weight at any one time. A heavily concentrated schedule, on the other hand, suffers from excessive exposures during the advertising period and a complete absence of advertising at all other times.

Advertisers have three general alternatives related to allocating the budget over the course of the campaign: continuous (and uniform), pulsing, and flighting schedules. To understand the differences among these three scheduling options, consider the advertising decision faced by a small, regional manufacturer of a product such as hot dogs. Figure 13.3 shows how advertising allocations might differ from month to month depending on the use of continuous, pulsing, or flighting schedules. For illustration, assume the advertising budget for this hypothetical brand of hot dogs is $3 million.

Continuous Schedule.   In a **continuous** advertising schedule, a relatively equal amount of ad dollars are invested throughout the campaign. The illustration in Panel A of Figure 13.3 shows an extreme case of continuous advertising in which the hypothetical hot dog advertiser allocates the $3 million advertising budget in equal amounts of exactly $250,000 each month.

Such an advertising allocation would make sense only if hot dogs were consumed in essentially equal quantities throughout the year. Although hot dogs are

[10]Leonard M. Lodish, *The Advertising and Promotion Challenge: Vaguely Right or Precisely Wrong?* (New York: Oxford University Press, 1986).

FIGURE 13.3

Continuous, Pulsing, and Flighting Advertising Schedules for a Hypothetical Brand of Hot Dogs

A. Continuous Schedule

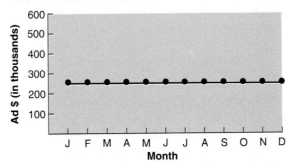

B. Pulsing Schedule

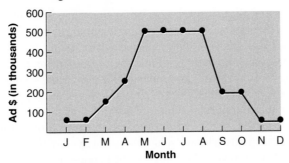

C. Flighting Schedule

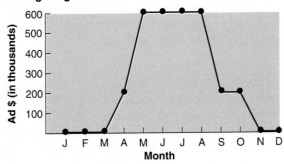

consumed year round, consumption is particularly high during May, June, July, and August. This calls for a discontinuous allocation of advertising dollars throughout the year.

Pulsing.   In a **pulsing** advertising schedule, some advertising is used during every period of the campaign, but the amount of advertising varies considerably from period to period. In Panel B of Figure 13.3 a pulsing schedule for our hypothetical hot dog manufacturer shows the company advertising especially heavy during the high-consumption months of May through August (spending $500,000 each month), but continuing to advertise in every month throughout the year. The minimum advertising expenditure is $50,000 even in the slow months of January, February, November, and December.

Flighting.   In a **flighting** schedule, the advertiser varies expenditures throughout the campaign and allocates zero expenditures in some months. Panel C in Figure 13.3 illustrates a flighting schedule. The hot dog company allocates $600,000 to each of the four high-consumption months, $200,000 each to moderate-consumption months (April, September, and October), but zero dollars to five low-consumption months (January, February, March, November, and December).

Thus, pulsing and flighting are similar in that they both involve *discontinuous expenditures* throughout the advertising campaign, but are different in that some advertising takes place in every period with pulsing but not with flighting. The following analogies may help to eliminate any confusion between pulsing and flighting. Pulsing in advertising is similar to an individual's heart beat, or pulse. One's pulse changes continuously between some lower and upper bounds but it is always present in a living person. Think of a flighting schedule in terms similar to the expression *flight of fancy*, which means soaring above ordinary limits or bounds. Thus, a pulsed advertising schedule is always *beating*, whereas a flighted schedule soars at times to very high levels but is nonexistent on other occasions.

Flighting and pulsing have become matters of necessity because of the tremendous increases in media costs, especially network television (more on this later in the chapter). Few advertisers can afford to advertise heavily throughout the year. They are forced to select periods when advertising stands the greatest chance of accomplishing communication and sales objectives.

C OST CONSIDERATIONS.   Media planners attempt to allocate the advertising budget in a cost-efficient manner subject to satisfying other objectives. One of the most important and universally used indicators of media efficiency is the cost-per-thousand criterion. **Cost per thousand** (abbreviated CPM, with the M being the Roman numeral for 1,000) is the cost of reaching 1,000 people. The measure can be refined to mean the cost of reaching 1,000 members of the target audience, excluding those people who fall outside the target market. This refined measure is designated CPM-TM.[11]

CPM and CPM-TM are calculated by dividing the cost of an advertisement by a medium's circulation within the total market (CPM) or target market (CPM-TM). By definition, CPM and CPM-TM are:

$$\text{CPM} \ = \ \frac{\text{Cost of Ad}}{\text{No. of total contacts (expressed in thousands)}}$$

$$\text{CPM-TM} \ = \ \frac{\text{Cost of Ad}}{\text{No. of TM contacts (expressed in thousands)}}.$$

The term *contacts* is used here in a general sense to include any type of advertising audience (television viewers, magazine readers, radio listeners, etc.).

To illustrate how CPM and CPM-TM are calculated, consider the following unconventional advertising situation. Every football Saturday at a major university a local airplane advertising service flies messages on a trailing device that extends behind the plane. The cost is $150 per message. The football stadium holds 75,000 fans and is filled to capacity every Saturday. Hence, the CPM in this situation is $2—i.e., the cost per message ($150) divided by the number of thousands of people (75) who potentially are exposed to any particular advertisement. Now assume that a new university bookstore uses the airplane advertising service to announce its opening to the 15,000 students who are in attendance at the game. Because the target market in this instance is only a fraction of the total audience, CPM-TM is a more appropriate cost-per-thousand statistic. CPM-TM in this instance is $10 ($150/15), which of course is five-times higher than the CPM statistic because the target audience is only one-fifth as large as the total audience.

To further illustrate how CPM and CPM-TM are calculated, consider a more conventional advertising situation on television. Suppose an advertiser promoted its brand on the sitcom *Cheers*, which, with a rating of 21.6, was the top-rated program based on Nielsen's Television Index for September 1990 to April 1991.[12] This means that 21.6 percent of 94 million U.S. households, or approximately 20,300,000 households, were tuned in to *Cheers* on a given Thursday evening. At a cost of $260,000 per 30-second commercial during the 1991 season, the CPM is as follows:

Total viewership   = 20,300,000 households
Cost of :30 commercial = $260,000.

[11]Charles H. Patti and Charles F. Frazer, *Advertising: A Decision-Making Approach* (Hinsdale, IL: The Dryden Press, 1988), 369.

[12]"Blacks Reveal TV Loyalty," *Advertising Age*, November 18, 1991, 28.

Thus,

$$CPM = \$260,000/20,300^{13}$$
$$= \$12.81.$$

If we assume that the target market consists only of women between the ages of 18-49 and that this market represents 35 percent of the total audience, or 7,105,000, then the CPM-TM is

$$CPM\text{-}TM = \$260,000/7,105$$
$$= \$36.59.$$

The CPM and CPM-TM statistics are useful for comparing different advertising schedules. They must be used cautiously, however, for several reasons. First, these are measures of cost efficiency—not of effectiveness. A media schedule may be extremely efficient but totally ineffective because it (1) reaches the wrong audience (if CPM is used rather than CPM-TM) or (2) is inappropriate for the product category advertised. For instance, compare CPM to using miles-per-gallon calculations for different automobiles. A Hyundai Excel may be more efficient than a BMW but less effective for one's purposes.[14]

A second limitation with CPM and CPM-TM measures is that it is inappropriate to compare CPMs across different media. CPMs differ across media because, as will be elaborated on later, the various media perform different roles and are therefore priced differently. A lower CPM for radio does not mean that buying radio is better than buying a more expensive (CPM-wise) television schedule.

Finally, CPM statistics can be misused unless vehicles within a particular medium are compared on the same basis. For example, the CPM for a daytime-television advertising schedule is less than a prime-time schedule, but this amounts to comparing apples with oranges. The proper comparison is between two daytime schedules or between two prime-time schedules. Similarly, it would be inappropriate to compare the CPM for a black and white magazine ad against a four-color magazine ad.

Tradeoffs, Tradeoffs, Tradeoffs

The various media-planning objectives (reach, frequency, continuity, and cost) have now been discussed in some detail. Each was introduced without direct ref-

---

[13]REMEMBER: The denominator in a CPM or CPM-TM calculation is expressed in thousands. In this situation, there are 20,300 thousands of viewers.

[14]This analogy is adapted from Patti and Frazer, ibid.

erence to the other objectives. It is important to recognize, however, that these objectives are actually *somewhat at odds with one another*. That is, given a fixed advertising budget (e.g., $10 million for the Toyota Paseo), the media planner *cannot* simultaneously optimize reach, frequency, and continuity objectives. Tradeoffs must be made because media planners operate under the constraint of fixed advertising budgets. Hence, to optimize one objective (e.g., minimizing CPM or maximizing GRPs) means that other objectives cannot simultaneously be optimized. This simply is due to the mathematics of constrained optimization: multiple objectives cannot simultaneously be optimized when constraints (like limited budgets) exist.

For example, with a fixed advertising budget, the media planner can choose to maximize reach or frequency, but not both. With increases in reach, frequency is sacrificed, and vice versa—if you want to reach more people, you cannot reach them as often with a fixed advertising budget; if you want to reach them more often, you cannot reach as many.[15] Similarly, with a fixed advertising budget, an advertiser cannot simultaneously increase advertising continuity and also increase reach or frequency.

What is the solution? There is no simple solution. Each media planner must decide what is best given the particular circumstances surrounding the advertising decision. However, considering just the tradeoff between reach and frequency, there are some general parameters to guide the decision of which to emphasize.[16] Let us distinguish between a reach strategy, which focuses on contacting as many audience members as possible, and a frequency strategy, which focuses on reaching fewer people more often.

In general, a **reach strategy** should be emphasized in the following situations: (1) for *new brands* (it is important to create widespread awareness, thus demanding a high level of reach); (2) for products/brands with *undefined markets* (when the market is undefined or diffused, the budget must be spread widely to reach as many people as possible); (3) for brands with *strong brand franchises* (brands with large market shares and more loyal customers can expand their markets only by reaching prospective new customers, thus calling for emphasis on reach over frequency); and (4) for product categories characterized by *infrequent purchase cycles* (when products are purchased infrequently, it is unnecessary to reach consumers frequently).

A **frequency strategy** is called for in situations counter to the preceding circumstances. In particular, emphasis on frequency over reach is suggested when: (1) *competitors are strong*, (2) a *complex message* has to be conveyed to the

---

[15] This discussion may remind you of the lesson in basic statistics about the tradeoff between committing Type I and Type II errors while holding sample size constant. You learned that with a fixed sample size, decisions to decrease a Type I error (say, from alpha=.05 to .01) must inevitably result in an increase in the Type II, or beta, error.

[16] This discussion is based on Don E. Schultz, Dennis Martin, and William P. Brown, *Strategic Advertising Campaigns* (Lincolnwood, IL: NTC Business Books, 1987), chap. 12.

target audience, (3) the product/brand is *purchased frequently*, (4) *brand loyalty is weak*, (5) the *target market is well-defined*, and (6) consumers are *resistant to the product/brand*.

Formal Media Models

The media planner is faced with the difficult task of trying to accomplish multiple objectives (reach, frequency, etc.) while at the same time having to make intelligent tradeoffs among them. On top of this, there literally are thousands of possible advertising schedules that could be selected depending on how the various media and media vehicles are combined. Fortunately, this daunting task can be facilitated by *computerized models* that assist media planners in making media-selection decisions. These models essentially attempt to optimize some goal, or objective function (e.g., select a schedule that yields a lower CPM than any other schedule), subject to satisfying constraints such as the upper limit on the advertising budget. A computer program then searches through the possible solutions, ultimately selecting a particular media schedule that optimizes the objective function and satisfies all specified constraints.[17]

The functioning of computerized media models will be illustrated with ADplus™, a model developed for personal computer usage. ADplus™ has been described by its developer as "the most comprehensive personal computer program available anywhere that allows you to evaluate all major advertising media categories and subcategories and also permits you to find optimum schedules involving multiple media categories."[18]

The following steps are involved in using ADplus™ for developing a media schedule:

1. First, the user must develop a *media database.* This is the strategic aspect of media planning and involves selecting which advertising vehicles will be used and specifying their cost (e.g., a magazine's page rate) and ratings.

2. Next, the user selects the *criterion for schedule optimization.* The available optimization alternatives include reach, effective reach, average frequency, and GRPs.

3. Then the user specifies the *budget constraint* (both the minimum and maximum amounts to be spent) and the *minimum and maximum number of ad placements, or insertions, for each vehicle.*

---

[17]These models go by names such as MEDIAC and ADMOD. For further discussion, see David A. Aaker and John G. Myers, *Advertising Management* (Englewood Cliffs, NJ: Prentice-Hall, 1987), 450–463; and Roland T. Rust, *Advertising Media Models: A Practical Guide* (Lexington Books, Lexington, MA: 1986).

[18]Kent Lancaster, *ADplus™: For Multi-media Advertising Planning* (Gainesville, FL: Media Research Institute, Inc., 1990), iii.

4. Once the user has provided the information required in steps 1 through 3, the ADplus™ algorithm seeks out the optimum media schedule in view of the objective function specified and subject to satisfying the budget and number-of-insertion constraints.

Illustration. An illustration of a hypothetical magazine schedule for the Toyota Paseo will be helpful to better understand how media models, ADplus™ in particular, are implemented. Let us assume that a media planner for the Toyota Paseo is in process of choosing an optimum, four-week schedule from among ten magazines considered appropriate for reaching young male readers aged 21–34. The Simmons Market Research Bureau (SMRB) estimates that as of 1990 there are 34,134,000 males in the 18–34 category.[19] Assuming further that only 50 percent of these 34+ million males satisfy the Paseo's income target of $25,000 or more, the target market is, accordingly, reduced downward to 17,067,000. All subsequent planning is based on this target size.

The media planner has prepared a database consisting of ten magazines considered suitable for reaching the target audience (see Table 13.3).

Here is how the table was constructed. First, the *ratings* column represents each magazine's audience size divided by the base audience size of 17,067,000.[20]

Database for the Hypothetical Toyota Paseo Media-Scheduling Decision   TABLE 13.3

MAGAZINE	RATING	COST	MAXIMUM INSERTIONS
Sports Illustrated	48.4	$120,950	4
Playboy	28.6	68,545	1
Popular Mechanics	23.6	54,065	1
Rolling Stone	15.2	43,040	2
Sports Afield	15.2	26,600	1
Hot Rod	15.0	36,750	1
Ebony	11.6	38,103	1
Golf Digest	11.2	64,730	1
Golf Magazine	9.8	46,235	1
GQ	9.4	29,390	1

[19]Cited in *Mediaweek's Guide to Media: 1991 Second Quarter* (New York: A/S/M Communications, Inc., 1991, 14, 2).

[20]In constructing Table 13.3, magazine audience sizes were based on the *larger* of the estimated audience sizes provided by the Simmons Marketing Research Bureau and Mediamark Research, Inc. Figures were obtained from *Mediaweek's Guide to Media: 1991 Second Quarter*, 108–112. Because many of the readers of these magazines undoubtedly do not satisfy the income requirement of $25,000+ or fall outside of the 18–34 age category targeted for the Paseo, each magazine's total audience size was arbitrarily cut in half prior to being divided by the target audience size of 17+ million.

Second, the *cost* column reflects the price charged by each magazine for a one-time placement of a full-page, four-color advertisement.[21] Finally, the *maximum insertions* column simply reflects each magazine's publication cycle. All magazines except *Rolling Stone* and *Sports Illustrated* are published once per month, whereas *RS* and *SI* are published bimonthly and weekly, respectively. Hence, it is possible to place only one ad during the four-week period in eight of the magazines, whereas two ads will be placed in *Rolling Stone* and four ads in *Sports Illustrated*.

The information in Table 13.3 was input into the ADplus™ program by including each magazine's name, cost, rating, and maximum insertions.[22] With this information, the ADplus™ program was instructed to *maximize GRPs and not to exceed a budget of $800,000* for this hypothetical four-week campaign.

Given 10 magazines and different numbers of maximum insertions in each, there literally are thousands of media schedules possible. However, in a matter of seconds, the ADplus™ algorithm identified that single combination of magazines that maximizes GRPs for an expenditure of $800,000 or less. The solution is shown in Table 13.4.

Table 13.4 shows that the optimum schedule consists of one ad each in *Sports Afield*, *Popular Mechanics*, *Playboy*, *Hot Rod*, and *Ebony*, two ads in *Rolling Stone*, and four ads in *Sports Illustrated*. The total cost is $793,943, which is just under the specified upper limit of $800,000. This schedule yields 318 GRPs, which is the maximum number of GRPs that any possible combination of magazines could have yielded given a budget constraint of $800,000. This optimum schedule reaches 68.7 percent of the audience with an average frequency of 4.6 exposures. Effective reach (i.e., 3+) is 55.7 percent. The cost per thousand is $14.63, which translates into a cost-per-rating point of $2,497.

Note carefully at the top of Table 13.4 that two frequency distributions are presented: a vehicle distribution and a message distribution. The distinction is an important one. *Vehicle distribution* refers to the estimated potential delivery of the magazine vehicles themselves. Comparatively, *message distribution* reflects smaller percentages of audience members who are expected to be exposed to the Paseo advertising message placed in the magazines. It should be apparent that the likelihood of being exposed to an advertisement in a magazine is lower than the likelihood of being exposed to the magazine per se. The ratio of message-to-vehicle exposure used to generate Table 13.4 is 52.5 percent, which, in other words, suggests that the average consumer magazine reader is about one-

---

[21]This information was obtained from *Mediaweek's Guide to Media: 1991 Second Quarter*, 91–94. In actuality, a large advertiser such as Toyota would receive quantity discounts and, thus, would pay only about 70–75 percent as much per full-page ad as the costs listed in Table 13.3.

[22]A users' manual and operating diskettes for the ADplus™ program are available for approximately $40 from Media Research Institute, Inc., 9414 N.W. 59th Lane, Gainesville, FL, 32606. Telephone: (904) 372-7173. The program is extremely user friendly.

ADplus™ Optimum Schedule for Toyota Paseo Media Decision

TABLE 13.4

ADplus™ RESULTS: CONSUMER MAGAZINES
Hypothetical Example
Toyota Paseo
Typical Month

Target: 17,067,000
Males, 18–34. $25+K

Message/vehicle = 52.5%

FREQUENCY (F) DISTRIBUTIONS

f	VEHICLE % f	VEHICLE % f+	MESSAGE % f	MESSAGE % f+
0	31.3	100.0	55.4	100.0
1	6.3	68.7	3.3	44.6
2	6.8	62.4	4.0	41.3
3	5.3	55.7	3.3	37.3
4	10.0	50.3	6.5	34.0
5	15.6	40.3	10.4	27.5
6	13.5	24.7	9.3	17.1
7	7.5	11.2	5.2	7.9
8	2.9	3.7	2.0	2.6
9	0.7	0.8	0.5	0.6
10+	0.1	0.1	0.1	0.1

SUMMARY EVALUATION

Reach (1+)	68.7%	44.6%
Effective reach (3+)	55.7%	37.3%
Gross rating points (GRPs)	318.0	213.1
Average frequency (f)	4.6	4.8
Gross impressions (000s)	54,273.1	36,368.9
Cost-per-thousand (CPM)	$14.63	$21.83
Cost-per-rating point (CPP)	$2,497	$3,726

VEHICLE LIST	RATING	AD COST	CPM-MSG	ADS	TOTAL COST	MIX
Sports Afield	15.20	$26,600	$19.53	1	$26,600	3.4%
Popular Mechanics	23.60	54,065	25.57	1	54,065	6.8
Playboy	28.60	68,545	26.75	1	68,545	8.6
Hot Rod	15.00	36,750	27.34	1	36,750	4.6
Sports Illustrated	48.40	120,950	27.89	4	483,800	60.9
Rolling Stone	15.20	43,040	31.60	2	86,080	10.8
Ebony	11.60	38,103	36.66	1	38,103	4.8
	Totals	$21.83		11	$793,943	100.0%

Maximum GRPs, budget: $800,000, time (mm:ss): 00:01
File(s): B:PASEO

half as likely to be exposed to an advertisement as she or he is to be exposed to a magazine carrying the advertisement.[23]

Is the media schedule in Table 13.4 a good schedule? In terms of GRPs, the schedule is the very best possible out of thousands of possibilities. Whether it satisfies other objectives (e.g., effective reach) is a matter that only the media planner and her associates can determine. As noted earlier, a variety of subjective considerations enter into a media choice. Media models such as ADplus™ do not make the ultimate media-scheduling decision. All they can do is efficiently perform the calculations needed to determine which single media schedule will optimize some objective function such as maximizing GRPs. Armed with the answer, it is up to the media planner to determine whether the media schedule satisfies other, nonquantitative objectives such as those described in the following section.

MEDIA AND VEHICLE SELECTION

We have reviewed the various objectives (reach, frequency, continuity, and cost considerations) that direct media choice and have described a model for selecting a mathematically optimum media schedule. However, the choice of general *media categories* (television, radio, magazines, etc.) and *specific vehicles* (particular television programs, magazines, etc.) involves more than pure mathematical considerations. Indeed, a variety of creative considerations must be taken into consideration.

Each medium and vehicle has a set of unique characteristics and virtues (see Figure 13.4). Advertisers attempt to select those media and vehicles whose characteristics are most compatible with the advertised product and which will enhance the product's image.

If the objective is to demonstrate product features, *television* is the best medium to use, followed by magazines, newspapers, radio, and outdoor advertising (see Figure 13.4). Television is also particularly strong in terms of its entertainment and excitement value and its ability to have an impact on the viewer. *Magazines* are strong in terms of elegance, beauty, prestige, and tradition. *Newspapers* are particularly good in terms of newsworthiness and price. *Radio*, which is especially personal, allows for the listener's imagination to play a part, while *outdoor* advertising is particularly good for package identification. Subsequent sections offer detailed descriptions of all five major media: television, radio, magazines, newspapers, and outdoor advertising.

---

[23]This estimate is based on research that asked media directors to specify the ratios they use in practice. See Kent M. Lancaster, Peggy J. Kreshel, and Joya R. Harris, "Estimating Describe Weighting and Timing Factors," *Journal of Advertising Research*, 15 (September 1986), 21–29.

Which Media Do It Best? FIGURE 13.4

	Television	Magazines	Newspapers	Radio	Outdoor
Demonstration					
Elegance					
Features					
Intrusion					
Quality					
Excitement					
Imagination					
Beauty					
Entertainment					
Sex Appeal					
Personal					
One-On-One					
Snob Appeal					
Package I.D.					
Product-In-Use					
Recipe					
Humor					
Tradition					
Leadership					
Information					
Authority					
Intimacy					
Prestige					
Bigger-Than-Life					
News					
Event					
Impact					
Price					

Best   Worst

Source: Courtesy of Needham Harper Worldwide, Inc.

Television

Television is practically ubiquitous in the United States and throughout the rest of the industrialized world. Television sets are present in over 98 percent of all American households. As an advertising medium, television is uniquely personal and demonstrative, yet it is also expensive and subject to considerable competitive clutter.

Television's specific strengths and weaknesses are elaborated upon in a later section. First it will be instructive to examine two specific aspects of television advertising: (1) the different programming segments, or so-called day parts and (2) the alternative outlets for television commercials (network, spot, local, and cable).

TELEVISION PROGRAMMING SEGMENTS.   Advertising costs, audience characteristics, and programming appropriateness vary greatly at different times of the day and during different days of the week. In television parlance, the times of day are referred to as *day parts*. The three major day parts are prime time, daytime, and fringe time. Each day part has its own strengths and weaknesses.[24]

Prime Time.   The period between 8:00 p.m. and 11:00 p.m. is known as *prime time* in most parts of the country. The best and most expensive programs are scheduled during this period. Audiences are largest during prime time, and the networks naturally charge the highest rates during this time.

Daytime.   The period that begins with the early morning news shows and extends to 4:00 p.m. is known as *daytime*. Early daytime appeals first to adults with news programs and then to children with special programs designed for this group. Afternoon programming, with its special emphasis on soap operas, appeals primarily to people working at home and, according to rumor, college students in dormitories.

Fringe Time.   The period preceding and following prime time is known as *fringe time*. Early fringe starts with afternoon reruns and is devoted primarily to children but becomes more adult oriented as prime time approaches. Late fringe appeals primarily to young adults.

NETWORK, SPOT, LOCAL, AND CABLE ADVERTISING. Television messages are transmitted by local stations, which are either locally owned cable television systems or are affiliated with the three major commercial

---

[24]The following discussion is adapted from Anthony F. McGann and J. Thomas Russell, *Advertising Media: A Managerial Approach* (Homewood, IL: Irwin, 1988), 141–143.

networks (ABC, CBS, and NBC) or with an independent cable network (such as WTBS, the Turner Broadcasting System). This arrangement of local stations and networks makes possible different ways of buying advertising time on television.

Network Television Advertising.   Companies that market products nationally often use network television to reach potential customers throughout the country. The advertiser, typically working through an advertising agency, purchases desired time slots from one or more of the major networks and advertises at these times on all local stations that are affiliated with the network.

The cost of such advertising depends on the time of day when an ad is aired as well as on the popularity of the television program in which the ad is placed. For example, network TV prime time rates for 30-second commercials during the 1991 season ranged from a low of $60,000 (on programs such as *FBI: Untold Stories* and *The Young Riders*) to a high of $260,000 for the ever-popular *Cheers.*[25]

Network television advertising, although expensive in terms of per-unit cost, can be a cost-efficient means to reach mass audiences. Consider the $260,000 cost for *Cheers.* This program, with a rating of 21.6 during the 1990–1991 television season, was viewed by approximately 19,700,000 households when it was aired by NBC from 9:00 until 9:30 on Thursday evenings.[26] Thus, an advertiser on this program would have paid approximately only $13.20 for a 30-second advertising message to reach every 1,000 households.

Network advertising is inefficient, and in fact infeasible, if the national advertiser chooses to concentrate efforts only on select markets. For example, some brands, though marketed nationally, are directed primarily at consumers in certain geographic locales. In this case, it would be wasteful to invest in network advertising, which would reach many areas where target audiences are not located.

Spot Television Advertising.   The national advertiser's alternative to network television advertising is spot advertising. As the preceding discussion intimated and as the name suggests, this type of advertising is placed (spotted) only in selected markets.

In some situations network advertising is completely infeasible for the national advertiser, who must then rely on spot television advertising. Spot advertising is particularly desirable when a company rolls out a new brand market by market before it achieves national distribution, or when a company's product distribution is limited to one or a few geographical regions. Also, spot advertising is useful even for those advertisers who use network advertising but need to

---

[25]Joe Mandese, "Prime-Time Rates Take a Tumble," *Advertising Age,* September 16, 1991, 6.

[26]"Blacks Reveal TV Loyalty," *Advertising Age,* November 18, 1991, 28.

supplement the national coverage with greater amounts of advertising in select markets that have particularly high brand potential. Greater use of spot television advertising is to be expected in the future inasmuch as consumer package goods companies are using more regionalized marketing and more sophisticated geodemographic segmentation practices. (See discussion of geodemographic clustering in the *Focus on Promotion*.)

Local Television Advertising.   Television advertising historically has been dominated by national advertisers, but local advertisers are turning to television in ever greater numbers. Local advertisers often find that the CPM advantages of television, plus the advantage of product demonstration, justify the choice of this advertising medium. Local television advertising is particularly inexpensive during the fringe times preceding and following prime-time programming.

Cable Advertising.   Cable television has been available for a number of years, but only recently have advertisers turned to cable as a potentially valuable advertising medium. Though some national advertisers are still somewhat uncertain about the advertising potential of cable television, growing numbers of national advertisers are using cable—companies such as Procter & Gamble, General Mills, Anheuser-Busch, Philip Morris, General Motors, and RJR Nabisco annually spend over $20 million on cable TV advertising.[27] Cable television's household penetration is expected to increase from only 22.6 percent in 1980 to a level exceeding 65 percent in 1994.[28]

Cable advertising is attractive to national advertisers for several reasons. First, advertisers are able to reach more finely targeted audiences (in terms of demographics and psychographics) than when using network or spot advertising. Second, the combination of high network rates and declining audiences has compelled advertisers to experiment with media alternatives such as cable. A third reason for cable advertising's growth is the demographic composition of cable audiences. Cable subscribers are more economically upscale and younger than the population as a whole.[29] By comparison, the heaviest viewers of network television tend to be more economically downscale. It is little wonder that the upscale characteristics of cable viewers have great appeal to many national advertisers.

TELEVISION ADVERTISING: STRENGTHS AND PROBLEMS. Each advertising medium possesses relative strengths in comparison with other media. These involve both quantitative considerations (the number of target

---

[27]"And Now, a Word from Our Sponsors," *Advertising Age*, May 13, 1991, sec. S, 32.

[28]"Cable TV Facts," *Advertising Age*, (advertising supplement), February 11, 1991, Cable-22.

[29]Ibid., Cable-27.

customers a particular medium reaches, its cost, and so on) and qualitative matters (e.g., how elegant or personal a medium is). The qualitative factors, though inherently more subjective, often play the determining role in advertisers' media decisions. Figure 13.4, which was introduced earlier, illustrates the types of qualitative considerations that advertising practitioners consider when making media selections and shows the relative strengths of television as well as the other major advertising media.

Television's Strengths.   Beyond any other consideration, television possesses the unique capability to *demonstrate* a product in use. No other medium has the ability to reach consumers simultaneously through both auditory and visual senses. Viewers can see and hear a product being used, identify with the product's users, and imagine themselves using the product.

Television also has *intrusion value* unparalleled by other media. That is, television advertisements engage one's senses and attract attention even when one would prefer not to be exposed to an advertisement. In comparison, it is much easier to avoid a magazine or newspaper ad by merely flipping the page or to avoid a radio ad by changing channels. But it is often easier to sit through a television commercial rather than attempting to avoid it either physically or mentally.

A third relative advantage of television advertising is its combined ability to *provide entertainment and generate excitement*. Advertised products can be brought to life or made to appear even bigger than life. Products advertised on television can be presented dramatically and made to appear more exciting and less mundane than they actually are.

Television also has the unique ability to *reach consumers one on one*, as is the case when a spokesperson or endorser espouses the merits of a particular product. Like a personal sales presentation, the interaction between spokesperson and consumer takes place on a personal level.

More than any other medium, television is able to use *humor* as an effective advertising strategy.

In the final analysis, the greatest relative advantage of television advertising is its ability to achieve *impact*. Impact is that quality of an advertising medium that activates a "special condition of awareness"[30] in the consumer and that "enlivens his mind to receive a sales message."[31]

Problems with Television Advertising.   As an advertising medium, television suffers from three distinct problems. First, and perhaps most serious, is the *rapidly escalating advertising cost*. The cost of network television advertising

[30]Richard C. Anderson, "Eight Ways to Make More Impact," *Advertising Age*, May 17, 1982, sec. M, 23.

[31]Raymond Rubicam quoted in Anderson, ibid.

FOCUS ON PROMOTION

INCREASED ADVERTISING EFFICIENCY VIA GEODEMOGRAPHIC CLUSTERING

Suppose your company markets a product that is used by only a fraction of the total market. Suppose further that the heavy users of this product tend to congregate in certain geographic areas rather than being equally dispersed throughout the United States. Facing such a situation, why advertise on network television?

This is precisely the circumstance confronted by a maker of a baking product used in making cakes and cookies from scratch. The company's objective was to advertise only in those markets where audiences contain large proportions of consumers who regularly bake from scratch. Using ClusterPLUS, a product of Donnelley Marketing Information Services, the company was able to accomplish its advertising-efficiency objective.

ClusterPLUS divides the United States' 250,000 census block groups into 47 geodemographic clusters, where each cluster consists of people with demographic and socioeconomic similarities. For example, Cluster 1, the Established Wealthy, contains the elite, affluent neigh-

(continued)

has more than tripled over the past two decades. A dramatic illustration of this is the increasing cost of buying advertising time during the Super Bowl. In 1975, the cost was $110,000 for a 30-second commercial. By 1991, ABC was asking $850,000 for the same commercial on Super Bowl XXV.[32]

A second problem is the *erosion of television viewing audiences*. Videocassette recorders, syndicated programs, cable television, and other leisure and recreational alternatives have diminished the number of people viewing network television.[33] The three major networks' share of television audiences during prime time fell from 91 percent in 1979 to 63 percent in 1991.[34]

---

[32]John McManus, "Super Bowl Rate Up 17%," *Advertising Age*, April 16, 1990, 3.

[33]For further discussion of options available to viewers, see Dean M. Krugman, "Evaluating the Audiences of the New Media," *Journal of Advertising*, 14, 4 (1985), 21-27; and Dean M. Krugman, "Telecommunication Services and Advertising: A Review of the Audiences and Research," in *Current Issues & Research in Advertising*, 11, eds. James H. Leigh and Claude R. Martin, Jr. (Ann Arbor, MI, Division of Research, Graduate School of Business Administration, University of Michigan, 1988), 331–349.

[34]"Neck and Neck At the Networks," *Business Week*, May 20, 1991, 36.

borhoods in places such as Greenwich, Connecticut and Beverly Hills, California.

Using the ClusterPLUS scheme along with product-usage data from Simmons Market Research Bureau, the baking-goods company identified its target cluster as those people who bake from scratch three or more times per month. ClusterPLUS's Cluster 23, Low-Mobility Rural Families, was identified as the best target group. Thirty-nine percent of the people in this cluster are heavy from-scratch bakers, compared with the national average of 17 percent. Nine other clusters also were considered appropriate targets for the company's advertising efforts.

The baking-goods company aimed its advertising at consumers in the combined 10 clusters. These are individuals who are older, rural, blue-collar, and reside predominantly in the South and Midwest. Spot advertising was placed in these geographic areas, and ads were aired on programs that Nielsen television-usage data revealed as being heavily viewed by these individuals—programs such as *America's Funniest Home Videos, Major Dad*, and *In the Heat of the Night*.

This illustration indicates that by utilizing a combination of modern information services (i.e., ClusterPLUS, Simmons, Nielsen) an advertiser can use spot television as an efficient, targeted marketing tool. Television is no longer just a mass advertising medium.

Source: This description is based on information provided in "Clusters Plus Nielsen Equals Efficient Marketing," *American Demographics*, September 1991, 16.

Third, even when people are viewing television, cable as well as network, much of their time is spent switching from station to station and *zapping* commercials. The remote control "zapper" has been referred to (only partially with tongue in cheek) as the greatest threat to capitalism since Karl Marx.[35]

Clutter is a fourth serious problem with television advertising. Clutter refers to the growing amount of nonprogram material—commercials, public service messages, and promotional announcements for stations and programs. Clutter has been created by the network's increased use of promotional announcements to stimulate audience viewing of heavily promoted programs and by advertisers' increased use of shorter commercials. Whereas 60-second commercials once were prevalent, now the vast majority of commercials are 30 seconds or less.

[35]"The Toughest Job in TV," *Newsweek*, October 3, 1988, 72; Dennis Kneale, "'Zapping' of TV Ads Appears Pervasive," *The Wall Street Journal*, April 25, 1988, 21.

The effectiveness of television advertising has suffered from the clutter problem, which creates a negative impression among consumers about advertising in general and turns viewers away from the television set.[36]

A series of experiments aimed at studying the consequences of television clutter revealed that the amount of attention devoted to commercials, the degree of content recall, and the extent of brand-name recognition all suffer from increased levels of clutter. For example, the percentage of subjects who pay full attention to any part of the tested commercials decreases from 56 percent in the least-cluttered experimental condition to 46 percent in the most-cluttered condition. Correct brand-name recognition drops from 22 percent in the least-cluttered version to 10 percent in the most-cluttered version. The extent to which clutter has negative effects on commercial effectiveness depends on a commercial's position in a series or stream of continuous commercial messages. The middle position is worst, the first position is best, and the last position is next best.[37]

Radio

Like television, radio is a nearly ubiquitous medium: 99 percent of all homes in the United States have radios, 77 percent of the homes contain four or more radios, 95 percent of all cars have a radio, and more than 50 million radios are purchased in the United States each year.[38] These impressive figures indicate radio's strong potential as an advertising medium.

Promotion efforts by the Radio Advertising Bureau, an industry trade association, claim that radio gets results. The point of this self-promotion is that radio is an effective medium for creating buying action. Puffery aside, radio is indeed an effective advertising medium. Although radio has always been a favorite of local advertisers, it is only in recent years that national advertisers have begun to appreciate radio's advantages as an advertising medium. The following section examines these advantages and also explores some of the problems with radio advertising.

R ADIO ADVERTISING: STRENGTHS AND PROBLEMS.   Like television, radio advertising has its own set of strengths and problems.

---

[36]Verne Gay, "Clutter is Ad Pollution," *Advertising Age*, October 10, 1988, 56; Joe Mandese, "Rival Spots Cluttering TV," *Advertising Age*, November 18, 1991, 6.

[37]For a review of these studies, see Peter H. Webb and Michael L. Ray, "Effects of TV Clutter," *Journal of Advertising Research*, 19 (June 1979), 7–12.

[38]Burt Manning, "Friendly Persuasion," *Advertising Age*, September 13, 1982, sec. M, 8; Marc Beauchamp, "Radio Days," *Forbes*, November 30, 1987, 200, 204.

Radio's Strengths.   The first major strength of radio is that it is second only to magazines in its *ability to reach segmented audiences.* Radio personifies the notion of **narrowcasting** in that it can be used to pinpoint advertisements to specific groups of consumers: teens, Hispanics, sports nuts, news enthusiasts, and so on. An extensive variety of radio programming enables advertisers to pick specific formats and stations to be optimally compatible with both the composition of their target audience and their creative message strategies. One media director explains radio's narrowcasting versatility this way:

> There's classical music to reach the same kind of educated, high income adults [who] read *Smithsonian* or *Travel and Leisure,* only at less cost. You've got a yen to reach working women? Try an all news station in a.m. drivetime. Blacks? Stations like WBLS in New York reach them more efficiently than TV's "Soul Train" or black magazines such as *Ebony* and *Essence.* You've got teen stations, old lady stations, stations which reach sports nuts, young adults and middle-of-the-roaders. So don't think of radio as a mass medium unless sheer tonnage at the lowest CPM is your game. The radio networks are made up of hundred of stations with different formats, audiences, signal strengths, coverage, etc.[39]

A second major advantage of radio advertising is its *ability to reach prospective customers on a personal and intimate level.* Local store merchants and radio announcers sometimes are extremely personable and convincing. Their messages come across as if they were personally speaking to each audience member.

The CEO of J. Walter Thompson USA, one of the largest advertising agencies in the United States, has metaphorically described radio as a "universe of private worlds," and a "communication between two friends."[40] In other words, people select radio stations in much the same way that they select personal friends. People listen to those radio stations with which they closely identify. Because of this, radio advertising is likely to be received when the customer's mental frame is most conducive to persuasive influence. Radio advertising, then, is a personal and intimate form of "friendly persuasion."[41]

Economy is a third advantage of radio advertising. In terms of CPM per target audience, radio advertising is considerably cheaper than other mass media. Over the past quarter century, radio's cost per thousand has increased less than any other advertising medium.[42]

---

[39]Cyril C. Penn, "Marketing Tool Underused," *Advertising Age,* September 25, 1978, 122.

[40]Manning, "Friendly Persuasion."

[41]Ibid.

[42]Beauchamp, "Radio Days," 204.

Flexibility is another relative advantage of radio advertising. Because radio production costs are typically inexpensive and scheduling deadlines are short, copy changes can be made quickly to take advantage of important developments and changes in the marketplace. For example, a sudden weather change may suggest an opportunity to advertise weather-related products. A radio spot can be prepared quickly to accommodate the needs of the situation.

Problems with Radio Advertising.   Radio shares some of television advertising's weaknesses and problems. Foremost is that both broadcast media are *cluttered* with competitive commercials and other forms of noise, chatter, and interference. Radio listeners frequently switch stations, especially on their car radios, to avoid commercials.[43]

A second limitation is that radio is the only major medium that is *unable to employ visualizations*. However, radio advertisers attempt to overcome the medium's visual limitation by using sound effects and choosing concrete words to conjure up images in the listener's mind's eye. It is important to note that many advertising campaigns use radio as a supplement to other media rather than as a stand-alone medium. This reduces radio's task from one of creating visual images to one of reactivating images that already have been created via television or magazines.

A third problem with radio advertising results from the *difficulty of buying radio time*. This problem is particularly acute in the case of the national advertiser who wishes to place spots in different markets throughout the country. With more than 10,000 commercial radio stations operating in the United States, buying time is complicated by unstandardized rate structures that include a number of combinations of fixed and discount rates.

A NOTE ON BUYING RADIO TIME.   Radio advertisers are interested in accomplishing reach, frequency, and GRP requirements while ensuring that the station format is compatible with the advertised product and its creative message strategy. Several considerations influence the choice of station. Station format (classical, progressive, country, top 40, etc.) is a major consideration. Certain formats are obviously inappropriate for particular products and brands.

A second consideration is the choice of geographic areas to cover. National advertisers buy time from stations whose audience coverage matches the advertiser's geographic areas of interest. This typically means locating stations in preferred Metropolitan Statistical Areas (MSAs) or in so-called Areas of Dominant Influence (ADIs), which are approximately 200 areas in the United States that correspond to the major television markets.

---

[43]A thorough study of this behavior was conducted by Avery M. Abernethy, "Determinants of Audience Exposure to Radio Advertising" (Ph.D. diss., University of South Carolina, 1988).

COLOR IN ADVERTISING

This section contains sixteen color reproductions of various marketing communications, mostly advertisements, that have appeared throughout the text as black and white images. The section has been included to illustrate some points that are missed in black and white. Some brief commentary about the use of color is offered now as prelude to the more in-depth descriptions that follow for each of the sixteen color inserts.

Advertisements and other printed forms of marketing communications come in three forms: black and white (b&w); b&w along with one other color; and four colors—black plus the three primary colors of yellow, red, and blue, which, when blended together, make it possible to capture the full palette of color alternatives. The use of color in advertising has grown steadily since the 1940s and now represents well over two-thirds of magazine ad pages. The reasons for using color are several: First and perhaps foremost, color is an effective attention getter that serves to increase readership. Second, the use of color creates moods and conveys emotions that run the gamut from a sense of frivolity to a state of intense excitement. Third, color makes advertised products appear more realistic, more appetizing, and therefore more desirable.

Figure 1.1, SAFARI.
This advertisement captures a sense of elegance and prestige. The sparkling perfume bottle has the look of leaded crystal, and the deep, rich earthtones along with the surrounding jewels convey a feeling of grandeur.

Figure 1.5, HUMMEL.
Compare the black and white version of this ad with the four-color version. In color, everything is more realistic and, at the same time, more evocative. The sun rising over the horizon forms a vivid, attention-getting contrast against the pale blue ocean. The subdued colors of the morning beach scene are in perfect harmony with the contemplative mood of the mother-to-be. Notice also how the visual design leads the eye from the protagonist over to the text copy and down to the figurine.

Figure 2.2, LINCOLN.
The elegance of the Faberge egg nestled against green velvet dramatically conveys the beauty of this unique item. Only in color is it possible to see how splendid a Faberge egg is. In turn, the Lincoln is itself more magnificent by virtue of its association with the Faberge egg.

The Encyclopedia of Summer Classics, Illustrated:

Adirondack chair. Elegantly simple cottage and resort chair designed at the turn of the century, using smooth-planed wood in place of the unmilled saplings typical of Adirondack furniture. The flat, broad arms accommodate a good vacation book or perhaps an ice-cold lemonade.

Alfa Romeo Spider Veloce.
The Pininfarina-designed, fuel-injected DOHC 2.0-liter, 5-speed classic roadster. With power-assisted four-wheel disc brakes, power-assisted steering, driver's side airbag and a premium sound system. Often referred to as "the official car of summer." For additional information, call **1-800-245-ALFA.**

©1991 Alfa Romeo Distributors of North America.

The legendary marque of high performance.

Figure 2.5, ALFA ROMEO.
The Alfa Romeo Spider Veloce ("the official car of summer") virtually jumps off the page with its bright-red color contrasted against the deep-white background. Notice, by comparison, that the Adirondack chair is stark white, so that even though it is a key point of reference, it does not deflect attention from the Alfa Romeo.

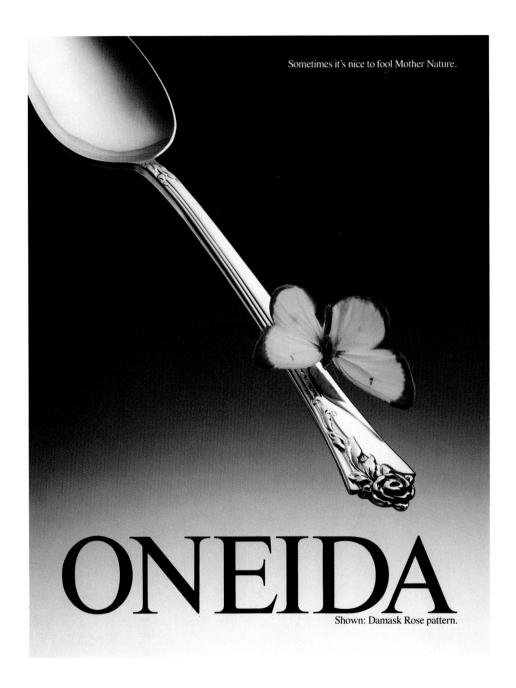

Figure 3.3, ONEIDA.
This advertisement illustrates the attention-getting power of color. The bright yellow butterfly provides a vivid contrast to the background of silver and dark shades. Attention is drawn first to the butterfly and then, intentionally, to the rose pattern, and finally to the Oneida name.

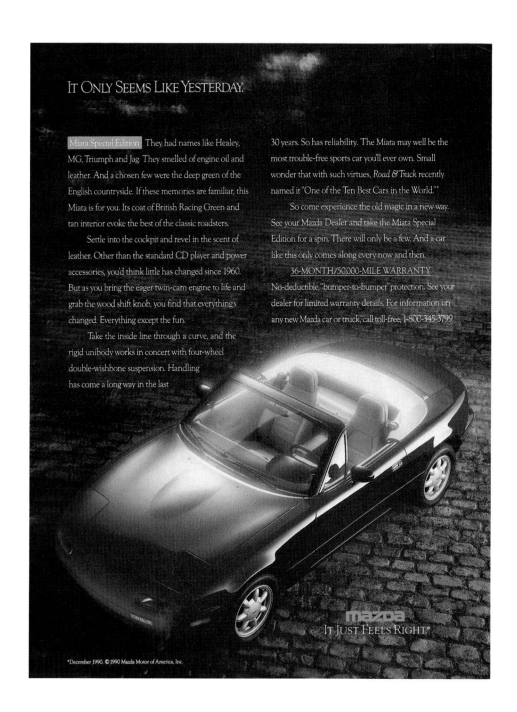

IT ONLY SEEMS LIKE YESTERDAY.

Miata Special Edition They had names like Healey, MG, Triumph and Jag. They smelled of engine oil and leather. And a chosen few were the deep green of the English countryside. If these memories are familiar, this Miata is for you. Its coat of British Racing Green and tan interior evoke the best of the classic roadsters.

Settle into the cockpit and revel in the scent of leather. Other than the standard CD player and power accessories, you'd think little has changed since 1960. But as you bring the eager twin-cam engine to life and grab the wood shift knob, you find that everything's changed. Everything except the fun.

Take the inside line through a curve, and the rigid unibody works in concert with four-wheel double-wishbone suspension. Handling has come a long way in the last

30 years. So has reliability. The Miata may well be the most trouble-free sports car you'll ever own. Small wonder that with such virtues, *Road & Track* recently named it "One of the Ten Best Cars in the World."*

So come experience the old magic in a new way. See your Mazda Dealer and take the Miata Special Edition for a spin. There will only be a few. And a car like this only comes along every now and then.

36-MONTH/50,000-MILE WARRANTY

No-deductible, "bumper-to-bumper" protection. See your dealer for limited warranty details. For information on any new Mazda car or truck, call toll-free, 1-800-345-3799.

mazda
IT JUST FEELS RIGHT.

*December 1990. © 1990 Mazda Motor of America, Inc.

Figure 6.2, MIATA.
The Miata in British racing green is lustrous when contrasted against a dark background. The glimmering light is an excellent attention getter, and a quaint sense of British civility and sportiness is created by displaying the Miata on a cobblestone road.

Figure 6.7, Diet Coke.
In this appeal to sophisticated career women, a mood of early evening tranquility is created with the use of rose tones. The entire setting (flickering candle, wrought iron gate) conveys an atmosphere of elegance and sophistication, just like the women professionals targeted by this ad.

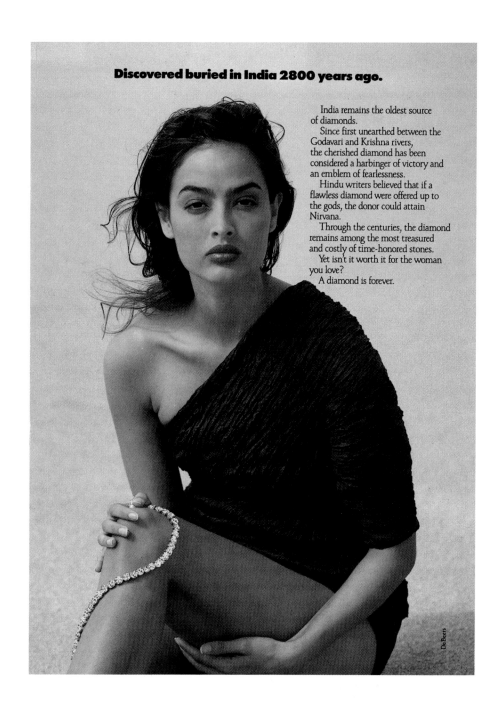

Discovered buried in India 2800 years ago.

India remains the oldest source of diamonds.

Since first unearthed between the Godavari and Krishna rivers, the cherished diamond has been considered a harbinger of victory and an emblem of fearlessness.

Hindu writers believed that if a flawless diamond were offered up to the gods, the donor could attain Nirvana.

Through the centuries, the diamond remains among the most treasured and costly of time-honored stones.

Yet isn't it worth it for the woman you love?

A diamond is forever.

De Beers

Figure 6.8, DIAMONDS.
The diamond necklace is lustrous when contrasted against the skin of the Asian Indian woman. India, according to the ad, is the oldest source of diamonds, and portraying products in the presence of beautiful women is one of the oldest forms of advertising.

Figure 7.3, AMWAY.
This delightful advertising supplement displays environmentally oriented artwork of the type children would create as part of a school project. The use of color captures the way children use color, creating an effective appeal to parents and teachers, who are encouraged to have their children and students enter an environmentally oriented contest.

Figure 11.7, MOUNTAIN DEW.

"Keep It Cool With Dew" is a catchy advertising slogan that requires visual support by depicting "cool" characters who represent the intended target for the brand. How better to demonstrate what being cool is all about than to show a group of accomplished rollerbladers in hot neon colors zipping along a smooth road? The bladers' sense of movement naturally directs the reader's eye flow to the cans of Mountain Dew and Diet Mountain Dew.

Figure 12.2, TIMEX.
An apparently very healthy Lisa Boyer, the protagonist in this minidrama, is shown suntanned and wearing her ever-faithful Timex watch. The special lighting attracts attention to Lisa's face, and then the eye naturally moves down her arm to the Timex watch. Imagine how dull and uninspiring this ad would be without color.

Figure 12.4, h.i.s.®

In a takeoff of the name of a famous airplane, "The Spirit of St. Louis," h.i.s.® jeans are sloganeered as "the spirit of jeans." The attractive model—perhaps the modern embodiment of the spirit captured by early airplane pilots—is shown seated on the wing of an early twentieth-century airplane. The model's suntanned skin and the bright colors in the h.i.s.® brand name provide vivid, attention-capturing contrasts to the stark silver background.

Figure 12.5, GIORGIO RED FOR MEN.

Red, the color of heat and passion, is an appropriate name for a product designed to capture the interest of a young male audience for whom passion is a hot commodity. The clever use of the red swatch against a black and white background provides a great attention getter while reinforcing the brand name and its primary benefit, the promise of passion. (Note that the male model in this ad is displayed as the recipient of passion rather than the aggressor, presumably because in the fantasy world of Madison Avenue, products like Red make one irresistible.)

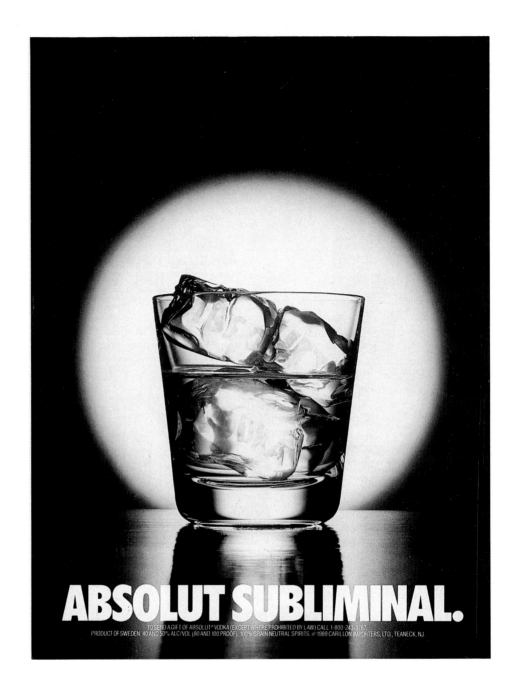

Figure 12.6, ABSOLUT.
This ad, which parodies the practice of embedding, uses color and other cues to draw attention to the word ABSOLUT airbrushed into the icecube. The soft yellow color is an appropriate backdrop for the focal glass and the accompanying statement: Absolut Subliminal.

Figure 17.6, KELLOGG'S.

This is not a standard advertisement but rather a free-standing insert from the Sunday newspaper. The bright neon yellow headline (Save 50¢) is a key feature of this coupon offer and ties in nicely with the neon yellow racing cap that is offered as a self-liquidating premium.

Figure 18.4, COORS LIGHT.
The dancing can is an outstanding point-of-purchase display. The shimmering humanoid can bedecked in neon pink sunglasses and earphones is a delightful eye-catcher as it gyrates to the music that hypothetically is being transmitted into its earphones.

A third consideration in buying radio time is the choice of day part. Most stations offer anywhere from two to five day parts. The following is a typical radio time schedule, with different day parts designated by letter combinations:

AAAA— Monday through Saturday, 5:30 to 10:00 a.m.
AAA— Monday through Saturday, 3:00 to 8:00 p.m.
AA— Monday through Friday, 10:00 a.m. to 3:00 p.m.; Saturday and Sunday, 6:00 a.m. to 8:00 p.m.
A—Monday through Sunday, 8:00 p.m. to midnight.
B—Tuesday through Sunday, midnight to 5:30 a.m.

Rate structures vary depending on the attractiveness of the day part; for example, AAAA is priced higher than B in the preceding schedule. Information about rates and station formats is available in *Spot Radio Rates and Data*, a source published by the Standard Rate and Data Services.

Magazines

Magazines use to be considered a mass medium. Today, however, there are literally hundreds of special-interest magazines, each appealing to audiences that manifest specific interests and lifestyles. In fact, *Standard Rate and Data Services*, the technical information source for the magazine industry, identifies nearly 1,300 consumer magazines and divides these into dozens of specific categories such as automotive (e.g., *Motor Trend*), general editorial (e.g., the *New Yorker*), sports (e.g., *Sports Illustrated*), women's fashions, beauty, and grooming (e.g., *Glamour*), and many others. In addition to consumer magazines, there are hundreds of other publications classified as farm magazines or business publications. Advertisers obviously have numerous options when selecting magazines to promote their products.

BUYING MAGAZINE SPACE.   A number of factors influence the choice of magazine vehicles in which to advertise. Most important is selecting magazines that reach the type of people who constitute the advertiser's target market. However, because the advertiser typically has several vehicle alternatives that satisfy the target-market objective, cost considerations also play an extremely important role.

The cost-per-thousand (CPM) measure introduced earlier is used by advertisers to compare different magazine buys. Cost-per-thousand information for each magazine is available from two syndicated magazine services: Mediamark Research, Inc. (MRI), and Simmons Market Research Bureau (SMRB). These services provide CPM figures for general categories (e.g., "total men") and also break out CPMs for subgroups (e.g., "men aged 18 to 49," "male homeowners"). These more specific subgroupings enable the advertiser to compare different magazine vehicles in terms of cost per thousand for reaching the target audience (i.e., CPM-TM) rather than only in terms of gross CPMs. Cost-per-thousand data are useful in making magazine-vehicle selection decisions, but many other factors must be taken into account. (Are thoughts of vaguely right versus precisely wrong decision making entering your mind?)

MAGAZINE ADVERTISING: STRENGTHS AND PROBLEMS. As an advertising medium, magazines have strengths and problems that are quite different from those of television and radio.

Magazine's Strengths. Some magazines reach very large audiences. For example, magazines like *TV Guide, Modern Maturity, Reader's Digest,* and *National Geographic* are circulated to over 10 million people.[44]

However, the *ability to pinpoint specific audiences* (termed *selectivity*) is the feature that most distinguishes magazine advertising from other media. If a potential market exists for a product, there most likely is at least one periodical that reaches that market. Selectivity enables an advertiser to achieve effective, rather than wasted, exposure. This translates into more efficient advertising and lower costs per thousand target customers.

Magazines are also noted for their *long life.* Unlike other media, magazines are often used for reference and kept around the home for several weeks or even longer. Magazine subscribers often pass along their copies to other readers, further extending a magazine's life.

In terms of qualitative considerations (refer again to Figure 13.4), magazines as an advertising medium are exceptional with regard to *elegance, quality, beauty, prestige,* and *snob appeal.* These features result from the high level of reproduction quality and from the surrounding editorial content that often transfers to the advertised product. For example, food items advertised in *Bon Appetit* always look elegant; furniture items in *Better Homes and Gardens* look tasteful; and clothing items in *Esquire* appear especially fashionable.

Magazines are also a particularly good source for providing *detailed product information* and for conveying this information with a sense of authority.

A final and especially notable feature of magazine advertising is its *creative ability to get consumers involved in ads.* Recent years have witnessed a variety of dramatic and highly successful efforts in magazine advertising to enhance reader involvement. For example, Revlon and Estée Lauder have offered eyeshadow and blusher samples on the pages of fashion magazines. Rolls-Royce included a scent strip in one of its ads that imitated the smell of the leather interior of its cars. Two liquor brands, Canadian Mist whiskey and Absolut vodka, used ads with microchips to play songs when the page opened. (A New York woman reported a case of "Absolut chaos" when she walked into her apartment

---

[44]"Rising above the Crowd," *Advertising Age,* April 18, 1988, sec. S, 13.

building to a chorus of noisy mailboxes full of magazine ads gone haywire.[45]) TransAmerican included a pop-up ad in *Time* magazine that featured the insurance company's distinctive pyramidal-shaped building set against the San Francisco skyline.

A very creative magazine advertising effort to enhance reader involvement was Toyota's use of three-dimensional viewfinders in 14 million copies of *Time, People,* and *Cosmopolitan* magazines. The ads were designed to show off the new look of the redesigned Corolla. Readers looked into the view finder and saw a very realistic three-dimensional portrayal of the Corolla. The ad received exceptionally high recall scores. Recall levels were 83 percent among males and 76 percent among females as compared with average recall rates for a four-page auto ad of 39 percent for males and 31 percent for females.[46]

Problems with Magazine Advertising. Several limitations are associated with magazine advertising. First, unlike TV and radio, magazine advertising is *not intrusive;* readers control whether they choose to be exposed to a magazine ad.

A second limitation is *lack of flexibility.* In newspapers and the broadcast media, it is relatively easy to change ad copy on fairly short notice and in specific markets. Magazines, by comparison, have *long closing dates* that require advertising materials to be on hand for eight weeks or longer.

As with other advertising media, *clutter* is a problem with magazine advertising. In certain respects clutter is a worse problem with magazines than, say, television, because readers can become engrossed in editorial content and skip over advertisements so as not to have their reading disrupted.

Newspapers

Newspapers are the leading advertising medium. Advertising expenditures in newspapers exceeded $32 billion in 1990 and represented over 25 percent of total advertising expenditures.[47] Table 13.5 compares newspaper advertising revenues with other media. Comparatively, it can be seen that television is the second largest advertising medium with $28.3 billion advertising revenues in 1990.

Newspaper advertising receipts are from local retail advertising (approximately 50 percent), classified ads (approximately 38 percent), and national ads (approximately 12 percent).[48]

[45]"The Escalating Ads Race," *Newsweek,* December 7, 1987, 65.

[46]"3-D Glasses Double Ad's Impact," *Marketing Communications,* January 1988, 10.

[47]"1991 Advertisers' Guide to Newspapers," *Advertising Age,* May 20, 1991, sec. N, 6.

[48]Tamara Goldman, "Big Spenders Develop Newspaper Strategies," *Marketing Communications,* January 1988, 24.

TABLE 13.5	Estimated 1990 Advertising Expenditure in Newspapers and Other Media

MEDIUM	AD DOLLARS (IN BILLIONS)
Newspapers	32.6
Television	28.3
Direct Mail	23.6
Radio	8.8
Yellow Pages	8.8
Magazines	6.9
Outdoor	1.2
Miscellaneous	19.6
Total	129.7

Source: Newspaper Advertising Bureau.

Local advertising is clearly the mainspring of newspapers. However, newspapers have become more active in their efforts to increase national advertising. These efforts have been facilitated by the Newspaper Advertising Bureau (NAB), a nonprofit sales and research organization. The NAB offers a variety of services that assist both newspapers and national advertisers by simplifying the task of buying newspaper space and by offering discounts that make newspapers a more attractive medium. Moreover, the trend toward regional marketing has led to greater use of newspaper advertising by major consumer package-good companies.

B UYING NEWSPAPER SPACE.   Whereas buying space in magazines is done on the basis of full and fractional pages, space in newspapers is identified in terms of *agate lines* and *column inches*. An agate line is 1/14 inch in depth and one column wide, regardless of the width of the column. The formula for transforming rates charged by different newspapers to a common denominator is called the *milline rate*, which stands for cost per line of advertising space per million circulation.

$$\text{Milline rate} \ = \ \frac{\text{Line rate}}{\text{Circulation (in millions)}}$$

This formula adjusts individual line rates in terms of a newspaper's circulation. Obviously, a higher line rate in one newspaper may well be a better value than a lower line rate in another paper if the circulation in the former newspaper is large enough to offset its higher line rate.

The choice of an advertisement's position must also be considered when buying newspaper space. Agate line rates apply only to advertisements placed *ROP* (run of press), which means that the ad appears in any location, on any page, at the discretion of the newspaper. Premium charges may be assessed if an advertiser has a preferred space positioning, such as at the top of the page in the financial section. Whether premium charges are actually assessed is a matter of negotiation between the advertiser and the newspaper.

NEWSPAPERS' STRENGTHS.   Because people read newspapers for news, they are in the *right mental frame to process advertisements* that present news of store openings, new products, sales, and so forth.

Mass audience coverage is a second strength of newspaper advertising. Coverage is not restricted to specific socioeconomic or demographic groups but rather extends across all strata. However, newspaper readers on average are considerably more economically upscale than television viewers. Special-interest newspapers also reach large numbers of potential consumers. For example, it is estimated that over 80 percent of all college students read a campus newspaper.[49]

Flexibility is perhaps the greatest strength of newspapers. National advertisers can adjust copy to match the specific buying preferences and peculiarities of localized markets. Local advertisers can vary copy through in-paper inserts targeted to specific zip codes. Short closing times, which permit advertisers to tie in advertising copy with local market developments or newsworthy events are another element of newspaper flexibility. In addition, advertising copy can be placed in a newspaper section that is compatible with the advertised product. Retailers of wedding accessories advertise in the bridal section, sporting-goods stores advertise in the sports section, and so forth.

The *ability to use long copy* is another strength of newspaper advertising. Detailed product information and extensive, editorial passages are used in newspaper advertising to an extent unparalleled by any other medium.

Timeliness is a final significant strength of newspaper advertising. Short scheduling deadlines make it possible for advertisers to develop copy or make copy changes quickly and thereby take advantage of dynamic marketplace developments.

PROBLEMS WITH NEWSPAPER ADVERTISING.   *Clutter* is a problem in newspapers, as it is in all of the other major media.

A second limitation of newspaper advertising is that newspapers are *not a highly selective medium.* Newspapers are able to reach broad cross sections of people, but, with few exceptions (such as campus newspapers), are unable to reach specific groups of consumers effectively.

---

[49]"Mediawatch," *Marketing Communications*, February 1983, 9.

Occasional users of newspaper space (such as national advertisers who infrequently advertise in newspapers) *pay higher rates* than do heavy users and have difficulty in securing preferred, non-ROP positions.

Newspapers generally offer a *mediocre reproduction quality.* For this and other reasons, newspapers are not generally known to enhance a product's perceived quality, elegance, or snob appeal, as do magazines and television.

Buying difficulties is a particularly acute problem in the case of the national advertiser who wishes to secure newspaper space in a variety of different markets. Each newspaper must be dealt with individually, and on top of this, the rates charged to national advertisers are typically higher than those charged to local advertisers.

However, the Newspaper Advertising Bureau (NAB) is making great strides toward making it easier for national advertisers to buy newspaper space. One program, called Standard Advertising Units (SAUs), has established 25 basic ad sizes that can be used in all broad-sheet newspapers (not tabloids) regardless of their column format or page size. Over 1,400 newspapers have accepted this program.[50] Another NAB program is known by the acronym CAN DO, which stands for Computer Analyzed Newspaper Data On-Line System. This program provides national advertisers with pertinent information about newspapers in terms of CPMs and demographic information on age, household income, and household size.[51]

A final significant problem with newspaper advertising involves the *changing composition of newspaper readers.* Whereas most everyone used to read a daily newspaper, readership has declined progressively over the past two decades. The most faithful newspaper readers are individuals aged 45 and older, but the large and attractive group of consumers aged 30 to 44 read daily newspapers less than ever before.[52] Daily newspaper readership in this age group fell by 30 percent in less than two decades—from 75 percent in 1972 to 45 percent in 1989![53]

Outdoor Advertising

Out-of-home advertising, or *outdoor* for short, is the oldest form of advertising. Although billboard advertising is the major aspect of outdoor, this type of advertising encompasses a variety of other delivery modes: advertising on bus shel-

[50]"Shedding the Local Image," *Marketing Communications,* September 1982, 43.

[51]Ibid.

[52]Joe Schwartz and Thomas Exter, "The News from Here," *American Demographics,* June 1991, 50–53.

[53]"Pages and Pages of Pain," *Newsweek,* May 27, 1991, 39, 41.

GLOBAL FOCUS

NEWSPAPER ADVERTISING IN THE FORMER SOVIET UNION

The virtual disintegration of the Soviet Union and the crumbling of communism have led toward a more market-oriented economy, albeit slowly. Perhaps the most dramatic indication of this development is the fact that *Pravda*, the hitherto mouthpiece of the Communist Party, and *Izvestia*, the organ of the Soviet Parliament, now accept advertising. The thought of seeing advertisements in these famous (infamous) newspapers is astonishing. Lenin must be rolling over in his grave!

Pravda, faced with a dramatically declining circulation, had to begin accepting advertising as a matter of survival. Although ad rates are subject to negotiation, the asking price is $50,000 to $60,000 for a full page. At the top end of $60,000 and with a circulation of 2.5 million readers, this means that *Pravda*'s full-page CPM is expensive at $24. What makes this rate expensive is the fact that Soviet consumers are cash starved.

Izvestia, with a daily circulation of 4.7 million, has a full-page rate of $52,000. This translates into a more economical CPM of slightly over $11. Sony (TVs and tape decks), Hyundai (automobiles), Taiwan Computers, and Ricoh Co. (copiers) are some of the first companies to take advantage of advertising space in *Izvestia*.

Source: Betsy McKay, "'Pravda' Struggles Post-Coup," *Advertising Age*, October 21, 1991, 20.

ters, giant inflatables (e.g., the Goodyear blimp), various forms of transit advertising (e.g., ads painted on the sides of cars and trucks), skywriting, t-shirts emblazoned with brand logo or company name, and so on. The one commonality among these is that they are seen by consumers outside of their homes (hence the name) in contrast to television, magazines, newspapers, and radio, which are received in the home (or in other indoor locations).

Outdoor advertising is regarded as a supplementary, rather than primary, advertising medium. As shown in Table 13.5, outdoor received approximately $1.2 billion in advertising revenues in 1990. Product categories that historically have spent the most on outdoor advertising include tobacco products and alcohol. However, these two categories, which increasingly have come under fire for excessive outdoor advertising in inner city areas, have dramatically reduced outdoor advertising. For example, although still the largest outdoor advertiser, tobacco now represents just over 13 percent of outdoor revenues compared to 40 percent only 10 years ago.[54]

BUYING OUTDOOR ADVERTISING.   Outdoor advertising is purchased through individual operators called *plants*. There are approximately hundreds of plants nationwide that offer outdoor advertising in all major markets. National outdoor buying organizations enable national advertisers to purchase outdoor space at locations throughout the country.

Like television and radio, outdoor advertising space is sold in terms of gross rating points (GRPs). However, the notion of GRP is somewhat different in the case of outdoor advertising. Specifically, one outdoor GRP means reaching 1 percent of the population one time. Outdoor GRPs are based on the daily duplicated audience as a percentage of the total potential market. For example, if four billboards in a community of 200,000 population achieve a daily exposure to 80,000 persons, the result is 40 gross rating points. GRPs are sold in units of 25, with 100 and 50 being the two most-purchased levels.[55]

OUTDOOR ADVERTISING: STRENGTHS AND PROBLEMS. Outdoor advertising presents the advertiser with several unique strengths and problems.

Outdoor Advertising's Strengths.   A major strength of outdoor advertising is its *broad reach and high frequency levels*. Outdoor advertising is effective in reaching virtually all segments of the population. The number of exposures is especially high when signs are strategically located in heavy-traffic areas.

Another advantage is *geographic flexibility*. Outdoor advertising can be strategically positioned to supplement other advertising efforts in select geographic areas where advertising support is most needed.

Low cost per thousand is another advantage. Outdoor advertising is the least expensive advertising medium on a CPM basis.

Because outdoor advertising is literally bigger than life, *product identification* is substantial. The ability to use large representations offers marketers excellent opportunities for brand and package identification.

Outdoor advertising also provides an excellent opportunity to reach consumers as a *last reminder before purchasing*. This explains why frequently purchased products (like cigarettes and beer) are the heaviest users of outdoor advertising. Advertisers in these categories hope to have their brands seen just prior to the consumer's brand choice.

---

[54]Adam Snyder, "Outdoor, Forecast: Sunny, Some Clouds," *Adweek's Marketing Week*, July 8, 1991, 18–19.

[55]McGann and Russell, *Advertising Media*, 272.

Problems with Outdoor Advertising.   A significant problem with outdoor advertising is *nonselectivity*. Outdoor advertising can be geared to general groups of consumers (e.g., inner-city residents) but cannot pinpoint specific market segments (say, professional black men between the ages of 25 and 39).

Short exposure time is another drawback. "Now you see it, now you don't" appropriately characterizes the fashion in which outdoor advertising engages the consumer's attention. For this reason, outdoor messages that have to be read are less effective than predominantly visual ones.

It also is *difficult to measure outdoor advertising's audience.* The lack of verified audience measurement is regarded by some as a significant impediment that must be overcome if outdoor advertising is to become a more widely used advertising medium.[56]

A final outdoor advertising problem involves *environmental concerns.* Billboards, the so-called "pollution on a stick," have been banned in some way by six states and more than 1,000 local governments.[57]

AGENCY-CLIENT RELATIONS

The subject of agency-client relations is a fitting chapter conclusion because the media strategies and decisions discussed to this point are most often the joint work of advertisers (clients) and their advertising agencies. This section first will examine the advertising-agency role and then the issue of agency compensation.

The Role of an Advertising Agency

Advertisers have three alternative ways to perform the advertising function. First, a company can maintain its own, *in-house* advertising operation. This necessitates employing an advertising staff and absorbing the overhead required to maintain the staff's operations. Such an arrangement is unprofitable unless a company does a relatively large and continuous amount of advertising.

An alternative arrangement is to contract for advertising services with a *full-service advertising agency.* Full-service agencies perform research, creative services, media planning and buying services, and a variety of client services. They also may be involved in the advertiser's total marketing process and, for a

---

[56]See Snyder, "Outdoor, Forecast: Sunny, Some Clouds."

[57]Ibid.

fee, may perform other marketing services including sales promotion, publicity, package design, strategic marketing planning, and sales forecasting.

Why would an advertiser want to employ the services of a full-service agency? The *advantages* include (1) acquiring the services of specialists with in-depth knowledge of current advertising and marketing techniques, (2) obtaining negotiating muscle with the media, and (3) being able to coordinate advertising and marketing efforts. The major *disadvantages* are that (1) some control over the advertising function is lost when it is performed by an agency rather than in-house, (2) agencies sometimes cater to larger clients and neglect smaller clients, and (3) agencies sometimes are inefficient in media buying.[58]

A third alternative is to purchase advertising services *a la carte*. That is, rather than depending on a single full-service agency to perform all advertising and related functions, an advertiser may recruit the services of a variety of firms with particular specialties in creative work, media selection, production, advertising research, sales promotion, publicity, new-product development, and so on. The *advantages* of this arrangement are (1) the ability to contract for services only when they are needed, (2) availability of high-caliber creative talent, and (3) potential cost efficiencies. The *disadvantages* include (1) a tendency for specialists (so-called *boutiques*) to approach client problems in a stereotyped rather than innovative fashion, (2) lack of cost accountability, and (3) the financial insta-bility of many smaller boutiques.[59]

Many advertisers actually employ a combination of the different advertising options rather than using one exclusively. For example, a firm may have its own in-house agency but contract with boutiques for certain needs. Although in-house agencies and boutiques experienced considerable growth during the late 1960s and early 1970s, the trend today is toward full-service agencies and away from in-house agencies—especially among larger advertisers.

Agency Compensation

Advertising agencies have three sources of compensation.[60]

1. The primary source is *commissions* from media (TV, magazines, etc.) for advertisements aired or printed on behalf of the agency's clients. The standard commission charged by U.S. agencies is *15 percent* of the gross amount of the billing.[61] To illustrate, suppose the XYZ Advertising Agency

---

[58]George Donahue, "Evaluating Advertising Services: Part II," *Marketing Communications*, April 1982, 61.

[59]Ibid., 64.

[60]Wes Perrin, *Advertising Realities: A Practical Guide to Agency Management* (Mountain View, CA: Mayfield Publishing, 1992), 74–75.

[61]The discount paid to advertising agencies for outdoor advertising is typically 16.67 percent.

buys $100,000 of space in a certain magazine for its client, ABC Company. When the invoice for this space comes due, XYZ would submit payment of $85,000 to the magazine ($100,000 less the 15 percent discount) and then bill ABC for the full $100,000. The $15,000 revenue realized by XYZ Advertising Agency historically has been regarded as a fair amount of compensation to the agency for its creative expertise, media-buying insight, and ancillary functions performed in behalf of its client, ABC Company.

The 15 percent compensation system has, as one may suppose, been a matter of some controversy between company marketing executives and managers of advertising agencies.[62] The primary area of disagreement is the matter of whether 15 percent compensation is too much (marketing executives' perspective) or too little (ad agencies' perspective). The disagreement has spurred the growth of an alternative compensation system, called the *fee system*. This system involves price negotiations between advertisers and agencies such that the actual rate of compensation, which may be more or less than 15 percent, is based on mutual agreement concerning the worth of the services rendered by the advertising agency. Although the fee system is being increasingly used, the conventional 15 percent compensation still dominates.[63] Despite the growth of the fee system, most agency executives believe that the 15 percent commission system will never die. The following quote from an agency executive summarizes the argument in favor of the traditional commission system:

> The best part about the commission system is that it is easy to understand and operates almost automatically. It can be reviewed periodically. Service can be improved or increased. Or concessions can be made. But the commission system actually reduces the chance of friction, which sooner or later can destroy even a productive agency-client relationship.[64]

2. The second form of agency compensation is *hourly fees* for specific services rendered for clients. For example, a focus group study performed on behalf of the client would be charged on an hourly basis.

3. The third form of compensation is *markups* on the cost of outside purchases. Outside purchases include an agency's acquisition of photographic and broadcast-production services on behalf of its clients. For example, suppose

[62]For an insightful review of different perspectives on the issue, see Herbert Zeltner, "Sounding Board: Clients, Admen Split on Compensation," *Advertising Age*, May 18, 1981, 63–76.

[63]"The 15% Media Commission Plans," *Marketing News*, June 10, 1983, 9.

[64]Merle Kingman, "To Fee or Not to Fee," *Advertising Age*, August 29, 1983, sec. M, 24.

XYZ Advertising Agency had a television commercial production company produce a commercial for its client, ABC Company, and assume a production cost of $75,000. XYZ would typically charge ABC a 17.65 percent markup, which in this case would amount to over $13,000.

In many respects, the matter of agency compensation boils down to an issue of what is fair and workable. Agencies and clients are not in complete harmony on this issue. A survey of members (agency representatives and clients) of an influential group called the Sounding Board offers insight into perceptions concerning the fairness and workability of various compensation systems. Agencies' and clients' views are somewhat divergent with regard to the fairness/workability of various compensation plans. In general, agencies prefer standard media commissions with additional fees for extra services rendered, whereas advertisers prefer the standard media commission system with maximum (ceiling) and minimum (floor) percentage adjustments for additional services rendered or not rendered.[65]

SUMMARY

Selection of advertising media and media vehicles is one of the most important and complicated of all marketing communications decisions. Media planning must be coordinated with marketing strategy and with other aspects of advertising strategy. The strategic aspects of media planning involve four steps: (1) selecting the target audience toward which all subsequent efforts will be directed; (2) specifying media objectives, which typically are stated in terms of reach, frequency, gross rating points (GRPs), or effective rating points (ERPs); (3) selecting general media categories and specific vehicles within each medium; and (4) buying media.

Media and vehicle selection are influenced by a variety of factors, the most important being target audience, cost, and creative considerations. Media planners select media vehicles by identifying those that will reach the designated target audience, satisfy budgetary constraints, and be compatible with and enhance the advertiser's creative messages. There are numerous ways to schedule media insertions over time, but media planners are increasingly using some form of pulsed or flighted schedule whereby advertising is on at times, off at others, but never continuous.

Five major media are available to advertising media planners: television, radio, magazines, newspapers, and outdoor advertising. Each medium has its

---

[65]Zeltner, "Sounding Board," 63.

unique qualities and strengths and weaknesses. The chapter provides a detailed analysis of each medium.

The chapter concludes with a discussion of the role of an advertising agency. Companies basically have three ways to perform the advertising function: set up an in-house advertising operation, use a full-service advertising agency, or buy advertising services on an a la carte basis from specialized advertising services called boutiques.

Discussion Questions

1. Why is target-audience selection the critical first step in formulating a media strategy?

2. Explain the problems associated with using GRPs as a media-selection criterion. In what sense is the concept of ERPs superior?

3. Why is reach also called net coverage or unduplicated audience?

4. Table 13.4 presents the ADplus™ output for the hypothetical media schedule for the Toyota Paseo. Show how the following values were obtained:
    (1) Vehicle reach = 68.7%; Message reach = 44.6%
    (2) Vehicle frequency = 4.6
    (3) CPM = $14.63
    (4) CPM-MSG (*Sports Afield*) = $19.53
    (5) CPP = $2,497
    (6) GRPs = 318.0

5. As noted in the text, it cost advertisers $260,000 for 30 seconds of advertising on *Cheers* during the 1990-1991 season. This price is over four times more expensive than the $60,000 charge to advertise on *The Young Riders*. Does this mean that *Cheers'* viewing audience would have to be over four times larger than the *The Young Riders'* audience for an advertiser to justify buying time on *Cheers?*

6. What are the advantages and disadvantages of cable television advertising? Why are more national advertisers turning to cable television as a viable advertising medium?

7. Assume you are brand manager for a product line of thermos containers. Your products range from thermos bottles to small ice chests. Assume you have $3 million to invest in a four-week magazine advertising campaign. What magazines would you choose for this campaign? Justify your choices.

8. It was noted in the text that cigarettes and liquor are credited with a very large percentage of all billboard advertising. Why do you think these two product categories dominate the billboard medium?

9. Present your views on whether you think VideOcarts will be an effective advertising medium. Are there any particular product categories with which you expect VideOcarts to be especially effective or ineffective?

10. Assume you are a manufacturer of various jewelry items; graduation rings for high-school and college students are one of the most important items in your product line. Suppose you are in the process of developing a media strategy aimed specifically at high-school students. You have an annual budget of $5 million. What media and vehicles would you use and how would you schedule the advertising over time?

11. Examine a copy of the most recent *Spot Radio Rates and Data* available in your library and compare the advertising rates for three or four of the radio stations in your hometown or university community.

12. Select any five magazines and apply the criteria in Figure 13.4 that are especially relevant to magazines (e.g., elegance). On the basis of this application, construct a rank ordering from best magazine to worst. Justify your rankings.

13. Pick your favorite clothing store in your university community (or hometown) and justify the choice of one radio station that the clothing store should select for its radio advertising. Do not feel constrained by what the clothing store may already be doing. Focus instead on what you think is most important. Be certain to make explicit all criteria used in making your choice and all radio stations considered.

CHAPTER FOURTEEN

Assessing Advertising Effectiveness

THE PEOPLE METER CONTROVERSY

A 30-second commercial on prime-time television can cost upwards of $260,000 or as little as $60,000. Why such a disparity? In a word, ratings! Generally speaking, higher-rated programs command higher prices. Because prices and ratings go hand in hand, the accurate measurement of program audience size, or ratings, is a critically important, multimillion dollar industry. Advertising researchers continuously seek ways to more accurately measure the size of program audiences. The people meter, by the well-known A.C. Nielsen Co., is the most important research innovation since the advent of television audience measurement. It has not been adopted without considerable controversy, however. A brief review of television audience measurement will set the stage for the controversy surrounding the use of people meters.

Historically, the A.C. Nielsen Co. measured television program ratings by combining two data-collection methods. One involved attaching electronic meters to the television sets of a national sample of households (the electronic-meter panel). These electronic meters (called black boxes) determined the number of households attuned to particular programs. Statistical inference techniques were used to estimate program ratings on a national basis. A separate national panel of households (the diary panel) maintained diaries of their on-going viewing habits and supplied pertinent demographic information on household size, income, education, race, and so on. When combined, the data from the two panels indicated the program ratings and demographic characteristics of each program's audience. This information was used by networks to set advertising rates and by advertisers to select programs on which to advertise their products.

This method worked well during a simpler time when fewer program options were available to television viewers. It became less suitable as independent stations, cable networks, and VCRs increased the number of choices available to viewers. Diary data diminished in accuracy because people became less willing or able to maintain precise accounts of their viewing behavior. Enter the people meter.

The people meter was developed by a British research firm, Audits Great Britain (AGB Television Research). This firm introduced people meters to the United States in late 1984. Nielsen followed with its own people-meter system shortly thereafter.

What is a people meter? The people meter is nothing more than a hand-held device slightly larger than a typical television channel selector. The meter has eight buttons for family members and two additional buttons for visitors. A family member (or visitor) must push his or her designated button each time he or she selects a particular program. The meter automatically records what programs are being watched, how many households are watching, and which family members are watching. Information from each household's people meter is fed daily into a central computer via telephone lines. This viewing information is combined with each household's pertinent demographic profile to provide a single source of data.

Why the controversy? Contemporaneous with the transition from diary panels to people meters, a substantial decline in network ratings occurred—declines of almost 10 percent. The big three networks (ABC, CBS, and NBC) have lost millions of dollars in advertising revenues because smaller-rated programs are unable to command higher prices. The networks have placed much of the blame on people meters, claiming that the meters have fundamental faults responsible for erroneous ratings data.

People meters are here to stay—and probably so is the controversy surrounding their use. Nonetheless, it is generally agreed that the people-meter system produces more accurate data than the combined black box/diary panel system it replaced.

Note: Many articles have been written about people meters and the surrounding controversy. See Verne Gay, "Vindication?" *Advertising Age*, May 30, 1988, 66; Ira Teinowitz, "People Meters Miss Kids: JWT," *Advertising Age*, July 18, 1988, 35; Joe Mandese, "Groups Propose TV Rating Changes," *Advertising Age*, September 9, 1991, 33. For a technical analysis, see Roland Soong, "The Statistical Reliability of People Meter Ratings," *Journal of Advertising Research*, 28 (February/March 1988), 50–56.

Hundreds of billions of dollars are spent worldwide annually to advertise products and services. Sound business practice requires that efforts be made to determine whether these expenditures are justified. Accordingly, much effort and investment are made to test advertising effectiveness. The people meter is just one of many techniques used in the advertising-research business. This chapter introduces you to advertising research by describing many of the research techniques used and explaining when and why they are used as well as the problems and issues involved in their use.

OVERVIEW OF ADVERTISING RESEARCH

Measuring advertising effectiveness is a difficult and expensive task. Nonetheless, the value gained from undertaking the effort typically outweighs the expense and difficulty. In the absence of formal research, most advertisers would not know whether their advertising is doing a good job, nor could they know what should be changed so that their future advertising could do even better. Advertising research enables management to increase advertising's contribution toward achieving marketing and corporate goals.

What Does Advertising Research Research?

Advertising research involves a wide variety of purposes, methods, measures, and techniques. Effectiveness is measured in terms of achieving awareness, conveying copy points, influencing attitudes, creating emotional responses, and affecting purchase choice.

Sometimes research is done under natural advertising conditions and other times in simulated or laboratory situations. Measures of effectiveness range from paper-and-pencil instruments (e.g., attitude scales) to physiological devices (e.g., pupillometers).

It should be clear that there is no such thing as a single form of advertising research. Rather, the measurement of advertising effectiveness is exceptionally diverse because the questions asked are themselves diverse.

Although, as will be seen shortly, there are a variety of research methods used to investigate advertising effectiveness, two general forms of advertising research are conducted. First, **message research,** also called **copytesting,** is needed to test the effectiveness of creative messages. Copytesting involves both *pretesting* a message during its development stages (prior to its actually being placed in an advertising medium) and *posttesting* the message for effectiveness after it has been aired or printed. Pretesting is performed to eliminate ineffective ads before they are ever run, while posttesting is conducted to determine whether the message achieved the objectives established for it.

Media research is the second general category of advertising research. Whereas copytesting asks questions about the message per se, media research attempts to ascertain the audience size of advertising vehicles so that ratings can be determined. For example, people-meter research (as discussed in the opening vignette) is performed to estimate television program ratings.

Idealism Meets Reality in Advertising Research

The role, importance, and difficulty of assessing advertising effectiveness can perhaps best be appreciated by first examining what an ideal system of advertising measurement would entail and then comparing this against the reality of advertising research.

First, an ideal measure would provide an *early warning signal*, that is, a *reading* of ad effectiveness at the earliest possible stage in the advertisement development process. The sooner an advertisement is found to be ineffective, the less time, effort, and financial resources will be wasted. Early detection of effective advertisements, on the other hand, enables marketers to hasten the developmental process so that the ads can generate return on investment as quickly as possible.

Second, an ideal measurement system would evaluate advertising effectiveness in terms of the *sales volume generated by advertising*, which is, according to the logic of vaguely-right-versus-precisely-wrong objective setting (see Chapter 10), the only bona fide advertising objective.[1] A measure of advertising effectiveness becomes less valuable the further removed it is from an advertisement's potential for generating sales volume. Hence, a measure of awareness is less valuable than an attitude measure because the former is further removed than the latter from the act of purchasing the advertised product.

Third, an ideal measurement system would satisfy the standard research requirements of *reliability and validity*. Advertising measures are reliable when the same results are obtained on repeated occasions, that is, the results are replicable. Measures are valid when they predict actual marketplace performance.

Finally, an ideal system would permit *quick and inexpensive measurement*. The longer it takes to assess advertising effectiveness and the more it costs, the less valuable is the measuring system.

The ideal conditions just discussed are rarely satisfied. In fact, several are inconsistent. For example, a measurement system capable of predicting sales potential is likely to be expensive. Similarly, one that provides an early warning signal is less likely to be reliable and valid. Advertising research must necessarily deviate from the ideal circumstances described previously. However, the gap between idealism and reality in advertising research is narrowing with advances in technology and greater ingenuity in developing testing procedures.

---

[1]Leonard M. Lodish, *The Advertising and Promotion Challenge: Vaguely Right or Precisely Wrong?* (New York: Oxford University Press, 1986).

ADVERTISING RESEARCH METHODS

Literally dozens of methods for measuring advertising effectiveness have appeared over the years. The following sections discuss some of the most frequently used procedures in media research and copytesting. Table 14.1 organizes the methods to be discussed in terms of media research and copytesting methods. The media research methods are separated into those that are used to calculate audience sizes for magazines, radio stations, and television programs. Copytesting methods are classified into those that measure recognition and recall, persuasion, emotions, physiological arousal, and sales response.

Before beginning our coverage of the various research methods, it is important to realize that advertising effectiveness measures generally are *not* interchangeable with one another. In other words, the choice of method is tied inextricably to the advertising objective that precipitated the ad campaign in the first place. If the ad objective is, say, primarily one of creating awareness, then a different method is called for in comparison to when, for example, the objective is to create a strong emotional reaction.

Illustrative Advertising Research Methods — TABLE 14.1

MEDIA RESEARCH METHODS

Magazine Audience Measurement
■ Simmons Market Research Bureau (SMRB)
■ Mediamark Research, Inc. (MRI)

Radio Audience Measurement
■ Arbitron Ratings Co. (Arbitron)

Television Audience Measurement
■ Nielsen People Meters
■ Arbitron's ScanAmerica

COPYTESTING METHODS

Measures of Recognition and Recall
■ Starch Readership Service
■ Burke Day-After Recall

Measures of Persuasion
■ ASI Theater Testing
■ AHF Competitive Environment Testing

Measures of Emotion
■ The Warmth Monitor
■ TRACE
■ BBDO's Emotional Measurement System

Measures of Physiological Arousal
■ Psychogalvanometer
■ Pupillometer
■ Voice-Pitch Analysis (VOPAN)

Measures of Sales Response
(Single-Source Systems)
■ IRI's BehaviorScan
■ Nielsen's SCANTRACK

Media Research Methods

The initial task an advertiser faces is to ensure that sufficient numbers of potential customers are actually exposed to its advertisements. This requires that (1) media vehicles (television programs, magazine issues, etc.) be distributed, (2) customers be exposed to these vehicles (by watching the television program, reading a specific magazine issue, etc.), and (3) customers be exposed to the advertiser's specific advertisement(s) carried in these vehicles.

MAGAZINE AUDIENCE MEASUREMENT.   It may seem at first that determining the size of a particular magazine's readership would be an easy task. All that is needed is to tally the number of people who subscribe to the magazine, right? Wrong!

Several complicating factors make subscription counting an inadequate way of determining a magazine's readership. First, magazine subscriptions are collected through a variety of middlemen, making it difficult to obtain accurate lists of which people subscribe to which magazines. Second, magazine purchases often are made from newsstands, in supermarkets, and from other retail outlets rather than through subscriptions, thus completely eliminating knowledge of who purchases which magazines. Third, a single magazine issue at a public location (doctors' offices, barber shops) is read by numerous people. Finally, magazine subscribers often share magazines with other people.

For all of these reasons, the number of subscriptions to a magazine and the number of people who actually read the magazine are nonequivalent. Companies began specializing in magazine readership analysis in order to determine audience size. Simmons Market Research Bureau (SMRB) and Mediamark Research Inc. (MRI) are the dominant firms in this area of media research.

Simmons Market Research Bureau (SMRB).   This research firm assesses magazine vehicle exposure for over 100 consumer magazines. A national probability sample of approximately 20,000 individuals are interviewed, and their magazine-reading habits are examined. Here is how SMRB's research is performed. SMRB's research staff goes into the field and shows interviewees representations of the logos of more than 100 magazines. Interviewees are asked to identify those magazines (by their logos) they may have read or looked through during the last six months. This recognition-assisted method is called the *through-the-book-technique,* or TTB for short. Respondents then are asked to look through a stripped-down version of a recent magazine issue. Through a series of questions, SMRB's interviewers attempt to determine whether respondents have truly been exposed to the particular magazine issue. Statistical inference procedures are used to generalize total vehicle exposure from the sample results. In addition to measuring magazine exposure, SMRB also asks respondents about their product/brand usage and their age, occupation, and other demographic variables. Advertisers and media planners use the readership information along with detailed demographic and product-usage data to evaluate the absolute and relative value of different magazines.

Mediamark Research Inc. (MRI).   Critics have challenged the TTB methodology, claiming the technique tends to understate audience size and fails to yield consistent results from year to year. Mediamark Research Inc. (MRI) was created to provide advertisers and agencies with an alternative magazine-readership source. MRI interviews 20,000 adults per year and, like SMRB, obtains readership statistics for over 100 magazines along with product/brand usage and demographic information. However, MRI's measurement technique differs from SMRB's approach. MRI gives each participant a *deck of magazine logo cards.* The participant then sorts the logo cards into three piles based on whether she or he has read the magazine, has not read it, or is not sure. The claimed advantage of MRI's procedure is that the participant can control the pace of evaluating whether he or she has read a particular magazine.

Because these two readership services use different research methods, their results are often discrepant. An extreme case, for example, was the 1990 estimate of the total audience for *Better Homes & Garden* magazine. SMRB estimated the audience to be 22.31 million readers, whereas MRI's estimate was 33.27 million readers.[2] Media planners are faced with the task of determining which service is right or whether both are wrong in their estimates of magazine audience size.[3]

Much useful information is obtained from SMRB and MRI in addition to information on magazine-audience size. Beyond measuring magazine audience sizes, each service also acquires detailed information on respondents' product- and brand-usage patterns and demographic characteristics. Advertisers use this information for selecting particular magazines that best match their intended target markets.

An example will illustrate the valuable information that these readership services provide. The illustration is potato-chip usage as reported by female homemakers in response to the following questions posed by Simmons Market Research Bureau: "Do you or other members of your household use potato chips?" "About how many bags, boxes or cannisters of potato chips were used by your entire household in the last 30 days?"[4]

[2]Based on *Mediaweek's Guide to Media*, 14, 2, (1991), 105.

[3]For additional information on magazine audience measurement, see Thomas C. Kinnear, David A. Horne, and Theresa A. Zingery, "Valid Magazine Audience Measurement: Issues and Perspectives," in *Current Issues and Research in Advertising*, eds. James H. Leigh and Claude R. Martin, Jr. (Ann Arbor, MI: Division of Research, Graduate School of Business, University of Michigan, 1986), 251–270. See also Joanne Lipman, "Readership Figures for Periodicals Stir Debate in Publishing Industry," *The Wall Street Journal*, September 2, 1987, 21.

[4]This and all following statistics are from Simmons Market Research Bureau, Inc., vol. P-22, 1986, 631–649.

Responses to the first question, when extrapolated from the sample to the total population, reveal that of the 82,369,000 American households with a female homemaker present, 76.1 percent (nearly 63 million households) reported that potato chips are a product they consume at least occasionally. Slightly over 19 percent of all the households are heavy users (buying four or more bags, boxes, or cannisters of potato chips in the last 30 days), approximately 35 percent are moderate users (buying two or three units of potato chips during this same period), 22 percent are light users (having bought none or one unit in the last 30 days), and the remainder never buy potato chips.

Media decision makers benefit greatly when product-usage information is combined with demographic characteristics and with media consumption habits. We learn from the SMRB report that potato-chip usage is disproportionately higher among white than black families, in the Midwest and the South compared to the Northeast and the West, and in middle-income compared to low-income households. Also, readers of different magazines are disproportionately heavy or light users of potato chips. For example, readers of the following magazines tend to be disproportionately heavy potato-chip users: *Esquire, Essence, Field & Stream, Gentlemen's Quarterly, Hot Rod, Jet, Playboy, Sports Afield,* and *Sports Illustrated.* In comparison, readers of magazines such as *The New Yorker, Scientific American, Smithsonian,* and *The Wall Street Journal* tend to be disproportionately light users or nonusers of potato chips.[5]

This information has obvious implications for potato-chip advertisers when choosing magazines in which to insert their advertisements. SMRB also provides data showing the relationship of product usage with television program viewing, radio-program listening, and newspaper reading. Thus, vehicle-selection information is provided for these media as well as magazines.

RADIO AUDIENCE MEASUREMENT.   There use to be two major research services that measure local and spot radio audience sizes: Arbitron Ratings Co. (Arbitron) and Birch Scarborough Research (Birch). However, in 1991 Birch discontinued operations, leaving Arbitron as the sole supplier of radio ratings data.

Arbitron.   Arbitron measures radio listening patterns in over 250 local markets based on data from 250 to 13,000 individuals aged 12 or older who are randomly selected in each market. Respondents are compensated for maintaining *diaries* of their listening behavior for a *seven-day period.* Subscribers to the Arbitron

---

[5]Statements about disproportionately heavy or light usage are based on index numbers presented in SMRB's reports. For example, of the total 82,369,000 households with a female homemaker, 62,701,000 (or 76.1 percent) of these households consume potato chips. This percentage, 76.1 percent, is called *base 100.* Of the 1,497,000 households reported by SMRB to read *Field & Stream* magazine, 1,242,000 (or 83.0 percent) consume potato chips. *Field & Stream's* index is thus 109 (83.0/76.1), which indicates that readers of this magazine are disproportionately more likely (by 9 percent) than the population at large to consume potato chips.

service (over 5,000 radio stations, advertisers, and agencies) receive detailed reports involving listening patterns, station preferences, and demographic breakdowns. This information is invaluable for selecting stations whose listener composition matches the advertiser's target market.

Arbitron is working on a new *electronic-diary* technology to overcome criticisms that the present diary procedure places excessive faith in listeners' abilities to remember which stations they listened to. The electronic diary is a hand-held minicomputer resembling a personal calculator. Listeners are simply required to punch in the call letters of the radio station they are listening to. This prevents the recallability problem associated with the diary-recording method.[6]

TELEVISION AUDIENCE MEASUREMENT.   As shown in Table 14.1, Nielsen People Meters and Arbitron's ScanAmerica are two research services that assess the audience sizes and ratings for television programs. The opening vignette described Nielsen's people meters, so no further discussion of that source is undertaken here. It is advisable, however, to return now to the opening vignette if you did not read that section carefully when beginning your study of this chapter.

Arbitron's ScanAmerica.   In late 1991 Arbitron introduced ScanAmerica to compete with Nielsen's rating system. The initial launch involved collecting data from 1,000 households in each of five cities (New York, Los Angeles, Chicago, Atlanta, and Dallas). Whereas Nielsen's people-meter procedure simply measures respondents' television viewing patterns and gathers their demographic characteristics, ScanAmerica also collects product-usage behavior from the same families who supply viewership data. Hence, by matching television viewing with product-usage data, Arbitron is able to supply advertisers and advertising agencies with a richer source of information than the traditional age and sex data they have relied upon in the past when buying advertising time on network television.

The ScanAmerica procedure involves two forms of data collection. On the one hand, participating households record their television viewing behavior by using a people meter much like Nielsen's people meter. In addition, they record their product purchases by running a handheld, electronic scanning wand (that looks like a large ballpoint pen) over the universal product codes (bar codes) that appear on packaged goods. The ScanAmerica system was just launched by Arbitron at the time of this writing, so detailed information regarding its success is unavailable.[7]

---

[6]"Media & Measurement Technologies," *Direct Marketing* (March 1991), 26.

[7]Kevin Goldman, "Arbitron Launches TV Ratings Service," *The Wall Street Journal*, November 1, 1991, sec. B, 6; Joe Mandese, "ScanAmerica Rolls with CBS," *Advertising Age*, November 4, 1991, 3, 49.

Copytesting Methods

As previously noted, copytesting methods are numerous and diverse. The following presentation discusses illustrative methods in the order they are presented in Table 14.1.

MEASURES OF RECOGNITION AND RECALL.   Several levels of awareness may occur after a consumer is exposed to an advertisement. At the most basic level, the consumer may simply notice an ad without noticing specific executional elements. However, the advertiser hopes that the consumer will become aware of specific parts, elements, or features of an ad and associate these with the specific product, brand, or service being advertised.[8]

Several commercial research firms provide advertisers with information on how well their ads perform in terms of generating awareness, which typically is measured in terms of recognition or recall. Communicus Inc., Gallup & Robinson, Inc., McCollum/Spielman, Starch Message Report Service, and Burke Day-After Recall Tests are some of the well-known commercial research services that have testing programs for measuring the awareness-generating ability of advertisements.[9] The research services performed by Starch and Burke are described in the following sections.

The Starch Readership Service.   Starch measures the effectiveness of an ad's primary objective, namely to be seen and read. Starch examines reader awareness of advertisements in consumer magazines and business publications. Over 75,000 advertisements are studied annually based on interviews with more than 100,000 people involving over 140 publications. Sample sizes range from 100 to 150 individuals of each sex per issue, with most interviews conducted in respondents' homes or, in the case of business publications, in offices or places of business. Interviews are conducted during the early life of a publication. Following a suitable waiting period after the appearance of a publication to give readers an opportunity to read or look through their issue, interviewing continues one week for a weekly publication, two weeks for a biweekly, and three weeks for a monthly publication.

Starch interviewers locate eligible readers of each magazine issue studied. An eligible reader is one who has glanced through or read some part of the issue

---

[8]Ivan L. Preston, "The Association Model of the Advertising Communication Process," *Journal of Advertising*, 11, 2 (1982), 3–15.

[9]For details, see David W. Stewart, David H. Furse, and Randall P. Kozak, "A Guide to Commercial Copytesting Services," in *Current Issues and Research in Advertising* eds. James H. Leigh and Claude R. Martin, Jr., (Ann Arbor, MI: Division of Research, Graduate School of Business, University of Michigan, 1983), 1–44; Surendra N. Singh and Catherine A. Cole, "Advertising Copy Testing in Print Media," in *Current Issues and Research in Advertising* eds. James H. Leigh and Claude R. Martin, Jr., (Ann Arbor, MI: Division of Research, Graduate School of Business, University of Michigan, 1988), 215–284.

prior to the interviewer's visit and who meets the age, sex, and occupation requirements set for the particular magazine. Once eligibility is established, interviewers turn the pages of the magazine, inquiring about each advertisement being studied. Respondents are first asked, "Did you see or read any part of this advertisement?" If a respondent answers "Yes," a prescribed questioning procedure is followed to determine the respondent's awareness of various parts of the ad (illustrations, headline, etc.). Respondents are then classified as follows:

- *Nonreader*—A person who did not remember having previously seen the advertisement in the issue.

- *Noted Reader*—A person who remembered having previously seen the advertisement in the issue.

- *Associated Reader*—A person who not only noted but also saw or read some part of the advertisement that clearly indicates the brand or advertiser.

- *Read-Most Reader*—A person who read half or more of the written material in the ad.

Figure 14.1 illustrates a Starch-rated advertisement with actual scores for a Slice soft drink ad that ran in the April 9, 1990, issue of *Sports Illustrated.* Sixty-two percent of the *M* respondents (signifying men) remembered having previously seen (or noted) the ad, 57 percent associated it, and 7 percent read most of it. (The minus sign to the right of the 7 is Starch's way of signifying that this ad contains fewer than 50 words). The scores also show that 39 percent read the headline, 62 percent remember seeing Magic Johnson, and so on.

A basic assumption of the Starch procedure is that respondents in fact do remember whether they saw a particular ad in a particular magazine. The Starch technique has sometimes been criticized because in so-called bogus ad studies that use pre-publication or altered issues, respondents report having seen ads that actually never ran. The Starch organization does not consider such studies valid because of the failure of researchers to follow proper procedures for qualifying issue readers and questioning respondents. Research by the Starch organization demonstrates that when properly interviewed, most respondents are able to identify the ads they have seen or read in a specific issue with a high degree of accuracy; false reporting of ad noting is minimal.[10]

Due to inherent frailties of people's memories, it is almost certain that Starch scores do not provide exact percentages but rather are biased to some degree by people reporting they have seen or read an ad when in fact they have

[10]D. M. Neu, "Measuring Advertising Recognition," *Journal of Advertising Research*, 1 (1961), 17–22. For an alternative view, see George M. Zinkhan and Betsy D. Gelb, "What Starch Scores Predict," *Journal of Advertising Research*, 26 (August/September 1986), 45–50.

FIGURE 14.1   Illustration of a Starch™-Rated Magazine Ad

not. Nonetheless, it is not exact scores that are critical but rather comparisons between scores for the same ad placed in different magazines or comparative scores among different ads placed in the same magazine issue. For example, compared to all other advertisements run in the same magazine issue, the Slice ad in Figure 14.1 obtained readership index scores of 119 (noted), 116 (associated), and 88 (read most). These indexes mean that the Slice ad performed 19 percent better than the median noted score for all ads tested, 16 percent better than the median associated score, but 12 percent worse than the median read-most score. Comparatively, the only other soft drink advertisement in this magazine issue had indexes of 100, 104, and 125 (for noted, associated, and read most, respectively). Because Starch has been performing these studies for well over 50 years and has compiled a wealth of baseline data, or norms, advertisers and media planners can make informed decisions concerning the relative merits of different magazines.

Burke Day-After Recall.   Various companies copytest new television commercials to determine whether viewers have been sufficiently influenced to recall having seen the copytested commercial. One well-known research service is Burke's day-after recall (DAR) procedure. Test commercials are embedded within normal television programming. The following day Burke's telephone staff conducts interviews with a sample of 150 consumers. Contacted individuals are first qualified as having watched the program in which the test commercial was placed and as having been physically present at the time the commercial was aired. Once qualified, individuals receive a product or brand cue, are asked whether they saw the test commercial in question, and then are asked to recall all they can about it.

Findings are reported as (1) *claimed-recall scores*, which indicate the percentage of respondents who recall seeing the ad, and (2) *related-recall scores*, which indicate the percentage of respondents who accurately describe specific advertising elements.

Advertisers and agencies use this information, along with verbatim statements from respondents, to assess the effectiveness of test commercials and to identify a commercial's strengths and weaknesses. On the basis of this information, a decision is made to advertise the commercial nationally, to revise it first, or possibly even to drop it.

The Recall Controversy.   Considerable controversy has surrounded the use of DAR testing. David Ogilvy, a famous advertising practitioner, contends that recall testing "is for the birds."[11] Coca-Cola executives reject recall as a valid

---

[11]David Ogilvy, *Ogilvy on Advertising* (New York: Crown Publishers, 1983).

measure of advertising effectiveness because, in their opinion, recall simply measures whether an ad is received but not whether the message is accepted.[12]

The strongest challenge to day-after recall testing comes from a study performed by Foote, Cone & Belding (FCB), a major advertising agency. The FCB agency claims that DAR copy tests significantly *understate the memorability* of commercials that employ *emotional or feeling-oriented themes.*[13] This is because the test procedures emphasize respondents' ability to verbalize key copy points, thereby biasing the results in favor of rational or thought-oriented commercials and against emotional or feeling-oriented commercials, which rarely make explicit selling points.

To test the assertion that DAR testing is biased against emotionally oriented commercials, FCB conducted a study that compared three thinking and three feeling commercials. The six commercials were copytested with two methods: the standard DAR measurement described previously and a *masked-recognition test.* The latter test involves showing a commercial to respondents on one day, telephoning them the next, requesting that they turn on their television sets to a given station where the commercial is shown once again (but this time masked, i.e., without any brand identification), and then asking them to identify the brand. FCB defines correct brand-name identification by this masked-recognition procedure as "proven recognition" or "true remembering."[14]

The results from FCB's research, shown in Table 14.2, demonstrate clearly the bias in day-after recall procedures against emotional, feeling commercials. It can be seen that the thinking commercials (coded A, D, and E in Table 14.2) perform only slightly better under masked-recognition measurement than under the standard DAR test. For example, commercial A obtained a DAR score of 49 percent and a masked-recognition score of 56 percent, thereby yielding a ratio of 114 (i.e., 56/49). In fact, as shown in Table 14.2, the average ratio for the three thinking commercials is 119. This indicates that an average of only 19 percent more people recognized the advertised brand when prompted by again seeing the product advertised with the brand masked compared to recalling the brand entirely from memory.

Comparatively, Table 14.2 shows that the feeling commercials (B, C, and F) performed considerably better under masked-recognition than day-after-recall procedures. Overall, the masked-recognition method reveals that proven recognition for the three feeling commercials is 68 percent higher than the day-after recall scores (see ratio of 168 in Table 14.2).

The implication is clear: day-after recall tests *are biased* against emotional or feeling commercials. A different research method, such as masked recognition, is

---

[12]"Recall Not Communication: Coke," *Advertising Age*, December 26, 1983, 6.

[13]Jack Honomichl, "FCB: Day-After-Recall Cheats Emotion," *Advertising Age*, May 11, 1981, 2; David Berger, "A Retrospective: FCB Recall Study," *Advertising Age*, October 26, 1981, sec. S, 36, 38.

[14]Honomichl, "FCB," 82.

Day-After Recall versus Masked-Recognition Research Findings

TABLE 14.2

THINKING COMMERCIALS	DAY-AFTER RECALL	MASKED RECOGNITION	RATIO OF MASKED RECOGNITION TO RECALL
A	49%	56%	114
D	24	32	133
E	21	24	114
Average	31	37	119
FEELING COMMERCIALS			
B	21%	37%	176
C	25	36	144
F	10	23	230
Average	19	32	168

Source: "FCB Says Masked-Recognition Test Yields Truer Remembering Measures Than Day-After Recall Test," *Marketing News*, June 12, 1981, 1.

needed when testing whether this type of commercial accomplishes suitable levels of awareness.[15]

MEASURES OF PERSUASION.   Measures of persuasion are used when the advertising objective is to influence consumers' attitudes toward and preference for the advertised brand. Advertising effectiveness can be assessed using the persuasiveness criterion by measuring attitudes/preferences both before and after an advertisement is run and determining whether attitudes have become more favorable or preference has shifted toward the advertised brand.

These procedures generally involve (1) recruiting a sample of representative consumers and having them meet at a central location (a movie theater, a room in a shopping mall, a conference room), (2) initially measuring their attitudes/preferences for a target brand (i.e., the brand paying for the research), (3) possibly measuring attitudes/preferences toward one or more competitive brands, (4) exposing consumers to a new television commercial for the target brand in context of a television pilot program or some other realistic viewing context, and (5) again measuring attitudes/preferences toward the target and competitive brands following the program and advertising exposure. Commercial effectiveness is assessed by determining the amount of attitude change or preference shift for the target brand.

Commercial research firms doing this type of research include ASI Market Research, Inc., AHF Marketing Research's competitive-environment testing,

---

[15]Ibid.

Gallup & Robinson, Inc., McCollum/Spielman, Mapes and Ross, and Research Systems Corp.[16] ASI's theater testing and AHF's competitive-environment testing illustrate the type of attitude/preference testing provided by commercial research firms.

ASI Theater Testing.   ASI performs theater testing of new television commercials. A total of 250 consumers are recruited and invited to attend a preview of new television programs. Once they are in the ASI theater, consumers are told that prizes from various product categories will be awarded in a drawing, and they are asked to identify for each product the specific brand they would prefer receiving if their name should happen to be drawn. They are then exposed to a pilot television program followed by test commercials for each of the product categories mentioned in the drawing. After being exposed to a second pilot television program, the participants are led to believe that one product was inadvertently omitted from the list of products for which the drawing will be held and that they will have to complete a new brand-preference sheet that includes the omitted product as well as the others.

Commercial effectiveness is determined by comparing the two sets of brand preferences. A commercial is considered effective to the extent that more consumers indicate a higher preference for the test product on the second preference sheet (i.e., after they have been exposed to a commercial for the brand) than on the first sheet (before they were exposed to the test commercial). Based on numerous past studies, ASI has been able to develop norms indicating the actual magnitude of shifting in brand preferences that advertisers in particular product categories should expect. In addition to the brand-preference measurement, ASI theaters are equipped with electronic Instantaneous Reaction Profile Recorder dials, which permit respondents to register continuously their likes and dislikes regarding the pilot programs and the test commercials. These specific likes and dislikes concerning commercial elements are used to explain the brand-preference shifts.

AHF Competitive Environment Testing.   AHF's competitive environment test represents an adaptation of the ASI methodology. Between 150 and 250 respondents are recruited from shopping centers and directed to an adjacent research test site (such as a specially equipped mobile trailer). Once they are at the test location, respondents are asked to allocate ten hypothetical purchases among competitive brands in the test-product category. They then are exposed to a test commercial for one of the brands (which, unbeknown to respondents, is the one being tested) and to commercials for two or three competitive brands. (The ASI method, by comparison, does not expose respondents to competitive commercials.) Following the commercial exposure, respondents are again asked to

---

[16]For details, see Stewart, Furse, and Kozak, "A Guide to Commercial Copytesting Services."

allocate ten hypothetical purchases among the competing brands in the product category.

Advertising effectiveness is determined by the shift in brand preference, just as it was in the ASI test. However, the difference here is that the competitive-environment test portrays reality more accurately by exposing respondents to several commercials within a product category rather than to a single commercial.

MEASURES OF EMOTIONS.   In recent years advertisers have increased their efforts to influence consumers' feelings and emotions. Along with the trend toward more advertising directed at emotions, there has been a corresponding increase in efforts to measure consumers' emotional reactions to advertisements.[17]

The Warmth Monitor.   Warmth is one of various emotional responses that consumers have to advertisements. Warmth from viewing a television commercial occurs when the viewer experiences a positive emotional reaction, albeit one which is mild and short-lived. This emotion is precipitated by experiencing a sense of love, family, or friendship.[18]

Research has shown that warmth in advertising increases physiological arousal in response to an advertisement, increases how much consumers like the ad, and is correlated with the likelihood of purchasing the advertised product.[19]

A technique called the **warmth monitor** is used to measure emotional warmth in television commercials. The warmth monitor is nothing more than a sheet of paper containing four vertical lines running from top to bottom. From left to right these lines are labeled *absence of warmth, neutral, warmhearted/tender,* and *emotional (moist eyes).* While viewing a test commercial, respondents move a pencil down the paper, moving it to the left and right to continuously reflect their feelings about the commercial. Respondents are instructed to chart how warm they feel and how warm or good they think the commercial is. They are directed to maintain a constant rate of speed in moving their pencils down the page while keeping their eyes fixed on the commercial and not on the page. Most respondents do not need to look down at all and others do so only rarely.[20]

---

[17]Judie Lannon, "New Techniques for Understanding Consumer Reactions to Advertising," *Journal of Advertising Research,* 26 (August/September 1986), RC6-RC9; Judith A. Wiles and T. Bettina Cornwell, "A Review of Methods Utilized in Measuring Affect, Feelings, and Emotion in Advertising," in *Current Issues and Research in Advertising* eds. James H. Leigh and Claude R. Martin, Jr., (Ann Arbor, MI: Division of Research, Graduate School of Business, University of Michigan, 1991), 241–275.

[18]David A. Aaker, Douglas M. Stayman, and Michael R. Hagerty, "Warmth in Advertising: Measurement, Impact, and Sequence Effects," *Journal of Consumer Research,* 12 (March 1986), 366.

[19]Ibid. See Studies 2 and 3, 371–377.

[20]This description is based on ibid., 368.

Market Fact's TRACE Method.   A more technologically sophisticated measure of consumers' feelings toward advertisements is a technique called TRACE that is used by the research firm Market Facts, Inc. TRACE enables consumers to reveal their feelings toward what they are seeing in a television commercial by pressing a series of buttons on a hand-held microcomputer. Responses are synchronized with commercial content, and the microcomputer then plays back the consumer's feelings, expressed as a TRACEline across the television screen. The TRACEline moves up when the consumer feels good about what is shown and down when he or she feels bad about it. At points of critical change in the TRACEline, consumers are asked to discuss why their feelings changed at that point.[21]

Another new approach used in measuring consumers' emotional reactions to advertisements is the use of photos to reflect different emotions. The *Focus on Promotion* describes a research procedure devised by the advertising agency, BBDO Worldwide.

MEASURES OF PHYSIOLOGICAL AROUSAL.   Advertising researchers have also turned to a variety of physiological testing devices to measure consumers' affective reactions to advertisements. These include such techniques as the psychogalvanometer (which measures minute levels of perspiration in response to emotional arousal), pupillometric tests (pupil dilation), and voice-pitch analysis. Psychologists have concluded that these physiological functions are indeed sensitive to psychological processes of concern in advertising.[22]

All of the bodily functions cited are controlled by the *autonomic nervous system*. Because individuals have little voluntary control over the autonomic nervous system, changes in bodily functions can be used by advertising researchers to indicate the actual, unbiased amount of arousal resulting from advertisements.

In order to appreciate the potential value of such physiological measurement, consider the case of an advertisement directed toward men that promotes the advertised product by associating it with a scantily clad female model. In pretesting this ad, some men, when asked what they think of it, may indicate that they dislike the ad because they consider it sexist and insulting to women. Others may respond that they really like it and find it appealing. Still others may feign disgust or aggravation in order to make a favorable impression to the interviewer. That is, this latter group of men may actually enjoy the ad but say otherwise in response to an interviewer's query, thereby disguising their true evaluation. Here is where measures of physiological arousal have a potential role to play in

[21]"New Technology 'TRACES' Reaction to TV Ads," *Marketing News*, May 25, 1984, 3.

[22]Paul J. Watson and Robert J. Gatchel, "Autonomic Measures of Advertising," *Journal of Advertising Research*, 19 (June 1979), 15–26.

FOCUS ON PROMOTION

BBDO'S EMOTIONAL MEASUREMENT SYSTEM

A major problem in measuring consumers' emotional reactions is that many people find it difficult to articulate their feelings. Words may not be readily available to describe how we feel, or we may be reluctant to share our feelings using words that may make us look excessively sentimental. BBDO Worldwide, a major New York advertising agency, recently developed a nonverbal data-collection technique with hopes of overcoming the articulation problem.

BBDO spent three years testing hundreds of photos and refining its nonverbal procedure. This research culminated in a final collection of 53 photos that represent 26 universal emotional reactions—shame, fear, happiness, disgust, etc. (See Figure 14.2 for two examples.) The Emotional Measurement System is simple to use. After consumers have been exposed to a test commercial, they are given the deck of 53 photos and asked to set aside any or all of the photos that reflect how they felt after viewing the commercial. The frequency with which a particular photo is chosen by the 150 to 600 respondents is then recorded and a perceptual map is constructed. The perceptual map provides a vivid graphical representation of the emotions which characterize a set of tested commercials and provides a convenient way to show how the commercials compare against one another in terms of emotions evoked.

Source: Abstracted from "Ad-testing Technique Measures Emotions," *Marketing News*, April 16, 1990, 9; Gary Levin, "Emotion Guides BBDO's Ad Tests," *Advertising Age*, January 29, 1990, 12.

advertising research, namely to prevent self-monitoring of feelings and emotional reactions.

The Psychogalvanometer.   The psychogalvanometer is a device for measuring *galvanic skin response.* (Galvanic refers to electricity produced by a chemical reaction.) When the consumer's autonomic nervous system is activated by some element in an advertisement, one physical response occurs in the *sweat glands* in the palms and fingers, which open in varying degrees depending on the intensity of the arousal. Skin resistance drops when the sweat glands open.

By sending a very fine electric current through one finger, out the other, and completing the circuit through an instrument called a *galvanometer*, it is possible to measure both the degree and frequency with which an advertisement

FIGURE 14.2   Illustrative Photos Used by BBDO's EMS to Reflect Disgust or Happiness

activates emotional responses.[23] Simply, the psychogalvanometer indirectly assesses the degree of emotional response to an advertisement by measuring minute amounts of perspiration. There is evidence to indicate that galvanic skin response is a valid indicator of the amount of warmth generated by an advertisement.[24]

Pupillometer.   Pupillometric tests in advertising are conducted by measuring respondents' *pupil dilation* as they view a television commercial or focus on a printed advertisement. Respondents' heads are in a fixed position to permit continuous electronic measurement of changes in pupillary responses. Responses to

[23]"Psychogalvanometer Testing 'Most Predictive'," *Marketing News,* June 17, 1978, 11.

[24]Aaker, Stayman, and Hagerty, "Warmth in Advertising: Measurement, Impact, and Sequence Effects."

specific elements in an advertisement are used to indicate positive reaction (in the case of greater dilation) or negative reaction (smaller relative dilation). Although not unchallenged, there has been scientific evidence since the late 1960s to suggest that pupillary responses are correlated with people's arousal to stimuli and perhaps even with their likes and dislikes.[25]

Voice-Pitch Analysis (VOPAN).   A complaint leveled against the psychogalvanometer, pupillometric tests, and other physiological measurement devices is that they are capable of indicating the amount of emotional arousal but *not the direction of arousal.* One advertising commentator stated it this way: "The problem . . . is that once you have the data, you don't know what to do with it. All you have is a reading of physiological changes in a person. You have to get from there to whether that is good or bad."[26]

Voice-pitch analysis (VOPAN) is a physiological measurement device that purportedly overcomes the preceding criticism.[27] A specially programmed computer analyzes a person's voice pitch in response to a question about a test commercial and determines how much the pitch differs in relation to the individual's normal, or baseline, pitch level. When an individual has emotional commitment, the vocal chord, which is regulated by the autonomic nervous system, becomes abnormally taut, and the pitch is higher than normal.

Thus, the voice-pitch reading indicates the *amount* of emotional involvement. Moreover, unlike other psychophysiological measures, the *direction* of an individual's emotional response—i.e., whether she or he likes or dislikes the test commercial—can be determined by simply recording whether the individual responds in the affirmative or negative to a question of whether she or he liked the commercial just seen. *Truthfulness* of response is established by comparing changes in voice pitch over the respondent's preinterview levels. Changes greater than a certain range indicate conscious or unconscious lies or confused responses.[28]

---

[25]For detailed discussion of pupil dilation and other physiological measures, see Joanne M. Klebba, "Physiological Measures of Research: A Review of Brain Activity, Electrodermal Response, Pupil Dilation, and Voice Analysis Methods and Studies," in *Current Issues and Research in Advertising,* eds. James H. Leigh and Claude R. Martin, Jr. (Ann Arbor MI: Division of Research, Graduate School of Business, University of Michigan, 1985), 53-76. See also John T. Cacioppo and Richard E. Petty, *Social Psychophysiology* (New York: The Guilford Press, 1983).

[26]Comment by William Wells as quoted in Mark Liff, "Cataloging Some Tools," *Advertising Age,* October 31, 1983, sec M, 54.

[27]The following discussion is based on material from several sources: Glen A. Brickman, "Voice Analysis," *Journal of Advertising Research,* 16 (June 1976), 43–48; Ronald G. Nelson and David Schwartz, "Voice Pitch Gives Marketer Access to Consumer's Unaware Body Responses," *Marketing News,* January 28, 1977, 21; Ronald G. Nelson and David Schwartz, "Voice-Pitch Analysis," *Journal of Advertising Research,* 19 (October 1979), 55–59.

[28]Nelson and Schwartz, "Voice-Pitch Analysis," 55.

Voice-pitch analysis is potentially a valuable research technique; unfortunately, research purporting its virtues and validity is without scientific merit. Thus, it is not yet known whether VOPAN is a valuable addition to the advertising researcher's repertoire or a case of commercial hype.[29]

MEASURES OF SALES RESPONSE (SINGLE-SOURCE SYSTEMS). The ultimate issue in measuring advertising effectiveness is whether advertising leads to increased sales activity. Measuring anything other than sales response is considered by some to represent another case of substituting precisely wrong for vaguely right action.[30] Awareness measures have the appearance of being precisely right. However, the statement "research shows that the advertising campaign is responsible for making 75 percent of the target market aware of our new brand" might be in actuality precisely wrong if the awareness level and the volume of sales are not closely related.

Determining the sales impact of advertising is, as explained in Chapter 10, a most difficult task. However, substantial efforts have been made in recent years toward developing research procedures that are able to assess the sales-generating ability of advertising.

The most fascinating of the new techniques are so-called **single-source systems** that have become possible with the advent of two electronic-monitoring tools: television meters and optical laser scanning of universal product codes (UPC symbols). Single-source systems gather purchase data from panels of households using optical scanning equipment and merge it with household demographic characteristics and, most important, with information about causal marketing variables that influence household purchases (i.e., television commercials, coupons, in-store displays, trade promotions, etc.). The following sections describe two single-source systems: Information Resource Inc.'s BehaviorScan and Nielsen's SCANTRACK.

IRI's BehaviorScan. Information Resource, Inc.'s BehaviorScan pioneered single source data collection in 1979. BehaviorScan operates panel households in 27 markets around the United States with approximately 2,500 panel members in each market. Of the 70,000 total BehaviorScan households, 10,000 are installed with electronic television meters.[31] Panel members provide IRI with information about the size of their families, their income, number of televisions owned, the types of newspapers and magazines they read, and who in the household does most of the shopping.[32] IRI then combines all of these data into a single source and thereby determines which households purchase what products/brands and how responsive they are to advertising and other purchase-causing variables.

---

[29]For further discussion, see Klebba, "Physiological Measures of Research," 70–73.

[30]Lodish, *The Advertising and Promotion Challenge: Vaguely Right or Precisely Wrong?*

[31]Joe Schwartz, "Back to the Source," *American Demographics* (January 1989), 22–26.

[32]"What the Scanner Knows about You," *Fortune*, December 3, 1990, 51-52.

BehaviorScan markets are located in relatively small cities, because all grocery stores in these cities have to be equipped with automatic scanning devices that read UPC symbols from grocery packages. Each household receives a *coded identification card* that must be used every time a shopper visits the supermarket. Panel members are eligible for prize drawings as remuneration for their participation.

To better understand how BehaviorScan's single-source data can be used to show the relationship between advertising and sales activity, consider a situation where a manufacturer of a new snack food is interested in testing the effectiveness of a television commercial promoting this product. BehaviorScan would do the following: (1) stock the manufacturer's product in supermarkets in two or three markets; (2) selectively broadcast the new commercial using special *split-cable television* so that the commercial is received by only a portion of the panel members in each market; (3) record electronically (via optical scanners) grocery purchases made by all panel members; and (4) compare the purchase behavior of those panel members who were potentially exposed to the new commercial with those who were not exposed.

If the advertising is effective, a greater proportion of the panel members exposed to the test commercial should buy the promoted item in comparison to those members not exposed to any advertising. The percentage of panel members who undertake a trial purchase behavior would thereby indicate the effectiveness of the television commercial and the percentage who repeat purchase the product would indicate how much the product is liked.

This type of research is not restricted to testing the effects of advertising. It can be used to examine other marketing-mix variables such as coupons, cents-off deals, trade allowances, and in-store merchandising activity. The technology also permits forecasts of product success. For example, when G. D. Searle introduced Equal, a low-calorie sweetener, BehaviorScan predicted annual initial sales of $50 million after a national rollout. This prediction proved to be 100 percent correct.[33]

Nielsen's SCANTRACK.   The A.C. Nielsen company entered into a joint venture with another research firm, the NPD Group, in 1989 to form the SCANTRACK single-source system. SCANTRACK differs from BehaviorScan in a couple of interesting respects. First, and most important, where BehaviorScan collects purchase data from optical scanners located *only in supermarkets*, SCANTRACK collects purchase data by having its 15,000 panel households use hand-held scanners that are similar to the previously described scanners used in Arbitron's ScanAmerica system. These scanners are located in panel members' homes, usually mounted to a kitchen or pantry wall. Hence, with SCANTRACK panelists record purchases of *every bar-coded product purchased* regardless of

[33]Grace Conlon, "Closing in on Consumer Behavior," *Marketing Communications*, November 1986, 56.

the store where purchased—a major grocery chain, independent supermarket, mass merchandiser, wholesale club, or even department store.[34]

A second distinguishing characteristic of SCANTRACK is that panel members also use their hand-held scanners to enter any coupons used and to record all store deals and in-store features that influenced their purchasing decisions. Panel members transmit purchases and other data to Nielsen every week by calling a toll-free number and holding up their scanner to the phone, which records the data via a series of electronic beeps.

The *Global Focus* describes some of Nielsen's single-source systems now available in Europe.

Copytesting Principles

Copytesting research is in wide use throughout North America, Europe, and elsewhere. Yet, it may be a bit sobering to note that much copytesting is not of the highest caliber. Sometimes it is unclear exactly what research is attempting to measure; measures often fail to satisfy basic reliability and validity requirements; and results have little to say about whether copytested ads stand a good chance of being effective.

Members of the advertising-research community have been mindful of these problems and have sought a higher standard of performance from advertising researchers. A major statement prepared jointly by 21 leading U.S. advertising agencies typifies the concern and offers steps toward remedying the problem of mediocre or flawed advertising research. This document, called **Positioning Advertising Copytesting (PACT),** represents a consensus of the advertising community on fundamental copytesting principles. The PACT document is directed primarily at television advertising but is relevant to the testing of advertising in all media.

The PACT document consists of nine copytesting principles.[35] These principles are more than mere pronouncements; they are useful guides to how copytesting research should be conducted or supervised. It is useful to review these principles, not so that the student should be expected to memorize all nine but rather with the intent that these principles will be reviewed when one is actually engaged in copytesting.

P R I N C I P L E 1 .   A good copytesting system needs to provide *measurements that are relevant to the advertising objectives.* The specific objective(s)

---

[34]Information from this description is from Schwartz, "Back to the Source," and from Andrew M. Tarshis, "The Single Source Household: Delivering on the Dream," *AIM* (a Nielsen publication) 1, 1 (1989).

[35]Material for this section is extracted from the PACT document, which is published in its entirety in the *Journal of Advertising*, 11, 4 (1982), 4–29.

GLOBAL FOCUS

SINGLE-SOURCE SYSTEMS IN EUROPE

In France, Nielsen has a nationwide consumer panel of 7,000 households who have identification cards (such as used by BehaviorScan in the United States) to electronically record their purchases in supermarkets. Nearly one-fourth of these households are metered for television viewing, thereby making it possible to assess what impact television commercials have on panel members' grocery purchasing decisions.

In the United Kingdom, Nielsen has a national grocery consumer panel called HOME SCAN that records consumer purchases with in-home scanners like those used in SCANTRACK. A joint venture with a regional television network makes it possible to transmit different television commercials to panel members or vary the frequency of transmissions in different areas and thereby test the impact television commercials have on panel members' purchasing behavior.

By the mid-1990s Nielsen will have a 4,000-member Italian household panel installed with in-home scanners. Because advertising is more important in Italy than sales promotions, the primary application of the single-source research will be test advertising effectiveness and to evaluate alternative media plans.

Source: Schwartz, "Back to the Source" and Tarshis, "The Single Source Household."

that an advertising campaign is intended to accomplish (creating brand awareness, influencing brand image, creating warmth) should be the first consideration in determining the copytesting methods to assess advertising effectiveness. For example, if the objective for a particular campaign is to evoke strong emotional reactions, a measure of day-after recall would be inappropriate.

PRINCIPLE 2. A good copytesting system is one that requires *agreement about how the results will be used in advance of each specific test.* Specifying how research results will be used *before* data are collected ensures that all parties involved (advertiser, agency, and research firm) agree on the research goals and reduces the chance of conflicting interpretations of test results. This principle's intent is to encourage the use of *decision rules or action standards* that, before actual testing, establish the test results that must be achieved for the test advertisement to receive full media distribution. Consider the following illustrative action standard: Commercial X must receive a minimum Burke-rated day-after recall score of 40, or the commercial will not be run.[36]

PRINCIPLE 3.   A good copytesting system provides *multiple measurements* because single measurements are generally inadequate to assess the performance of an advertisement. Because the process by which advertising influences customers is complex, multiple measures are more likely to capture the various advertising effects and are therefore preferred over single measures.

PRINCIPLE 4.   A good copytesting system is *based on a model of human response to communications*—the reception of a stimulus, the comprehension of the stimulus, and the response to the stimulus. Because advertisements vary in the impact they are intended to achieve, a good copytesting system is capable of answering questions that are patterned to the underlying model of behavior. For example, if consumers purchase a particular product for primarily emotional reasons, then the copytest should use a suitable measure of emotional response rather than simply measuring recall of copy points.

PRINCIPLE 5.   A good copytesting system allows for consideration of whether the *advertising stimulus should be exposed more than once*. This principle addresses the issue of whether a single test exposure (showing an ad or commercial to consumers only once) provides a sufficient test of potential impact. Because multiple exposure is often required for advertisements to accomplish their full effect, copytesting procedures should expose a test ad to respondents on two or more occasions when the communication situation calls for such a procedure.[37] For example, a single-exposure test is probably insufficient to test whether an advertisement successfully conveys a complex benefit. On the other hand, a single exposure may be adequate if an advertisement is designed solely to create name awareness for a new brand.

PRINCIPLE 6.   A good copytesting system recognizes that the more finished a piece of copy is, the more soundly it can be evaluated; therefore, a good system requires, at minimum, that *alternative executions be tested in the same degree of finish*. Test results can often vary depending on the degree of finish of the test executions. Sometimes the amount of information lost from testing a less-than-finished ad may be inconsequential; sometimes it may be critical.

PRINCIPLE 7.   A good copytesting system *provides controls to avoid the bias normally found in the exposure context*. The context in which an adver-

---

[36]A score of 40 would indicate that 40 percent of the queried respondents correctly recalled the test commercial the day after it was aired on television.

[37]Herbert E. Krugman, "Why Three Exposures May be Enough," *Journal of Advertising Research*, 12 (December 1972), 11–14.

tisement is contained (e.g., the clutter or lack of clutter in a magazine) will have a substantial impact on how the ad is received, processed, and accepted. For this reason, copytesting procedures should attempt to duplicate the actual context that an advertisement or commercial may eventually have. This is why the competitive-environment test, discussed previously under affect measures of persuasion, is superior to other tests that fail to incorporate competitive commercials into the testing program.

P R I N C I P L E 8.   A good copytesting system is one that takes into account *basic considerations of sample definition*. Any good research requires that the sample be representative of the target audience to which test results are to be generalized and that the sample size be sufficiently large to permit reliable statistical conclusions.

P R I N C I P L E 9.   A good copytesting system is one that can *demonstrate reliability and validity*. Reliability and validity are basic requirements of any research endeavor. As applied to copytesting, a reliable test is one that yields consistent results each time an advertisement is tested, and a valid test is one that is predictive of marketplace performance.

The foregoing principles establish a high set of standards for the advertising-research community. Yet, they should not be regarded in the same sense that the earlier discussion of research ideals were. Rather, these principles should be viewed as mandatory if advertising effectiveness is to be tested in a meaningful way.

SUMMARY

Though difficult and often expensive, measuring advertising effectiveness is essential so that advertisers can better understand how well their ads are performing and what changes need to be made to improve performance.

Advertising research consists of media research and copytesting. Media research measures audience sizes for media vehicles as a basis for determining ratings. The text discusses two magazine audience measurement services (Simmons Market Research Bureau and Mediamark Research, Inc.), one radio audience service (Arbitron), and two television audience measurement systems (Nielsen's people meters and Arbitron's ScanAmerica).

Copytesting research evaluates the effectiveness of advertising messages. Dozens of copytesting techniques for measuring advertising effectiveness have evolved over the years. The reason for this diversity is that advertisements perform a variety of functions and multiple methods are needed to test different indicators of advertising effectiveness.

Starch Readership and Burke Day-After Recall Tests are techniques for measuring recognition and recall. ASI theater and AHF competitive environment testing are used to measure attitudinal responses and preference shifts to advertising. Consumers' emotional reactions to advertisements are measured using techniques such as the warmth monitor, TRACE, and the photograph-based Emotional Measurement System. Various physiological measures (such as galvanic skin response, pupil dilation, and voice pitch) are used to assess physiological arousal activated by advertisements. The impact of advertising on actual purchase behavior is assessed with single-source data collection systems (IRI's BehaviorScan and Nielsen's SCANTRACK) that obtain optical-scanned purchase data from household panels and then integrate this with television viewing behavior and other marketing variables.

No single copytesting technique is ideal, nor is any particular technique appropriate for all occasions. The choice of technique should depend on the specific objective an advertising campaign is intended to accomplish. Moreover, it is typically preferable to use multiple measurement methods rather than any single technique in order to answer the diversity of questions that are typically involved in attempts to assess advertising effectiveness.

Discussion Questions

1. It is desirable that the measurement of advertising effectiveness focus on sales response rather than on some precursor to sales, yet measuring sales response to advertising is typically difficult. What complicates the measurement of sales response to advertising?

2. PACT principle 2 states that a good copytesting system should establish how results will be used in advance of each copy test. Explain the specific meaning and importance of this copytesting principle. Construct illustrations of an anticipated result lacking a sufficient action standard and one with a suitable standard.

3. In reference to PACT principle 9, explain in your own words what *valid* measurement means. Suppose a research firm offers television advertisers an inexpensive method of testing commercials in which consumers merely evaluate photographed pictures of key commercial scenes. Comment about the probable validity of this approach.

4. Advertising research often measures vehicle exposure to indicate advertising exposure. What is the difference between these two types of exposure, and why do researchers measure the former when advertising decision makers are really interested in the latter?

5. If you were an account executive in an advertising agency, what would you tell clients to convince them to use (or not to use) the Starch Message Report Service?

6. An advertising agency is in the process of arranging research services to assess advertising effectiveness for two clients: one advertising campaign is for a unique financial service that is advertised with a number of specific selling points; the other campaign involves a very touching family scene used to advertise another client's food product. The agency proposes that day-after recall tests be conducted for both clients. Comment.

7. As advertising manager for a brand of toothpaste, you are considering using a physiological measurement technique to assess consumers' evaluative reactions to your new advertisements. Present an argument in favor of using VOPAN rather than pupil dilation testing or galvanic skin-response measurement.

8. Present an argument in favor of using the AHF's competitive-environment test rather than the ASI's theater testing procedure.

9. A test of television advertising effectiveness performed by BehaviorScan will cost you, as brand manager of a new brand of cereal, approximately $200,000. Why might this be a prudent investment in comparison to spending $50,000 to perform an awareness study?

10. The chapter's opening vignette noted that network representatives claim people meters are flawed. What are some of the reasons why people meters may not yield precise information about the number of households tuned into a specific television program?

11. Select three national television commercials, identify the objective(s) each appears to be attempting to accomplish, and then propose a procedure for how you would go about testing the effectiveness of each commercial. Be specific.

12. Locate a recent SMRB or MRI publication in your library and select a product that is consumed by large numbers of consumers (soft drinks, cereal, candy bars, etc.). Pick out the index numbers for the 18 to 24, 25 to 34, 35 to 44, 45 to 54, 55 to 64, and 65 and older age categories based on "All Users" columns. Show how the index numbers in column "D" were calculated. Also, identify some magazines that would be especially suitable for advertising to the "Heavy Users" of your selected product category.

SALES PROMOTION

Part 6 discusses the increasing practice of sales promotion. **Chapter 15** overviews sales promotion by explaining the targets of sales promotion, the reasons for its growth, and the tasks sales promotion is and is not capable of performing. The chapter also explains the conditions under

which sales promotion is and is not profitable.

    Chapter 16 focuses on trade-oriented sales promotions. The chapter describes the most important and widely used forms of trade promotions: trade allowances, contests and incentives, trade-oriented point-of-purchase materials, retailer-training programs, cooperative advertising and vendor support programs, specialty advertising programs, and trade shows.

    Consumer-oriented sales promotion is the subject of **Chapter 17.** Primary focus is placed on the major forms of sales promotions that are directed at consumers. These include sampling, couponing, premiums, price-offs, bonus packs, refunds and rebates, contests and sweepstakes, and overlay and tie-in promotions. The chapter concludes with a three-step procedure for evaluating sales promotion ideas.

CHAPTER FIFTEEN

Overview of Sales Promotion

WETPROOF BY ALMAY: THE ROLE OF SALES PROMOTION IN INTRODUCING A NEW BRAND

Almay, a division of Revlon, Inc., is a maker of hypoallergenic cosmetics that have mostly appealed to middle-aged and medically minded consumers. One of Almay's products, waterproof mascara, reached a point where sales volume leveled off, thereby forcing the marketing staff to consider ways to invigorate the product. Almay's marketers made the resourceful move to introduce a new mascara brand, named Wetproof, to a market—teens and women in their early twenties—that Almay had not had much success with in the past.

Some substantial marketing changes were needed to attract this market. Because mass-merchandise cosmetics are typically purchased on impulse, in-store displays are a crucially important promotional vehicle. Almay came up with a bold color combination, neon yellow and black, to use in both product packages and merchandise displays. This combination appealed to the youthful market and also differentiated Wetproof from competitive mascaras. However, although the use of attention-getting packaging and displays would increase the likelihood that consumers might spot Wetproof at the point of purchase, it would take more than this to encourage retailers to stock Wetproof and to entice consumers to try it. Sales promotion incentives were needed. Here is the program that Almay undertook.

First, to encourage retailers to handle Wetproof and to support the brand's sales performance, a free gift of a floating air mattress—a product that tied into Wetproof's waterproof feature—was offered to the head buyer on all accounts.

To further encourage retail support, a contest offered store managers the opportunity to win 35-millimeter cameras, cordless telephones, and other attractive items.

Next, to entice consumers to purchase Wetproof, Almay launched a sweepstakes in which the grand-prize winner received a free vacation to Aruba and $500 spending money. Secondary prize winners, like the store managers, received cameras, cordless telephones, divers' watches, and other items. Additionally, consumers who purchased Wetproof received a free cosmetic bag with a sample size container of Waterproof Sunblock.

A final effort to successfully introduce Wetproof involved the use of incentives to create excitement among the sales force. All quota-meeting salespersons received prizes of cordless telephones, watches, or air mattresses. They also had their names entered into a sweepstakes for another free trip to Aruba.

This promotional activity paid off. In a matter of months Wetproof found its way into 16,000 retail outlets, and sales to consumers were vigorous.

Source: Adapted from "Almay Catches the Wave with Wetproof Mascara," *Adweek's Marketing Week,* March 25, 1991, 26, 28.

AN INTRODUCTION TO SALES PROMOTION

The opening vignette illustrates how sales promotion can effectively appeal to different parties: retailers, consumers, and the salesforce. The vignette also introduces some terminology you have not previously been exposed to in this textbook. The objective of this chapter and the two chapters that follow is to provide a thorough introduction to the sales-promotion function. You will see how sales promotion complements other elements of the promotion mix along with performing its own unique functions. Sales promotion's role in influencing wholesaler and retailer behavior, on the one hand, and its role in influencing consumer behavior, on the other, are covered in detail in the two chapters that follow.

What Exactly Is Sales Promotion?

From your introductory marketing course and possibly from other courses, you no doubt have at least a general understanding of sales promotion. You probably are a bit uncertain, however, as to exactly what it is. Join the crowd! The fact is that sales promotion is a term often used rather indiscriminately to encompass all promotional activities other than advertising, personal selling, or public relations.

In this text, **sales promotion** will be understood to mean the use of any *incentive* by a manufacturer to induce the *trade* (wholesalers and retailers) and/or *consumers* to buy a brand and to encourage the *salesforce* to aggressively sell it. The incentive is *additional to the basic benefits* provided by the brand and *temporarily changes* its *perceived price or value*.[1]

The italicized features require comment. First, by definition, sales promotions involve incentives—that is, a bonus or reward for purchasing one brand rather than another. Second, these incentives (sweepstakes, coupons, premiums, display allowances, etc.) are additions to, not substitutes for, the basic benefits a purchaser typically acquires when buying a particular product or service. For example, getting 50 cents off the price of a new brand of shampoo would be little consolation if the shampoo failed to work properly. Third, the target of the incentive is the trade, consumers, the salesforce, or all three parties. Finally, the incentive changes a brand's perceived price/value, but only temporarily. This is to say that a sales-promotion incentive for a particular brand applies to a single purchase or perhaps several purchases during a period, but not to every purchase a consumer would make over an extended period.

The Targets of Sales Promotion

To more fully appreciate the role of sales promotion, consider the promotional imperatives faced by the brand management for a consumer packaged good—for example, Almay's Wetproof that was highlighted in the opening vignette. For this brand to meet its marketing objectives (sales volume, market share, etc.), several things had to happen (see Figure 15.1): First, Almay's sales force had to enthusiastically and aggressively sell the product to the trade. Second, retailers had to be encouraged to allocate sufficient store space to the product and provide merchandising support to enable Wetproof to stand out from competitive brands. Third, consumers needed reasons for selecting Wetproof over competitive brands.

All three groups are targets of sales-promotion efforts. Allowances, contests, and advertising-support programs encourage retailers to stock and promote a particular brand. Coupons, samples, premiums, cents-off deals, sweepstakes, and other incentives encourage consumers to purchase a brand on a trial or repeat basis. Trade- and consumer-oriented sales promotions also provide salespeople with the necessary tools for aggressively and enthusiastically selling to wholesale and retail buyers.

---

[1]This definition combines the author's thoughts with those from two sources: Roger A. Strang, "Sales Promotion Research: Contributions and Issues," unpublished paper presented at the AMA/MSI/PMAA Sales Promotion Workshop, Babson College, May 1983; and James H. Naber in his James Webb Young address at the University of Illinois, Urbana-Champaign, IL, October 21, 1986.

Brand-Level Promotional Imperatives   FIGURE 15.1

THE BIG SHIFT FROM ADVERTISING TO SALES PROMOTION

Advertising spending as a percentage of total promotional expenditures has declined in recent years, while sales promotion, direct marketing, telemarketing, and other forms of promotion have increased. In fact, annual studies have shown that media advertising expenditures as a proportion of companies' total promotional expenditures have declined steadily for over a decade. Whereas media advertising averaged 42 percent of companies' promotional budgets in 1977, by 1990 media advertising's portion of the total budget had fallen to just 30.6 percent.[2]

Reasons for the Shift

A variety of factors account for the shift in the allocation of promotion budgets away from advertising toward sales promotion and other forms of nonadvertising promotions. Before describing the reasons for this shift, it first will be beneficial to briefly review the concepts of push and pull marketing strategies.

---

[2]The 1977 figure is based on Nathaniel Frey, "Ninth Annual Advertising & Sales Promotion Report," *Marketing Communications*, August 1988, 11. The 1990 figure is from Michael Burgi, "Trade Spending Tops," *Advertising Age*, April 15, 1991, 36. Both figures are based on annual surveys conducted by Donnelly Marketing. The 1991 study, on which the 1990 figure is based, surveyed marketing executives from package goods, health and beauty aids, and household products companies.

PUSH AND PULL STRATEGIES.   As noted in Chapter 8, the concepts of push and pull are physical metaphors that characterize the promotional activities manufacturers undertake to encourage channel members (the trade) to handle products. **Push** implies a forward thrust of effort whereby a manufacturer directs personal selling, trade advertising, and trade-oriented sales promotion to wholesalers and retailers. **Pull** suggests a backward tug from consumers to retailers. This tug, or pull, is the result of a manufacturer's successful advertising and sales-promotion efforts directed at the consumer. Successful marketing involves a combination of forces: exerting push to the trade and creating pull from consumers.

Table 15.1 illustrates the differences between push-and-pull-oriented promotional strategies based on two companies' allocations of $20 million among different promotional activities. Company A emphasizes a *push strategy* by allocating most of its promotional budget to personal selling and sales promotions aimed at retail customers. Company B, on the other hand, utilizes a *pull strategy* by investing the vast majority of its budget in consumer advertising.

It should be clear that pushing and pulling are not mutually exclusive. Both efforts occur simultaneously. Manufacturers promote to consumers (creating pull) and to trade members (accomplishing push). The issue is not which strategy to use, but rather, *which to emphasize.*

Historically, at least through the mid-1970s, the emphasis in consumer packaged-goods marketing was on promotional pull (such as Company B's budget). Manufacturers advertised heavily, especially on network television, and literally forced retailers to handle their products by virtue of the fact that consumers demanded heavily advertised brands. However, over the past two decades, pull-oriented marketing has become less effective. Along with this reduced effectiveness has come an increase in the use of push-oriented sales promotion practices (such as company A's budget).[3]

Increased investment in sales promotion, *especially trade-oriented sales promotion,* has gone hand-in-hand with the growth in push marketing. Major developments that have given rise to sales promotion follow. As will become apparent, these factors are interrelated and *not* mutually exclusive.

BALANCE OF POWER TRANSFER.   Until recently, national manufacturers of consumer packaged goods generally were more powerful and influential than the supermarkets, drug stores, and mass merchandisers that carried the manufacturers' brands. The reason was twofold. First, manufacturers were able to create consumer pull by virtue of heavy network-television advertising, thus effectively requiring retailers to handle their brands whether retailers wanted to

---

[3]Alvin A. Achenbaum and F. Kent Mitchel, "Pulling Away from Push Marketing," *Harvard Business Review,* 65, May–June 1987, 38–40; Robert J. Kopp and Stephen A. Greyser, "Packaged Goods Marketing—'Pull' Companies Look to Improved 'Push'," *The Journal of Consumer Marketing,* 4 (Spring 1987), 13–22; F. Kent Mitchel, "Strategic Use of A&P," *Marketing Communications,* April 1986, 34–36.

	TABLE 15.1

Push versus Pull Promotional Strategies

	COMPANY A (PUSH)	COMPANY B (PULL)
Advertising to Consumers	$1,200,000	$13,700,000
Advertising to Retailers	1,600,000	200,000
Personal Selling to Retailers	9,000,000	4,000,000
Sales Promotion to Consumers	200,000	2,000,000
Sales Promotion to Retailers	8,000,000	100,000
Total	$20,000,000	$20,000,000

Source: Arnold M. Barban, Steven M. Cristol, and Frank J. Kopec, *Essentials of Media Planning: A Marketing Viewpoint* (Lincolnwood, IL: NTC Business Books, 1987), 15.

or not. Second, retailers did little research of their own and, accordingly, were dependent on manufacturers for information such as whether a new product would be successful. A manufacturer's sales representative could convince a buyer to carry a new product using test-market results suggesting a successful product introduction.

The balance of power began shifting *when network television dipped in effectiveness* as an advertising medium and, especially, with the advent of *optical scanning equipment.* Armed with a steady flow of data from optical scanners, retailers now know within days which products are selling and which advertising and sales promotion programs are working. Retailers no longer need to depend on manufacturers for facts. Retailers possess the facts and use them to demand terms of sale rather than merely accepting manufacturers' terms. The consequence for manufacturers is that for every promotional dollar used to support retailers' advertising or merchandising programs, one less dollar is available for the manufacturer's own advertising.

INCREASED BRAND PARITY AND PRICE SENSITIVITY. In earlier years when truly new products were being offered to the marketplace, manufacturers could effectively advertise unique advantages over competitive offerings. As product categories have matured, however, most new offerings represent slight changes from existing products, thus resulting, more often than not, in greater similarities between competitive brands than differences. With fewer distinct product differences, consumers have grown more reliant on price and price incentives (coupons, cents-off deals, refunds, etc.) as a way of differentiating alternative parity brands.[4] Because real, concrete advantages are often

---

[4]Bud Frankel and J. W. Phillips, "Escaping the Parity Trap," *Marketing Communications,* November 1986, 93–100.

difficult to obtain, firms have turned increasingly to sales promotion as a means of achieving at least *temporary advantages* over competitors.

REDUCED BRAND LOYALTY. Consumers have become less brand loyal than they once were. This is partly due to the fact that brands have grown increasingly similar, thereby making it easier for consumers to switch among brands. Also, marketers have effectively trained consumers to expect that at least one brand in a product category will always be on deal with a coupon, cents-off offer, or refund; hence, many consumers rarely purchase brands other than those on deal. The upshot of all of this dealing activity is that marketers have created a monster. That is, their extensive use of sales promotions has reduced brand loyalty and increased switching behavior, thereby requiring evermore dealing activity to feed the monster's (i.e., consumers') insatiable desire for more deals.

SPLINTERING OF THE MASS MARKET AND REDUCED MEDIA EFFECTIVENESS. Advertising efficiency is directly related to the degree of homogeneity in consumers' consumption needs and media habits. The more homogenous are these needs and habits, the less costly it is for mass advertising to reach target audiences. However, as consumer lifestyles have become more diverse and advertising media have become more narrow in their appeal, mass-media advertising is no longer as efficient as it once was. On top of this, advertising effectiveness has declined with simultaneous increases in *ad clutter* and *escalating media costs*. These combined forces have influenced many brand managers to devote proportionately larger budgets to sales promotions.

SHORT-TERM ORIENTATION AND CORPORATE REWARD STRUCTURES. Although several large companies have recently turned to regionalized organizational structures and category-management systems (see Chapter 8), the brand management structure remains dominant in U.S. packaged-goods firms. The brand-management system and sales promotion are perfect partners. The reward structure in firms organized along brand-manager lines emphasizes *short-term sales response* rather than slow, long-term growth, and sales promotion is incomparable when it comes to generating quick sales response. In fact, for many brands of packaged goods, the majority of their sales are associated with some kind of promotional deal.[5]

CONSUMER RESPONSIVENESS. A final force that explains the shift toward sales promotion at the expense of advertising is that consumers respond favorably to money-saving opportunities. A national survey of more than 7,500 households revealed that over 90 percent of consumers had taken

---

[5]Robert C. Blattberg and Scott A. Neslin, "Sales Promotion: The Long and the Short of It," *Marketing Letters*, 1, 1 (1989), 81–97.

advantage of some form of promotion in the past month. Coupons in particular have nearly universal acceptance with over 80 percent of respondents acknowledging that coupons increase shopping value.[6]

Allocating the Promotion Budget Between Advertising and Sales Promotion

Sales promotion likely will continue to grow. However, excessive promotional activity may damage a product's image, diminish brand loyalty, and possibly even reduce consumption.[7] The important point stressed throughout the text is that the various promotional tools must be blended together to achieve communication functions without inordinate emphasis on any one tool.

Advertising and sales promotion both play important roles in most companies' promotional mixes. What determines which receives greater budgetary support? A study based on interviews with marketing executives who represent a variety of grocery, personal care, toiletry, and household products determined that

1. Advertising plays a dominant role in the promotional mixes of *more profitable brands.*

2. Advertising also plays a dominant role in the promotion of *premium-priced brands.*

3. However, marketers of *low-growth brands* place greater emphasis on sales promotion.

These findings taken together suggest that managers of successful brands support success with advertising, while managers who desire greater success (faster growth, larger market shares, etc.) attempt to achieve it with relatively greater emphasis on sales promotion.[8]

It should be apparent that the allocation of the promotional mix between advertising and sales promotion varies from situation to situation; there is no best solution in general. Rather, the best allocation depends on the specific conditions a brand encounters in the marketplace.

---

[6]Scott Hume, "Coupons Score with Consumers," *Advertising Age*, February 15, 1988, 40.

[7]Roger A. Strang, *The Promotional Planning Process* (New York: Praeger Publishers, 1980), 7. It is important to realize that sales promotions do not invariably have negative effects. There is some evidence to suggest that sales promotion's negative impact on consumer perceptions may be limited only to consumers who have rarely, if ever, tried the promoted brand. See Gwen Ortmeyer and Joel Huber, "Brand Experience as a Moderator of the Negative Impact of Promotions," *Marketing Letters*, 2, 1 (1990), 35–45.

[8]Strang, *The Promotional Planning Process.*

WHAT SALES PROMOTION CAN AND CANNOT DO

Every promotion-mix element is capable of accomplishing certain objectives and not others. Sales promotion is well suited for accomplishing certain tasks but incapable of achieving others.[9] It is instructive to examine first the tasks that sales promotion cannot accomplish.

What Tasks Sales Promotion Cannot Accomplish

Sales promotion *cannot* . . .

COMPENSATE FOR A POORLY TRAINED SALES FORCE OR FOR A LACK OF ADVERTISING.   When suffering from poor sales performance or inadequate growth, some companies consider sales promotion to be the solution. However, sales promotion will provide at best a temporary fix if the underlying problem is due to a poor sales force, a lack of brand awareness, a weak brand image, or other maladies that only proper sales management and advertising efforts can overcome.

GIVE THE TRADE OR CONSUMERS ANY COMPELLING LONG-TERM REASON TO CONTINUE PURCHASING A BRAND. The trade's decision to continue stocking a brand and consumers' decision to repeat purchase are based on continued satisfaction with the brand. Satisfaction results from the brand's meeting profit objectives (for the trade) and providing benefits (for consumers). Sales promotion cannot compensate for a fundamentally flawed or mediocre product.

PERMANENTLY STOP AN ESTABLISHED PRODUCT'S DECLINING SALES TREND OR CHANGE THE BASIC NONAC-CEPTANCE OF AN UNDESIRED PRODUCT.   Declining sales over an extended period indicate poor product performance or the availability of a superior alternative. Sales promotion cannot reverse the basic nonacceptance of an undesired product. A declining sales trend can be reversed only through product improvements or perhaps an advertising campaign that breathes new life into an aging product. Sales promotion used in combination with advertising effort or product improvements may reverse the trend, but sales promotion by itself is a waste.

---

[9]The discussion is guided by Charles Fredericks, Jr., "What Ogilvy & Mather Has Learned About Sales Promotion," *The Tools of Promotion* (New York: Association of National Advertisers, 1975), and Don E. Schultz and William A. Robinson, *Sales Promotion Management* (Lincolnwood, IL: NTC Business Books, 1986), chap. 3.

What Tasks Sales Promotion Can Accomplish

Sales promotion cannot work wonders but it is well-suited to accomplishing various tasks. Specifically, sales promotion *can* . . .

STIMULATE SALES-FORCE ENTHUSIASM FOR A NEW, IMPROVED, OR MATURE PRODUCT.   There are many exciting and challenging aspects of personal selling; there also are times when the job can become dull, monotonous, and unrewarding. For example, imagine what it would be like to repeatedly call on a customer if you never had anything new or different to say about your products or the marketing efforts supporting your products. Maintaining enthusiasm would be difficult, to say the least. Exciting sales promotions give salespeople extra ammunition to use when interacting with buyers; they revive enthusiasm and make the salesperson's job easier and more enjoyable.

INVIGORATE SALES OF A MATURE PRODUCT.   As mentioned earlier, sales promotion cannot reverse the sales decline for an undesirable product. However, sales promotion can invigorate sales of a mature product that requires a shot in the arm. A case in point is Quaker Oats's efforts with Cap'n Crunch. After nearly a quarter of a century on the market, Cap'n Crunch dropped from a 3.2 percent market share to a 2.8 percent share in less than two years. This may appear to be a miniscule drop but in actuality amounted to a $16 million loss in annual sales in the huge ready-to-eat-cereal business where annual U.S. sales exceed $4 billion.

A major promotional effort was needed to invigorate Cap'n Crunch sales. Accordingly, promotional planners at Quaker Oats undertook an effort to increase brand interest among children between the ages of 6 and 12 and to encourage repeat purchasing. The "Find the Cap'n" sales promotion game was developed. Cap'n Horatio Crunch's picture was temporarily dropped from the cereal package; in his place appeared the question "Where's the Cap'n?" Package directions informed children that they could share in a *$1 million reward* for finding the Cap'n. Consumers had to buy three boxes of Cap'n Crunch to get clues to Horatio Crunch's whereabouts. At the game's end, 10,000 children's names were drawn from the pool of thousands of correct answers, and each child received $100.

The "Find the Cap'n" promotion involved heavy television and magazine advertising along with the sales-promotion effort. In addition to the cash giveaway, coupons and cents-off deals were used to stimulate consumer purchasing. The result: an incredible 50 percent increase in sales during the promotion.[10]

---

[10]"Quaker Oats Finds Cap'n Crunch Loot with Hide-and-Seek," *Advertising Age*, May 26, 1986, 53.

FACILITATE THE INTRODUCTION OF NEW PRODUCTS TO THE TRADE.   In order to achieve sales and profit growth objectives, marketers continuously introduce new products. For example, in 1991 approximately 15,000 new products were introduced to U.S. supermarkets.[11] Sales promotions to wholesalers and retailers are often necessary to encourage the trade to handle new products. In fact, many retailers refuse to carry new products unless they receive extra compensation in the form of trade allowances, display allowances, and slotting allowances. The following chapter discusses each of these various forms of allowances. The *Focus on Promotion* describes the role of sales promotion in successfully introducing the Schick Tracer shaving system.

INCREASE ON- AND OFF-SHELF MERCHANDISING SPACE. Trade-oriented sales promotions enable a manufacturer to obtain extra shelf space for a temporary period. This space may be in the form of extra *facings* on the shelf or off-shelf space in a gondola or end-aisle display.[12]

NEUTRALIZE COMPETITIVE ADVERTISING AND SALES PROMOTION.   Sales promotions can be used to offset competitors' advertising and sales-promotion efforts. For example, one company's 50 cents-off coupon loses much of its appeal when a competitor simultaneously comes out with a $1 cents-off coupon.

OBTAIN TRIAL PURCHASES FROM CONSUMERS.   Marketers, such as Warner-Lambert, depend on free samples, coupons, and other sales promotions to encourage *trial purchases* of new products. Many consumers would never try new products without these promotional inducements.

It is important to note in this regard that most consumer-goods marketers have operated under the assumption that heavy sales promotion is essential for generating high levels of trial purchases. However, only recently are marketers beginning to challenge this belief. For example, the chairman and CEO of Procter and Gamble contends that advertising produces "a higher quality of trial for *new* P&G brands than any form of price promotion."[13] The point he makes is that consumers who purchase a new brand due to learning about the brand from advertising are more likely to become repeat purchasers than are those who try the item based on a price promotion.

Whether P&G's experience with advertising generalizes to other companies is uncertain. Nevertheless, such a bold position presented by the top person in one of the world's top consumer-goods companies demands our attention. We

---

[11]"Another 15,000 New Products Expected for U.S. Supermarkets," *Marketing News*, June 10, 1991, 8.

[12]A facing is a row of shelf space. Brands typically are allocated facings proportionate to their profit potential to the retailer. Manufacturers must pay for extra facings by offering display allowances or providing other inducements that increase the retailer's profit.

[13]Edwin L. Artzt, "The Lifeblood of Brands," *Advertising Age*, November 4, 1991, 32.

FOCUS ON PROMOTION

USING SALES PROMOTIONS TO INTRODUCE THE SCHICK TRACER

Warner-Lambert Co. invested $30 million in marketing to introduce the Schick Tracer shaving system. Approximately 60 percent of this amount went toward sales promotions with the remainder invested in media advertising. The innovative Tracer was advertised as the first razor with a blade that flexes. (See eye-catching advertisement in Figure 5.3 on page 134.)

Aggressive sales promotional measures were required in order to successfully compete against Gillette's Sensor razor, which was introduced to the United States one year before the Tracer and was supported with a marketing budget more than twice as large as Tracer's. First, to stimulate trial purchases, Warner-Lambert distributed 50 million free-standing inserts that offered consumers $1 coupons and two free razor cartridges. Then, to stimulate repurchasing of blades, all Tracer razor packs contained a 25-cent coupon for refill cartridges. Finally, Warner-Lambert also included $1 Tracer coupons in bottles of its Listerine mouthwash.

The combination of an innovative product, eye-catching advertising, and aggressive sales promotions resulted in a successful product introduction for the Tracer.

Source: Adapted from Allison Fahey, "Schick Sharpens Razor Promotions," *Advertising Age,* February 25, 1991, 12.

might expect that many other companies will reconsider their advertising and sales promotions budgets and perhaps in the future reallocate proportionately more to advertising.

HOLD CURRENT USERS BY ENCOURAGING REPEAT PURCHASES. Brand switching is a fact of life faced by all brand managers. The strategic use of certain forms of sales promotion can encourage at least short-run repetitive purchasing. Premium programs, refunds, and various other devices (discussed in Chapter 17) are used to encourage repeat purchasing.

INCREASE PRODUCT USAGE BY LOADING CONSUMERS. Consumers tend to use more of certain products (e.g., snack foods and soft drinks) when they have more of them available in their homes. Thus, sales-promotion efforts that *load* consumers generate temporary increases in product usage. Bonus packs and two-for-the-price-of-one deals are particularly effective loading devices.

PREEMPT COMPETITION BY LOADING CONSUMERS.   When consumers are loaded with one company's brand, they are temporarily out of the marketplace for competitive brands. Hence, one brand's sales promotion serves to preempt sales of competitive brands.

REINFORCE ADVERTISING.   A final can-do capability of sales promotion is to reinforce advertising. An advertising campaign can be strengthened greatly by a well-coordinated sales promotion effort. The Cap'n Crunch and Schick Tracer examples illustrate this feature of sales promotion. Both Quaker Oats and Warner-Lambert would not have been nearly as successful in accomplishing their objectives had they relied exclusively on advertising to enhance consumer interest in the Cap'n Crunch name or to successfully introduce the Tracer. Another instance of sales promotion reinforcing advertising is the case of Coke's European advertising campaign that appears in the *Global Focus*.

WHEN IS SALES PROMOTION DEALING PROFITABLE?

A brand's *sales volume* is almost always increased during the period of a coupon offering or cents-off deal. However, increases in sales volume do not necessarily lead to increased *profits*. Indeed, many sales promotion deals spur sales but not profits. When is a promotional deal likely to be profitable?

As we will see, whether or not a sales promotion is profitable *depends on consumers' deal responsiveness within a particular product category*. (The term **deal** refers to any form of sales promotion that delivers a price reduction to consumers; coupons and cents-off offers are the most frequent forms of deals.) For example, if consumers are *insensitive* to deals, sales promotions are necessarily unprofitable. This is because per-unit profit margin is reduced during a sales promotion and no additional sales volume is realized to offset the reduction in profit margin. To fully appreciate this, it is important that you recall the concept of *contribution margin* from basic accounting. Contribution margin, or simply *margin*, is a brand's selling price minus its per-unit variable cost. When a brand is on deal, its price typically remains the same as prior to the promotion but its variable cost increases due to the expense of offering, say, a coupon worth 50 cents. This results in a reduced margin.

Consumer Responsiveness to Sales-Promotion Deals

The market for any product category is made up of consumers who differ in their responsiveness to deals. Some consumers are loyal to a single brand in a category and buy only that brand. Other consumers have absolutely no brand loyalty and

GLOBAL FOCUS

EURO DISNEY AND COCA-COLA

Mickey Mouse, Snow White, Donald Duck, and other Disney characters no longer are restricted to theme parks in California and Florida. Disney now has Euro Disney, and Coca-Cola is its only authorized soft drink marketer. Taking advantage of this enviable situation, Coca-Cola invested nearly $200 million in its 1991 European advertising campaign tauting Coca-Cola as "The soft drink of Europe." Television spots ran in the United Kingdom, the Netherlands, Denmark, Italy, Germany, Belgium, and France. The spots, varying in length from 20 to 35 seconds (in contrast with television spots in the United States that are typically 15 or 30-seconds long), included real-life and animated scenes and emphasized how Coke can transport people to Euro Disney.

The last 10 seconds of each television spot provided details of how consumers could win free trips to Euro Disney and other gifts. The free-trip and gift opportunities were promoted on Coca-Cola packages at the point of purchase. The specific execution of on-package promotions varied from country-to-country, because promotional conventions and government regulations vary among the seven European countries targeted. For example, in the United Kingdom, Coke containers were marked with visible numbers. Consumers won trips to Euro Disney when the visible numbers matched concealed numbers on the can or bottle. In Belgium, Coke packages were marked with concealed stars. Consumers were entered into a drawing for Euro Disney trips if their can or bottle had a set minimum number of stars.

The heavy advertising campaign and implementation of an exciting and attractive sales promotion combined to move Coke toward achieving its claim of being *the* soft drink of Europe.

Source: Adapted from Elena Bowes, "Coke Rides Disney," *Advertising Age,* December 2, 1991, 31.

will purchase only those brands that are on deal.[14] Most consumers lie somewhere between these extremes. Figure 15.2 presents a framework showing various segments of consumers in terms of their deal proneness.[15]

---

[14]Research has shown that consumers possess a good understanding of when deals are offered by manufacturers and have a reasonably good understanding of how much savings they can enjoy by purchasing on deal. See Aradhna Krishna, Imran S. Currim, and Rober W. Shoemaker, "Consumer Perceptions of Promotional Activity," *Journal of Marketing,* 55 (April 1991), 4–16.

[15]The following discussion is based on the work of Leigh McAlister, "Continued Research into Sales Promotion: Product Line Management Issues," a research report and proposal prepared for the Marketing Science Institute and other sponsors (circa 1986); also, Leigh McAlister, "A Model of Consumer Behavior," *Marketing Communications,* April 1987, 27–30.

FIGURE 15.2   ## A Segmentation Model of Consumer Response to Sales-Promotion Deals

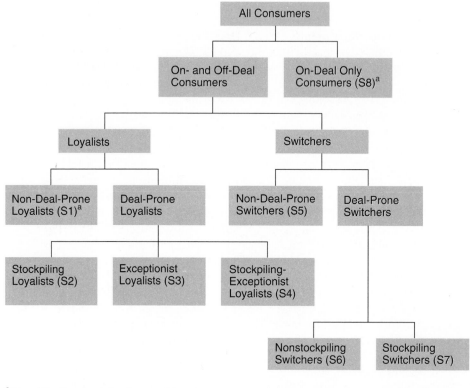

[a]S1 – S8 = Segment 1 – Segment 8.

Source: Adapted from Leigh McAlister, "Continued Research into Sales Promotion: Product Line Management Issues," A Research Report and Proposal Prepared for the Marketing Science Institute and Other Sponsors (circa 1986). Adapted with permission.

As shown in Figure 15.2, a market can be segmented into eight groups based on the pattern of consumers' deal responsiveness. There are two critical points about these groupings and the purchase patterns on which they are based: First, the patterns are obtained from *optically scanned purchase data* obtained from consumers who are members of household panels such as IRI's BehaviorScan (as described in the previous chapter). Second, the eight segments are based on consumers' purchase patterns *within a single product category*. The segmentation of consumers into deal-responsiveness segments is meaningful only on a product-by-product basis inasmuch as consumers exhibit different deal-responsiveness patterns across product categories.

Returning to the eight segments in Figure 15.2, the most general distinction is between consumers who purchase *only when a brand is on deal* (Segment 8) and all remaining consumers who do *not* restrict their purchasing to times when a product is on deal. These *on- and off-deal consumers* fall into two general categories, loyalists and switchers. The distinction between loyalists and switchers is based on purchase behavior when *no brands in a product category are on deal.*

Loyalists are consumers whose purchase patterns reflect that they buy the *same brand* over and over *when no brands are on deal* (when the category is off promotion). Looking again at Figure 15.2, you can see that some loyalists are deal prone and some are not. **Switchers,** on the other hand, are consumers who even when all brands in a category are off promotion nonetheless switch among different brands. Like loyalists, switchers may or may not be deal prone. Now let's track the various types of loyalist consumers and then the switchers.

Non-deal-prone loyalists (Segment 1) are consumers who invariably buy a single brand in a product category and are not influenced by that brand's deals or the deals from competitive brands. Segment 1 represents consumers who are truly brand loyal. Most brands today have relatively few consumers who are non-deal-prone loyalists. *Non-deal-prone switchers* (Segment 5) are like their loyalist counterparts insofar as they are not responsive to deals. They switch among brands, but this is due to a need for novelty and not to avail themselves of deals.

Deal-prone loyalists come in three varieties: (1) *stockpiling loyalists* (Segment 2) purchase only the single brand to which they are loyal but take advantage of savings by stockpiling when that brand is on deal (e.g., buying three instead of the customary one box of their favored cereal when a 50 cents-off deal is offered); (2) *exceptionist loyalists* (Segment 3), though loyal to a single brand when all brands in the category are off deal, will make an exception and purchase another, nonpreferred brand when it, but not their preferred brand, is on deal; (3) *stockpiling-exceptionist loyalists* (Segment 4) not only make exceptions by choosing nonpreferred brands but also stockpile quantities of other brands when they are on deal.

Deal-prone switchers break into two groups: *nonstockpiling switchers* (Segment 6) are responsive to deals but do not purchase extra quantities when any of their acceptable brands are on deal; *stockpiling switchers* (Segment 7) exploit deal opportunities by purchasing multiple units when any acceptable brand is on deal.

Because several of the loyalist and switcher segments are conceptually overlapping, we can eliminate any further need to distinguish between Segments 1 and 5, Segments 3 and 6, and Segments 4 and 7. All subsequent discussion is based on the following five categories of purchase patterns:

1. Promotion Insensitives (Segments 1 and 5)

2. Stockpiling Loyalists (Segment 2)

3. Nonstockpiling Promotion Sensitives (Segments 3 and 6)

4. Stockpiling Promotion Sensitives (Segments 4 and 7)

5. On-Deal-Only Consumers (Segment 8)

Profit Implications for Each Category

The profit implications of dealing in each category will be based on a hypothetical brand of shampoo called "HairRelief."[16] (For the moment, return to Figure 15.2 and identify which segment of the shampoo market you belong to on the basis of your responsiveness, or lack of responsiveness, to shampoo deals.)

PROMOTION INSENSITIVES (SEGMENTS 1 AND 5).   Assume that the market for shampoo consists entirely of consumers who are insensitive to promotional deals. Would it be profitable in such a situation to place HairRelief on deal? Your answer should be a resounding NO! The reason is depicted in Figure 15.3, which portrays the sales pattern that would result from a market made up entirely of promotion insensitives.

Note first in Figure 15.3 the labels for the horizontal and vertical axes. The horizontal axis is a time dimension, which indicates that HairRelief, like most real brands, is off deal for a period of time, then on deal, then off, and so on. The vertical axis graphs HairRelief's sales volume. The line marked "HairRelief's Market Share" represents the amount of sales volume that HairRelief normally would be expected to garner in the shampoo category.

The reason it would be unprofitable to place HairRelief on deal is because promotion insensitives will *not*, by definition, alter their purchase behavior in response to HairRelief's dealing activity. As a result, when HairRelief is placed on deal the same number of units are sold that would have been sold without the promotion; however, these units are now being sold *at a lower profit margin*. The total amount of loss from the sales promotion would equal the number of units sold when HairRelief is on deal times the cost per unit of running the deal.

STOCKPILING LOYALISTS (SEGMENT 2).   These shampoo purchasers are loyal to HairRelief and will stockpile quantities of that brand when it is on deal. Should HairRelief be placed on deal if all consumers were stockpiling loyalists? The answer again is NO. It would be *unprofitable* for HairRelief to use a deal if the shampoo market were made up entirely of stockpiling loyalists.

The reason is shown in Figure 15.4. Note first from the vertical axis that *sales depression* results from HairRelief's own sales promotions when the brand

---

[16]Shampoo is an appropriate product category because it is characterized by both switching and loyal purchase patterns. For a fascinating set of experiments using shampoo as the experimental product, see Barbara E. Kahn and Therese A. Louie, "Effects of Retraction of Price Promotions on Brand Choice Behavior for Variety-Seeking and Last-Purchase-Loyal Consumers," *Journal of Marketing Research*, 27 (August 1990), 279–289.

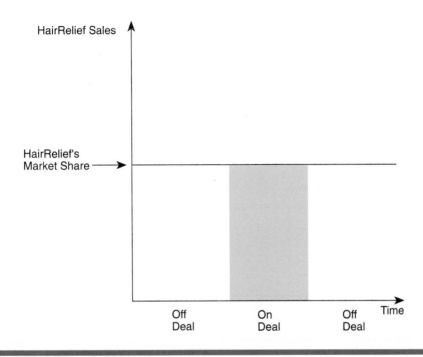

Promotion Insensitives' Deal Responsiveness

FIGURE 15.3

Source: Adapted from Leigh McAlister, "Continued Research into Sales Promotion: Product Line Management Issues," A Research Report and Proposal Prepared for the Marketing Science Institute and Other Sponsors (circa 1986), 7. Adapted with permission.

is off deal. In other words, during off-deal periods sales are below the Hair-Relief's regular sales volume because consumers who stockpiled in response to past promotions have no need to now purchase HairRelief at its regular, non-deal price. When HairRelief *is* on deal, sales bump up considerably because stockpiling loyalists avail themselves of the deal (see Figure 15.4). However, when HairRelief is on deal, it is simply *borrowing from future sales*. The promotion results in a sales bump, but it is unprofitable for two reasons: (1) sales made when HairRelief is on deal are made at a lower profit margin, and (2) when HairRelief is off deal, fewer sales are made at the full margin.

NONSTOCKPILING PROMOTION SENSITIVES (SEGMENTS 3 AND 6).   This segment consists of loyalists and switchers who *take advantage of promotional deals but do not stockpile*. In terms of shampoo purchasing, these

FIGURE 15.4	Stockpiling Loyalists' Deal Responsiveness

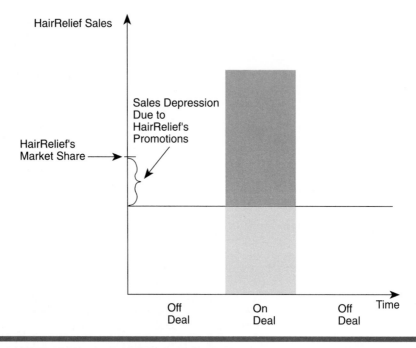

Source: Adapted from Leigh McAlister, "Continued Research into Sales Promotion: Product Line Management Issues," A Research Report and Proposal Prepared for the Marketing Science Institute and Other Sponsors (circa 1986), 7. Adapted with permission.

consumers will *switch* among several brands of acceptable shampoos depending on which brand is on deal on any particular shopping occasion. They do not choose to stockpile, however. This segment represents a large percentage of consumers in many product categories. For example, one study determined that increases in coffee sales from promotions were due almost entirely to brand switching (84 percent) rather than from accelerated purchasing (14 percent) or stockpiling (2 percent).[17]

How profitable would a promotional offering by HairRelief be if the market for shampoo consisted entirely of consumers who switch among shampoo brands but do not stockpile? Figure 15.5 displays this situation. As in the case of stockpiling loyalists, a sales depression exists between HairRelief's market share and its non-deal, or baseline, sales level. However, in the present case the depression is *due entirely to competitive promotions*. When HairRelief is on deal its sales

[17]Sumil Gupta, "Impact of Sales Promotion on When, What, and How Much to Buy," *Journal of Marketing Research*, 25 (November 1988) 342–355.

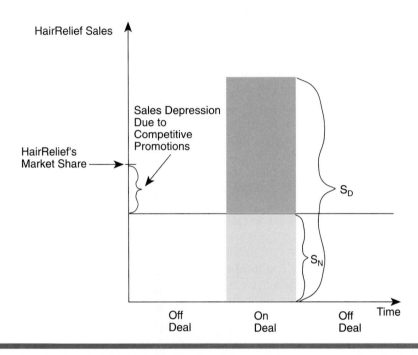

Nonstockpiling Promotion Sensitives' Deal Responsiveness   FIGURE 15.5

Source: Adapted from Leigh McAlister, "Continued Research into Sales Promotion: Product Line Management Issues," A Research Report and Proposal Prepared for the Marketing Science Institute and Other Sponsors (circa 1986), 7. Adapted with permission.

are bumped up measurably over the baseline level. This, of course, is due to capturing purchases from consumers who have switched from competitive shampoo brands.

HairRelief's sales during the promotional period are made at a margin M_D, which stands for the per-unit profit margin (M) during the period when HairRelief is on deal (D). If HairRelief did not promote, its sales volume would remain at a level equal to the light green portion in Figure 15.5 (labeled S_N, or the sales volume when HairRelief is *not* on deal). These sales would have been made at a margin M_N. (HairRelief's profit margin is, of course, greater when it is not on deal compared to when it is; i.e., $M_N > M_D$.) Total sales due to the deal are shown in Figure 15.5 by S_D, which includes incremental sales from the promotion (darker green area) plus regular nonpromotional sales (S_N).

Let us define R as the ratio of sales volume when HairRelief is on deal to when it is not on deal (i.e., R equals the ratio of S_D to S_N). We conclude that it will be *profitable* to put HairRelief on deal only if $(R \times M_D) > M_N$. An example will clarify the point. Assume HairRelief's sales volume (S_N) is 2,000,000 units when it is *off deal* and its profit margin (M_N) is 25 cents. *On deal* assumes that HairRelief's sales volume (S_D) increases to 4,200,000 units at a reduced profit margin (M_D) of 15 cents. Hence, in this case R equals 2.1 (4,200,000/2,000,000). It thus would be profitable to promote HairRelief because R × M_D is greater than M_N; that is, 2.1 × 15 = 31.5 > 25.

STOCKPILING PROMOTION SENSITIVES (SEGMENTS 4 AND 7).   This segment switches among brands depending on which is on deal and stockpiles extra quantities when an attractive deal is located. In this case, HairRelief's baseline sales are depressed both by its own dealing activity *and* by competitive dealing. If HairRelief's dealing activity is profitable when consumers do not stockpile (the situation in the previous case), then stockpiling behavior will lead to even greater profitability. This is because HairRelief will profit both by taking consumers away from competitors during the period HairRelief is on deal *and* by preempting competitors' sales in subsequent off-deal periods when consumers are "working off" their stockpiles of HairRelief.

ON-DEAL-ONLY CONSUMERS (SEGMENT 8).   Because, by definition, HairRelief makes no sales to these consumers *unless it is on deal*, it follows that promotions to a market made up exclusively of on-deal-only consumers will be *profitable*. The total amount of profit would equal the number of units sold (Q) times the profit margin when the brand is on deal (M_D).

In Conclusion

The discussion to this point has provided several guidelines regarding sales promotion.

1. Putting a brand on deal is *unprofitable* if the market is composed of either promotion-insensitive consumers or stockpiling loyalists.

2. Putting a brand on deal is *profitable* if the market contains on-deal-only consumers.

3. Putting a brand on deal *may or may not be profitable* if the market consists of nonstockpiling or stockpiling promotion-sensitive consumers.

The preceding statements are based on the assumption that a brand's market consists *exclusively of one or another type of consumer*—for example, promotion insensitives or stockpiling loyalists. This obviously is an untenable assumption. The market for any product (such as our illustrative shampoo brand, HairRelief) contains consumers from all segments. The matter of whether promotion is profitable or not thus depends on the relative composition of customer types.

Fortunately, the availability of scanner data makes it possible for marketing researchers to identify the percentage of consumers who fall into each of the categories that were just described. Armed with this information, brand managers can determine whether dealing activity is profitable or whether it merely results in a revenue-increasing but profit-losing endeavor.

SUMMARY

The topic of sales promotion is introduced in this first of three chapters devoted to the topic. The precise nature of sales promotion is described, and specific forms of trade- and consumer-oriented sales promotion are discussed. Sales promotion is explained as having three targets: the trade (wholesalers and retailers), consumers, and a company's own sales force.

The chapter proceeds to explain the reasons underlying a significant trend in U.S. marketing toward greater sales promotion in comparison with advertising. This shift is part of the movement from pull- to push-oriented marketing, particularly in the case of consumer packaged goods. Underlying factors include a balance-of-power transfer from manufacturers to retailers, increased brand parity and growing price sensitivity, reduced brand loyalty, splintering of the mass market and reduced media effectiveness, a growing short-term orientation, and favorable consumer responsiveness to sales promotions.

The specific tasks that sales promotion can and cannot accomplish are discussed. For example, sales promotion cannot give the trade or consumers compelling long-term reasons to purchase. However, it is ideally suited to generating trial-purchase behavior, facilitating the introduction of new products, gaining shelf space for a brand, encouraging repeat purchasing, and performing a variety of other tasks.

Detailed discussion is devoted to the conditions under which the use of dealing activities in sales promotions is profitable. Various segments of consumers based on their responsiveness to promotional deals are described. It is concluded that sales promotion is unprofitable if a brand's market is composed of promotion insensitive or brand-loyal stockpilers; sales promotion is always profitable if the market contains consumers who buy only on deal; and sales promotion may be profitable if the market consists primarily of consumers who switch from brand to brand depending on which brand is on deal.

The following chapter continues with a detailed treatment of sales promotion's role in influencing trade behavior, while Chapter 17 examines its role in influencing the behavior of ultimate consumers.

Discussion Questions

1. The term promotional inducement has been suggested as an alternative to sales promotion. Explain why this new term is more descriptive than the established term.

2. Describe the factors that have accounted for sales promotion's rapid growth. Do you expect sales promotion to continue to grow through the remainder of the 1990s?

3. Explain in your own words the meaning of push- versus pull-oriented promotional strategies. Using for illustration a well-known supermarket brand of your choice, explain which elements of this brand's promotion mix embody push and which embody pull.

4. Assume you are the vice president of marketing for a large, well-known manufacturer of consumer packaged goods (e.g., Procter & Gamble, Lever Brothers, Johnson & Johnson). What steps might you take to restore a balance of power favoring your company in its relations with retailers?

5. Are sales promotions able to reverse a brand's temporary sales decline and/or a permanent sales decline? Be specific.

6. The allocation of promotional dollars to advertising and sales promotion is influenced by a variety of factors, including life-cycle stage, the degree of brand differentiation, and the degree of brand dominance. Explain how these factors influence the allocation decision.

7. How can sales-promotion techniques generate enthusiasm and stimulate improved performance from the sales force?

8. Offer a specific explanation of why you think the "Find the Cap'n" promotional campaign for Cap'n Crunch cereal was so successful.

9. What is the logic underlying Warner-Lambert's decision to use one of its brands (Listerine mouthwash) as a medium for distributing coupons for the Schick Tracer? (Refer to the *Focus on Promotion*.)

10. If a market for a brand were composed entirely of brand-loyal stockpilers, why would promotional deals for this brand necessarily be unprofitable? Why are promotional deals profitable when a market consists of on-deal-only consumers?

11. Why is it critical that objectives be clearly specified when formulating a sales-promotion program?

12. In the opening vignette describing Almay's introduction of Wetproof mascara, a sweepstake offered consumers the opportunity to receive a free vacation to Aruba along with $500 spending money. Why do you think so many companies offer vacations to exotic places as the grand prize in their sweepstake offers?

CHAPTER SIXTEEN

Trade-Oriented Sales Promotion

STREET MONEY

Imagine yourself for the moment as the vice president of marketing and sales for a regional manufacturer of canned goods headquartered in Massachusetts. Your company has a fine reputation for high-quality seafood products such as clam chowder. Your market includes grocery stores throughout New England. Unfortunately, sales growth has been minimal in recent years, averaging only two percent annually. A marketing research study performed by a Boston consulting firm shows that many consumers are not purchasing your products because they perceive them to be too fattening, canned as they are in creamy sauces. The consulting firm recommends a new line of low-calorie items. This should pose quite a challenge for your company, since you have not introduced a single new product for over ten years.

After months of planning and testing, you are prepared to introduce the new line of low-calorie canned goods. Knowing that retailer support is absolutely critical for product success, you decide to personally call several major grocery chains to sell them on the new product idea.

The first person you see, a buyer for a 250-store regional chain, is excited about the new product and considers the price reasonable. She agrees to carry your new low-calorie canned seafood in all 250 stores, subject to one condition: Your company will have to pay a fee of $100 for each store in the chain, for a total of $25,000. The buyer explains that this is a typical charge necessary to compensate her company for the extra expenses it incurs when taking on new products.

You leave the buyer's office in a state of disbelief. You've never heard of such an arrangement—$25,000 just to get one of numerous accounts to handle your new product line. A quick call to your Boston consulting firm verifies that arrangements such as this are not restricted to this one chain but in fact have become widespread in grocery marketing. You learn that such arrangements go by different names, such as *slotting allowances, stocking allowances,* or just plain *street money.*

You're between a rock and a hard place. If you *don't* go along with the offer, you won't be able to get your new product distributed. If you *do* go along with the offer, you'll go broke because your budget can't afford this amount of trade support.

INTRODUCTION TO TRADE PROMOTION

The growth of slotting allowances is just one of the various reasons spending on sales promotions has increased while advertising spending has declined as a percentage of the total promotion budget. A survey of major packaged-goods marketers reveals that allocations of promotion dollars among consumer-oriented sales promotions, trade-oriented promotions, and media advertising were 25.1 percent, 44.3 percent, and 30.6 percent respectively.[1] In other words, trade promotions represent over $44 out of every $100 invested to promote new and existing products. It is estimated that trade promotions including slotting allowances account, on average, for 16 percent of manufacturers' new-product introduction costs.[2] This translates into an average cost of $222 per stock-keeping unit (SKU) for introducing a product into a single store.[3]

The General Nature and Objectives of Trade Promotion

As discussed in the previous chapter, manufacturers use some combination of push and pull strategies to accomplish both retail distribution and consumer pur-

[1]Michael Burgi, "Trade Spending Tops," *Advertising Age*, April 15, 1991, 36.

[2]Julie Liesse, "Slotting Bites New Products," *Advertising Age*, November 5, 1990, 16.

[3]Retailer's designate each size and form of manufacturers' brands with specific SKU codes, standing for stockkeeping units. For example, six packs of 12-ounce Coca-Cola cans and single one-liter Coke bottles represent two SKUs.

chasing. Trade promotions, which are directed at wholesalers, retailers, and other marketing intermediaries, represent the first step in any promotional effort. Consumer promotions are likely to fail unless trade-promotion efforts have succeeded in getting wholesalers to distribute the product and retailers to stock adequate quantities.

A manufacturer has various objectives for using trade-oriented sales promotions: (1) to introduce new or revised products, (2) to increase distribution of new packages or sizes, (3) to build retail inventories, (4) to maintain or increase the manufacturer's share of shelf space, (5) to obtain displays outside normal shelf locations, (6) to reduce excess inventories and increase turnover, (7) to achieve product features in retailers' advertisements, (8) to counter competitive activity, and, ultimately, (9) to sell as much as possible to final consumers.[4]

To accomplish these myriad objectives, several ingredients are critical to building a successful trade-promotion program.[5]

FINANCIAL INCENTIVE.   The trade promotion must offer retailers increased profit margins and/or increased sales volume.

CORRECT TIMING.   Sales promotions to the trade are appropriately timed when they are (1) tied in with a seasonal event during a time of growing sales (such as candy sales during Halloween), (2) paired with a consumer sales-promotion effort, or (3) used strategically to offset competitive promotional activity.

MINIMIZE THE RETAILER'S EFFORT AND COST.   The more effort and expense required, the less likely it is that retailers will cooperate in a program they see as benefiting the manufacturer but not themselves.

QUICK RESULTS.   The most effective trade promotions are those that generate immediate sales or increases in store traffic.

IMPROVE RETAILER PERFORMANCE.   Promotions are effective when they help the retailer do a better selling job or improve merchandising methods (like superior display devices).[6]

---

[4]These objectives are adapted from a consumer-promotion seminar conducted by Ennis Associates, Inc., and sponsored by the Association of National Advertisers, Inc., New York, undated. See also Chakravarthi Narasimhan, "Managerial Perspectives on Trade and Consumer Promotions," *Marketing Letters*, 1, 3, (1989), 239–251.

[5]Don E. Schultz and William A. Robinson, *Sales Promotion Management* (Lincolnwood, IL: NTC Business Books, 1986), 265–266.

[6]For further reading see Kenneth G. Hardy, "Key Success Factors for Manufacturers' Sales Promotions in Package Goods, *Journal of Marketing*, 50 (July 1986), 13–23.

Types of Trade Promotions

Manufacturers employ various trade-oriented promotional inducements. Following sections discuss these widely used and important forms of trade promotions:

- Trade Allowances

- Cooperative Advertising and Vendor Support Programs

- Trade Contests and Incentives

- Point-of-Purchase Materials

- Training Programs

- Specialty Advertising

- Trade Shows

TRADE ALLOWANCES

Trade allowances, or *trade deals*, come in a variety of forms and are offered to retailers for performing activities in support of the manufacturer's brand.[7] These allowances/deals are needed to encourage retailers to stock the manufacturer's brand, discount the brand's price to consumers, feature it in advertising, or provide special display or other point-of-purchase support.[8]

Buying Allowances

Buying allowances provide deals to the trade in the form of *free goods or price reductions* in return for the purchase of specific quantities of goods. For example, Shell offered dealers of its Fire & Ice Motor Oil five free cases (120 free quarts) with every purchase of 45 cases. The makers of ACTIFED, a nasal decongestant/antihistamine, provided a trade allowance of 16 2/3 percent off the retail invoice price for all purchases during the deal period.

By using buying allowances, manufacturers hope to accomplish two interrelated objectives: (1) increase retailers' purchasing of the manufacturer's brand,

---

[7]Rajiv Lal, "Manufacturer Trade Deals and Retail Price Promotions," *Journal of Marketing Research*, 27 (November 1990), 428–444.

[8]Ronald C. Curhan and Robert J. Kopp, "Obtaining Retailer Support for Trade Deals: Key Success Factors," *Journal of Advertising Research*, 27 (December 1987/January 1988), 51–60.

and (2) increase consumers' purchasing from retailers. This latter objective is based on the expectation that consumers are receptive to price reductions, and that retailers will in fact pass along to consumers the discounts they receive from manufacturers. This, unfortunately, does not always happen. Some retailers take advantage of allowances without performing the services for which they receive credit. In fact, it has been estimated that retailers often put as much as *30 percent* of trade-allowance dollars into their own bottom lines without passing the savings along to consumers.[9]

One study determined that large chain retailers are particularly likely to take advantage of manufacturers' trade allowances *without passing the savings along to consumers*. Table 16.1 shows that large chains account for 29 percent of all retail sales but only 17 percent of sales for items featured in advertisements at below-normal prices. In other words, large chains sell *disproportionately less* than their share of products at reduced prices (as indicated by the trade-performance index of 59 in Table 16.1). This is another way of saying that large chains often keep the manufacturer's trade allowance without passing the savings along to consumers. By comparison, medium-sized chains' sales of featured merchandise is exactly proportionate to their nondeal sales (providing a trade performance index of 100), and small chains and independent retailers sell proportionately more than their share at reduced prices.[10]

One major reason large chains are disproportionately less likely to pass price reductions from manufacturers along to consumers is that, unlike smaller chains and independents, they are able to promote and sell their own *private brands*. Because private brands can be sold at lower prices than manufacturers' comparable brands, large chains are able to use private brands to satisfy the needs of

Deal versus Nondeal Sales by Store Size   TABLE 16.1

STORE SIZE	NONDEAL SALES (1)	FEATURE SALES (2)	TRADE PERFORMANCE INDEX (2÷1)
Large chains	29%	17%	59
Medium chains	7	7	100
Small chains and independents	64	76	119
	100%	100%	

Source: Adapted from *Insights: Issues 1-13, 1979-1982* (New York: NPD Research, 1983), 9.

[9]Jennifer Lawrence and Judann Dagnoli, "P&G's Low-Price Strategy Cuts Trade Fees, Irks Retailers," *Advertising Age*, December 23, 1991, 3.

[10]*Insights: Issues 1-13, 1979-1982* (New York: NPD Research, 1983), 8.

price-sensitive consumers while selling manufacturers' brands at their normal price and pocketing the trade allowance as extra profit. This certainly is not meant to imply that all large chains exploit manufacturers and consumers. It does point out, however, a serious problem that manufacturers must contend with when offering trade deals. In fact, many manufacturers have responded to this problem by tightening performance requirements and requiring retailers to do more to earn their allowances.

A second major problem with manufacturers' trade allowances is that they often *induce the trade to stockpile products* in order to take advantage of the temporary price reduction. This merely shifts business from the future to the present. Two prevalent practices are forward buying and diverting.

FORWARD BUYING.   Manufacturers' trade allowances are typically available every four weeks of each business quarter (which translates to about 30 percent of the year). Retailers take advantage of manufacturers' deals by buying larger quantities than needed for normal inventory and warehousing the excess quantity, thereby avoiding purchasing the product at full price. Retailers often purchase enough product on one deal to carry them over until the manufacturer's next regularly scheduled deal. This is the practice of **forward buying,** which, for obvious reasons, is also called *bridge buying.*

When a manufacturer marks down a product's price by, say, 10 percent, wholesalers and retailers commonly stock up with a 10 to 12 week supply.[11] A conservative estimate would place the amount of forward buying by wholesalers and retailers at about one-quarter of their inventories.[12] A number of manufacturers sell 80 to 90 percent of their volume on deal.[13]

The practice of forward buying has given rise to computer models that enable wholesale and retail buyers to estimate the profit potential from a forward buy and the optimum weeks of inventory to purchase. The models take into consideration the amount of savings from a deal and then incorporate into their calculations the various added costs from forward buying: warehouse storage expenses, shipping costs, and the cost of money.

It may appear that forward buying benefits all parties to the marketing process, but this is not the case. First, retailers' savings from forward buying often are not passed on to consumers. Second, forward buying leads to increased distribution costs since wholesalers and retailers pay greater carrying charges in inventorying larger quantities. Third, manufacturers experience reduced margins due to the price discounts that they offer as well as the increased costs that result from factors illustrated in the *Focus on Promotion.* It is estimated that

[11]Ronald Alsop, "Retailers Buy Far in Advance to Exploit Trade Promotions," *The Wall Street Journal*, October 9, 1986, 37.

[12]Monci Jo Williams, "The No-Win Game of Price Promotion," *Fortune*, July 11, 1983, 92–102.

[13]Willard R. Bishop, Jr., "Trade Buying Squeezes Marketers," *Marketing Communications*, May 1988, 50–54.

FOCUS ON PROMOTION

FORWARD BUYING OF CAMPBELL'S CHICKEN NOODLE SOUP

The Campbell Soup Company is one of the most respected packaged-goods marketers in the United States, but like many other companies, it suffers from forward-buying practices. Campbell's chicken noodle soup, a staple item in many homes and in most supermarkets, provides a telling example of this problem. Sometimes the company sells as much as 40 percent of its annual chicken noodle soup production to wholesalers and retailers in just six weeks!

When wholesalers and retailers forward buy chicken noodle soup in large quantities, Campbell must schedule extra work shifts and pay overtime to keep up with the accelerated production and shipping schedules. Later, layoffs result when demand for chicken noodle soup falls.

These problems can be partially avoided with the use of a *bill and hold* program. In other words, the manufacturer invoices (bills) the retailer as soon as the order is placed but delays shipping (holds) the order until desired quantities are requested by the retailer. Such programs smooth out production and shipping schedules by allowing retailers to purchase large amounts at deal prices but delay receiving shipments until inventory is needed.

Source: Adapted from Alsop, "Retailers Buy Far in Advance to Exploit Trade Promotions."

forward buying costs manufacturers between 0.5 to 1.1 percent of retail prices, which translates into hundreds of millions of dollars annually.[14]

DIVERTING.   Another growing buying practice, diverting, occurs when a manufacturer restricts a deal to a limited geographical area rather than making it available nationally. The manufacturer's intent is that only wholesalers and retailers in that area will benefit from the deal. However, what happens with diverting is that wholesalers and retailers buy abnormally large quantities at the deal price and then *transship the excess quantities to other geographical areas.* It

---

[14]Robert D. Buzzell, John A. Quelch, and Walter J. Salmon, "The Costly Bargain of Trade Promotion," *Harvard Business Review,* March–April 1990, 145.

is estimated that the volume of merchandise involved amounts to at least $5 billion a year.[15]

Diverting has been practiced for a number of years, but until recently diverting operations were run in bookie-type fashion. That is, shady characters working in small offices wheeled and dealed in lining up sellers of diverted products in one geographical area with buyers in another. Recently, diverting has taken on the appearance of a high-tech business. There now are sophisticated electronic diverting networks in the United States doing millions of dollars of diverting business.[16]

The practice of diverting probably is no less unethical than it ever was, but now it is more out in the open. Many retailers blame the manufacturers for offering irresistible deals; the retailers argue that they must take advantage of the deals in any way legally possible in order to remain competitive with other retailers. Manufacturers could avoid the problem by placing brands on national deal only. This solution is more ideal than practical, however, since regional marketing efforts are expanding (as discussed in Chapter 8), and local deals and regional marketing go hand in hand.

Slotting Allowances

Slotting allowances are a special form of trade deal that apply specifically to *new products*. As noted in the chapter's opening vignette, slotting allowances are also called stocking allowances or simply, *street money*. A **slotting allowance** is defined as the fee a manufacturer pays a supermarket chain or other retailer to get that retailer to handle the manufacturer's new product. The allowance is called *slotting* in reference to the slot, or location, that the retailer must make available in its distribution center to accommodate the manufacturer's product.

You probably are thinking "This sounds like bribery." You also may be wondering "Why do manufacturers tolerate slotting allowances?" Let's examine each issue.[17]

First, slotting allowances are indeed a form of bribery. The retailer who demands slotting allowances denies the manufacturer shelf space unless the manufacturer is willing to pay the upfront fee, the slotting allowance, to acquire that space for its new product. Second, manufacturers tolerate slotting allowances because they are confronted with a classic dilemma: Either they pay the fee and eventually recoup the cost through increased sales volume, or they refuse to pay

---

[15]Buzzell, Quelch, and Salmon, "The Costly Bargain of Trade Promotion," 143.

[16]Bishop, "Trade Buying Squeezes Marketers," 52–53.

[17]For discussion of the legal issues surrounding the use of slotting allowances, see Joseph P. Cannon and Paul N. Bloom, "Are Slotting Allowances Legal Under the Antitrust Laws?" *Journal of Public Policy and Marketing*, 10, 1 (1991).

the fee and in so doing accept a fate of not being able to successfully introduce new products.

The expression "between a rock and a hard place" is as appropriate here as it was in the opening vignette. Consider, for example, Eastman Kodak Co.'s introduction of Supralife alkaline batteries, which entered stores in 1986 to compete against the likes of Duracell, Eveready and Ray-O-Vac. As of 1990, Supralife's performance was so weak that Kodak decided to discontinue all advertising and, in effect, to accept its destiny as a minor player in the alkaline battery business. Analysts estimate Kodak's battery-business losses at somewhere between $100 million and $200 million. Among other reasons for Supralife's losses is the fact that Kodak in the first year or so had to pay slotting allowances estimated at $75 million![18]

In certain respects, slotting allowances are a legitimate cost of doing business. When, for example, a large multi-store supermarket chain takes on a new product, it incurs several added expenses. These expenses arise because the chain must make space for that product in its distribution center, create a new entry in its computerized inventory system, redesign store shelves, and notify individual stores about the new product.[19] In addition to these expenses, the chain takes the risk that the new product will fail. This is a likely result in the grocery industry, where at least half of the 15,000 products introduced annually fail. Hence, the slotting allowance serves as an *insurance policy* against product failure.

It is questionable, however, whether the actual expenses incurred by retailers are anywhere near the slotting allowances they charge. Actual charges are highly variable. Some supermarkets charge as little as $5 per store to stock a new item, while others charge as much as $50 or $100 per store. Some Northeastern grocery chains charge as much as $15,000 to $40,000 for a single new product.

Large companies can afford to pay slotting allowances, because their volume is sufficient to recoup the expense. However, brands with small consumer franchises are frequently unable to afford these fees. For example, one grocery chain demanded $1,000 per store to introduce Frookie cookies in its 100 stores. To have paid this fee would have required the retail price for a package of Frookie cookies to jump by 50 cents from $1.79 to $2.29. The makers of Frookie cookies were forced to turn down the opportunity to sell their product in this chain.[20]

HOW CAN THEY GET AWAY WITH IT?   This question has probably entered your mind. How, in fact, are retailers able to charge such huge fees?

[18]Julie Liesse, "Kodak Brand Calls Retreat in the Battery War," *Advertising Age*, October 15, 1990, 3, 69.

[19]Laurie Freeman and Janet Meyers, "Grocer 'Fee' Hampers New-Product Launches," *Advertising Age*, August 3, 1987, 1.

[20]Richard Gibson, "Supermarkets Demand Food Firms' Payments Just to Get on the Shelf," *The Wall Street Journal*, November 1, 1988, sec. A, 1, 9.

The reason is straightforward: As noted in the previous chapter, the balance of power has shifted away from manufacturers and toward retailers. Power means being able to call the shots, and increasing numbers of retailers are doing this. Also, manufacturers have hurt their own cause by introducing thousands of new products each year, most of which are trivial variants of existing products rather than distinct new offerings with meaningful profit opportunities for the retailer. As such, every manufacturer competes against every other manufacturer for limited shelf space, and slotting allowances are simply a mechanism used by retailers to exploit the competition among manufacturers. Furthermore, many grocery retailers find it easy to rationalize slotting allowances on the grounds that their net-profit margins in selling groceries are minuscule (typically 1 to 1.5 percent) and that slotting allowances enable them to earn returns comparable to what manufacturers earn.

Further understanding of the rationale and dynamics underlying slotting allowances is possible by drawing an analogy with prices for apartments in any college community. When units are abundant, different apartment complexes compete aggressively with one another and force prices down. On the other hand, when apartments are scarce (which typically is the case on most college campuses), prices are often inflated. The result: You may be forced to pay an arm and a leg to live in a miserable, albeit conveniently located, apartment.

This is also the case in today's marketing environment. Each year retailers are confronted with requests to stock thousands of new products (potential tenants). The amount of shelf space (the number of apartments) is limited because relatively few new stores are being built. Hence, retailers are able to command slotting allowances (higher rent), and manufacturers are willing to pay the higher rent to "live" in desirable locations.

AVOIDING SLOTTING ALLOWANCES.   What can a manufacturer do to avoid paying slotting allowances? Sometimes nothing. But powerful manufacturers like Procter & Gamble and Kraft, for example, are less likely to pay slotting fees than are weaker national and particularly regional manufacturers. Retailers know that P&G's and Kraft's new products probably *will* be successful. This is because P&G and Kraft invest heavily in research in order to develop meaningful new products; they spend heavily on advertising to create consumer demand for these products; and they use extensive sales promotions (e.g., couponing) that serve to create strong consumer pull.

And Now, Exit Fees

Whereas slotting allowances represent a form of *entry fee* for getting a new product entered in a grocery chain's distribution center, now some chains have begun charging an *exit fee* to remove unsuccessful new products from their distribution centers. These **exit fees** could just as well be called *deslotting allowances*. Here is how they operate: When introducing a new product to a supermarket chain, the vendor (manufacturer or wholesaler) and chain enter into a contractual arrangement. This arrangement stipulates the *average volume of weekly product movement* during a specified period, say six months, that must be achieved for the vendor's product to be permitted to remain in the chain's distribution center. Then, if the six months have elapsed and the product has *not met the stipulated average weekly movement*, the chain will issue a deslotting charge to the vendor. This charge, or exit fee, is intended to cover the handling costs for the chain to remove the item from its distribution center. One chain has a deslotting charge of $1,200.

This practice may appear to represent a marketplace application of the old saying about having salt rubbed into a wound. However, what it really represents is the fact that retailers, especially in the supermarket industry, no longer are willing to pay for manufacturers' new-product mistakes. There clearly is some economic logic to deslotting charges. Indeed, these charges are simply another form of insurance policy to protect grocery chains from slow-moving and unprofitable new products. To continue the apartment-rental analogy, a deslotting charge operates in much the same fashion as the stipulation between apartment owner and tenant regarding property damage. If as a tenant you damage an apartment, the apartment owner is fully justified in forfeiting all or part of your rental deposit. As such, your deposit provides the apartment owner with an insurance policy against your potential negligence. This is precisely how an exit fee, or deslotting charge, operates.

COOPERATIVE ADVERTISING AND VENDOR SUPPORT PROGRAMS

Another form of trade promotion occurs when manufacturers of branded merchandise pay for part of the expense that retailers incur when advertising manufacturers' brands. Both cooperative advertising and vendor support programs deal with *the advertising relation between manufacturers and retailers*. A fundamental distinction between the two is that cooperative advertising programs are *initiated by the manufacturer*, whereas vendor support programs are *retailer initiated*. The significance of this distinction will become clear in the following discussion.

Cooperative Advertising

As the name suggests, **cooperative (co-op) advertising** is a cooperative arrangement between a manufacturer and retailer. Co-op programs permit retailers to place ads promoting the manufacturer's product and its availability at the retailer's place of business. (For example, see the ad for Nike's Aqua Sock in

Figure 16.1.) The cost of the ad placement is shared by the manufacturer and retailer according to the terms specified in the cooperative contract.

Though cooperative advertising programs vary, *five elements are common to all.* These elements are illustrated with the co-op advertising program from La-Z-Boy®, a well-known manufacturer of reclining chairs and sofas.

1. **Specified Time Period.** Co-op funds typically apply to a specified time period. La-Z-Boy®'s program applies to funds accrued between January 1 and December 31. These funds can be applied only to advertising that is run during the same period.

2. **Accrual.** The retailer receives from the manufacturer an advertising fund, called an *accrual account,* against which advertising costs are charged. The accrual typically is based either on a fixed amount or a percentage of a retailer's net purchases from the manufacturer during the term of the co-op contract. In the case of La-Z-Boy®, which applies a *fixed accrual,* the retailer accrues $3 on each chair purchased from La-Z-Boy® and $6 on each sofa.

   To illustrate a percentage accrual, suppose a certain appliance retailer purchases $200,000 from a manufacturer in one year. Suppose further that the manufacturer's cooperative program allows 3 percent of purchases to accrue to the retailer's cooperative advertising account. Thus, the retailer would have accrued $6,000 worth of cooperative advertising dollars.

3. **Payment Share.** This is the amount of advertising reimbursement the manufacturer pays the retailer. Manufacturers generally agree to pay a set percentage ranging from 50 to 100 percent of the cost for each advertisement placed by the retailer. La-Z-Boy® pays 50 percent of each advertisement.

   Continuing the preceding example of the appliance manufacturer, now suppose the manufacturer's co-op program pays 50 percent of individual advertising charges and that the retailer places a $1,000 newspaper ad featuring the manufacturer's brand of appliances. The manufacturer would pay 50 percent of this amount, that is, $500; the retailer would pay the remaining $500 and would have $5,500 remaining in its accrual account for future advertising.

4. **Performance Guidelines.** These are the manufacturer's requirements that the retailer must satisfy in order to qualify for advertising reimbursement. Guidelines typically deal with suitable media, size and type of logos, the use of trademarks, copy and art directions, and product content. For example, La-Z-Boy® requires the following (1) The name La-Z-Boy® must never be used as a noun (e.g., a retailer could not say "Looking for a La-Z-Boy®? We have it!"); the purpose of this requirement is to prevent the name La-Z-Boy® from becoming generic, that is, being used synonymously with the product category. (2) A trademark symbol (i.e., ®) must follow the name La-Z-Boy at least once in the advertising copy, preferably the first time the name appears. (3) Competitive products cannot appear or be mentioned in the retailer's advertising.

Illustration of Cooperative Advertisement FIGURE 16.1

Aqua Sock Classic.

Five years later and the world is still trying to catch up to the original: Aqua Sock Classic.
With hundreds of uses ranging from aqua aerobics to washing the car to a walk on the beach,
the Aqua Sock Classic is designed to get you there in style-and comfort.
Men's, Ladies'. Children's sizes available.

Todd & Moore

Harbison Blvd.	620 Huger St.	225 Onell Ct.
781-1837	765-0150	1 Block From Columbia Mall
		788-9000

38410-68

5. **Billing for Reimbursement.** This prescribes how the retailer is to be reimbursed. To receive reimbursement from La-Z-Boy®, the retailer must present a copy of the invoice from the newspaper or other medium where the ad was placed along with evidence of the actual advertising copy.

WHY IS COOPERATIVE ADVERTISING USED? There are several reasons.[21] First, consumers of infrequently purchased goods (appliances, apparel, chairs and sofas) are responsive to retailer advertisements, especially preceding a major buying decision. In the absence of co-op dollars, however, most retailers would *not* emphasize a specific manufacturer's products/brands in their advertisements but would rather simply mention the variety of products/brands that the retailer handles. Hence, co-op advertising enables manufacturers to achieve advertising support on a local-market basis and provides them a way to *get their products associated in the consumer's mind with specific retail outlets.*

Second, manufacturers have found that cooperative advertising *stimulates greater retailer buying and merchandising support.* Retailers, knowing they have accrued co-op dollars, are more likely to aggressively promote and merchandise a specific manufacturer's products. From the manufacturer's perspective, this amounts to greater stocking and more display space for its brands as well as more retail advertising support.

A third advantage of co-op advertising is that it *enables manufacturers to have access to local media at an advertising rate lower than would be paid if the manufacturer advertised directly rather than through retailers.* This cost savings reflects the fact that local media, particularly newspapers, charge lower advertising rates to local advertisers than to national advertisers. For example, average national rates for advertising in major U.S. newspapers were found to be over 66 percent higher than the average local rates.[22] Hence, by using cooperative advertising, a manufacturer gets exposure in local markets at a reduced rate.

From the retailer's perspective, cooperative advertising is a relatively inexpensive form of advertising. The advertising is not truly free, however, because the manufacturer's cooperative advertising costs are built into the price of the merchandise. Failure to take advantage of accrued co-op dollars means that the retailer is effectively paying more for the same merchandise than retailers who do utilize co-op funds.

Much cooperative advertising accruals are never spent by retailers. Over $11 billion is available annually in co-op funds and fully one-third of that amount goes unspent each year.[23] Research by the Newspaper Advertising Bureau

[21]Stephen A. Greyser and Robert F. Young, "Follow 11 Guidelines to Strategically Manage Co-op Advertising Program," *Marketing News*, September 16, 1983, 5.

[22]*Newspaper Rate Differentials 1987* (New York: American Association of Advertising Agencies, 1988).

[23]Martin Everett, "Co-op Advertising and Computers," *Sales and Marketing Management*, May 1987, 56.

shows that only about 40 percent of all retailers take advantage of co-op accruals.[24]

Some manufacturers have implemented cooperative advertising programs that make it easier and more lucrative for retailers to utilize co-op funds. The objective is to make the program instructions simpler to read and easier to implement. Advertising media are also offering new programs to attract more co-op dollars. For example, the Newspaper Advertising Bureau has developed a program whereby salespeople of newspaper space are able to identify all the products in a retailer's store that carry co-op, determine how much the retailer has accrued for each product, and then run an ad for the retailer that will use the accrued co-op funds.[25]

OPEN-ENDED CO-OP ADVERTISING.   The cooperative advertising programs discussed to this point relate the amount of co-op funds to the amount of product purchased by a retailer from a particular manufacturer. The more product purchased, the more co-op funds that accrue to the retailer. Open-ended co-op advertising involves paying for part of the retailer's advertising cost without relating the reimbursement to the amount of product purchased from the manufacturer.[26]

Open-ended programs make considerable sense when the manufacturer (1) wants to encourage the use of co-op funds by *smaller retailers* or (2) when the manufacturer *sells through intermediaries* and does not have access to retailers' purchase figures. Major advantages of open-ended programs involve simplifying the record-keeping task and, more importantly, making it possible to use advertising for generating sales rather than relying on sales to generate advertising.

Vendor Support Programs

In contrast to cooperative advertising, **vendor support programs (VSPs)** are *initiated by retailers*. A retailer, such as a supermarket chain, develops an advertising program in consultation with local advertising media and then invites its suppliers to pay for a specific percentage of the media cost for the proposed campaign. In other words, the retailer creates advertising dollars by exerting its power over a manufacturer, or vendor, who depends on the retailer for its marketplace success.

To illustrate, consider a hypothetical 250-store grocery chain called BuyRight. BuyRight's advertising agency recommends that the chain undertake

[24]Renee Blakkan, "Savory Deals Tempt Hungry Retailers," *Advertising Age*, March 7, 1983, sec. M, 11.

[25]Ibid.

[26]Ed Crimmins, "Why Open-Ended Co-op Is on the Rise," *Sales and Marketing Management*, December 1986, 64, 67.

a heavy advertising campaign in April. The campaign will cost BuyRight $200,000. Where is the money to come from? Solution: Get 10 vendors (manufacturers) to contribute $20,000 each to BuyRight's April campaign. In return for their participation, manufacturers will receive *feature time and space* in BuyRight's advertisements as well as extra display space. Extra sales volume, BuyRight assures the manufacturers, will more than compensate for their advertising support funds.

VSPs have clear advantages for the retailer. Indeed, these programs seem to benefit everyone (retailers, ad agencies, media), except perhaps the manufacturers who provide the financial support.[27] Often a manufacturer pays a large sum to support a retailer's advertising efforts but receives very little actual promotion of its own brands to end users. The manufacturer's products may be lost amid the clutter of the other brands featured in, say, a supermarket chain's newspaper advertisement.

W H Y   D O   M A N U F A C T U R E R S   P A R T I C I P A T E   I N   V S P s ? Vendor support programs are most likely used when the retailer's channel power is greater than that of manufacturers who compete against one another for the retailer's limited shelf space. This is particularly true in the case of smaller, regional manufacturers who have not created strong consumer franchises for their brands. These weaker manufacturers cannot afford to invest in consumer-pull programs, because their promotion funds are almost fully consumed by retailers' vendor support programs. As such, it becomes an irrevocable cycle: The less powerful a manufacturer, the more susceptible it is to retailers' demands for advertising support funds. In turn, the more the manufacturer invests in the retailers' advertising programs, the less funds available for building demand for the manufacturer's own brands.

TRADE CONTESTS AND INCENTIVES

Contests and incentive programs are developed by manufacturers to encourage better performance from retail-management personnel and their salespersons. A **trade contest** typically is directed at store-level or department managers and generally is based on managers *meeting a sales goal* established by the manufacturer. For example, in the previous chapter's discussion of Almay's promotion of Wetproof mascara, it was noted that a sales contest offered store managers the opportunity to win 35-millimeter cameras, cordless telephones, and other attractive items.

---

[27]Ed Crimmins, "Dispelling the Hype of 'Vendor Support'," *Sales and Marketing Management*, December 9, 1985, 54–57.

Whereas contests are typically related to meeting sales goals, **trade incentives** are given to retail managers and salespeople for performing certain tasks. For example, when running sweepstakes or contests directed to final consumers (discussed fully in the following chapter), manufacturers often encourage retailers to display the object of merchandise that is being offered to consumers (e.g., a soccer ball). As an incentive to encourage retailer participation, the manufacturer gives the item to the store manager when the sales promotion is completed. Bigger prizes in the form of vacations and other high-ticket items are sometimes used as incentives.

Another form of incentive is directed at retail salespeople. Called **push money,** or *spiffs*, the manufacturer provides cash to salespeople to encourage them to push certain products in the manufacturer's line. For example, a manufacturer may pay retail salespeople $10 for every unit of a particular compact disc player that they sell. Of course, the purpose of the push money is to encourage salespeople to favor the manufacturer's model over competitors' offerings.

When structured properly, trade contests and incentives can serve the manufacturer's interests very well. These programs may not serve the retailer's or the consumer's interests however. For example, push money can cause retail salespeople to be overly aggressive in pushing products on consumers. For this reason, many stores have policies that prevent their managers and salespeople from accepting any form of incentives from manufacturers.

POINT-OF-PURCHASE MATERIALS

Anything a manufacturer can do to assist the retailer in using store space more efficiently, in expanding product-category sales volume, or in increasing store traffic will likely meet with retailer acceptance. Manufacturers supply a variety of point-of-purchase materials to achieve these objectives: dump bins, motion pieces, stand-up racks, end-of-counter displays, posters, shelf cards, and a variety of other materials. All of these items are designed to attract consumer attention by enhancing either the conspicuousness or attractiveness of the displayed merchandise.

Manufacturers generally must use a price discount (called a **display allowance**) to obtain trade support for displays, especially elaborate ones such as the center-of-aisle or end-of-aisle displays seen in grocery stores and other outlets. For example, assume a manufacturer's regular price to the retailer is $18 per 12-item case. This price is reduced to $15.75, a 12.5 percent display allowance, if the retailer constructs and merchandises the manufacturer's products from a special display. Display allowances are particularly effective for brands that the trade accepts as good display brands, namely, those with strong consumer franchises. Display promotions are relatively ineffective for small-volume brands.

Because point-of-purchase materials are frequently developed by manufacturers without considering the retailer's needs, the materials (especially posters, shelf cards, and other smaller items) *often go unused.* They are delivered to retailers but are never brought out of storage areas or, worse yet, immediately end up in retailers' trash bins. It has been estimated that only 25 percent of all point-of-purchase materials sent by manufacturers are eventually used in retail stores. The reasons for this are that (1) display materials often are poorly planned by manufacturers and are unsuitable for retailers, (2) the materials take up too much space for the amount of sales generated, and (3) they are too difficult to set up.[28]

The discussion of point-of-purchase materials has been intentionally brief, because Chapter 18 is devoted exclusively to this increasingly important form of marketing communications. However, for the time being, read the case in the *Global Focus* section for an interesting illustration of point-of-purchase materials working with other marketing communications to achieve great success.

TRAINING PROGRAMS

Many products at the retail level are sold on a self-service basis due to their simplicity and because they have been presold by manufacturers' advertising efforts. Numerous other products require sophisticated selling assistance in the retail outlet. Cosmetics, machinery, appliances, jewelry, and other (typically high-ticket) items require knowledgeable salespeople who can present consumers with relevant information about a product's performance and its relative advantages compared with competitive offerings. Lamentably, retail salespeople often are not adequately trained in how to properly sell a particular product or brand. Hence, it is in both the manufacturer's and retailer's best interest to provide this training.

Manufacturer's sales representatives typically perform this function as part of their routine sales calls on retail accounts. Training is time well spent, because the more knowledge retail salespeople have about a particular product, the greater their confidence and the more effort they will devote to that item compared to its competition.

In addition to face-to-face training conducted by the manufacturer's own sales representatives, training can also be accomplished through literature mailed to retail clerks and, increasingly, through videocassettes. Videocassettes provide

---

[28]Schultz and Robinson, *Sales Promotion Management*, 278–279.

GLOBAL FOCUS

HOW AN UNKNOWN BRAND IN THE UNITED STATES BECAME NUMBER ONE IN JAPAN

If you are like most Americans, you probably have never tasted bourbon whiskey and have no desire to try it. In an earlier era, however, bourbon was one of the major alcoholic drinks in the United States. When bourbon fell out of favor in this country (starting in the late 1970s) and was replaced by increased consumption of wine and beer, many lesser brands went out of production and distribution. One such brand was United Distillers' I.W. Harper. This brand is virtually unknown in the United States among young people, but it has become the leading brand of bourbon in Japan. Here is how this happened.

The market for bourbon started exploding in Japan in the 1980s inasmuch as younger Japanese have a fascination with American and other Western lifestyles and products. Bourbon sales in Japan have been growing by 70 percent annually since the mid-1980s. United Distillers', the marketer of I.W. Harper, was one of the first companies to exploit the Japanese thirst for bourbon. The company decided to pull I.W. Harper from American distributors and ship available quantities entirely to Japan. United Distillers positioned I.W. Harper as a premium brand in Japan, although in the United States it certainly never had that reputation.

Advertising and point-of-purchase displays in Japan feature a hip American, Mr. Harper, who represents the epitome of Japanese consumers' fantasy of the United States as a society of excitement, bright lights, and New York City dynamism. Mr. Harper has become one of the most well-known ad characters in Japan. Now Japanese consumers are willing to pay $15 to $20 for a single tumbler of I.W. Harper Kentucky bourbon!

Could something like this happen in the United States, Canada, or other Western countries? Not only is it possible but, in fact, it has happened. Absolut vodka's success in the United States far outstrips its performance in its native Sweden.

Source: Adapted from Eric Hollreiser, "The Toast of Tokyo," *Adweek's Marketing Week,* December 9, 1991, 20.

the manufacturer with an ideal medium for supplying retail salespeople with detailed product information, product-use demonstrations, and selling tips.

Merely making videocassettes or other forms of training materials available is no assurance that they will be reviewed or will have any effect. A fundamental requirement for successful training materials is that they be readily understandable and interesting. As with any form of promotion, this requires the creative development of persuasive and interesting messages.

SPECIALTY ADVERTISING

Specialty advertising is a hybrid form of marketing communications. On one hand, it is very much like direct-mail advertising in that both pinpoint their communication efforts toward specifically defined audiences. On the other hand, specialty advertising is like public relations in that both engender goodwill. In another respect, specialty advertising is like sales promotion in that both involve the use of incentives given to recipients to encourage certain forms of behavior.

Specifically, **specialty advertising** is "that advertising/sales promotion medium which utilizes useful articles to carry the advertiser's identification and advertising message to its target audience."[29] Specialty advertising complements other forms of promotion by providing another way to keep a company's name before customers and prospects.[30] Specialty-advertising expenditures are small in comparison with other forms of trade promotion, yet annual expenditures in the United States on specialty merchandise exceed $5 billion.

This form of promotion can help companies achieve a variety of marketing communications objectives, including (1) promoting new store openings, (2) introducing new products, (3) motivating salespeople, (4) establishing new accounts, (5) developing trade-show traffic, (6) improving customer relations, and (7) activating inactive accounts.[31]

Specialty advertising generally takes two forms. One is the *random distribution of items to prospects and customers as a type of reminder advertising.* Typical specialty items in this category include matchbooks, calendars, ballpoint pens, and T-shirts—all of which are inscribed with a company or brand name and other relevant information. A second form of specialty advertising is the *struc-*

---

[29]*Success Stories: 40 Award-Winning Specialty Advertising Promotions* (Irving, TX: Specialty Advertising Association International, 1991), 1.

[30]George L. Herpel and Richard A. Collins, *Specialty Advertising in Marketing* (Homewood, IL: Dow Jones-Irwin, 1972).

[31]"The Case for Specialty Advertising," Specialty Advertising Association International, Irving, TX, undated. See also Dan S. Bagley, III, *Understanding Specialty Advertising* (Irving, TX: Specialty Advertising Association International, 1990).

tured promotion, which calls for planning and analyzing promotion objectives, identifying target audiences, creating promotional themes, budgeting, and developing systems for distributing specialty items.[32] It is this latter, more sophisticated use of specialty advertising that is pertinent to the present discussion. It can be considered a form of trade promotion when the target audience is a company's wholesaler, distributor, retailer, or other intermediate customer. The following case illustrates how specialty advertising works as a form of structured trade promotion.

Xerox undertook a specialty-advertising program to generate sales leads for its printing systems. The designated target audience was 3,800 information-services and data-processing managers. Based on research showing this audience to be composed largely of upscale individuals with sophisticated tastes, the creative appeal centered around a music theme. A promotion was assembled showing how Xerox could orchestrate a system to meet corporate requirements. The first of five music-theme mailings consisted of a record-album package with an imprinted pencil housed in blueprint graphics with copy stating: "For a perfect arrangement, Xerox presents products that work in perfect harmony with your system." A second mailing depicted an orchestra conductor and included a conductor's baton and a response card promising a free gift (a recording of Vivaldi's "The Four Seasons") to those who replied. Later mailings tied the music theme to the idea that Xerox could orchestrate a system meeting the buyer's needs. The promotion generated a very high response rate: over one-third of all recipients responded. Salespersons found the promotion to be a helpful "door opener" in acquiring appointments.[33]

TRADE SHOWS

A **trade show** is a temporary forum (typically lasting several days) where sellers of a product category (small appliances, toys, clothing, furniture, industrial tools, food products, etc.) exhibit and demonstrate their wares to present and prospective buyers.[34] It is estimated that nearly 150,000 U.S. companies participate in trade shows each year.[35]

---

[32]Richard G. Ebel, "Specialties: Gifts of Motivation," *Marketing Communications*, April 1986, 75–80.

[33]*Success Stories: 25 Award-Winning Specialty Advertising Promotions* (Irving, TX: Specialty Advertising Association International, 1988), 15.

[34]The trade show is not strictly sales promotion. It, nonetheless, is appropriate to discuss trade shows in context of sales promotions inasmuch as trade shows, like certain forms of sales promotions, provide an extremely effective mechanism for assisting customers in learning about and trying new products.

[35]Edward M. Mazze, *Trade Shows in Black and White: A Guide for Marketers* (New Canaan, CT: Trade Show Bureau, 1986), 3.

Trade-show attendees include most of an industry's important manufacturers and major customers. This encapsulated marketplace enables the trade-show exhibitor to accomplish both selling and nonselling functions. Specific functions include (1) servicing present customers, (2) identifying prospects, (3) introducing new or modified products, (4) gathering information about competitors' new products, (5) taking product orders, and (6) enhancing the company's image.[36]

Trade shows are an excellent forum for introducing new products. Products can be demonstrated and customer inquiries can be addressed at a time when customers are actively soliciting information. This allows companies to gather useful feedback. Positive information can be used in subsequent sales presentations and advertising efforts, while negative information can guide product improvements or changes in the marketing program. Trade shows also provide an ideal occasion to recruit dealers, distributors, and sales personnel.

SUMMARY

This chapter presents the topic of trade-oriented sales promotions and describes the various forms widely in use. Trade-oriented sales promotions represent over 44 percent of consumer packaged-good companies' promotional budgets. These programs perform a variety of objectives.

Trade allowances, or trade deals, are offered to retailers for performing activities supporting the manufacturer's brand. Manufacturers find allowance promotions attractive for several reasons: They are easy to implement, can successfully stimulate initial distribution, are well accepted by the trade, and can increase trade purchases during the allowance period. However, two major disadvantages of buying allowances are that they (1) often are not passed along by retailers to consumers and (2) may induce the trade to stockpile a product in order to take advantage of the temporary price reduction. This merely shifts business from the future to the present. Two prevalent practices in current business are forward buying and diverting. Another form of trade deal, called a slotting allowance, applies to new-product introductions. Manufacturers of grocery products typically are required to pay retailers a slotting fee for the right to have their product carried by the retailer. Exit fees, or deslotting charges, are assessed manufacturers whose products do not achieve pre-arranged levels of sales volume.

Cooperative advertising and vendor support programs are trade promotions in which manufacturers and retailers jointly pay for the retailer's advertising

---

[36]Roger A. Kerin and William L. Cron, "Assessing Trade Show Functions and Performance," *Journal of Marketing*, 51 (July 1987), 88.

that features the manufacturer's product. Co-op advertising is initiated by the manufacturer, whereas vendor support programs are initiated by retailers.

Trade contests and incentives encourage retailer performance by offering gifts for meeting sales goals or for performing certain tasks deemed important for the success of the sponsoring manufacturer's products. Push money is one form of trade incentive used to encourage special selling effort from retail salespeople.

Point-of-purchase materials are another form of trade promotion that serve both the manufacturer's and retailer's economic interests. Display allowances are provided by manufacturers to obtain trade support for center-of-aisle or end-of-aisle displays.

Training programs are undertaken by manufacturers to facilitate distributors' and retail salespersons' efforts in selling the manufacturer's products. Training is typically performed by the manufacturer's own sales force, but written literature and videocassettes are additional training media.

Specialty advertising is a hybrid form of marketing communications that uses articles of merchandise to carry a company's message to its target audience. Specialty advertising is a form of trade-oriented sales promotion when the audience consists of the manufacturer's distributors or other intermediate customers.

A final sales-promotion type practice is *trade shows*. Over 150,000 U.S. companies participate in trade shows each year. Specific functions of trade shows include (1) servicing present customers, (2) identifying prospects, (3) introducing new or modified products, (4) gathering information about competitors' new products, (5) taking product orders, and (6) enhancing the company's image.

Discussion Questions

1. A number of retailers have explicit policies that prevent their managers or salespeople from receiving any form of incentives from manufacturers. Are these policies wise? Under what conditions might manufacturer-sponsored incentives benefit the retail firm above and beyond the obvious benefit that they hold for individual managers or salespeople?

2. You are the marketing manager of a company that manufacturers a line of paper products (tissues, napkins, etc.). Your market share is 7 percent in a market where you are considering offering retailers an attractive allowance for giving your brand special display space. Comment on this promotion's chances for success.

3. Identify concepts in Chapter 12 ("Message Appeals and Endorsers in Advertising") that would be relevant to a furniture company in its efforts to develop an effective exhibition at a trade show attended by major furniture retailers from around the country.

4. In your own words, explain the practices of forward buying and diverting. Also, describe the advantages and disadvantages of bill and hold programs.

5. Assume you are a buyer for a large supermarket chain and that you have been asked to speak to a group of marketing students at a nearby university. During the question-and-answer session following your comments, one student remarks: "My father works for a grocery-product manufacturer, and he says that slotting allowances are nothing more than a form of larceny!" How would you respond to this student's comment in defense of your company's practice?

6. Explain why selling private brands often enables large retail chains to pocket trade deals instead of passing their reduced costs along to consumers in the form of lower product prices.

7. It is estimated that at least one-third of the billions of co-op advertising dollars offered by manufacturers go unspent. Why? What could a manufacturer do to encourage greater numbers of retailers to spend co-op dollars? Do you think some manufacturers may not want their retail customers to spend co-op funds?

8. In discussing open-ended co-op programs, the text stated that this type of cooperative advertising makes it possible to use advertising for generating sales rather than relying on sales to generate advertising. Explain precisely what this means.

9. You are the Midwest sales manager for a product line marketed by a large, highly respected national manufacturer. Most of your products hold market shares of 30 percent or higher. The promotion manager for a big Midwestern grocery chain approaches you about a vendor support program his company is in the process of putting together. It will cost you $50,000 to participate. What would be the reasons for and against your participation? On balance, would it be in your company's long-term interest to participate in this or other VSPs?

10. Assume that you are the marketing director for a hospital located in your home town or college/university community. Your birthing center is operating far below capacity, so your objective is to gain visibility for the center and greater usage. Design a specialty advertising program to accomplish this objective.

CHAPTER SEVENTEEN

Consumer-Oriented Sales Promotion

SOME AWARD-WINNING CONSUMER PROMOTIONS

The Promotion Marketing Association annually selects the 10 best sales promotions. Following are three 1990 award-winning promotions. These will provide a sample of the material to follow in the chapter.

Kraft Singles Outrageous Sandwich Contest. This contest was aimed at developing a relationship with the kids' market and boosting slice-cheese sales. Kids aged 6–14 were invited to enter a contest in which they would develop and name an "Outrageous" sandwich using at least one slice of Kraft Singles cheese. A free-standing insert coupon offer was used to reach mothers and have them encourage their children to enter the contest. The Sunday comics and *Disney Channel* magazine were used to directly reach kids. Free trips to Disney World were awarded as contest prizes. Thousands of kids entered the contest making this Kraft's most successful promotion of all time. With a sales jump of over 20 percent above base sales, this contest will become an annual event.

Gillette's Right Guard and Nascar. Gillette formulated a "Halfway Challenge" sweepstakes whereby consumers entered themselves into the sweepstakes by calling a 900 telephone number anytime during a Nascar race up until the halfway point. During the second half of a race, company representatives called randomly selected entrants and asked them who was leading the race at the halfway point. People who knew the race leader at halftime were eligible to win a car. Winners' names were broadcast on ESPN at the conclusion of the televised race. Gillette's Right Guard realized triple-digit market-share increases in markets where the promotion ran.

The Pillsbury Doughboy. In celebration of the doughboy's 25th birthday, Pillsbury developed a birthday theme that included product coupons, a sweepstakes offer, and a tie-in with Sears stores. The tie-in provided Pillsbury with product visibility outside the usual advertising and point-of-purchase channels.

Source: Adapted from Laurie Petersen, "Reggie Winners Shy Away from Radical Innovations," *Adweek's Marketing Week,* March 25, 1991, 12, 13.

INTRODUCTION TO CONSUMER-ORIENTED SALES PROMOTION

The opening vignette identifies some very successful sales promotions and introduces a sampling of the promotion methods that will be discussed throughout the chapter—practices such as contests, sweepstakes, coupons distributed via freestanding inserts, and tie-in offers. This chapter builds on the base developed in Chapter 16 and focuses exclusively on consumer-oriented sales promotions. The unique character of each sales-promotion technique is described and specific objectives that each technique is intended to accomplish are explained.

Consumer Rewards and Manufacturer Objectives

Why do consumers respond to coupons, contests, sweepstakes, and other sales-promotion techniques? What objectives do manufacturers hope to accomplish by using these techniques? Answers to these interrelated questions are the core of this chapter's purpose.

CONSUMER REWARDS.   Consumers would not be responsive to sales promotions unless there was something in it for them—and, in fact, there is. All sales-promotion techniques provide consumers with *rewards* (incentives or inducements) that encourage certain forms of behavior desired by marketers. Rewards are typically in the form of cash savings or free gifts. Sometimes rewards are immediate, while other times they are delayed.

An *immediate reward* is one that delivers the savings or gift as soon as the consumer performs a marketer-specified behavior. For example, you receive cash savings at the time you redeem a coupon; pleasure is obtained immediately when you try a free candy bar. *Delayed rewards* are those that follow the behavior by a period of days, weeks, or even longer. For example, you may have to wait weeks before a free-in-the-mail premium object can be enjoyed. Generally speaking, *consumers are more responsive to immediate rather than delayed rewards.* Of course, this is in line with the natural human tendency to seek immediate rather than delayed gratification.

MANUFACTURER OBJECTIVES. As discussed in Chapter 16, manufacturers use sales promotions to accomplish various objectives. There are three general categories of objectives: trial impact, franchise holding/loading, and image reinforcement.

Some sales promotions (such as samples and coupons) are used primarily for *trial impact.* A manufacturer employs these techniques to induce nonusers to try a brand for the first time or to encourage retrial for consumers who have not purchased the brand for an extended period. At other times, manufacturers use sales promotions to hold on to their franchise of current users by rewarding them for continuing to purchase the promoted brand or to load them so they have no need to switch to another brand. This is sales promotions' *franchise holding/loading* objective. Sales promotions also can be used for *image-reinforcement purposes.* For example, the careful selection of the right premium object or appropriate sweepstake prize can serve to reinforce a luxury brand's high-quality image.

Classification of Sales-Promotion Methods

It is insightful to consider each consumer-oriented sales-promotion technique in terms of the type of reward provided and the nature of objective accomplished. Table 17.1 presents a six-cell typology that was constructed by cross-classifying the two forms of consumer rewards with the manufacturers' three objectives for using promotions.

Cell 1 includes three sales-promotion techniques—sampling, instant coupons, and shelf-delivered coupons—that are used to induce trial purchase behavior by

---

Major Consumer-Oriented Forms of Sales Promotions   TABLE 17.1

	MANUFACTURER'S OBJECTIVE		
CONSUMER REWARD	TRIAL IMPACT	FRANCHISE HOLDING/LOADING	IMAGE REINFORCEMENT
IMMEDIATE	(1) ■ Sampling ■ Instant coupons ■ Shelf-delivered coupons	(3) ■ Price-offs ■ Bonus packs ■ In-, on-, and near-pack premiums	(5)
DELAYED	(2) ■ Media- and mail-delivered coupons ■ Free-in-the-mail premiums ■ Scanner-delivered coupons	(4) ■ In- and on-pack coupons ■ Refunds and rebates	(6) ■ Self-liquidating premiums ■ Contests and sweepstakes

providing consumers with an immediate reward. The reward is either monetary savings, in the case of instant coupons, or a free product, in the case of sampling. Media- and mail-delivered coupons, free-in-the-mail premiums, and scanner-delivered coupons—all found in Cell 2—are techniques that produce trial impact yet delay the reward to consumers.

Cells 3 and 4 contain franchise holding/loading tools. Marketing communicators design these techniques to keep existing customers (a brand's franchise) from switching to competitive brands, to reward present customers, and to encourage repeat purchasing in general. Immediate reward/franchise holding methods (Cell 3) are price-offs, bonus packs, and in-, on-, and near-pack premiums. Delayed reward/franchise holding techniques, in Cell 4, are in- and on-pack coupons and refund and rebate offers.

Building a brand's image is primarily the task of advertising; however, sales-promotion tools may support advertising efforts by reinforcing a brand's image. By nature, these techniques are incapable of providing consumers with an immediate reward; therefore, Cell 5 is empty. Cell 6 contains self-liquidating premiums and contests/sweepstakes; these techniques serve to strengthen a brand's image in addition to performing other tasks.

Several concluding observations concerning Table 17.1 are needed before proceeding. First, although the Table classifies each technique under a specific objective it is *primarily* responsible for accomplishing, it is important to recognize that *most forms of sales promotions perform more than a single objective.* For example, refunds and rebates are classified as franchise holding/loading techniques but on some occasions they may also encourage trial purchasing. Second, note that two techniques, coupons and premiums, have multiple entries. This is because these techniques achieve different objectives depending on the specific form of delivery vehicle. Coupons delivered through the media (e.g., newspapers) or in the mail offer a form of delayed reward, whereas so-called instant coupons that can be peeled from a package at the point of purchase offer an immediate reward. Similarly, premium objects that are delivered in, on, or near a product's package provide an immediate reward, while those requiring mail delivery yield a reward only after some delay.

The remainder of the chapter will explore each of these techniques in detail.

SAMPLING

The baby-food division of Heinz foods developed a rather revolutionary product idea—a powdered instant baby food. Although Heinz's management was optimistic about instant baby food, they knew consumers would resist trying the product because of the natural inertia people have in making any dramatic product shift and for fear of treating their new babies as guinea pigs. A further complication was the difficulty of communicating the product's benefits by advertising alone.

Heinz needed a way to get mothers to try instant baby food. The solution was to employ the services of Giftpax, a company that annually delivers over 3.5 million product samples to mothers of newborn infants. This form of sampling avoided waste distribution and gave mothers firsthand experience with preparing and feeding their babies instant food. Many sample users became loyal users.[1]

This case illustrates the power of sampling as a promotional technique. Most practitioners agree that sampling is the *premier sales-promotion device for generating trial* product or brand usage. In fact, some observers believe that sample distribution is almost a necessity when introducing truly new products.

By definition, **sampling** includes any method used to deliver an actual- or trial-size product to consumers. Marketers deliver samples in a variety of ways: (1) by *direct mail*, either alone or in cooperation with other brands; (2) through *flat samples* included *in print media;* (3) *door to door* by special distribution crews; (4) *in or on the package of another product* that serves as the sample carrier; (5) at *high-traffic locations*, such as shopping centers, movie theaters, airports, or special events; and (6) *in store*, where demonstrator samples are available for trial.

When the objective is to reach *a broad cross section* of consumers, door-to-door and mail delivery are the most effective means. The other sampling methods cost substantially less but do not reach nearly as many consumers.

Sampling Problems

There are several problems with the use of sampling. First, sampling is *expensive*. Second, mass mailings of samples can be *mishandled* by the postal service or other distributors. Third, samples distributed door to door or in high-traffic locations may suffer from *wasted distribution* and not reach the hands of the best potential customers. Fourth, in- or on-package sampling *excludes consumers* who do not buy the carrying brand. Fifth, in-store sampling often *fails to reach sufficient numbers of consumers* to justify the expense.

A sixth problem with samples is that they may be misused by consumers. Consider the case of Sun Light dishwashing liquid, a product of Lever Brothers. This product, which smells like lemons and contains 10 percent lemon juice, was extensively sampled to more than 50 million households. Nearly 80 adults and children became ill after consuming the product, having mistaken the dishwashing liquid for lemon juice! According to a Lever Brothers' marketing research

---

[1]"Products on Trial," *Marketing Communications*, October 1987, 73–74.

director, there is always a potential problem of misuse when a product is sent to homes rather than purchased with prior product knowledge at a supermarket.[2]

A final sampling problem, *pilferage*, can result when samples are distributed in the mail. A case in point is presented in the *Global Focus*, which describes a sampling problem in Poland that is rarely seen in economies where samples are regularly available.

Due to its expense and because of waste and other problems, the use of sampling fell out of favor for a period of time as many marketers turned to coupons as a cheaper alternative. However, with the development of creative solutions and innovations, promotion managers have again become enthusiastic about sampling. Sampling has become more efficient in reaching specific target groups, results are readily measurable, and the rising costs of media advertising have increased its relative attractiveness.

Sampling Trends

Two major trends have evolved in conjunction with the renewed use of sampling: increased targeting and innovative distribution methods.

INCREASED TARGETING.   Sampling services that specialize in precision distribution (*targeting*) have emerged in recent years. Giftpax's distribution of Heinz baby food to mothers of newborns is one example.

Another form of targeting is delivering samples to consumers who are either *product nonusers or users of competitive brands*. The Gillette Co. mailed 400,000 Sensor razors to men who use competitive wet razors. (Figure 2.1 on p. 32 contains an advertisement for the Sensor.)

John Blair Marketing's "JBM Sample Pack" illustrates how targeted sampling operates. Sample recipients are surveyed initially by questionnaire and identified by demographic and product/brand-usage characteristics. Individual sample packs are then assembled specifically for each person: he or she receives only products that match his or her product and brand consumption patterns. Sampled products are delivered directly by mail to recipients' homes.

Suppose you wanted to distribute coupons to blue-collar employees. How would you reach them? The MarketSource Corporation offers the Bonus Pak, a hand-delivered package of product samples and coupons, that is delivered to blue-collar employees at workplace sites.[3]

How would you reach high-school males? This is one of the most inaccessible markets because they are not particularly heavy television viewers or magazine

---

[2]Lynn G. Reiling, "Consumers Misuse Mass Sampling for Sun Light Dishwashing Liquid," *Marketing News*, September 3, 1982, 1, 2.

[3]"Targeting the Blue Collar Market," *Marketing Communications*, May 1987, 10.

GLOBAL FOCUS

THE HAZARDS OF SAMPLING FOR THE FIRST TIME

In October 1991, Procter & Gamble mailed 580,000 samples of Vidal Sassoon Wash & Go shampoo to consumers in Poland, the first ever mass mailing of free samples in that country. The mailing was a big hit, so big in fact that about 2,000 mailboxes were broken into by people who wanted the samples for their own use or to sell.

The shampoo samples, although labeled "Not for sale," turned up on open markets and were in high demand at a price of 60 cents each.

P&G paid nearly $40,000 to the Polish Post, Poland's mail service, to deliver the samples. In addition to the cost of distribution, P&G paid thousands more to have mailboxes repaired.

Source: Maciek Gajewski, "Samples: A Steal in Poland," *Advertising Age,* November 4, 1991, 54.

readers. A company called MarketSource developed a program that reaches teenage males by distributing gift packages of product samples (shaving cream, razor, mouthwash, candy, etc.) at tuxedo-rental shops. Recipients pick up their sample pack when they arrange to rent a prom tuxedo. A follow-up phone survey four weeks later provides information on product usage and purchase intentions.[4]

Finally, suppose you wanted to reach young children with free samples. Where would you gain access to this group? One company hands out sample packs at Toys 'R' Us stores.[5]

NEW DISTRIBUTION METHODS.   Numerous creative ideas are being applied in an effort to get sample merchandise into the hands of targeted consumers. Any college student who has traveled to Florida over spring break is familiar with the product sampling techniques used by a variety of companies.

An especially creative product distribution took place recently in Brazil. In trying to grab market share from Coca-Cola, Pepsi-Cola hired male students to walk the beaches of Rio de Janeiro and distribute free Pepsi samples from refrigerated containers carried on their backs. The objective was to reach the

[4]Scott Hume, "Prom Night: Free Samples with Tux," *Advertising Age,* March 13, 1989, 53.

[5]Russ Bowman, "Freebie Follow-Through," *Marketing and Media Decisions,* February 1989, 102.

prime market of consumers under the age of 20, who represent 50 percent of Brazil's population.[6]

Movie theaters are becoming a particularly attractive outlet for sample distribution. The benefit of using movie theaters is that they enable marketers to reach the hardest-to-reach active consumers, namely those who are in their teens and twenties.[7] United Artists Entertainment, the largest theater chain in the United States with about 2,500 screens in over 500 locations, has started an in-theater sampling program. The program costs advertisers $45 per thousand samples distributed during a four-week cycle. Over nine million samples are distributed during the cycle.[8]

How Effective Is Sampling?

How effective is sampling in influencing trial purchase behavior? What influence does it have on stimulating repeat purchase behavior? NPD Research, Inc., a firm that collects data from a panel of over 30,000 households who maintain continuous diaries of their packaged goods purchases, has shed light on these questions. Their composite results for eight brands show that of the households who did *not* receive free samples (the control group), an average of about 11 percent made trial purchases of the eight brands. By comparison, 16 percent of the *recipients of free samples* made trial purchases. Moreover, nearly 36 percent of the families who made purchases after receiving a sample repurchased the brand, whereas only 32 percent of the control-group triers repurchased.[9]

These results are particularly interesting because they run somewhat contrary to more theoretically based research, which has detected a tendency for sampling to diminish repeat purchasing.[10] According to *attribution theory*, sampling should diminish repeat purchasing because the sample users should infer that the only reason they consumed the sampled product was because it was free. The users are said to make an *external attribution*, that is, to discount their personal liking for a sampled item in favor of the alternative explanation that they tried it only because it was free. Comparatively, those who try a product without

---

[6]Tania Anderson, "Pepsi Rescues Parched Beachgoers," *Advertising Age*, May 2, 1988, sec. S, 9.

[7]Laurie Petersen, "Showtime for Product Samples," *Adweek's Marketing Week*, November 11, 1991, 28.

[8]Marcy Magiera, "A Real Movie Treat," *Advertising Age*, December 10, 1990, 6.

[9]*Insights: Issues 1-13, 1979-1982* (New York: NPD Research, 1983), 6–7.

[10]Carol Scott, "Effects of Trial and Incentives on Repeat Purchase Behavior," *Journal of Marketing Research*, 13 (August 1976), 263-269. See also Joe A. Dodson, Alice M. Tybout, and Brian Sternthal, "Impact of Deals and Deal Retraction on Brand Switching," *Journal of Marketing Research*, 15 (February 1978), 72–81.

first receiving a sample are more likely to attribute their trial to a personal liking for the item (an *internal attribution*). This internal attribution fosters a positive attitude and is hypothesized to enhance the probability of repeat purchasing.[11]

In sum, there absolutely is no doubt that sampling is an effective stimulant to trial purchasing. However, no single answer is possible regarding the matter of whether sampling increases or decreases repeat purchase behavior. As always, the answer depends on the specific circumstances of the situation. All that can be said is that the impact of sampling on repeat purchase behavior probably is moderated by *the quality of the sampled product.* In other words, if consumers sample a new product and learn that it is demonstrably superior to alternatives on the market, it stands to reason that the sample-use experience will facilitate further purchasing. If, on the other hand, the product is found wanting in quality or has no relative advantage, sampling is likely to retard subsequent purchasing.

When Should Sampling Be Used?

Promotion managers use sampling to induce consumers to try either a brand that is new or one that is moving into a different market. While it is important to encourage trial usage for new brands, sampling is not appropriate for all new or improved products. Ideal circumstances include the following:[12]

1. Sampling should be used when a new or improved brand is either *demonstrably superior* to other brands or when it has *distinct relative advantages* over brands that it is intended to replace. If a brand does not possess superiority or distinct advantages, it probably is not economically justified to give it away.

2. Sampling should be used when the product concept is so innovative that it is *difficult to communicate by advertising alone.* The earlier example of Heinz instant baby food illustrates this point. In general, sampling enables consumers to learn about product advantages which marketers would have difficulty convincing them of via advertising alone.

3. Sampling should be used when promotional *budgets can afford to generate consumer trial quickly.* Broad-scale sampling is extremely expensive. Imagine the expense incurred by Lever Brothers when it distributed samples

4.) You can demonstrate an effect.

[11]For more discussion of applications of attribution theory in marketing and consumer behavior, see Richard W. Mizerski, Linda L. Golden, and Jerome B. Kernan, "The Attribution Process in Consumer Decision Making," *Journal of Consumer Research*, 6 (September 1979), 123-140; Valerie S. Folkes, "Recent Attribution Research in Consumer Behavior: A Review and New Directions, *Journal of Consumer Research*, 14 (March 1988), 548–565.

[12]Charles Fredericks, Jr., "What Ogilvy & Mather Has Learned about Sales Promotion," in *The Tools of Promotion* (New York: Association of National Advertisers, 1975).

of the previously mentioned lemon-scented Sun Light dishwashing liquid to over 50 million households.

COUPONING

A **coupon** is a promotional device that provide cents-off savings to consumers upon redeeming the coupon. Coupons are delivered through a variety of modes, including newspapers, magazines, free-standing inserts, direct mail, in or on packages, and, increasingly, at the point-of-purchase. *Not all delivery methods have the same objective.* Coupons distributed at the point of purchase provide immediate rewards to consumers and encourage trial purchases. Mail- and media-delivered coupons delay the reward, although they also generate trial purchase behavior. In comparison, package-delivered coupons are used to accomplish franchise holding rather than product trial. Later sections discuss all of the coupon delivery modes in detail. Before discussing any specific delivery mode, it will be instructive to examine the growth of couponing, its economic impact, and consumer redemption patterns.

Growth and Trends in Coupons

In 1970 U.S. marketers distributed fewer than 17 billion coupons.[13] The number had increased to nearly 143 billion coupons by 1983.[14] By 1990, almost 307 billion coupons were distributed in the United States via mail and print media and another 30 billion coupons were available on or inside packages.[15] Just considering the 307 billion mail- and media-delivered coupons, this means over 1200 coupons were distributed in 1990 to every man, woman, and child in the United States!

The average face value of coupons in 1990 was approximately 50 cents, up by 20 cents from the average value just three years earlier.[16] Surveys indicate that over 95 percent of American consumers use coupons at least on occasion.[17] However, research has established that consumers vary greatly in terms of their

---

[13]Roger A. Strang, "The Economic Impact of Cents-off Coupons," *Marketing Communications*, March 1981, 35–44.

[14]Nathaniel Frey, "Sales Promotion Analysis," *Marketing Communications*, August 1988, 14–20.

[15]Garrie Goerne, "Clutter Anyone?" *Adweek's Marketing Week*, April 8, 1991, 22, 24.

[16]Ibid.

[17]Ira Teinowitz, "Coupons Gain Favor with U.S. Shoppers," *Advertising Age*, November 14, 1988, 64.

psychological inclination to use coupons, and that this *coupon proneness* is predictive of actual coupon redemption behavior.[18]

Coupons appeal not just to American consumers. A major international couponing study learned that coupons are valued by consumers in every country studied. Although vastly more coupons are distributed in the United States than elsewhere, *redemption rates* (the percentage of all distributed coupons that are taken to stores for price discounts) are higher in all countries surveyed except Canada. Whereas redemption rates average around *2.5 percent* in the United States, redemption rates elsewhere in 1990 averaged the following: Canada (1%), the United Kingdom (7.5%), Italy (16%), Spain (16%), and Belgium (a whopping 56%).[19]

The massive increase in the number of coupons distributed reflects the growing importance of couponing to marketers and the growing number of marketers using coupons as an integral part of their promotional activities. Fully 95 percent of packaged-goods marketers used coupons in 1990.[20]

While packaged-goods manufacturers are major users of coupons, coupon use has spread to producers of appliances and other durables, apparel, and numerous other products. Perhaps the most innovative of all couponing applications in recent years was by United Airlines following a devastating 55-day labor strike. By offering passengers half-fare coupons, United regained its prestrike market share in only 11 days rather than the seven months company financial executives feared it would take for recovery.[21]

Along with the rising trend in the use of coupons, there have been significant developments in how coupons are distributed. Changes have been made primarily because of the need to *avoid competitive clutter and to reduce distribution costs.* Coupons must stand out so that they will be clipped and ultimately redeemed by consumers. Accordingly, the preferred mode for delivering coupons is the *free-standing insert (FSI)*, which accounts for about 80 percent of all coupons distributed in the United States.[22] This is a dramatic change from slightly more than a decade ago when only 15 percent of coupons were

[18]Donald R. Lichtenstein, Richard G. Netemeyer, and Scot Burton, *Journal of Marketing*, 54 (July 1990), 54–67.

[19]Betsy Spethmann, "Countries Crave Coupons," *Advertising Age*, July 15, 1991, 26.

[20]Michael Burgi, "Trade Spending Tops," *Advertising Age*, April 15, 1991, 36.

[21]"The Toothpaste Tube That Saved United," *Advertising Age*, October 29, 1979, 14. This article's interesting title provides a clue as to the reason United decided on its couponing campaign. It seems that corporate executives were having difficulty coming up with a major promotional program to regain market share until one employee entered a meeting with a tube of toothpaste in his hand and claimed that just that morning he had gone to the store to get toothpaste and rather than buying the regular brand he switched to another brand that offered a 50 cents-off coupon. Why couldn't United do the same to get customers to switch back to it?

[22]Scott Hume and Patricia Strnad, "FSI Coupon Redemption Hits Wall," *Advertising Age*, March 18, 1991, 41.

distributed by FSI and nearly 75 percent were distributed via newspapers and magazines as run-of-paper coupons (ROPs).[23] The reason for these changes should be obvious: Freestanding inserts capture the consumer's attention more readily and therefore are superior in overcoming competitive clutter.

Another major trend in coupon distribution has been the establishment of *cooperative coupon programs*. These are programs in which a couponing distribution service distributes coupons for a single company's multiple brands or brands from multiple companies. Cooperative programs enable companies to expand coupon reach and gain the economies of scale resulting from shared distribution costs. Some illustrative cooperative programs are Newspaper Co-op Couponing by the Marketing Corporation of America (a daily newspaper distribution program); Blair Inserts, Valassis Inserts, Quad Marketing, and Product Movers (all Sunday insert programs); Thermatics by Synergistic Marketing (a magazine insert program); Intercept by Stratmar Systems (store handouts); and Carol Wright by Donnelley Marketing and Val-Pak by Val-Pak Direct Marketing Systems (direct mail programs).

Donnelley Marketing's "Carol Wright" service provides a good illustration of how cooperative couponing services operate. Donnelley Marketing mails questionnaires to millions of households and collects information on product and brand usage. Figure 17.1 shows one page from a three-page questionnaire mailed to millions of consumers. Please note that questions ask respondents about their general product usage and specific brand usage. Donnelley enters returned surveys into a huge data base containing names and addresses of more than 80 million unduplicated households. Coupons and samples are then mailed to product/brand nonusers and competitive brand users. With regard to question 3 (brands of pain relievers used), the makers of Advil, for example, would find it advantageous to mail coupons to people who are *heavy users of other brands*.

Economic Impact

The growth in coupon offers has not occurred without criticism. Some critics contend that coupons are wasteful and may actually increase prices of consumer goods.

Whether coupons are wasteful and inefficient remains problematic. However, it is undeniable that coupons are an expensive proposition. For better understanding of coupon costs, consider the case of a rather typical coupon with a face value of 50 cents. The coupon's actual cost to the manufacturer for each redeemed coupon is considerably more than the 50-cents face value. Table 17.2 details the full cost per redeemed coupon. The actual cost of 97.5 cents per

---

[23]"Couponing Distribution Trends and Patterns," *PMAA Promotion Update '82* (New York: Promotion Management Association of America, Inc., 1983). Note: run of paper, or run of press, means that an advertisement carrying a coupon is part of the regular newspaper/magazine pages and not a separate section or insert.

Questionnaire from Donnelley Marketing's "Carol Wright" Cooperative Service

FIGURE 17.1

Even if you've answered before, please help with this NEW SURVEY

Plus FREE!!! Carol Wright's All New Coupon Wallet

America's leading manufacturers want to know what smart shoppers like you are looking for when they go to the store. So, when you send us your answers to this survey, they'll say "Thanks" with a pack of discount coupons, special offers, FREE samples plus your FREE Carol Wright COUPON WALLET. Thanks.

Carol Wright

Please help us to read your survey by answering within the squares.

1. Which brand(s) of toothpaste was used most often by your household in the past three months?
1. ☐ Aim   3. ☐ Close-Up   5. ☐ Crest
2. ☐ Aqua-Fresh   4. ☐ Colgate   6. ☐ Other

1A. Which form of toothpaste do you use most often?
7. ☐ Paste   8. ☐ Gel

1B. Do you have a child twelve years or younger living in your household?   09. ☐ Yes   10. ☐ No

2. Do you use milk additive products to make cold chocolate milk?   1. ☐ Yes   2. ☐ No

2A. If yes, which of the following milk additive products do you use most often to make cold chocolate milk?
3. ☐ Hershey's Syrup   5. ☐ Nestle Powder
4. ☐ Nestle's Syrup   6. ☐ Other

3. Which brand(s) of pain relievers are used in your home regularly?
01. ☐ Advil   07. ☐ Datril   12. ☐ Nuprin
02. ☐ Anacin   08. ☐ Excedrin   13. ☐ Panadol
03. ☐ Anacin-3   09. ☐ Tylenol   14. ☐ Store Brand
04. ☐ Bayer   10. ☐ E.S. Tylenol   15. ☐ Other
05. ☐ Max. Bayer   11. ☐ Medipren   16. ☐ None
06. ☐ Bufferin

3A. How many tablets of pain relievers are used in your household each month?
17. ☐ 1-4   18. ☐ 5-10   19. ☐ 11-20   20. ☐ 21+

3B. Did you ever use non-prescription pain relievers in capsule form?   21. ☐ Yes   22. ☐ No

4. How many times did you or any member of your household purchase eye drops in the past 6 months?
1. ☐ 1   2. ☐ 2 to 4   3. ☐ 5 or more   4. ☐ None

4A. Which of the following brands of eye drops have you or any member of your household purchased in the past 6 months?
05. ☐ Clear Eyes   08. ☐ OcuClear   10. ☐ Visine A.C.
06. ☐ Murine   09. ☐ Visine   11. ☐ Other
07. ☐ Murine Plus

5. Do you use an air freshener or carpet deodorizer?
1. ☐ Yes   2. ☐ No

5A. If yes, how often do you make a purchase?
3. ☐ Once a month   5. ☐ Less than every
4. ☐ Once every three months   three months

6. Do you own an automatic dishwasher?
1. ☐ Yes   2. ☐ No

6A. If yes, about how many loads of dishes do you do in your automatic dishwasher in an average week?
3. ☐ 7+   4. ☐ 3-6   5. ☐ 1-2   6. ☐ Less than 1

6B. Which brands of automatic dishwasher detergents have you used in the past year? (Check all that apply.) Which brand do you buy most often? (Check only one.)

	Have Used	Use Most Often (Check only one)
Cascade Powder		
Regular	07. ☐	17. ☐
Lemon	08. ☐	18. ☐
Liquid Cascade	09. ☐	19. ☐
Electrasol Powder	10. ☐	20. ☐
Liquid Electrasol	11. ☐	21. ☐
Liquid Palmolive Automatic		
Regular	12. ☐	22. ☐
Lemon	13. ☐	23. ☐
Sunlight Powder	14. ☐	24. ☐
Liquid Sunlight	15. ☐	25. ☐
Other	16. ☐	26. ☐

7. Over the past 2 years which of the following all purpose spray cleaners have you purchased?
1. ☐ Formula 409   6. ☐ Pine Sol
2. ☐ Fantastik   7. ☐ Lysol Direct
3. ☐ Lemon Fantastik   8. ☐ Pine Magic
4. ☐ Scrub Free Kitchen   9. ☐ Other
5. ☐ Scrub Free Pine

8. Do you or does anyone in your household have thinning hair, that is, hair that is now not as full and dense as it once was when you were younger?
1. ☐ Yes   2. ☐ No

8A. Which one of the following statements best describes the feelings you or another household member have about his or her own thinning hair?
3. ☐ Not at all concerned about thinning hair
4. ☐ Somewhat concerned about thinning hair
5. ☐ Very concerned about thinning hair
6. ☐ Extremely concerned about thinning hair

8B. Would you or the person in your household who has thinning hair use a scientifically formulated shampoo to gently, but effectively clean thinning hair?
7. ☐ Yes   8. ☐ No

9. Which best describes your dress size?
1. ☐ Petite   3. ☐ Misses   5. ☐ Women   7. ☐ Tall
2. ☐ Junior   4. ☐ Maternity   6. ☐ Half-size

10. Which of these pads and/or tampons is your usual brand?

TAMPONS (check one)
01. ☐ Tampax Slender
02. ☐ Tampax Regular
03. ☐ Tampax Super
04. ☐ Tampax Super Plus
05. ☐ Kotex Security Regular
06. ☐ Kotex Security Super
07. ☐ Playtex Slender
08. ☐ Playtex Regular
09. ☐ Playtex Super
10. ☐ Playtex Super Plus
11. ☐ Other _____

PADS (check one)
12. ☐ Always Plus Super
13. ☐ Kotex Overnites
14. ☐ Stayfree Super Maxi
15. ☐ Stayfree Maxi
16. ☐ Other _____

11. Do you, or anyone in your household use a laxative?
1. ☐ Yes   2. ☐ No

11A. If yes, which brand is used most often? (Check One)
03. ☐ Citrucel   07. ☐ Dulcolax   16. ☐ Naturacil
04. ☐ Correctol Powdered   08. ☐ Effer-Syllium   17. ☐ Nature's Remedy
Fiber   09. ☐ Ex-Lax
Laxative   10. ☐ Feen-A-Mint   18. ☐ Perdiem
   11. ☐ Fiberall   19. ☐ Phillips' Milk
05. ☐ Correctol Tablets or   12. ☐ Fibercon   of Magnesia
Liquid   13. ☐ Fiberway   20. ☐ Prompt
   14. ☐ Haley's M-O   21. ☐ Serutan
06. ☐ Doxidan   15. ☐ Metamucil   22. ☐ Other

11B. When a laxative is used, how many days during a one-month period is it taken? (Check One)
23. ☐ Less than one day per month   26. ☐ One day per week
24. ☐ One day per month   27. ☐ 2-3 days per week
25. ☐ 2-3 days per month   28. ☐ 4 or more days per week

11C. On those days when this product is used, how many times a day do you use it? (Check One)
29. ☐ More than once a day   30. ☐ Once a day

12. How many times have you shopped by mail in the last six months? In total, what did you spend?
1. ☐ Once or twice   3. ☐ Under $50
2. ☐ 3 or more times   4. ☐ Over $50

Please answer questions on inside. ▶

Source: Courtesy Donnelley Marketing.

TABLE 17.2	Full Coupon Cost per Redeemed Coupon[a]

Important

1. Distribution cost:
   10,000,000 coupons circulated at $5 per thousand — $ 50,000
2. Redemption rate = 2.5% — 250,000 redeemed coupons
3. Redemption cost:
   250,000 redemptions at 50¢ face value — $125,000
4. Handling cost:
   250,000 redemptions at 8¢ each[b] — $ 20,000
5. Total program cost: 1 + 3 + 4 — $195,000
6. Cost per redeemed coupon:
   $195,000/250,000 — 78¢
7. Actual product sold on redemption:
   With misredemption estimated at 20%, product
   sold by redemption = 250,000 × 80% — 200,000 coupons
8. Actual cost per redeemed coupon:
   Total program cost ($195,000)/actual amount
   of redeemed coupons (200,000) — 97.5¢

[a]Adapted from Louis J. Haugh, "How Consumers Measure Up," *Advertising Age*, June 1981, 58.

[b]A handling charge is the amount paid by manufacturers to retailers to compensate for their costs incurred while handling coupons.

redeemed coupon, which is nearly twice the face value, indicates that coupon activity requires substantial investment to accomplish desired objectives. (To make sure you fully understand the cost derivation in Table 17.2, answer question 8 at the end of the chapter.)

Obviously, programs that aid in reducing costs, such as cooperative delivery programs, are eagerly sought. Creative and innovative couponing programs are constantly being developed. One such development is described in the *Focus on Promotion*.

Coupons are indeed costly, some are clearly wasteful, and other promotional devices may be better. However, the extensive use of coupons either suggests that there are a large number of incompetent marketing executives or that better promotional tools are not available or are economically infeasible. The latter explanation is the more reasonable when considering how the marketplace operates. If a business practice is uneconomical, it will not continue to be used for long. When a better business practice is available, it will replace the previous solution. Conclusion: It appears that coupons are extensively used because marketers have been unable to devise more effective and economical methods for accomplishing the objectives achieved with couponing.

Is Couponing Profitable?

You will recall the discussion in Chapter 15 where we examined when promotional dealing is profitable and when it is not. Among other conclusions, it was

FOCUS ON PROMOTION

A COUPON PROGRAM THAT REWARDS NONUSERS

Research shows that one problem with distributing coupons via free-standing inserts is that approximately *70 percent* of the people who redeem coupons are already *users of the brand*. Considering that 80 percent of all coupons in the United States are delivered via FSI, this indicates that approximately 56 percent of the coupons redeemed are by users of the couponed brand.

This isn't all bad provided the objective is to reward consumers for their continued brand usage. However, what if the objective is to reach nonusers of your brand? How could you get coupons in these peoples' hands, or how could you deliver higher-value coupons to nonusers than to users? Marketers at Larry Tucker, Inc., a direct marketing company, have developed a method that identifies nonusers of a brand and provides them with a higher-value coupon than that given to current brand users.

Tucker's Variable Incentive Promotion delivers a coupon to consumers that shows on the face of the coupon two competing brands and presents consumers with an opportunity to pull one of two tabs. Consumers are instructed to pull the blue tab if they regularly buy Brand A (the coupon-sponsoring company, say Wisk laundry detergent) or pull down the green tab if they buy Brand B (a competitive brand, say Tide detergent).When the consumer pulls one or the other tab, a cents-off coupon for one brand is revealed while the coupon for the other brand is simultaneously torn across and destroyed. The coupons have different face values. For example, consumers who indicate they are regular brand users (by pulling the blue tab for Wisk) would receive a lower-value coupon for Wisk worth, say, 25 cents, whereas consumers who indicate being Tide users when pulling the green tab would receive a more valuable coupon for Wisk worth, say, $1.

Tucker began using this couponing program in 1991 in its targeted co-op mailing program. Lawry's Foods was the first user. Consumers pulling the tab indicating they are users of Lawry's garlic salt received a 25-cent coupon, and those users of other brands received a 75-cent coupon for Lawry's.

Source: Adapted from Scott Hume, "Coupon Rewards Non-Users," *Advertising Age*, May 6, 1991, 31.

determined that putting a brand on deal is *unprofitable* if the market is composed entirely of promotion-insensitive consumers or entirely of stockpiling loyalists. On the other hand, dealing a brand is *profitable* if the market consists entirely of on-deal-only consumers.

Of course, markets never consist entirely of just one type of consumers. However, there is evidence showing that households most likely to redeem are those that were the most likely to buy the brand in the first place. It has been estimated that as much as 70 to 80 percent of coupons are redeemed by a brand's current users.[24] Moreover, most consumers revert to their precoupon brand choice immediately after making a coupon redemption.[25]

Hence, when the consumers who redeem are those who would have bought the brand anyway, the effect of couponing, at least on the surface, is to merely increase costs and reduce the per-unit profit margin. However, the issue is more involved than this. Although it is undeniable that most coupons are redeemed by current brand users, competitive dynamics force companies to continue offering coupons to prevent losing consumers to other brands that do offer coupons.

Couponing is a fact of life that will continue to remain an important part of marketing in North America and elsewhere. The real challenge is for promotion managers to continuously seek ways to increase couponing profitability and to target coupons to those consumers who may otherwise not purchase their brands.

The following sections describe the major forms of couponing activity, the objectives each is intended to accomplish, and the innovations designed to increase couponing profitability. The presentation of couponing delivery methods is ordered along the lines of the framework presented earlier in Table 17.1.

Point-of-Purchase Couponing

A major trend in couponing distribution is to increase the delivery of coupons at the point-of-purchase. As will be examined in detail in the following chapter, purchase decisions are frequently made while in the store. It thus makes sense to deliver coupons at the point where decisions are made. Point-of-purchase coupons come in three forms: instant, shelf-delivered, and electronically delivered by optical scanner.

INSTANT COUPONS.   Most coupon-distribution methods have delayed impact on consumers because the coupon is received in the consumer's home and held for a period of time before it is redeemed. **Instant coupons,**

---

[24]Nathaniel Frey, "Targeted Couponing: New Wrinkles Cut Waste," *Marketing Communications*, January 1988, 40.

[25]Kapil Bawa and Robert W. Shoemaker, "The Effects of a Direct Mail Coupon on Brand Choice Behavior," *Journal of Marketing Research*, 24 (November 1987), 370–376.

which are *peelable from the package* at the point of purchase, represent an *immediate reward* that can spur the consumer to undertake a trial purchase of the promoted brand. A Wheaties cereal campaign illustrates the use of instant couponing. General Mills, the maker of Wheaties, wanted a promotional program that would provide a significant price reduction and an immediate point-of-purchase incentive for consumers. Rather than use a price-off deal, which often creates problems for retailers, General Mills offered a peel-off coupon attached to the front of the Wheaties package. The coupons were designed to be removed by the consumer and redeemed when checking out. The program gained strong retailer acceptance and high coupon-redemption levels.[26]

Although the instant coupon is a *minor* form of couponing, it has emerged in recent years as an alternative to price-off deals (in which case every package must be reduced in price). The redemption level for instant coupons (around 25 percent) is considerably higher than the level for other couponing techniques.[27] It may surprise you to learn that the average redemption rate for instant coupons is *only* 25 percent. One would think that most all purchasers would remove instant coupons at the time of making a purchase so as to receive the savings immediately. Some consumers no doubt do, but most apparently do not.

Figure 17.2 is an instant coupon for $1 off the price of Glad® trash bags. Although designed to be removed in the store (see "Redeem Now" at top), the marketers of this brand realize that some consumers will not remove the coupon until later at their homes; in fact, the back side of the coupon (which, of course, would be undetectable in the store) identifies a variety of other Glad® products for which this coupon can be redeemed.

S H E L F - D E L I V E R E D   C O U P O N S .   Actmedia, Inc., recently introduced an on-shelf coupon machine (nicknamed the "red hot coupon machine") that is available in nearly 10,000 grocery stores. The machine is attached to the shelf beside the coupon-sponsoring brand. Consumers can pull out a maximum of two coupons and then a 20-second delay is in effect before the next coupon is exposed. Sponsoring brands pay $55 per machine for a four-week cycle. The maximum number of coupons a machine will dispense during this cycle is 1,500, which amounts to a cost-per-thousand distributed coupons of $36.67 (i.e., $55/1.5).

Actmedia's research has revealed that the average redemption rate is slightly over 24 percent and that the product movement of couponing brands during test marketing increased by nearly one-third during the course of the four-week test period. Moreover, and of particular importance, a shopper survey indicated that *66 percent of machine users had not planned to buy the couponed*

[26]Richard H. Aycrigg, *Promotion Update '82*, a publication of the Promotion Marketing Association of America, Inc., New York, 1982.

[27]Ed Meyer, "It's on the Package," *Advertising Age*, May 17, 1982, sec. M, 27.

| FIGURE 17.2 | Illustration of an Instant (Peelable) Coupon |

brand.[28] It thus would appear that shelf-delivered couponing is a profitable way to generate trial purchase behavior from product/brand nonusers by offering an *immediate reward* that is realizable at the checkout counter. Given the infancy of this coupon-delivery mode, only time will tell whether shelf delivery remains appealing to consumers and profitable for marketers.

SCANNER-DELIVERED COUPONS.   Several electronic systems for dispensing coupons at the point of purchase have been introduced in recent years. Most have failed due to poor technology and costs to the manufacturer that are much higher than FSIs.[29] One system that appears to be a success is a program named "Checkout Coupon" from Catalina Marketing Corporation.

As of 1991, Catalina's couponing system was available in over 4,000 super-markets nationwide.[30] Catalina's couponing system delivers coupons contingent on the products and brands a shopper has purchased as revealed electronically

[28]"Actmedia Cites Coupon Machines 'Red Hot' Results," *POPAI News*, April/May 1991, 11.

[29]Liz Murphy, "Redemption Isn't Always Salvation in Couponing," *Sales and Marketing Management*, January 13, 1986, 45–47.

[30]Laurie Petersen, "The Checkout Kings," *Adweek's Marketing Week*, October 21, 1991, 22, 23.

by an optical scanner. Once the scanner records that the shopper has purchased a *competitor's brand*, a coupon from the participating manufacturer is dispensed. For example, a consumer who has just purchased Heinz ketchup receives a coupon for Hunt's ketchup. By targeting competitors' customers, Catalina's couponing system ensures the manufacturer of reaching people who buy the product category but are not currently purchasing the manufacturer's brand. The redemption rate is said to exceed 14 percent, which far exceeds the rate for all forms of media- and mail-delivered coupons.[31]

Another couponing program from Catalina, called "Checkout Direct," enables marketers to deliver coupons only to those consumers who satisfy the coupon-sponsoring manufacturer's demographic requirements (e.g., families with incomes greater than $25,000) or who exhibit a predictable purchase pattern for a particular product (e.g., who purchase toothpaste every six weeks). Once the couponing requirements are established, Catalina's computer operators can identify coupon-target households by analyzing two data bases: (1) optical-scanned purchase data and (2) household demographic variables acquired by supermarkets when requiring shoppers to complete a form to receive check-cashing privileges. (Nearly two-thirds of all supermarket transactions are made with check-cashing cards.[32]) When shoppers who satisfy the coupon-sponsoring manufacturer's requirement make a purchase (as indicated by their check-cashing ID number), a coupon for the sponsoring manufacturer's brand is automatically dispensed for use on the shopper's next purchase occasion.[33]

Both Catalina programs are used to encourage trial purchasing. However, because coupons are distributed to consumers when they are checking out of a store and cannot be used until their next visit, the reward offered is *delayed* rather than immediate as in the case of instant or shelf-delivered coupons. Nevertheless, these scanner-delivered couponing methods are potentially *very effective and cost efficient* because they provide a way to carefully *target* coupon distribution. Targeting, in the case of Checkout Coupon, is directed at *competive-brand users*, and, in the case of Checkout Direct, is directed at users who satisfy a manufacturer's prescribed *demographic or product-usage requirements*.

Mail- and Media-Delivered Coupons

These coupon delivery modes initiate *trial purchase* behavior by offering consumers *delayed rewards*. Mail-delivered coupons represent only about five

[31]Lori Kesler, "Catalina Cuts Couponing Clutter," *Advertising Age*, May 9, 1988, sec. S, 30.

[32]Laurie Petersen, "Catalina Launches Two New Coupon Programs," *Adweek's Marketing Week*, November 12, 1991, 11.

[33]Bradley Johnson, "Catalina Adds Coupon Options," *Advertising Age*, November 26, 1990, 58; Petersen, "The Checkout Kings," 23.

percent of all manufacturer-distributed coupons. Mass-media modes (newspapers and magazines) are clearly dominant, carrying well over 80 percent of all coupons distributed; the bulk of this is in the form of freestanding inserts (FSIs).

MAIL-DELIVERED COUPONS.　Marketers typically use mail-delivered coupons to *introduce new or improved products*. Mailings can be directed either at a broad cross section of the market or *targeted* to specific demographic segments. Mailed coupons achieve the *highest household penetration*. Coupon distribution via magazines rarely reaches more than 60 percent of all homes, whereas mail can reach as high as 95 percent. Moreover, when consumers receive coupon offers in the mail, they are able to make a purchase decision at home, away from the competitive influences of the supermarket. Furthermore, direct mail achieves the *highest redemption rate* of all mass-delivered coupon techniques. There also is empirical evidence to suggest that direct-mail coupons increase the amount of product purchases, particularly when coupons with higher face-values are used and among households that own their homes, have larger families, and are more educated.[34]

The major disadvantage of direct-mailed coupons is that they are *relatively expensive* compared with other coupon-distribution methods. Another disadvantage is that direct mailing is especially inefficient and expensive for brands that enjoy a high market share. This is because a large proportion of the coupon recipients may already be regular users of the coupon brand, thereby defeating the primary purpose of generating trial purchasing. Mass-mailing inefficiencies account for the rapid growth of efforts to target coupons to narrowly defined audiences such as users of competitive brands.

MEDIA-DELIVERED COUPONS.　Most coupon distribution is achieved through magazines or various newspaper delivery modes—especially ROP solo during the week and freestanding inserts on Sundays. The major advantage of media coupons is their *broad exposure;* they are limited only by media circulation. While magazines and newspapers both permit *geographical selectivity*, magazines also permit demographic and psychographic pinpointing. Moreover, the *cost-per-thousand* for freestanding inserts is only about 50 to 60 percent of that for direct-mail coupons, which largely explains why FSIs are the dominant coupon-delivery mode.

The disadvantages of media-delivered coupons are that they generate *relatively low levels of redemption;* they do not, with the exception of freestanding inserts, generate much trade interest; and they suffer from *considerable misredemption*. The latter problem is so significant to all parties involved in couponing that it deserves a separate discussion later.

---

[34]Kapil Bawa and Robert W. Shoemaker, "Analyzing Incremental Sales from a Direct Mail Coupon Promotion," *Journal of Marketing Research*, 53 (July 1989), 66–78.

In- and On-Pack Coupons

In- and on-pack coupons are distributed by inclusion either inside a product's package or as a part of a package's exterior. This form of couponing should not be confused with the previously discussed instant, or peelable, coupon. Whereas the latter is removable at the point of purchase and redeemable *for that particular purchase while the shopper is in the store*, an in- or on-pack coupon cannot be removed until it is in the shopper's home or redeemed until a subsequent purchase occasion.

Frequently, a coupon for one brand is promoted by another brand. For example, General Mills promoted its brand of granola bars by placing cents-off coupons in cereal boxes. Practitioners call this practice *crossruffing*, a term borrowed from bridge and bridge-type card games where partners alternate trumping one another when they are unable to follow suit.

Though marketers use crossruffing to create trial purchases or to stimulate purchase of products such as granola bars that are not staple items, in- and on-pack coupons carried by the same brand are generally intended to stimulate *repeat purchasing*. (Note that in Table 17.1 in- and on-pack coupons are positioned as performing franchise holding objectives for manufacturers while providing consumers with delayed rewards.) That is, once consumers have exhausted the contents of a particular package, they are more likely to repurchase that brand if an attractive inducement, such as a cents-off coupon, is available immediately. A package coupon has *bounce-back value*. An initial purchase, the *bounce*, may stimulate another purchase, the *bounce back*, when a hard-to-avoid inducement such as an in-package coupon is made available.

A major advantage of in- and on-pack coupons is that there are *virtually no distribution costs*. Moreover, redemption rates are much higher because most of the package-delivered coupons are received by brand users. The major limitations of these coupons are that they offer *delayed value* to consumers, they *do not reach nonusers* of the carrying brand, and *trade interest is relatively low* due to the delayed nature of the offer.

Coupon Misredemption

As alluded to earlier, misredemption is a major problem, especially in the use of media-delivered coupons. The best way to understand how misredemption occurs is to examine the redemption process.

The process begins with a shopper presenting the checkout clerk with coupons that are then subtracted from the shopper's total purchase cost. For the shopper to legitimately be entitled to the coupon discount, certain conditions and restrictions must be met: The consumer must buy the merchandise specified on the coupon in the size, brand, and quantity directed; only one coupon can be redeemed per item; cash may not be given for the coupon; and the coupon must be redeemed before the expiration date.

Retailers, in turn, redeem the coupons they have received in order to obtain reimbursement from the manufacturers that sponsored the coupons. Retailers typically hire another company, called a *clearinghouse*, to sort and redeem the coupons in return for a fee. Clearinghouses, acting on behalf of a number of retail clients, consolidate coupons before forwarding them. Clearinghouses maintain controls by ensuring that their clients legitimately sold products in the amounts they submitted for redemption.

Clearinghouses forward the coupons to *redemption centers*, which serve as agents of the coupon-issuing manufacturers. The redemption center pays off on all properly redeemed coupons. If a center questions the validity of certain coupons, it may go to its client, a manufacturer, for approval on redeeming suspected coupons.[35]

The system is not quite as clear-cut as it may appear from this description. Some large retailers act as their own clearinghouses, some manufacturers serve as their own redemption centers, and some independent firms, such as the A. C. Nielsen Co., offer both clearinghouse and redemption-center services.

However, regardless of the specific mechanism by which a coupon is ultimately redeemed (or misredeemed), the retailer is reimbursed for the amount of the face value paid to the consumer and for payment of a handling charge, which currently is 8 cents per coupon. Herein rests the potential for misredemption: A single coupon with, say, a face value of 50 cents pays the unscrupulous person 58 cents. One thousand such misredeemed coupons are worth $580! Exacerbating the potential for misredemption is the fact that some coupons now have face values worth as much as $2 or $3. (See Figure 17.3 and the $2.50 coupon for Purina® dog foods.)

With an understanding of the redemption mechanism, questions arise as to how misredemption occurs and who participates in it. Estimates of the misredemption rate range from a low of 15 percent to a high of 40 percent. Many product managers estimate a 20 to 25 percent rate of misredemption when budgeting for coupon events.[36] A. C. Nielsen estimates the amount of annual coupon misredemption as at least $250 million.[37]

Misredemption occurs at every level of the redemption process. Sometimes *consumers* present coupons that have expired, coupons for items not purchased, or coupons for a smaller-sized product than that specified by the coupon. Some *clerks* take coupons to the store and exchange them for cash without making a purchase. At the *store management level*, retailers may boost profits by submitting extra coupons in addition to those redeemed legitimately. A dishonest retailer can buy coupons on the black market, age them in a clothes dryer, mix

---

[35]"The Route to Redemption," *Advertising Age*, May 30, 1983, 57.

[36]Louis J. Haugh, "What Are the Added Costs of Coupon Misredemption?" *Advertising Age*, February 6, 1978, 42.

[37]"Computers Help Foil Coupon Fraud," *Marketing News*, August 15, 1986, 1.

Illustration of High Face-Value Coupon

FIGURE 17.3

WHAT'S YOUR BAG?

CHOOSE TWO. SAVE $2.50

Save $2.50 when you purchase any TWO (12 lb. or smaller) bags of the above Purina® Dog Food.

Helping pets live longer, healthier lives.

© 1992, Ralston Purina Company

$2.50 OFF any TWO 12 lb. or smaller bags

EXPIRATION DATE 1/31/92

$2.50 off the regular price when you buy any TWO bags, 12 lb. or smaller, Dog Chow,® Purina® Kibbles and Cheezy Chews, Purina® Kibbles and Chunks, Purina® Hi Pro, Puppy Chow,® Lucky Dog,® Chuck Wagon® or Grrravy® brand Dog Foods.

VR 57   030163

CONSUMER: Required purchase necessary. Coupon may not be copied or transferred. No other coupon may be used to purchase the same package(s).

RETAILER: Ralston Purina Company, P.O. Box 18003, Nogales, AZ 85662, will redeem this coupon per our Coupon Redemption Policy, available upon request (in the case of free goods, shelf price). Consumer must pay sales tax. Good only in USA, APO's, FPO's. Void where prohibited. Cash value: 1/20¢. Printed in U.S.A.

© 1992, Ralston Purina Company

030163

them with legitimate coupons, and then mail in the batch for redemption.[38] Shady *clearinghouses* engage in misredemption by combining illegally purchased coupons with real ones and certifying the batch as legitimate.

The major source of coupon misredemption is *large-scale professional misredeemers* who either (1) recruit the services of actual retailers to serve as conduits through which coupons are misredeemed, or (2) operate phony businesses that exist solely for the purpose of redeeming huge quantities of illegal coupons.[39] Illegal coupons typically are obtained from *gang cutting or tearing* mint-condition coupons from numerous copies of the same issue of a newspaper or magazine.

The following examples reveal how professional misredeemers operate. "Jimmy's Coupon Redemption Center" was the front for a six-man misredemption ring. Jimmy's acquired bulk coupons from sources such as scrap dealers, newspapers, and charity groups, and then designated fictitious stores as payees for redeemed coupons. The gang managed to acquire $750,000 from nearly 200 manufacturers before they were caught.[40]

Another case involving coupon fraud was discovered by employees of Colgate-Palmolive's coupon redemption center in Kentucky. The redemption center received coupons that had been printed but had never been used in a promotion. The discovery of these stolen coupons led investigators to uncover a large-scale fraud scheme run by four supermarket operators who, during an 11-month period, defrauded companies of about $500,000.[41]

A Los Angeles accountant recruited coupon clippers from California charities and paid $5 for each pound of coupons they collected. He accumulated huge quantities of coupons and was able to redeem millions of dollars before the scheme was detected.[42]

THE STING.   Due to the pervasiveness of the coupon-misredemption problem and especially because of the role played by organized crime, postal authorities and local governments have taken retaliatory action. Two celebrated *sting operations* have attempted to identify fraudulent coupon redemption schemes. In both cases, *coupons for fictitious brands* were advertised heavily in newspapers.

The first undercover operation was undertaken by the Brooklyn district attorney's office and involved a fictitious detergent brand, "Breen," that was

---

[38]Vincent Coppola and David Friendly, "Coupon Caper," *Newsweek*, November 27, 1978, 89–90.

[39]Ibid.

[40]Louis J. Haugh, "Feds Smash Profitable Coupon Fraud Operation," *Advertising Age*, June 9, 1975, 27.

[41]Coppola and Friendly, "Coupon Caper," 89–90.

[42]Ibid.

advertised with 25 cents-off coupons. Of course, because Breen was a fictitious brand, any redemption would have entailed misredemption. Twenty-six retailers, who collected more than $122,000 from a variety of coupon refunds including over $100,000 paid out by A. C. Nielsen, were indicted on various charges of larceny and fraud.[43]

A second sting operation took place in Florida. U.S. Postal Service (USPS) inspectors finally busted a well-organized misredemption ring, but not before the ring had bilked manufacturers out of an astounding $186 million. The ring had organized between 700 and 800 otherwise legitimate grocery retailers through which they redeemed gang-clipped coupons.

In order to catch the ring in action, the USPS used a coupon for a nonexistent bug killer named "Broach." Broach ads carrying 25 cents-off coupons (see Figure 17.4) were run in three Florida newspapers as part of a cooperative free-standing-insert package. Coupon misredemptions for this fictitious product led to the arrest of dozens of retailers and four independent newspaper distributors, who sold freestanding-coupon inserts in bulk to the misredemption ring.

FOILING COUPON FRAUD. In addition to government-sponsored sting operations, companies have taken steps to reduce the loss from coupon misredemption. Quaker Oats, for example, maintains a computerized database of the coupon-redemption histories of over 100,000 retail grocers. The data file for

The Bait: Coupon for Fictitious "Broach" **FIGURE 17.4**

Source: "Coupon Fraud Indictments Termed 'Only Tip of Iceberg'," *Advertising Age,* December 18, 1986, 1, 77.

[43]"Coupon Fraud Indictments Termed 'Only Tip of Iceberg'."

each retailer contains information on whether the retailer has a history of misredemption along with data on normal redemption patterns. Hence, an abnormally large coupon submission from a particular retailer signals the possibility of a misredemption attempt.[44]

Another method of reducing coupon misredemption is the use of actual *bank checks* instead of traditional coupons. With this method, the customer receives a check from a manufacturer through the mail. The check permits the customer to receive a cash discount when purchasing the manufacturer's product. The retailer deposits redeemed checks into its bank account and does not have to go through a clearinghouse, with the accompanying delay, to get reimbursed—reimbursement is immediate with the deposit. While it is too early to know how extensively bank checks will be used in lieu of conventional coupons, preliminary evidence indicates that the misredemption rate is reduced from upwards of 20 percent for coupons to 4 percent or less with checks.[45]

Another recent contributor to misredemption is the advent of color copiers that create virtually undetectable counterfeit coupons. A company named Comark Merchandising is marketing an anti-copying security system called Copy-Stop. Copy-Stop uses a special printing process that covers a coupon's face with a virtually undetectable pattern of the word *VOID*. When the coupon is duplicated with a copier the VOID pattern emerges, thereby preventing redemption. Major companies such as Colgate-Palmolive, Johnson & Johnson, Nestle USA, Procter & Gamble, Ralston Purina, and RJR Nabisco are using the Copy-Stop system. Figure 17.5 illustrates the Copy-Stop method.[46]

PREMIUMS

Broadly defined, **premiums** are articles of merchandise or services (e.g., travel) offered by manufacturers to induce action on the part of the sales force, trade representatives, or consumers. This section focuses on consumer motivation. Several forms of premium offers are used to motivate consumers: free-in-the-mail premiums; in-, on-, and near-pack premiums; and self-liquidating premiums. All three forms serve fundamentally different purposes. Free-in-the-mail premiums are useful primarily for generating initial brand trial or retrial; in-, on-, and near-pack premiums serve franchise-holding purposes; and self-liquidators perform image-reinforcement functions (see Table 17.1).

[44]"Computers Help Foil Coupon Fraud."

[45]Len Strazewski, "Checks May Replace Some Coupons," *Advertising Age*, October 12, 1987, 30.

[46]Figure 17.5 and the preceding description are based on Scott Hume, "Redeeming Feature," *Advertising Age*, February 4, 1991, 35.

Example of the Copy-Stop Coupon Security Method   FIGURE 17.5

Free-in-the-Mail Premiums

By definition, a **free-in-the-mail premium** is a promotion in which consumers receive a premium item from the sponsoring manufacturer in return for submitting a required number of proofs of purchase. For example, Kellogg's offered a free racing cap with purchases of its corn flakes brand and designated quantities of proofs of purchases (see Figure 17.6).

In addition to stimulating consumer trial, free-in-the-mail premiums can achieve other objectives. When directed at adult audiences, these premiums can accomplish *franchise-holding* objectives by rewarding consumers' brand loyalties and encouraging repeat-purchase behavior.

Relatively few consumers who are exposed to free mail-in offers actually avail themselves of these opportunities. The national average redemption rate is estimated to be between 2 and 4 percent.[47] However, these premiums can be extremely effective if the premium item is appealing to the target market, as is probably the case with Kellogg's offer.

[47]William R. Dean, "Irresistible But Not Free of Problems," *Advertising Age*, October 6, 1980, sec. S, 1, 12.

FIGURE 17.6   Illustration of Free-in-the-Mail Premium

In-, On-, and Near-Pack Premiums

In- and on-pack premiums offer a premium item inside a package, attached to a package, or the package itself is reusable. For example, in a delightful promotional program for Cap'n Crunch cereal, the box was labeled "Christmas Crunch" and Captain Horatio was shown on the package dressed like Santa Claus. The package advertised a free Christmas tree ornament inside the box—a premium offer with much appeal to small children. In general, in- and on-package premiums offer consumers *immediate value* and thereby encourage increased product consumption.

Contrary to what you probably think, this form of premium is not restricted to children. For example, Ralston Purina offered tiny sports-car models in about 11 million boxes of six cereal brands. Ten of these boxes contained scale-model red Corvettes. Lucky consumers turned in the models for real Corvettes, each valued at about $29,000 at the time of the promotion.[48]

Near-pack premiums provide the retail trade with specially displayed premium pieces that retailers then give to consumers who purchase the promoted product. Near-pack premiums have the added advantage of being less expensive than on-pack premiums because additional packaging is not required. Furthermore, near-pack premiums can build sales volume in stores that put up displays and participate fully.

Self-Liquidating Premiums

The **self-liquidating premium** gets its name from the fact that the consumer mails in a stipulated number of proofs of purchase along with *sufficient money to cover the manufacturer's purchasing, handling, and mailing costs of the premium item*. In other words, the actual cost of the premium is paid for by consumers; from the manufacturer's perspective the item is cost free, or, in other words, self-liquidating.

An illustrative self-liquidating premium is presented in Figure 17.7. Kodak, as an Olympic Games' sponsor, offered a commemorative Olympic watch valued at $30 for a charge of only $3.50 to consumers along with proofs of purchase from selected Kodak products. In addition to *reinforcing and strengthening a brand's image* by associating it with an attractive premium object, self-liquidating premiums are an effective means of obtaining store displays and *encouraging trade support* for the brand.

---

[48]"Ralston-Purina Offers Adult Incentive in Kids' Cereal Boxes," *Marketing News*, April 25, 1988, 1.

FIGURE 17.7   Illustration of Self-Liquidating Premium

However, very few consumers ever send for a premium.[49] Companies generally expect only 0.1 percent of self-liquidators to be redeemed.[50] A circulation of 20,000,000, for example, would be expected to produce only about 20,000 redemptions.

Industry specialists generally agree that the most important consideration in developing a self-liquidator program is that the premium be appealing to the target audience and *represent a value.* Most sources agree that consumers look for a savings of at least 50 percent of the suggested retail price.[51]

PRICE-OFFS

Price-off promotions entail a reduction in a brand's regular price. A price-off is clearly labeled as such on the package. Price-offs typically range from 10 to 25 percent. This type of promotion is effective when the marketer's objective is any of the following: (1) to reward present brand users; (2) to get consumers to purchase larger quantities of a brand than they normally would (i.e., to load them), thereby effectively preempting the competition; (3) to establish a repeat purchase pattern after an initial trial; (4) to ensure that promotional dollars do, in fact, reach consumers (no such assurance is possible with trade allowances); (5) to obtain off-shelf display space provided that display allowances are offered to retailers; and (6) to provide the sales force with an incentive to obtain retailer support.[52]

Price-offs cannot reverse a downward sales trend, produce a significant number of new users, or attract as many trial users as sampling, coupons, or premium packs. Furthermore, *retailers often dislike price-offs* because they create inventory and pricing problems, particularly when a store has a brand in inventory at both the price-off and regular prices. Despite trade problems, price-offs have strong consumer appeal.

FTC Price-Off Regulations

Manufacturers cannot indiscriminately promote their products with continuous or near-continuous price-off labeling. To do so would deceive consumers into

[49]William A. Robinson, "What Are Promos' Weak and Strong Points?" *Advertising Age*, April 7, 1980, 54.

[50]Francine Schore, "Inflation Hurts Cheaper Items," *Advertising Age*, October 6, 1980, sec. S, 19, 20.

[51]Ibid.

[52]Fredericks, "What Ogilvy & Mather Has Learned about Sales Promotion."

thinking the product is on sale when in fact the announced sale price is actually the regular price.

The Federal Trade Commission controls price-off labeling with the following regulations:

1. Price-off labels may only be used on brands already in distribution with established retail prices;

2. There is a limit of three price-off label promotions per year per brand size;

3. There must be a hiatus period of at least 30 days between price-off label promotions on any given brand size;

4. No more than 50 percent of a brand's volume over a 12-month period may be generated from price-off label promotions;

5. The manufacturer must provide display materials to announce the price-off label offer; and

6. The dealer is required to show the regular shelf price in addition to the new price reflecting the price-off label savings.[53]

BONUS PACKS

Bonus packs are extra quantities of a product that a company gives to consumers at the regular price. For example, in Figure 17.8 Carnation offers consumers 25 percent more hot cocoa mix at the regular price. Bonus packs are sometimes used as an *alternative to price-off deals* when the latter are either overused or resisted by the trade. The extra value offered to the consumer is readily apparent and for that reason can be effective in *loading current users* and thereby removing them from the market—a defensive tactic that is used against aggressive competitors.

A potential drawback of bonus packs is that a large proportion of the bonus-packed merchandise will be *purchased by regular customers* who would have purchased the brand anyway. Of course, this is *not* a drawback if the explicit purpose of the bonus-pack offer is to reward a brand's present customers.

---

[53]*ANA Consumer Promotion Seminar Fact Book,* 7.

REFUNDS AND REBATES

The terms refund and rebate both refer to the practice in which manufacturers give *cash discounts or reimbursements* to consumers who submit proofs of purchase. Though often used interchangeably, a **refund** typically refers to cash reimbursement for *packaged goods*, whereas a **rebate** more often refers to reimbursements for *durable goods* (especially small appliances and automobiles).

Both refunds and rebates offer consumers *delayed* rather than immediate value since the consumer has to wait to receive the reimbursement. In using these programs, manufacturers achieve *franchise holding* objectives by encouraging consumers to make multiple purchases or by rewarding previous users with a cash discount for again purchasing the manufacturer's brand.

Packaged-good marketers are fond of refund offers because they *stimulate purchase behavior* and provide an alternative to the use of coupons.[54] Overall, refunds represent a useful technique: They reinforce brand loyalty, provide the sales force with something to talk about, and enable the manufacturer to flag the package with a potentially attractive deal.

However, because of the delayed reward, there is limited interest among many consumers and much of the retail trade. Many consumers consider using refunds or rebates to be too much of a hassle, and some even think that manufacturers only use these programs when their products are not selling well.[55]

CONTESTS AND SWEEPSTAKES

Contests and sweepstakes offer consumers the opportunity to win cash, merchandise, or travel prizes. In a **sweepstakes,** winners are determined *purely on the basis of chance.* Accordingly, proofs of purchase cannot be required as a condition for entry. In a **contest,** the consumer *must solve the specified contest problem* (e.g., a puzzle) and may be required to submit proofs of purchase.

Because they require less effort from consumers and generate greater response, *sweepstakes are much preferred to contests.* Moreover, contests have the added disadvantage of sometimes going awry. For example, the Beatrice Company, makers of many consumer packaged goods, initiated a contest involving *Monday Night Football.* Contestants scratched silver-coated footballs off

---

[54]Ronnie Telzer, "Rebates Challenge Coupons' Redeeming Values," *Advertising Age*, March 23, 1987, sec. S, 18.

[55]Peter Tat, William A. Cunningham III, and Emin Babakus, "Consumer Perceptions of Rebates," *Journal of Advertising Research*, 28 (August/September 1988), 45–50.

cards to reveal numbers, hoping to win the prize offered if the numbers on the cards matched the number of touchdowns and field goals scored in the weekly Monday night NFL game. Contest planners intended the chances of getting a match to be infinitesimal. However, to Beatrice's great surprise, a salesman for rival Procter & Gamble put in a claim for a great deal more money than they had planned on paying out.

A computer buff, the salesman cracked the contest code and determined that 320 patterns showed up repeatedly in the cards. By scratching off just one line, he could determine which numbers were underneath the rest. With knowledge of the actual numbers of TDs and field goals scored on a particular Monday night, he would start scratching cards until winning numbers were located. He enlisted friends to assist in collecting and scratching the cards. Thousands of cards were collected, mostly from Beatrice salespeople. The P&G salesman and friends identified 4,000 winning cards worth $21 million in prize money! Beatrice discontinued the game and refused to pay up.[56]

Beatrice is not the only company that has been burned with a contest gone awry. For example, PepsiCo ran a spell-your-surname contest with letters printed on bottle caps. Because very few caps bore vowels, PepsiCo assumed that only a small number of people would win the contest. What the contest planners failed to realize, however, was that many Asian names contain only consonants (such as Ng).[57]

These and other problems lead many companies to shy away from contests. Sweepstakes, on the other hand, have experienced a tremendous increase in popularity. Compared with many other sales-promotion techniques, sweepstakes are *relatively inexpensive, simple to execute,* and are *able to accomplish a variety of marketing objectives.*[58] In addition to reinforcing a brand's image and attracting attention to advertisements, well-designed sweepstakes can promote distribution and retailer stocking, increase sales-force enthusiasm, and reach specific groups, such as ethnic markets, through a prize structure that is particularly appealing to those groups.[59]

The majority of sweepstakes offer a prize or group of prizes to entrants, who mail an entry blank along with a proof of purchase (or a facsimile, since purchase cannot legally be required) to the manufacturer's judging agency. For example, a Duracell sweepstake offered a grand prize of $100,000 (see Figure 17.9).

The effectiveness and appeal of a sweepstakes is generally limited if the sweepstakes is used alone. However, when tied in with advertising, point-of-

---

[56]Laurie Baum, "How Beatrice Lost At Its Own Game," *Business Week,* March 2, 1987, 66.

[57]Ibid.

[58]Thomas J. Conlon, "Sweepstakes Rank As Tops," *Advertising Age,* October 6, 1980, sec. S, 6, 7; Don Jagoda, "It's Not What You Give But What You Get," *Marketing Communications,* April 1984, 27–31.

[59]Stanley N. Arnold, "Consumer Sweepstakes and Contests," in *The Tools of Promotion* (New York: Association of National Advertisers, 1975), 4, 5.

FIGURE 17.9   An Appealing Sweepstakes

purchase displays, and other promotional tools, sweepstakes can work effectively to produce significant results.

OVERLAY AND TIE-IN PROMOTIONS

Discussion to this point has concentrated on individual sales promotions. In practice, sales-promotion techniques are often used in combination to accomplish a number of objectives that any one tool could not accomplish alone. Furthermore, these techniques, individually or in conjunction with one another, are frequently used to simultaneously promote two or more brands either from the same company or from different firms.

The use of *two or more sales-promotion techniques* in combination with one another is called an **overlay,** or combination, program. The *simultaneous promotion of multiple brands in a single promotional effort* is called a **tie-in,** or joint, promotion. In other words, overlay refers to the use of multiple sales promotion *tools*, whereas tie-in refers to the promotion of multiple *brands* from the same or different companies. Overlay and tie-ins often are used together, as the following sections illustrate.

Overlay Programs

Media clutter, as noted repeatedly in past chapters, is an ever-growing problem facing marketers. When used individually, sales-promotion tools, particularly coupons, may never be noticed by consumers. A combination of tools—such as the use of a coupon offer with another promotional device (see Figures 17.6, 17.7, and 17.9)—increases the likelihood that consumers will attend a promotional message and process the sales-promotion offer. In addition, the joint use of several techniques in a well-coordinated promotional program *equips the sales force with a strong sales program* and *provides the trade with an attractive incentive* to purchase in larger quantities (in anticipation of enhanced consumer response) and to increase display activity.

A campaign by Welch's Jam & Jelly illustrates the use of overlay and tie-in promotions in conjunction with one another. Welch's primary objectives were to load existing customers and to induce users of competitive brands to make a trial purchase. Their strategy consisted of overlaying coupons with a self-liquidating premium. At the same time, the promotion was tied in with two natural partners, the Quality Bakers of America and the American Dairy Association.

Welch's selected a family-oriented vehicle, the Sunday comics, for delivering the coupon and announcing a free milk offer. Consumers would receive a free half-gallon of milk for submitting the net weight statements from any three jars of Welch's grape jelly or strawberry jam and from any Quality Bakers of

America brand bread. In addition, display materials in stores offered consumers a soccer ball (with a retail value of $27) in return for only $11.95 and the UPC codes from any two jars of Welch's jam or jelly. Moreover, a trade-oriented contest was run in an effort to stimulate retailer support. Prizes included a Nassau vacation for two people and 500 soccer balls for store managers to give to their children.

As a result of this creative and well-coordinated program, initial sales exceeded levels forecasted to the trade by 30 percent, the increase in in-store display activity was double that originally estimated, and Welch brands experienced a 3.9 percent increase in market share over the eight weeks following the promotion.[60]

Tie-In Promotions

Growing numbers of companies are using tie-ins (group promotions) to generate increased sales, to stimulate trade and consumer interest, and to gain optimal use of their promotional budgets, especially during recessionary periods.[61] Tie-in promotions are cost effective because the cost, say, of distributing coupons is shared among multiple brands. For example, Kraft's Cheez Whiz® and Oscar Mayer weiners, two natural partners, share the expense of distributing the coupons in Figure 17.10.

TYPES OF TIE-IN PROMOTIONS.   By definition, a tie-in promotion involves the *pooling of resources* between two or more products, brands, or services. The exact nature of the pooling can take various forms.[62] Two major forms are intra- and inter-company tie-ins.

Intra-company pooling involves a joint sales promotion for two or more distinct brands from a single company. For example, PepsiCo spent about $20 million on its Halloween "Monster Match" promotion to jointly promote two of its brands, Pepsi-Cola and Doritos. The promotion involved placing halves of game pieces in bags of chips and in soft-drink packages. Consumers who located correctly matched halves of pieces from the chips and cola were eligible to receive hundreds of thousands of cash awards, including three $1 million grand prizes.[63]

---

[60]Adapted from Joseph S. Maier, *Promotion Update '82*, a publication of the Promotion Marketing Association of America, Inc., New York, 1982.

[61]Alison Fahey and Scott Hume, "Marketers Team in Time of Trouble," *Advertising Age*, February 18, 1991, 36.

[62]Melvin Scales, "What Tie-in Promotions Can Do for You," *Outlook*, a publication of the Promotion Marketing Association of America, 12, Fall 1988, 10–11; P. "Rajan" Varadarajan, "Horizontal Cooperative Sales Promotion: A Framework for Classification and Additional Perspectives," *Journal of Marketing*, 50 (April 1986), 61–73.

[63]Michael J. McCarthy, "PepsiCo Will Tout Doritos, Pepsi Sodas for Halloween Sales," *The Wall Street Journal*, August 21, 1991, sec. B, 6.

A Tie-In Promotion between Two Natural Partners

FIGURE 17.10

Inter-company tie-ins involve coordinated activities between products from *distinct companies* that are not in direct competition with one another and which, typically, complement one another (such as in Figure 17.10). Thomas J. Lipton, Inc., wanted a promotion that would attract consumer attention to its Lipton tea, Wish-Bone salad dressings, and other Lipton products and would generate retail display space in the competitive pre-summer holiday period. A tie-in was arranged with Walt Disney Productions, which was looking for a way to build awareness for the 50th anniversary re-release of the motion picture *Snow White.* Lipton distributed freestanding inserts to 21 million households. The FSI overlayed coupons with a special premium item for children—a personalized birthday tale from *Snow White* that imprinted the child's name, age, and hometown. The promotion was supported by heavy advertising to retailers and an incentive program for the sales force that offered all-expense trips to Disney World for successful sales performance. The promotion was extremely appealing to retailers and consumers and satisfied both Lipton's and Walt Disney Production's objectives.[64]

IMPLEMENTATION PROBLEMS.   Tie-in promotions are capable of accomplishing useful objectives, but not without potential problems.[65] Promotion *lead time is lengthened* because two or more entities have to coordinate their separate promotional schedules. *Creative conflicts and convoluted messages* may result from each partner trying to receive primary attention for its product/service.

To reduce problems as much as possible and to accomplish objectives, it is important that (1) the *profiles of each partner's customers be similar* with regard to pertinent demographic or other consumption-influencing characteristics; (2) the partners' *images should reinforce one another* (e.g., Lipton iced tea and *Snow White* both have wholesome images); and (3) partners *must be willing to cooperate* rather than imposing their own interests to the detriment of the other partner's welfare.[66]

EVALUATING SALES-PROMOTION IDEAS

It should be apparent by this point that numerous alternatives are available to sales-promotion planners. There also are a variety of objectives that effective

---

[64]Adapted from Ronnie Telzer, "Dickering Done, Tie-ins Prove Worth," *Advertising Age*, May 2, 1988, sec. S, 4.

[65]Scales, "What Tie-in Promotions Can Do for You," 11.

[66]"Creating Synergy through Tie-in Promotions," *Marketing Communications*, April 1988, 45.

sales-promotion programs are able to achieve. The combination of numerous alternatives and diverse objectives leads to a staggering array of possibilities. A straightforward three-step procedure has been recommended by promotion experts as an aid in determining which sales promotion ideas and approaches have the best chance of succeeding.[67]

Step 1: Identify the Objectives

The most basic yet important step toward successful sales promotions is the clear identification of the specific objectives that are to be accomplished. Objectives should be specified as they relate *both to the trade and to ultimate consumers;* for example, the objectives may be to generate trial, to load consumers, to pre-empt competition, to increase display space, and so on.

In this first step, the promotional planner must commit the objectives to writing and state them specifically and in measurable terms. For example, the objective "to increase sales" is too general. In comparison, the objective "to increase display space by 25 percent over the comparable period last year" is specific and measurable.

Step 2: Achieve Agreement

Everyone involved in the marketing of a product category or brand must agree with the objectives developed. Failure to achieve agreement on objectives results in various decision makers (such as the advertising, sales, and sales-promotion managers) pushing for different programs because they have different objectives in mind. Also, a specific sales-promotion program can more easily be evaluated in terms of a specific objective than in terms of a vague generalization.

Step 3: Evaluation System

With specific objectives established and agreement achieved, the following five-point evaluation system should be used to rate any sales-promotion program or idea:

1. **How good is the general idea?** Every idea should be evaluated against the promotion's objectives. For example, if the objective is to increase product

---

[67]Don E. Schultz and William A. Robinson, *Sales Promotion Management* (Lincolnwood, IL: NTC Business Books, 1986), 436–445.

trial, a sample or a coupon would be rated favorably, while a sweepstake would flunk this initial evaluation.

2. **Will the sales-promotion idea appeal to the target market?** A contest, for example, might have great appeal to children, but for certain adult groups it would have disastrous results. In general, remember that the target market represents the bedrock against which all proposals should be judged.

3. **Is the idea unique or is the competition doing something similar?** The prospects of receiving both trade and consumer attention depend on developing promotions that are not ordinary. Creativity is every bit as important to sales-promotion success as it is with advertising.

4. **Is the promotion presented clearly so that the intended market will notice, comprehend, and respond to the deal?** Sales-promotion planners should start with one fundamental premise: Most consumers are not willing to spend much time and effort figuring out how a promotion works. It is critical to a promotion's success that instructions be user friendly. Let consumers know quickly and clearly what the offer is and how to respond to it.

5. **How cost-effective is the proposed idea?** This requires an evaluation of whether or not the proposed promotion will achieve the intended objectives at an affordable cost. Sophisticated promotion planners cost out alternative programs and know in advance the likely bottom-line payoff from a promotion.

SUMMARY

This chapter focuses on consumer-oriented sales promotions. The various sales-promotion tools available to marketers are classified in terms of whether the reward offered consumers is immediate or delayed and in terms of whether the manufacturer's objective is to achieve trial impact, franchise holding/loading, or image reinforcement. Specific sales-promotion techniques fall into one of five general categories: immediate reward/trial impact, delayed reward/trial impact, immediate reward/franchise holding, delayed reward/franchise holding, and delayed reward/image reinforcement.

Specific topics addressed in the chapter include the following: sampling effectiveness; conditions when sampling should be used; coupon usage and growth; couponing costs; coupon misredemption; reasons for using in- and on-pack premiums and self-liquidators; FTC price-off regulations; differences between refunds and rebates and when each is used; the role of contests and sweepstakes; the nature of overlay and tie-in promotions, and various other topics.

The first and most critical requirement for a successful sales promotion is that it be based on clearly defined objectives. Second, the program must be designed with a specific target market in mind. It should also be realized that many consumers, perhaps most, desire to maximize the rewards gained from participating in a sales promotion while minimizing the amount of time and effort invested. Consequently, an effective sales promotion, from a consumer-response perspective, must make it relatively easy for consumers to obtain their reward, and the size of the reward must be sufficient to justify the consumer's efforts. A third essential ingredient for effective sales promotions is that programs must be developed with the interests of retailers in mind—not just the manufacturer's interests.

Discussion Questions

1. Sales promotions offer consumers immediate or delayed rewards. The former is more effective in inducing behaviors desired by the marketer. Explain why and back it up with a specific, concrete illustration from your own experience.

2. Explain in your own terms the meaning of franchise holding and loading objectives.

3. One of the major trends in product sampling is selective sampling of targeted groups. Assume you work for a company that has just developed a new candy bar substitute which tastes almost as good as a regular candy bar but is much lower in calories. Marketing research has identified the target market as economically upscale consumers, aged 34 to 55, who reside in urban areas. Explain specifically how you might selectively sample over 5 million such consumers.

4. Compare and contrast sampling and media-delivered coupons in terms of objectives, consumer impact, and overall roles in marketing-communications strategies.

5. A packaged-goods company plans to introduce a new bathroom soap that differs from competitive soaps by virtue of a distinct new fragrance. Should sampling be used to introduce the product?

6. Present your personal views concerning the number of coupons distributed annually in the United States. Is widespread couponing in the best interest of consumers? Could marketers use other promotional methods to more effectively and economically achieve the objectives accomplished with coupons?

7. Present a position on the following statement: "I can't understand why in Table 17.1 free-in-the-mail premiums are positioned as accomplishing just a trial-impact function. It would seem that this form of promotion also accomplishes franchise holding objectives."

8. Using Table 17.2 as a guide, calculate the full cost per redeemed coupon given the following facts: (1) face value = 75 cents; (2) 20,000,000 coupons distributed at

$7 per thousand; (3) redemption rate = 3%; (4) handling cost = 10 cents; and (5) misredemption rate = 15%.

9. Can you envision any potential problems with Tucker's Variable Incentive Promotion described in the *Focus on Promotion?*

10. Your company markets hot dogs, bologna, and other processed meats. You wish to offer a self-liquidating premium that would cost consumers approximately $25, would require 10 proofs of purchase, and would be appropriately themed to your product category during the summer months. Your primary market segment is families with school-aged children crossing all socio-economic strata. Suggest two premium items and justify your choice.

11. What is the purpose of the FTC price-off regulations?

12. Compare bonus packs and price-off deals in terms of consumer impact.

13. What is crossruffing in sales promotion, and why is it used?

14. How can sales promotion reinforce a brand's image? Is this a major objective of sales promotion?

15. Compare contests and sweepstakes in terms of how they function and in terms of relative effectiveness.

16. Your company markets antifreeze. Sales to consumers take place in a very short period, September through December. You want to tie in a promotion between your product and the product of another company that would bring more visibility to your brand and encourage retailers to provide more shelf space. Recommend a partner for this tie-in promotion and justify the choice.

17. Go through a Sunday newspaper and select 5 FSIs. Analyze each in terms of what you think the marketer's objectives are in using this particular promotion.

INTEGRATING MEDIA ADVERTISING AND SALES PROMOTIONS WITH POINT-OF-PURCHASE COMMUNICATIONS, DIRECT MARKETING, PUBLIC RELATIONS, AND SPONSORSHIP MARKETING

Part 7 covers three topics that are growing in importance in today's promotion management and marketing communications programs. Point-of-purchase communications, direct-marketing com-munications, and public relations and sponsorship marketing com-bine many fea-tures of media advertising and sales promo-tions; however, their distinct features and indi-vidual importance deserve separate coverage.

Chapter 18 discusses the ever-growing practice of point-of-purchase communications. The growth is explained in terms of the valuable functions that P-O-P performs for consumers, manufacturers, and retailers. Specific topics include unplanned purchasing and electronic retailing.

Chapter 19 describes the phenomenal growth that direct-response advertising and direct selling—the two major aspects of direct-marketing communications—have experienced in recent years. In addition, the chapter dis-cusses in particular detail direct-mail advertis-ing and telephone marketing.

Finally, the related topics of public relations and sponsorship marketing are examined in **Chapter 20.** The section on public relations includes a discussion of the historically entrenched practice of reactive public relations as well as the more recent practice of proactive public relations. A special section is devoted to negative publicity, including the issue of rumors and how to handle them. The last major section covers both cause and event marketing—the two specific aspects of sponsorship marketing.

CHAPTER EIGHTEEN

Point-of-Purchase Communications

INCREASING CHEESE SALES WITH POINT-OF-PURCHASE MATERIALS

The American Dairy Association (ADA), a trade association for producers of cheese and other dairy products, employed the services of A.C. Nielsen to investigate a very important question: Do stores which promote cheese sales using point-of-purchase (POP) materials enjoy higher sales levels?

To test this question, the A.C. Nielsen Company monitored more than 700 grocery stores in 13 major U.S. markets over a three-week period. During this time the ADA had designed a football-related promotion (named "Kick Off the Season with Cheese") that used in-store promotions along with a television campaign featuring prime and daytime advertising spots with weatherman Willard Scott. But the test dealt not with the advertising but with the effectiveness of the point-of-purchase materials.

The ADA's in-store "Kick Off" promotion used a football motif including small banners, varsity letters, case flags, and helmet mobiles. Over half of the 700 monitored stores used these point-of-purchase materials, while the remaining stores used no in-store promotions. Some of the stores that chose to use ADA's promotional materials also created their own displays to further attract consumer attention.

Test results convincingly established the effectiveness of P-O-P materials in this particular application. Figure 18.1 presents the test results. In the stores that did *not* participate in the "Kick Off" promotion, cheese sales averaged $4,184. Stores that used the ADA promotional package (banners, mobiles, etc.) experienced average sales of $5,392—a 29 percent increase over the non-promoting stores. Stores which supplemented the promotional package with

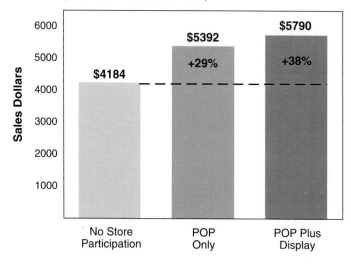

FIGURE 18.1

Results from the American Dairy Association POP Study

American Dairy Association Fall 1989 Promotion

Average Store Retail Cheese Sales (Per Million $ Total Store Sales)

Source: A.C. Nielsen Custom Store Audits of Fall 1989 Cheese Sales

their own displays enjoyed 38 percent greater sales than the non-promoting stores, or average sales of $5,790 per store.

These results, according to an ADA marketing executive, prove "beyond a shadow of a doubt" that point-of-purchase materials are an effective way to increase sales volume.

Source: "A.C. Nielsen Research Reveals Cheese Sales Skyrocket with In-Store Promotions," *POPAI News*, Marketplace 1990, 19.

OVERVIEW OF POINT-OF-PURCHASE COMMUNICATIONS

The example in the opening vignette epitomizes the value of point-of-purchase materials and the impact they can have in increasing sales volume. The point of purchase is an ideal time to communicate with consumers, because this is the time at which many product- and brand-choice decisions are made. It is the time and place at which all elements of the sale (consumer, money, and product) come together.[1]

Marketers attempt to influence buying decisions at the point of purchase using various communication vehicles—displays, shelf talkers, packaging graphics, brand names, sales promotions, and salespeople. This chapter's objective is to instill an enhanced appreciation of the increasingly important role played by communication devices at the point of purchase. Two aspects of point-of-purchase communications are spotlighted: (1) packaging and brand naming, and (2) the use of various types of in-store displays.

PACKAGING AND BRAND NAMING

A product is more than merely a physical object. Although functional product features play important roles in consumers' purchase and repurchase decisions, choices also are influenced by product features such as the package shape, design, color, and brand name. A growing number of marketing communicators appreciate the crucial roles performed by packaging and brand naming.

Packaging

The package is a vital element in the marketing communications mix.[2] The increasingly important communications role of packaging has given rise to expressions such as "Packaging is the least expensive form of advertising"; "Every package is a five-second commercial"; and "The package *is* the product."[3]

The growth of supermarkets and other self-service retail outlets has necessitated that the package assume marketing functions beyond the traditional role of merely containing and protecting the product. The package serves to (1) draw attention to a brand, (2) break through competitive clutter at the point of purchase, (3) justify price/value to the consumer, (4) signify brand features and benefits, and (5) ultimately motivate consumers' brand choices. Packaging is particularly important for differentiating homogenous or unexciting brands from

---

[1]John A. Quelch and Kristina Cannon-Bonventre, "Better Marketing at the Point-of-Purchase," *Harvard Business Review*, November-December 1983, 162–169.

[2]Laura Bird, "Romancing the Package," *Adweek's Marketing Week*, January 21, 1991, 10, 11, 14.

[3]Michael Gershman, "Packaging: Positioning Tool of the 1980s," *Management Review*, August 1987, 33–41.

available substitutes. Packaging accomplishes this by working uninterruptedly to say what the brand is, how it is used, and what it can do to benefit the user.[4]

There is a tendency for consumers to impute characteristics from a package to the brand itself. This tendency is called **sensation transference.** A package communicates meaning about a brand via its various symbolic components: color, design, shape, size, physical materials, and information labeling. All of these components must interact harmoniously to evoke within buyers the set of meanings intended by the company. The notion underlying good packaging is *gestalt.* That is, people react to the whole, not to the individual parts.

THE USE OF COLOR IN PACKAGING.   Colors have the ability to communicate many things to prospective buyers, including quality, taste, and the product's ability to satisfy various psychological needs. Research studies have documented the important role that color plays in affecting our senses. In one study researchers tested color's cueing role using *vanilla pudding* as the experimental product. The researchers altered the color of vanilla pudding by adding food colors to create dark brown, medium brown, and light brown "flavors."

The pudding, which actually was identical in all three experimental versions (namely vanilla), was perceived as tasting like chocolate. Moreover, the *dark brown* pudding was considered to have the best chocolate flavor and to be the thickest. The *light brown* pudding was perceived to be the creamiest, possibly because cream is white in color.[5]

The strategic use of colors in packaging is effective, because colors affect people emotionally. For example, the so-called high-wavelength colors of red, orange, and yellow possess strong excitation value and induce elated mood states.[6] *Red* is often described in terms such as active, stimulating, energetic, and vital. Close-up toothpaste is one well-known brand that effectively uses red in its packaging. *Orange* is an appetizing color that is often associated with food. Popular food brands using orange packaging include Wheaties, Uncle Ben's rice, and Sanka coffee. *Yellow*, a good attention getter, is a warm color that has a cheerful effect on consumers. Cheerios, Kodak, and Pennzoil are just a few of the many brands that use yellow packages.

Green connotes abundance, health, calmness, and serenity. Green packaging is sometimes used for beverages (e.g., Heineken beer, Seven-Up), often for

---

[4]John Deighton, "A White Paper on the Packaging Industry," Dennison Technical Papers, December 1983, 5.

[5]Gail Tom, Teresa Barnett, William Lew, and Jodean Selmants, "Cueing the Consumer: The Role of Salient Cues in Consumer Perception," *The Journal of Consumer Marketing*, 4 (Spring 1987), 23–27.

[6]This comment and parts of the following discussion are based on statements appearing in Joseph A. Bellizzi, Ayn E. Crowley, and Ronald W. Hasty, "The Effects of Color in Store Design," *Journal of Retailing*, 59 (Spring 1983), 21–45. Many of the brand-name examples in this section were suggested in "Color Is Prime 'Silent Communicator'," *Marketing News*, April 25, 1986, 15.

vegetables (e.g., Green Giant), and most always in packaging for mentholated products (e.g., Salem cigarettes). *Blue* suggests coolness, refreshment, and water. Blue is often associated with laundry and cleaning products, including brands such as Windex and Downey fabric softener. Finally, *white* signifies purity, cleanliness, and mildness. Gold Medal flour, Special-K cereal, and Lean Cuisine are a few food brands that feature white packages.

In addition to the emotional impact that color brings to a package, *elegance and prestige* can be added to products by the use of polished reflective surfaces and color schemes using white and black or silver and gold.[7] An example of the effective use of a white and black color scheme is found in the elegantly simple package utilized by Chanel No. 5 perfume. Another prestige-enhancing packaging is that for LeSueur peas, which for years have stood out on grocery shelves with their metallic silver labels.

DESIGN AND SHAPE CUES IN PACKAGING.   Variations in the design and shape of a package communicate differences in the product to consumers. Design refers to the organization of the elements on a package. An effective package design is one that permits good eye flow and provides the consumer with a point of focus.

Package designers bring various elements together in a package to help define a *brand's image*. These elements include shape, size, and label design. One way of evoking different feelings is through the choice of slope, length, and thickness of lines on a package. *Horizontal lines* suggest restfulness and quiet, evoking feelings of tranquility. There appears to be a physiological reason for this reaction—it is easier for people to move their eyes horizontally than vertically; vertical movement is less natural and produces greater strain on eye muscles than horizontal movement. *Vertical lines* evoke feelings of strength, confidence, and even pride. Various baseball teams convey these feelings by wearing packages in the form of vertically striped jerseys, including the New York Yankees and the Minnesota Twins. *Slanted lines* suggest upward movement to most people in the Western world, who read from left to right and thus view sloped lines as ascending rather than descending. Diet Coke's packaging illustrates the use of upward-slanting lines.

Shapes, too, arouse certain emotions and have specific connotations. Generally, round, curving lines connote femininity, whereas sharp, angular lines suggest masculinity. The oval shape of the famous L'eggs pantyhose package is an example of true femininity. The egg-shaped package elicits perceptions of a fragile yet protected product and connotes fashion and perhaps even sex appeal.[8]

---

[7]Dennis J. Moran, "Packaging Can Lend Prestige to Products," *Advertising Age*, January 7, 1980, 59–60.

[8]"Packaging Remains an Underdeveloped Element in Pushing Consumer Buttons," *Marketing News*, October 14, 1983, 3.

A package's shape also affects the apparent volume of the container. In general, if two packages have the same volume but a different shape, the taller of the two will appear to hold a greater volume inasmuch as height is usually associated with volume.

PHYSICAL MATERIALS IN PACKAGING.   An important consideration in packaging is the materials that make up a package. Some marketers are inclined to emphasize cost over all other considerations. The selection of package materials based primarily on cost considerations may be the result of a misguided engineer or accountant; the most important consideration should be the marketing-communications implications of the materials chosen. Increased sales and profits often result when upgraded packaging materials are used to design more attractive and effective packages.

Packaging materials can arouse consumer emotions, usually subconsciously. Packages constructed of *metal* evoke feelings of strength, durability, and coldness; *plastics* connote newness, lightness, cleanliness, and perhaps cheapness.[9] Materials that are *soft*, such as velvet, are associated with femininity. *Foil* has a high-quality image and can evoke feelings of prestige.[10] *Wood* arouses feelings of masculinity. The men's cologne English Leather, for example, has enjoyed much success using a wooden box and a bottle with a large wooden knob as a cap. English Leather's name and rectangular package present an overall image of masculinity by blending design, shape, brand name, and materials in a consistent fashion.

PRODUCT INFORMATION ON PACKAGES.   Product information can come in several forms. In a sense, all of the previous package components (such as color and design) inform consumers (or convey meaning) about what is inside the package. However, when used in the more restricted sense (for our purposes) *product information* refers to key words on the package, information on the back panel, ingredients, warnings, pictures, and illustrations. An example of the effectiveness of information included on packages comes from a field experiment that measured weekly sales of bread. When a "Made with 100% Natural Ingredients: No Artificial Additives" statement was affixed to the package, sales volume increased. When the message was removed, sales returned to their prior level.[11]

The words *new, improved,* and *free* frequently appear on packages. These words stimulate immediate trial purchases or restore a brand purchase pattern

[9]Burleigh B. Gardner, "The Package as Communication," in *Marketing for Tomorrow . . . Today*, eds. M. S. Moyer and R. E. Vosburgh (Chicago: American Marketing Association, 1967), 117–118.

[10]Kevin Higgins, "Foil's Glitter Attracts Manufacturers Who Want Upscale Buyers," *Marketing News*, February 3, 1984, 1.

[11]William H. Motes and Arch G. Woodside, "Field Test of Package Advertising Effects on Brand Choice Behavior," *Journal of Advertising Research*, 24 (February–March 1984), 39–45.

for previous consumers who have switched to other brands. Furthermore, these key words presumably offer consumers what they want—something new, improved, or free.

There is some question whether the key words just cited have been overworked in the marketplace. One study suggests that the new and improved claims on packages do not significantly affect consumer evaluations of certain household and personal care products.[12] More research is necessary to support or refute this point. Perhaps there is a need for new motivating words. Some examples may be the use of numerals, as in Gleem II (toothpaste) and Clorox 2 (laundry bleach). These names inform consumers that there is a new and improved version of an old brand without directly using hackneyed words such as new and improved.[12]

In some instances, putting a short, memorable *slogan* on a package is a good marketing tactic. Slogans on packages are best used when a strong association has been built between the brand and the slogan through extensive and effective advertising. The slogan on the package, a concrete reminder of the brand's advertising, can facilitate the consumer's retrieval of advertising content and thereby enhance the chances of a trial purchase. For example, the classic Ray Charles advertisement for Diet Pepsi ("You got the right one, baby, uh-huh!") carried over to the package when the uh-huh! slogan was printed on cans and bottles of Diet Pepsi.

Not only is the package a critical communication device in the store, it also provides a focus for much advertising effort in television commercials. Research has revealed that television commercials feature packages about 40 percent of the time.[13]

EVALUATING THE PACKAGE: THE VIEW MODEL.   A number of individual features have been discussed in regard to what a package communicates to buyers. It now is fitting to address this issue: What constitutes a good package? Although, as always, no single response is equally suitable across all packaging situations, four general features can be used to evaluate whether a particular package is a good package. These are visibility, information, emotional appeal, and workability, which are conveniently remembered with the acronym **VIEW**.[14]

Visibility signifies the ability of a package to attract attention at the point of purchase. The objective is to have a package stand out on the shelf yet not be so garish that it detracts from a brand's image. Brightly colored packages are especially effective attention getters. Novel packaging graphics, sizes, and shapes

[12]Edward H. Asam and Louis P. Bucklin, "Nutrition Labeling for Canned Goods: A Study of Consumer Response," *Journal of Marketing*, 37 (April 1973), 36–37.

[13]"Packaging Plays Starring Role in TV Commercials," *Marketing News*, January 30, 1987, 6.

[14]Dik Warren Twedt, "How Much Value Can Be Added Through Packaging," *Journal of Marketing*, 32 (January 1968), 61–65.

also may enhance a package's visibility. Brands such as Pepsi, Diet Pepsi, and Cap'n Crunch cereal alternate packages throughout the year with special seasonal and holiday packaging as a way of attracting attention.[15] By aligning the brand with the shopping mood fitting the season or holiday, companies provide consumers with an added reason for selecting the specially packaged brand over more humdrum brands which never vary their package design.

Technological innovations in packaging—such as using holograms on packages and incorporating voice chips into packages—represent another class of attention-getting devices. These technologies are under development and will be appearing on store shelves in the near future.[16]

The second consideration, *information*, deals with product usage instructions, claimed benefits, slogans, and supplementary information (such as cooking recipes and sales promotion offers) that are presented on or in a package. Package information is useful for (1) stimulating trial purchases, (2) encouraging repeat purchase behavior, and (3) providing correct product-usage instructions. The objective is to provide the right type and quantity of information without cluttering the package with excessive information which could interfere with the primary information or cheapen the look of the package.

Emotional appeal, the third component, is concerned with the ability of a package to evoke a desired feeling or mood. Package designers attempt to evoke specific feelings (elegance, prestige, cheerfulness, fun, nostalgia, etc.) through the use of color, shape, packaging materials, and other devices. Packages for some brands contain virtually no emotional content and emphasize instead informational content, while packages of other brands emphasize emotional content and contain very little information.

What determines whether information or emotion is emphasized in a brand's package? The major determinant is the nature of the product category and the underlying consumer behavior involved. With recognition of the distinction drawn in Chapter 3 between the consumer processing model (CPM) and the hedonic, experimental model (HEM), it should be expected that greater informational influence in packaging would go along with CPM-oriented consumer behavior, whereas more emotional influence would be associated with HEM-oriented behavior.

In other words, if consumers make brand-selection decisions based on objectives such as obtaining the best buy or making a prudent choice (CPM-type objectives), then packaging must provide sufficient concrete information to facilitate the consumer's need to make an informed choice. When, however, product and brand selections are made in the pursuit of amusement, fantasies, or sensory stimulation (HEM-type objectives), packaging must contain the requisite emotional content to activate purchase behavior. This discussion should *not* be taken as suggesting that all packaging emphasizes information or emotion. Although

---

[15]Patricia Winters, "Rapt Up in Packages," *Advertising Age*, December 3, 1990, 4.

[16]Cyndee Miller, "Hey, Listen to This: A Talking Package!" *Marketing News*, April 15, 1991, 1, 25.

the packaging of brands in some categories does emphasize one or the other content, there are many product categories where it is necessary for packaging to blend informational and emotional content so as to simultaneously appeal to consumers' rational and symbolic needs.

The final component of the VIEW model is *workability*, which involves how a package functions rather than how it communicates. Several workability issues are prominent: (1) Does the package protect the product contents? (2) Does it facilitate easy storage on the part of both retailers and consumers? (3) Does it simplify the consumer's task in accessing and using the product? (4) Is the package environmentally friendly?

Numerous packaging innovations in recent years have enhanced workability. These include pourable-spout containers for motor oil and sugar, microwavable containers for many food items, aseptic cartons, zip-lock packaging, and less-mess toothpaste containers (e.g., Crest's Neat Squeeze).

There also have been a host of environmentally safe packaging innovations that serve to increase what might be called societal workability. Many of the changes have involved moves from plastic to recyclable paper packages; for example, fast-food chains eliminated the use of foam packaging and L'eggs panty hose removed its famous egg-like plastic container in favor of cardboard packaging. Another significant environmental initiative has been the increase in spray containers as substitutes for ozone-harming aerosol cans.

Workability is, of course, a relative matter. The objective is to design a package that is as workable as possible yet is economical for the producer and consumer. For example, consumers prefer food packages that completely prevent food from getting stale or spoiling, but the manufacturer's ability to provide this degree of workability is limited by cost. At the other extreme, some marketers skimp in their package design and use inexpensive packages that are unsuitable because they are difficult to use and frustrate consumers.

In conclusion, most packages do not perform well on all of the VIEW criteria, but packages need not always be exemplary on all four VIEW components because the relative importance of each criterion varies greatly from one product category to another. Emotional appeal dominates for some products (e.g., perfume), information is most important for others (e.g., staple food items), while visibility and workability are generally important for all products. In the final analysis, the relative importance of packaging requirements depends, as always, on the particular market and the competitive situation.

Brand Naming

A brand is a company's unique designation, or *trademark*, which distinguishes its offering from other product category entries.[17] Many marketing executives

---

[17]For a thorough discussion of the technical and legal aspects of trademarks, see Dorothy Cohen, "Trademark Strategy Revisited," *Journal of Marketing*, 55 (July 1991), 46–59.

consider brand naming to be one of the most important aspects of marketing management.[18] The brand name certainly is the single most important element found on the package. It identifies the product and differentiates it from others on the market. The brand name and package graphics work together to communicate and position the brand's image. A good brand name can evoke a feeling of trust, confidence, security, strength, durability, speed, status, and many other desirable associations.

Through brand names, a company can create excitement, elegance, exclusiveness, and various sensory perceptions. For example, ninety-nine percent of the customers of Polo brand clothing have never seen nor will ever play a match of polo, yet Ralph Lauren through the wise choice of the Polo name was able to endow this brand with a high-status cachet.[19]

Creating a strong brand name and a strong reputation is invaluable for several reasons: First, a strong brand generates consistent sales volume and revenue year after year. Names like McDonald's, Coca-Cola, Sony, IBM, and Levi's are known, respected, and insisted upon around the world. (For a humorous illustration of brand insistence, see Figure 18.2.) Second, a strong brand commands a higher price and larger gross margin. Third, a strong brand provides a platform for introducing new brands. Indeed, the dominant brand strategy in recent years has been to extend well-known brands into other product categories (so-called *brand extensions*). In the first five months of 1991, for example, only five percent of the over six thousand new products introduced to U.S. stores bore new brand names.[20] Fourth, a strong brand provides the manufacturer with leverage when dealing with distributors and retailers. Finally, without a strong brand, the marketer is forced to compete on the basis of price, to be a low-cost producer.[21]

SELECTING A BRAND NAME.   What determines whether a brand name is a good name and how do firms go about developing brand names? These are complex questions and straightforward answers are unavailable. Researchers, however, have investigated the determinants of good brand names.[22] Although the accumulated knowledge is nowhere close to the point of specifying scientific principles, there is some consensus regarding the fundamental

[18]Mark Landler and Zachary Schiller, "What's in a Name: Less and Less," *Business Week*, July 8, 1991, 66–67.

[19]Moran, "Packaging Can Lend Prestige," 59.

[20]Landler and Schiller, "What's in a Name: Less and Less," 67.

[21]Graham Phillips, "The Role of Advertising—Or, the Importance of a Strong Brand Franchise," from a talk in 1986 to senior U.S. marketing executives under the auspices of The Conference Board.

[22]See for example Bruce Vanden Bergh, Keith Adler, and Lauren Oliver, "Linguistic Distinction Among Top Brand Names," *Journal of Advertising Research*, 27 (August/September 1987), 39-44; George Zinkhan and Claude R. Martin, Jr., "New Brand Names and Inferential Beliefs: Some Insights on Naming New Products," *Journal of Business Research*, 15 (1987), 157–172.

A Humorous Illustration of Brand Insistence   FIGURE 18.2

THE FAR SIDE   By GARY LARSON

"Hey! Not this new stuff. ... Me want Jurassic Coke."

requirements that should guide brand name selection. It generally is agreed that a good brand name should accomplish the following tasks:[23]

1. The name must obviously *distinguish the product from competitive brands.* The failure to clearly distinguish a brand from competitive offerings creates consumer confusion and increases the chances that consumers mistakenly will select another brand. Of course, some marketers attempt to hitchhike on the success of better known brands by using names that are similar to the well-known brands, but this is a deceptive and unethical practice that should be condemned.

2. The name should *describe the product or its benefits.* It is important to note in this regard that a brand name need *not* state a specific benefit; rather, it is important that the name provide consumers with an *abstract promise*, not necessarily an actual benefit.[24] Post-It (note pads), I Can't Believe It's Not Butter (margarine), and Healthy Choice (a line of frozen food for health-conscious consumers) illustrate brand names that do outstanding jobs in describing their respective products.

    A recent trend in brand naming is the creation of words which heretofore did not exist as part of people's vocabularies or appear in dictionaries. Many automobile names are of this nature (Acura, Geo, Lumina, and Sentra). Compaq computers and Zapmail are additional examples. All of these names have been created by a company called NameLab, whose sole business is developing brand names for clients. The names developed at NameLab are designed to communicate an image desired by the client. Names are created from *morphemes*, which are the semantic kernels of words. For example, Compaq, which combines two morphemes (com and paq), is an excellent name for suggesting the product's benefits of *com*munication and *com*pactness. The automobile name Acura suggests precision in product design and engineering, while Zapmail evokes an image of superiority by zapping (destroying) the competition.

3. A good brand name should be *compatible with the product.* A good brand name is compatible with a brand's image, its product design, and its packaging. For example, Teddy Grahams Bearwich's (see Figure 18.3) is an ideal name for this product (mini, creme-filled graham crackers). The name resonates the playful image associated with the product and captures the sandwich-like product design (Bearwich's).

---

[23]These requirements represent a summary of views from a variety of sources including Daniel L. Doden, "Selecting a Brand Name That Aids Marketing Objectives," *Advertising Age*, November 5, 1990, 34; and Walter P. Margulies, "Animal Names on Products May Be Corny, but Boost Consumer Appeal," *Advertising Age*, October 23, 1972, 78.

[24]Doden, "Selecting a Brand Name That Aids Marketing Objectives."

A Product-Compatible Brand Name   FIGURE 18.3

Because marketplaces are dynamic and consumer preferences and desires change over time, some brand names lose their effectiveness and have to be changed to avoid negative images. A case in point is Kentucky Fried Chicken. This name was compatible with the product for well over two decades, but a name change was needed when consumers became more health conscious. A change from Kentucky Fried Chicken to simply KFC was undertaken with hopes of preventing the negative implications associated with the word fried.

4. Finally, a good brand name is one that is *memorable and easy to pronounce.* This is why so many brand names are short, one-word names (Tide, Bold, Shout, Edge, Bounce, Cheer, etc.). Probably few words are as memorable as those learned in early childhood, and among the first words learned are animal names. This probably explains marketers penchant for using animals as brand names; for example, automobile companies have used names such as Mustang, Thunderbird, Bronco, Cougar, Lynx, Skyhawk, Skylark, Firebird, Jaguar, and Ram.

In addition to being memorable, animal names can also conjure up vivid images. This is very important to the marketing communicator because, as discussed in Chapter 3, concrete and vivid images facilitate consumer information processing. Dove soap, for example, suggests softness, grace, gentleness, and purity.

POINT-OF-PURCHASE SIGNS AND DISPLAYS

Spectrum of P-O-P Materials

Marketers use a variety of items in point-of-purchase communications. These include various types of signs, mobiles, plaques, banners, shelf tapes, mechanical mannequins, lights, mirrors, plastic reproductions of products, checkout units, full-line merchandisers, wall posters, and numerous other materials.

Many of these materials are *temporary items*, with useful life spans of only weeks or months. Others are relatively *permanent* fixtures that can be used for months or years. Whereas temporary signs and displays are particularly effective for promoting impulse purchasing, permanent P-O-P units compartmentalize and departmentalize a store area to achieve high product visibility, facilitate customer self-service, prevent stock-outs, and help control inventory.

P-O-P's Dramatic Growth

Companies are increasingly investing promotional dollars in point-of-purchase materials. P-O-P expenditures have been growing in the United States by ap-

GLOBAL FOCUS

A LESSON IN HOW TO BEAT GRAY MARKETERS

Gray marketing is big business in the United States, estimated, in fact, to exceed $6 billion per year.[1] Gray-market goods are foreign-manufactured items which bear valid U.S. trademarks and are imported without the consent of the U.S. trademark owner. Items such as this are called gray-marketed goods and not black-marketed because, unlike the latter, they are not counterfeited or stolen. Rather, gray-marketed goods are trademarked brands that are sold through channels of distribution not authorized by the trademark holder.[2]

Procter & Gamble's *Ariel* brand of detergent is a case in point. Until recently this brand was available only in Latin America and Europe. However, even before P&G began officially marketing Ariel in U.S. stores, the brand was widely available in Southern California. The many Mexican and other Hispanic immigrants to California knew Ariel from their native countries. They preferred Ariel to such a degree that a small industry had developed to import gray-marketed versions of Ariel from Tijuana, Mexico.

Seeing an opportunity, P&G executives decided to officially introduce Ariel Ultra to grocery stores in the Los Angeles area. A P&G spokesperson explained that Hispanics were familiar with Ariel and could not be convinced to purchase P&G's American brands of laundry detergents. Hence, P&G responded to consumers' wishes by making Ariel available at their local grocery stores.[3]

[1]Paul I. J. Fleischut, "The Current State of the United States Gray Market: The Common-Control Exception Survives for Now," *Missouri Law Review*, 54 (Spring 1989), 414–423. Cited in Cohen, "Trademark Strategy Revisited," 54.

[2]For further discussion see Cohen, "Trademark Strategy Revisited," 54.

[3]Dan Koeppel, "P&G Tests Foreign Brands in L.A.," *Adweek's Marketing Week*, June 24, 1991, 4.

proximately 12 percent each year. As of 1992, expenditures on in-store promotional materials exceeded $20 billion. This impressive growth is due to the fact that point-of-purchase materials provide a useful service for all participants in the marketing process.

For *manufacturers*, P-O-P keeps the company's name and the brand name before the consumer and reinforces a brand image that has been previously established through advertising. P-O-P calls attention to special offers such as sales promotions and helps stimulate impulse purchasing—as, no doubt, was the case in the American Dairy Association case described in the opening vignette where sales volume in stores with point-of-purchase materials were 29 percent greater than in stores without.

P-O-P serves *retailers* by attracting the consumer's attention, increasing his or her interest in shopping, and extending the amount of time spent in the store—all of which mean increased sales. P-O-P helps retailers utilize available space to the best advantage by displaying several manufacturers' products in the same unit (e.g., many varieties of vitamins and other medicinal items all in one well-organized unit). It enables retailers to better organize shelf space and to improve inventory control, volume, stock turnover, and profitability.

Consumers are served by point-of-purchase units that deliver useful information and simplify the shopping process by setting products apart from similar items.

In addition to benefiting all participants in the marketing process, point-of-purchase plays another important role: It serves as the capstone for an *integrated marketing-communications program*. P-O-P by itself may have limited impact, but when used in conjunction with advertisements and sales promotions, P-O-P can create a synergistic effect.

Functions Performed by P-O-P Materials

P-O-P materials perform four important marketing functions: informing, reminding, encouraging, and merchandising.

INFORMING.   *Informing* consumers is P-O-P's most basic communications function. Signs, posters, displays, and other P-O-P materials alert consumers to specific items and provide potentially useful information.

Displays that move (i.e., *motion displays*) are especially effective for this purpose. Motion displays, though typically more expensive than static displays, represent a sound business investment because they attract significantly higher levels of shopper attention. Evidence from three studies shows that motion displays are often worth the extra expense.[25]

Researchers tested the relative effectiveness of motion and static displays for Olympia beer by placing the two types of displays in a test sample of liquor stores and supermarkets in California. Each of the sampled stores was stocked either with static or motion displays. Another sample of stores, serving as the control group, received no displays. Over 62,000 purchases of Olympia beer were recorded during the four-week test period.

Static displays in liquor stores increased Olympia sales by 56 percent over stores with no displays (the control group). In supermarkets, static displays improved Olympia sales by a considerably smaller, though nonetheless substantial,

---

[25]"The Effect of Motion Displays on the Sales of Beer"; "The Effect of Motion Displays on Sales of Baked Goods"; "The Effect of Motion Displays on Sales of Batteries." All from the Point-of-Purchase Advertising Institute, New York, undated.

amount (18 percent). More dramatic, however, was the finding that motion displays increased Olympia sales by 107 percent in liquor stores and by 49 percent in supermarkets.

A second test of the effectiveness of motion displays used S. B. Thomas English muffins as the focal product. Two groups of 40 stores each were matched by store volume and customer demographics. One group was equipped with an S. B. Thomas English muffin post sign that moved from side to side. The other 40 stores used regular floor displays with no motion. Records of product movement revealed that sales in the stores stocked with motion displays were over 100 percent greater than in stores with static displays.

A study of motion displays for Eveready batteries was conducted in Atlanta and San Diego. In each city, six drugstores, six supermarkets, and six mass merchandisers were studied. The stores were divided into two groups, like the English muffin study. Some newspaper advertising appeared during the test period, but special pricing was the primary promotional element. For mass merchandisers, the static display increased sales during the test period by 2.7 percent over the base period, but surprisingly, sales in the drug and food outlets utilizing the static displays were slightly less (each 1.6 percent lower) than those not using the static displays. By comparison, the motion displays uniformly increased sales by 3.7 percent, 9.1 percent, and 15.7 percent in the drugstore outlets, supermarkets, and mass merchandisers, respectively.

All three sets of results convincingly demonstrate the effectiveness of motion displays. The consumer information-processing rationale (see Chapter 3) is straightforward: Motion displays attract attention. Attention, once attracted, is directed toward salient product features, including recognition of the displayed brand's name. Brand name information activates consumers' memories pertaining to brand attributes previously processed from media advertising. Information on brand attributes, when recalled, supplies a reason for the consumer to purchase the displayed brand.

Hence, a moving display performs the critical in-store function of bringing a brand's name to active memory. The probability of purchasing the brand increases, perhaps substantially (as in the case of S. B. Thomas' English muffins), if the consumer is favorably disposed toward the brand. The Eveready display was less effective apparently because the selling burden was placed almost exclusively on the display. Without prior stimulation of demand through advertising, the static display was ineffective and the motion display was not as effective as it might have been.

Motion displays are widely used for introducing new products and to provide tie-ins with seasonal or holiday advertising campaigns. An especially creative display is the award-winning Coors Light dancing can (see Figure 18.4). The 42" beer-can character was powered by a battery-operated motor that gave the can a real, gyrating appearance, thus providing an extremely effective attention getter.[26]

[26]Joe Fish, "Moving Toward Motion Displays," *POPAI News*, Marketplace 1991, 14.

FIGURE 18.4   A Creative Motion Display

R E M I N D I N G .   A second point-of-purchase function is *reminding* consumers of brands they have previously learned about via broadcast, print, or other advertising media. This reminder role serves to complement the job already performed by advertising before the consumer enters a store.

To fully appreciate the reminder role served by point-of-purchase materials, it is important at this point to address a key principle from cognitive psychology called the **encoding specificity principle.** In simple terms, this principle states that information recall is enhanced when the context in which people attempt to *retrieve* information is the same or similar to the context in which they originally *encoded* the information.[27] (Encoding is the placing of information items into memory.)

A nonmarketing illustration—one that may bring back some unpleasant memories—will serve to clarify the exact meaning and significance of the encoding specificity principle. Recall a time when you were studying for a crucial exam which required problem-solving skills. You may have been up late at night trying to solve a particularly difficult problem, perhaps in accounting, calculus, or statistics. Eventually the solution came to you and you felt well prepared for the next morning's exam. Sure enough, the exam has a problem very similar to the one you worked on just last night. Now, disappointingly and surprisingly, you are unable to solve the problem. Your mind goes blank. But after the exam, back in your room, the solution hits you like the proverbial ton of bricks.

Encoding specificity is the culprit. Specifically, the context (your room) in which you originally encoded a solution to the problem was different than the context (your classroom) in which you subsequently were asked to solve a similar problem. Hence, contextual retrieval cues were unavailable to readily facilitate your recall of how you solved the problem originally.

Returning to the marketplace, consider the situation in which consumers encode information about a brand and its unique features and benefits from television commercials. The advertiser's expectation is that consumers will be able to retrieve this information at the point of purchase and use it to select the advertiser's brand over competitive offerings. It doesn't always work like this, however. Our memories are fallible, especially since we are exposed to the incredible amount of information provided to consumers. Hence, although we may have encoded advertising information at one time, we may not be able to retrieve it without a reminder at the point of purchase.

Take the pink-bunny-pounding-a-drum advertising campaign mentioned in Chapter 11. Most everyone is aware of this campaign but many consumers have difficulty remembering the advertised brand. (Think for a moment, which brand is it?) When facing brands of Duracell, Eveready, and Energizer on the shelf, the consumer may not connect the pink-bunny advertising with any specific brand. Here is where point-of-purchase materials can perform a critically important

[27]Margaret W. Matlin, *Cognition* (New York: Holt, Rinehart and Winston, Inc., 1989), 109.

role. Energizer (the pink-bunny brand) can facilitate encoding specificity by using shelf displays that present the bunny and the Energizer name together (just as they were presented together in advertisements). Accordingly, by providing consumers with encoding-specific retrieval cues, chances are that consumers will recall from earlier advertisements that Energizer is the battery brand that powers the drum-pounding bunny that never stops.

ENCOURAGING.   *Encouraging* consumers to buy a specific item or brand is P-O-P's third communications function. Effective P-O-P materials influence product and brand choices at the point of purchase and can encourage impulse buying.

Consider the case of Isotoner gloves, a product that realizes nearly 75 percent of its annual sales in the five-week shopping period between Thanksgiving and Christmas.[28] Consequently, it is absolutely crucial that Isotoner provide department stores with attractive displays—they put the product on the selling floor in high-traffic locations and encourage shoppers, perhaps on impulse, to consider Isotoner gloves as an appropriate gift item. Figure 18.5 shows the effective displays used by Isotoner.

MERCHANDISING.   The *merchandising* function is served when point-of-purchase displays enable retailers to utilize floor space effectively and boost retail sales by assisting consumers in making product and brand selections.

The merchandising role is well-illustrated with the information-center displays developed by Clairol to merchandise women's hair-coloring products and to answer questions concerning these products. Product information appears on large, colorful header signs above Clairol products placed on the display's shelves. The information center makes product selection easy: Color-coded labels identify product subcategories and shelf dividers separate the various products. When the information center displays were first introduced to retail accounts, Clairol's sales increased an average of 32 percent and shelf space devoted to Clairol products averaged 15 percent more linear feet.[29]

Interactive Point-of-Purchase Displays

One of the major developments of in-store promotions is the interactive display. **Interactive displays** are computerized units that allow consumers to answer questions pertaining to their product-category needs and help them make well-informed product choices. Examples of interactive displays abound.

---

[28]Howard Riell, "Isotoner Has to Stretch Its Tactics to Exploit Brief Selling Season," *Marketing News*, April 1, 1991, 12.

[29]Adapted from "Marketing Textbook: Clairol's Haircoloring Information Center," *POPAI News*, 7, 1 (1983), 3.

The Use of Displays to Encourage Product Choice

FIGURE 18.5

L'eggs Products has an interactive unit called the Pantyhose Advisor that is available in 2,000 food and drug chains and mass merchandisers. The 14" units ask shoppers questions about their height, weight, the occasion for which they are buying pantyhose, and the style of shoes they will be wearing. The unit then recommends two styles of pantyhose and the appropriate size from the L'eggs and Just My Size brands of pantyhose. This unit has reduced the confusion women face when choosing among a wide variety of styles and shades.[30]

Kal Kan, makers of Expert pet food, has introduced the Select-A-Diet interactive unit to assist pet owners in choosing the right nutritional formula of Expert pet food. The unit, attached to supermarket shelves, asks a series of questions regarding a pet's age, weight, and activity level. The unit then recommends the best formula of food for the pet.[31]

The Kelly-Springfield interactive unit is a liquid crystal display that presents questions on car type, driving habits, and tire style performance. Consumers input their answers via a touch key pad and then the unit recommends three tire choices for the consumer to choose among.[32]

---

[30]"The L'eggs Egg Goes Interactive," *POPAI News*, March/April 1990, 28.

[31]"Interactive Unit Is Pet Project for Dog and Cat Food Marketer," *POPAI News*, June/July 1991, 9.

[32]"Kelly-Springfield Electronic Performance Tire Fitment Center," *POPAI News*, Marketplace 1991, 35.

Video Merchandising Centers

A particularly sophisticated version of interactive unit is the *video merchandising center (VMC)*, which displays and sells entire product lines through audio and video presentations. VMCs perform both *informational* and *transactional* functions. That is, they inform and educate consumers about product features and process orders for delivery.

This technology offers important benefits to all participants in the marketing process. A major advantage for *manufacturers* is the ability to broaden product lines at the point of purchase without requiring retailers to increase inventory. For example, Pantene, a Procter & Gamble line of hair care products, had experienced weak distribution and poor in-store visibility. Sales were being lost due to these problems and because retail sales personnel were not always well-informed about Pantene's advantages.

The solution was the Pantene video merchandising center. This VMC included a video monitor that continuously showed animated graphics to attract customer traffic. After being instructed to touch the screen, customers were guided through a series of multiple-choice questions to find out what products had been designed for their particular hair condition. A printout of Pantene's hair-care prescription was automatically provided; the customer then selected the recommended product directly from the display below the monitor. Initial testing in two markets revealed sales increases in excess of 400 percent.[33]

For *retailers*, VMCs broaden product lines without increasing inventories, turn shoppers into buyers, increase sales per square foot, supplement the selling-floor staff, and create on-line inventory replenishment systems.[34] For example, the Florsheim Shoe Company's "Express Shops" enable Florsheim dealers to carry limited assortments of styles and sizes while using the video center to supplement in-store offerings. (See the *Focus on Promotion* for more details.)

The Result of P-O-P: Increased Unplanned Purchasing

Studies of consumer shopping behavior have shown that a high proportion of all purchases in supermarkets, drugstores, and other retail outlets are *unplanned*. In a general sense, this means that many product- and brand-choice decisions are made while the consumer is in the store rather than before he or she arrives

---

[33]This description is based on trade literature from Intermark Corporation, the developers of Procter & Gamble's Pantene merchandising center (1985).

[34]"Interactive Videodiscs Combine Technology with Simplicity to be Consumer Friendly," *POPAI News*, 11 (October 15, 1987), 15.

FOCUS ON PROMOTION

THE WORLD'S SMALLEST SHOE STORES

ByVideo, Inc., the developers of the Florsheim Express Shops, describes them as "the world's smallest shoe stores with the world's largest selection of shoes." Over 17,000 combinations of styles, sizes, and widths are available through the Express Shop. This helps retailers avoid losing sales due to a store not having a particular style, size, or color in stock. The customer merely touches the screen, explores different styles and sizes, makes a selection, and slides a credit card through a reader or pays at the cash register. Orders are transmitted electronically to a central warehouse, and the shoes are delivered to the customer's home within a week. (See Figure 18.6.)

Source: "Florsheim's Pushbutton Sales Force," *Sales and Marketing Management,* June 1987, 23.

at the store. Point-of-purchase materials play a role, perhaps the major role, in influencing unplanned purchasing. The remainder of this section explains unplanned purchasing and describes the research revealing the high incidence of this type of purchase behavior.

The Supermarket Consumer Buying Habits Study, conducted by the Point-of-Purchase Advertising Institute (POPAI), determined that approximately *two-thirds* of all grocery purchase decisions are made while the consumer is in the supermarket aisle (see Table 18.1). The study measured the behavior of 4,000 shoppers nationwide who made over 65,000 purchases. Explanations of study procedures and terminology are needed to fully appreciate these results.

The periodic Supermarket Buying Habits studies are conducted in the following manner. Upon entering a supermarket, a shopper is queried about his or her purchase plans. This initial questioning is used to identify which specific product and brand purchases are planned. Then, actual purchases are compared against planned purchases. This comparison leads to the classification of four types of purchase behaviors:

1. *Specifically planned.* This category represents purchases where the consumer indicates an intent to purchase a specific brand and in fact proceeds to buy that brand. For example, the purchase of Diet Pepsi would be considered a **specifically planned purchase** if a consumer mentioned her intention to purchase that brand and in fact bought Diet Pepsi. As shown in Table 18.1, specifically planned purchases represented just over one-third of all classified purchases in the Supermarket Buying Habits study.

FIGURE 18.6   Illustration of a Video Merchandising Center

Study Results of Supermarket Buying Habits		TABLE 18.1
1. Specifically Planned Purchases		33.9%
2. Generally Planned Purchases	10.6%	
3. Substitute Purchases	2.9	
4. Unplanned Purchases	52.6	
In-Store Decisions (2 + 3 + 4)		66.1%

Source: Point-of-Purchase Advertising Institute's 1986 Supermarket Buying Habits Study.

2. *Generally planned.* This classification applies to purchases for which the shopper indicates an intent to buy a particular product (say, a soft drink) but has no specific brand in mind. The purchase of Diet Pepsi in this case would be classified as a **generally planned purchase** rather than a specifically planned purchase. Generally planned purchases constituted 10.6 percent of the classifications.

3. *Substitute purchases.* Purchases where the shopper does not buy the product or brand he or she indicates constitute **substitute purchases.** For example, if a consumer says she will buy Diet Pepsi but actually purchases Tab, or no diet soft drinks at all, her behavior would be classified as a substitute purchase. These represented just 2.9 percent of all classified purchases.

4. *Unplanned purchases.* Under this heading are purchases for which the consumer had no prior purchase intent. If, for example, she buys Diet Pepsi without having informed the interviewer of this intent, the behavior would be recorded as an **unplanned purchase.** Slightly over half (52.6 percent) of all purchases were classified as unplanned.

A technical point needs to be addressed at this time. Specifically, it is important to recognize that not all purchases recorded as unplanned by POPAI interviewers are truly unplanned. Rather, some purchases are recorded as such simply because shoppers are unable or unwilling to inform interviewers of their exact purchase plans.

This is not to imply that the POPAI research is seriously flawed, but rather that the measurement of unplanned purchases probably is somewhat overstated due to the unavoidable bias just described. Other categories may be biased also. For example, by the same logic, the percentage of specifically planned purchases is probably somewhat understated. In any event, POPAI's findings are important even if they are not precisely correct.

Notice in Table 18.1 that the generally planned, substitute, and unplanned purchases are summed to form total **in-store decisions.** In other words, the three categories representing purchases that are not specifically planned all represent decisions influenced by in-store factors.

The number of in-store decisions totals 66.1 percent. To the extent that the figure is accurate, this indicates that nearly two out of every three supermarket decisions are influenced by in-store factors. It is apparent that P-O-P materials represent a very important determinant of consumers' product- and brand-choice behaviors.

The Use and Nonuse of P-O-P Materials

Various reasons alluded to earlier explain why retailers would want to use the point-of-purchase materials supplied by manufacturers. The fact remains, however, that a large percentage of all signs, posters, wall units, racks, displays, and other P-O-P materials supplied by manufacturers are never used.

WHY P-O-P MATERIALS GO UNUSED.   Four major reasons explain why retailers choose not to use P-O-P materials. First, there is no incentive for the retailer to use certain P-O-P materials because their designers do not consider the retailer's needs. Second, some displays take up too much space for the amount of sales they generate. Third, some materials are too unwieldly, too difficult to set up, too flimsy, or have other construction defects.[35] A fourth reason many signs and displays go unused is because they lack eye-appeal.

WAYS TO GET RETAILERS TO USE P-O-P MATERIALS. Getting retailers to use P-O-P materials is a matter of basic marketing. Persuading the retailer to enthusiastically use a display or other P-O-P device means that the manufacturer must view the material from the retailer's perspective. First and foremost, P-O-P materials must satisfy the retailer's needs and the needs of the retailer's customer (the consumer) rather than just the manufacturer's needs. This is the essence of marketing, and it applies to encouraging the use of P-O-P materials just as much as it applies to promoting the acceptance of their products.

P-O-P materials must be designed so that:

1. they are the right size and format;

2. they fit the store decor;

3. they are "user friendly"—that is, easy for the retailer to attach, erect, or otherwise use;

[35]Don E. Schultz and William A. Robinson, *Sales Promotion Management* (Lincolnwood, IL: NTC Business Books, 1982), 279.

4. they are sent to stores when they are needed (e.g., at the right selling season);

5. they are properly coordinated with other aspects of the marketing communications program (they should tie-in to a current advertising or sales-promotion program); and

6. they are attractive, convenient, and useful for consumers.[36]

SUMMARY

The point-of-purchase is an ideal time to communicate with consumers. Accordingly, anything that a consumer is exposed to at the point of purchase can perform an important communications function. It is for this reason that packaging and brand naming are increasingly important activities. Both inform consumers and influence perceptions and emotions.

The package is perhaps the most important component of the product as a communications device. It reinforces associations established in advertising, breaks through competitive clutter at the point of purchase, and justifies price/value to the consumer. Package design relies upon the use of symbolism to support a brand's image and to convey desired information to consumers. A number of package cues are used for this purpose, including color, design, shape, brand name, physical materials, and product information labeling. These cues must interact harmoniously to evoke within buyers the set of meanings intended by the marketing communicator. Package designs can be evaluated by applying the verbal VIEW model, which contains the elements of visibility, informativeness, emotionality, and workability.

The brand name is the single most important element found on a package. The brand name works with package graphics and other product features to communicate and position the brand's image. The brand name identifies the product and differentiates it from others on the market. A good brand name can evoke feelings of trust, confidence, security, strength, durability, speed, status, and many other desirable associations. A good brand name must satisfy several fundamental requirements: It must describe the product's benefits, be compatible with the product's image, and be memorable and easy to pronounce.

Another class of point-of-purchase communication devices, signs and displays, perform both communications and merchandising functions. A variety of P-O-P materials are used. These are distinguished broadly as either temporary (e.g., signs) or permanent (e.g., integrated merchandising systems). Permanent displays are becoming more common for two principal reasons: They offer the

---

[36]Adapted from Schultz and Robinson, *Sales Promotion Management*, 278–279.

manufacturer substantial savings and they enable the retailer to merchandise the product more effectively.

Research has documented the high incidence of consumers' in-store purchase decision making and the corresponding importance of P-O-P materials in these purchase decisions. The POPAI Supermarket Consumer Buying Habits Study classified all consumer purchases into four categories: specifically planned, generally planned, substitutes, and unplanned decisions. The combination of the last three categories represent in-store decisions that are influenced by P-O-P displays and other store cues. In-store decisions represent nearly two out of every three purchase decisions.

Discussion Questions

1. One of packaging's jobs is to "drive associations established in advertising into the consumer's mind." Give a specific explanation of what this means and use several marketplace illustrations to support your explanation.

2. What is sensation transference? Provide two specific examples to support your answer.

3. In your opinion, why do so many marketers use the words *new* and *improved* on their product packages? Justify why you think this usage is effective or ineffective.

4. With reference to the encoding specificity principle, explain the probable rationale underlying PepsiCo's printing the uh-huh! slogan from its classic Ray Charles advertisement ("You got the right one, baby, uh-huh!") on cans and bottles of Diet Pepsi.

5. Select a packaged goods product category and apply the VIEW model to three competitive brands within that category. Do the following:
   (a) Discuss all four components of the model (define each component and how it applies to your selected product).
   (b) Weigh each component in the model in terms of your perception of its relative packaging importance in your chosen product category; do this by distributing ten points among the four components, with more points signifying more importance and the sum of the allocated points totaling exactly 10. (Note: this weighting procedure involves what marketing researchers refer to as a constant sum scale.)
   (c) Next, evaluate each brand in terms of your perception of its performance on each packaging component by assigning a score from 10 (performs extremely well) to 1 (does not perform well).
   (d) Combine the scores for each brand by multiplying the brand's performance on each component by the weight of that component and then summing the products of these four weighted scores.

The summed score for each of your three chosen brands will reflect your perception of how good that brand's packaging is in terms of the VIEW model—the higher the score, the better the packaging in your opinion. Summarize the scores for the three brands for an overall assessment of each brand's packaging.

6. Select yet another product category and analyze the brand names for three competitive brands in that category. Analyze each brand name in terms of the fundamental requirements that were described in the text. Order the three brands in terms of which has the best, next best, and worst brand name. Support your ranking with specific reasons.

7. Assume you operate a company that competes directly against NameLab and that your company, like NameLab, creates brand names by using a morpheme, or combination of morphemes, that best captures the primary selling feature a client wishes to convey with its new product. Your first client is a company that plans to go into business to compete against Dunkin' Donuts. However, the company's unique advantage is that its donuts are made with a fat substitute (simplesse) and hence are fat-free. The client wants a name for its future donut shops which conveys the idea that its donuts are fat-free but tasty. Create two names you consider appropriate and justify the logic underlying each.

8. What functions can point-of-purchase materials accomplish that mass-media advertising cannot?

9. Explain why the POPAI Supermarket Consumer Buying Habits Study probably overestimates the percentage of unplanned purchases and underestimates the percentage of specifically planned and generally planned purchases.

10. Although not presented in the chapter, the POPAI Supermarket Consumer Buying Habits Study revealed that the percentage of in-store decisions for pet foods and supplies was 55.7 percent, whereas the comparable percentage for herbs and spices was 81.5 percent. What accounts for the 26 percent difference in in-store decision making for these two products? Go beyond these two product categories and offer a generalization as to what product categories likely have high and low proportions of in-store decision making.

11. The discussion of the S. B. Thomas English muffin study pointed out that in stores using motion displays, sales increased by 473 percent. By comparison, sales of Eveready batteries, when promoted with motion displays, increased anywhere from 3.7 percent to 15.7 percent, depending on the type of store in which the display was placed. How would you account for the tremendous disparity in sales impact of motion displays for English muffins compared to batteries?

12. Why were motion and static displays considerably more effective in increasing Olympia beer sales in liquor stores than in supermarkets?

13. What types of product categories do you think are most appropriate for the use of video merchandising centers? Provide a rationale for your response.

CHAPTER NINETEEN

Direct Marketing Communications

IS ROADMASTER ON THE ROAD TO SUCCESS WITH DATABASE MARKETING?

Reminiscent of its automobiles from earlier decades, the Buick Division of General Motors reintroduced the name Roadmaster when it launched the Roadmaster station wagon in 1991. A major decision facing Buick was how to reach the best target customers without wasting advertising dollars. With the help of its advertising agency, McCann-Erickson Worldwide, Buick used the unprecedented approach of targeting Roadmaster magazine ads to potential customers located in select ZIP-code areas. Although magazines have previously offered advertisers the opportunity to direct ads to specific geographic areas, Buick's targeted advertising is the first known case where an advertiser has selected its own list of geographic targets.

Initial magazine ads for the Roadmaster ran in *Time, Newsweek, U.S. News & World Report, People, Sports Illustrated, Entertainment Weekly,* and *Money.* However, what made this advertising campaign revolutionary is that Roadmaster ads were directed at just the 4,940 ZIP codes (out of more than 40,000 national ZIP codes) containing the most likely prospects for Roadmaster station wagons. The targeted ZIP codes were mostly upscale suburbs in the Northeast and Midwest. Though representing only about 20 percent of U.S. households, these ZIP-code areas represent 50 percent of the buyers of large station wagons. This targeted advertising was necessary because Buick expects to sell only about 40,000 Roadmaster station wagons per year.

McCann-Erickson combined information from several different data bases to identify these best-prospect postal areas. Included in each magazine issue was an ink-jet-printed card personally addressed to the subscriber that invited him or her to send for more information about the Roadmaster station wagon. Hence, unlike traditional magazine advertising which has a mass appeal, Buick's ads established a relationship of sorts between the company and specifically named individuals.

Source: Raymond Serafin and Cleveland Horton, "Buick Ads Target ZIP Codes," *Advertising Age,* April 1, 1991, 1, 36.

Earlier chapters introduced various aspects of advertising management with emphasis on the major advertising media: television, magazines, newspapers, radio, and outdoor advertising. Advertising in these media is designed primarily to create brand awareness, convey product information, and to build or reinforce a brand's image.

Historically, these conventional media have been used to reach *mass audiences* and have been judged in terms of cost efficiencies. Marketers now are turning increasingly to techniques such as those described in the opening vignette to fine-tune their customer selection, better serve customer needs, and better serve their own needs by achieving advertising results that are measurable in terms of actual sales response.

This chapter covers the related topics of database marketing and direct marketing, which collectively include direct-response advertising, telemarketing, and direct selling. An overview of direct marketing is provided before turning to each specific topic.

DIRECT MARKETING

Only a few short years ago direct marketing was considered a specialty form of marketing and advertising appropriate only for "book publishers, record clubs, magazines seeking subscriptions, correspondence schools, and sellers of kitchen gadgets and low-priced fashions."[1] Most Fortune 500 firms now are enthusiastic users of database marketing and/or direct marketing. Indeed, direct marketing is one of the growth areas in business.[2] But what precisely is direct marketing?

[1] Edward L. Nash, *Direct Marketing: Strategy, Planning, Execution,* 2d. ed. (New York: McGraw-Hill, 1986), 2.

[2] Stan Rapp and Thomas L. Collins, *MaxiMarketing* (New York: McGraw-Hill, 1987).

The Direct Marketing Association, a trade group whose members practice various forms of direct marketing, offers the following definition:

> **Direct marketing** is an *interactive system* of marketing which uses *one or more advertising media* to effect a *measurable response* and/or transaction *at any location.*[3]

Note the special features in this definition. First, direct marketing involves *interactive marketing* in that it entails personalized communications between marketer and prospect. Second, direct marketing is not restricted to just direct mail but rather involves *one or more media* (e.g., direct mail with telephone marketing). Third, marketing via media such as direct mail allows for relatively greater *measurability of response* in comparison to indirect media such as television advertising. Greater measurability is possible because purchase responses to direct marketing (1) typically are more immediate than responses to mass-media advertising and (2) can be tracked to specific customers. For example, Buick knows precisely which recipients of each ink-jet-printed ad eventually purchase a Roadmaster station wagon. Finally, direct marketing takes place at a *variety of locations*—by phone, at a kiosk, by mail, or by personal visits.

You now have a general understanding of direct marketing; however, you probably remain a little confused because the terminology of direct marketing is somewhat of a semantic jungle because the word *direct* is used in several different ways: direct marketing, direct selling, direct-response advertising, and direct mail.

Figure 19.1 provides a framework to help clarify the distinctions among these various D words. The figure depicts the total marketing process as consisting of indirect and direct marketing and delineates the latter into its various forms.

Indirect marketing includes the use of middlemen in the channel of distribution; examples include distributors or dealers in industrial-goods marketing and retailers in consumer-goods marketing. Indirect marketing is what typically comes to mind when one thinks of marketing.

With *direct marketing* the marketer's purpose is to establish a direct relationship with a customer in order to initiate immediate and measurable responses. Direct marketing is accomplished using direct-response advertising, direct mail (including catalogs), telemarketing, and direct selling.

Direct-response advertising involves the use of any of several media to transmit messages that encourage buyers to purchase directly from the advertiser. *Direct mail* is the most important direct-advertising medium, but certainly not the only one. Direct-response advertising also uses television, magazines,

---

[3]*Fact Book on Direct Response Marketing* (New York: Direct Marketing Association, Inc., 1982), xxiii. Italics not in original.

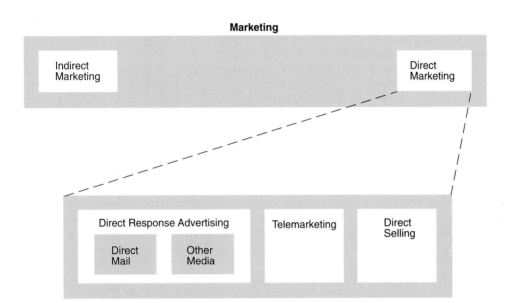

Distinctions Among Various "Direct" Concepts   FIGURE 19.1

and other media with the intent of creating immediate action from customers. *Telemarketing*, the dominant form of direct marketing, involves both using outbound calls from telephone salespersons and handling inbound orders, inquiries, and complaints. *Direct selling* is the use of in-person salespeople (for example, Avon or Tupperware representatives) to sell directly to the final consumer.

As a final preliminary matter, we need also to introduce the practice of database marketing. **Database marketing,** used both by indirect and direct marketers, involves collecting and electronically storing (in a database) information about present, past, and prospective customers. Typical databases include purchase data and other types of relevant customer information (demographic, geographic, and psychographic). The information is used to profile customers and to develop effective and efficient marketing programs by communicating with individual customers and by establishing long-term communication relationships.[4]

Although database marketing and direct marketing are *not* equivalent, the increased sophistication of database marketing has been largely responsible for

[4]This description is adapted from Don E. Schultz, "The Direct/DataBase Marketing Challenge to Fixed-Location Retailing," in Robert A. Peterson (ed.), *The Future of U.S. Retailing: An Agenda for the 21st Century* (New York: Quorum Books, 1992), 165–184.

the growing use and effectiveness of direct marketing. Moreover, indirect marketers (such as Buick in the opening vignette) also have increased their use of database marketing.

Direct Marketing's Phenomenal Growth

Historically, direct marketing represented a relatively small part of most companies' marketing efforts. However, American consumers now spend well over $200 billion annually through mail- and telephone-order sales. Experts place the annual growth rate between 10 and 16 percent.[5] Direct mail is the leading medium used by national advertisers, accounting for nearly one-third of all advertising expenditures. In fact, mail order is the fastest growing form of product distribution in the United States.

A variety of factors help to explain direct marketing's growth. Fundamental *societal changes* (including more women in the work force, greater time pressures, increased use of credit cards, and more discretionary income) have created a need and opportunity for the convenience of direct-marketed products and services. Direct marketing provides shoppers with an easy, convenient, and relatively hassle-free way to buy. This is particularly important to working women and other time-pressured consumers.[6]

Major advances in *computer technology and database management* have made it possible for companies to maintain huge databases containing millions of prospects/customers. *Niche marketing* can be fully realized by targeting promotional efforts to a company's best prospects (based on past product-category purchasing behavior), and who can be identified in terms of specific geographic, demographic, and psychographic characteristics. Indeed, companies have become so proficient with data bases that many consumers are concerned about their privacy being invaded. The *Focus on Promotion* section elaborates on some of these concerns.

The Growth of Business-to-Business Direct Marketing

In addition to the growth of consumer-oriented direct marketing, there has been a tremendous increase in applications of direct marketing for businesses that market to other businesses (business-to-business marketers). Nearly one-third

---

[5]William A. Cohen, "The Future of Direct Marketing," Retailing Issues Letter, vol. 1, published by Arthur Andersen & Co. in conjunction with the Center for Retailing Studies, Texas A&M University, November 1987.

[6]Larry J. Rosenberg and Elizabeth C. Hirschman, "Retailing Without Stores," *Harvard Business Review*, July–August 1980, 103–112.

FOCUS ON PROMOTION

YOU'RE INVADING MY PRIVACY

There is a growing wariness among American consumers that they "have lost all control over how personal information about them is circulated and used by companies.[1] A 1990 Harris poll showed that nearly 80 percent of respondents were concerned that companies were invading their personal privacy. A similar poll in 1977 had identified the percent of concern at less than 50 percent.[2]

The fact is that anytime the consumer charges anything, rents anything, or gives his or her name and address for any reason, there is a good chance that information will end up in some company's data base. Names and addresses then are sold to companies which specialize in the business of compiling and selling mailing lists. Ultimately, the consumer's name appears on multiple lists and the consumer becomes a target for direct-mail and telemarketing efforts.

Consumers' concerns about having their privacy invaded was dramatically revealed in 1991 when an executive of the 1,500-store Blockbuster Entertainment Corp. was quoted in *The Wall Street Journal* as suggesting that Blockbuster was considering selling information about consumers' video rentals to direct marketers. Blockbuster quickly changed any plans it may have had when hundreds of consumers called with complaints. In fact, a Gallup Organization poll indicated that over 75 percent of consumers would take their business elsewhere if they learned that a video rental store was selling information about their rental habits.[3]

[1]Laura Bird, "Marketing in Big Brother's Shadow," *Adweek's Marketing Week*, December 10, 1990, 27.
[2]John Schwartz, "How Did They Get My Name?" *Newsweek*, June 3, 1991, 40–42.
[3]Scott Hume, "Consumers Target Ire At Data Bases," *Advertising Age*, May 6, 1991, 3.

of all money invested in business-to-business marketing goes to direct marketing, especially telemarketing.[7]

A major reason for this trend is the cost of a personal industrial-sales call, which is estimated to exceed $250 per call. Direct marketing through telemarketing and direct mail actually replaces the sales force in some companies,

[7]Kevin Brown, "Mail, Phone Sell Business-to-Business," *Advertising Age*, May 18, 1987, Sec. S, 1.

whereas in other cases it is used to supplement the sales force's efforts by building goodwill, generating leads, and opening doors for salespeople. Over 90 percent of the respondents to a recent survey indicated that direct marketing is an important tool in their business-to-business marketing efforts.[8]

Mail-order selling, telemarketing, and other forms of direct marketing provide attractive options for firms who either prefer to avoid the tremendous expense of a traveling sales force or desire to supplement sales-force effort with supportive marketing communications. Business-to-business direct marketing can reduce marketing costs substantially and provide firms with larger potential markets. Consider the case of General Binding Corporation (GBC), a marketer of printing-related machines and other printing products. GBC's sales force consisted of more than 300 salespersons who sold to tens of thousands of small, medium, and large businesses throughout the country. Escalating sales costs forced the company to find ways other than in-person sales contact to do business with its many smaller customers. GBC found that mail order proved an efficient distribution method for serving the many customers that make small purchases individually but represent huge sales potential collectively.[9]

DIRECT-RESPONSE ADVERTISING

As shown in Figure 19.1, direct-response advertising includes direct mail and other media. Direct mail is by far the dominant direct advertising medium, but some of the advertising placed in conventional mass media (newspapers, magazines, and television) is of the direct-response variety. In general, three distinct features characterize direct-response advertising: (1) it makes a *definite offer*, (2) it contains *all the information necessary to make a decision*, and (3) it contains a *response device* (coupon, phone number, or both) to facilitate immediate action.[10]

An illustration of direct-response advertising is the advertisement for the A-2 leather flying jacket shown in Figure 19.2. This ad satisfies the requirements of a direct-response advertisement in its appeal to readers of the various magazines in which the ad was placed. Note the detailed information and the conspicuous toll-free number. The ad provides prospective customers with interesting background information and solid reasons to buy a Cooper A-2 flying jacket. The ad also offers readers with convenient mechanisms to actualize their purchase

---

[8]*1990/91 Statistical Fact Book* (New York: Direct Marketing Association), 211.

[9]Jack Miller, "Several Factors Converge to Spawn Mail Order's Business-to-Business Sales Growth," *Marketing News*, July 8, 1983, 8.

[10]Bob Stone, "For Effective Direct Results," *Advertising Age*, March 28, 1983, sec. M, 32.

Illustration of Direct-Response Advertising

FIGURE 19.2

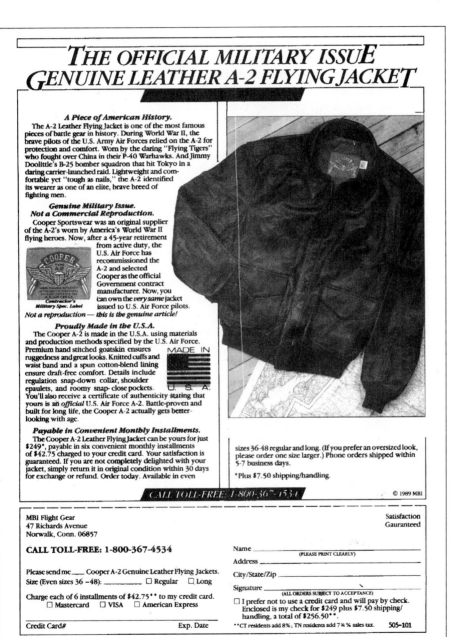

desires—a toll-free number and the opportunity for payment over time in five installments. In addition, the purchaser can return the jacket within 30 days if not fully satisfied. It appears the consumer has little to lose when responding to this offer, which is essential for successful direct marketing.

The direct marketer's objective is to select a medium (or multiple media) that provides maximum ability to segment the market at a reasonable cost. Effective direct-response media selection demands that the marketer have a clearly defined target market in mind. For example, the target market for the Cooper A-2 flying jacket (which was advertised shortly after the U.S.'s Desert Storm conflict with Iraq) probably consists of patriotic young-to-middle-aged men.

Direct Mail

Although direct-response advertisers use various media (such as the magazine ad just described) direct mail is vastly the most important direct-response medium. **Direct mail** advertising is any advertising matter sent through the mail directly to the person whom the marketer wishes to influence; these advertisements can take the form of letters, postcards, programs, calendars, folders, catalogs, blotters, order blanks, price lists, or menus. Direct mail's primary advantages are that it targets specific market segments and measures success immediately by knowing how many customers actually respond.

Additional positive features of direct mail are that it permits greater personalization than does mass media advertising; it can gain the prospect's undivided attention because it is not subject to competing adjacent ads (as is the case with advertising in other printed and broadcast media); it has no constraints in terms of form, color, or size (other than those imposed by cost and practical considerations); and it is relatively simple and inexpensive to change direct-mail ads.[11]

An alleged disadvantage of direct mail is that it is more expensive than other media. On a cost-per-thousand (CPM) basis, direct mail *is* more expensive. For example, the CPM for a particular direct mailing may be as high as $250, whereas a magazine's CPM might be as low as $4. However, compared with other media, direct mail is much less wasteful and will usually produce the highest percentage of responses. Thus, on a *cost per order basis*, direct mail is often less expensive and a better bargain.

WHO USES DIRECT MAIL ADVERTISING?   As noted earlier, direct mail used to be restricted to fairly specialized businesses—book publishers, record clubs, etc. But now all types of marketers are using direct mail as a strategically important advertising medium. *Business Week* magazine claims,

---

[11]Richard Hodgson, *Direct Mail and Mail Order Handbook* (Chicago: Dartnell Publishing Corporation, 1974).

albeit with some hyperbole, that marketers of all types of consumer goods "are turning from the TV box to the mailbox."[12] Some automobile manufacturers, for example, are budgeting as much as 10 percent of their advertising expenditures to direct mail.[13] Cadillac direct mailed brochures of its Seville and Eldorado models to 180,000 prospects who were offered eight-minute videocassettes of each model.[14]

At least four factors account for the trend toward widespread use of direct mail by all types of marketers. First, the rising expense of television advertising along with increased audience fragmentation has led many advertisers to reduce investments in television advertising. Second, direct mail enables unparalleled targeting of messages to desired prospects. Why? Because, according to one expert, it is "a lot better to talk to 20,000 prospects than 2 million suspects."[15] Third, increased emphasis on measurable advertising results has encouraged advertisers to use that medium—namely, mail—which best lends itself to a clear identification of how many prospects purchased the advertised product. Finally, consumers are responsive—surveys indicate that Americans like mail advertisements. For example, Louis Harris & Associates learned that 40 percent of consumers would be "very or somewhat upset" if they could not get mail offers or catalogs.[16]

THE ROLE OF ELECTRONIC DATABASES. Success with direct mail depends greatly upon the quality of mailing lists. Mailing lists of past customers (either of the company's own customers or customers of related products) enable direct marketers to pinpoint the best candidates for future purchases. One observer has aptly dubbed mailing lists "windows to our pocketbooks."[17]

As mentioned in the chapter introduction, the success of modern direct marketing is largely due to the availability of huge computer databases. *Database management* is the construction and maintenance of data lists containing customer and/or prospect names and detailed information for each listing. There are two broad categories of lists: internal (house lists) and external (public lists).[18]

---

[12]"What Happened to Advertising," *Business Week*, September 23, 1991, 69.

[13]Rebecca Fannin, "Detroit's Direct Route," *Marketing and Media Decisions*, February 1989, 41–44.

[14]David Kiley, "A Bold Push for Cadillac's New Models," *Adweek's Marketing Week*, August 26, 1991, 7.

[15]Don Schultz as quoted in Gary Levin, "Going Direct Route," *Advertising Age*, November 18, 1991, 37.

[16]Annetta Miller, "My Postman Has a Hernia!" *Newsweek*, June 10, 1991, 41.

[17]Robert J. Samuelson, "Computer Communities," *Newsweek*, December 15, 1986, 66.

[18]Rose Harper, *Mailing List Strategies: A Guide to Direct Mail Success* (New York: McGraw-Hill, 1986); Bob Stone, *Successful Direct Marketing Methods* (Lincolnwood, IL: NTC Business Books, 1988).

HOUSE LISTS.   A company's own internal records are used to generate house lists. For example, Nintendo of America has a two-million-name data base developed from past purchasers of Nintendo products.[19] Because house lists contain the names of customers who previously responded to a company's offering, they are generally more valuable than external lists. Useful house lists are segregated by the *recency* (R) of a customer's purchase, the *frequency* (F) of purchases, the *monetary value* (M) of each purchase, and the type of products purchased.

Companies typically assign point values to accounts based on the recency, frequency, and monetary value of the consumers' purchases. Each company has its own customized procedure for point assignment (i.e., its own R-F-M formula), but in every case more points are assigned to more recent, more frequent, and larger monetary purchases. The R-F-M system offers tremendous opportunities for database manipulation and direct-mail targeting. For example, a company might choose to send out free catalogs only to those accounts whose point totals exceed a certain amount. In addition to R-F-M information, house lists often categorize customers by geographic, demographic, or psychographic characteristics.

Maintaining a database of current customers is advantageous for several reasons.[20] It provides a company with an opportunity to practice *relationship marketing*—that is, working toward building long-term relations with existing customers rather than focusing solely on cultivating new customers. (See the *Global Focus* for an application of relationship marketing in Great Britain.) It enables a firm to build *customer loyalty and encourage repeat purchasing* by directing promotions to known customers of its products or services. (Airline frequent-flyer programs typify this application.) An additional advantage of maintaining customer lists is the *possibility for cross promotions*. Cross promotions encourage customers of one product to purchase other products marketed by the same company.

EXTERNAL LISTS   There are two types of **external lists.** The first type—*house lists of other companies*—is bought by a firm to promote its own products. These lists are effective because they comprise the names of people who have responded to another company's direct-response offer. The greater the similarity of the products offered by both the buyer and the seller of the list, the greater the likelihood that the purchased list will be effective.

For example, imagine a company that markets coverings that protect automobile exteriors from exposure to the elements. New automobile purchasers who do not have a garage are the best market for this company's products. The

---

[19]Laura Loro, "Data Bases Seen As 'Driving Force,'" *Advertising Age*, March 19, 1991, 39.

[20]Rapp and Collins, *MaxiMarketing*, 216ff.

GLOBAL FOCUS

TAILS MAGAZINE: A BRITISH APPLICATION OF RELATIONSHIP MARKETING

Friskies Petcare, a division of Nestlè, is a small-share company in the $2 billion petfood industry in England. With its major competitors spending heavily on television advertising, marketing personnel at Friskies decided they could use their limited promotional funds in a more efficient way than attempting to compete on television against much heavier spenders. Fortunately, Friskies had built up a five-million-name data base of pet owners.

After considering a number of possible uses for the data base, Friskies and its direct-marketing agency came upon the idea of developing a magazine that would be mailed periodically to consumers in the database. *Tails* magazine was born to position Friskies Petcare among consumers as a caring, high-quality, nutritious brand. The magazine is an excellent vehicle for promoting dialogue between Friskies Petcare and pet owners. It also provides a mechanism for introducing new products and offering promotional inducements for existing products.

Source: "An Animal Instinct for Going Direct," *Marketing Week*, May 2, 1991, 25-26.

coverings marketer could purchase mailing lists from automobile manufacturers and specify names of only those buyers who have purchased an automobile within, say, the last six months and who rent an apartment rather than own their own home.

Compiled lists, the second type of external list, include lists compiled by a company for its own purposes or lists purchased from another company that specializes in list compilation. The first type of compiled list is illustrated by a direct-marketing effort at Kimberly-Clark, makers of Huggies disposable diapers. Each year, Kimberly-Clark's data base identifies by name 75 percent of the 3.5 million new mothers in the United States. (The names are obtained from hospitals and doctors.) Kimberly-Clark sends the new mothers personalized letters, educational literature about caring for a new baby, and cents-off coupons for Huggies.[21] Huggies' database program has been extremely effective, resulting

---

[21]Rapp and Collins, *MaxiMarketing*, 216ff.

in market share growth to 33 percent from 26 percent and an accompanying decrease in media expenses.[22]

The other type of compiled list comes from businesses that specialize in compiling lists and selling them to other companies. List compilers are typically involved in businesses that give them access to millions of consumer names and vital statistics. For example, The Lifestyle Selector, a service of National Demographics and Lifestyles, Inc., is a data-list service provided by a company that originally handled processing of warranty cards for dozens of manufacturers. For each of the millions of names on file, the database contains 10 demographic characteristics (for example, age, sex, and education) and 50 lifestyle characteristics (sports participation, travel activities, etc.).

The Lifestyle Selector enables a direct-mail marketer to order a list containing names and addresses that have been identified based on any combination of lifestyle and demographic characteristics. A manufacturer of men's sporting goods, for example, would be able to request a list matching its desired target market. A possible description of the target market could be the following: males between the ages of 35 and 54 who play golf and enjoy fashion clothing, who are business executives, professionals, or technicians earning $40,000 or more annually, and who possess an American Express credit card.

Donnelly's Share Force program compiles names by including a questionnaire in its coupon mailings (under the name Carol Wright) that go out twice a year to 45 million households. Recipients are households with above-average incomes and greater-than-average numbers of children. Identified as the Carol Wright Super Saver Gift, the mailing offers free gifts, coupons, and product samples to consumers who answer approximately 50 questions related to usage in select product categories and brand preferences. The information is then used to target users of competing brands with coupons and/or samples.[23]

Another example is the Lists-on-Disc™ database of 9.2 million U.S. businesses available on a single CD-ROM disk. The list is compiled by a company called American Business Information, which records company names and addresses from over 4,800 telephone directories from every town and city in the United States. Users can tap into all 9.2 million names or selectively choose companies based on geographic, business type, or other pertinent delineations. Figure 19.3 provides further information about the Lists-on-Disc™ database.

Compiled lists play an important role for marketers of packaged-good products, because these companies are obviously much less able than business-to-business marketers to maintain customer lists. For example, General Foods and R. J. Reynolds Tobacco Co. have compiled databases with 25 million and 30

---

[22]Lynn G. Coleman, "Data-Base Masters Become King of the Marketplace," *Marketing News*, February 18, 1991, 13.

[23]This description is based on "Donnelley Seems to Be Asking All the Right Questions," *Advertising Age*, May 16, 1988, sec. S, 5.

The Lists-on-Disc™ Database FIGURE 19.3

A Complete Business Database — on your PC!

Now there's a single source for information on every U.S. Business. "**Lists-On-Disc**" is the ultimate desktop marketing tool.

Lists-On-Disc was compiled from the Yellow Pages of over 4,800 telephone directories, covering every city and town in the country. Yellow Pages are the most complete source for business information, since virtually every company is listed in its home-town Yellow Pages. And the data is continually updated and telephone verified as the new phone directories are published.

The immense storage capacity of the CD-ROM allows you to access this total U.S. database . . . **over 9.2 million business listings** . . . right on your PC. Retrieve and print lists, perform market research, find out more about a particular company — the uses go on and on.

Lists-On-Disc puts you in control . . .

Get the information you need — when **you** need it! Our easy-to-use software gives you the flexibility to retrieve information in seconds. And only the information you want; you make the decisions on what types of businesses and what markets to select.

We also give you maximum flexibility to select the output format that works best for you:

- Prospect Lists
- Mailing Labels
- Telemarketing Cards
- Diskette Formats

With **Lists-On-Disc** unique record key system, you'll have unlimited screen-viewing of the company name city, state, and telephone number. When you need complete information — such as full address, S.I.C. Code, number of employees — the record key "counts" only what you print or download from the disc. Your first 1,000 records are included in the annual license fee.

This system allows you to use the entire database of 9.2 million businesses for such things as doing market research, previewing lists prior to purchase, or getting counts . . . all for an extremely affordable price. No other desktop marketing product allows you this type of flexibility on a PC.

million names, respectively.[24] Compiled lists are not as desirable as house lists, however, because they do not contain information about the willingness of a person to purchase by mail. The characteristics of the members of compiled lists may also be too diversified to serve the purposes of the direct mailer. However, some compiled lists are put together with considerable care and may serve the direct mailer's specific needs.

Catalog Marketing

Though a form of direct mail, catalog marketing deserves a separate section due to its distinctiveness and tremendous growth in recent years. For clarity, it should be noted that there are actually four types of catalogs: (1) *retail catalogs* designed by retailers to increase store traffic; (2) *full-line merchandise catalogs* (including Sears and J.C. Penney); (3) *consumer specialty catalogs* (like the L. L. Bean sporting goods and ready-to-wear catalog); and (4) *industrial specialty catalogs*, which are used by business-to-business marketers to reach smaller customers while freeing up the sales force's time to devote to larger, more promising accounts.

The greatest growth in cataloging is consumer specialty catalogs. Name the product, and at least one company is probably marketing that item via catalog—food items (cheese, candy, pastry, steaks), clothing, furniture . . . the list goes on and on.

The growth rate for catalog sales in the United States far exceeds the growth rate for retailers.[25] Various factors account for this growth. From the *marketer's perspective*, catalog selling provides an efficient and effective way to reach prime prospects. From the *consumer's perspective* (1) catalogs save time because people do not have to find parking spaces and deal with in-store crowds; (2) catalog buying appeals to consumers who are fearful of shopping due to rising crime rates; (3) catalogs allow people the convenience of making purchase decisions at their leisure and away from the pressure of a retail store; (4) the availability of toll-free 800 numbers and credit-card purchasing has made it easy for people to order from catalogs; and (5) people are confident in purchasing from catalogs because merchandise quality and prices are often comparable to what is available in stores and guarantees are attractive.

As examples of this last point, consider the policies of two very successful catalog marketers, Lands' End and L. L. Bean. Lands' End's Fair Pricing Policy states:

> We price our products fairly and honestly. We do not, have not, and will not participate in the common retailing practice of inflating markups to set up a future phony "sale."

[24]Howard Schlossberg, "Marketers Moving to Make Data Bases Actionable," *Marketing News*, February 18, 1991, 8.

[25]Ed Fitch, "Election Year Frenzy Bane of Catalogers," *Advertising Age*, August 1, 1988, sec. S, 2.

L. L. Bean's guarantee claims:

All of our products are guaranteed to give 100% satisfaction in every way. Return anything purchased from us at any time if it proves otherwise. We will replace it, refund your purchase price or credit your credit card, as you wish. We do not want you to have anything from L. L. Bean that is not completely satisfactory.

Although catalog marketing is pervasive, signs indicate it has reached the mature life-cycle stage. A variety of factors point to this fact. First, according to industry observers, the novelty of catalog scanning has worn off for many consumers. Second, as is typically the case when a product or service reaches the maturity stage, the costs of catalog marketing have increased dramatically. A primary reason is that firms have incurred the expenses of developing more attractive catalogs and compiling better mailing lists in the effort to out-perform their competitors. Costs have been further strained by third-class postal rate increases in recent years and sharp increases in paper prices.

Some catalog companies have responded to the slow down by sending out even more catalogs than they mailed in the past. Other companies are scaling back their efforts. Many marginal companies are beginning to drop out, which invariably is the case when an industry reaches the maturity stage.

In sum, the best days in U.S. catalog marketing are history for most catalog companies. Some companies will continue to flourish, but many others will find it unprofitable to remain in the catalog business.[26]

TELEMARKETING AND TELEMEDIA

Telephone marketing is *the* dominant form of direct marketing. Telephone marketing consists of both telemarketing and telemedia. Where **telemarketing** deals primarily with selling products over the phone, **telemedia** uses the phone to merchandise, advertise, and market products and services.[27]

Telemarketing

As earlier noted, many companies use the telephone to support or even replace their conventional sales forces. Telemarketing uses *outbound calls* from

[26]Francine Schwadel, "Catalog Overload Turns Off Consumers," *The Wall Street Journal*, October 28, 1988, sec. B, 1.

[27]Alison Fahey, "Fledgling 'Telemedia' Fights for Respect," *Advertising Age*, November 19, 1990, 50.

telephone salespersons for purposes of (1) opening new accounts, (2) qualifying advertising leads, and (3) servicing existing business, including reorders and customer service. Telemarketing is used in conjunction with advertising, direct mail, catalog sales, and face-to-face selling.

Telemarketing's versatility applies to both consumer-oriented products and business-to-business marketing. IBM, for example, uses telemarketing to cover its small- to medium-size accounts, generate incremental sales, enhance the productivity of traditional sales representatives via the leads and information that it provides, and ensure customer satisfaction and buying convenience. IBM has a fully integrated system of mail, catalog, and inbound and outbound telephone activity for its hardware, software, supplies, and services. The strategy is to transform a prospect or a dormant account into an active account, then to service the account with as little in-person sales contact as possible.[28]

WHO SHOULD USE TELEMARKETING?   Telemarketing is not appropriate for all sales organizations. The following eight factors should be considered when evaluating the suitability of introducing a telephone sales force.[29]

1. An initial consideration is an evaluation of *how essential face-to-face contact is;* the more essential it is, the less appropriate is telemarketing.

2. A second consideration is *geographical concentration.* Telephone selling may represent an attractive alternative to in-person selling if customers are highly dispersed; if however, customers are heavily concentrated (such as apparel makers in Manhattan, or automobile manufacturers in Detroit), minimal travel time is required and personal selling is probably preferable.

3. *Economic considerations* involving average order size and total potential should be estimated to determine whether in-person sales is cost-effective. In cases of small and marginal accounts, customers may be served more economically by telephone.

4. A fourth area for evaluation is *customer decision criteria.* Telephone sales may be sufficient if price, delivery, and other quantitative criteria are paramount, but in-person sales may be essential in instances where product quality, dealer reputation, and service are uppermost in importance.

5. A fifth factor is the *number of decision makers* typically involved in purchasing a company's product. Face-to-face contact is typically necessary when several decision makers are involved—for example, when an industrial

---

[28]This description is an adaptation of remarks from Peter DiSalvo in "3 Telemarketers Tell How to Hire, Train, Organize for this Profitable Direct Medium," *Marketing News*, July 8, 1983, 4.

[29]Hubert D. Hennessey, "Matters to Consider Before Plunging into Telemarketing," *Marketing News*, July 8, 1983, 2.

engineer, a purchasing agent, and financial representative all have input into a purchase decision.

6. Another consideration is the *nature of the purchase.* Routine purchases (such as office supplies) can be handled easily by phone, whereas more complex purchasers will likely require face-to-face interactions.

7. The *status of the major decision maker* is a seventh consideration. The telephone is acceptable for buyers, purchase agents, and engineers, but probably not for owners, presidents, and vice presidents.

8. A final consideration is an *evaluation of the specific selling tasks* that telemarketing is or is not capable of performing. For example, telephone representatives may be particularly effective for prospecting and postsale follow-ups, whereas in-person sales effort is needed for the intervening sales task—preapproach, approach, presentation, objection handling, and closing.

These eight factors make it apparent that telephone selling is appropriate and effective in certain situations but not others. Systematic application of this eight-step process should enable a company to determine whether and to what extent telemarketing is appropriate for serving its customers.

Telemedia

Telemedia involves the use of *inbound* telephone marketing. It includes both the toll-free, or 800, number option and the Dial-It, or 900, number service, which is not a free call for the user.

TOLL-FREE (800 NUMBER) TELEMEDIA. 800 numbers are virtually everywhere, in fact there are more than one-half million 800 numbers in the United States.[30] Every time you open a magazine, turn on the television, or pick up a newspaper, you hear, "Call 1-800-XXX-XXXX." An 800-number telecommunication program uses an incoming WATS (wide area telecommunication service) telephone system to encourage potential customers to phone a publicized number (an 800 number) in response to media advertising or other marketing communications. This 800 number, correctly inserted in advertisements, can be used by motivated, self-qualified consumers to request product or service information, place direct orders, express complaints or grievances, request coupons or other sales-promotion materials, and inquire about the nearest dealers or outlets.

Customer-service representatives who receive 800 calls can provide immediate responses to requests for merchandise and product information and can

---

[30]Terry Lefton, "Toll-Free Turf Wars," *Adweek's Marketing Week,* January 27, 1992, 28.

handle complaints. Additionally, representatives can record callers' names and addresses to initiate immediate follow-ups by sending promotional materials. Also, the effectiveness of an advertising campaign can be measured quickly.

Toll-free numbers are widely used because they are valuable adjuncts to marketing communications programs. Although there are distinct benefits with 800 numbers, there also are potential problems. One problem is that 800 service communicators are sometimes improperly trained or unskilled. A second potential problem is that there may be an insufficient number of lines to handle incoming calls. Third, failure to integrate the 800 number carefully into a company's marketing program can be extremely wasteful. Advertising, sales promotions, and 800 numbers need to be coordinated carefully to achieve their maximum, synergistic effects.

DIAL-IT (900 NUMBER) TELEMEDIA. The Dial-It, or 900 number, service was introduced by AT&T to permit callers, who pay a fee, to phone a central number and register an opinion on a particular issue. The 900 service is the only national communication medium that can accept simultaneous calls by large numbers of people at a flat rate. The first major use of the Dial-It service was during the Carter-Reagan debate in 1980, when over 700,000 people spent 50 cents each to call a 900 number and register their opinions about who won the debate. Since then, the use of 900-number telemedia activity has increased substantially.

Sleazy sex operations, contest scams, and other unscrupulous efforts have dominated 900-number telemedia usage; nonetheless, there are legitimate uses for 900-number technology.[31] One use is to update customers about services that are subject to frequent changes. For example, the American Bankers Association has sponsored a 900-number service to inform callers of the most recent interest rates on various financial instruments. Dial-It numbers are also used as sources of sports information, weather updates, and travel information. Companies have also used 900 numbers in concert with sweepstake offers. For example, Revlon ran a sweepstake as part of a freestanding insert carried in newspapers. Recipients of the FSI were instructed to call a 900 number and recite a four-digit code to learn if they were instant winners.

Telephone Marketing under Attack

The dramatic increase in the use of telephone marketing, both telemarketing and telemedia, has inevitably included some untoward practices. Consumers are besieged by calls from telemarketers at undesirable times, particularly during

---

[31]Cyndee Miller, "It's Not Just for Sleaze Anymore: Serious Marketers Want Consumers to Dial 1-900," *Marketing News*, October 15, 1990, 1-2; Scott Hume, "900 Numbers: The Struggle for Respect," *Advertising Age*, February 18, 1991, sec. S, 1.

the dinner hour. More extreme are telemarketing scams that deceive credulous individuals into thinking they are dealing with legitimate businesspeople. Vitamin-pill ripoffs, travel scams, fake AIDS cures, and phony art reproductions are just some of the fraudulent telemarketing practices used in recent years.[32] It is estimated that American consumers lose over $1 billion annually to telephone scam artists.[33]

Many consumers are disgusted with all forms of telephone marketing except 800 numbers. Likewise, in response to consumer complaints, government regulators have taken action in hopes of preventing further abuses.[34] Telephone marketers will eventually have to clean up their acts or suffer reprisals from irate customers and legislators.

DIRECT SELLING

An important though relatively minor aspect of direct marketing is direct selling. Direct selling involves the personal explanation and demonstration of products and services to consumers in their homes or at their jobs. Amway, Avon, Mary Kay Cosmetics, and Tupperware are just a few of the hundreds of companies that market directly to consumers.

Annual direct sales in the United States exceed $9 billion. Japan, where annual direct sales exceed $16 billion, is the only country where direct-selling activity is greater than in the United States. Nearly everything is sold direct in Japan—including products ranging from condoms to automobiles. Over 75 percent of all automobiles sold in Japan are sold by direct salespeople!

Returning to the United States, approximately 6 million Americans (5 percent of the labor force) work in direct sales.[35] The number and quality of direct salespeople varies inversely with the economic cycle. More people gravitate toward direct selling when the economy suffers, such as during the recession of 1991-1992.[36] The vast majority of direct salespeople work part-time. For the

[32]"Dial M for Marketing Fraud," *Newsweek*, May 16, 1988, 56.

[33]Ann Lallande, "The Teletroublemakers," *Marketing and Media Decisions*, May 1989, 128.

[34]Amy E. Gross, "Regulators Push the Hot Button on 900," *Adweek's Marketing Week*, October 15, 1990, 52, 54; Eric Weissenstein and Steven W. Colford, "Close Calls for 900," *Advertising Age*, May 13, 1991, 45.

[35]Thomas R. Wotruba and Pradeep K. Tyagi, "Met Expectations and Turnover in Direct Selling," *Journal of Marketing*, 55 (July 1991), 24–36.

[36]Elaine Underwood, "Building the Recovery, Door-to-Door," *Adweek's Marketing Week*, January 27, 1992, 16.

most part, direct salespeople are *independent contractors* and not employees of the firms whose products they represent. In fact, 98 percent of all direct salespeople work as independent contractors. The rate of salesperson turnover is very high, over 100 percent annually.[37]

Three primary types of direct-selling programs are practiced: (1) *repetitive person-to-person selling* occurs when salespeople visit homes or job sites to sell frequently purchased products/services (e.g., Avon cosmetics); (2) *nonrepetitive person-to-person selling* is used for infrequently purchased products/services (e.g., encyclopedias); and (3) *party plans* are used in which salespeople offer products to groups of people at homes or job sites (e.g., Tupperware parties).

Direct Selling Moves to the Office

In past years, when fewer women worked outside the home, door-to-door direct selling was effective. Now, however, with huge numbers of American women in the work force, in-home selling has diminished due to both fewer customers and fewer salespeople. Tupperware alone lost over 10,000 salespeople during the early-to-mid 1980s. As a result, more and more direct selling is taking place in the workplace. Avon, for example, now gets over 25 percent of its sales from buyers at businesses.[38] Many of the direct-selling industry's current sales representatives are themselves in the work force, and their customers are work associates.

On-the-job direct selling is not restricted to cosmetics and food containers. For example, the clothier Alfred Dunhill of London sends tailors with fabric swatches to fit executives on the job. The average Dunhill sale is $4,000. (Top-of-the-line Dunhill suits are priced at about $3,000)[39]

Whether door-to-door or office-to-office, direct selling has a promising future in the United States and elsewhere. The industry has begun to adapt to social changes and is showing signs of growing sophistication. One remaining negative that needs to be overcome is the presence of a relatively small number of shysters such as those who operate pyramid schemes.[40]

---

[37]For an interesting study of turnover in the direct selling industry, see Wotruba and Tyagi, "Met Expectations and Turnover in Direct Selling."

[38]Kate Ballen, "Get Ready for Shopping at Work," *Fortune*, February 15, 1988, 95, 98.

[39]Ibid.

[40]The Direct Selling Association defines pyramid schemes as "illegal scams in which large numbers of people at the bottom of the pyramid pay money to a few people at the top. Each new participant pays for the chance to advance to the top and profit from payments of others who might join later." DSA distinguishes between illegitimate pyramid schemes and legitimate multi-level marketing involving different levels of product distributorships.

However, most direct-selling operations are legitimate businesses. The day of the quick-talking, high-pressure salesman ended in the 1970s with the enactment of *cooling-off laws*. Consumers were given three business days to back out of a purchase (i.e., to cool off) and obtain a full refund.

SUMMARY

Direct marketing is the most rapidly growing aspect of marketing activity in the United States. Direct mail is the dominant direct-marketing advertising medium. The outstanding advantages of this medium are that marketers can target messages to specific market segments and determine success (or failure) virtually immediately. Direct mail also permits greater personalization than mass media advertising and is not subject to the clutter of competing ads such as those that appear in other print and broadcast media. On a cost-per-order basis, direct mail is often less expensive and more efficient than alternative media.

Magazines, newspapers, and television are additional media used by direct marketers. Catalog marketing is a form of direct marketing that has enjoyed spectacular success but is now abating. Factors that account for this growth include consumer time savings, buying freedom, greater disposable income, and increased confidence in mail-order buying.

Telephone marketing is a special form of direct marketing in which the telephone is the major direct-marketing medium. Two forms of telephone marketing are practiced. One, *telemarketing*, involves outbound calls from telephone salespersons to customers and prospects; the other, *telemedia*, involves handling inbound calls for orders, inquiries, and complaints. The growth of outbound telemarketing is attributable in large part to the enormous expense of in-person sales contacts, which exceed $250 on average. Telemarketing can be used to support or even replace a conventional sales force.

Inbound telemedia activities include the well-known toll-free, or 800 number, programs and the lesser-known Dial-It, or 900 number, service. Toll-free programs have experienced tremendous growth and now consist of over 500,000 toll-free numbers in the United States. Dial-It (900 number) telemedia was introduced initially by AT&T to permit callers to pay a fee for a phone call to register an opinion on a particular issue. Many unscrupulous operators began using 900 numbers shortly thereafter. Nonetheless, there are numerous potential uses of 900 numbers by legitimate telephone marketers.

Direct selling is the final topic covered in the chapter. Direct selling has changed rather dramatically in recent years, largely due to growing numbers of women in the workforce. Direct selling is increasingly taking place in offices and factories rather than in the home.

Discussion Questions

1. Explain the differences among direct marketing, direct sales, direct-response advertising, and direct mail.

2. Why has direct marketing enjoyed such rapid growth in recent years?

3. Direct selling plays a much bigger role in Japan than elsewhere in the world. Salespeople go door-to-door and office-to-office to make sales. What is it about Japanese society compared to U.S. society that explains the greater importance of direct selling in Japan?

4. As noted in the chapter, direct marketing constitutes around 75 percent of the automobile sales in Japan. Could direct selling be used in the United States for selling automobiles? Justify your response.

5. Your company, Computer Supplies, Inc., sells computer supplies (paper, ribbons, diskettes, etc.) to thousands of business and nonbusiness organizations. Because most orders are relatively small, selling costs are extremely high relative to revenues. The vice president of sales is evaluating the implementation of a telemarketing program directed at all accounts whose annual purchases are less than $10,000. What factors should the V.P. consider? Be specific.

6. Figure 19.2 in the text was an ad for the Cooper A-2 leather flying jacket. Assume the manufacturer of this product chose to use direct mail to market the jacket in addition to advertising it in magazines. Explain how you, as vice president of marketing for this company, would acquire a mailing list. What demographic and lifestyle factors would you select in generating the list?

7. Jewelry, clothing, electronics, toys, and exercise equipment are some of the products frequently featured on televised home-shopping programs. Why are these particular products suitable for this form of direct marketing? Profile the typical consumer who buys products via home-shopping programs.

8. John Deere, a major company in the lawn-tractor business, includes an 800 number at the bottom of its advertisement. A relatively unknown competitor, Kubota, includes this statement at the bottom of its ads: "To learn more about our tractors and other power products, please write Kubota Tractor Corporation [address followed]." How responsive do you think consumers would be in writing for more information? How could a company like Kubota justify not installing an 800-number service?

9. What should government regulators do to prevent telemarketing abuses? Should prohibitions be placed on telemarketing?

10. Assume you are a direct marketer of a line of merchandise imprinted with major university logos. These items are targeted to the fans and supporters of

the universities' athletic programs. Detail how you would compile a mailing list. Use your college or university for illustration.

11.   Conduct five to ten interviews with nonstudent adults regarding their attitudes toward telemarketing. Are they hassled often? Do they mind having telephone salespeople call them? What specific complaints do they have?

12.   Go through a recent consumer magazine and list every advertiser that employs a toll-free 800 number. Describe the specific function that the 800 number is apparently intended to serve for each advertiser.

CHAPTER TWENTY

Public Relations and Sponsorship Marketing

NEGATIVE PRODUCT SAFETY NEWS

Every five years or so it seems that charges of unsafety are brought against some automobile company. The first major outcry occurred in the 1960s when the Chevrolet Corvair was accused of being a dangerous and poor-handling automobile. When Ralph Nader's famous book, *Unsafe at Any Speed*, hit bookstore shelves in 1965, Corvair sales plummeted. In two years Corvair's submarket share declined from a high of 25.3 percent in 1965 to 4.2 percent in 1967.[1]

A more recent negative publicity case involves the Suzuki Samurai. American Suzuki Motor Corporation, marketers of the Samurai, achieved tremendous success upon introducing the Samurai to the United States. Over 160,000 Samurais were sold in just three years. The Samurai appealed primarily to youthful consumers who identified with the product's inexpensive and fun-oriented positioning.

Samurai's future looked positive, to say the least. But the situation changed dramatically when NBC-TV aired a report that revealed the Samurai's high propensity to tip over. Then, Consumers Union, publishers of *Consumer Reports*, announced it had found the Samurai "not acceptable." No vehicle had received that rating in nearly 10 years. Consumers Union's testing revealed that the Samurai toppled repeatedly when making sharp turns at about 40 miles per hour. The U.S. Government's Office of Defects Investigation had identified 67 rollover accidents involving the Samurai. Those accidents had resulted in 20 deaths and 87 injuries.[2]

A Suzuki spokesman defended the Samurai record, claiming, "We have absolute confidence that we are selling a safe and stable vehicle."[3] The company also held a news conference challenging Consumers Union's report, but nonetheless, sales of the Samurai immediately fell. Suzuki eventually settled law suits with seven states (California, Massachusetts, Minnesota, Missouri, New York, Texas, and Washington) and agreed to announce in future advertising that the Samurai could roll over if turned too sharply.

[1]This statistic is based on Marc G. Weinberger, Jean B. Romeo, and Azhar Piracha, "Negative Product Safety News: Coverage, Responses, and Effects," *Business Horizons*, 34 (May/June 1991), 23–31.

[2]"Follow-Up: Some Suzuki Rollovers," *Consumer Reports*, August 1988, 487.

[3]"A Tough Turn for the Suzuki Samurai," *Newsweek*, June 13, 1988, 49.

The opening vignette points out a potential problem that all companies may face—the possibility of negative publicity and the disastrous consequences that may follow. Handling negative publicity is one of the roles relegated to public relations. This chapter explores the multiple roles performed by the public-relations function.

The chapter also treats the related topics of event and cause marketing as part of the more general practice known as sponsorship marketing. These growing aspects of the promotion mix are conceptually aligned with public relations and in some organizations are administratively part of the public-relations department.

PUBLIC RELATIONS

Public relations, or **PR,** is that aspect of promotion management uniquely suited to fostering *goodwill* between a company and its various publics. PR efforts are aimed at various publics, primarily the following: consumers, employees, suppliers, stockholders, governments, the general public, labor groups, and citizen action groups (see Figure 20.1).

When effectively integrated with advertising, personal selling, and sales promotion, public relations is capable of accomplishing objectives other than goodwill. It can also increase brand awareness, build favorable attitudes toward a company and its products, and encourage purchase behavior.

FIGURE 20.1   The Various Publics with Which Public Relations Interacts

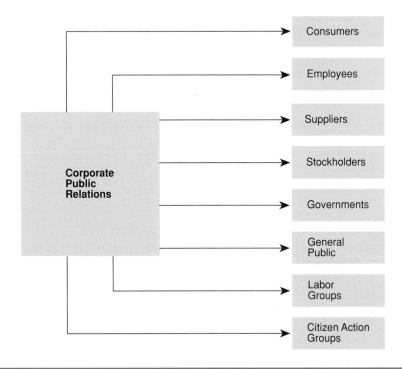

Public Relations Activities and Functions

Public relations entails a variety of specific functions and activities, of which the following are most important.

ADVICE AND COUNSEL.   Public-relations input is required in any decision that has significant implications for any of an organization's publics. For example, a decision to construct a new manufacturing facility in a geographic area where wildlife may be disturbed would require PR advice and counsel to determine how best to deal with environmentalists and other concerned citizens groups.

PUBLICATIONS.   Public-relations personnel prepare a variety of publications: newsletters for employees, pamphlets and brochures for stockholders, reports for governmental agencies on matters involving corporate interests, and so on.

PUBLICITY.   The public-relations department serves as the prime source of an organization's contact with the news media. News releases and press conferences are two of the most important avenues for corporate publicity. Publicity activities take two extreme forms: (1) disseminating *positive publicity* (news about product innovations, announcements of corporate philanthropic activities and so on), or (2) dealing with *negative publicity* during periods of corporate crisis (such as the situation with the Suzuki Samurai). More information on the important topic of publicity will be offered in a later section.

RELATIONS WITH PUBLICS.   Public-relations personnel deal with various publics in matters involving any company decisions, policies, or impending actions that have ramifications for these publics. Dealing with employees in matters of plant closings, with stockholders during times of financial exigency (such as a takeover crisis), with environmentalists during periods of ecological conflict (such as the massive Exxon Valdez oil spill in Alaska), and with governments in matters of public policy are some of the major forms of public relations.

CORPORATE IMAGE ADVERTISING.   This form of advertising, which was discussed in Chapter 11, is often the work of the public-relations department in coordination with the organization's advertising department.

PUBLIC OPINION.   Public-relations departments work closely with marketing-research departments on matters involving public opinion. Because public opinion is often volatile, it is important that PR departments spot emerging trends that have relevance for corporate policies and actions.

MISCELLANEOUS.   Public-relations departments are sometimes responsible for handling speaker's bureaus, corporate donations, scholarships and awards programs, and other specialized programs.

Specific Forms of Public Relations

It is important now to make some finer distinctions so that the promotion management and marketing communications aspects of public relations are brought into sharper focus and distinguished from the more general aspects of public relations.

As just described, PR involves relations with all of an organizations' relevant publics—employees, stockholders, governments, etc. Most PR activities do *not* involve marketing per se, but rather deal with general management concerns. This more encompassing aspect of public relations can be called *general PR*. Interactions with employees, stockholders, labor groups, citizen action groups, and suppliers are typically part of a company's general, nonmarketing public relations.

Our concern is only with the more narrow aspect of public relations involving an organization's interactions with consumers or with other publics (such as governments) regarding marketing matters (like product safety). The marketing-oriented aspect of public relations is called *marketing PR*, or *MPR* for short.

Marketing PR can be further delineated as involving either proactive or reactive public relations.[1] **Proactive MPR** is *dictated by a company's marketing objectives.* It is offensively rather than defensively oriented and opportunity-seeking rather than problem-solving. Proactive MPR is another tool in addition to advertising, sales promotion, and personal selling for promoting a company's products and services.

Reactive MPR, by comparison, is the conduct of public relations *in response to outside influences.* It is undertaken as a result of external pressures and challenges brought by competitive actions, changes in consumer attitudes, changes in government policy, or other external influences. Reactive MPR typically deals with changes that have *negative consequences* for the organization. Reactive MPR attempts to repair a company's reputation, prevent market erosion, and regain lost sales.

Proactive MPR

The major role of proactive MPR is in the area of *product introductions or product revisions.* Proactive MPR is integrated with other promotional devices to give a product additional exposure, newsworthiness, and credibility. This last factor, *credibility,* largely accounts for the effectiveness of proactive MPR. Whereas advertising and personal selling claims are sometimes suspect—because we question salespeople's and advertisers' motives, knowing they have a personal stake in persuading us—product announcements by a newspaper editor or television broadcaster are notably more believable. Consumers are less likely to question the motivation underlying an editorial-type endorsement.

Publicity is the major tool of proactive MPR. Like advertising and personal selling, the fundamental purposes of marketing-oriented publicity are to engender brand awareness, enhance attitudes toward a company and its brands, and possibly influence purchase behavior.

Companies obtain publicity using various forms of news releases, press conferences, and other types of information dissemination. News releases concerning new products, modifications in old products, and other newsworthy topics are delivered to editors of newspapers, magazines, and other media. Press conferences announce major news events of interest to the public. Photographs, tapes, and films are useful for illustrating product improvements, new products,

---

[1]Jordan Goldman, *Public Relations in the Marketing Mix* (Lincolnwood, IL: NTC Business Books, 1984).

advanced production techniques, and so forth. Of course, all forms of publicity are subject to the control and whims of the media. However, by disseminating a large volume of publicity materials and by preparing materials that fit the media's needs, a company increases its chances of obtaining beneficial publicity.

SOME TOOLS OF PROACTIVE MPR.   Three widely used forms of publicity in marketing-oriented PR are product releases, executive-statement releases, and feature articles.

Product releases announce new products, provide relevant information about product features and benefits, and tell how additional information can be obtained. A product release is typically aired on television networks or published in a product section of trade magazines and business publications such as *Business Week, Forbes, Fortune, The Wall Street Journal,* or in the business section of consumer magazines such as *Time* or *Newsweek.*

Audio-visual product releases (called video news releases, or VNRs) have gained wide usage in recent years. For example, Hershey introduced its new Hershey Kisses with almonds by showing a 6-foot, 500-pound replica of a Hershey Kiss covered in gold sequins and foil being dropped from a Times Square building (much like the neon apple is dropped on New Year's Eve). Hershey's PR agency videotaped the event, distributed tapes to New York networks, and the same evening the event was seen on TV by millions of Americans. For less than $100,000, Hershey's new product received tremendous exposure.

Executive-statement releases are news releases quoting a corporate executive such as the CEO. Unlike a product release, which is restricted to describing a new product or product improvement, an executive-statement release may deal with a wide variety of possible issues relevant to a corporation's publics. Topics covered include the following:

■ Statements about industry developments and trends.

■ Company sales forecasts.

■ Views on the economy.

■ Comments on R&D developments or market-research findings.

■ Announcements of new marketing programs launched by the company.

■ Views on foreign competition (e.g., former Chrysler CEO Lee Iacocca talking about unfair Japanese competition).

■ Comments on environmental issues.

Whereas product releases are typically published in the business or product section of a publication, executive-statement releases are published in the news section. This location carries with it a significant degree of credibility. Note that any product release can be converted into an executive-statement release by changing the way it is written.

Feature articles are detailed descriptions of products or other newsworthy programs that are written by a PR firm for immediate publication or airing by print or broadcast media. For example, Edelman Public Relations, an international public relations firm, wrote a detailed feature article about a deodorant imported from France called Le Crystal Naturel. The article was mailed to approximately 400 newspapers with circulations exceeding 45,000 and to top beauty magazines such as *Glamour* and *Cosmopolitan*. Materials such as this are inexpensive to prepare, yet they can provide companies with tremendous access to many potential customers.

Reactive MPR

Unanticipated marketplace developments can place an organization in a vulnerable position which demands reactive marketing PR. The Suzuki Samurai episode presented in the opening vignette is a vivid example. In general, *product defects and failures* are the most dramatic factors underlying the need for reactive MPR. A number of negative-publicity cases have received widespread media attention in recent years.

THE AUDI CASE.   Audi of America had realized record sales in 1985 and was moving toward recognition alongside Mercedes-Benz and BMW as one of the Big 3 manufacturers of German luxury performance cars. Then consumers started complaining and the media (including CBS's *60 Minutes*) started reporting that the Audi 5000-S sometimes lunged out of control when shifted into drive or reverse gears. Sales plummeted from approximately 74,000 units in 1985 to projected sales of only 12,000 in 1991.[2]

Audi represents a classic illustration of how *not* to respond to negative publicity. Audi's response to consumer complaints and to the *60 Minutes* report was to deny any product problems and instead to blame drivers. As one auto-industry analyst put it: "[For Audi to announce] to the world that the reason people are accelerating through their garages is because they're hitting the accelerator instead of the brake is not exactly going to make you a lot of friends."[3]

PRODUCT TAMPERINGS: TYLENOL AND SUDAFED.   In 1982, seven people in the Chicago area died from cyanide poisoning after ingest-

---

[2]David Kiley, "After Peugeot and Sterling, Who's Next?" *Adweek's Marketing Week*, August 19, 1991, 9.

[3]Fannie Weinstein, "One Foot in the Junkyard," *Advertising Age*, October 19, 1987, 92.

ing Tylenol capsules. Many analysts predicted that Tylenol would never regain its previously sizable market share. Some observers even questioned whether Johnson & Johnson ever would be able to market anything under the Tylenol name.

Johnson & Johnson's handling of the Tylenol tragedy was near brilliant. Rather than denying a problem existed, J&J acted swiftly by removing Tylenol from retail shelves. Spokespersons appeared on television and cautioned consumers not to ingest Tylenol capsules. A tamper-proof package was designed, setting a standard for other companies. As a final good-faith gesture, J&J offered consumers free replacements for products they had disposed of in the aftermath of the Chicago tragedy. Figure 20.2 shows a Tylenol advertisement that offered consumers a $2.50 certificate for obtaining a free bottle of Tylenol. Tylenol regained its market share shortly after this campaign began.

In a tragic replay of the Tylenol case, two people in Washington state died in 1991 after ingesting cyanide-laced Sudafed capsules. Following Tylenol's lead, Burroughs Wellcome Co., Sudafed's maker, immediately withdrew the product from store shelves, suspended advertising, established an 800-number phone line for consumer inquiries, and offered a $100,000 reward for information leading to the arrest of the product tampering. Industry analysts predicted that Burrough's quick and effective response would result in only a brief sales slump for Sudafed.[4]

THE PERRIER CASE.   Perrier was the leading brand of bottled water in the United States until 1990 when Source Perrier, the manufacturer, announced that traces of a toxic chemical, benzene, had been found in some of its products. Perrier recalled 72 million bottles from U.S. supermarkets and restaurants and subsequently withdrew the product from distribution elsewhere in the world. The total cost of the global recall was about $166 million. Moreover, Perrier's sales in the U.S. declined by 40 percent and Evian replaced it as the leading imported bottled water.[5]

SECTION SUMMARY.   Negative publicity can hit any company at any time. The lesson to be learned is that quick and positive responses to negative publicity are imperative. Negative publicity is something to be dealt with head-on, not denied. When done effectively, reactive MPR can virtually save a product or a company. A corporate response immediately following negative publicity can lessen the inevitable loss in sales.

---

[4]Judann Dagnoli, "Brief Slump Expected for Sudafed," *Advertising Age*, March 18, 1991, 53.

[5]The facts in this description are from Annetta Miller, Fiona Gleizes, and Elizabeth Bradburn, "Perrier Loses Its Fizz," *Newsweek*, February 27, 1990, 53; Laura Bird, "Perrier Imports New Image from France," *Adweek's Marketing Week*, June 10, 1991, 9; and "Perrier: Heavy Users Came Back," *Advertising Age*, October 21, 1991, 36.

FIGURE 20.2   Johnson & Johnson's Efforts to Retain Customers

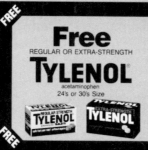

The makers of TYLENOL®
want to say

"ThankYou America"

for your continuing confidence and support.

Since the recent tragic criminal tampering incident in Chicago involving Extra-Strength TYLENOL Capsules, we've talked with many people all over the country.

The attitude toward TYLENOL is overwhelmingly positive. People tell us they have trusted the TYLENOL name for many, many years, that they still have the highest regard for TYLENOL, and that they will continue to use TYLENOL. We are delighted by this response, because for over 20 years we have worked hard to earn your trust. We are now working even harder to keep it.

Following the Chicago tragedy, we know that many of you disposed of your TYLENOL product. We want to help you replace that product—*at our expense*. Just tear out the attached $2.50 certificate and redeem it at your local store.

You have made TYLENOL a trusted part of your health care program for over 20 years. This offer is a token of our appreciation for your loyalty, understanding, and continued trust.

Free!

A $2.50 certificate to purchase a free bottle of Regular Strength or Extra-Strength TYLENOL (24's/30's size) or to apply against the purchase of any other TYLENOL product. Just tear it out and take it to your local store.

Free
REGULAR OR EXTRA-STRENGTH
TYLENOL®
acetaminophen
24's or 30's Size

Take this coupon to your local store for ONE free package of either Regular Strength tablet/capsule 24's or Extra-Strength TYLENOL® tablet 30's/capsule 24's size up to a retail price of $2.50. If your store does not carry this size, you may redeem this coupon for credit up to $2.50 toward the purchase of a larger size of Regular or Extra-Strength TYLENOL® tablets or capsules. You may also redeem this coupon for up to $2.50 toward the purchase of any Children's TYLENOL®, Children's or Adult COTYLENOL®, or Maximum-Strength TYLENOL® sinus medication product. You must pay any applicable sales tax.

Dealer: See reverse side for redemption

©McN 1982

The Special Case of Rumors

You have heard them and probably helped spread them since you were a small child in elementary school. They are often vicious and malicious. Sometimes they are just comical. Most always they are false. We are talking about rumors.

Commercial rumors are widely circulated but unverified propositions about a product, brand, company, store, or other commercial target.[6] Rumors are probably the most difficult problem public-relations personnel deal with. What makes rumors so troublesome is that they spread like wildfire and most always state or imply something very undesirable, and possibly repulsive, about the target of the rumor.

Consider the case of the persistent rumor that surrounded the Procter & Gamble Company for years. The rumor involved P&G's famous man-in-the-moon logo, which was claimed to be a symbol of the devil. The logo on the left side of Figure 20.3 is the old P&G logo. According to the rumor mongers, when the stars in the old logo are connected (as has been done in the figure), the number 666 (a symbol of the Antichrist) is formed. Also, the curls in the man-in-the-moon's beard, which have been circled, also supposedly form 666 when held up to a mirror.

Old and New Procter & Gamble Logos   FIGURE 20.3

[6]This definition is adapted from Fredrick Koenig, *Rumor in the Marketplace: The Social Psychology of Commercial Hearsay* (Dover, MA: Auburn House Publishing Company, 1985), 2.

Although nonsensical, this rumor spread for years throughout the Midwest and South. P&G eventually decided to drop the old logo and change to the new logo on the right side of Figure 20.3. The new logo retains the 13 stars, which represent the original United States colonies, but eliminates the curly hairs in the beard that appeared to form the number 666. It is interesting to note that in 1991 P&G won a $75,000 monetary judgment against two Amway product distributors who were distributing leaflets urging people to boycott P&G products and claiming P&G was linked with the devil.

Following are some other rumors you may have heard at one time or another. (Some of these rumors are pretty old, so you might want to ask someone else about them.) None are true, but all have been widely circulated.

- The McDonald's Corporation makes sizable donations to the Church of Satan.

- Wendy's hamburgers contain something other than beef, namely red worms. (Other versions of this rumor have substituted McDonald's or Burger King as the target.)

- "Pop Rocks" (a carbonated candy-type product made by General Foods) explode in your stomach when mixed with soda.

- "Bubble Yum" chewing gum contains spider eggs.

- A woman was bitten by a poisonous snake in a Kmart store when trying on a coat imported from Taiwan.

- A boy and his date stopped at a Kentucky Fried Chicken restaurant on their way to a movie. Later the girl became violently ill and the boy rushed her to the hospital. The examining physician said the girl appeared to have been poisoned. The boy went to the car and retrieved an oddly shaped half-eaten piece from the KFC bucket. The physician recognized it to be the remains of a rat. It was determined that the girl died from consuming a fatal amount of strychnine from the rat's body.[7]

The preceding examples illustrate two basic types of commercial rumors: conspiracy and contamination.[8] **Conspiracy rumors** involve supposed company policies or practices that are threatening or ideologically undesirable to consumers. For example, a conspiracy rumor circulated in New Orleans in 1990

---

[7]These rumors, all of which are false, have been in circulation at one time or another since the 1970s. All are thoroughly documented and analyzed in the fascinating book by Koenig, ibid.

[8]Ibid., 19.

claiming that the founder of the Popeyes restaurant chain, Al Copeland, supported David Duke, the politician with Ku Klux Klan and Nazi connections. Copeland immediately called a press conference and vehemently denied any connections with Duke. In addition he offered a $25,000 reward for information leading to the source of the rumors. This swift response squashed the rumor before it gained momentum.[9] (For another example of a conspiracy rumor, see the *Focus on Promotion.*)

Contamination rumors deal with undesirable or harmful product or store features. For example, in 1987 a rumor started in Reno, Nevada, that Mexican-import beer, Corona, was contaminated with urine. The rumor was started by a beer distributor in Reno who handled Heineken, a competitive brand. Corona sales fell by 80 percent in some markets. The rumor was hushed when an out-of-court settlement against the Reno distributor required a public statement declaring that Corona is not contaminated.

What Is the Best Way to Handle a Rumor?

When confronted with a rumor, some companies believe that doing nothing is the best way to handle it. This cautious approach is apparently based on the fear that an anti-rumor campaign will call attention to the rumor itself.[10]

An expert on rumors claims that rumors are like fires, and like fires, time is the worst enemy. His advice is to not merely hope that a rumor will simmer down but rather to combat it swiftly and decisively to PUT IT OUT![11] Recommended steps for rumor control are presented in Table 20.1. It will be well worth your time to review these recommendations.

SPONSORSHIP MARKETING

A rapidly growing aspect of U.S. marketing is the practice of corporate sponsorships. Sponsorships range from supporting athletic events (golf and tennis tournaments, college football bowl games, etc.) to underwriting rock concerts (e.g., Reebok spent $10 million as the sole sponsor for "Human Rights Now!" a 20-city tour organized by Amnesty International).

---

[9]Amy E. Gross, "How Popeyes and Reebok Confronted Product Rumors," *Adweek's Marketing Week*, October 22, 1990, 27.

[10]Koenig, *Rumor in the Marketplace*, 163.

[11]Ibid., 167.

FOCUS ON PROMOTION

A BIZARRE CONSPIRACY RUMOR

The Brooklyn Bottling Corp. in 1990 introduced an inexpensive line of soft drinks under the name Tropical Fantasy. Priced at 49 cents for a 20-ounce bottle, Tropical Fantasy quickly gained sales momentum and was heading toward becoming the top-selling brand in small grocery stores in many Northeastern markets. But then the rumor peddlers went to work. Leaflets started appearing in low-income neighborhoods warning minorities away from Tropical Fantasy and claiming that the brand was manufactured by the Ku Klux Klan and "contain[s] stimulants to sterilize the black man."

Angry Tropical Fantasy drinkers threatened distributors with baseball bats and threw bottles at delivery trucks. Some stores stopped accepting shipments. Sales of Tropical Fantasy immediately plummeted.

Source: Adapted from "A Storm Over Tropical Fantasy," *Newsweek*, April 22, 1991, 34.

Sponsorships involve investments in *events* or *causes* for the purpose of achieving various corporate objectives: increasing sales volume, enhancing a company's reputation or a brand's image, increasing brand awareness, and so on.[12]

At least four factors account for the growth in sponsorships.[13] First, by attaching their names to special events and causes, companies are able to *avoid the clutter* inherent in advertising media. Second, sponsorships help companies *respond to consumers' changing media habits*. For example, with the decline in network television viewing, sponsorships offer a potentially effective and cost-efficient way to reach customers. Third, sponsorships help companies *gain the approval of various constituencies*, including stockholders, employees, and society at large. Finally, the sponsorship of special events and causes enables marketers to *target their communication and promotional efforts* to specific geographic regions and/or to specific lifestyle groups. For example, General Foods

---

[12]Meryl Paula Gardner and Phillip Joel Shuman, "Sponsorship: An Important Component of the Promotions Mix," *Journal of Advertising*, 16, 1 (1987), 11–17.

[13]The first three are adapted from ibid., 12.

Recommended Steps for Rumor Control	**TABLE 20.1**

A. Alert Procedure

   1. On first hearing a rumor, note the location and wording of the allegation and target.

   2. Keep alert for any other rumors to see if the original report was spurious.

   3. If rumors increase to ten or more, send requests to distributors, franchise managers, and whoever else meets the public to find out who told the rumor to the person reporting it. It is important to specify the regional boundaries of the problem and the characteristics of the participating population. Distribute forms that can be filled out for the above information, as well as fact sheets rebutting the rumor.

   4. Check with competitors to see if they share the problem. Try to find out if the target has moved from your company to them or from them to yours, or if it has spread throughout the industry.

B. Evaluation

   1. Check for a drop in sales or a slowdown in sales increase.

   2. Monitor person-hours required to answer phone calls and mail.

   3. Keep tabs on the morale of the company personnel meeting people in the corporation. Do they feel harassed? Do they feel that management is doing enough to help them?

   4. Design a marketing survey to find out what percentage of the public believes any part of the rumor.

   5. Make an assessment of the threat or potential threat the rumor poses to profits. Is the corporation in danger of appearing to be an inept, impotent, and passive victim of the rumor problem? How much is management's image affected by the way things are going? The next move is a judgment call. If it seems that something more should be done, then it is time to move to the next square.

C. Launch a Media Campaign

   1. Assemble all facts about the extent of the problem to present to co-workers and superiors. Be prepared for resistance from people who support the myth that "pussyfooting is the best policy."

   2. Based on information gathered in the previous phases, decide on the geographical regions for implementing the campaign. If it is a local rumor, treat it locally; if it is a national rumor, treat it nationally.

   3. Based on information gathered in the previous phases, decide on the demographic features of the carrying population.

   4. Select appropriate media outlets and construct appropriate messages.

   5. Decide on what points to refute. (Don't deny *more* than is in the allegation.) If the allegation is of the contamination variety, be careful not to bring up any offensive association or to trigger potential "residuals" in the refutation.

   6. Two important points to make in any campaign are that the allegations are *untrue* and *unjust*. It should be implied that the company's business is not suffering, but that "what's right is right" and that people who pass on the rumor are "going against the American sense of fair play!"

   7. Line up spokespeople such as scientists, civic and/or religious leaders, rumor experts—whoever you think appropriate—to make statements on the company's behalf.

If all of the above is done properly, the problem is well on the way to being solved.

Source: From Fredrick Koenig, *Rumor in the Marketplace: The Social Psychology of Commercial Hearsay* (Dover, MA: Auburn House Publishing Company, 1985), 171-173. Reprinted with permission.

Corporation (GFC) sponsored "March Across America" to benefit Mothers Against Drunk Driving (MADD). In sponsoring this cause, GFC was able to reach a relatively narrow segment of people who identify with MADD's laudable efforts. GFC raised $100,000 for MADD and in so doing experienced a 13 percent increase in the sales of Tang drink mix.[14]

Cause-Related Marketing

As mentioned, sponsorships involve both events and causes. **Cause-related marketing (CRM)** is a relatively narrow aspect of overall sponsorship. CRM involves an amalgam of public relations, sales promotion, and corporate philanthropy; however, the distinctive feature of CRM is that a company's contribution to a designated cause is linked to customers' engaging in revenue-producing exchanges with the firm.[15] Cause-related marketing, in other words, is based on the idea that a company will contribute to a cause every time the customer undertakes some action. The contribution is contingent on the customer performing a behavior (such as buying a product or redeeming a coupon) that benefits the firm.

The following examples illustrate how cause-related marketing operates. For each Heinz baby-food label mailed in by consumers, H. J. Heinz Company contributed six cents to a hospital near the consumer's home. Nabisco Brands donated one dollar to the Juvenile Diabetes Foundation for each one dollar donation certificate that was redeemed with a Ritz brand proof of purchase. Hershey donated 25 cents to local Hospitals for Children for each Hershey coupon redeemed (see Figure 20.4).

Cause-related marketing is corporate philanthropy based on profit motivated giving.[16] Corporate interests are served while helping worthy causes. In addition to helping worthy causes, corporations satisfy their own tactical and strategic objectives when undertaking cause-related efforts. By supporting a deserving cause, a company can (1) enhance its corporate or brand image, (2) thwart negative publicity, (3) generate incremental sales, (4) increase brand awareness, (5) broaden its customer base, (6) reach new market segments, and (7) increase a brand's level of merchandising activity at the retail level.[17] The *Global Focus* describes a fascinating use of cause-related marketing in Canada.

---

[14]Laurie Freeman and Wayne Walley, "Marketing with a Cause Takes Hold," *Advertising Age*, May 16, 1988, 34.

[15]P. Rajan Varadarajan and Anil Menon, "Cause-Related Marketing: A Coalignment of Marketing Strategy and Corporate Philanthropy," *Journal of Marketing*, 52 (July 1988), 58-74.

[16]Ibid., 58.

[17]Varadarajan and Menon, "Cause-Related Marketing."

Illustration of Cause-Related Marketing   **FIGURE 20.4**

GLOBAL FOCUS

A CEREAL WITH A CAUSE

Kellogg Canada in 1991 introduced a new brand of cereal to Canadian grocery stores without investing any money in advertising. Such an introduction is virtually unheard of in this era of intense competition and spectacular marketing. Over one million boxes of Kellogg's Nutrific, the new brand, were shipped to stores without the benefit of advertising or even product testing. The brand was launched solely on the strength of a sponsorship relation between Kellogg Canada and the Canadian Breast Cancer Foundation.

Kellogg promised to donate 50 cents for each box of Nutrific it sold with hopes of raising $500,000 for breast cancer research. Not only does this benefit an extremely important cause and in so doing enhance Kellogg's image, but this innovative form of product innovation was able to inexpensively achieve product trial among the targeted audience of women. Also, because grocers were supportive of Kellogg's cause-oriented efforts, the marketers of Nutrific were able to gain shelf space without having to pay listing allowances (the name in Canada for slotting allowances).

Source: Adapted from Fara Warner, "Kellogg Launches a Cereal for Charity," *Adweek's Marketing Week,* November 11, 1991, 6.

Event Marketing

Though relatively small compared to the major components of the promotions mix, expenditures on event sponsorship are increasing. Thousands of companies invest in some form of event sponsorship. Defined, **event marketing** is a form of brand promotion that ties a brand to a meaningful cultural, social, athletic, or other type of high-interest public activity. Event marketing is separate from advertising, sales promotion, point-of-purchase merchandising, or public relations, but it generally incorporates elements from all of these promotional tools.

Event marketing is growing rapidly because it provides companies alternatives to the cluttered mass media, an ability to segment on a local or regional basis, and opportunities for reaching narrow lifestyle groups whose consumption behavior can be linked with the local event. For example, Procter & Gamble sponsors racing cars emblazoned with P&G's Tide, Crisco, and Folgers brands because auto-racing audiences in the Southeast and Midwest are heavy consumers of these brands. Sara Lee Corp. sponsors the Ice Capades with designs of promoting two brands of hosiery simultaneously: Sheer Energy hose to women and Little L'eggs for children.[18]

USING EVENT MARKETING EFFECTIVELY.   As with every other marketing and promotion-management decision, the starting point for effective event sponsorship is to clearly specify the *objectives* that an event is designed to accomplish. Event marketing has no value unless it accomplishes these objectives. Two examples of effective event marketing follow.

Procter & Gamble sponsored the Mexican Festival weekend of Cinco de Mayo, the May 5th anniversary of Mexico's victory in its war against France. The objective was to strengthen P&G's relations with Hispanic retailers and consumers in the Los Angeles and Santa Ana areas of California. Over 100 festivals in supermarket parking lots were conducted during and after the official Cinco de Mayo celebration. The result: More than 4 million Hispanic consumers were reached through various Spanish-language media, and nearly 85 percent of the retailers participated in the promotion. By supporting an important community event P&G was able to increase its standing with Hispanic consumers and community leaders.[19]

General Food's Crystal Light Drink Mix was the beneficiary of another successful application of event marketing. General Food's objective was to sponsor an event compatible with Crystal Light's image and appropriate for its target market, women aged 18 to 34 who are concerned with health and fitness. The event selected was an aerobic dance competition. The Crystal Light National Aerobic Championship consists of regional aerobic dance competitions in nine malls around the country, topped off by a national championship from among the regional winners. Crystal Light backed up each regional aerobic dance competition with point-of-purchase merchandising support and product sampling. Extensive media exposure for Crystal Light was obtained through interviews with touring aerobic experts about the event on local television, radio, and in newspapers and magazines. Crystal Light also made available a videotape of the national championship as a self-liquidating premium item.[20] This event sponsorship has provided General Foods with an effective way to reach prime consumers and to enhance the brand's image.[21]

---

[18]Cara Appelbaum, "L'eggs Signs Up with the Ice Capades," *Adweek's Marketing Week*, June 3, 1991, 10.

[19]Adapted from William A. Robinson, "Adweek's First Annual Achievements in Event Marketing," Promote section of *Adweek*, November 16, 1987, 12.

[20]As will be recalled from Chapter 17, a self-liquidating premium is one in which the consumer buys the item at a price much lower than what it would cost at retail. The manufacturer recovers its cost but earns no direct profit from the premium item.

[21]"Special Events as a Growing Marketing Tool," *DFS Promotion Report* (a publication of the Dancer Fitzgerald Sample, Inc.), 7 (July 1986), C, D.

SUMMARY

This chapter covers two major topics: public relations and sponsorship marketing. *Public relations (PR)* involves a variety of functions and activities directed at fostering harmonious interactions with an organization's publics (customers, employees, stockholders, governments, etc.). An important distinction is made between general public relations (*general PR*), which deals with overall managerial issues and problems (e.g., relations with stockholders and employees), and marketing-oriented public relations (*MPR*). The chapter focuses on MPR.

Marketing PR consists of proactive MPR and reactive MPR. *Proactive MPR* is another tool, in addition to advertising, personal selling, and sales promotion, for promoting a company's products and brands. Proactive MPR is dictated by a company's marketing objectives. It seeks opportunities rather than solving problems. *Reactive MPR* responds to external pressures and typically deals with changes that have negative consequences for an organization. Handling negative publicity and rumors are two areas in which reactive PR is most needed.

The other major topic covered in this chapter is *sponsorship marketing*. Sponsorships involve investments in events or causes in order to achieve various corporate objectives. *Cause-related marketing (CRM)* is a narrow aspect of overall sponsorship. The distinctive feature of CRM is that a company's contribution to a designated cause is linked to customers' engaging in revenue producing exchanges with the firm. Cause-related marketing serves corporate interests while helping worthy causes.

Event marketing is a rapidly growing aspect of the promotional mix. Though small in comparison to advertising and other major promotional elements, expenditures on event promotions are growing. Event marketing is a form of brand promotion that ties a brand to a meaningful cultural, social, athletic, or other type of high-interest public activity. Event marketing is growing because it provides companies with alternatives to the cluttered mass media, an ability to segment on a local or regional basis, and opportunities for reaching narrow lifestyle groups whose consumption behavior can be tied in to the local event.

Discussion Questions

1. What role might sponsorship marketing perform for a nationally distributed consumer-goods product such as a brand of soft drink?

2. Explain how a local business in your area (a bank, manufacturer, etc.) might use event marketing to its advantage. Be specific in describing the objectives that event marketing would satisfy and the type of event that would be compatible with these objectives.

3. You are the owner of a restaurant in your college/university community. A rumor about your business is circulating; the rumor concerns your head chef who is allegedly suffering from AIDS. Your business is falling off. What would you do?

4. Explain the similarities and differences among general public relations, marketing PR, and publicity.

5. What are the advantages of publicity in comparison to advertising? What are some of the objectives that both of these marketing communications techniques fulfill?

6. Some marketing practitioners consider publicity to be too difficult to control and measure. Evaluate these criticisms?

7. As the brand manager of Planter's Peanuts, an old and mature brand, how might you use proactive MPR to create some inexpensive brand exposure and incremental sales?

8. Assume you are the athletic director of your college or university's athletic department. A major story hits the news claiming that a high proportion of the school's athletes use steroids. How would you handle this negative publicity? Describe the specific steps you would follow.

9. With reference to the negative publicity about the Suzuki Samurai (as described in the chapter's opening vignette), what would you have done if you had been the CEO of this firm?

10. Faced with the rumor about Corona beer being contaminated with urine, what course of action would you have taken if the Heineken distributor in Reno had *not* been identified as starting the rumor? In other words, if the source of the rumor were unknown, what steps would you have taken?

11. Classify the various rumors presented in the text (P&G's logo, McDonald's Church of Satan connection, etc.) as conspiracy or contamination rumors.

12. Identify three examples of event marketing other than those mentioned in the chapter. For each example, explain what the sponsoring company, or brand, would have hoped to accomplish. Also, specify the characteristics of the people who participate or spectate in each event and compare their characteristics with your interpretation of the characteristics of the sponsor's primary market.

13. Describe two or three commercial rumors other than those mentioned in the chapter. Identify each as either a conspiracy or a contamination rumor. Describe how you think this rumor started and why people apparently consider it newsworthy enough to pass along. (You may discuss rumors originating in your hometown or local area; you have probably heard more of these than rumors about national companies and brands.)

PERSONAL SELLING AND SALES MANAGEMENT

The two chapters in Part 8 examine the face-to-face communication, or personal selling, aspect of the promotion mix. **Chapter 21** introduces students to the job of the salesperson and its unique characteristics. The chapter covers a broad array of topics regarding the nature of personal  selling, including personal selling's role in the promotion mix, attractive features of a personal selling job, and the kinds of activities performed by a salesperson. The chapter also discusses factors that determine salesperson performance, requirements for becoming an outstanding salesperson, and the types of available selling jobs.

Chapter 22 overviews the managerial aspects of personal selling. The practice of sales management involves planning, organizing, staffing, directing, and evaluating/controlling an organization's selling function. Each of these sales-management activities is explored. Students will acquire a general understanding of the tasks involved in sales management and learn that organizational success greatly depends on how well the sales-management function is performed.

Part 8

CHAPTER TWENTY-ONE

Personal Selling

- -

WHAT QUALITIES ARE LIKED AND DISLIKED IN A SALESPERSON?

A national sample of purchasing agents was surveyed to determine what qualities buyers value most and least in a salesperson. Ratings from over 200 purchasing agents revealed the following:

Most Valued

Reliability/credibility	98.6%
Professionalism/integrity	93.7
Product knowledge	90.7
Innovativeness in problem solving	80.5
Presentation/preparation	69.7

Least Valued

Supplies market data	25.8%
Appropriate frequency of calls	27.3
Knowledge of competitor's products	31.2
Knowledge of buyer's business and negotiation skills (tie)	45.8

In purchasing agents' own words, here are some of the specific qualities and behaviors in salespeople that are most liked, disliked, and despised—the good, the bad, and the ugly.

THE GOOD	THE BAD	AND THE UGLY
"Honesty"	"No follow-up"	"Wise-ass attitude"
"Lose a sale graciously"	"Walking in without an appointment"	"Calls me 'dear' or 'sweetheart' (I am a female)"
"Admits mistakes"	"Begins call by talking sports"	"Gets personal"
"Problem-solving capabilities"	"Puts down competitor's products"	"Doesn't give purchasing people credit for any brains"
"Friendly but professional"	"Poor listening skills"	"Whiners"
"Dependable"	"Too many phone calls"	"Bullshitters"
"Adaptability"	"Lousy presentation"	"Wines and dines me"
"Knows my business"	"Fails to ask about needs"	"Plays one company against another"
"Well prepared"	"Lacks product knowledge"	"Pushy"
"Patience"	"Wastes my time"	"Smokes in my office"

Source: "PAS Examine the People Who Sell to Them," *Sales and Marketing Management,* November 11, 1985, 38–41.

A good sales force that embodies the positive qualities identified in the opening vignette is crucial to corporate success. Personal selling is the last promotion-mix element covered in this textbook, but it certainly is not the least important. Indeed, popular business wisdom holds that everything starts with selling. Personal selling provides the push (as in *push strategy*) needed to get customers to carry new products, increase their amount of purchasing, and devote more effort in merchandising a company's brand. At the retail level, personal selling can determine whether a purchase is made and how often consumers shop at a particular store.

This chapter's objective is to present the reader with a broad array of ideas about the nature of personal selling, encouraging a greater appreciation of the opportunities and challenges for career success in this field. Toward this end, the chapter explores several dimensions of personal selling. First, the chapter discusses personal selling's role in the promotional mix, its advantages and disadvantages, society's attitudes toward this activity, and the attractive characteristics of personal selling and opportunities in this field. A second section examines selling activities, duties, and types of selling jobs. Determinants of salesperson performance and effectiveness are covered in the third section. Finally, the characteristics of excellence in selling are examined.

OVERVIEW

Personal selling is a form of person-to-person communication in which a salesperson works with prospective buyers and attempts to influence their purchase needs in the direction of his or her company's products or services. The most important feature of this definition is the idea that personal selling involves *person-to-person interaction*. This contrasts with other forms of marketing communications in which the audience typically consists of many people, sometimes millions (as in the case of mass-media advertising).

Personal Selling's Role in the Promotion Mix

As explained at various points throughout the text, all elements of the promotion mix work together to achieve overall organizational objectives. Each promotional element has its own unique characteristics, purposes, and advantages. Personal selling's primary purposes include educating customers, providing product usage and marketing assistance, and providing after-sale service and support to buyers. Personal selling, in comparison to other promotional elements, is uniquely capable of performing these functions as a result of the person-to-person interaction mode that characterizes this form of marketing communications. Consequently, various advantages accrue to personal selling compared to other promotional tools.

1. Personal selling contributes to a *relatively high level of customer attention*, since in face-to-face situations it is difficult for a potential buyer to avoid a salesperson's message.

2. It enables the salesperson to *customize the message* to the customer's specific interests and needs.

3. The two-way communication characteristic of personal selling yields *immediate feedback*, so that an alert salesperson can know whether or not his or her sales presentation is working.

4. Personal selling enables a salesperson to *communicate a larger amount of technical and complex information* than could be communicated using other promotional methods.

5. In personal selling there is *a greater ability to demonstrate a product's functioning and performance characteristics*.

6. Frequent interactions with a customer permit the *opportunity for developing long-term relations* and effectively merging selling and buying organizations into a coordinated unit where both sets of interests are served.[1]

The primary disadvantage of personal selling is that it is *more costly* than other forms of promotion because sales representatives typically interact with

[1]Gilbert A. Churchill, Jr., Neil M. Ford, and Orville C. Walker, Jr., *Sales Force Management: Planning, Implementation, and Control* (Homewood, IL: Richard D. Irwin, 1985), 67.

only one customer at a time. Hence, when considering only the outcomes or results accomplished with the personal-selling effort (an effectiveness consideration), personal selling is generally *more effective* than other promotion elements. However, when considering the ratio of inputs to outputs (cost to results), personal selling is typically *less efficient* than other promotion tools. In practice, allocating resources to personal selling and the other promotion elements amounts to an effort at balancing effectiveness and efficiency.

Attitudes toward Selling

Personal selling historically has been held in low esteem. This reputation dates back at least to the time of the ancient Greek philosophers and continues to be perpetrated today by movie and television directors and playwrights. For example, Arthur Miller's classic *Death of a Salesman* and David Mamet's more recent *Glengarry Glen Ross* depict salesmen as rather pathetic characters who struggle for an existence and earn their living through ingratiation, deceit, and other unethical and immoral practices. In real life, there are indeed con men and women who rely on deception, false promises, trickery, and misrepresentation to persuade people to buy products and services they do not need or items that do not work. Although this still happens today, it represents a small percentage of the personal-selling business.

Fortunately, there is a continuing trend toward college students' holding more favorable attitudes toward selling. Table 21.1 compares results of two studies separated by a 30-year interval. It can be seen that student attitudes have improved rather dramatically.[2] Personal selling is a much more attractive career option than many students previously thought.

Attractive Features of Personal Selling

Numerous challenging and exciting job opportunities are available in this field. The attractive features of a sales job include freedom of action, variety and challenge, opportunities for advancement, and desirable financial and nonfinancial rewards.[3]

JOB FREEDOM. In field-sales positions (those outside of retail settings), the individual is primarily responsible for most of his or her day-to-day

---

[2]The 1958 study was conducted by the *American Salesman* magazine. The 1988 study was performed by Rosemary R. Lagace and Timothy A. Longfellow, "The Impact of Classroom Style on Student Attitudes toward Sales Careers: A Comparative Approach," *Journal of Marketing Education* (Fall 1989), 72–77.

[3]Churchill, Ford, and Walker, *Sales Force Management: Planning, Implementation, and Control.*

TABLE 21.1	College Students' Changing Attitudes Toward Personal Selling		

	1958 STUDY	1988 STUDY
I associate a job in personal selling with		
■ Insincerity and deceit	Agree	Disagree
■ Low status/low prestige	Agree	Disagree
■ Much traveling	Agree	Agree
■ Salespeople being money hungry	Agree	Disagree
■ High pressure forcing people to buy unwanted goods	Agree	Disagree
■ Low job security	Agree	Disagree
■ Just a job not a career	Agree	Disagree
■ Personality is crucial	Agree	Agree
■ Too little monetary reward	Disagree	Disagree
■ I prefer a nonsales position much more than sales	Agree	Disagree

Source: Adapted from Rosemary R. Lagace and Timothy A. Longfellow, "The Impact of Classroom Style on Student Attitudes toward Sales Careers: A Comparative Approach," *Journal of Marketing Education*, 1989 (Fall), 74.

activities. Many sales positions involve little direct supervision. Salespeople may go days or even weeks without seeing their supervisors. Of course, with freedom comes responsibility. The unsupervised salesperson is expected to conduct his or her business professionally and to achieve sales objectives.

VARIETY AND CHALLENGE.   Managing one's own time presents a challenge that professional salespeople enjoy. Much like the person who operates his or her own business, a salesperson can invest as much time and energy into the job as desired and can generate as many rewards as he or she is willing to work for.

OPPORTUNITIES FOR ADVANCEMENT.   More and more companies expect their middle- and upper-level managers to have had sales experience because they believe it helps an individual understand a business from the ground-level up. More corporate presidents come from the sales ranks than from any other position; sales experience provides them with a knowledge of the customers, the trade, the competition, and their own company.

ATTRACTIVE   COMPENSATION   AND   NONFINANCIAL REWARDS.   Personal selling is potentially both lucrative and rewarding. Nonfinancial rewards include feelings of self-worth for a job well done and the satisfaction that comes from providing a customer with a solution to a problem or with a product or service that best meets his or her needs.

MODERN SELLING PHILOSOPHY

Before *modern* selling philosophy, there must have been an earlier variety. Let us label this earlier version *antiquated* and place the two in stark contrast, realizing of course that any such comparison is necessarily simplified.

In a word, *antiquated selling* is *seller-oriented*. Selling practices in this older view are undertaken with the seller's interests paramount. Manifestations of this approach include high-pressure selling tactics, little effort to understand the customer's business, and little post-sale follow through and attention to customer satisfaction.

Are these antiquated practices truly antiquated in the sense that they no longer are practiced? Certainly not. Some firms are still antiquated; although they remain in business, they no longer thrive. Their selling practices lag behind contemporary forces that have imposed a higher standard on sales performance. These forces include intense competition, narrow profit margins, sophisticated buying practices, and expectations of reliable and dependable service from vendors.

In most prospering firms, modern selling philosophy has supplanted this seller-oriented approach. A *partner-oriented* selling mind-set exists in most successful firms. These firms realize that their own success rests with their customers' successes. Hence, modern partner-oriented wisdom makes customer satisfaction its highest priority. Modern selling practice is based on the following principles.[4]

1. *The sales process must be built on a foundation of trust and mutual agreement.*   Selling should not be viewed as something someone does to another; rather, it should be looked upon as something two parties agree to do for their mutual benefit. In fact, it is easy to argue that modern salespeople do not sell, but rather, facilitate buying. This difference is not merely semantics—it is at the root of the transformation from the antiquated to modern selling philosophies.

2. *A customer-driven atmosphere is essential to long-term growth.*   This is a corollary point to the preceding principle. Modern selling requires that the

[4]These points are adapted from two excellent practitioner-oriented books: Anthony Alessandra, James Cathcart, and Phillip Wexler, *Selling by Objectives* (Englewood Cliffs, NJ: Prentice-Hall, 1988); and Paul Hersey, *Selling: A Behavioral Science Approach* (Englewood Cliffs, NJ: Prentice-Hall, 1988).

customer's welfare, interests, and needs be treated as equal to the seller's in the partnership between seller and buyer. A customer-oriented approach means avoiding high-pressure tactics and focusing on customer satisfaction. Salespeople have to be trained to know the customer and to speak in a language that the customer understands. Perhaps the preceding points are best summed up in these terms: "Be product-centered, and you will make a few sales; be prospect-centered, and you will gain many customers."[5]

3. *Sales representatives should act as if they were on the customer's payroll.* The ultimate compliment a salesperson can receive is a comment from a customer to the sales supervisor along these lines: "I'm not sure whether your sales rep works for me or for you."[6] The closer salespeople are to the customer, the better they will be at providing solutions to the customer's problems.

4. *Getting the order is only the first step; after-sales service is what counts.* No problem a customer has should be too small to address. Modern selling philosophy calls for doing whatever is necessary to please the customer in order to ensure a satisfying long-term relationship. (See the *Global Focus*.)

5. *In selling, as in medicine, prescription before diagnosis is malpractice.* This principle holds that no one solution is appropriate for all customers any more than any single diagnosis is appropriate for all patients. Customers' problems have to be analyzed by the modern salesperson and solutions customized to each problem. The days of "one solution fits all" are gone. Moreover, because most people like to make their own decisions or at least be involved in making them, a salesperson should treat the customer as a partner in the solution.

6. *Salesperson professionalism and integrity are essential.* Customers expect high standards of conduct from their salespeople and dislike unprofessional, untrustworthy, and dishonest behavior. (As evidence of this, reexamine the Bad and the Ugly in the chapter's opening vignette.)

SELLING ACTIVITIES AND TYPES OF PERSONAL-SELLING JOBS

To this point in the chapter, personal selling has been treated rather generally as if all selling jobs are identical. This section describes the various kinds of activities that salespeople perform and then identifies six types of selling jobs.

---

[5]C. Conrad Elnes, *Inside Secrets of Outstanding Salespeople* (Englewood Cliffs, NJ: Prentice-Hall, 1988), 6.

[6]Hersey, *Selling: A Behavioral Science Approach*, xi.

GLOBAL FOCUS

SELLING JAPANESE STYLE

Modern selling philosophy and modern selling practice are not the same thing. That is, what *ought* to be and what *is* may be worlds apart. The incommensurability of philosophy and practice is perhaps particularly acute in the United States, where organizational structures and personalities make it difficult for many Americans to behave in the fashion laid out in the six principles underlying modern selling practice. For example, the individualistic style and competitive spirit that are part of the American psyche make it difficult for some salespeople to consider their customers' needs as important as their own.

Japanese salespeople's personalities are perhaps better suited to implementing modern selling philosophy. *Respect* is the foundation of Japanese selling. Being respectful (deferential to their customers and dedicated to their needs) is easy for Japanese businesspeople insofar as the feudal roots of Japan placed businessmen at the bottom of the societal hierarchy. As one writer observes, "today's Japanese sales reps, if they're good, still behave as if they're at the bottom of the social ladder, respecting and trying to satisfy their customers."

The Japanese selling style is sometimes referred to as "wet," implying that it is flexible, accommodating, caring, and human. The American style is more likely to be "dry," or more inflexible, logical, and cut-and-dried. A notable distinction in how the wet and dry styles are manifest is in the area of customer service. Upon being informed of a customer problem, an American sales representative might simply just pass the problem along to the technical support staff with hopes that the problem will be resolved. Japanese sales reps, on the other hand, will personally become involved in solving the problem, work with the support staff, and submit a report to the customer explaining why the product failed and what has been done to prevent that failure from happening again.

Source: George Leslie, "U.S. Reps Should Learn to Sell 'Japanese Style'," *Marketing News*, October 29, 1990, 6.

Selling Activities

What exactly does a salesperson do? The specific activities and their range of performance vary greatly from sales job to sales job. Nonetheless, the following ten activities are common to nearly all selling jobs.[7]

SELLING FUNCTION.   This is the typical activity envisioned when thinking of personal selling. Selling-function activities include planning the sales presentation, making the presentation, overcoming objections, trying to close the sale, and so on.

WORKING WITH ORDERS.   Much of a salesperson's time is spent writing up orders, working with lost orders, handling shipment problems, expediting orders, and handling back orders.

SERVICING THE PRODUCT.   These activities are performed primarily by people who sell technical products (e.g., an industrial machine). Activities include testing a newly sold product to ensure that it is working properly, training customers to use the product, and teaching safety procedures.

INFORMATION MANAGEMENT.   These activities involve receiving feedback from customers and then relaying the information to management. Much of this is done in the course of day-to-day selling, but some information-management work requires the salesperson to serve in the capacity of a field marketing researcher.

SERVICING THE ACCOUNT.   These activities include inventory control, stocking shelves, handling local advertising, and setting up and working with point-of-purchase displays. Such activities are primarily performed by salespeople who call on retail customers such as supermarkets and drugstores.

CONFERENCE/MEETINGS.   Attending conferences, working at trade shows, and attending sales meetings are activities nearly all salespeople participate in to some extent.

TRAINING/RECRUITING.   Salespeople who are in more advanced stages of their careers often become involved in training new salespeople, traveling with trainees, and similar duties.[8]

---

[7]William C. Moncrief III, "Selling Activity and Sales Position Taxonomies for Industrial Selling," *Journal of Marketing Research*, 23 (August 1986), 261–270.

[8]For a discussion of different stages of sales careers, see William L. Cron, Alan J. Dubinsky, and Ronald E. Michaels, "The Influence of Career Stages on Components of Salesperson Motivation," *Journal of Marketing*, 52 (January 1988), 78–92.

ENTERTAINING.   Some sales positions involve entertaining customers through activities such as dining and playing golf. Parenthetically, the antiquated view of selling would hold that you can buy customers by wining and dining them. Modern selling philosophy includes a role for customer entertainment but recognizes that customers are earned (through loyal, efficient, dependable service) rather than bought.

OUT-OF-TOWN TRAVEL.   Although sales jobs involve some traveling, the amount of time spent out of town is highly variable, ranging from virtually no travel to journeying thousands of miles each month.

WORKING WITH DISTRIBUTORS.   A final category of selling activity is selling to or establishing relations with distributors and collecting past-due accounts.

Types of Sales Jobs

The following six categories encompass the major types of sales jobs.[9]

TRADE SELLING.   A sales representative for a food manufacturer who sells to the grocery and drug industries typifies trade selling. The primary task of trade salespeople is to build sales volume by providing customers with promotional assistance in the form of advertising and sales promotion. Trade selling requires limited prospecting and places greater emphasis on *servicing accounts*. Trade salespeople, who typically are hired out of college, may work for companies such as Noxell, Beecham Products, Johnson & Johnson, Campbell's Soup, Procter & Gamble, and many other consumer packaged-goods companies.

MISSIONARY SELLING.   Like trade salespeople, missionary salespeople typically are employees of manufacturers. However, the difference is that trade salespeople sell *through* their direct customers, whereas a missionary sales force sells *for* its direct customers.[10]

The pharmaceutical industry typifies missionary selling. Nearly two-thirds of all pharmaceutical sales to retailers are through wholesalers. In other words, manufacturers of pharmaceuticals typically market their products to wholesalers who in turn market to pharmacies and other retailers. Thus, the wholesaler is the pharmaceutical manufacturer's direct customer. Sales representatives for

---

[9]Ronald B. Marks, *Personal Selling: An Interactive Approach* (Boston: Allyn and Bacon, 1988), 39.

[10]Ibid., 45.

pharmaceutical manufacturers (called detail reps or detailers) nonetheless call on physicians and pharmacies to detail (explain) the advantages of the manufacturer's brands compared to competitive offerings. Detail reps are not selling directly to physicians (i.e., selling in the sense that a physician will place an order with the salesperson's company); rather, they are trying to get physicians to prescribe their brands. In so doing, they benefit both the manufacturer (via increased sales volume) and their direct customers (wholesalers).

TECHNICAL SELLING.   Technical salespeople are present in industries such as chemicals, machinery, mainframe computers, and sophisticated services (e.g., complicated insurance and other financial programs). They are typically trained in technical fields such as chemistry, engineering, computer science, and accounting. For example, in the chemical division of Du Pont, 95 percent of the company's salespeople start out in a technical field and then are recruited into sales.[11] Later, many sales technicians attain advanced training in business administration. Good technical salespeople must be especially knowledgeable about their company's product lines and must be able to communicate complicated features to prospective customers.

NEW-BUSINESS SELLING.   This type of selling is prevalent with products such as office copiers, data-processing equipment, personal computers, business forms, and personal insurance. Practitioners use terms such as bird-dogging, cold calling, and canvassing to characterize this type of selling. These terms capture the idea that new-business salespeople must call on new accounts continuously. Salespeople involved in any of the previous categories of sales jobs do some prospecting for new customers, but most of their time is spent working with and servicing existing accounts. New-business salespeople continually work to open new accounts, because sales to most customers are infrequent.

RETAIL SELLING.   The distinguishing characteristic of retail selling is that the customer comes to the salesperson. Many retail sales jobs require limited training and sophistication, but others demand salespeople who have considerable product knowledge, strong interpersonal skills, and an ability to work with a diversity of customers.

TELEMARKETING.   Telemarketing was discussed in some detail in Chapter 19. Suffice it to say again that telemarketing is a rapidly growing form of selling activity. Telephone salespeople perform essentially the same types of selling activities as do salespeople who meet customers face to face.

---

[11]"Du Pont Turns Scientists into Salespeople," *Sales and Marketing Management*, June 1987, 57.

SALESPERSON PERFORMANCE AND EFFECTIVENESS

Regardless of the type of sales job, certain aptitudes and skills are needed to perform effectively. Indeed, people in all facets of life are ultimately judged in terms of their performance and effectiveness. Typically these evaluations are based on quantitative assessments: number of arrests by a police officer, number of indictments by a prosecuting attorney, number of hits by a baseball player, number of units produced by a factory worker, number of articles published by a professor, and so on. Likewise, salespeople are typically judged in terms of the number of units sold or dollar volume.

Academic and business researchers have long been intrigued with explaining and predicting salesperson performance. The fundamental issue is one of identifying the specific factors that determine salesperson effectiveness—the factors that distinguish the outstanding salesperson from the good, the mediocre, and the bad salespeople. (Stop reading for a few moments and think about your own ideas on this issue. Jot down what you think are the most important determinants of salesperson success and later compare your thoughts with the ideas presented.)

Before a specific discussion of the determinants of salesperson performance and effectiveness, two general points require careful attention. The first is that *no single factor is able to adequately explain salesperson performance.* In a very thorough and insightful analysis of sales research conducted over a 40-year span, researchers examined over 100 separate studies and over 1,500 correlations in these studies relating salesperson performance with a wide variety of potential predictors. Their analyses revealed that, on average, no single predictor explained more than *four percent* of the variability in salesperson performance![12] The conclusion to be drawn is clear: Sales performance is based on various considerations; to expect any single factor (or even several factors) to adequately explain a complex behavior is expecting too much.

A second general conclusion is that salesperson performance and effectiveness are *contingent on a host of factors;* indeed, selling performance and effectiveness depend on the total situation in which sales transactions take place. Specifically, salesperson performance is contingent upon (1) the salesperson's own resources (product knowledge, analytical skills, etc.), (2) the nature of the customer's buying task (e.g., whether it is a first-time or repeat decision), (3) the customer-salesperson relationship (relative power, level of conflict, etc.), and interactions among all three of these general sets of factors.[13]

---

[12]Gilbert A. Churchill, Jr., Neil M. Ford, Steven W. Hartley, and Orville C. Walker, Jr., "The Determinants of Salesperson Performance: A Meta Analysis," *Journal of Marketing Research*, 22 (May 1985), 103–118

[13]Barton A. Weitz, "Effectiveness in Sales Interactions: A Contingency Framework," *Journal of Marketing*, 45 (Winter 1981), 85–103.

Specific Determinants of Salesperson Performance

You now appreciate the fact that salesperson performance and effectiveness are contingent on various factors. Detailing all of these factors would take us beyond the scope of this overview. We will examine in greater detail six characteristics that have been hypothesized to determine salesperson performance: (1) aptitude, (2) skill level, (3) motivational level, (4) role perceptions, (5) personal characteristics, and (6) adaptability.[14]

A P T I T U D E .   An individual's ability to perform certain tasks depends greatly on his or her aptitude, which includes interests, intelligence, and personality characteristics. Because different salespeople have different tasks and activities to perform, some people are better suited to one type of sales job than another. Technical sales positions require individuals with the strong analytical aptitude and technical knowledge needed for explaining complex product features to customers. Trade selling requires individuals who have good interpersonal skills and are highly adaptive, because they meet with many different types of customers.

Regardless of the specific type of sales position, all professional salespeople must be customer oriented and empathetic. They must be able to view the world from the outside in and not just in terms of their own limited perspective.

S K I L L   L E V E L .   Whereas aptitude is a matter of native ability, skill level refers to an individual's *learned proficiency* at performing necessary selling tasks. These skills include salesmanship skills (such as knowing how to make a sales presentation), interpersonal skills (such as how to cope with and resolve conflict), and technical skills (such as knowledge about a product's features, performance, and benefits). These skills are partially brought to a sales job as a function of an individual's educational preparation, but are also learned and fostered on the job.

Companies with effective sales programs instill in their sales force the skills needed for success. In fact, many sales organizations prefer to recruit salespeople directly out of college rather than from other sales positions so that they do not have to retrain sales candidates to overcome bad habits and conflicting skills learned elsewhere.

For example, Armstrong World Industries, a maker of carpeting and other products, is legendary for hiring salespeople directly from college and sending them through the same basic training program that all Armstrong salespeople have undergone for over 60 years. In explaining the company's attitude toward sales training, Armstrong's director of human resources explains: "We prefer to

---

[14]The following discussion of the first five factors is based on Gilbert A. Churchill, Jr., Neil M. Ford, and Orville C. Walker, Jr., *Sales Force Management: Planning, Implementation, and Control* (Homewood, IL: Richard D. Irwin, 1985).

hire people without any biases, conflicting opinions, or bad traits—and then we train them ourselves. We've had great success doing things our way, and if we're doing it that way and other companies aren't, well, then they're doing it wrong."[15] This may sound arrogant, but it merely represents the belief that it is often easier to train than it is to retrain.

M O T I V A T I O N A L   L E V E L .   Motivational level refers to the *amount of time and energy* a person is willing to expend performing tasks and activities associated with a job. These tasks typically include filling out reports, calling on new accounts, creating new sales presentations, following up on sales, and so forth. An interesting thing about motivation is that it is *reciprocally related to performance*. That is, motivation is a determinant of performance and also is determined by performance—we often become even more motivated after we have enjoyed some success.

Another important characteristic of salesperson motivation is the distinction between *working hard and working smart*. Motivation is not simply the amount of effort but also how the effort is directed. Salespeople who work smart are typically more effective than those who just work hard.[16] Of course, a truly dynamite combination for a salesperson is to work both smart and hard.

R O L E   P E R C E P T I O N S .   In order to perform their jobs well, salespeople must know what is expected of them and have accurate perceptions of their role. Their jobs are defined by people both within and outside the organization, including family, sales managers, company executives, and customers. Thus, how well people perform in sales jobs depends on the accuracy of their perceptions of management's stated goals, demands, policies, procedures, and organizational lines of authority and responsibilities.

Very often salespeople face *role conflicts* that inhibit their sales performance. For example, a customer may want special price or advertising concessions that the company has policies against. Salespeople have been trained to meet customers' needs; however, they have also learned to follow company policies. They play the role of customer satisfier but also of company satisfier. What do sales representatives do? If a salesperson can negotiate differences between the two parties he or she may be able to resolve the conflict and make the sale. In general, accurate role perceptions are a very important determinant of sales performance, effectiveness, and organizational commitment. Research has shown that role ambiguity in the early stage of employment decreases

[15]"Armstrong Salespeople Are to the Manor Born," *Sales and Marketing Management*, June 1987, 46.

[16]Harish Sujan, "Smarter Versus Harder: An Exploratory Attributional Analysis of Salespeople's Motivation," *Journal of Marketing Research*, 23 (February 1986), 41–50.

salesperson commitment to their companies and increases turnover.[17] Accurate perceptions are instilled during initial sales training and over time during periodic sales meetings and through periodic interactions with sales supervisors.

PERSONAL CHARACTERISTICS. Another determinant of salesperson effectiveness is an individual's personal characteristics—his or her age, physical size, appearance, race, and gender are some of the personal characteristics expected to affect sales performance. Research has shown that these personal factors may be even more important than the other factors in determining sales performance.[18]

It would be erroneous, however, to conclude that one's personal characteristics ensure sales success or failure. To the contrary, personal characteristics merely may make it more or less difficult to succeed in sales. Performance by any individual depends ultimately on his or her ability, skill, and motivation level. One can either misuse personal advantages or overcome disadvantages. For example, women and blacks were at one time perceived to be less qualified for sales positions than white males. The number of sales opportunities for both groups have increased significantly in recent years, however, partly because both groups have overcome what used to be perceived as sales-related disadvantages.[19]

Speaking of gender, recent years have seen increasing numbers of women in sales positions. The percentage has risen to nearly 15 percent.[20] The idea that women might make better salespersons has also increased in popularity. Yet, the question of who is better—men or women—is a fruitless one. No doubt, some women are better salespersons than some of their male colleagues and vice versa. The real determinant of sales success is not dependent on one's gender but rather the ability to adapt oneself to situational circumstances and to call upon a repertoire of both male and female traits. This ability is called **androgyny,** which is "the degree to which individuals feel that they are characterized by traits associated with both men and women."[21] The *Focus on Promotion* elaborates on the role of androgyny and presents some recent research evidence.

[17]Mark W. Johnston, A. Parasuraman, Charles M. Futrell, and William C. Black, "A Longitudinal Assessment of the Impact of Selected Organizational Influences on Salespeople's Organizational Commitment During Early Employment," *Journal of Marketing Research*, 27 (August 1990), 333–344.

[18]Churchill, Ford, Hartley, and Walker, "The Determinants of Salesperson Performance: A Meta Analysis."

[19]See, for example, Michelle Block Morse, "Rich Rewards: For Ambitious Blacks, Selling Can Mean Pride, Power, and High Pay," *Success*, 35 (March 1988), 50–61.

[20]"Women Keep Coming On," *Sales & Marketing Management*, February 1989, 26.

[21]Rosemary R. Lagace and Jacquelyn L. Twible, "The Androgyny of Salespeople: Gooses and Ganders, or All Geese?" *Journal of Social Behavior and Personality*, 5, 6 (1990), 641–650.

FOCUS ON PROMOTION

THE ANDROGYNOUS SALESPERSON

Salespeople are generally considered to exhibit a variety of traits, some of which might be thought of as stereotypically male traits and some that are considered stereotypically female traits. These include being empathetic (which is stereotypically female, or F), competitive (stereotypically male, or M), sensitive (F), ambitious (M), and so on. Because adaptability is critical for success in selling and because androgynous people are more adaptable, it follows that salespeople are likely to be androgynous—that is, possess both male and female traits. Two marketing scholars performed an interesting study to test this proposition.

The researchers obtained a sample of 177 salespeople (40 percent men and 60 percent women) and administered a 16-item, semantic-differential instrument to measure androgyny. The instrument measured 8 "masculine" and 8 "feminine" traits. Respondents indicated the degree to which they possessed each trait. The researchers then classified respondents as masculine if they scored above the mean score on the masculine items, as feminine if they scored above the mean score on the feminine items, as androgynous if they scored above the sample mean on *both* the masculine and feminine items, and as undifferentiated if they scored below the sample mean on both the masculine and feminine items.

The results of these classifications revealed that the highest percentage of salespeople were in fact androgynous (41 percent). The next highest percentage were classified as masculine (24 percent), then feminine (19 percent), and undifferentiated (16 percent). The study also found that saleswomen were more androgynous than salesmen.

Unfortunately, the researchers did not measure salesperson effectiveness so that it might have been possible to determine whether androgynous salespeople are more effective than their nonandrogynous counterparts. It might be surmised, however, that saleswomen, on average, are likely to be more successful than salesmen because they are disproportionately more androgynous. The study results also might be interpreted as indicating that women who possess stereotypical male traits (assertiveness, competitiveness, independence, etc.) are more likely to choose a sales career than are women not possessing these traits.

Source: Ibid.

ADAPTABILITY.   A final determinant of salesperson effectiveness is one's ability to adapt to situational circumstances. This ability is due in part to personal aptitude but also includes learned skills. Researchers have built a compelling case that adaptability is an absolutely essential characteristic for success in selling.[22]

Formally, **adaptive selling** is "the altering of sales behaviors during a customer interaction or across customer interactions based on perceived information about the nature of the selling situation."[23] A low level of adaptability is manifest when a salesperson uses the same presentation approach and methods during a single sales encounter or across encounters. Effective salespeople adapt their presentation to fit the situation; they are able to pick up signals and *read* the situation. For example, a brief, matter-of-fact presentation may be called for when meeting with a time-pressured and impatient customer, whereas a longer, more-detailed presentation is appropriate when interacting with a customer who wants all the details before making a decision.

Hence, adaptive selling involves (1) recognizing that different selling approaches are needed in different sales situations; (2) having confidence in one's ability to use a variety of sales approaches *across* selling encounters as called for by the specifics of the situation; (3) having confidence in one's ability to alter the sales approach *during* a sales encounter; and (4) actually using different approaches in different situations.[24]

EXCELLENCE IN SELLING

What does it take to be a truly outstanding salesperson, to be a high performer, to excel in sales? As is always the case, there are no simple answers. Moreover, achieving excellence in one type of sales endeavor, say selling personal insurance, undoubtedly requires somewhat different aptitude and skills than achieving excellence when selling sophisticated information systems to corporate buyers.

---

[22]See Siew Meng Leong, Paul S. Busch, and Deborah Roedder John, "Knowledge Bases and Salesperson Effectiveness: A Script-Theoretic Analysis," *Journal of Marketing Research*, 26 (May 1989), 164–178; Rosann L. Spiro and Barton A. Weitz, "Adaptive Selling: Conceptualization, Measurement, and Nomological Validity," *Journal of Marketing Research*, 27 (February 1990), 61–69; Weitz, "Effectiveness in Sales Interactions: A Contingency Framework"; Barton A. Weitz, Harish Sujan, and Mita Sujan, "Knowledge, Motivation, and Adaptive Behavior: A Framework for Improving Selling Effectiveness," *Journal of Marketing*, 50 (October 1986), 174–191.

[23]Weitz, Sujan, and Sujan, "Knowledge, Motivation, and Adaptive Behavior: A Framework for Improving Selling Effectiveness."

[24]Adapted from Spiro and Weitz, "Adaptive Selling: Conceptualization, Measurement, and Nomological Validity."

However, although there are differences from sales job to sales job, there also are similarities.

High-performing salespeople generally differ from other salespeople in terms of some general attitudes they have about the job and the manner in which they conduct their business. High-performing salespeople do the following:

- Represent the interests of their companies and their clients simultaneously to achieve *two-way advocacy*.

- Exemplify *professionalism* in the way they perform the sales job.

- Are *committed to selling* and the sales process, because they believe the sales process is in the customer's best interest.

- Actively *plan and develop strategies* that will lead to programs benefiting the customer.[25]

Specific Characteristics of High-Performers

In addition to these general practices, excellence in selling is associated with a variety of specific characteristics that are reflected in the salesperson's personal features and job behavior. These include the first impression a salesperson makes, his or her depth of knowledge, breadth of knowledge, adaptability, sensitivity, enthusiasm, self-esteem, extended focus, sense of humor, creativity, risk taking, and sense of honesty and ethics.[26]

THE FIRST IMPRESSION.   The outcome of a sales call is greatly influenced by the first impression a salesperson makes on the customer. The likelihood that a salesperson's ideas will be accepted depends largely on the initial encounter. Determinants of the first impression include personal looks, dress, body language, eye contact, handshake, punctuality, and courtesy.

DEPTH OF KNOWLEDGE.   A salesperson's depth of knowledge reflects how well he or she understands the business, products, company, competitors, and general economic climate related to the sales job. Depth of knowledge

---

[25]Thayer C. Taylor, "Anatomy of a Star Salesperson," *Sales and Marketing Management*, May 1986, 49–51.

[26]These characteristics and the following discussion are based on Alessandra, Cathcart, and Wexler, *Selling by Objectives*, 59–76. A related perspective is provided by Lawrence W. Lamont and William J. Lundstrom, "Identifying Successful Industrial Salesmen by Personality and Personal Characteristics," *Journal of Marketing Research*, 14 (November 1977), 517–529.

is obtained in part through an individual's self-study efforts. Knowledgeable salespeople stay alert to what is going on by listening carefully to customers, reading general business publications (*The Wall Street Journal*, *Business Week*, etc.), and getting the most out of company sales meetings and conferences. Another source of company knowledge is the initial training a salesperson receives.

BREADTH OF KNOWLEDGE.   Salespeople who have a wide breadth of knowledge are conversant on a broad spectrum of subjects and, therefore, are able to interact effectively with a variety of customers. Salespeople who possess a broad scope of knowledge make customers feel relaxed and are able to share common interests (via comments or discussions concerning world events, athletics, cultural affairs, or whatever the customer's interests may be). One acquires this facet of excellence through expansive reading, taking a variety of courses while in college, continuous studying, and good listening skills. In general, breadth of knowledge is a matter of being alert, attentive, and interested in different people and events.

At a minimum, any college graduate who expects to be conversant and effective in a selling position should read a daily newspaper and a weekly magazine such as *Newsweek* or *Time*.

ADAPTABILITY.   As already discussed, this fourth characteristic of excellence is the willingness and ability to adapt your interactional style to match the other person's. Because salespeople interact with a wide variety of customers, those who are more adaptable tend to be more effective. Adaptability in this sense is not to be misinterpreted as suggesting that a salesperson should alter his or her presentation to accommodate what each prospect might want to hear, regardless of the truth. Rather, the point is that people differ in terms of how open, sociable, and communicative they are, and a salesperson must adjust his or her interactional style to the customer's preferred style.

SENSITIVITY.   The essence of this fifth characteristic of excellence is *empathy*, or the ability to place oneself in the other person's position. That is, the successful sales representative shows a genuine interest in the prospect's needs, problems, and concerns. Also, the salesperson demonstrates respect for customers and does not patronize them. Most people are quick to notice a sales representative's positive attitude toward them, and they react favorably to it.

Good listening skills are another facet of sensitivity. Listening enables the salesperson to understand the needs of the customer and to adjust the sales message accordingly. Listening is a rare skill. But why? One reason is that people are usually absorbed in their own lives and activities and listening to someone else becomes boring for them. Most of us enjoy a conversation only when the other person is finished talking and we can start talking. The fact that so many people look upon listening as something irksome reflects the scarcity of good listeners.

ENTHUSIASM. Enthusiasm, the sixth characteristic of excellence, reflects a salesperson's *deep-seated commitment to his or her company's products and to customers' needs*. Enthusiastic salespeople tend to be more motivated than less enthusiastic people, and customers are responsive to the salesperson's enthusiastic efforts.

SELF-ESTEEM. This involves feelings of *self-worth and personal confidence*. A salesperson is more successful if he or she has a positive self-concept, likes his or her product and company, and looks forward to meeting prospects. A salesperson who does not have self-confidence will seldom be successful in selling. Furthermore, a salesperson must have a positive attitude toward the product, company, and sales message. A person who does not fully believe in what he or she sells will be seen as insincere. After all, if the salesperson does not believe in the product, how can the customer?

EXTENDED FOCUS. Excellent people in any endeavor have specific goals and purpose, that is, a sense of focus. Said another way, "Most people aim at nothing in life and hit it with amazing accuracy."[27] The term extended focus means the ability to *simultaneously focus on the specific and look at the big picture*. This eighth characteristic of excellence is based on the idea that salespeople must focus their efforts into achieving specific goals; they must not permit themselves to be distracted.

SENSE OF HUMOR. This ninth characteristic of excellence stresses the ability to laugh with others as well as to laugh at yourself. Humor helps customers relax. It also helps customers remember you. There is a difference, however, between having a sense of humor and being a clown or buffoon.

CREATIVITY. Salespeople who exhibit this tenth characteristic have an ability to connect seemingly unrelated ideas and to arrive at unique solutions to problems. This ability is critical in many selling positions, such as trade selling and technical selling, where the salesperson is often selling a total system rather than a single product. Often competing companies' basic products and nonproduct offerings (e.g., promotional programs) are very similar; hence, what distinguishes one company from the next are the creative solutions that salespeople devise for addressing customers' needs or solving problems. Creativity does not stop with merely coming up with an idea; rather, "it is the quality of the action that puts the idea into being."[28]

---

[27]Alessandra, Cathcart, and Wexler, *Selling by Objectives*, 73.

[28]Ibid., 75.

TAKING RISKS.   Closely related to creativity is the eleventh characteristic of excellence, the willingness to take risks. To be creative you must be willing to take risks, recommend solutions that might backfire or be ridiculed, and seek change rather than sameness. Excellent salespeople are always looking for new ideas, new methods, and new solutions that will benefit their customers, themselves, and their companies.

SENSE OF HONESTY AND ETHICS.   This twelfth characteristic is last but certainly not least. Contrary to widespread myths about personal selling, excellence in personal selling requires as high a degree of honesty and ethical behavior as in any of life's lasting relationships. The key word is *relationship*. There are some sales jobs where a single transaction between buyer and seller takes place; however, most personal-selling interactions involve building long-term relationships with customers. This is not accomplished with deceit, misrepresentation, or undependable behavior. The excellent salesperson is seen by the customer as trustworthy and dependable. We expect these qualities in our friends, and the same expectations carry over on a professional level to the marketplace. You may recall the opening vignette identifying the qualities most and least valued by purchasing agents in salespeople. The two most valued qualities are reliability/credibility and professionalism/integrity.

SUMMARY

This chapter presents a broad array of ideas about the nature of personal selling. Personal selling's role in the promotion mix includes educating customers, encouraging product usage and marketing assistance, and providing after-sale service and support to the buyer. As a personal career, sales includes the attractive features of freedom of action, variety and challenge, opportunities for advancement, and desirable financial and nonfinancial rewards.

A *partner-oriented* selling mind-set is in operation in most successful firms today. These firms realize that their success rests with their customers' successes. Hence, modern partner-oriented philosophy makes *customer satisfaction* its highest priority. Modern selling practice is based on the following principles: trust and mutual agreement must exist between buyer and seller; getting the order is only the first step—after-sales service is what counts; and professionalism and integrity are essential in a salesperson.

Personal selling is a broad field consisting of a variety of different types of sales jobs entailing different activities, including: making sales presentations, working with orders, servicing the product and the account, managing information, participating in conferences and meetings, training, entertaining, traveling, and working with distributors. Sales jobs include trade selling, missionary selling, technical selling, new-business selling, retail selling, and telemarketing.

A contingency model of the selling process is presented to explain that salesperson performance and effectiveness are dependent on a variety of factors. Specific determinants of salesperson performance include (1) aptitude, (2) skill level, (3) motivational level, (4) role perceptions, (5) personal characteristics, and (6) adaptability.

A final section examines excellence in selling. Twelve basic characteristics of excellence include the first impression a salesperson makes, his or her depth of knowledge, breadth of knowledge, adaptability, sensitivity, enthusiasm, self-esteem, extended focus, sense of humor, creativity, risk taking, and sense of honesty and ethics.

Discussion Questions

1. Personal selling is more effective than advertising but less efficient. Explain.

2. Many people hold personal selling in low esteem. Many students rebel at the idea of taking a sales job out of college. Why do you think these attitudes persist?

3. Comment on the following statement: Salespeople must lie and be deceitful in order to succeed.

4. Contrast antiquated and modern selling practices. In rethinking your response to question 2, what additional insight can you offer by taking into consideration the antiquated-modern distinction?

5. One form of sales presentation is called a *canned presentation*. This means that a salesperson uses the identical presentation time after time. How would you evaluate the canned sales presentation? What are the advantages and disadvantages of this form of presentation?

6. "Sales representatives should act as if they were on the customer's payroll." Evaluate this statement by explaining in your own words what it means and by describing the advantages and disadvantages that may result when a salesperson acts in this manner.

7. In view of the different types of sales jobs described in the chapter (such as trade selling and technical selling), identify the job types you would or would not be willing to take as a first job out of college. Provide your rationale for each decision.

8. No single factor is able to adequately explain salesperson performance. Comment.

9. Clearly distinguish among aptitude, skill, and personal characteristics as unique determinants of salesperson performance. Considering only aptitude and personal characteristics, provide an assessment of whether you possess the aptitude and personal features for a successful career in (1) computer sales for a

company like IBM, and (2) trade sales for a company such as Procter & Gamble. Offer reasons why you think you would (or would not) succeed.

10. Distinguish between working hard and working smart. As a student, which behavior better characterizes your own performance? What behaviors would a salesperson manifest in demonstrating an ability to work smart rather than simply hard? Be specific.

11. Based on the 12 characteristics of personal excellence described in the text, which of these do you think most salespeople with whom you have come in contact lack? Do you possess the potential for excellence in selling? Why or why not?

12. Interview three sales representatives and describe the differences in their philosophies and approaches to personal selling. Compare your findings with the ideas presented in the text.

13. Studies of college students' views toward personal selling were mentioned in the chapter and summarized in Table 21.1. Interview five students and ask them to rate each of the statements on a five-point scale labeled strongly agree, agree, neither agree nor disagree, disagree, and strongly disagree. Summarize the results from your small survey and draw implications based on the assumption that the five students you queried hold representative views.

14. Write a two- to three-page essay on why you would or would not be a good salesperson.

Sales Management

SELECTING TOP-PERFORMING SALESPEOPLE

Q: As a sales manager, I know I've hired the best when a salesperson sells the most, but how do I know how to find this kind of person again?

A: You identify what you've learned that can apply the next time you hire a salesperson. That is, you need a system that keeps track of what it is about a person's background, experience, and abilities that is relevant to picking another like that. For example, what qualities does a person have before joining your organization that lead to success? You will not be able to find duplicate people, but you can find persons with approximately the same characteristics. In short, we're talking about the ability to identify specific qualities that contribute to success and to apply this information to your next selection decision. Obviously everyone can't be the best. But you can expect the average performance per salesperson to get better if you have a system that tracks performance and constantly identifies success characteristics—and you use this information when hiring in the future. This approach translates into increased productivity and sales revenues.

Q: Can't psychologists simply provide a test that predicts sales success?

A: There is no single psychological test or set of characteristics that assures that you will get the best person for a position. And even if you could find one, it would not work across all companies or industries; there is no way to determine a single generic standard to pick what is best for all companies. Top performance in one company can't assure success in another. There is no single golden person who will perform best everywhere. Each organization must develop its own model of what is best based upon everything in its recruiting and selection process.

Q: Why can't sales success be defined generically?

A: It is vital for you to know what is best for your own company, because sales success is much more dependent upon an individual's background and experience relevant to a company's products and services than it is upon personality types. It is true that some generalized characteristics are needed for all sales jobs. You need to find people who are willing to talk to prospects, and to answer questions about the commodity they sell.

Note: These questions were posed by interviewers for *Sales and Marketing Management* and were answered by Dr. David W. Merrill, chairman of Tracom Corp., a psychological consulting firm located in Denver. Source: "New England Life Takes Steps to Insure Its Future," *Sales and Marketing Management,* August 12, 1985, 77. Copyright 1985; reprinted by permission of *Sales & Marketing Management.*

The opening vignette deals with one of the most important yet difficult tasks sales managers confront, namely, selecting salespeople who have the potential to become top performers. However, a sales manager's overall responsibilities encompass much more than the staffing function.

In general, **sales management** involves acquiring, directing, and stimulating competent salespeople to perform tasks that move the organization toward accomplishment of its objectives and mission. Sales management provides a significant link between an organization's corporate and marketing strategies and the salespeople who actuate the marketing transaction. A sales manager is

the tactician who translates plans into action. He or she implements the various programs for market analysis, direction of sales effort, training, performance appraisal and compensation. . . [and] also has a longer-term responsibility for planning market development and account coverage in his/her area. He or she provides management with information on the organization's effectiveness and conditions in the marketplace as inputs to management's analysis, planning and control activities.[1]

In an overall sense, sales management involves the performance of five basic functions: (1) planning, (2) organizing, (3) staffing, (4) directing, and (5) evaluat-

---

[1]John P. Steinbrink, "Field Sales Management," in *Marketing Manager's Handbook,* eds. Stuart Henderson Britt and Norman F. Guess (Chicago: Dartnell Corporation, 1983), 984.

ing and controlling sales-force performance and satisfaction. Each function is discussed in the following sections.

PLANNING THE SALES FUNCTION

Planning is the process of establishing a broad set of goals, policies, and procedures for achieving sales and marketing objectives. Three of the most important planning activities undertaken by sales managers are (1) developing sales budgets, (2) designing sales territories, and (3) setting sales-force quotas.

Developing Sales Budgets

The budgeting process for selling has been described in these terms:

> The salesforce budget is the amount of money available or assigned for a definite period of time, usually a year. It is based on estimates of expenditures during that period of time . . . [and] depends on the sales forecast and the amount of revenue expected to be generated for the organization during that time period.[2]

The first step in developing a budget is to analyze market opportunity and forecast sales potential. Then management must estimate the amount of money required to accomplish the tasks necessary to achieve its forecasted sales. Two basic procedures for allotting funds are (1) the line-item budget and (2) the program-budget method.

In **line-item budgeting,** management allocates funds in meticulous detail to each identifiable cost center. For example, the sales department may budget funds for areas such as office supplies, wages, research, and travel.[3] This budgeting procedure requires management to forecast and account for each item in great detail. **Program budgeting** avoids many of the problems of line-item budgeting. With this approach, management provides each administrative unit with a lump sum of money that each administrative head can use as he or she sees fit to accomplish the stated objectives. This method provides considerable flexibility by allowing managers to shift funds as deemed necessary. For example, funds for travel and/or entertainment can be shifted to recruitment in the event that one or more salespersons change jobs, retire early, and so on.

---

[2]Charles Futrell, *Sales Management*, 3d. ed. (Chicago: The Dryden Press, 1991), 128–129.

[3]William J. Stanton and Richard H. Buskirk, *Management of the Salesforce* (Homewood, IL: Richard D. Irwin, 1983), 431.

Designing Sales Territories

A **sales territory** consists of present and prospective customers assigned to a salesperson, sales branch, or distributor for a specified period.[4] The ideal situation is to create sales territories of *equal potential and equal workload*. In this way, the sales manager can more easily evaluate and control each salesperson's performance. Also, having equal workloads among the sales representatives leads to greater salesforce motivation and morale. Unfortunately, achieving this ideal situation is rare, if not impossible.

Although each company has its own unique procedures for designing sales territories, the design process generally adheres to the following steps: (1) selecting a basic control unit, (2) estimating the market potential in each control unit, (3) combining control units into tentative territories, (4) performing a workload analysis, (5) adjusting tentative territories to allow for differences in potential sales and workload across territories, and (6) assigning salespeople to territories (see Figure 22.1).[5] Each of these steps will now be discussed in detail.

SELECTING A BASIC CONTROL UNIT.   Sales managers design territories along lines of elemental geographical areas: regions, states, regions within states, counties, cities, parts of cities, and so on. The *basic control unit* selected depends on the size of the company, the products the company sells, and the nature of the customers called on. For example, larger geographical units (e.g., states rather than counties) could serve as the basic unit for an industrial-goods company whose salespeople each call on relatively few large accounts. Comparatively, individual counties, or even ZIP-code areas, might represent a superior control unit for a company selling personal insurance.

ESTIMATING MARKET POTENTIAL.   The second step is to estimate the market potential of each basic control unit. Previous sales records, emerging sales opportunities, and competitive concentration help the sales manager determine these estimates.

FORMING TENTATIVE TERRITORIES.   In step three, the sales manager combines contiguous control units (e.g., five adjoining counties) into a tentative territory. Again, the objective is to develop sales territories of equal potential.

PERFORMING A WORKLOAD ANALYSIS.   In step four, the sales manager must consider the amount of work that is necessary to attain the

---

[4]Gilbert A. Churchill, Jr., Neil M. Ford, and Orville C. Walker, Jr., *Salesforce Management: Planning, Implementation and Control* (Homewood, IL: Richard D. Irwin, Inc., 1985), 175.

[5]These steps and related discussion are based on ibid., 187–204.

Stages in Territory Design

FIGURE 22.1

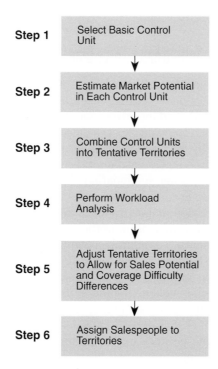

Step 1	Select Basic Control Unit
Step 2	Estimate Market Potential in Each Control Unit
Step 3	Combine Control Units into Tentative Territories
Step 4	Perform Workload Analysis
Step 5	Adjust Tentative Territories to Allow for Sales Potential and Coverage Difficulty Differences
Step 6	Assign Salespeople to Territories

Source: Gilbert A. Churchill, Jr., Neil M. Ford and Orville C. Walker, Jr., *Sales Force Management,* Third Edition (Homewood, IL: Richard D. Irwin, 1990), 221. Copyright 1990 by Richard D. Irwin, Inc. Reprinted with permission.

territory's potential. Although two salespeople may have equal sales potential in their respective territories, the workloads necessary to reach those potentials could be unequal. For example, one salesperson may have to travel longer distances, endure more severe weather conditions, and have many small accounts to call on.

ADJUSTING TENTATIVE TERRITORIES. In step five, the sales manager attempts to equalize sales potentials and workloads across all territories. In this stage the sales manager often must rely on a combination of quantitative tools, subjectivity, and trial and error.

ASSIGNING SALESPEOPLE TO TERRITORIES. Finally, the sales manager must assign salespeople to the various sales territories. If we assume that all territories have the same workload and have the same sales potential, and we further assume that all salespeople have the same selling skills, product knowledge, and so on, then the territorial assignment task would be simple. However, all salespeople are not the same; the sales manager must devise a method that is fair to all and that optimizes the firm's profits.

Setting Sales-Force Quotas

Sales quotas are specific performance goals that management sets for territories, branch offices, and individual sales representatives. The primary functions of quotas are to establish goals and incentives for the salesforce and to give management yardsticks by which to evaluate each salesperson's performance on the job, thus providing a basis for job promotion and/or salary raises.

Sales managers most frequently base quotas on (1) sales volume, (2) profit, (3) activities performed, or (4) some combination of the preceding methods.[6]

The most typical method for developing quotas is by the use of **sales-volume quotas.** These quotas are based on geographical areas, product lines, individual customers, time periods, or a combination of these factors. For example, a quota for a particular sales representative might be to sell at least 20 units of product X in region Z during the next quarter. The major advantage of basing quotas on sales volume is these quotas are easy to understand and simple to use. A disadvantage, however, is that sales-volume quotas, if used alone, can encourage selling behaviors that disregard expenses and neglect nonselling activities. In other words, in attempting to meet and exceed sales-volume quotas, sales might be made that are not profitable because expenses are excessive, accounts are not adequately serviced, and so on.

Profit quotas are based on the profits (sales minus expenses) generated rather than amount of sales per se. Since sales representatives often prefer to sell low-profit, fast-moving items rather than harder-to-sell products that often contribute greater amounts to company profits, profit quotas offer an obvious advantage over sales-volume quotas for sales management. However, whereas measurement of sales-volume-quota achievement is a straightforward matter of simply tabulating the number of units or dollars sold by a salesperson, measurement of profit-quota achievement also requires calculating the expenses incurred in generating the sales volume. Two potential problems result: (1) calculating profit quotas can require inordinate amounts of clerical and administrative efforts; and (2) sales representatives may have problems with profit-based quotas since some of the expenses that go into their calculation are perceived to be beyond the salesperson's direct control.

Activity quotas are used to encourage sales representatives to perform specific activities such as calling on new accounts, making product demonstrations,

---

[6]Futrell, *Sales Management*, 3d. ed., 176–180.

building displays, and so forth. Although in principle these types of quotas stimulate a balanced approach to sales representatives' jobs, in actuality they may encourage little more than perfunctory effort to satisfy the activity quota without any effort to do it well or effectively. Sales manager supervision is needed to assure that salespeople are satisfying the spirit of an activity quota rather than merely meeting the letter of the quota.

In summary, sales quotas are an extremely important aspect of the sales-management function. If set fairly and realistically, they can encourage highly motivated salesperson performance and reward quota achievers for their efforts. On the downside, quotas set too low may fail to provide sufficient challenge or incentive for the salesforce; or quotas set too high may serve as a disincentive because salespeople feel they cannot possibly meet what is expected of them. Setting challenging yet realistic quotas is truly an art that only the most effective sales managers ever accomplish.

ORGANIZING THE SALES FUNCTION

Most companies organize or specialize their sales departments in one of four ways: (1) geographically, (2) by product types, (3) by market or customer classes, or (4) by function.

Geography-Based Sales Organization

Specialization by geographical territories is probably the most common form of sales management organization. Figure 22.2 provides an illustrative organizational chart that is based on geographical specialization. Depending on the size of the business, the manager who runs a geographical sales unit is called a regional, divisional, or district sales manager. In the organizational arrangement in Figure 22.2, regional sales managers supervise zone managers, who in turn supervise the district sales managers to whom salespeople report. In many cases the sales manager, regardless of the title he or she is given, is basically running his or her own business within a business. That is, he or she is like the president of his or her own firm.

As discussed in Chapter 8, the trend toward regional marketing has encouraged many firms to reorganize their sales departments along geographical lines. Campbell Soup is one of the many consumer package-good companies that has reorganized geographically. For many years, the sales function at Campbell Soup was organized along product lines. Each of four product lines (canned foods, frozen foods, special products, and fresh foods) had its own vice president of sales. Reporting to each vice president was a chain of sales managers and sales representatives. This arrangement created a major problem: up to four

| FIGURE 22.2 | Geographic Sales Organization |

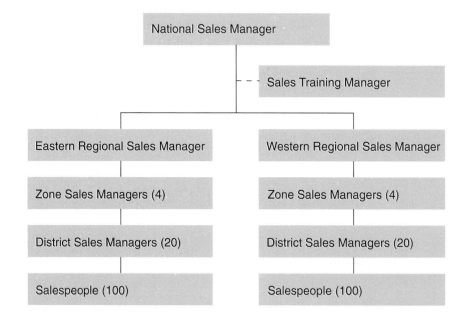

Source: Thomas N. Ingram and Raymond W. LaForge, *Sales Management: Analysis and Decision Making* (Chicago: The Dryden Press, 1989), 228.

different Campbell sales representatives, one from each product line, called on a single retail account. Duplicated efforts made the selling costs excessive, and the rigid sales structure was unable to accommodate new product introductions. These factors along with the growing power of supermarket chains and the increased sophistication in their buying practices necessitated sales reorganization.

Campbell reorganized along geographical lines. General sales managers head up sales departments in each of four U.S. regions: west, central, south, and east. Reporting to these four general managers are 22 regional managers. Directors of retail operations report to each regional manager. The director of retail operations is responsible for the field salesforce. Sales representatives now sell all Campbell products rather than only a single product line as they did in the past.

Another fundamental change at Campbell Soup involves the manner in which sales-promotion decisions are made. Under the product-organization structure, promotion decisions were made at corporate headquarters and then delegated to the salesforce. In effect, this meant that all areas of the country were told to use the same promotions. Now, local salesforces in each region have their own promotion budgets, develop promotion ideas, get approval from head-quarters, execute the promotion, and are held accountable for the results.[7]

Product-Line Sales Organization

Although a company's sales organization can be very effective for one product line, the same type of organizational structure may not be effective for a company that carries *diverse product offerings*. Gillette, for example, has separate salesforces for its personal care and writing products.[8] A company that offers a set of unrelated or heterogeneous products should consider organizing or reorganizing by product types or groups. Figure 22.3 shows a basic example of a sales organizational structure used in product specialization. In this case, the company has separated sales activity between its office-equipment and office-supply products.

Management's idea is that sales representatives should use their particular knowledge about specific products to increase company profits. This organizational structure works well if the customers the sales representatives call on do

Product-Line Sales Organization   FIGURE 22.3

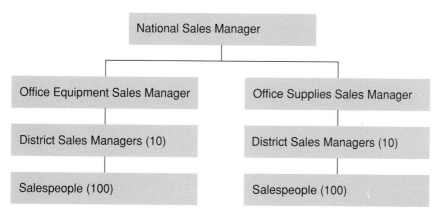

Source: Ingram and LaForge, 230.

<hr />

[7]Adapted from Rayna Skolnik, "Campbell Stirs Up Its Salesforce," *Sales and Marketing Management*, April 1986, 56–58.

[8]Ingram and LaForge, 229.

not overlap, which was the problem with Campbell Soup's old product-based sales structure.

Market-Based Sales Organization

This structure emphasizes specific markets rather than products. A market-based sales structure is needed when a company sells to multiple customers whose buying needs and procedures differ greatly. Figure 22.4 illustrates an organization based on market-based specialization. In this instance, a company has separated its salesforce into one group calling on commercial accounts and another group that caters to government customers.

Companies may find that specialization by market is to their advantage when the needs of customer groups differ significantly, when the customer groups are geographically concentrated, and/or when the company uses different channels of distribution and therefore wants to minimize friction among them.[9]

FIGURE 22.4   **Market-Based Sales Organization**

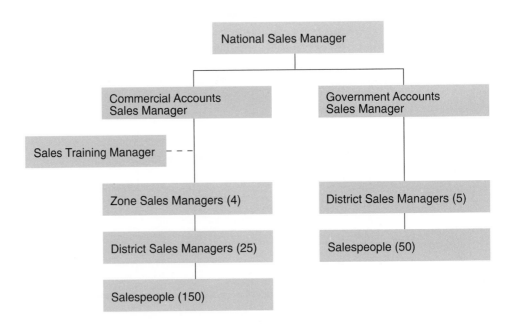

Source: Ingram and LaForge, 232.

[9]Stanton and Buskirk, *Management of the Salesforce*, 67–68.

We can understand why an automobile manufacturer, for example, may want to have different salesforces (and in fact, a different marketing plan) when selling to the government market (post office, military, etc.), to the industrial market, and to the ultimate consumer (through dealers). Each market's buying behavior is different and therefore requires a different approach and a different sales organization.

Function-Based Sales Organization

Figure 22.5 illustrates a sales organization that separates its salesforce into field sales and telemarketing sales. As discussed in Chapter 19, increasing numbers of companies—especially in the case of business-to-business marketing—have established telemarketing salesforces. In this particular case (Figure 22.5) the role of the field salesforce is to generate sales and that of the telemarketing salesforce is to perform account-servicing activities.

Which Organizational Arrangement Is Best?

You know by now that there is no simple answer to questions such as this; rather, the answer always is contingent on the circumstances. In short, it depends. It is possible, however, to examine the comparative advantages and

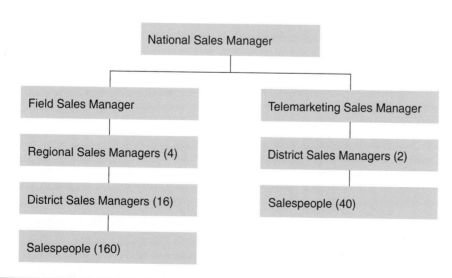

Function-Based Sales Organization   FIGURE 22.5

Source: Ingram and LaForge, 233.

disadvantages of each form of organization structure. These are summarized in Table 22.1.

STAFFING THE SALES FUNCTION

To staff any organization properly, the manager must understand fundamental principles in the recruiting and selection process. Several steps should be followed in creating or reorganizing a sales staff.[10]

First, the sales manager must perform a job analysis. A **job analysis** identifies the activities, duties, responsibilities, knowledge, selling skills, and personal attributes a sales representative should have in order to function effectively in the organization.

Next, the sales manager needs to write a **job description.** This document is a written statement of the job analysis described in step 1. The job description includes a job title, the specific duties and responsibilities of the sales representative, the authoritative relationships with other immediate members of the organization, and the opportunities for advancement. Good job descriptions include the following:

1. A description of the products or services the sales representative will sell.

2. The types of customers the sales representative must call on, the desired frequency of sales calls, and the specific personnel the sales representative should contact.

3. The specific tasks and responsibilities the sales representative must carry out, including customer service, clerical work, reports, information collection, and promotional activities.

4. The authoritative relationships between the sales representative and other positions within the company. This statement provides information regarding who the sales representative reports to and under what circumstances he or she interacts with other departmental personnel.

Table 22.2 provides a typical job description for a field sales representative.

Finally, the sales manager should develop a statement of job qualifications. Whereas the job description provides information on the salesperson's activities, responsibilities, assignments, and authorities, the **job-qualifications document** describes the personal features, characteristics, and abilities that management

---

[10]Adapted from Churchill, Ford, and Walker, *Salesforce Management: Planning, Implementation, and Control*, 362–364.

	Comparison of Sales Organization Structures		TABLE 22.1

ORGANIZATION STRUCTURE	ADVANTAGES	DISADVANTAGES
Geographic	■ Low cost ■ No geographic duplication ■ No customer duplication ■ Fewer management levels	■ Limited specialization ■ Lack of management control over product or customer emphasis
Product	■ Salespeople become experts in product attributes and applications ■ Management control over selling effort allocated to products	■ High cost ■ Geographic duplication ■ Customer duplication
Market	■ Salespeople develop better understanding of unique customer needs ■ Management control over selling effort allocated to different markets	■ High cost ■ Geographic duplication
Functional	■ Efficiency in performing selling activities ■ Customer duplication	■ Geographic duplication ■ Need for coordination

Source: Thomas N. Ingram and Raymond W. LaForge, *Sales Management: Analysis and Decision Making* (Chicago: The Dryden Press, 1989), 239.

believes a salesperson needs in order to perform the job effectively and efficiently. These qualifications may include educational background, business experience, personality, perceived attitude toward the work ethic, ability to get along with others, personal appearance, and so forth.

Developing a Recruiting System

The purpose of a recruiting system is to match people who have the specific and desired qualifications with management's written job descriptions in order to meet sales, marketing, and company objectives.

To locate potentially qualified applicants for a sales job, recruiters use advertising, employment agencies, employee referrals, internal training programs, educational institutions, internal transfers, unsolicited applications, competitors' employees, and those people with whom management deals—from suppliers of products or information (such as an account executive from an advertising agency) to customer salespeople (someone in a wholesale or retailing business, for example).

TABLE 22.2	Job Description for a Sales Representative

I.   Basic Function

The sales representative is charged with building profitable volume, broadening distribution, and maintaining a professional image with assigned accounts.

II.   Specific Duties

   A. Sells sufficient profitable products to customers to reach assigned objectives.
   B. Calls on selected commercial consumers in order to convert them to the use of our products.
   C. Organizes and plans territory coverage for the most effective use of time.
   D. Gains commitment from assigned accounts for our promotions.
   E. Conducts effective organized product knowledge and promotional sales meetings with assigned accounts.
   F. Prospects for new business at the distributor and consumer levels.
   G. Maintains an awareness of competitive activity and opportunities.
   H. Submits concise and accurate reports on time; maintains records and responds to assignments.
   I. Transmits marketing and sales intelligence relating to competition and changes in the marketplace.
   J. Works within assigned expense budget.

III.   Relationships

   A. Reports to and is accountable solely to regional/district sales manager.
   B. Has a close working relationship with other members of the region and district.
   C. Develops effective relationships with decision makers in assigned accounts.

Interviewing, Testing, and Hiring

In the final stage of the staffing function, the manager must determine whether applicants match the company's job specifications and which applicant(s) will do the best job. Several methods for accomplishing this objective are available to the sales manager, including interviews, reference checks, and various types of intelligence, aptitude, and personality tests.

The initial source of information typically available to a sales manager is an applicant's *resume*. Applicants who pass the initial resume inspection are *personally interviewed*. The interview allows sales management to verify the information in the prospect's application form and gives the interviewer the opportunity to evaluate the prospect in person. The recruiter can evaluate the applicant's verbal skills—vocabulary, grammar, and general conversational ability—and can observe the prospect's mannerisms, physical appearance, voice quality, and eye contact to gain insights into the candidate's personal and persuasive skills.

Sales managers often use *references* as an additional source of information in the evaluation of prospective sales representatives. However, it must be noted that the references suggested by the candidate are often highly biased in his or her favor because they are typically friends and relatives. For this reason, sales managers or their staffs often check with sources that are probably more impartial, such as the prospect's present and former employers and professors. The best way for an interviewer to obtain solid references is through face-to-face contact or voice-to-voice contact on the telephone with each referent. More open dialogue occurs in these ways rather than by letter.

Psychological tests are another valuable input to a sales manager's selection decision. The four most common tests are (1) personality tests, (2) sales-aptitude tests, (3) interest tests, and (4) intelligence tests. **Personality tests** attempt to measure a person's affability, confidence, poise, aggressiveness, and other job-related attributes. **Sales-aptitude tests** are designed to measure a person's verbal ability, tactfulness, persuasiveness, tenacity, memory, and social extroversion/introversion, among many other traits. **Interest tests** are designed to identify a person's vocational and avocational inclinations. **Intelligence tests** attempt to measure memory ability, critical-reasoning ability, and ability to draw inferences.

Sales managers should consider these tests as useful inputs to their decisions, but not as final hiring decisions. The sales manager's *judgment* is the final test. A good sales manager tempers the results of measurement tools with his or her judgment and intuition. This is absolutely essential, because as noted in the opening vignette, there is no such thing as an all-purpose test that will ensure the selection of a top-performing salesperson.

DIRECTING THE SALESFORCE

This sales-management function involves the training of new recruits, the continuing education of existing personnel, and motivational and incentive plans for all sales personnel. This section describes briefly the elements of sales-force direction.

Training the Salesforce

Training programs vary considerably from company to company, but all successful sales organizations have excellent training programs for new members of the salesforce as well as periodic refresher courses for current salespeople.

OBJECTIVES OF TRAINING. The general objectives of sales training should be to (1) provide new salespeople with product, customer, and competitor knowledge; (2) improve salesperson morale and reduce turnover;

(3) establish expected salesperson behavior; (4) improve customer relations; (5) lower selling costs; and (6) show salespeople how to use time efficiently.

These broad sales-management objectives for a sales-training program should then be broken down into specific objectives for the sales representatives. These objectives may include training sales representatives to fill out reports, demonstrating how management uses reports, providing salespeople with methods for keeping records, training salespeople how to allocate their selling time with and among customers, suggesting ways to improve prospecting, and explaining how to handle objections.[11]

CONTENT OF TRAINING.   The content of the sales training program varies from company to company depending on the level of sophistication among the firm's sales personnel. Also, the content varies according to whether new sales personnel or veteran sales personnel are the audience. However, the content generally focuses on corporate policies, selling techniques, product knowledge, and self-management skills.

TRAINING PERSONNEL.   There are three basic sources of trainers: *line personnel* (e.g., district sales manager), *staff trainers* (people hired for the exclusive purpose of training sales personnel), and *outside training specialists* (hired consultants who either provide general training programs or specialize in particular aspects of personal selling).

LOCATION OF TRAINING.   Some initial training is conducted in the classroom, and additional training is done in the field. The classroom setting is usually in the home or district office.

TIMING OF TRAINING.   Companies vary in their philosophies regarding when training should take place. Some companies feel that extensive training in basic product knowledge, sales techniques, company policies, and so on should be concentrated in the first several weeks after a person is hired. After this period of training, the person is qualified to go out and sell. Other companies prefer to give new hirees a quick, basic course, have the applicants go into the field and gain some practical experience, and then provide them with an intensive period of training. Some companies schedule several one- to two-day training seminars per year, whereas others schedule several intensive one- to two-week annual training programs.

TRAINING TECHNIQUES.   The training techniques a company uses depend on the objectives that sales managers want to accomplish and on the amount of time that the trainer has to achieve these objectives. Lectures,

---

[11]Stanton and Buskirk, *Management of the Salesforce*, 186–188.

discussion, demonstration, role playing, and on-the-job training are the basic training techniques.

The *lecture method* is the most efficient way to present company policies, procedures, and selling concepts and principles. Lectures provide the new salesperson with an introduction to the company and the subject of selling. The *discussion method* provides salespeople with the opportunity to state their ideas and opinions on a variety of subjects related to personal selling and company policies. These thoughts are most often expressed through pedagogical devices such as cases, round-table discussions, and panels. By using the discussion method, the group leader can draw out experiences from the new sales representatives that are informative and useful to other members who have had or are having similar problems in the field.

Demonstration involves showing rather than explaining the best way to sell a product. Sales representatives can see how their job should be performed instead of merely hearing an explanation. *Role playing* places sales trainees closer to the actual sales situation by having them sell a product in a hypothetical situation. If the situation and the prospect are presented realistically, the trainee learns how to translate lectured concepts and principles into real-life presentations. Sales trainers often videotape the sales trainees as they role-play, because seeing and reviewing one's nonverbal behavior in a selling situation and listening to one's voice and presentation mode can be very enlightening. Finally, in *on-the-job training*, the sales trainer accompanies the sales trainee in actual selling situations. Feedback is provided immediately after the fledgling salesperson has performed admirably or made mistakes.

Various forms of training techniques are illustrated in the *Focus on Promotion*, which describes the outstanding sales-training program used by Merck Sharp & Dohme.

Motivating the Salesforce

In motivating the salesforce, sales management can use both financial and nonfinancial incentives. As the following sections explain, financial rewards are extremely important but usually are not enough.

FINANCIAL INCENTIVES. Sales managers use three basic compensation plans: salary plan, commission plan, and a combination plan (salary plus commission). Within the three basic plans, there are many possible combinations involving base earnings and incentive pay. Six of the most common methods of paying the salesforce are:

■ Straight salary

■ Straight commission

■ Draw against commission

FOCUS ON PROMOTION

SALES TRAINING AT MERCK SHARP & DOHME

Merck Sharp & Dohme is a pharmaceutical company that is known for its outstanding sales-training programs. Merck's philosophy is that a well-trained salesperson is the absolute key to building a relationship of trust with the customer. The vice president of sales proclaims: "We have an obsession about it. Training drives the whole salesforce and it separates us from everybody else."

Merck's training program involves three phases of instruction. The first phase is a primer on medicine basics such as anatomy and physiology. Phase two lasts from one-half to one full year and consists of an in-depth program on the presentation of products in the field. The third phase concentrates on providing Merck's sales reps with knowledge of the diseases and maladies that the company's products treat.

Merck's training involves more than this initial in-depth program. Once every two years each salesperson is sent to medical school for detailed instruction concerning the latest developments in diseases and in medicine in general. In addition, each representative works with a physician/mentor in a hospital setting and learns practical aspects of medicine and the effects of pharmaceutical products. Beyond this, every two months district meetings are held that focus on specific topics dealing with state-of-the-art developments in the treatment of diseases and maladies.

It comes as little surprise that Merck's salespeople are among the best trained in any industry. Customers are extremely pleased, and the turnover rate of top salespeople is much lower at Merck than at other companies.

Source: Based on "Merck's Grand Obsession," *Sales and Marketing Management*, June 1987, 65.

■ Salary plus commission

■ Salary plus bonus

■ Salary plus bonus plus commission

Figure 22.6 presents statistics on the frequency that each form of salesforce compensation is used in different industry groups. Among manufacturing firms,

Frequency of Sales Force Compensation

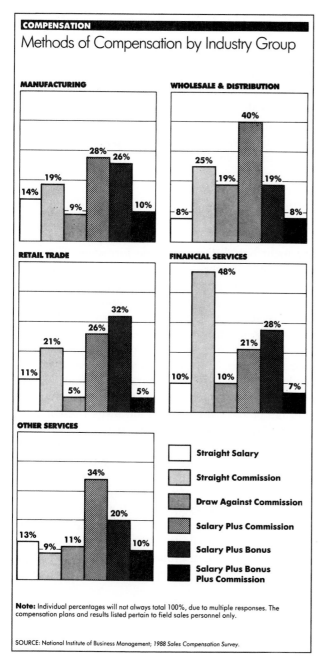

COMPENSATION
Methods of Compensation by Industry Group

MANUFACTURING

14% | 19% | 9% | 28% | 26% | 10%

WHOLESALE & DISTRIBUTION

8% | 25% | 19% | 40% | 19% | 8%

RETAIL TRADE

11% | 21% | 5% | 26% | 32% | 5%

FINANCIAL SERVICES

10% | 48% | 10% | 21% | 28% | 7%

OTHER SERVICES

13% | 9% | 11% | 34% | 20% | 10%

☐ Straight Salary

▢ Straight Commission

▢ Draw Against Commission

▢ Salary Plus Commission

■ Salary Plus Bonus

■ Salary Plus Bonus Plus Commission

Note: Individual percentages will not always total 100%, due to multiple responses. The compensation plans and results listed pertain to field sales personnel only.

SOURCE: National Institute of Business Management; *1988 Sales Compensation Survey.*

Source: Sales & Marketing Management, February 20, 1989, 20. Copyright 1989 Survey of Selling Costs. Reprinted by permission of Sales & Marketing Management.

for example, 14 percent use a straight salary compensation method, 19 percent offer straight commission, 9 percent draw against commission, and so on. It can be seen in Figure 22.6 that *combination plans* (salary plus commission, salary plus bonus, and salary plus bonus plus commission) are most commonly used by sales managers because they provide sales representatives with a broader range of earnings opportunities. Regardless of which specific compensation plan is selected, it is critical that the plan be (1) competitive within the industry, (2) equitable within the company, and (3) fair among members of the salesforce.[12]

A **straight salary** plan provides sales representatives with a *fixed amount of income* regardless of sales productivity. This method of compensation gives management maximum control over the salesforce's activities because management can dictate the activities salespeople must perform in servicing current customers, creating new merchandise displays, and filling out reports for the home or district office. Thus, this plan is best for companies who have a large amount of work devoted to *nonselling activities and routine selling tasks*. Such selling jobs are found in the grocery and pharmaceutical industries.

Straight salary provides little incentive for sales representatives to increase sales. However, it is a good plan for new salespeople who are still learning the ropes.

A **commission plan** is payment based directly on performance. There are two basic commission plans: straight commission or draw against commission. *Straight commissions* can be based on a fixed percentage of a sales representative's dollar sales or product units sold or can be based on a multiple percentage rate that increases as dollar sales volume or some other performance measure increases. The *draw against commission* method is based on draw accounts, which are accounts from which the sales representative receives (or draws) a fixed sum of money on a regular time basis. The money in a draw account comes from either earned or unearned commissions. A salesperson, for example, may draw $1,000 per pay period but may have earned $800 or $1,200 during the same period. In the case of an underage ($800), the salesperson owes the company money. In the case of an overage ($1,200), the salesperson may take the extra commission, apply it against past underages, or defer the amount to the future.

A **bonus** is usually a lump-sum payment that the company makes to sales representatives who have exceeded a set sales quota. However, management may use bases other than sales, such as number of new accounts opened, reduction in expenses, and divisional profits, to set the requirements for a bonus.

In sum, straight salary provides sales managers with maximum control over the sales representative's routine duties, whereas the straight-commission plan provides the sales representatives with maximum financial incentive to sell the company's line of products. As noted above, most companies use some combination of salary plus commission (or bonus).

---

[12]Steinbrink, "Field Sales Management," 992.

NONFINANCIAL INCENTIVES.   Job satisfaction and motivation rest strongly on nonfinancial rewards. Achievement or recognition awards are commonly presented to sales representatives at sales meetings and award banquets as a means of giving sales representatives psychological rewards. Companies also frequently use newsletters, publicity in local media, published sales results, personal letters of commendation, and other psychological rewards to encourage sales performance. Sales managers also motivate sales-force members with face-to-face encouragement, telephone calls of commendation, and by providing assistance when the salesperson requires help in closing a sale or performing other job responsibilities. Some companies also award honorary job titles to outstanding sales representatives, induct them into honor societies, and present distinguished sales awards, often in the form of plaques or certificates.

Sales managers frequently conduct annual sales meetings in attractive vacation sites as another incentive to the salesforce. A company may take its sales representatives to a beach retreat and schedule sales meetings in the morning and recreation in the afternoon. Sales managers use meetings to generate enthusiasm for new product lines and marketing/selling programs. Generally, the sales representatives remain extremely enthusiastic for weeks following these meetings.

Overall, sales managers must find ways to meet not only the immediate financial needs of their sales representatives but also (and perhaps more important) their employees' security needs, opportunities for advancement, personal ego and status needs, personal power needs, desires for a meaningful job, beliefs in self-determination, and requirements for pleasant working conditions. These sales-management considerations both attract and maintain a salesforce. The *Global Focus* offers an interesting parallel between Japanese and American businesspeople. It reveals that fundamental cultural differences necessitate different motivational techniques.

EVALUATING AND CONTROLLING SALESFORCE PERFORMANCE AND SATISFACTION

This management function requires the sales manager to monitor actual salesperson performance, to reward the performance when it meets expectations, and to take corrective action when performance is below the preestablished standard. The basic objective is to determine how well salespeople have performed so as to make corrective changes if necessary and to maintain salesperson satisfaction. Salesperson performance evaluations are used for at least five reasons:

1. To ensure that rewards given salespeople are consistent with their actual performance.

GLOBAL FOCUS

ARE JAPANESE BETTER MARKETERS THAN AMERICANS?

Sales & Marketing Management magazine conducted a nonscientific survey of American sales managers who work for Japanese companies to learn whether Japanese marketing and sales personnel are different, and perhaps better, than their American counterparts. Some of the key findings are these:

1. Because individuality and independence are not as highly valued in Japan as America, Japanese marketing and salespeople are less inclined to take credit for successes or blame others for failures.

2. Japanese companies, even those located in the United States, rarely use nonfinancial incentives to recognize, praise, or reward salespeople for successful performance. Good performance is simply expected, and special praise is deemed unnecessary.

3. Because loyalty to one's employer is a fundamental characteristic of Japanese society, commissions are generally an unnecessary component of compensation packages. Salespeople consider it their duty to create business for their companies; it is the honorable thing to do, and no special compensation is required for doing what duty demands.

4. Because Japanese typically stay with one company for their entire professional lives, there is a greater tendency than in the United States to focus on long-term results. American businesspeople, by comparison, frequently switch jobs; hence, compensation and incentive packages are tied to short-term results.

5. Japanese businesspeople are more dedicated to their companies than are Americans. Accordingly, Japanese tend to work longer hours, oftentimes working (at least entertaining) until midnight.

Source: Adapted from Bill Kelley, "Culture Clash: West Meets East," *Sales & Marketing Management,* July 1991, 28–34.

2. To identify salespeople who deserve promotions.

3. To identify salespeople who should be terminated.

4. To determine specific training and counseling needs of individual salespeople.

5. To identify criteria for the future recruitment and selection of salespeople.[13]

Performance standards include the salespersons' sales volume, percentage of quota met, selling expenses, profit contributions, and customer services rendered. Through sales analysis, cost analysis, and personal evaluations, sales managers can determine whether a salesperson's performance meets preestablished standards.

When the actual and planned performances of a salesperson differ significantly, the sales manager must determine the underlying reasons and take appropriate corrective actions if necessary. Sometimes performance is not up to par due to extenuating circumstances. For example, a union strike in a particular territory may have affected sales; a salesperson may have suffered from an extended illness; he or she may be experiencing marital difficulties; or the sales quota may be unattainable.

When attempting to correct inadequate salesperson performance, it is important that the sales manager avoid excess negativity. In fact, research evidence (and common sense) suggest that managers should seek opportunities to *provide positive feedback* to salespeople rather than accentuating deficiencies.[14] Negative feedback does not motivate salespeople as much as positive feedback does. Moreover, positive feedback serves to clarify what behaviors are expected of salespeople.[15]

SUMMARY

Sales management involves the process of planning, organizing, staffing, directing, and evaluating/controlling a company's salesforce. A sales manager determines sales opportunities, analyzes his or her resources, sets goals and objectives, develops good recruiting and selection procedures, sets up clear lines of authority and responsibilities, creates sales training programs, utilizes sound motivational approaches, and thoroughly analyzes sales and costs, among many other activities. All of these functions must be performed within the context of

---

[13]Adapted from Ingram and LaForge, *Sales Management: Analysis and Decision Making.*

[14]Bernard J. Jaworski and Ajay K. Kohli, "Supervisory Feedback: Alternative Types and Their Impact on Salespeople's Performance and Satisfaction," *Journal of Marketing Research,* 28 (May 1991), 190–201.

[15]Ibid.

both external and internal environments of the firm. Furthermore, these functions must be coordinated with the other elements of the firm's overall marketing communications strategy.

A good sales manager must have a clear understanding of what determines a salesperson's performance. These determinants include the salesperson's view of his or her job requirements as well as his or her aptitude, skill level, and motivational level.

Finally, the sales manager must evaluate the performance of the salesforce by examining the outcomes of their efforts. This stage of the sales management process includes an analysis of sales volume, selling expenses, customer-service reports, and overall profitability. These and other performance evaluations help the sales manager to control and therefore direct (or redirect) the salesforce.

Discussion Questions

1. Management-science tools can be used for establishing sales territories. Models such as linear programming attempt to maximize an objective function subject to satisfying various constraints. Explain why such a model would be unsuitable by itself for establishing sales-force territories.

2. Although sales quotas are most often based on sales volume, they can also be based on profit or activities performed. Explain why salespeople prefer to have quotas established in terms of sales volume, whereas sales managers prefer to establish quotas for their salesforces in terms of nonsales criteria.

3. Explain the rationale favoring market-, product-, and geographically-based selling organizations. Assume you are the vice president of sales for a sporting-goods firm that markets several product lines (apparel, shoes, equipment) to large and small retail stores and to schools and other institutions. How might you organize your salesforce?

4. What are the shortcomings of evaluating sales representatives' performance solely in terms of unit sales?

5. Discuss the relationship between sales-territory design and salesforce morale.

6. One often hears the advice that a college student's resume should never exceed one page in length. What is the rationale underlying this advice? Is it sound?

7. Sometimes salespeople are placed in conflicts that result from customers having expectations that are counter to a sales manager's expectations. How can sales training help to reduce this conflict?

8. What are the possible drawbacks to using sales contests to motivate salespeople?

9. As a salesperson, would you prefer to work on a straight-salary or straight commission basis? Why? As a sales manager, would you prefer to pay your salespeople on a straight-salary or straight-commission basis? Why?

10. Compared to Campbell Soup's previous product-based organizational structuring of its salesforce, comment on the expanded authority the salesforce now has under the new geographic-based structure.

11. Both the product-based and market-based salesforce organization structures suffer from high cost and geographic duplication (see Table 22.1). Given such significant disadvantages, how could any company possibly justify using these structures?

12. Interview someone such as a local football coach, basketball coach, tennis coach, baseball coach, or band director and find out the methods they use in their sales-management efforts. That is, how do they recruit personnel, motivate team members, evaluate performance, and so on. Compare their methods with those of a sales manager for a profit-oriented business.

PHOTO CREDITS

1.1: Ralph Lauren Fragrance. 1.3: Oldsmobile Division, General Motors Corporation. 1.4: Courtesy Philips Consumer Electronics Co. 1.5: Courtesy of Goebel Marketing Corp. 1.6: TOMBSTONE is a registered trademark of Kraft General Foods, Inc. Reproduced with permission. 1.7: Kraft is a registered trademark of Kraft General Foods, Inc. Reproduced with permission.

2.1: The Gillette Company. 2.2: Courtesy Lincoln Mercury Division, Ford. 2.3: Courtesy Tandy Corporation. 2.5: Courtesy of Alfa Romeo Dealers Association of America. 2.6: Ralph Lauren. 2.7: Nabisco. 2.8: Courtesy of the Jekyll Island Authority. 2.9: Courtesy Southwest Toyota Distributors, Inc.

3.2: Leaf, Inc.–Client; Ayer Chicago–Agency; Dave Jordano–Apple, package, product photos; Jon Riley/Tony Stone Worldwide–Manhattan skyline photo. 3.3: Courtesy Oneida Ltd. All Rights Reserved. 3.4: Photo © 1991 Tim Bieber. 3.8: Courtesy of Oscar Mayer Foods Corporation. Claussen is a registered trademark of Oscar Mayer Foods Corporation, Madison, Wisconsin. 3.9: Courtesy Lincoln-Mercury Division of Ford Motor Company. 3.10: Reprinted courtesy Miller Brewing Co. Ad produced by Frankenberry, Laughlin & Constable. 3.11: Courtesy of Oscar Mayer Foods Corporation. Louis Rich is a registered trademark of Oscar Mayer Foods Corporation, Madison, Wisconsin. 3.12: Courtesy of Campbell Soup Company. 3.13: Southeast United Dairy Industry Association, Inc. (SUDIA)

4.1: America West Airlines. 4.2: Light n' Lively is a registered trademark of Kraft General Foods, Inc. Reproduced with permission. 4.3: American Express. 4.5: Reprinted with the permission of Subaru of America, Inc. 4.6: McNeil Consumer Products. 4.7: FREE is a registered trademark of Kraft General Foods, Inc. Reproduced with permission.

5.3: Courtesy of Warner-Lambert Company. 5.4: Courtesy of Anheuser Busch Co. 5.5: Courtesy of Deere & Company.

6.2 Courtesy Mazda Motor of America, Inc. Photo by Sean Thonson. 6.3: Reprinted courtesy of the Wm. Wrigley Jr. Company. 6.5: Campbell Taggart, Inc. 6.7: Caffeine free diet Coke and the Dynamic Ribbon device are registered trademarks owned and used with permission of The Coca-Cola Company. 6.8: DeBeers.

7.2: Procter & Gamble. 7.3: Courtesy Creative Resources, Inc.

9.2: Courtesy E. I. DuPont DeNemours & Company, Inc.

10.2: © 1991 Hitachi Home Electronics (America) Inc.

11.1 Reproduced with the permission of Clairol, Inc. 11.2: Advertisement created by Carillon Importers Ltd. and TBWA Advertising Inc. 11.4: Armstrong World Industries. 11.5: Canon USA, Inc. 11.7: Reproduced with permission of Pepsico, Inc. 1992, Purchase, NY. 11.8: Courtesy Pioneer Electronics (USA), Inc. 11.9: © 1991 Toyota Motor Sales USA, Inc. 11.10 Reprinted with permission of State Farm Insurance Companies. 11.11: Reprinted by permission of Philip Morris Incorporated.

12.1: Whitehall Laboratories. 12.2: Reprint permission granted by Timex Corporation. 12.3: Michelin. 12.4: h.i.s. 12.5: © 1992 Giorgio. 12.6: Advertisement created by Carillon Importers Ltd. and TBWA Advertising.

13.1: American Marketing Association.

14.1 Slice is a registered trademark of Pepsico, Inc. Reproduced with permission of Pepsico, Inc. 1992, Purchase, NY. 14.2: Reproduced with permission of BBDO Worldwide, Inc. © 1988.

16.1: Reprinted with permission of Nike, Inc., and Pete Stone Photography.

17.3: Courtesy Ralston Purina. Flowershop photo © 1992 Jay Silverman Productions L.A. 17.6: Kellogg Co. 17.7: © Eastman Kodak Company, 1991. 17.8: Nestle Foods. 17.9: Duracell Inc. 17.10: KRAFT and CHEEZ WHIZ are registered trademarks of Kraft General Foods, Inc. OSCAR MAYER is a registered trademark of Oscar Mayer Foods Corporation. Reproduced with permission.

18.1: American Dairy Association®. 18.3: Printed with the permission of Nabisco, Inc. 18.4: Courtesy Coors Marketing Services. 18.5: Fredrichman-Aris Isotoner Inc. 18.6: Courtesy Florsheim.

19.2: © MBI. 19.3: Courtesy American Business Information.

20.2: Courtesy of Johnson & Johnson. 20.4: Hershey Foods.

GLOSSARY

Ability   Consumers are more able to process message claims when they possess prior familiarity about the topic and when there is little interference to interrupt message processing.

Active-synthesis   The second stage of perceptual encoding, active-synthesis involves a more refined perception of a stimulus than simply an examination of its basic features. The context of the situation in which information is received plays a major role in determining what is perceived and interpreted.

Activity quotas   Salesperson performance goals that emphasize such tasks as (1) daily calls, (2) new customers called on, (3) orders from new accounts, (4) product demonstrations made, and (5) displays built. This type of quota stimulates a balanced approach to sales representatives' jobs; however, it fails to show whether the activity was actually performed or whether it was done effectively.

Adoption process   The mental stages through which an individual passes in accepting and becoming a repeat purchaser of an innovation.

Advertising   A form of either mass communication or direct-to-consumer communication that is nonpersonal and is paid for by various business firms, non-profit organizations, and individuals who are in some way identified in the advertising message and who hope to inform or persuade members of a particular audience.

Advertising objectives   Motives or goals that advertising efforts attempt to achieve. Examples include the following: to increase sales volume, consumer brand awareness, or favorability of attitudes.

Advertising plans   Provide the framework for the actual execution of advertising strategies.

Advertising strategy   A plan of action that is guided by corporate and marketing strategies. Corporate and marketing strategies determine how much can be invested in advertising, at what markets advertising efforts need to be directed, how advertising must be coordinated with other marketing elements, and, to some degree, how advertising is to be executed.

Affective component of attitude   The emotional component of an attitude.

Affordability method   An advertising budgeting method that sets the budget by spending on advertising those funds that remain after budgeting for everything else.

Allegory   A form of figurative language that equates the objects in a particular narrative (such as an advertised brand in a television commercial) with meanings lying outside of the narrative itself.

AMO factors   The three factors of ability, motivation, and opportunity which determine each individual's elaboration likelihood for a particular message.

Androgyny   The ability to adapt oneself to situational circumstances and to call upon a repertoire of both male and female traits.

Attention   The act of focusing on and thinking about a message that one has been exposed to.

Attitude   A general and enduring positive or negative feeling about some person, object, or issue.

Attributes   In the means-end conceptualization of advertising strategy, attributes are features or aspects of the advertised product or brand.

Awareness class   The first step in product adoption. Four marketing-mix variables influence the awareness class: samples, coupons, advertising, and product distribution.

Baby boom   Demographers refer to the 74 million Americans born between 1947 and 1964 as the baby-boom generation.

Basic offer   Mode 1 of the three modes of marketing. Consists of the product itself and associated terms of sale. In general, the basic offer consists of the benefits the marketer offers to the target market as a solution to some problem.

Beliefs   The consumer's subjective probability assessments regarding the likelihood that performing a certain act will lead to a certain outcome.

Bonus   Usually a lump-sum payment that a company makes to sales representatives who have exceeded a set sales quota.

Bonus packs   Extra quantities of a product that a company gives to consumers at the regular price.

Brand concept   The specific meaning that marketing managers create for a brand and then communicate to the target market.

Brand-concept management   The planning, implementation, and control of a brand concept throughout the life of the brand.

Brand equity   The goodwill (equity) that an established brand has built up over the period of its existence.

Brand-image strategy   A creative advertising strategy that involves psychological rather than physical differentiation. The advertiser attempts to develop an image for a brand by associating it with symbols.

Category management   A new system established by Procter & Gamble whereby each product category within a company is managed by a category manager who has direct profit responsibility.

Cause-related marketing (CRM) A relatively narrow aspect of overall sponsorship which involves an amalgam of public relations, sales promotion, and corporate philanthropy. The distinctive feature of CRM is that a company's contribution to a designated cause is linked to customers' engaging in revenue-producing exchanges with the firm.

Central route The message-processing strategy, or pathway, in the elaboration likelihood model that occurs when consumers are involved in a communication topic and diligently process message arguments contained in the communications. If the message arguments are sound, consumers' attitudes will be influenced. See **Peripheral route.**

Cognitive component of attitude The intellectual component of attitude. In marketing, it is the consumer's knowledge, thoughts, and beliefs about an object or issue.

Cognitive response A self-generated thought that consumers produce in response to persuasive efforts. Includes counter arguments, support arguments, and source derogation.

Commercial rumors Widely circulated but unverified propositions about a product, brand, company, store, or other commercial topic. Rumors pose a difficult public-relations problem.

Commission Payments to salespeople based directly on performance. Commissions take the form of either straight commissions or a draw against commission.

Communications Process whereby individuals share meaning and establish a commonness of thought.

Compatibility The degree to which an innovation is perceived to fit into a person's ways of doing things. The more compatible an innovation is with a person's need structure, personal values and beliefs, and past experiences, the more rapid the rate of adoption.

Compensatory heuristic A choice strategy in which the customer ranks each of the criteria he or she would like to be met, decides how well each alternative will satisfy these criteria, and integrates this information to arrive at a "score" for each alternative. Theoretically the consumer selects the alternative with the highest overall score. This procedure is likely to be used in risky (high-involvement) circumstances; that is, when a decision involves considerable financial, performance, or psychological risk.

Compiled list A compiled direct-mail list contains prospect names that are gathered from a variety of data sources such as census reports, telephone directories, and car registrations.

Complexity The degree of perceived difficulty of an innovation. The more difficult an innovation is to understand or use, the slower the rate of adoption.

Compliance The source attribute of power influences message receivers via a process of compliance; that is, a receiver complies with the persuasive efforts of the source because the source has the power to administer rewards or punishments.

Comprehension The ability to understand and create meaning out of stimuli and symbols.

Conative component of attitude The action component of an attitude; a person's behavioral tendency toward an object. In marketing, it is the consumer's intention to purchase a specific item. Also called *behavioral component.*

Conditional value This consumption value is acquired when an alternative is perceived as having greater utility due to situational factors that enhance its functional or social value.

Confirmation stage The stage in the new-product adoption process after a decision has been made in which postdecisional dissonance, regret, and dissonance reduction occur.

Conjunctive heuristic One of three noncompensatory choice strategies in which the consumer establishes cutoffs, or minima, on all pertinent criteria; an alternative is retained for further consideration only if it meets or exceeds all minima.

Consequences In the means-end conceptualization of advertising strategy, consequences represent the desirable or undesirable results from consuming a particular product or brand.

Consumer information processing (CIP) perspective A model of consumer choice behavior in which marketers view the consumer as a logical, highly cognitive, and systematic decision maker. See **Hedonic-experiential model (HEM).**

Consumption values Five forms of perceived utility (functional value, social value, emotional value, epistemic value, and conditional value) which influence consumers' choices and are individually or collectively acquired when choosing an alternative.

Contamination rumors Unconfirmed statements dealing with undesirable or harmful product or store features.

Contest A form of consumer-oriented sales promotion in which consumers have an opportunity to win cash, merchandise, or travel prizes. Winners become eligible by solving the specified contest problem.

Continuity A media planning consideration that involves the matter of how advertising should be allocated during the course of an advertising campaign.

Continuous advertising schedule In a continuous schedule, a relatively equal amount of ad dollars are invested in advertising throughout the campaign.

Continuous innovation A new product or product change that represents a minor alteration from existing products and has limited impact on customers' consumption patterns. See **Discontinuous innovation.**

Cooperative (co-op) advertising Co-op programs are initiated by manufacturers and permit retailers to place ads promoting the manufacturer's product and receive partial or full reimbursement from the manufacturer.

Copytesting Advertising research undertaken to test the effectiveness of creative messages. Also called *message research.*

Corporate advertising This form of advertising focuses not on specific products or brands but on a corporation's overall image or on economic/social issues relevant to the corporation's interests.

Corporate image advertising A specific form of corporate advertising that attempts to gain name recognition for a company, establish goodwill for it and its products, or identify itself with some meaningful and socially acceptable activity. See **Issue advertising.**

Cost per thousand (CPM) A measure of advertising efficiency based on the cost of reaching 1,000 people.

Counter argument A form of cognitive response that occurs when the receiver challenges message claims. See **Source derogation** and **Supportive argument.**

Coupon A promotional device that provides cents-off savings to consumers upon redeeming the coupon.

CPM-TM A refinement of CPM that measures the cost of reaching 1,000 members of the target market, excluding those people who fall outside of the target market.

Customer satisfaction The ultimate goal of all marketing and promotional activities.

Database management Used in direct marketing, database management is the construction and maintenance of data lists containing customer and prospect names and detailed information for each listing.

Database marketing Used both by indirect and direct marketers, database marketing involves collecting and electronically storing (in a database) information about present, past, and prospective customers.

Deceptive advertising Advertising is considered deceptive by the Federal Trade Commission if there is a representation that misleads reasonable consumers by influencing their product preferences and choices.

Decision stage The stage of new-product adoption that represents the period during which a person mentally chooses either to adopt or reject an innovation.

Decoding The mental process of transforming message symbols into thought; consumers' interpretations of marketing messages. See **Encoding.**

Demographic variables Measurable characteristics of populations, including characteristics such as age, income, minority population patterns, and regional population statistics.

Diffusion In a marketing communications sense, diffusion means that a product or idea is adopted by more and more customers as time passes. In other words, a new product "spreads out" through the marketplace. See **Adoption Process.**

Direct advertising objectives Objectives that seek an overt behavioral response (e.g., product purchase) from the audience. See **Indirect advertising objectives.**

Direct mail The use of mail deliveries sent to current or prospective customers. Examples include letters, postcards, programs, calendars, folders, catalogs, order blanks, and price lists.

Direct marketing Activities by which products and services are offered to market segments in one or more media for informational purposes or to solicit responses from present or prospective customers or contributors by mail, telephone, or other access.

Direct-response advertising The use of any medium (direct mail, television, etc.) with the intent of creating immediate action from customers. Three distinct characteristics of direct-response advertising are (1) it makes a definite offer, (2) it contains all of the information necessary to make a decision, and (3) it contains a response device (coupon, phone number, or both) to facilitate immediate action.

Direct selling Involves the personal explanation and demonstration of products and services to consumers in their homes or at their jobs.

Discontinuous innovation A new product or product change that requires substantial relearning and fundamental alterations in basic consumption patterns. See **Continuous innovation.**

Disjunctive heuristic One of three noncompensatory choice strategies in which the consumer accepts an alternative if it meets any one of his or her minimum standards; that is, an alternative is acceptable if it meets or exceeds choice criterion 1, choice criterion 2, or choice criterion n.

Display allowance A price discount used by manufacturers to obtain trade support for displays.

Diverting This practice takes place when a manufacturer offers a trade deal that is restricted to a limited geographical area. Wholesalers and retailers often buy abnormally large quantities at the deal price and then transship the excess quantities to other geographical areas.

Dual-coding theory A theory of memory that states that pictures are stored in an individual's memory in both verbal and visual form, whereas words are less likely to have visual representations.

Dynamically continuous innovation   A new product or product change that requires some disruption in established consumer behavior patterns rather than fundamental alterations.

Effective rating points (ERPs)   A statistical measure of an advertising campaign based on the idea that each exposure to an advertisement is not of equal value. ERPs are used in media planning to achieve the maximum impact for a product; what is effective (or ineffective) for one product may not necessarily be so for another. Hence, ERPs represent an alternative media selection criterion to gross rating points (GRPs).

Effective reach   Based on the idea that an advertising schedule is effective only if it does not reach members of the target audience too few or too many times. What exactly is too few or too many depends on the specific advertising situation, but many media planners consider fewer than three exposures as too few and more than ten as too many.

Elaboration   The mental activity associated with a consumer's response to a persuasive message. Elaboration involves thinking about what the message is saying, evaluating the arguments in the message, agreeing with some, disagreeing with others, and so on.

Elaboration likelihood model (ELM)   A theory of persuasion and attitude change that predicts two forms of message processing and attitude change: central and peripheral routes. The former occurs under high involvement and leads to a more permanent attitude change than does the latter.

Emotional responses   Various forms of self-generated thoughts that consumers produce in response to persuasive efforts.

Emotional strategy   A creative advertising strategy that uses appeals to the consumer's emotions.

Emotional value   A value acquired by a consumption alternative when it precipitates or perpetuates specific feelings in the consumer.

Encoding   The process of putting thoughts into symbolic form. See **Decoding.**

Encoding specificity principle   A principle of cognitive psychology which states that information recall is enhanced when the context in which people attempt to retrieve information is the same or similar to the context in which they originally encoded the information.

Environmental management   The idea that through its promotional efforts and other marketing activities, a firm can attempt to modify existing environmental conditions.

Environmental monitoring   A process involving continual monitoring of competitors, societal events, economic developments, regulatory activity, and a company's internal situation in order to facilitate the development of successful marketing communications.

Epistemic value   When an alternative is perceived as yielding utility by arousing curiosity, providing novelty, or satisfying a desire for knowledge, it acquires epistemic value.

Ethics   Matters of right and wrong, or *moral,* conduct pertaining to any aspect of marketing communications.

Evaluate the results   The act of measuring the results of promotional programs against the objectives that were established at the outset. The results are typically measured in terms of communication outcomes rather than sales.

Evaluations   The subjective value or importance that consumers attach to consumption outcomes.

Event marketing   A form of brand promotion that ties a brand to a meaningful cultural, social, athletic, or other type of high-interest public activity.

Executive-statement release   A tool of proactive marketing PR that quotes a corporate executive in a news release on matters of interest to prospective customers and other interested parties such as stockholders.

Experiential needs   Represent desires for products that provide sensory pleasure, variety, and stimulation.

Exposure   The consumer information processing stage in which consumers come in contact with the marketer's message.

External lists   Mailing lists bought from other companies rather than being based on a company's own internal list of customers.

Feature analysis   The initial stage of perceptual encoding whereby a receiver examines the basic features of a stimulus (brightness, depth, angles, etc.) and from this makes a preliminary classification.

Feature article   A form of proactive marketing PR that consists of a full-length article about a company and its products that is suitable for publication in a newspaper or other media.

Federal Trade Commission (FTC)   The U.S. governmental agency that has primary responsibility for regulating unfair and deceptive promotion.

Feedback   Affords the source of marketing communications with a way of monitoring how accurately the intended message is being received and offers some measure of control in the communications process.

Figurative language   Includes simile, metaphor, and allegory.

Flighting   A form of discontinuous advertising schedule in which some periods in the campaign receive zero expenditures. See **Pulsing.**

Food and Drug Administration   The federal body responsible for regulating information on the packages of food and drug products.

Forward buying   The practice whereby retailers take advantage of manufacturers' trade deals by buying larger quantities than needed for normal inventory. Retailers often buy enough product on one deal to carry them over until the manufacturer's next scheduled deal; hence, forward buying also is called *bridge buying.*

Free-in-the-mail premium   A promotion in which consumers receive a premium item from the sponsoring manufacturer in return for submitting a required number of proofs of purchase.

Frequency   The number of times, on average, within a four-week period that members of the target audience are exposed to the advertiser's message. Also called *average frequency.*

Frequency strategy   A strategy used by media planners when a product's advertisements must reach people as many times as possible.

Functional needs   Those needs involving current consumption-related problems, potential problems, or conflicts.

Functional value   Represents the consumer's perception of an alternative's capacity to fulfill utilitarian or functional requirements.

Generally planned purchase   A form of purchase behavior based on POPAI's supermarket buying-habits study in which a shopper indicates an intent to buy a particular product but has no specific brand in mind.

Generic strategy   A creative advertising strategy in which the advertiser makes a claim about its brand that could be made by any company that markets the product.

Geographical territories   The most common form of sales-management organization.

Gross rating points (GRPs)   A statistic that represents the mathematical product of reach multiplied by frequency. The number of GRPs indicates the total weight of advertising during a time frame, such as a four-week period. The number of GRPs indicates the gross coverage or duplicated audience that is exposed to a particular advertising schedule.

Hedonic-experiential model (HEM)   This perspective of consumer behavior views consumers as driven not by rational and purely logical considerations but, rather, by emotions in pursuit of fun, fantasies, and feelings. See **Consumer information processing (CIP) perspective.**

Hedonistic consumption   The consumer's multisensory images, fantasies, and emotional arousal elicited when purchasing and using products.

Hierarchy-of-effects models   There are numerous hierarchy-of-effects models, all of which are predicated on the idea that advertising moves people from an initial state of unawareness about a product/brand to a final stage of purchasing that product/brand.

House list   Names of customers that are generated from a company's own internal records. Customers' names are often grouped into active, recently active, long-since-active customers, or inquiry categories. A list may be subdivided by the recency of a customer's purchase, the frequency of a customer's purchase, the monetary value of each purchase, or the type of products purchased. Customers may be categorized by geographic, demographic, or psychographic characteristics.

Identification   The source attribute of attractiveness influences message receivers via a process of identification, that is, receivers perceive a source to be attractive and therefore identify with the source and adopt the attitudes, behaviors, interests, or preferences of the source.

Imagery   A mental event involving visualization of a concept or relationship.

Implementation stage   The stage in the new-product adoption process in which a person puts the new product or idea to use.

In- and on-pack premiums   Programs which offer a premium item inside a package, attached to a package, or the package itself is reusable.

Indirect advertising objectives   Those objectives aimed at communication tasks (e.g., awareness, knowledge) that need to be accomplished before overt behavioral responses can be achieved. See **Direct advertising objectives.**

Innovation   An idea, practice, product, or service that an individual perceives to be new. The consumers' view of the product is the critical factor.

In-store decisions   The sum total of generally planned, substitute, and unplanned purchases.

Integrated information-response model   This model takes its name from the idea that consumers integrate information from two sources—advertising and direct product-usage experience—in forming attitudes and purchase intentions toward products and brands.

Integrated marketing communications   The coordination of advertising, publicity, sales promotion, point-of-purchase communications, direct marketing, and event marketing with each other and with other elements of a brand's marketing mix.

Intelligence tests   Tests which attempt to measure a person's memory ability, critical-reasoning ability, and ability to draw inferences.

Interactive displays   Computerized units that allow consumers to answer questions pertaining to their product-category needs and help them make well-informed product choices.

Interest tests   Tests which are designed to identify a person's vocational and avocational inclinations.

Internalization The source attribute of credibility influences message receivers via a process of internalization; that is, receivers perceive a source to be credible and therefore accept the source's position or attitude as their own. Internalized attitudes tend to be maintained even when the source of the message is forgotten and even when the source switches to a new position.

Involuntary attention One of three forms of attention that requires little or no effort on the part of the message receiver; the stimulus intrudes upon a person's consciousness even though he or she does not want it to. See **Nonvoluntary attention** and **Voluntary attention.**

Issue advertising A form of corporate advertising that takes a position on a controversial social issue of public importance. It does so in a manner that supports the company's position and best interests. Also called *advocacy advertising.* See **Corporate image advertising.**

Job analysis Identifies the activities, duties, responsibilities, knowledge, selling skills, and personal attributes a sales representative should have in order to function effectively in an organization.

Job description Includes a job title, the specific duties and responsibilities of the sales representative, the authoritative relationships with other company personnel, and other pertinent information about the sales job.

Learning Changes in the content or organization of information in consumers' long-term memories.

Lexicographic heuristic One of three noncompensatory consumer strategies in which the consumer ranks his or her criteria according to relative importance. Alternatives are then evaluated on each criterion, starting with the most important. An alternative is selected if it is judged superior on the most important criterion. If two or more alternatives are judged equal on the most important criterion, the consumer examines these alternatives on the next most important criterion, then on the next most important, and so on until a tie is broken.

Limited processing capacity The most outstanding characteristic of STM whereby individuals can process only a limited amount of information at any one time.

Line-item budgeting With this form of budgeting, management allocates funds in meticulous detail to each identifiable cost center. See **Program budgeting.**

Loyalists Consumers whose purchase patterns reflect that they buy the same brand over and over when no brands are on deal. Loyalists may or may not be deal prone.

Market maven An individual who has information about many kinds of products and places to shop and shares this information with fellow consumers.

Marketing Process whereby businesses and other organizations facilitate exchanges, or transfers of value, between themselves and their customers and clients.

Marketing communications The collection of all elements in an organization's marketing mix that facilitates exchanges by establishing shared meaning with the organization's customers or clients.

Marketing concept Philosophy in which the marketer adapts to the customers' needs and wants. This is usually accomplished by satisfying the customers' needs and by offering superior value. See **Promotion concept.**

Marketing mix Consists of four sets of decision spheres: product, pricing, distribution, and promotion decisions.

Marketing objectives Objectives for marketing actions include setting overall sales levels, establishing marketing cost requirements, and setting performance requirements for specific market segments and geographical locales.

Marketing strategy A plan of action that is an extension of corporate strategy and involves plans, budgets, and controls needed to direct a firm's product, promotion, distribution, and pricing activities.

Marketing structure The organizational arrangement employed in a company to achieve its overall marketing and promotional objectives.

Match-competitors method An advertising budgeting method that sets the ad budget by basically following what competitors are doing.

Mature market Although there is disagreement about what age group constitutes this market, this text adopts the U.S. Bureau of the Census' designation, which classifies mature people as those who are 55 and older.

Meaning The set of internal responses and resulting predispositions evoked within a person when presented with a sign or stimulus object.

Means An organization's wherewithal or resources represent its means for accomplishing the motives it has established for its various promotional tools.

MECCAS An acronym for Means-End Conceptualization of Components for Advertising Strategy, MECCAS is a model which provides a procedure for applying the concept of means-end chains to the creation of advertising messages.

Media The agency or instrument for transmission of all marketing communications. The term is typically applied to advertising media (television, magazines, radio, and so on), but it is relevant to all promotional tools.

Media planning The process of designing a course of action that shows how advertising time and space will be used to contribute to the achievement of marketing objectives.

Media research   Advertising research undertaken to test the effectiveness of creative media.

Message   A symbolic expression of a sender's thoughts; the instrument (e.g., advertisement) used to share thought with a receiver. More practically, the term *message* refers to the verbal and nonverbal persuasive techniques that are used in all forms of marketing communications.

Message channel   The path through which the message moves from source to receiver; for example, from a marketer via a magazine to consumers.

Message content   Includes the types of appeals used in marketing-communications messages. Examples include the use of humor, fear appeals, sex appeals, and subliminal techniques.

Message research   Also known as copytesting, message research is a technique which tests the effectiveness of creative messages. Copytesting involves both pretesting a message during its development stages and posttesting the message for effectiveness after it has been aired or printed.

Message structure   The organization of elements in a message. Three structural issues have particular relevance to marketing communicators: (1) message-sidedness, (2) order of presentation, and (3) conclusion drawing.

Metaphor   A form of figurative language that applies a word or a phrase to a concept or object, such as a brand, that it does not literally denote in order to suggest a comparison with the brand (e.g., Budweiser is "the king of beers").

Micromarketing   The customizing of products and communications to small segments of consumers.

Milline rate   Used for comparing the cost of advertising in different newspapers, the milline rate is the cost per line of advertising space per million circulation.

Momentum   The word momentum refers to an object's force or speed of movement. When applied to marketing communications, momentum determines the effectiveness of a message. It is a campaign's timing (speed) and force (amount of effort) that make it successful.

Morals   The set of principles and standards that individual managers bring to the job and that the corporate culture encourages.

Motivation   One of the factors which determines each individual's elaboration likelihood for a particular message.

Motives   The underlying objectives or goals on which promotion managers base their general and specific choices.

Narrowcasting   The pinpointing of advertising exposures to specific groups of consumers such as teens, Hispanics, and news enthusiasts.

National Advertising Review Board (NARB)   Part of the National Advertising Division (NAD) of the Council of Better Business Bureaus, NARB is a court of appeals in the self-regulation of deceptive advertising cases.

National Association of Attorneys General (NAAG)   Includes attorneys general from all 50 states. In recent years this group has played an increasingly active role in regulating advertising deception and other business practices.

Near-pack premiums   Specially displayed premium pieces that retailers give to consumers who purchase the promoted product.

Noise   Extraneous and distracting stimuli that interfere with reception of a message in its pure and original form. Noise occurs at all stages of the communications process.

Noncompensatory heuristics   Choice behavior based on strategies such as conjunctive, disjunctive, or lexicographic heuristics. Contrasts with the compensatory heuristic to choice.

Nonvoluntary attention   One of three forms of attention that occurs when a person is attracted to a stimulus and continues to pay attention because it holds interest for him or her. A person in this situation neither resists the stimulus nor willingly attends to it initially; however, once his or her attention is attracted, the individual continues to give attention because the stimulus has some benefit or relevance. Also called *spontaneous attention*. See **Involuntary attention** and **Voluntary attention.**

Normative influence   Represents the influence that important others, or referent groups, have on us. See **Theory of reasoned action.**

Objective-and-task method   This budgeting method establishes the advertising budget by determining the communication tasks that need to be established. See **Percentage-of-sales method.**

Observability   The degree to which other people can observe one's ownership and use of a new product. The more a consumption behavior can be sensed by other people, the more observable it is and typically the more rapid is its rate of adoption.

Opinion leader   A person who frequently influences other individuals' attitudes or overt behavior.

Opportunity   A term referring to whether it is physically possible for a person to process a message.

Outcomes   The aspects of brand ownership that the consumer either desires to obtain or to avoid.

Overlay   The use of two or more sales-promotion techniques in combination with one another.

Percentage-of-sales method This budgeting method involves setting the budget as a fixed percentage of past or anticipated (typically the latter) sales volume. See **Objective-and-task method.**

Perceptual encoding The process of interpreting stimuli, which includes two stages: feature analysis and active-synthesis.

Peripheral route In the peripheral route of the elaboration likelihood model, persuasion occurs not as a result of a consumer's processing salient message arguments but by virtue of his or her attending to relevant (though peripheral to the main message argument) persuasion cues. See **Central route.**

Personal selling A form of person-to-person communication in which the seller attempts to persuade prospective buyers to purchase his or her company's (organization's) product or service.

Personality test A psychological test that attempts to measure a prospective salesperson's affability, confidence, poise, aggressiveness, and so on.

Persuasion In marketing, persuasion is an effort by a marketing communicator to influence the consumer's attitude and behavior in some manner.

Persuasive communications Mode 2 of the three modes of marketing. Consists of various forms of marketing-communications messages designed to enhance customers' impressions of the basic offer.

Phased strategies Procedure in which consumers use a combination of choice heuristics in sequence or in phase with one another to make decisions.

Planning The process of establishing a broad set of goals, policies, and procedures for achieving sales and marketing objectives.

Point-of-purchase (P-O-P) communications Promotional elements, including displays, posters, signs, and a variety of other in-store materials, that are designed to influence the customer's choice at the time of purchase.

Point-of-purchase coupons Coupons that are simultaneously distributed and redeemable at the point of purchase.

Positioning advertising copytesting (PACT) A set of nine copytesting principles developed by leading U.S. advertising agencies.

Positioning strategy A creative advertising strategy in which an advertiser implants in the consumer's mind a clear understanding of what the brand is and how it compares to competitive offerings.

Preemptive strategy A creative advertising strategy in which the advertiser that makes a particular claim effectively prevents competitors from making the same claim for fear of being labeled a copycat.

Premiums Articles of merchandise or services offered by manufacturers to induce action on the part of the sales force, trade representatives, or consumers.

Price-off promotions A promotion which entails a reduction in the brand's regular price.

Proactive MPR A form of PR that is offensively rather than defensively oriented and opportunity-seeking rather than problem-solving. See **Reactive marketing PR.**

Product release A tool of proactive marketing PR that announces a new product, provides relevant information, and tells how additional information can be obtained.

Product types or groups Companies that offer a set of unrelated or heterogeneous products should consider organizing by product type or group.

Profit quotas Performance goals based on the total amount of revenue generated by a salesperson for the organization rather than on the number of items sold.

Program budgeting A procedure that provides each administrative unit with a lump sum of money that each administrative head can use as he or she sees fit in order to accomplish the stated objectives. See **Line-item budgeting.**

Promotion The aspect of general marketing that promotion management deals with explicitly. Promotion includes the practices of advertising, personal selling, sales promotion, publicity, and point-of-purchase communications.

Promotion concept Marketing practices that attempt to adapt the customer to the marketer's needs and wants. See **Marketing concept.**

Promotion management The practice of coordinating the various promotional-mix elements, setting objectives for what the elements are intended to accomplish, establishing budgets that are sufficient to support the objectives, designing specific programs to accomplish objectives, evaluating performance, and taking corrective action when results are not in accordance with objectives.

Promotional inducements Mode 3 of the three modes of marketing. More commonly referred to as *sales promotion,* promotional inducements comprise extra benefits beyond the basic offer that are intended to motivate particular customer actions.

Promotional management The practice of coordinating the various promotional mix elements, setting objectives for what the elements are intended to accomplish, establishing budgets that are sufficient to support the objectives, designing specific programs to accomplish objectives, evaluating performance, and taking corrective action when results are not in accordance with objectives.

Promotional mix An organization's blend of advertising, personal selling, sales promotion, publicity, and point-of-purchase communications elements.

Psychogalvanometer A device for measuring galvanic skin response that is used as an indicator of advertising effectiveness, specifically by determining whether the consumer's autonomic nervous system is activated by some element in an advertisement.

Psychological reactance A theory that suggests that people react against any efforts to reduce their freedoms or choices. When products are made to seem less available, they become more valuable in the consumer's mind.

Public relations (PR) A practice that includes all nonadvertising and nonselling activities that are designed explicitly to engender a desired corporate image. This corporate-image engineering is directed at promoting harmonious relations with various publics: consumers, employees, suppliers, stockholders, governments, the general public, labor groups, and citizen-action groups.

Publicity Nonpersonal communication to a mass audience that is not paid for by an organization. Examples include news items or editorial comments about an organization's products or services.

Pull strategy Marketing efforts directed to ultimate consumers with the intent of influencing their acceptance of the manufacturer's brand. Manufacturers hope that the consumers will then encourage retailers to handle the brand. Typically used in conjunction with *push strategy.*

Pulsing A form of discontinuous advertising-schedule in which some advertising is used in every period of the campaign, but the amount of advertising varies considerably from period to period. See **Flighting.**

Pupillometric tests A measure of advertising effectiveness that records a consumer's pupil dilation, an autonomic response, as the consumer views a television commercial or printed advertisement. Greater pupil dilation is thought to indicate greater arousal from attending the advertisement.

Push money Cash provided to salespeople by the manufacturer to encourage them to push certain products in the manufacturer's line. Also called spiffs.

Push strategy A manufacturer's selling and other promotional efforts directed at gaining trade support from wholesalers and retailers for the manufacturer's product.

Rating The proportion of the target audience exposed to a single issue of an advertising vehicle such as a television program or a particular magazine.

Reach The percentage of an advertiser's target audience that is exposed to at least one advertisement over an established time frame (a four-week period represents the typical time frame for most advertisers). Reach represents the number of target customers who see or hear the advertiser's message one or more times during the time period. Also called *net coverage, unduplicated audience,* or *cumulative audience (cume).*

Reach strategy A marketing strategy which focuses on contacting as many consumers as possible.

Reactive MPR Undertaken as a result of external pressures and challenges brought by competitive actions, changes in consumer attitudes, or other external influences. It typically deals with changes that have negative consequences for the organization. See **Proactive MPR.**

Rebate A cash reimbursement to consumers from the manufacturer whose product the consumer has purchased. Typically refers to cash reimbursement for durable goods. See **Refund.**

Receiver The person or group of people with whom the sender of a communication shares thoughts. In marketing, the receivers are the prospective and present customers of an organization's product or service.

Refund A cash reimbursement to the consumer by the manufacturer whose product the consumer has purchased. Typically refers to cash reimbursement for packaged goods. See **Rebate.**

Relative advantage The degree to which an innovation is perceived as better than an existing idea or object in terms of increasing comfort, saving time or effort, and increasing the immediacy of reward.

Repeater class This third stage in the adoption process is influenced by four marketing-mix variables: advertising, price, distribution, and product satisfaction.

Resonance strategy A creative advertising strategy that structures an advertising campaign to pattern the prevailing lifestyle orientation of the intended market segment.

Sales-aptitude test A psychological test that is designed to measure a person's verbal ability, tactfulness, persuasiveness, tenacity, memory, and social extroversion/introversion, among other traits.

Sales management The process of planning, organizing, staffing, directing, and controlling an organization's selling function within the context of environmental limitations and corporate and marketing constraints. The purpose is to acquire, direct, and stimulate competent salespeople to perform tasks that move the company or organization toward its objective and mission.

Sales promotion Marketing activities intended to stimulate quick buyer action by offering extra benefits to customers. Examples include coupons, premiums, free samples, and sweepstakes. Also called *promotional inducements.*

Sales quotas Specific performance goals that management sets for sales representatives, sales territories, organizational branches, middlemen, and other marketing units.

Sales territory Consists of present and prospective customers assigned to a salesperson, sales branch, or distributor for a specified period.

Sales-volume quotas Performance goals that are based on geographical areas, product lines, individual customers, time periods, or a combination of these factors. Sales-volume quotas do not, however, measure or control expenses, profits, nonselling activities, and so on.

Sampling The use of various distribution methods to deliver actual- or trial-size products to consumers. The purpose is to initiate trial-usage behavior.

Self-liquidating premium A promotion whereby the consumer mails in a stipulated number of proofs of purchase along with a fee to cover the manufacturer's purchasing, handling, and mailing costs of the premium item; thus the actual cost of the premium is paid for by consumers and from the manufacturer's perspective, the item is cost-free, or self-liquidating.

Self-regulation A form of private government whereby peers establish and enforce voluntary rules of behavior.

Semiotics The study of meaning and the analysis of meaning-producing events.

Sensation transference The consumer's tendency to equate a brand with an information cue such as the package; that is, the consumer imputes characteristics to the product from the package.

Sign (1) Something physical and perceivable by our senses that represents or signifies something (the referent) to somebody (the interpreter) in some context. (2) Specifically, when both a product/brand and referent belong to the same cultural context.

Signal A product or specific brand is a signal of something if it is causally related to it either as the cause of something or the effect of something.

Simile A form of figurative language that uses a comparative term such as *like* or *as* to join items from different classes of experience (e.g., "love is like a rose").

Single-source systems Systems which gather purchase data from panels of households using optical scanning equipment and merge it with household demographic characteristics and, most important, with information about causal marketing variables that influence household purchases.

Slotting allowance The fee a manufacturer pays a supermarket or other retailer to get that retailer to handle the manufacturer's new product. The allowance is called *slotting* in reference to the slot, or location, that the retailer must make available in its warehouse to accommodate the manufacturer's product.

Social value The perceived utility acquired when an alternative has been associated with a stereotyped group such as a demographic group, an ethnic group, a group based on some distinct cultural characteristic, or some other type of group.

Source In marketing communications, a source is a person, group, organization, or label that delivers a message. Marketing communications sources influence receivers by possessing one or more of three basic attributes: power, attractiveness, and credibility.

Source derogation A form of cognitive response that occurs when the receiver disputes the source's ability to make certain message claims. See **Counter argument** and **Supportive argument.**

Specialty advertising A hybrid form of marketing communications that combines elements of advertising and, at times, trade-oriented sales promotion. Specialty advertisers imprint merchandise with an advertiser's message and distribute the merchandise without obligation to designated recipients. Specialty advertising complements other forms of advertising by providing another way to keep a company's name before customers and prospects.

Specifically planned purchase A form of purchase behavior based on POPAI's supermarket buying-habits study in which the consumer indicates an intent to purchase a specific brand and in fact proceeds to buy that brand.

Sponsorship A form of marketing whereby a company invests in special events or causes for the purpose of achieving various promotional and corporate objectives.

Straight commission Payment based directly on sales performance. Straight commission can be based on a fixed percentage of a sales representative's dollar sales, product units sold, type of product sold, season sales, dollars of profit, and so on, or can be based on a multiple percentage rate that increases as dollar sales volume or some other performance measure increases.

Straight salary Payment that provides a sales representative with a fixed amount of income regardless of sales productivity. Also called *base salary.*

Substitute purchases A form of purchase behavior based on POPAI's supermarket buying-habits study in which the shopper does not buy the product or brand he or she indicates will be purchased.

Supportive argument A form of cognitive response that occurs when a receiver agrees with a message's arguments. See **Counter argument** and **Source derogation.**

Sweepstake A form of consumer-oriented sales promotion in which winners receive cash, merchandise, or travel prizes. Winners are determined purely on the basis of chance.

Switchers Consumers who even when all brands in a category are off promotion nonetheless switch among different brands. Switchers may or may not be deal prone.

Symbol A product and referent put together arbitrarily or metaphorically with no prior intrinsic relationship.

Symbolic needs Those involving internal consumer needs such as the desire for self enhancement, role position, or group membership.

Telemarketing The use of the telephone for direct-marketing purposes. Telemarketing represents nearly one-half of all direct marketing.

Telemedia The practice of using the phone to merchandise, advertise, and market products and services.

Theory of reasoned action A theory that predicts behavior based on the idea that normative influences and attitudes influence behavior indirectly by directly influencing people's behavioral intentions.

Three modes of marketing Consists of the basic offer (Mode 1), persuasive communications (Mode 2), and promotional inducements (Mode 3).

Tie-in The simultaneous promotion of multiple brands in a single sales-promotion effort.

Trade allowances Also called *trade deals,* trade allowances are offered to retailers for performing activities in support of the manufacturer's brand.

Trade contest A form of trade-oriented sales promotion that is directed at store-level or department managers and generally is based on managers meeting a sales goal established by the manufacturer.

Trade incentives In contrast to trade contests, trade incentives are given to retail managers and salespeople for performing tasks such as displaying merchandise or selling certain lines of merchandise.

Trade show A temporary forum where sellers of a product category exhibit and demonstrate their wares to present and prospective buyers.

Trialability The extent to which an innovation can be used on a limited basis. Trialability is tied closely to the concept of perceived risk. In general, products that lend themselves to trialability are adopted at a more rapid rate.

Trier class The group of consumers who actually try a new product; the second step in which an individual becomes a new brand consumer. Coupons, distribution, and price are the variables that influence consumers to become triers.

Unfair advertising The Federal Trade Commission regards advertising as unfair if it is immoral, unethical, oppressive, or unscrupulous and causes substantial injury to consumers, competitors, or other businesses.

Unique-selling proposition (USP) strategy A creative advertising strategy that promotes a product attribute that represents a meaningful, distinctive consumer benefit.

Unplanned purchase A form of purchase behavior based on POPAI's supermarket buying-habits study in which the consumer purchases a product or brand for which he or she had no prior purchase intent.

Values In the means-end conceptualization of advertising strategy, values represent important beliefs that people hold about themselves and that determine the relative desirability of consequences.

Vendor support programs (VSPs) A form of cooperative advertising program initiated by retailers whereby the retailer features one or several manufacturers' products in local advertising media and has the manufacturer(s) pay for the advertising.

Vicarious modeling A type of behavior modification in which advertisers attempt to influence consumers' perceptions and behaviors by having them observe the actions of others and the resulting consequences.

Video merchandising centers (VMCs) Electronic devices that display and sell entire product lines through audio and video presentations. VMCs perform both informational and transactional functions.

Visibility The degree to which other people can observe one's ownership and use of a new product. The more a consumption behavior can be sensed by other people, the more visible it is and typically the more rapid is its rate of adoption.

Voice-pitch analysis (VOPAN) A physiological measurement device that assesses the consumer's physiological reaction to an advertisement by using a specially programmed computer to analyze a person's voice pitch in response to questions about a test advertisement.

Voluntary attention One of three forms of attention that occurs when a person willfully notices a stimulus. See **Involuntary attention** and **Nonvoluntary attention.**

Warmth One of the various emotional responses that consumers have to advertisements. This emotion involves physiological arousal and is precipitated by experiencing a sense of love, family, or friendship.

Warmth monitor A technique which measures emotional warmth in television commercials.

NAME INDEX

SUBJECT INDEX